End User Computing Challenges Technologies:
Emerging Tools and Applications

Steve Clarke
The University of Hull, UK

INFORMATION SCIENCE REFERENCE

Hershey · New York

Acquisitions Editor:	Kristin Klinger
Development Editor:	Kristin M. Roth
Assistant Development Editor:	Meg Stocking
Senior Managing Editor:	Jennifer Neidig
Managing Editor:	Sara Reed
Assistant Managing Editor:	Carole Coulson
Copy Editor:	April Schmidt
Typesetter:	Cindy Consonery
Cover Design:	Lisa Tosheff
Printed at:	Yurchak Printing Inc.

Published in the United States of America by
Information Science Reference (an imprint of IGI Global)
701 E. Chocolate Avenue, Suite 200
Hershey PA 17033
Tel: 717-533-8845
Fax: 717-533-8661
E-mail: cust@igi-global.com
Web site: http://www.igi-global.com

and in the United Kingdom by
Information Science Reference (an imprint of IGI Global)
3 Henrietta Street
Covent Garden
London WC2E 8LU
Tel: 44 20 7240 0856
Fax: 44 20 7379 0609
Web site: http://www.eurospanonline.com

Library of Congress Cataloging-in-Publication Data

End-user computing : concepts, methodologies, tools, and applications / Steve Clarke, editor.

p. cm.

Summary: "This collection compiles the most authoritative research in this area, . It provides libraries with definitive studies covering all of the salient issues of the field, it gives researchers, managers, and other professionals the knowledge and tools they need to properly understand the role of end-user computing in the modern organization"--Provided by publisher.

Includes bibliographical references and index.

ISBN-13: 978-1-59904-945-8 (hardcover)

ISBN-13: 978-1-59904-946-5 (e-book)

1. End-user computing. I. Clarke, Steve.

QA76.9.E53E44 2008

004.01'9--dc22

2007041257

British Cataloguing in Publication Data
A Cataloguing in Publication record for this book is available from the British Library.

All work contributed to this book set is new, previously-unpublished material. The views expressed in this book are those of the authors, but not necessarily of the publisher.

Advances in End User Computing Series (AEUC)

ISBN: 1537-9310

Editor-in-Chief: Steve Clarke, University of Hull, UK

End User Computing Challenges and Technologies: Emerging Tools and Applications
Edited by: Steve Clarke, University of Hull, UK

Information Science Reference ◘ copyright 2008 ◘ 300pp ◘ H/C (ISBN: 978-1-59904-295-4) ◘ US $180.00 (our price)

Advances in information technologies have allowed end users to become a fundamental element in the development and application of computing technology and digital information. End User Computing Challenges & Technologies: Emerging Tools & Applications examines practical research and case studies on such benchmark topics as biometric and security technology, protection of digital assets and information, multilevel computer self-efficacy, and end-user Web development. This book offers library collections a critical mass of research into the advancement, productivity, and performance of the end user computing domain.

Contemporary Issues in End User Computing
Edited by: M. Adam Mahmood, University of Texas, USA

IGI Publishing ◘ copyright 2007 ◘ 337pp ◘ H/C (ISBN: 1-59140-926-8) ◘ US $85.46 (our price) ◘ E-Book (ISBN: 1-59140-928-4) ◘ US $75.96 (our price)

Contemporary Issues in End User Computing brings a wealth of end user computing information to one accessible location. This collection includes empirical and theoretical research concerned with all aspects of end user computing including development, utilization, and management. Contemporary Issues in End User Computing is divided into three sections, covering Web-based end user computing tools and technologies, end user computing software and trends, and end user characteristics and learning. This scholarly book features the latest research findings dealing with end user computing concepts, issues, and trends.

Other books in this series include:

Advanced Topics in End User Computing, Volume 1
Edited by: M. Adam Mahmood, University of Texas, USA
IGI Publishing ◘ copyright 2002 ◘ 300pp ◘ H/C (ISBN: 1-930708-42-4) ◘ US $67.46 (our price)

Advanced Topics in End User Computing, Volume 2
Edited by: M. Adam Mahmood, University of Texas, USA
IGI Publishing ◘ copyright 2003 ◘ 348 pp ◘ H/C (ISBN: 1-59140-065-1) ◘ US $71.96 (our price) ◘ E-Book (ISBN: 1-59140-100-3) ◘ US $63.96 (our price)

Advanced Topics in End User Computing, Volume 3
Edited by: M. Adam Mahmood, University of Texas, USA
IGI Publishing ◘ copyright 2004 ◘ 376 pp ◘ H/C (ISBN: 1-59140-257-3) ◘ US $71.96 (our price) ◘ E-Book (ISBN: 1-59140-258-1) ◘ US $51.96 (our price)

Advanced Topics in End User Computing, Volume 4
Edited by: M. Adam Mahmood, University of Texas, USA
IGI Publishing ◘ copyright 2005 ◘ 333pp ◘ H/C (ISBN: 1-59140-474-6) ◘ US $76.46 (our price) ◘ E-Book (ISBN: 1-59140-476-2) ◘ US $55.96 (our price)

DISSEMINATOR OF KNOWLEDGE

Hershey • New York

Order online at www.igi-global.com or call 717-533-8845 x10 –
Mon-Fri 8:30 am - 5:00 pm (est) or fax 24 hours a day 717-533-8661

Table of Contents

Detailed Table of Contents

This chapter advances IT ethics research by surveying the literature regarding IT ethical behavior models and proposes an IT ethical behavioral model for further research. A proposed conceptual ethical behavior model is based on an initial meta analysis of most of the ethical research. The proposed model suggests that ethical behavioral intention is influenced by an individual's attitude (which in turn is influenced by a variety of other factors such as perceived importance of the issue, consequences of the action and beliefs), as well as other elements from the theory of planned behavior, equity theory, the environment, control, norms, past ethical behavior, and individual characteristics. This proposed model provides a basis for additional research that should foster a better understanding regarding ethical/unethical behavior and determinants of that behavior. Results from further research in ethical behavior will provide a better understanding of unethical behavior and inappropriate acts allowing organizations to develop realistic training programs for IT professionals, users, and managers as well as incorporate effective deterrent and preventive measures that can curb the rising tide of undesired misuse and unethical behavior in the IT arena.

This chapter reports research concerning privacy, risk perceptions, and online behavior intentions on a sample of expert household end users. Findings include identification of (1) an e-privacy typology, consisting of "privacy aware", "privacy suspicious", and "privacy active" types, and (2) an e-privacy hierarchy of effects. Results suggest the presence of a privacy hierarchy of effects where awareness leads to suspicion, which subsequently leads to active behavior. Perceived risk was found to interact with the e-privacy hierarch and to have a strong negative influence on the extent to which respondents participated in online subscription and purchasing. A key finding was that privacy active behavior which was hypothesised to increase the likelihood of online subscription and purchasing was not found to be significant. The chapter concludes with a number of important implications for managers, and directions for future research are discussed.

Identifying factors affecting effectiveness of computer training remains a key issue in information systems (IS) research and practice. To this end, the current study builds upon IS and training literatures to develop and test a research model to examine the impact of multilevel computer self-efficacy (CSE) on effectiveness of computer training. The model distinguishes between general and application-specific CSE and posits that both levels of CSE will have positive effects on: perceived ease of use, near-transfer learning, and far-transfer learning of computer skills and a negative effect on computer anxiety. The results of a field experiment conducted to empirically test the model revealed that general CSE had positive effects on far-transfer learning and perceived ease of use, whereas application-specific CSE demonstrated positive effects on near-transfer learning and perceived ease of use. The results also showed that general and application-specific CSE had negative effects on computer anxiety. This study provides better insights into the relationships between the two levels of CSE and computer training outcomes and offers valuable research and practical implications.

This chapter illustrates how to optimize the return on investment (ROI) of enterprise architecture. Enterprise architecture is a blueprint for defining the structure and operation of organizations, such as local, state, and federal agencies. Done well enterprise architecture results in leaner and more effective information systems that satisfy organizational goals and objectives. This chapter introduces a suite of simple metrics and models for measuring the ROI of enterprise architecture. This chapter also introduces real options, which is a contemporary approach to measuring ROI. Whereas typical measures tend to underestimate ROI, real options have the ability to unearth business value hidden deep within the economics of investments in enterprise architecture.

Protection of physical assets and digital information is of growing importance to society. The need for development and use of security technologies is ever increasing. As with any new technology, user acceptance of new software and hardware devices is often hard to gauge, and policies to introduce and ensure adequate and correct usage of such technologies are often lacking. Security technologies have widespread applicability to different organizational contexts that may present unusual and varied adoption considerations. This study adapts the technology acceptance model and extends it to study the intention to use security devices, more specifically biometrics, across a wide variety of organizational contexts. Due to the use of physiological characteristics, biometrics present unique adoption concerns. The extension of the technology acceptance model for biometrics is useful, as biometrics encompass many of the same adoption concerns as traditional security devices, but include a level of invasiveness that is obvious to the user. Through the use of vignettes, this study encompasses a systematically varied set of usage contexts for biometric devices to provide a generalizable view of the factors impacting intention to use over all categories of situational contexts of the device's use. The technology acceptance model is extended in this study to include constructs for perceived need for privacy, perceived need for security, and perceived physical invasiveness of biometric devices as factors that influence intention to use. The model is shown to be a good predictor of intention to use biometric devices and implications of the results for biometric and security technology acceptance is discussed.

An integrative model explaining intentions to use an information technology is proposed. The primary objective is to obtain a clearer picture of how intentions are formed, and draws on previous research such as the technology acceptance model and the decomposed theory of planned behavior. The conceptual model was tested using questionnaire responses from 189 subjects, measured at two time periods approximately two months apart. The results generally supported the hypothesized relationships, and revealed strong influences of both personal innovativeness and computer self-efficacy.

The chapter presents a case study following the activities of super users and local developers during the adoption of a new business application by an accounting firm in Scandinavia (referred to as the Company). The Company launched a program to train super users to help with this process because of the complexity of the new system, a generic, multipurpose application system replacing several older, non-integrated systems. The system, Visma Business (VB,) is a comprehensive financial and accounting application delivered as a set of components that need to be configured for domain-specific tasks, depending on the clients the accountants will interact with. The super users and the local end user developer (also called the application coordinator) were asked to take part in this study. We documented their activities empirically and analytically, using interviews to gather data and drawing on aspects of activity theory for the conceptual framework for analysis. Our findings provide insight into end-user development (EUD) activities with VB: what roles were created by the Company, what roles emerged spontaneously during the process, what the various user groups (regular users, super users, and the application coordinator) did, and how EUD was coordinated between super users and the application coordinator. Our findings show that super users fill an important niche as mediators between regular users and local developers and can make a significant contribution to the success of EUD efforts in a non-technical application domain.

The development of applications by end users has become an integral part of organizational information provision. It has been established that there are both benefits and risks associated with end-user development, particularly in the areas of spreadsheets and databases. Web development tools are enabling a new kind of end-user development. The fact that Web page creation may impact not only locally but also globally, significantly raises the importance of this type of end-user application development. This chapter reports on the extent of Web page development amongst end users and investigates their perceptions of the benefits and risks of end user Web development relative to those associated with spreadsheet development and explores approaches to reducing the risks.

End-user development means the active participation of end users in the software development process. In this perspective, tasks that are traditionally performed by professional software developers at design time are transferred to end users at use time. This creates a new challenge for software engineers: designing software systems that can be evolved by end users. Metadesign, a new design paradigm discussed in this chapter, is regarded as a possible answer to this challenge. In this line, we have developed a meta-design methodology, called software shaping workshop methodology, that supports user work practice and allows experts in a domain to personalize and evolve their own software environments. We illustrate the software shaping workshop methodology and describe its application to a project in the medical domain. The work proposes a new perspective on system personalization, distinguishing between customization and tailoring of software environments. The software environments are customized by the design team to the work context, culture, experience, and skills of the user communities; they are also tailorable by end users at runtime in order to adapt them to the specific work situation and users' preferences and habits. The aim is to provide the physicians with software environments that are easy to use and adequate for their tasks, capable to improve their work practice and determine an increase in their productivity and performance.

(Chapters 7-10 were sourced by Nikolay Mehandjiev, Alistair Suttcliffe, and Trevor Wood-Harper, all of The University of Manchester, UK).

Many recently emerging component-based Web portal application platforms allow end users to compose dynamic Web dialogues on the fly. Experts predict that this paradigm will enable a class of new applications for Web-based content delivery in information-rich, agile business domains, such as health care. We present a conceptual analysis of the user-based composition paradigm currently used and argue that its usability is limited with respect to complex, dynamic applications. To overcome these limitations, we present an alternative composition paradigm, which is based on a semantic model of a portal's application domain. We evaluate this approach with an application scenario in the health care domain.

Grounded in uncertainty reduction theory, the present study analyzes the content of 50 privacy policies from well known commercial Web sites with a view to identifying starting points for improving the quality of online privacy policies. Drawing on traditional content analysis and computer-assisted textual analysis, the study shows that privacy policies often omit essential information and fail to communicate data handling practices in a transparent manner. To reduce Internet users' uncertainty about data handling practices and help companies build stable relationships with users, privacy policies need to explain not only the data collection and sharing practices a company engages in but also those practices companies do not engage in. Further, more exact lexical choice in privacy policies would increase the transparency of data handling practices and therefore user trust in WWW interactions. The results also call for less verbose texts and alternatives to the currently narrative presentation format.

Despite the fact that over half of U.S. residents are now online, Internet users hesitate to enter into transactions with e-retailers in the absence of certain assurances. Recent IS research shows that institution-based assurance structures, such as Web seals, are drivers of online trust. We extend the research in online trust to include the effect of third-party organization (TPO) credibility on both Internet users' perceptions of assurance structures and purchase risk. Findings indicate that TPO credibility is positively related to the value Internet users assign assurance structures and negatively related to perceptions of purchase risk. Furthermore, perceptions of TPO credibility are strongly associated with users' trusting attitudes toward the e-retailer. For some online consumers, trust may have less to do with privacy and security and more to do with the reputation of the TPO. These findings have important implications for the design of Web sites, the selection of assurance providers and services, and the reputation of both e-retailers and providers.

The leadership role facilitates group process by structuring group interaction. How leadership affects group performance in GSS settings remains one of the least investigated areas of GSS research. In this study, the presence of a group leader is found to make a significant difference in objective decision quality and satisfaction with the decision process. At the same time, perceived decision quality and consensus are not significantly different in groups with a leader and those without one. A content analysis of comments by group leaders shows that group leaders are effective when making comments on clear group objectives and interaction structure in the early stages of group interaction. In the later stages, however, it becomes more important for group leaders to offer comments encouraging interaction and maintaining group cohesion.

This study examines the formation of relationship quality and loyalty in the context of IT service, and a conceptual model is also proposed. In the model, expertise, relational selling behavior, perceived network quality, and service recovery indirectly influence a customer's loyalty through the mediation of relationship quality. Gender moderates each model path. The moderating effects are simultaneously examined using data from customers of Taiwan's leading ISP (internet service provider). The test results indicate that the influences of perceived network quality on relationship quality and of relationship quality on loyalty are stronger for males than females, while relational selling behavior influences relationship quality more for females than for males. Furthermore, service recovery influences relationship quality for both the male and female groups, but its influence does not differ significantly between the two groups. Finally, expertise exerts an insignificant influence on relationship quality for both groups. Implications of the empirical findings also are discussed.

This research examines electronic commerce participation and attitudes by older Americans. Questionnaires were distributed at a large retirement community and several senior centers located in Pennsylvania. The sample of 110 respondents ranged in age from 52 to 87. Fifty nine percent reported purchasing an item online in the last six months. The technology acceptance model (TAM) was used and modified to examine the impact attitudes concerning ease of use, usefulness, and trust had on electronic commerce usage. Usefulness and trust were found to have a positive, direct affect on usage. Ease of use had significant impacts on usefulness and trust had a significant impact on both ease of use and usefulness. The chapter concludes with a discussion of these results, study limitations, and directions for future research.

Until recent years, the end user computing ergonomic focus has primarily been on stationary computer use. A new trend for the end user is mobile computing. An increasing number of end users are working outside of the traditional office. Mobile computing devices allow for these workers to perform job functions while in the field, at home, or while traveling. The organizational and end-user benefits abound for the use of such enabling technology. However, the mobile computing environment introduces a new area of ergonomic concerns. Are businesses and end users monitoring the use of these devices from an ergonomic perspective?

The good news is the outcome can be influenced and/or determined with intentional efforts on the part of both end users and managers. This chapter includes an in-depth review of the current and emerging issues, especially the mobile end-user environment, that is important to the end user, manager, and organization as a whole. It also provides end user ergonomic suggestions and resources and addresses the management challenges rising from ergonomic issues.

Preface

We are pleased to bring you this latest volume of the *Advances in End-User Computing* (EUC) series. Few domains of computing progress at the pace of end-user issues, and research and practice into EUC needs a resource able to provide access to new concepts and applications within the domain. This 2007 Volume of *Advances in End-User Computing* presents a wide range of the most current research into a variety of aspects of EUC, and will assist researchers, educators, and professionals in understanding the most recent developments in the domain. A summary of the contents of the text is given below.

Chapter I, "A Proposed IT Ethical Behavioral Model", by Timothy Paul Cronan and David E. Douglas, of The University of Arkansas, USA, advances IT ethics research by surveying the literature regarding IT ethical behavior models and proposes an IT ethical behavioral model for further research. A proposed conceptual ethical behavior model is provided, and suggests that ethical behavioral intention is influenced by an individual's attitude (which in turn is influenced by a variety of other factors such as perceived importance of the issue, consequences of the action and beliefs), as well as other elements from the theory of planned behavior, equity theory, the environment, control, norms, past ethical behavior, and individual characteristics. The authors argue that results from further research in ethical behavior will provide a better understanding of unethical behavior and inappropriate acts allowing organizations to develop realistic training programs for IT professionals, users, and managers as well as incorporate effective deterrent and preventive measures that can curb the rising tide of undesired misuse and unethical behavior in the IT arena.

Chapter II, "Understanding the Impact of Household End Users' Privacy and Risk Perceptions on Online Behaviour", by Judy Drennan and Josephine Previte of Queensland University of Technology, Australia, and Gillian Sullivan Mort of Griffith University, Australia, reports research concerning privacy, risk perceptions and online behavior intentions on a sample of expert household end users. Findings include identification of an e-privacy typology, and an e-privacy hierarchy of effects. A key finding was that privacy active behavior which was hypothesized to increase the likelihood of online subscription and purchasing was not found to be significant. The chapter concludes with a number of important implications for managers, and directions for future research are discussed.

Chapter III, "The Impact of Multilevel Computer Self-Efficacy on Effectiveness of Computer Training", is by Bassam Hasan, The University of Toledo, USA. Bassam argues that identifying factors affecting the effectiveness of computer training remains a key issue in information systems (IS) research and practice. His study builds upon IS and training literature to develop and test a research model to examine the impact of multilevel computer self-efficacy (CSE) on effectiveness of computer training. The model distinguishes between general and application-specific CSE and posits that both levels of CSE will have positive effects on: perceived ease of use, near-transfer learning, and far-transfer learning of computer skills and a negative effect on computer anxiety. The results of a field experiment revealed that general CSE had positive effects on far-transfer learning and perceived ease of use, whereas application-specific CSE demonstrated positive effects on near-transfer learning and perceived ease of use. This study provides insights into the relationships between the two levels of CSE and computer training outcomes and offers valuable research and practical implications.

Chapter IV, "Optimizing the ROI of Enterprise Architecture Using Real Options", by David F. Rico, a computing consultant, illustrates how to optimize the return on investment or ROI of enterprise architecture. Enterprise architecture is a blueprint for defining the structure and operation of organizations, such as local, state, and federal agencies. Done well enterprise architecture results in leaner and more effective information systems that satisfy organizational goals and objectives. This article introduces a suite of simple metrics and models for measuring the ROI of enterprise architecture. This article also introduces real options, which is a contemporary approach to measuring ROI. Whereas, typical measures tend to underestimate ROI, real options have the ability to unearth business value hidden deep within the economics of investments in enterprise architecture.

Chapter V, "An Extension of the Technology Acceptance Model to Determine the Intention to Use Biometric Devices", is by Tabitha James and Reza Barkhi, Virginia Polytechnic Institute and State University, USA; Taner Pirim, Mississippi Center for Supercomputing Research, USA; Katherine Boswell, Middle Tennessee State University, USA; and Brian Reithel, University of Mississippi, USA. They argue that the protection of physical assets and digital information is of growing importance to society. The study adapts the technology acceptance model and extends it to study the intention to use security devices, more specifically biometrics, across a wide variety of organizational contexts. Through the use of vignettes, this study encompasses a systematically varied set of usage contexts for biometric devices to provide a generalizable view of the factors impacting intention to use over all categories of situational contexts of the device's use. The technology acceptance model is extended in this study to include constructs for perceived need for privacy, perceived need for security, and perceived physical invasiveness of biometric devices as factors that influence intention to use. The model is shown to be a good predictor of intention to use biometric devices and implications of the results for biometric and security technology acceptance is discussed.

Chapter VI, "Intentions to Use Information Technologies: An Integrative Model", by Ron Thompson, Wake Forest University, USA, and Deborah Compeau, Chris Higgins, and Nathan Lupton, University of Western Ontario, Canada, presents an integrative model explaining intentions to use an information technology. The primary objective is to obtain a clearer picture of how intentions are formed, and it draws on previous research. The conceptual model was tested using questionnaires. The results generally supported the hypothesized relationships, and revealed strong influences of both personal innovativeness and computer self-efficacy.

Chapter VII, "The Organization of End User Development in an Accounting Company", by Anders I. Mørch and Hege-René Hansen Åsand, University of Oslo, Norway, and Sten R. Ludvigsen, InterMedia, University of Oslo, Norway, uses activity theory as a conceptual analysis framework to analyze real-world tailoring practices in a sophisticated organizational context, explored through a case study where a complex business application is implemented in an accounting company. The organizational context embeds formally defined roles of end users, super users, and application coordinators, and the chapter offers interesting findings regarding the relationships and interactions between these roles, concluding that the role of super users fills an important niche in supporting organization-wide EUD. The analysis in the chapter provides insights into end-user development (EUD) activities with the "Visma Business" system, including the roles created by the Company and those which emerged spontaneously during the process, and information concerning what the various user groups (regular users, super users, and the application coordinator) did, and how EUD was coordinated between super users and the application coordinator. The recommendations of this chapter would benefit other organizations in their EUD efforts.

Chapter VIII, "End User Perceptions of the Benefits and Risks of End User Web Development", by Tanya McGill and Chris Klisc, Murdoch University, Australia, is concerned with organizational issues of supporting EUD, with a focus on approaches to alleviating risks of EUD. It compares perceptions and opinions regarding risk management within two contexts: end-user development of Web pages with end-user development of spreadsheets. The chapter uses a questionnaire-based survey to gather information regarding practices and perceptions of Web page development among end users. The importance of the Web page development context comes from the external nature of the Web pages as development artifacts, which means that consequences of end-user development are much wider than the conventional EUD activities such as spreadsheet development, and mistakes can affect core business processes involving customers and suppliers. The survey targets end users who are known to have developed spreadsheets, probing the extent to which they undertake Web page development, and using their experience of EUD in both contexts. One interesting finding is that training is perceived to be the most important approach to risk reduction, despite the lack of such training among the survey sample of end-user developers.

Chapter IX, "Advancing End User Development Through Metadesign", is by Maria Francesca Costabile, Rosa Lanzilotti, and Antonio Piccinno, Università di Bari, Italy; Daniela Fogli, Università di Bresica, Italy; and Piero Mussio and Loredana Parasiliti Provenza, Università di Milano, Italy. This chapter analyzes the richness of working practices, representations, and tacit knowledge found in professional communities, and explores the interactions between these and software tools at the levels of use, design, and metadesign. It proposes the SSW (software shaping workshops) methodology, which focuses on enabling the participation of end users in the development of their software environments to ensure the environment is tuned to their needs. The tools used in everyday work of users are gathered in environments called application workshops, while the tools necessary to design and customize those are gathered in system workshops, and so forth. This contribution is grounded in the medical domain, and a field study of physicians and their activities of customizing their workshops is reported in the chapter.

Chapter X, "Semantic Composition of Web Portal Components", by Jens H. Weber-Jahnke, Yury Bychkov, David Dahlem, and Luay Kawasme, University of Victoria, Canada, targets the health care domain, and proposes a novel approach to enabling end-user development of Web portals. Web portals have recently gained importance in information rich and agile domains such as health care. As the size and complexity of portal-based content delivery applications increases, current component-based technologies are no longer suitable because of their significant cognitive overload for end-user developers in terms of type checking, debugging, and complex metaphors. The core innovation reported in the chapter is the use of the semantic-based composition model, achieving integration of ontologies and component-based technology to simplify end-user development in this particular context. The proposed approach is implemented in a tool and evaluated using an application scenario.

Chapter XI, "Privacy Statements as a Means of Uncertainty Reduction in WWW Interactions", by Irene Pollach, Vienna University of Economics and Business Administration, Austria, analyzes the content of 50 privacy policies from well-known commercial Web sites with a view to identifying starting points for improving the quality of online privacy policies. The study shows that privacy policies often omit essential information and fail to communicate data handling practices in a transparent manner. The results also call for less verbose texts and alternatives to the current narrative presentation format.

Chapter XII, "Examining User Perception of Third-Party Organization Credibility and Trust in an E-Retailer", is by Robin L. Wakefield, Hankamer School of Business, Baylor University, USA, and Dwayne Whitten, Mays School of Business, Texas A&M University, USA. Despite the fact that over half of U.S. residents are now online, Internet users hesitate to enter into transactions with e-retailers in the absence of certain assurances. The authors extend the research in online trust to include the effect of third-party organization (TPO) credibility on both Internet users' perceptions of assurance structures and purchase risk. Findings indicate that TPO credibility is positively related to the value that Internet users assign to assurance structures and negatively related to perceptions of purchase risk. These findings have important implications for the design of Web sites, the selection of assurance providers and services, and the reputation of both e-retailers and providers.

Chapter XIII, "Supporting Distributed Groups with Group Support Systems: A Study of the Effect of Group Leaders and Communication Modes on Group Performance", is by Youngjin Kim, Fordham University, USA. In this study, the presence of a group leader is found to make a significant difference in objective decision quality and satisfaction with the decision process. At the same time, perceived decision quality and consensus are not significantly different in groups with a leader and those without one. A content analysis of comments by group leaders shows that group leaders are effective when making comments on clear group objectives and interaction structure in the early stages of group interaction. In the later stages, however, it becomes more important for group leaders to offer comments encouraging interaction and maintaining group cohesion.

Chapter XIV, "Evaluating Group Differences in Gender During the Formation of Relationship Quality and Loyalty in ISP Service", by Chieh-Peng Ling, Vanung University, Taiwan, and Cherng G. Ding, National Chiao Tung University, Taiwan, examines the moderating role of gender during the formation of relationship quality and loyalty in the context of IT service. In the proposed model, expertise, relational selling behavior, perceived network quality, and service recovery indirectly influence a customer's loyalty through mediation of relationship quality. Test results indicate that the influences of perceived network quality on relationship quality and of relationship quality on loyalty are stronger for males than females, while relational selling behavior influences relationship quality more for females than for males.

Chapter XV, "The Importance of Ease of Use, Usefulness, and Trust to Online Consumers: An Examination of the Technology Acceptance Model with Older Consumers", by Donna Weaver McCloskey, Widener University, USA, examines electronic commerce participation and attitudes by older Americans. Questionnaires were distributed at a large retirement community and several senior centers located in Pennsylvania. The technology acceptance model (TAM) was used and modified to examine the impact attitudes concerning ease of use, usefulness, and trust had on electronic commerce usage. Usefulness and trust were found to have a positive, direct affect on usage. Ease of use had significant impacts on usefulness and trust had a significant impact on both ease of use and usefulness. The article concludes with a discussion of these results, study limitations, and directions for future research.

Chapter XVI, "End User Computing Ergonomics: Facts or Fads?," is by Carol Clark, Middle Tennessee State University, USA. Until recent years, the end-user computing ergonomic focus has primarily been on stationary computer use. A new trend for the end user is mobile computing. However, the mobile computing environment introduces a new area of ergonomic concerns. This chapter includes an in-depth review of the current and emerging issues, especially the mobile end user environment, that is important to the end user, manager, and organization as a whole. It also provides end-user ergonomic suggestions and resources and addresses the management challenges rising from ergonomic issues.

CONCLUSION: CONTRIBUTION TO THE FIELD

The field of end-user computing has grown exponentially in recent years, and continues to expand rapidly. Professionals and educators alike will find that the *Advances in End-User Computing* series provides a constantly up-to-date resource for understanding and implementing EUC, which will be of value to professors, researchers, scholars, professionals, and all who have an interest in the domain. An outstanding collection of the latest research associated with EUC, the 2008 copyright volume of *Advances in End-User Computing* provides valuable recent thinking from the field.

We hope you enjoy reading it.

Steve Clarke
Editor-in-Chief
Advances in End User Computing, Copyright 2008

Acknowledgment

Chapters VII to X were sourced by Nikolay Mehandjiev, Alistair Suttcliffe and Trevor Wood-Harper, all of The University of Manchester, UK. My thanks go to Nikolay, Alistair and Trevor for their contribution to this volume.

Steve Clarke
Editor-in-Chief

Chapter I
A Proposed IT Ethical Behavioral Model[1]

Timothy Paul Cronan
University of Arkansas, USA

David E. Douglas
University of Arkansas, USA

ABSTRACT

This chapter advances IT ethics research by surveying the literature regarding IT ethical behavior models and proposes an IT ethical behavioral model for further research. A proposed conceptual ethical behavior model is based on an initial meta-analysis of most of the ethical research. The proposed model suggests that ethical behavioral intention is influenced by an individual's attitude (which in turn is influenced by a variety of other factors such as perceived importance of the issue, consequences of the action, and beliefs), as well as other elements from the Theory of Planned Behavior, equity theory, the environment, control, norms, past ethical behavior, and individual characteristics. This proposed model provides a basis for additional research that should foster a better understanding regarding ethical/unethical behavior and determinants of that behavior. Results from further research in ethical behavior will provide a better understanding of unethical behavior and inappropriate acts allowing organizations to develop realistic training programs for IT professionals, users, and managers as well as incorporate effective deterrent and preventive measures that can curb the rising tide of undesired misuse and unethical behavior in the IT arena.

IT UNETHICAL BEHAVIOR: COMMONPLACE

During the last decade, abundant research has been dedicated to the study of ethics and ethical behavior in business. Moreover, unethical behavior in businesses has underscored the need for a better understanding of this behavior as well as additional and better methods of preventing this unethical behavior. Ethical situations arise often in many different areas of business; this has been complicated by the integration of IT into business operations. Common ethical issues faced by IT professionals include piracy, accuracy, property, and accessibility (Mason, 1986). Among the issues in the news lately is the issue of intellectual property, and specifically software piracy, which has been identified as a major problem facing the $140 billion software market (Lau, 2003).

In spite of its undoubted value to users and organizations, information technology (IT) poses some risks and ethical issues, because its misuse results in serious losses to business and society (Marshall, 1999; Straub & Nance, 1990). From a social and professional perspective, most business professionals and IT users are concerned about unacceptable, inappropriate, illegal, and unethical use of IT. Many recognize the potential harm to society, the IT profession, and the economy (Cappel & Windsor, 1998).

While software piracy has received much interest (with an estimated $30 billion in lost revenues in 2003) (First Annual Business Software Alliance and IDC Global Software Piracy Study, 2004), a new form of piracy has taken the piracy spotlight and being called the next big piracy arena (Bhattacharjee, Gopal, & Sanders, 2003). Referred to as digital piracy, it is defined as "the illegal copying/downloading of copyrighted software and media files." According to the Forrester Research Group (http://www.forrester.com), lost revenues due to digital piracy could reach $5 billion alone from music and book publishers in the year 2005 (not counting losses from software companies or cinema studios). The current piracy target apparently will be Hollywood, as the Motion Picture Association of American (MPAA) estimates that around 400,000 to 600,000 movies are being copied/downloaded on the Internet everyday (MPAA Report, 2003).

To combat unethical behavior (piracy, privacy, etc.), two popular methods have been employed: preventives and deterrents. Preventives impede unethical acts by making it very difficult to commit

the act. The idea is to make the culprits expend so much effort that it will wear them down, and eventually they will not want to do it. Deterrents, on the other hand, use the threat of undesirable consequences (mostly legal sanctions) to prevent inappropriate and unauthorized behavior (Gopal & Sanders, 1997). Unfortunately, given the rise in inappropriate and unethical behavior; none of the current strategies appear to be working.

Instead of relying solely on existing preventives and deterrents, knowing what influences individuals to act unethically would be a more advantageous path. This is especially important because many studies have suggested that individuals do not see piracy (and other inappropriate behavior) as a crime or as unethical (Im & Van Epps, 1991; Reid, Thompson, & Logston, 1992). For example, Solomon and O'Brien (1990) examined attitude towards piracy among business students and found that they view piracy as socially and ethically acceptable, and that piracy is widespread among business students. Christensen and Eining (1991) also found that individuals do not perceive piracy as inappropriate and do not believe their friends and superiors think it is inappropriate.

With the goal of curbing unethical behavior, the overall objective of this research is to provide a conceptual model, via synthesis of the literature, of general ethical behavior which identifies and provides a better understanding of the factors that influence an individual's decision to act ethically or unethically in an effort to curb unethical behavior. While much of the previous research concentrated on the unethical behavior and how to control it (Conner & Rumlet, 1991; Moseley & Whitis, 1995; Glass & Wood, 1996; Gopal & Sanders, 1997), this chapter presents a survey of the ethics literature summarizing models of IT ethical behavior and presents a comprehensive ethical model based on an inceptive meta-analysis of those models. By examining and understanding the factors that influence such behavior, measures and policy to alter those factors can be implemented (and thus influence behavior indirectly) that would reduce losses to business and society.

UNDERSTANDING IT ETHICAL BEHAVIOR

Prior research has attempted to explain ethical behavior. Jones (1991) provides an excellent summary of ethical decision models from which many of the behavioral and ethical models explaining software piracy are derived. The theory of planned behavior (TPB) asserts that intention to perform a behavior is based on one's attitude towards the behavior, the social influence to perform/not perform the behavior (subjective norms), and one's control over performing such a behavior (perceived behavioral control) (Ajzen, 1991). Analogous to Simon's human decision-making model (Simon, 1960) in the information systems literature, the Fishbein and Ajzen (1975) and Ajzen and Fishbein (1977, 1982) consumer behavior model incorporates various learning theories into a model explaining consumer behavior. The theory of reasoned action (TRA) is prevalent in the consumer behavior literature and has been found consistent with expectancy value theories and exchange theory (Harder, 1991). Venkatesh, Morris, Davis, and Davis (2003) also provides a good summary of TRA and TPB in their discussion of models and theories of individuals' acceptance of technology.

Ethical behavior is one kind of general behavior that is usually studied using TPB. The attitude construct is the closest match to ethical judgment in the TPB model (compared to subjective norms, perceived behavioral control, intention, or behavior). Both attitude and ethical judgment have been used to explain intention/behavior, and the TPB has been used to explain ethical behavior (Banerjee, Cronan, & Jones, 1998; Dubinsky & Loken, 1989; Flannery & May, 2000; Randall & Gibson, 1991).

Banerjee, Cronan, and Jones (1998) developed the basis of an ethical research framework, based on the TPB, to model the ethical behavior intentions of information systems professionals. This framework incorporated much of the prior ethics research. Their model integrated factors that included attitude and personal normative beliefs (TPB), moral judgment (Kohlberg, 1969; Rest, 1986), ego strength, locus of control, organizational climate (Trevino, 1986), and environmental (Bommer, Gratto, Gravander, & Tuttle, 1987) and individual attributes. In an empirical test of the model, three variables were significant—personal normative beliefs, organizational climate, and an organization-scenario variable, which had been included as a control variable. Though many of the model's variables were not found to be statistically significant, the authors believed this could be due to the small sample size in their study.

Equity theory (Adams, 1963, 1965; Walster, Berscheid, & Walster, 1973; Walster, Walster, & Berscheid 1978) has served as the basis for fairness in IT decision making. Joshi (1989) considered the equity dimensions of reciprocal, procedural, and distributive fairness of providing IT services implying that the perception of nonfairness could lead to unethical behavior. Glass and Wood (1996) found equity theory significantly influences intention to pirate software.

Attitude has been long acknowledged as the most important construct in social psychology (Allport, 1935). This is evident by the overwhelming amount of research published in this area. The attitude component has also been found to be the most significant factor influencing behavioral intention. A review of the ethics research by Trafimow and Finlay (1996) found that attitude was the best predictor of intention in 29 out of 30 studies. For example, Peace, Galleta, and Thong (2003) found that attitude (explained by punishment and software costs) had the strongest effect on intention to pirate software. A compelling reason why attitude is so important is that attitude can be changed through persuasion and other means.

An abundance of research regarding attitude change and persuasion exists in the psychology literature (Olson & Zanna, 1993). If attitude can be changed, then intention may be influenced (and subsequently behavior may be influenced through attitude change and persuasion). A stream of literature regarding attitude change exists and, if applied to unethical acts, will prove to be an excellent choice that can be used to combat and deter unethical and inappropriate behavior.

Model Development and Further Directions

Table 1 details the selected literature (ethical research models that explain ethical behavior) to support the development of a proposed general ethical behavior model (Figure 1). This proposed conceptual model expands on the widely accepted behavioral models, TRA and TPB, which posit that attitude explains intention to behave and in-

Table 1. IT behavior research

Ethical Issue	Research	Factors that Influence Intention	Reference Theories	Method	Results
Ethical Decision Models	Jones (1991)	Multiple		Literature Summary	Source for subsequent research
Software Piracy	Peace et al. (2003)	Punishment Severity Software Costs Punishment Certainty Attitude Subject Norms Perceived Behavioral Control	Theory or Reasoned Action Theory of Planned Behavior Expected Utility Theory Deterrence Theory	Structural Modeling Partial Least Squares	$R^2 = .65$; software piracy predicted by attitude, subjective norms and perceived behavioral control
Computer Abuse	Harrington (1996)	Codes of Ethics Denial of responsibility	Corporate Codes of Ethics Deterrence Theory	ANOVA Multiple Comparisons	Codes affect abuse but related only to certain abuses
Privacy, accuracy, ownership, access	Banerjee et al. (1998)	Moral Judgment Attitude Personal Normative Beliefs Ego Strength Locus of Control Organizational Ethical Climate	Theory of Reasoned Action Theory of Planned Behavior	Multiple Regression Analysis	Ethical behavior intention strongly related to the computing concept (that is, organizational environment)— situational ethics and personal normative beliefs

continued on following page

Table 1. continued

Ethical Issue	Research	Factors that Influence Intention	Reference Theories	Method	Results
Fairness	Joshi (1989)	Equity Reciprocal Fairness Procedural Fairness Distributive Fairness	Reinforcement Theory Cognitive Consistency Theory Psychoanalysis Theory Exchange Theory	Framework Cross section survey Factor Analysis Measurement Development	Validated a Fairness Instrument
Software Piracy	Glass and Wood (1996)	Equity	Reinforcement Theory Cognitive Consistency Theory Psychoanalysis Theory Exchange Theory	ANOVA with Duncan's Three-way Multiple Comparisons	Piracy is related to ratio of outcomes/inputs
Software Piracy	Douglas, Cronan, and Behel (2006)	Equity Reciprocal Fairness Procedural Fairness Distributive Fairness	Equity Theory	Structured Equation Modeling (AMOS)	Equity significantly influences ethical behavior
Digital Piracy	Al-Rafee and Cronan (2005) Cronan and Al-Rafee (2007)	Individual Attributes Attitude Perceived Importance Moral Judgment Machiavellianism Cognitive Beliefs Affective Beliefs Subjective Norms Perceived Behavioral Control Past Piracy Behavior	Deontological and Teleological Theory Decision Making Theory Theory of Reasoned Action Theory of Planned Behavior Perceived Importance	Structured Equation Modeling (AMOS) Multiple Regression	$R^2 = .436$; Piracy Attitude is influenced by perceived importance, moral judgment, Machiavellianism, cognitive beliefs, affective beliefs, subjective norms, and age $R^2 = .708$; Piracy Intention is influenced by attitude, perceived behavioral control, moral obligation, and past piracy behavior

continued on following page

Table 1. continued

Ethical Issue	Research	Factors that Influence Intention	Reference Theories	Method	Results
Ethical Behavior	Leonard, Cronan, and Kreie (2004)	Moral Judgment Attitude Personal Normative Beliefs Ego Strength Locus of Control	Theory of Reasoned Action Theory of Planned Behavior Moral Development Stage Psychosocial ethical model	Multiple Regression	$R^2 = .61$ Attitude and Personal Norms Beliefs were significant in all models
Software Piracy/ Culture	Shin, Gopal, Sanders, and Whinston (2004) Hofstede (2003)	Economic Factors Cultural Factors	Economic Theory National Culture	Multiple Regression	Individualism-Collectivism plus country GDB explains 73.9% of software piracy
Ethical Behavior	Bommer, Gratto, Gravander, and Tuttle (1987)	Environment work, professional personal, social government/legal Individual Attributes	Environment	Conceptual Model	Identifies and relates environmental factors and individual attributes that influence ethical/unethical decision making
Information Ethics	Lin and Ding (2003)	Job insecurity Locus of control	Theory of Reasoned Action Theory of Planned Behavior	SEM	Partial support of joint moderating role of locus of control and job insecurity on ethical/ unethical decisions

continued on following page

Table 1. continued

Ethical Issue	Research	Factors that Influence Intention	Reference Theories	Method	Results
Ethical behavior in organizations	Trevino (1986)	Individual moderators Ego strength, locus of control Field dependence Situational moderators Job content Organizational culture Characteristics of work	Moral Development Stages (Kolberg)	Conceptual Only	Proposes the use of organizational culture as a variable affecting ethical behavior in an organization
Privacy, accuracy, ownership, access	Cronan, Leonard, and Kreie (2005)	Attitude Individual Characteristics (sex, age) Perceived Importance	Theory of Reasoned Action Theory of Planned Behavior Perceived Importance	Multiple Regression Factor Analysis	R^2 = .41 to .53 Intention is influential of attitude, perceived importance, age, and sex

tention influences actual behavior. Various other studies of behavior directly, or indirectly through intention to behave, have supported that the other factors in the proposed conceptual model significantly influence behavior. The model provides a synthesis of many important findings in ethical behavior research.

The preliminary meta-analysis of the ethics literature (Table 1) leads to a proposed conceptual model for general ethical behavior (Figure 1). The core of the proposed model is based on the TPB (Ajzen, 1991), that is, attitude, subjective norms, and perceived behavioral control intention which in turn explains behavior (illustrated in Figure 1). With that as a core, the model hypothesizes that general factors (attitude, culture, ego strength, equity, environment, locus of control, moral obligation, past piracy behavior, perceived behavioral control, perceived normative beliefs, and subject

norms) influence intention to behave which leads to the actual behavior. Further, it is hypothesized that an individual's moral judgment, individual attributes, affective beliefs, Machiavellianism, importance, cost, and punishment influences attitude and that equity (fairness) is composed of three factors of reciprocal fairness, distributive fairness, and procedural fairness. Model development is supported as follows:

- **Intention and behavior:** Theory of reasoned action and rheory of planned behavior – Ajzen (1991), Ajzen and Fishbein (1977, 1982), Fishbein and Ajzen (1975)
- **Attitude:** Ajzen (1991), Al-Rafee and Cronan (2005), Banerjee et al. (1998), Cronan and Al-Rafee (2007), Cronan et al. (2005), Peace

Figure 1. A proposed general ethic model

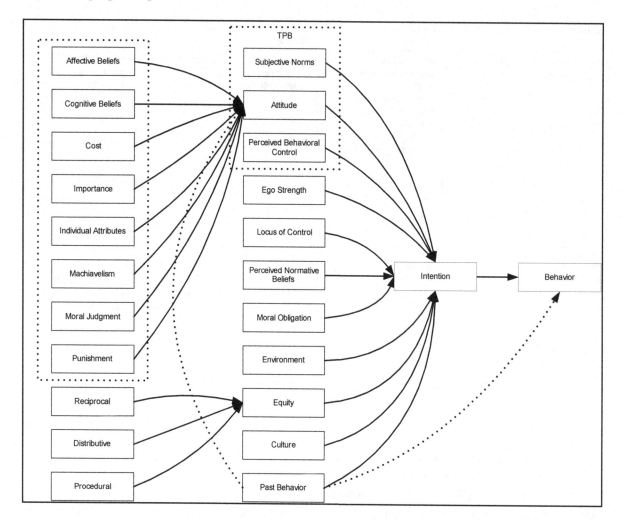

et al. (2003), Leonard et al. (2004)

- **Affective beliefs:** Al-Rafee and Cronan (2005)
- **Cognitive beliefs:** Al-Rafee and Cronan (2005)
- **Cost:** Shin et al (2004), Peace et al. (2003)
- **Individual attributes:** Al-Rafee and Cronan (2005), Bommer et al. (1987), Cronan et al. (2005)
- **Importance:** Al-Rafee and Cronan (2005), Cronan et al. (2005)
- **Machiavellianism:** Al-Rafee and Cronan (2005)

- **Moral Judgment:** Al-Rafee and Cronan (2005), Banerjee et al. (1998), Leonard et al. (2004)
- **Punishment:** Peace et al. (2003)
- **Culture** – Hofstede (2003), Shin et al. (2004)
- **Ego Strength:** Banerjee et al. (1998), Leonard et al. (2004), Trevino (1986)
- **Equity:** Douglas et al. (2006), Glass and Wood (1996), Joshi (1989)
- **Reciprocal:** Douglas et al. (2006), Joshi (1989)

- **Distributive** – Douglas et al. (2006), Joshi (1989)
- **Procedural** – Douglas et al. (2006), Joshi (1989)
- **Environment:** Banerjee et al. (1998), Bommer et al. (1987), Shin et al. (2004), Trevino (1986)
- **Locus of control:** Banerjee et al. (1998), Leonard et al. (2004), Trevino (1986)
- **Moral obligation:** Al-Rafee and Cronan (2005)
- **Past behavior:** Ajzen (2002), Cronan and Al-Rafee (2007), Hagger, Chatzisarantis, and Biddle (2002)
- **Perceived behavioral control:** Ajzen (1991), Peace et al. (2003)
- **Perceived normative beliefs:** Banerjee et al. (1998), Leonard et al. (2004)
- **Subjective norms:** Ajzen (1991), Al-Rafee and Cronan (2005), Peace et al. (2003)

The ethics literature, as well as worldwide attention, confirms that ethical behavior continues to be a very important global issue. A better understanding of the precedents and influences of ethical/unethical behavior may lead to approaches for positively influencing ethical behavior—a desirable outcome for business and society. The proposed conceptual model provides a foundation upon which alternative models can be researched in the quest for understanding ethical/unethical behavior. Given the proposed model (Figure 1) as a basis, additional empirical research is called for in order to better understand ethical behavior, as well as its determinants, and hence yield valuable information that can be used to curb unethical behavior.

REFERENCES

Adams, J.S. (1963). Towards an understanding of inequity. *Journal of Abnormal and Normal Social Psychology, 67*, 422-436.

Adams, J.S. (1965). Inequity in social exchange. In L. Berkowitz (Ed.), *Advances in experimental social psychology* (vol. 2, pp. 267-299). New York: Academic Press.

Ajzen, I. (1991). The theory of planned behavior. *Organizational Behavior and Human Decision Processes, 50*(1), 179-211.

Ajzen, I. (2002). Residual effects of past on later behavior: Habituation and reasoned action perspectives. *Personality and Social Psychology Review, 6*(2), 107-122.

Ajzen, I., & Fishbein, M. (1977). Attitude-behavior relation: A theoretical analysis and review of empirical research. *Psychological Bulletin, 84*(5), 888-918.

Ajzen, I., & Fishbein, M. (1982). *Understanding attitudes and predicting social behavior.* Englewood Cliffs, NJ: Prentice Hall.

Allport, G. (1935). Attitudes. In C. Murchison (Ed.), *Handbook of social psychology* (pp. 798-844). Worcester, MA: Clark University Press.

Al-Rafee, S., & Cronan, T.P. (2005). *Digital piracy: Factors that influence attitude toward behavior* (Working Paper). Information Systems Department, University of Arkansas, Fayetteville, AR.

Banerjee, D., Cronan, T.P., & Jones, T.W. (1998). Modeling IT ethics: A study in situational ethics. *MIS Quarterly, 22*(1), 31-60.

Bhattacharjee, S., Gopal, R.D., & Sanders, G.L. (2003). Digital music and online sharing: Software piracy 2.0? *Communication of the ACM, 46*(7), 107-111.

Bommer, M., Gratto, C., Gravander, J., & Tuttle, M. (1987). A behavioral model of ethical and unethical decision making. *Journal of Business Ethics, 6*(4), 265-280.

Cappel, J.J., & Windsor, J.C. (1998). A comparative investigation of ethical decision making: Information systems professionals versus students. *Database for Advances in Information Systems, 29*(2), 20-34.

Christensen, A.L., & Eining, M.M. (1991). Factors influencing software piracy: Implications for accountants. *Journal of Information Systems, 5*(1), 67-50.

Conner, K., & Rumlet, R. (1991). Software piracy: An analysis of protection strategies. *Management Science, 37*(2), 125-139.

Cronan, T.P., & Al-Rafee, S. (2007). Factors that influence the intention to pirate software and media. *Journal of Business Ethics.*

Cronan, T.P., Leonard, L.N.K., & Kreie, J. (2005). An empirical validation of perceived importance and behavior intention in IT ethics. *Journal of Business Ethics, 56*(3), 231-238.

Douglas, D.E., Cronan, T.P., & Behel, J.D. (2006). *Equity perceptions as a deterrent to software piracy behavior* (Working Paper). Information Systems Department, University of Arkansas, Fayetteville, AR.

Dubinsky, A., & Loken, B. (1989). Analyzing ethical decision making in marketing. *Journal of Business Research, 19*(2), 83-107.

First Annual BSA and IDC Global Software Piracy Study. (2004). Retrieved August 3, 2007, from *http://www.bsa.org/globalstudy/*

Fishbein, M., & Ajzen, I. (1975). *Attitude, intention, and behavior: An introduction to theory and research.* Reading, MA: Addison-Wesley.

Flannery, B., & May, D. (2000). Environmental ethical decision making in the U.S. metal-finishing industry. *Academy of Management Journal, 43*(4), 642-662.

Glass, R., & Wood, W. (1996). Situational determinants of software piracy: An equity theory perspective. *Journal of Business Ethics, 15*(11), 1189-1198.

Gopal, R., & Sanders, L. (1997). Preventive and deterrent controls for software piracy. *Journal of Management Information Systems, 13*(4), 29-47.

Hagger, M., Chatzisarantis, N., & Biddle, S. (2002). A meta-analytic review of the theories of reasoned action and planned behavior in physical activity: Predictive validity and the contribution of additional variables. *Journal of Sport & Exercise Psychology, 24*(1), 3-32.

Harder, J.W. (1991). Equity theory versus expectancy theory: The case of major league baseball free agents. *Journal of Applied Psychology, 76*(3), 458-464.

Harrington, S.J. (1996). The effects of codes of ethics and personal denial of responsibility on computer abuse judgments and intentions. *MIS Quarterly, 20*(3), 257-278.

Hofstede, G. (2003). *Culture's consequences, comparing values, behaviors, institutions, and organizations across nations* (2nd ed.). Newbury Park, CA: Sage Publications.

Im, J., & Van Epps, P. (1991). Software piracy and software security in business schools: An ethical perspective. *The DATABASE for Advances in Information Systems, 22*(3), 15-21.

Jones, T.W. (1991). Ethical decision making by individuals in organizations: An issue-contingent model. *Academy of Management Review, 16*(2), 366-395.

Joshi, K. (1989). The measurement of fairness or equity perception of management information systems users. *MIS Quarterly, 13*(3), 343-358.

Kohlberg, L. (1969). Stages and sequence: The cognitive-developmental approach to socialization. In D. Grosling (Ed.), *Handbook of socialization theory and research*. Chicago: Rand McNally.

Lau, E. (2003). An empirical study of software piracy. *Business Ethics, 12*(3), 233-245.

Lin, C., & Ding, C.G. (2003). Moderating information ethics: The joint moderaing role of locus of control and job insecurity. *Journal of Business Ethics, 48*(4), 335-346

Leonard, L.N.K., Cronan, T.P., & Kreie, J. (2004). What influences IT ethical behavior intentions: Planned behavior, reasoned action, perceived importance, or individual characteristics? *Information and Management, 42*(1), 143-158.

Marshall, K.P. (1999). Has technology introduced new ethical problems? *Journal of Business Ethics, 19*(1), 81-90.

Mason, R.O. (1986). Four ethical issues of the information age. *MIS Quarterly, 10*(1), 4-12.

Moseley, O., & Whitis, R. (1995, December). Preventing software piracy. *Management Accounting*, pp. 42-47.

MPAA Report. (2003). Thoughts on the digital future of movies, the threat of piracy, the hope of redemption. Encino, CA: Motion Picture Association of America.

Olson, J., & Zanna, M. (1993). Attitudes and attitude change. *Annual Review of Psychology, 44*(1), 117-154.

Peace, A., Galletta, D., & Thong, J. (2003). Software piracy in the workplace: A model and empirical test. *Journal of Management Information Systems, 20*(1), 153-177.

Randall, D., & Gibson, A. (1991). Ethical decision making in the medical profession: An application of the theory of planned behavior. *Journal of Business Ethics, 10*(2), 111-122.

Reid, R., Thompson, J., & Logston, J. (1992). Knowledge and attitudes of management students toward software piracy. *Journal of Computer Information Systems, 33*(1), 46-51.

Rest, J. (1986). *Moral development: Advances in research and theory*. New York: Praeger.

Simon, H. (1960). *The new science of management decisions*. New York: Harper and Row.

Shin, S.K., Gopal, R.D., Sanders, G.L., & Whinston, A.B. (2004). Global software piracy revisited. *Communications of the ACM, 47*(1), 103-107.

Solomon, S., & O'Brien, J. (1990). The effect of demographic factors on attitudes toward software piracy. *The Journal of Computer Information Systems, 30*(3), 45-45.

Straub, D.W., & Nance, W.D. (1990). Discovering and disciplining computer abuse in organizations: A field study. *MIS Quarterly, 14*(1), 45-60.

Trafimow, D., & Finlay, K. (1996). The importance of subjective norms for a minority of people: Between-subjects and within-subjects analyses. *Personality & Social Psychology Bulletin, 22*(8), 820-829.

Trevino, L.K. (1986). Ethical decision making in organizations: A person-situation interactionist model. *Academy of Management Review, 11*(3), 601-617.

Venkatesh, V., Morris, M.G., Davis, G.B., & Davis, F.D. (2003). User acceptance of information technology: Towards a unified view. *MIS Quarterly, 27*(3), 425-478.

Walster, E., Berscheid, E., & Walster, G.W. (1973). New directions in equity research. *Journal of Personality and Social Psychology, 25*, 151-176.

Walster, E., Walster, G.W., & Berscheid, E. (1978). *Equity theory and research*. Boston: Allyn & Bacon

ENDNOTE

[1]   Revised IT Ethical Behavior Model; original model proposed in "Information Technology Ethical Behavior: Toward a Comprehensive Ethical Behavior Model," *Journal of Organizational and End User Computing, 18*(1), 2006, i-xi.

Chapter II
Understanding the Impact of Household End Users' Privacy and Risk Perceptions on Online Behavior

Judy Drennan
Queensland University of Technology, Australia

Gillian Sullivan Mort
Griffith University, Australia

Josephine Previte
The University of Queensland, Australia

ABSTRACT

This chapter reports research concerning privacy, risk perceptions, and online behavior intentions on a sample of expert household end users. Findings include identification of (1) an e-privacy typology, consisting of "privacy aware," "privacy suspicious," and "privacy active" types, and (2) an e-privacy hierarchy of effects. Results suggest the presence of a privacy hierarchy of effects where awareness leads to suspicion, which subsequently leads to active behavior. Perceived risk was found to interact with the e-privacy hierarch and to have a strong negative influence on the extent to which respondents participated in online subscription and purchasing. A key finding was that privacy active behavior which was hypothesised to increase the likelihood of online subscription and purchasing was not found to be significant. The chapter concludes with a number of important implications for managers, and directions for future research are discussed.

INTRODUCTION

Advances in online technologies have raised new concerns about privacy. Worldwide, more people are moving to the online environment with the number of Internet users growing to a population of 1093 million as of December 2006 (Nua Internet Surveys, 2003). In addition, household users of the Internet are increasing rapidly with 136.60 million Americans and 8.79 million Australians having online access at home (Greenspan, 2004). As this burgeoning number of household end users of the Internet embark on new activities online, the issue of privacy and security becomes a major concern for consumers (Milne & Rohm, 2000; Sheehan & Hoy, 2000) and governments and consumer organisations (Consumer Reports Org, 2002; Federal Trade Commission, 1996, 2000a, 2000b; Office of the Federal Privacy Commissioner, 2001a). As a result, specific calls have emerged for end user research on security and privacy to be extended to household end users (Troutt, 2002). Businesses also recognise privacy as an important positioning tool with, for example, the ISP EarthLink positioning itself on privacy in its competition against the dominant company AOL (Sweat, 2001) and myspace.com, a site for developing personal friendships, carefully delineating its privacy policy (Myspace.com, 2007). As more household end users become increasingly expert in that environment, privacy in the electronic domain (e-privacy) needs specific research attention (Perri 6, 2002). Given the growing number of competent experienced Internet users, e-privacy issues need to be reframed and investigated in the context of their online expertise.

This chapter focuses on the expert household end user, defined as highly competent experienced Internet users who consistently spend time online, are likely to have subscribed to commercial and/or government Web sites, to have purchased online, and have Internet access via a home computer. The chapter proceeds as follows. First, privacy conceptualisations and typologies are examined. Second, theoretical approaches to consumers' online privacy and risk perceptions are addressed, together with the argument that privacy issues from the perspective of the expert online household user needs to be considered. Third, the methodology is explained, and the results of the two studies undertaken are provided. Finally, findings are discussed, management implications are drawn, and future research directions are identified.

CONCEPTUALISATION OF PRIVACY AND TYPOLOGIES

The protection of privacy has received growing attention in the literature (Buchholz & Rosenthal, 2002; Charters, 2002; Cook & Coupey, 1998; Hoy & Phelps, 2003; Milne & Rohm, 2000; Miyazaki & Fernandez, 2001) in conjunction with the advances in technology and its applications to the Internet (Sappington & Silk, 2003). There are a number of conceptualisations of privacy, but fundamentally privacy has been viewed as the right to be left alone (Warren & Brandeis, 1890), manifesting in the definition that other people, groups, or entities should not intrude on an individual's seclusion or solitude (McCloskey, 1980). For many people, there is now an expectation of privacy as a basic consumer right (Goodwin, 1991). The issue becomes problematic when violations to privacy occur where consumers' control over their private information is unwittingly reduced (Culnan, 1995; Nowak & Phelps 1995; Lwin & Williams 2003). However, privacy is not enshrined in constitutional rights, nor is it grounded as essential to the operation of a democracy, as free speech is held to be essential in countries like the United States of America. Privacy is thus a weak right (Charters, 2002) which may be easily over-ridden by other legislative rights. Privacy and anonymity are also associated for many with personal freedom and liberty. Specifically, privacy is considered to exist when consumers are able to control their personal information (McCloskey, 1980) or restrict the use of their personal information (Culnan, 1995; Nowak & Phelps, 1995). A recent study in the U.S. and Italy by Dinev, Bellotto, Hart, Russo, Serra, and Colautti (2006) found that an Internet user's decision to conduct e-commerce transactions is influenced by privacy concerns, as well as their perception of the need for government surveillance to secure the Internet environment from fraud, crime, and terrorism, which is then balanced against their concerns about government intrusion. The Internet was designed on the assumption of anonymity; however, the reality has been a shift away from this original premise (Nijboer, 2004; Shah, White, & Cook, 2007).

Some futurists, for example, George Orwell (1951) in *1984*, foreshadowed the interest of the state in observing the citizen, which has achieved new significance post-9/11. The motivation of business in monitoring and maintaining surveillance of customers, considered likely to undermine anonymity, privacy, and thus perhaps freedom, and consumers' reactions to loss of privacy is receiving continued attention (e.g., Retsky, 2001). For example, research indicates that consumers experience loss of privacy as being embarrassing (Grace, 2007). Implicit in the conceptualisation of privacy as the ability of individuals to restrict information is the recognition that there may emerge a community consensus regarding which type of personal information is not for public consumption and that there are rights and duties on both sides of the exchange (Charters, 2002).

It has been accepted (Westin for Federal Trade Commission, 1996) that consumers fall into three basic types with regard to privacy in the general sense: the privacy fundamentalists who always tend to choose privacy controls over consumer benefits; the privacy unconcerned who tend to forgo most privacy claims in exchange for service benefits; and the privacy pragmatists who weigh the benefits of various consumer opportunities and services against the degree of personal information sought. Recently, the Westin typology has been tested and extended to specifically apply to

the online consumer. The study (Sheehan, 2002) found that online consumers in the U.S. are better represented by a four-part typology consisting of the unconcerned, circumspect, wary, and alarmed Internet users. This four-part typology for online consumers was established as a result of the identification of the high percentage of pragmatists (81%) compared to the Westin study (50%). Pragmatists were thus divided into circumspect and the wary group. Fundamentalists were renamed alarmed Internet users.

The unconcerned Internet users rarely complain about privacy breaches, and when registering at Web sites rarely provide inaccurate information. The next group, termed circumspect Internet users, have minimal concerns about privacy overall, although there are some situations that may cause them to have higher levels of concern about privacy. In addition, they give incomplete information quite often when registering for Web sites. The third group, wary Internet users, have a moderate level of concern with most online situations. They experience higher than average concern for Internet privacy, including clandestine data collection practices. They occasionally complain about privacy breaches and are likely to provide incomplete information when they sporadically register for Web sites. The final group, consisting of alarmed Internet users, are most likely to complain about privacy breaches, rarely register for Web sites and, when they do, they are likely to provide incomplete and inaccurate data.

Sheehan and Hoy (2000) also conducted a survey using 15 privacy scenarios. Results from this study indicate that privacy dimensions are first related to control over, and collection of, information. The further two privacy dimensions refer to privacy within a short-term transactional relationship and an established long term relationship.

The typologies of Sheehan and Hoy (2000) and Sheehan (2002) relate to early types of technology use, such as e-mail, and construct the end user in a passive role where he or she only becomes aware of privacy issues after a breach has occurred. The studies are descriptive and do not link privacy types overtly to consequent online behaviors.

THEORETICAL APPROACHES TO CONSUMERS' ONLINE PRIVACY, RISK PERCEPTION, AND THE EXPERT ONLINE CONSUMER

Several studies have attempted to measure privacy concerns; however, most studies tend to focus on informational privacy and privacy scales are usually approached with a view of privacy as a one-dimensional construct (Buchanan, Paine, Joinson, & Reips, 2007). Recently, Malhotra, Kim, and Agarwal (2004) operationalised a multidimensional model of Internet users information privacy concerns (IUIPC). Their model considers multiple aspects of informational privacy and identifies attitudes towards the collection of personal information, control over personal information, and awareness of privacy practices of companies gathering personal information as being components of a second-order construct called IUIPC. Although this model does consider multiple aspects of privacy, all of these aspects still lie within the domain of informational privacy. Buchanan et al. (2007) attempted to broaden our understanding of privacy concerns by developing three measurement instruments to capture online consumers' privacy concerns and resulting behaviors. They argue that to understand the impact of privacy, it is important to understand the behaviors that result from various positions on privacy, such as purchasing and privacy protection actions. However, their results failed to elicit clear patterns related to attitudinal variables, and further research aimed at more fine-grained understanding of Internet users' real-life privacy concerns is necessary (Paine, Reips, Stieger, Joinson, & Buchanan, 2006). Moreover, the research and typologies have not focused on the issue of expert end users' privacy concerns.

A recent literature review has also criticised privacy typologies such as Sheehan (2002) based on the conventional segmentation of fundamentalist, unconcerned, and pragmatist on a number of grounds (Perri 6, 2002). These include criticisms that the typology bears no relationship to risk in other consumption practices and has no underlying theoretical rationale to explain the privacy types. Moreover, at a practical level, the criticism has been raised that the most common type, the pragmatic type, is too vague and likely to lead to business complacency. A new way of understanding privacy risk perception has been proposed (Perri 6, 2002) based on neo-Durkheimian institutionalist theory, using the social group as the unit of analysis. Perri 6 did not undertake empirical research to test the validity of the typology, and owing to unfamiliar theoretical framework in neo-Durkheimian institutionalist theory (rather than the more usual individual psychology paradigm), it has limited practical utility for online privacy research. However, the conceptualisation appears to offer some ability to understand how consumers may move in their privacy risk perception and offers marketers some insight into how privacy communication may be framed.

Consistent with Perri 6 (2002) and others (Buchanan et al., 2007; Ho & Ng, 1994; Hoy & Phelps, 2003; Miyazaki & Fernandez, 2001), we argue that perceived risk is fundamental to understanding consumer concerns about privacy online and the relationship among privacy, risk, and online purchase intentions is central to enhancing our understanding the behavior of expert online household end users.

The issue of perceived risk in consumer purchase has been addressed by a large number of studies over the years (e.g., Mitchell, 1999). Perceived risk can be defined as an expectation of loss (e.g., Stone & Winter, 1987) or "consumer's subjective belief of suffering a loss in pursuit of a desired outcome" (Pavlou, 2003, p. 109). Viewed in this way, risk is strongly negatively correlated with intentions and behavior (Stone & Winter, 1987). Pavlou (2003) suggests that behavioral uncertainty is created as a result of Web retailers misrepresenting products, leaking private information, providing misleading advertising, using false identities, and denouncing warranties. Specifically, consumers may perceive risks in terms of monetary losses (economic risk), the purchase of unsafe products and services (personal risk), imperfect monitoring of products (seller performance risk), and disclosure of private information (privacy risks). Environmental uncertainty is also an important issue leading consumers to fear theft of personal information online. Consumer intentions to transact business online are thus "contingent upon beliefs about Web retailers that are partly determined by behavioral and environmental factors", and therefore perceived risk is likely to negatively influence consumer's intentions to undertake transactions on Internet sites (Pavlou, 2003).

Risk has been studied in a number of contexts such as food technology (Frewer, 1994), banking (Ho & Ng, 1994), and retail patronage mode, for example, mail order, catalogue, and in-home shopping (Festerand, Snyder, & Tsalikis, 1986; Schiffman, Schus, & Winer, 1976). Different types of perceived risk have been identified, including functional, physical, financial, social, and psychological risk (Kaplan, Szybillo, & Jacoby, 1974). Saythe (1999) studied the risk referred to as "the security and reliability of transactions over the Internet", a type of physical risk, and found that this type of risk was a significant barrier to diffusion of Internet banking. Bhatnagar, Misra, and Rao (2000) examined financial and product risk in purchasing on the Web where financial risk is related to the possibility of credit card fraud. Product risk was not as important as financial risk in predicting likelihood of online purchase. Recently, Slyke, Shim, Johnson, and Jiang (2006) also found that concern for information privacy affects risk perceptions, trust, and willingness to transact for a well-known merchant, but not

for a less well-known merchant, suggesting that risk perception may be different depending on the company and the users experience in dealing with that company.

Perceived risk generally produces wariness or risk aversion and leads to a variety of risk handling behaviors which include buying well known, major brands, brand loyal behavior, seeking information, wider search, increased use of use of word of mouth information sources, a preference for congruent rather than incongruent products in a product category, or avoiding purchase altogether (Campbell & Goodstein, 2001; Dowling & Staelin, 1994; Roselius, 1971). Concerns about privacy were not found to affect online purchasing rates directly, neither was concern about online retailer fraud, such as nondelivery of goods or misrepresentation of goods (Miyazaki & Fernandez, 2001). Only the general perceived risk of online purchase and what was termed in the study "system security issues", such as unauthorised access to personal and credit card information, were found to directly affect rates of online purchase.

Empirical research examining privacy concerns and experienced online consumers is beginning to emerge. For example, Graeff and Harmon (2002) undertook a study of U.S. consumers and asked about their privacy concerns, use, and familiarity with loyalty cards and online purchase behavior. Those with online purchase experience were significantly more likely than nonpurchasers to consider that customers should be informed and have a say in such information gathering and selling practices. In addition, Koyuncu and Lien (2002) found that those with more online experience in a private and secure home environment were more likely to purchase on the Internet. This was also supported by Bellman, Johnson, Kobrin, and Lohse (2004) who found that privacy concerns diminished with increased online experience in a sample of Internet users from 38 countries. Research by Milne, Rohm, and Bahl (2004) suggests that the reason for this is that experienced online consumers tend to be more aware of privacy issues and therefore are more likely to take precautions in their online transactions (such as using anonymity techniques, encryption software, etc.), thereby decreasing their own concern, implying that this group of consumers may exhibit different behaviors than novice users (Armstrong & Forde, 2003; Bellman et al., 2004).

While there has been some attention to the experienced online consumer and privacy concerns, no research to date has empirically developed a typology of experienced "expert" household end users and sought to relate these typologies to online behavior. "Expert" end users are of particular interest because they are becoming the dominant group online. We are rapidly exiting the era when most online household end users were novices with low levels of knowledge and experience in the online environment. More often, a purposeful motivation has replaced random surfing of the Internet (Rodgers & Sheldon, 2002; Zhang et al., 2007). Experts are an important population sample to answer questions about consumer privacy protection strategies online because they are better able to distinguish between relevant and irrelevant information and have more differentiated and organised knowledge (Larkin, McDermott, Simon, & Simon, 1980).

This research addresses the need to develop an e-privacy typology of expert household end users and relate these privacy types to online behavior. Perceived risk is used as a central theoretical foundation. Informed by typologies developed in earlier research (Sheehan, 2002; Sheehan & Hoy, 2000; Perry 6, 2002), we integrate government privacy guidelines(www.dcita.gov.au) for end users to ascertain the dimensions of privacy concerns. The next section presents the method undertaken for two studies: Study 1 empirically derives a typology of e-privacy dimensions for expert household end users; Study 2 tests the causal relationships among these derived e-privacy dimensions, perceived risk, and online subscription and purchasing behavior.

Methodology

The Sample

A sample of 76 expert household end users was recruited for the present study by surveying an Internet marketing class of university, e-commerce students who all had access to the Internet via their home computers. There was a 91% response rate to the survey. 63% of respondents were male and 37% were female. 94% were in the age range 18-25 years while 6% were over 25 years. A convenience sample of college students was considered appropriate for the current study because demographically they share characteristics of the stereotypical user—young, university/college-educated males. Importantly, representation of women in the sample corresponds to the changing gender trend in user statistics over time that indicates a growing population of educated women online (Rainie & Kohut, 2000). It is argued therefore that university or college students are representative of a dominant cohort of online users for the following reasons: the tertiary student group is the most connected segment of the population in the United States with 93% of American college students regularly using the Internet (Nua Internet Surveys, 2002) and a similar trend is evident in the Australian population (Australian Bureau of Statistics, 2004). In addition, their visits to online shopping sites is growing dramatically (Nua Internet Surveys, 2002). Though no specific data were available for Australia, it has further been predicted that U.S. and European teenagers are likely to spend USD$10.6 billion online by 2005 (Nua Internet Surveys, 2002). Thus, a sample drawn from university students is appropriate as it is drawn from an active and rapidly growing segment of experienced and frequent users of the Internet.

Additionally, this sample was considered to be illustrative of expert household end users as it is descriptive of experiential behavior of Internet users based on the following criteria;

first, survey respondents were second year e-commerce students who had completed courses in introductory e-commerce business studies and Web-based design and development subjects. Therefore, they meet the criteria of competence and experience. Second, as e-commerce students, they are required by their studies to spend extensive time online (approximately 20 hours per week). They thus meet the criterion of consistent time spent online. Third, expert consumers are also more likely to have subscribed to a Web site and purchased online. Approximately 54% of the sample population had purchased goods or services over the Internet. This is well above the population average for online purchasing, where only 10% had done so (Australian Bureau of Statistics, 2001). In addition, 80% of the sample had subscribed to commercial or government Web sites by exchanging personal information for free services. Thus, the sample meets the criterion of having experience in subscribing to a Web page and purchasing online.

Collecting and interpreting data about Internet use is not straightforward because of inadequacies in sampling frame. A number of factors compromise random sampling statistical measures in Internet research such as users holding multiple e-mail accounts and maintaining different identifies to log into different commercial and noncommercial Web sites. Therefore, while numerous Internet directories are available online, their reliability is questionable compared to sampling frames such as the commercially controlled and updated telephone listings by telecommunication companies. Consequently, the Internet population typifies characteristics of a "hidden population" (Heckathorn, 1997). The defining characteristics of a "hidden population" are that no sample frame exists, as the size and boundaries of the population are unknown. Other researchers have identified similar problems in conducting Internet research (Aladwani, 2002; Wyatt, Thomas, & Terranova, 2002) and consider the appropriateness of university/college students a useful representative

sample of Internet and computer users (see Wierschem & Brodnax, 2003). Nevertheless, a convenience sample reduces the generalisability of the findings to the larger Internet population. However, this sample was considered adequate and useful for the current research to address "expert" Internet users' privacy concerns. Furthermore, it is argued that the "expert" online user will continue as the dominant Internet cohort in light of emergent research that indicates that less educated, younger Internet users are "logging off" (Katz & Rice, 2002). Arguably, education is a significant demographic indicator in continued Internet usage—combined with other access factors (income, etc.). Finally, when it is borne in mind that response rate to sample surveys are often low and declining, the research differences between random and convenience samples in terms of their representativeness is not always as great as some researchers wish to imply (Bryman & Cramer, 2001).

SURVEY MEASURES

Expert users were surveyed using a self-administered instrument including a participant's information sheet and instructions for participants. The survey instrument was developed from three main sources. First, questions relating to e-privacy issues were derived from the Australian Federal Government privacy fact sheet concerning consumers' shopping on the Internet (Department of Communications Information Technology and the Arts, 2002). This fact sheet was developed as a result of extensive research by the Australian Federal Government and reflects international best practice procedures for online consumer privacy. As such it identifies key privacy protection indicators applicable to household online users when interacting and purchasing on the Internet. These privacy protection indicators were particularly considered appropriate for use in this study, as they encompass both attitudes and behaviors towards online privacy protection.

Second, a three-item perceived risk scale (Jarvenpaa & Tractinsky, 1999) was modified to reflect risk relating to online purchasing and subscription. Specifically, two items (the first pertaining to safety of using a credit card to purchase online and the second to risk online compared to other ways of purchasing) were slightly modified to reflect online purchasing risk. A new item pertaining to perceptions of risk in revealing personal details online if requested was included to tap concerns relating to Web site subscription. While the original scale had a Cronbach's alpha of 0.65, the modified scale had a Cronbach's alpha of 0.58, which was a little low (Nunnally, 1989) but was accepted as satisfactory for the purposes of this exploratory research. Third, two questions were developed to ascertain whether respondents had purchased online or disclosed personal information to subscribe to a Web site. These items were aggregated into a single item termed "online subscription and purchasing" further discussed below. The preliminary instrument was pilot tested and reviewed for clarity by postgraduate students and the chapter's authors and accepted without further revision.

The survey instructions informed participants that the aim of the research was to assess awareness of online privacy issues regarding requested personal information when subscribing to Web sites or purchasing over the Internet and their perception of any risks involved in sharing information online. All privacy and risk items were measured using five-point Likert scales, and questions relating to online subscription and purchase behavior were dichotomous.

A construct, representing online subscription and purchasing transactions that involve disclosure of personal information, was developed. Online subscription is a form of consumer transaction that can be described as a "secondary exchange" where there is a nonmonetary exchange of personal information for perceived value from the online organisation in terms of quality service, prize incentives, or relationship building (Culnan

& Bies, 2003). Online purchasing, on the other hand, is the "first exchange" whereby money or other goods is given in exchange for goods or services (Culnan & Bies, 2003). Nonetheless, in the online environment, personal information must also be disclosed in the "first exchange." Two dichotomous variables: *online subscriptions* and *online purchasing*, which provided data relating to whether respondents actually subscribed and purchased online were combined to form a construct with ordinal properties representing "no online subscriptions or purchases," "online subscriptions only," "online purchases only," and "online subscriptions and purchases."

STUDY RESULTS

Study 1: Dimensionality of E-Privacy

Privacy dimensions were developed by submitting 12 privacy items to a principal components procedure with a varimax rotation. This analysis yielded three orthogonal factors with eigenvalues greater than 1.0, explaining 52.21% of the variance within these data. Factor loadings of less than 0.3 were omitted from the privacy factors illustrated in Table 1. The final analysis therefore included 11 items, as one did not load above 0.3 on any of the factors.

The grouping of statements provided insights into the interpretation of the three privacy factors. As shown in Table 1, four items loaded on factor 1, which explains 21.3% of total variance. Factor I, labeled *privacy aware*, is reflective of consumer knowledge and sensitivity regarding the risks of sharing selected personal information online. It consists of four items: selective about information provision, awareness of sensitivity of tax file number, and awareness of sensitivity of mother's maiden name and perception, companies require excessive personal information. The *privacy aware* factor is illustrative of users who guard information, such as their mother's maiden name, and are selective about the information they provide during online exchanges because they are aware of the risks involved. Significantly, these users feel companies in the current marketplace require excessive or unnecessary information to complete an online exchange.

Factor II, labeled *privacy active*, illustrates active behaviors users undertake relating to privacy. This factor explains 16.4% of the variance within the sample (Table 1). Four items load onto this factor, specifically: seeking detailed information

about privacy policies, demanding detailed information before purchasing online, requesting that firms do not share personal details provided by the consumer, and regularly changing passwords to guard their privacy. Those users who take action to guard their privacy are more likely to perceive reduced risk. If the benefits of disclosing information outweigh the risks, it is likely that they will divulge the personal information required for online subscription or purchasing transactions (Culnan & Bies, 2003). However, as

Table 1. Dimensionality of e-privacy factors

Privacy Statements	Mean*	S.D.	Privacy Factors		
			Factor Loadings I	II	III
Privacy Aware					
Selective about providing information requested for transactions	3.54	1.10	**.786**		.303
Aware of sensitivity of tax file number	3.39	1.61	**.743**		
Aware of sensitivity of mother's maiden name	2.38	1.62	**.713**		
Feel online companies require excessive personal inform	3.34	1.15	**-.538**		
Privacy Active					
Ask for detailed privacy policy information before purchasing online	2.41	1.44		**.740**	
Look for privacy policies	2.04	1.26		**.646**	.419
Request firms do not share personal information & details with other organisations	2.91	1.51		**.578**	
Do not regularly use the same password	3.03	1.18		**.425**	
Privacy Suspicious					
Aware companies plan to share consumers personal information with other companies	3.64	1.20		-.339	**.693**
Believe companies privacy policies are difficult to find	3.00	.99	-.415		**.673**
Before transacting with businesses online, they check to ensure e-mail and phone numbers are provided	3.40	1.52			**.570**
Eigenvalues % Variance–Factor % Variance–Cumulative			21.332 21.332	16.421 37.7543	14.457 52.210

*All item means display prodimension agreement. Factor loadings of less than .3 have been omitted, and those judged to constitute a factor (the dominant loadings) are in bold.

Graeff and Harmon (2002) found, experienced online purchasers demand to be informed and/or have a say in the sharing between organisations of their personal information.

Factor III, labeled *privacy suspicious*, highlights consumer concerns about company behavior and explains 14.45% of the total variance (Table 1). For example, these online household end users are concerned about how companies use personal information and potentially divulge users' details. Three items load onto this factor: awareness of companies' plans to share personal information, belief that company privacy policies are hard to find, and checking to ensure e-mail and online phone numbers are provided before transacting with a company. The *privacy suspicious* construct highlights the point that users' privacy concerns also extend to suspicions that commercial organisations may fail to guard consumer data and privacy. Previous privacy research (Sheehan & Hoy, 2000) found that users' concerns about privacy increased because of company management behavior such as disclosing a consumer's personal information without permission. In contrast, users' beliefs that firms use fair information practices will ease privacy concerns (Culnan & Bies, 2003) and should reduce perceived risk.

Study 2: Relationship Between E-Privacy Dimensions, Perceived Risk, and Online Subscription and Purchasing Behavior

Development of Hypotheses

Figure 1 illustrates a number of inferred causal relationships between the expert end user privacy dimensions empirically derived in Study 1, perceived risk, and online subscription and purchasing behaviors. These were tested in the second stage of this exploratory research using a probabilistic approach to causation. De Vaus (2001) defines probabilistic approaches to causation as the argument that a given factor increases

(or decreases) the probability of a particular outcome. We now develop the hypotheses that drive Study 2 and discuss the relationship between privacy concerns, risk, and outcome behavior in terms of the e-privacy dimensions of privacy awareness, privacy suspicion, and privacy active derived in Study 1. We present two lines of argument. In the first, we adopt a "hierarchy of effects" model of expert household end users' privacy concerns, relating awareness to suspicious to active. The hierarchy of effects is a well recognised marketing model (Lavidge & Steiner, 1961) which proposes that consumers move through subsequent stages of awareness (think), affection (feel), and conation (do). Moreover, this model has been specifically used in Internet related research (Huizingh & Hoekstra, 2003) to describe attitudinal changes of online consumers leading to behavioral changes after visiting a Web site. In the second line of argument, the relationships between the stages in the privacy hierarchy and perceived risk are proposed. We then propose a relationship between the end stage of the privacy hierarchy, privacy active, and online subscription and purchasing intentions. We conclude with a proposed relationship between perceived risk and online subscription and purchasing behavior. The proposed relationships are shown in Figure 1.

Privacy awareness and the extent of knowledge about privacy issues have been raised by a number of researchers (e.g., Graeff & Harmon, 2002). However, there has been little research to examine the impact of this awareness on subsequent privacy attitudes and protective behaviors. Dhillon and Moore's (2001) research suggest that as consumers become more aware of privacy issues, they question how firms use the information that is collected about them. These authors suggest that the provision by consumers of such information should be made discretionary. This questioning and apparent suspicion aroused in consumers leads us to hypothesise that higher levels of privacy awareness are positively related to increased levels of privacy suspicion (Hypothesis 1a).

Figure 1. A model depicting the relationships among privacy dimension, perceived risk, and online subscription and purchasing

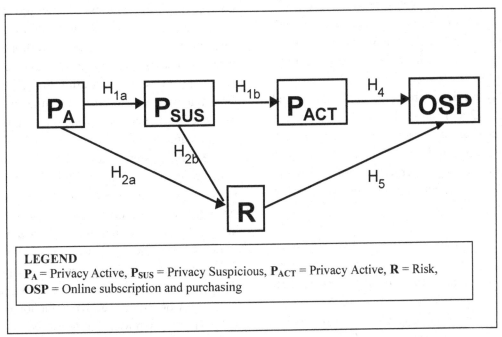

In proposing the next stage of the privacy hierarchy, a relationship between privacy suspicious attitudes and privacy active behaviors, we adopt a hierarchy of effects argument. We argue that privacy suspicion of company online behavior may lead to proactive behavior by expert household end users to protect their privacy and that higher levels of privacy suspicion lead to privacy active behavior (Hypothesis 1b). Moreover, consistent with our hierarchy of effects approach, whereby awareness leads to affect before action, we propose that there will be no direct link between privacy awareness and privacy active behavior. This leads to Hypothesis 1c that privacy awareness does not directly affect privacy active behavior.

We now consider the relationships between the stages of the privacy hierarchy and perceived risk. Research by Nowak and Phelps (1995) suggests that privacy awareness leads to a greater perception of threat to consumer privacy. We thus hypothesise higher levels of end user privacy awareness lead to heightened perceived risk (Hypothesis 2a).

Culnan and Bies (2003) argue that consumers will perceive disclosure of personal information to be low risk if they believe the company to be open and honest about their information practices. Conversely, it can be argued that if end users are suspicious of a company's honesty, their perceived risk is likely to be heightened. Therefore, we hypothesise that the extent of end user suspicion of a company will be positively related to perceived risk (Hypothesis 2b).

We have argued that a hierarchy of effects exists for privacy and that privacy awareness leads to privacy suspicion, which subsequently leads to privacy active behavior. It is further argued that privacy active behavior by expert end users is also influenced by perception of risk. Thus, a relationship between higher levels of perceived risk and privacy active behavior is proposed (Hypothesis 3).

Returning to the end stage of the privacy hierarchy, we suggest that privacy active behavior influences online subscription and purchasing.

We argue that expert household end users who take action to protect their privacy are then more likely to subscribe to Web sites and make online purchases. This leads us to hypothesise that high levels of privacy active behavior are positively related to online purchase and subscription (Hypothesis 4).

Finally, relying on research by Miyazaki and Fernandez (2001) and Pavlou (2003), which suggests that risk perceptions of Internet privacy relate to online purchasing behavior, we propose that higher levels of perceived risk negatively influence online subscription and purchasing (Hypothesis 5).

H1a: The extent of end users' awareness of threats to privacy in the online environment will be positively related to their privacy suspicious attitudes.

H1b: The extent of end users' privacy suspicious attitudes will be positively related to their online privacy active behavior.

H1c: No direct relationship will be found between privacy awareness and online privacy active behavior.

H2a: The extent of end users' awareness of threats to privacy in the online environment will be positively related to perceived risk.

H2b: The extent of end users' suspicious attitudes towards company online behavior will be positively related to perceived risk.

H3:   The extent of end users' perceived risk will be positively related to active online privacy protection behavior.

H4:   The extent of end users' active online privacy protection behavior will be positively related to online subscription and purchasing behavior.

H5:   The extent of end users' perceived risk will be negatively related to online subscription and purchasing behavior.

Regression Analyses

To test these hypotheses, simple and multiple regression analyses were employed to examine relationships among the privacy awareness, privacy suspicious, privacy active, and perceived risk constructs. Multinomial logistic regression analyses were used to examine the effect of these constructs on online subscription and purchasing.

Results of simple and multiple regression analyses are reported in Table 2. Simple regression was used to examine the influence of *privacy awareness* on *privacy suspicious* (H1a) and findings show that 16% of *privacy suspicious* is explained by *privacy awareness* (Beta = .417, p < 01). Thus Hypothesis 1a is supported. The influence of *privacy awareness* and *privacy suspicious* on privacy active behavior was also tested (H1b) and showed that 24% of *privacy active* behavior is explained with only *privacy suspicious* as statistically significant (Beta = .353, p < 01). Thus, Hypothesis 1b is supported and there is also support for the hierarchy of privacy effects model as there is no direct relationship between *privacy aware* and *privacy active* (H1c).

In the next step, multiple regression analysis was undertaken to test the influence of *privacy awareness* and *privacy suspicious* on *perceived risk* (H2a and H2b), and results show that 29% of variance is explained. However, only *privacy suspicious* (Beta = .535, p < 01) is statistically significant, thus only Hypothesis 2b is supported.

To test whether *privacy active* behavior was influenced by *perceived risk* (H3), simple regression was used, and results show that a positive relationship exists with 27% of *privacy active* behavior being explained by perceived risk (Beta = .353, p < 01), thus Hypothesis 3 is supported.

Multinomial logistic regression was then used to examine whether *privacy active* behavior was positively related to *online subscription and purchasing* (H4) and *perceived risk* was negatively related to *online subscription and*

Table 2. Results of regression analysis of e-privacy dimensions influencing perceived risk and privacy active behavior

(a) Effect of privacy awareness on privacy suspiciousness

			Sig .000
Adj R Square = .162	F= 14.549		
Variable	β	t	
Privacy Aware (H1a)	.417	3.814	.000

(b) Effect of privacy awareness and privacy suspiciousness on privacy active behavior

			Sig .000
Adj R Square = .217	F= 10.406**		
Variable	β	t	
Privacy Suspicious (H1b)	.353	3.001	.004
Privacy Aware (H1c)	.225	1.912	.060

(c) Effect of privacy awareness and privacy suspiciousness on perceived risk

			Sig .000
Adj R Square = .286	F= 15.039		
Variable	β	t	
Privacy Aware (H2a)	.041	.369	.713
Privacy Suspicious (H2b)	.535	4.819	.000

(d) Effect of perceived risk on privacy active behavior

			Sig .000
Adj R Square = .264	F= 27.148		
Variable	β	t	
Perceived risk (H3)	.523	5.210	.000

Table 3. Results of multinomial logistic regression of perceived risk and privacy active behavior on user subscription and consumer purchasing behavior online

(a) Effect of perceived risk and privacy active behavior on online subscription and purchasing behavior

Variables	-2 Log Likelihood	Chi Square	Sig
Intercept	135.780	16.308	.001
Privacy Active (H4)	122.114	2.642	.450
Perceived Risk (H5)	150.515	31.043	.000

(b) Effect of perceived risk, privacy active behavior, privacy suspiciousness, and privacy awareness on online subscription and purchasing behavior

Variables	-2 Log Likelihood	Chi Square	Sig
Intercept	135.917	14.593*	.002
Perceived Risk	145.856	24.532**	.000
Privacy Active	123.510	2.186	.535
Privacy Suspicious	123.941	2.618	.454
Privacy Aware	122.090	.767	.857

purchasing (H5). Results (Table 3) show that only the negative influence of *perceived risk* is statistically significant. To establish that there were no influences on *online subscription and purchasing* from *privacy awareness* and *privacy suspicious*, multinomial logistic regression was also undertaken that included all four constructs. Only *perceived risk* was found to be a significant influence. Table 4 provides a summary of the results of the hypotheses.

Discussion

This study provides new understanding of the typologies of e-privacy in the context of expert online household end users. Specifically, results indicated that different online privacy types exist: privacy aware, privacy suspicious, and privacy active. Importantly, the presence of a privacy hierarchy of effects has been identified where awareness leads to suspicion, which subsequently leads to active behavior. While Buchanan et al. (2007) have recently developed a psychometrically

valid scale of online privacy, we have contributed beyond the initial stages of conceptualisation in this domain to defining types and a suggested sequential relationship between these types. This development has implication for businesses that can use these findings to enhance satisfaction with their privacy policies through the hierarchy of effects model.

Next, we address the relationships within the hierarchy and the impacts on online behavior. The extent of end users' awareness of threats to privacy in the online environment was found to be positively related to their privacy suspicious attitudes, successfully establishing the initial relationship in the privacy hierarchy. Suspicion lessens the extent to which end users will be naïve to the dangers of online privacy infringements and likely increases appreciation of those Web sites that provide the credible assurances that they seek. Consequently, businesses themselves need to be aware of consumer privacy expectations and openly provide this information online. As the explanatory power of privacy awareness on

Table 4. Summary of results of hypotheses

H1a:	*The extent of end users' awareness of threats to privacy in the online environment will be positively related to their privacy suspicious attitudes.*	**Supported**
H1b:	*The extent of end users' privacy suspicious attitudes will be positively related to their online privacy active behavior.*	**Supported**
H1c:	*No direct relationship will be found between privacy awareness and online privacy active behavior.*	**Supported**
H2a:	*The extent of end users' awareness of threats to privacy in the online environment will be positively related to perceived risk.*	**Not Supported**
H2b:	*The extent of end users' suspicious attitudes towards company online behavior will be positively related to perceived risk.*	**Supported**
H3:	*The extent of end users' perceived risk will be positively related to active online privacy protection behavior.*	**Supported**
H4:	*The extent of end users' active online privacy protection behavior will be positively related to online subscription and purchasing behavior.*	**Not supported**
H5:	*The extent of end users' perceived risk will be negatively related to online subscription and purchasing behavior.*	**Supported**

suspicion is relatively low, however, other factors, such as personal attributes (Dowling & Staelin, 1994) and specific experiences may also need also to be considered in future research as additional triggers of perceived risk.

The extent of end users' privacy suspicious attitudes was positively related to their online privacy active behavior and suggests that a cognitive appraisal such as suspicion that often leads to fear-based emotions can have positive outcomes in terms of self protective behaviors online. End users may also have experienced the negative emotion of embarrassment, consistent with Grace's (2007) recent research. No direct relationship will be found between privacy awareness and online privacy active behavior consistent with the privacy hierarchy of effects.

A notable finding was that privacy active behavior which was hypothesised to increase the likelihood of online subscription and purchasing was not found to be significant. Similar findings were recently reported by Sykes et al. (2006) who found that consumer concern for information privacy did not directly affect willingness to transact online. It is also consistent with Donmeyer and Gross (2003) who found that those who took action to protect their privacy were also less likely to subscribe and purchase online. It seems that expert household end users feel that any privacy active behaviors that they undertake may be necessary but not sufficient to lead them to be more likely to engage in online subscription and purchasing. This is a possible explanation for the previous finding of Miyazaki and Fernandez's (2001) research on consumers.

Consistent with Sykes (2006) we identified the key role of perceived risk in online privacy and online behavior. In our study, perceived risk was heightened by privacy suspicion but no direct effect was identified between privacy awareness and risk. This finding indicates that there may be some threshold level that must be achieved in the privacy hierarchy of effects before risk is perceived. Perceived risk was itself found to

increase levels of privacy active behavior and decrease online subscription and purchasing behavior. Thus, it appears that it is not sufficient to consider privacy concerns alone but rather the inter-relationship between privacy concerns and perceived risk if we are to understand the drivers of online subscription and purchasing for the expert online household end user.

The results of this study show that the task of building online confidence in terms of privacy issues is a complex one. The results indicating that action by users to protect privacy do not positively impact on online and purchase behavior suggests that expert online household end users may feel that, at this stage, the options available to protect their privacy are not sufficient. This implies that companies may need to provide more effective privacy protective options to all online users. It is also possible that governments may need to legislate more effectively in this area and make available legal recourse to assist and protect end users.

This research has advanced our understanding of e-privacy by putting forward a new typology of expert online household end users' privacy concerns. The existing typologies (Sheehan, 2002; Sheehan & Hoy, 2000; Perry 6, 2002) are more appropriate to the earlier types of technology, such as e-mail, while our typology is relevant to more sophisticated uses, such as e-commerce. Moreover, the existing typologies construct the end user in a passive role where they only become aware of privacy issues after a breach has occurred, for example, when they receive e-mail from an unknown company. Our research acknowledges and incorporates a heightened sensitivity to privacy on the part of the end user resulting from expertise in the online environment. The previous studies are also largely descriptive and, unlike our study, do not conceptualise privacy in a hierarchy of effects, nor do they link privacy concerns specifically to online behaviors.

Management Implications and Future Research

Managers must increased their understanding of privacy issues and improve their response to consumer privacy concerns. The telephone, television, and now the Internet are just some of the technologies available to managers who are newly responsible for privacy related policies and initiatives. Internet technologies are, of course, especially important for managers because they transform the way in which goods and services are bought and sold and provide new opportunities for developing and maintaining longer term relationships with household end users. However, it these relationships are to be sustained, household end users need to be reassured that organisational collection and use of personal data will not involve invasions of privacy.

As suggested by the results in the present study, expert household end users may be concerned about how personal information is collected, shared, and used by companies in today's marketplace. The important question for managers in the future is how to respond to these issues. Currently, management reactions to privacy concerns include a range of activities such as adding privacy policies to Web sites, use of encryption methods, and security protocols to guard against misuse of sensitive and private information. Findings from this study suggest that managers need to consider whether technical security solutions are the answer to resolving consumer concerns about privacy online. As Katz and Rice (2002) states, a number of encryption methods are flawed and anonymous remailer and other anonymity-guaranteeing services have been compromised by browser software. It appears that expert users may have become aware of such weaknesses in current technical approaches to Internet security. Sykes et al.'s (2006) research is also supportive of more targeted initiatives in privacy protection development by firms.

Expert household end users may respond to the provisions of detailed information and clarification about the steps a company will take to guard their personal information. For example, if companies wish to develop a long-term relationship with expert end users, they may need to provide, for example, details during a transaction of how the information is to be used and then discarded after each individual transaction. Research is needed to investigate expert household end users' information requirements and their desired level of control over their personal information. It seems certain that the standard minimal privacy policy notices attached to Web sites will necessarily be superseded by much more targeted and sophisticated documents. Ultimately, improved privacy protection strategies and procedures are likely to enhance a company's competitive position because it will be able to retain customers who perceive lower levels of risk and are willing to enter longer term partnerships.

While this exploratory research has gone some way towards elucidating the dimensionality of privacy concerns of expert household end users and understanding the relationships among privacy concerns, perceived risk, and online subscription and purchasing, a more comprehensive study needs to be undertaken to confirm these findings. In addition, research is required to test the cross-national validity of the model. As highlighted above, research is also needed to understand expert household end users' information requirements and their desired level of control over the information provided during e-commerce and other transactions. Finally, the research agenda in this field would also benefit from a study on the perceived locus of risk and whether it is at the level of the vendor company, the product, or in the transaction medium itself. More specific information such as this will allow management to direct its risk minimisation strategies to the correct target and have greater impact for the expert end user.

REFERENCES

Aladwani, A.M. (2002). Organisational actions, computer attitudes, and end-user satisfaction in public organisations: An empirical study. *Journal of End User Computing, 14*(1), 42-50.

Armstrong, H.L., & Forde, P.J. (2003). Internet anonymity practices in computer crime. *Information Management & Computer Security, 11*(5), 209-215.

Australian Bureau of Statistics. (2001). *Use of the Internet by householder: Australia* (Catalogue: 8147.0). Canberra, Australia: Government Printing Office.

Australian Bureau of Statistics. (2004). *Measures of a knowledge-based economy and society: Australia information and communications technology indicators.* Retrieved August 4, 2007, from http://www. abs.gov.au

Bellman, S., Johnson, E., Kobrin, S., & Lohse, G. (2004). International differences in information privacy concerns: A global survey of consumers. *Information Society, 20*(5), 313-324.

Bhatnagar, A., Misra, S., & Rao, H.R. (2000). On risk, convenience and Internet shopping behaviour. *Communications of the ACM, 43*, 98-105.

Bryman, A., & Cramer, D. (2001). *Quantitative data analysis with SPSS Release 10 for Windows: A guide for social scientists.* London: Routledge.

Buchanan, T., Paine, C., Joinson, A.N., & Reips, U. (2007). Development of measures of online privacy concern and protection for use on the Internet. *Journal of the American Society for Information Science and Technology, 58*(2), 157-165.

Buchholz, R.A., & Rosenthal, S.B. (2002). Internet privacy: Individual rights and the common good. *SAM Advanced Manangement Journal, 67*(1), 34-41.

Campbell, M.C., & Goodstein, R.C. (2001). The moderating effect of perceived risk on consumers' evaluations of product incongruity: Preference for the norm. *Journal of Consumer Research, 28*(3), 439-450.

Charters, D. (2002). Electronic monitoring and privacy issues in business-marketing: The ethics of the double click experience. *Journal of Business Ethics, 35*(4), 243-255.

Consumer Reports Organization. (2002). Big browser is watching you. Retrieved August 4, 2007, from http://www.consumerreports/org/main/detailv2.jsp?CONTENT%3C%Ecnt_id=1 8207&FOLDER%3C%3Efolder_id=18151&bm UID=1057810848320

Cook, D.L., & Coupey, E. (1998, March). Consumer behavior and unresolved regulatory issues in electronic marketing. *Journal of Business Research, 41*(3), 231-238.

Culnan, M.J. (1995). Consumer awareness of name removal procedures: Implications for direct marketing. *Journal of Direct Marketing, 9*(2), 10-20.

Culnan, M.J., & Bies, R. (2003). Consumer privacy: Balancing economic and justice considerations. *Journal of Social Issues, 59*(2), 323-342.

De Vaus, D. (2001). *Research design in social research.* London: Sage Publications.

Department of Communications Information Technology and the Arts. (2002). Consumer privacy fact sheet. Retrieved August 4, 2007, from http://www.dcita.gov.au

Dinev, T., Bellotto, M., Hart, P., Russo, V., Serra, I., & Colautti, C. (2006). Internet users' privacy concerns and beliefs about government surveillance: An exploratory study of differences between Italy and the United States. *Journal of Global Information Management, 14*(4), 57-93.

Dowling, G.R., & Staelin, R. (1994). A model of perceived risk and intended risk handling activity. *Journal of Consumer Research, 21*(1), 119-154.

Federal Trade Commission. (1996). *Consumer information privacy hearings.* Retrieved August 4, 2007, from http://www.ftc.gov

Federal Trade Commission. (2000a). *FTC sues failed Website, Toysmart.com, for deceptively offering for sale personal information of Website visitors.* Retrieved August 4, 2007, from http://ftc.gov/opa/2000/07/toysmart.htm

Federal Trade Commission. (2000b, July 21). *FTC announces settlement with bankrupt Website, Toysmart.Com, regarding alleged privacy violations.* Retrieved August 4, 2007, from http://www.ftc.gov/opa/2000/07/toysmart2.htm

Festerand, T.A., Snyder, D.R., & Tsalikis, J.D. (1986). Influence of catalog versus store shopping and prior satisfaction on percieved risk. *Journal of the Academy of Marketing Science, 14*(4), 28-36.

Frewer, L., Shepherd, R., & Sparks, P. (1994). The interrelationship between perceived knowledge, control and risk associated with a range of food related hazards targeted at the self, other people and society. *Journal of Food Safety, 14,* 19-40.

Goodwin, C. (1991). Privacy: Recognition of a consumer right. *Journal of Public Policy and Marketing, 10*(1), 149-167.

Grace, D. (2007). How embarrassing! An exploratory study of critical incidents including affective reactions. *Journal of Service Research, 9*(3), 271-284.

Graeff, T., & Harmon, S. (2002). Collecting and using personal data: Consumers' awareness and concerns. *Journal of Consumer Marketing, 19*(4), 302-318.

Greenspan, R. (2004). Three-quarters of Americans have access from home (Click Z News

Formerly Internet Advertising Report). Retrieved August 4, 2007, from http://www.clickz.com/news/article.php/3328091

Ho, S.S.M., & Ng, V. (1994). A study of consumers risk perception of electronic payment systems. *International Journal of Bank Marketing, 12*(4), 26-38.

Hoy, M.G., & Phelps, J. (2003). Consumer privacy and security protection on church Web sites: Reasons for concern. *Journal of Public Policy & Marketing, 22*(1), 58-70.

Huizingh, E.K.R.E., & Hoekstra, J.C. (2003). Why do consumers like Websites? *Journal of Targeting, Measurement and Analysis for Marketing, 11*(4), 350.

Internet World Stats. (2007). Internet growth statistics. Retrieved August 4, 2007, from http://www.Internetworldstats.com/emarketing.htm

Jarvenpaa, S., & Tractinsky, N. (1999). Consumer trust in an Internet store: A cross-cultural validation. *JCMC, 5*(2).

Kaplan, L., Szybillo, G.J., & Jacoby, J. (1974). Components of perceived risk in product purchase: A cross validation. *Journal of Applied Psychology, 59,* 287-291.

Katz, J.E., & Rice, R.E. (2002). *Social consequences of Internet use: Access, involvement, and interaction.* Cambridge, MA: MIT Press.

Larkin, J., McDermott, J., Simon, D.P., & Simon, H.A. (1980). Models of competence in solving physics problems. *Cognitive Science, 208,* 317-345.

Lavidge, R.J., & Steiner, G.A. (1961). A model for predictive measurements of advertising effectiveness. *Journal of Marketing, 25,* 59-62.

Lwin, M.O., & Williams, J.D. (2003). Model integrating the multidimensional developmental theory of privacy and theory of planned behaviour to examine fabrication of information online. *Marketing Letters, 14*(4), 257-272.

Malhotra, N.K., Kim, S.S., & Agarwal, J. (2004). Internet users' information privacy concerns (IUIPC): The construct, the scale and a causal model. *Information Systems Research, 15*, 336-355.

Mascarenhas, O.A.J., Kesavan, R., & Bernacchi, M.D. (2003). Co-managing online privacy: A call for joint ownership. *The Journal of Consumer Marketing, 20*(7), 686-702.

McCloskey, H. (1980). Privacy and the right to privacy. *Philosophy, 55*(211), 17-38.

Milne, G.R., & Rohm, A.J. (2000). Consumer privacy and name removal across direct marketing channels: Exploring opt-in and opt-out alternatives. *Journal of Public Policy & Marketing, 19*(2), 238-249.

Milne, G.R, Rohm, A.J, & Bahl, S. (2004). Consumers protection of online privacy and identity. *The Journal of Consumer Affairs, 38*(2), 217-232.

Mitchell, V.-W. (1999). Consumer perceived risk: Conceptualisations and models. *European Journal of Marketing, 33*(1/2), 163-195.

Miyazaki, A., & Fernandez, A. (2001). Consumer perceptions of privacy and security risks for online shopping. *The Journal of Consumer Affairs, 35*(1), 27-44.

Myspace.com. (2007). *Privacy policy*. Retrieved August 4, 2007, from http://www.myspace.com/Modules/Common/Pages/Privacy.aspx

Nijboer, J. (2004). Big brother versus anonymity on the Internet: Implications for Internet service providers. *New Library World, 105*(7/8), 256-261.

Nowak, G.J., & Phelps, J. (1995). Direct marketing and the use of individual-level consumer informa-tion: Determining how and why privacy matters. *Journal of Direct Marketing, 9*(3), 46-60.

Nua Internet Surveys. (2002). How many online? Retrieved August 4, 2007, from http://Www.Nua.Com/Surveys/How_Many_Online/Index.html

Nua Internet Surveys. (2003). Nielsen Netratings: Global net population increases. Retrieved August 4, 2007, from http://www.Nua.Com/Surveys/Index

Office of the Federal Privacy Commissioner. (2001a). Privacy and the community (Roy Morgan Research). Retrieved August 4, 2007, from http://www.privacy.gov.au/publications/rcommunity.pdf

Orwell, G. (1951). *Nineteen eighty-four.* London: Secker and Warburg.

Paine, C., Reips, U.-D., Stieger, S., Joinson, A.N., & Buchanan, T. (2006). *Internet users' perceptions of "privacy concerns" and "privacy actions."* Manuscript submitted for publication.

Pavlou, P. (2003). Consumer acceptance of electronic commerce: Interrating trust and risk with the technology acceptance model. *International Journal of Electronic Commerce, 7*(3), 101-134.

Perri 6. (2002). Who wants privacy protection and what do they want? *Journal of Consumer Behaviour, 2*(1), 80-100.

Peslak, A.R. (2006). Internet privacy policies of the largest international companies. *Journal of Electronic Commerce in Organisations, 4*(3), 46-62.

Rainie, L., & Kohut, A. (2000). Tracking online life: How women use the Internet to cultivate relationships with family and friends.

Retsky, M.L. (2001). Just posting cookies agreement not enough. *Marketing News, 35*(20), 12-13.

Rodgers, S., & Sheldon, K.M. (2002). An improved way to characterize Internet users. *Journal of Advertising, 42(5), 85-84*

Roselius, T. (1971, January). Consumer rankings of risk reduction methods. *Journal of Marketing, 35*, 56-61.

Rust, R.T., Kannan, P.K., & Peng, N. (2002). The customer economics of Internet privacy. *Academy of Marketing Science Journal, 30*(4), 455-464.

Sappington, D., & Silk, A. (2003). Marketing's information technology revolution: Implications for consumer welfare and economic performance: Overview of the special issue. *Journal of Public Policy and Marketing, 22*(1).

Saythe, M. (1999). Adoption of Internet banking by Australian consumers. *International Journal of Bank Marketing, 17*(7), 324-334.

Schiffman, L.G., Schus, S., & Winer, L. (1976). Risk perception as a determinant of in-home consumption. *Journal of the Academy of Marketing Science, 4*(4), 753-763.

Shah, J.R., White, G.L., & Cook, J.R. (2007). Privacy protection overseas as perceived by USA-based IT professionals. *Journal of Global Information Management, 15*(1), 68-81.

Sheehan, K.B. (2002). Toward a typology of Internet users and online privacy concerns. *The Information Age, 18*, 21-32.

Sheehan, K.B., & Hoy, M.G. (2000). Dimensions of privacy concern among online consumers. *Journal of Public Policy and Marketing, 19*(1), 62-73.

Syke, C., Shim, J.T., Johnson, R., & Jiang, J. (2006). Concern for information privacy and online consumer purchasing. *Journal of the Association for Information Systems, 7*(6), 415-444.

Stone, R.N., & Winter, F.W (1987). Risk: It is still uncertainty times consequences? In R.W. Belk et al. (Eds.), *Proceedings of the American Marketing Association* (pp. 261-265).

Sweat, J. (2001). Earthlink: An ISP that customers can trust? *InformationWeek, 851*, 36.

Warren, S.D., & Brandeis, L.D. (1890, December). The right for privacy. *Harvard Law Review, 4*, 193-220.

Wyatt, S., Thomas, G., & Terranova, T. (2002). They came, they surfed, they went back to the beach: Conceptualizing use and new use of the Internet. In S. Woolgar (Ed.), *Virtual society? Technology, cyberbole, reality.* Oxford: Oxford University Press.

Chapter III
The Impact of Multilevel Computer Self–Efficacy on Effectiveness of Computer Training

Bassam Hasan
The University of Toledo, USA

ABSTRACT

Identifying factors affecting effectiveness of computer training remains a key issue in information systems (IS) research and practice. To this end, the current study builds upon IS and training literatures to develop and test a research model to examine the impact of multilevel computer self-efficacy (CSE) on effectiveness of computer training. The model distinguishes between general and application-specific CSE and posits that both levels of CSE will have positive effects on perceived ease of use, near-transfer learning, and far-transfer learning of computer skills and a negative effect on computer anxiety. The results of a field experiment conducted to empirically test the model revealed that general CSE had positive effects on far-transfer learning and perceived ease of use, whereas application-specific CSE demonstrated positive effects on near-transfer learning and perceived ease of use. The results also showed that general and application-specific CSE had negative effects on computer anxiety. This study provides better insights into the relationships between the two levels of CSE and computer training outcomes and offers valuable research and practical implications.

INTRODUCTION

In the current era of increased proliferation of computer technologies at all managerial levels and functional areas, individuals must possess adequate computing skills to enable them to do their jobs effectively. Moreover, changing computer technologies continue to alter the way individuals perform their work tasks, requiring employees to learn new computing skills and learn how to apply their new knowledge to their jobs (Tai, 2006). As a result, most organizations are faced with an incessant challenge to provide effective computer training to enable employees to learn the necessary skills and knowledge needed for effective use of computer systems. Thus, computer training remains a critical issue in information systems (IS) research and practice that deserves further examination and better understanding.

Much research attention has been given to computer training over the past few years (e.g., Davis & Bostrom, 1993; Harrison & Rainer, 1992; Johnson & Marakas, 2000; Lu, Yu, & Liu, 2003; Simon & Werner, 1996; Yi & Davis, 2001, 2001; Tai, 2006). Most of this research activity has focused on identifying factors that contribute to (or hamper) trainees' ability to learn and master the skills presented in training (e.g., Agarwal, Sambamurthy, & Stair, 2000; Bostrom, Olfman, & Sein, 1990; Simon et al., 1996; Yi & Davis, 2003). This line of research has shown that computer self-efficacy (CSE), one's confidence in his/her computing skills, represents a significant determinant of learning performance and other outcomes associated with computer training (Agarwal et al., 2000; Compeau & Higgins, 1995; Gist, Schwoerer, & Rosen, 1989; Johnson & Marakas, 2000; Yi & Davis, 2003).

However, a review of past studies concerning CSE and computer training reveals two significant voids. First, most prior studies have evaluated computer learning performance in general terms, without distinguishing between near-transfer and far-transfer learning (Haskell, 2001). Since the type of learning that a trainee accomplishes in training affects the extent to which he/she can apply and extend the newly learned skills (Cormier & Hagman, 1987) and transfer of learning knowledge represents a key objective of training (Holladay & Quiñones, 2003), it is important to understand factors that influence

each type of learning in order to enhance training transfer. Moreover, in addition to learning, effective training should lead to improvements in trainees' reactions (Kirkpatrick, 1959). Hence, it is important to assess reactions as an outcome in computer training (Tai, 2006).

Second, although CSE is a multilevel construct that operates at a general and application level (Agarwal et al., 2000; Johnson & Marakas, 2000; Marakas, Yi, & Johnson, 1998; Yi & Davis, 2003), most previous studies have focused on CSE as a general and system-independent construct. To date, very little research has examined the generality of CSE beliefs or the impact of application CSE on computer training outcomes.

Although general and application CSE represent similar concepts, there are genuine differences between the two constructs. While CSE at the general level is considered a trait-oriented efficacy (applicable to a variety computing tasks and achievements), CSE at the application level is considered a state-oriented efficacy (applicable to specific tasks and situations within the same computing domain) (Hsu & Chiu, 2004). Furthermore, the evaluation of CSE at the general and application level is more closely aligned with the generality dimension of self-efficacy which suggests that self-efficacy operates at general and task-specific levels (Bandura, 1986; Gist, 1987). Finally, this distinction allows the assessments of application CSE to exclude evaluations of cross-domain and distant skills necessary to perform a given computing task. For instance, using a spreadsheet application to prepare a financial forecast requires knowledge of forecasting and financial concepts and (Marakas et al., 1998).

The current study attempts to fill the aforementioned limitations. Thus, it attempts to provide better insights into the relationships among CSE beliefs (general and application-specific) and key computer training outcomes. Thus, the study proposes and empirically tests a research model that comprises the following variables: general CSE, application CSE, perceived ease of use, computer anxiety, near-transfer learning, and far-transfer learning.

RESEARCH MODEL AND HYPOTHESES

Figure 1 presents the research model guiding the present study. The development of this model was based on self-efficacy and learning theories, training literature, and empirical IS studies. As Figure 1 shows, the research model posits that general and application CSE will have positive effects on perceived ease of use, near-transfer learning, and far-transfer learning. In addition, the research model posits that general and application CSE will have negative effects on computer anxiety.

The present study extends previous research in several important aspects. First, the study makes a clear distinction between general and application CSE and examines both levels of CSE as determinants of computer training outcomes. Second, learning performance is examined in terms of near-transfer and far-transfer learning. Third, consistent with training literature which regards trainees' reactions as a major training outcome (e.g., Tai, 2006), reactions to training are examined relative to perceived ease of use and computer anxiety. The research variables and their relevant hypotheses are discussed and presented below.

COMPUTER SELF-EFFICACY

Self-Efficacy

The concept of self-efficacy is grounded in social cognitive theory (Bandura, 1986). It refers to people's confidence in their abilities to organize and execute the required skills to perform a behavior successfully. It is important to note that self-efficacy is not concerned about the actual skills that people may have, but it is concerned about people's confidence in their ability to use whatever skills they may have to perform a behavior successfully. Studies have shown that individuals who have more confidence in their abilities tend to exert more effort to perform a behavior, persist longer to overcome obstacles, and set more challenging goals than those who have less confidence in their abilities (Bandura, 1986, 1997).

Computer Self-Efficacy

Adapted from the general concept of self-efficacy, computer self-efficacy (CSE) refers to people's perceptions about their abilities to use a computer successfully (Compeau & Higgins, 1995). The CSE construct has been examined as an antecedent to various computer-related behaviors and outcomes (e.g., Gist et al., 1989; Venkatesh & Davis, 1996, Yi & Im, 2004).

In computer training, the results have been somewhat inconsistent. For example, several stud-

Figure 1. Research model

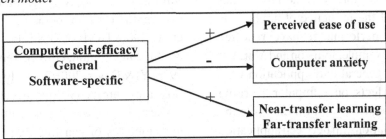

ies found that individuals with higher CSE beliefs demonstrated higher learning performance in computer training than individuals with lower CSE scores (e.g., Gist et al.,1989; Jawahar & Elango, 2001). In contrast, mixed results pertaining to the effect of CSE on learning performance have also been reported in the literature (e.g., Compeau & Higgins, 1995).

Multilevel Computer Self-Efficacy

Consistent with Bandura's (1986, 1997) suggestion that self-efficacy varies in its generality within the same or across domains of activities, Marakas et al. (1998) indicated that CSE was a multilevel construct that operates at a general and a specific computer application level. They defined general CSE as "an individual's judgment of efficacy across multiple computer application domains" (p. 129). They suggested that general CSE represents an accumulation of related experiences over a lifetime. General CSE is similar to the common CSE construct that is widely used in the literature.

Application CSE refers to individuals' perceptions of efficacy in performing specific computing tasks related to a particular system or computer application. Thus, unlike general CSE which refers to a generalized and system-independent individual trait, application CSE refers to judgments of self-efficacy toward a specific computer application or computing domain (Marakas et al., 1998) such as Internet self-efficacy (Torkzadeh, Chang, & Demirhan, 2006).

While studies of general CSE are abound, there is a dearth of research focusing on CSE at the application level. Moreover, the few studies which investigated the influence of application CSE on learning performance have reported mixed results. For example, Johnson and Marakas (2000) found that general and application CSE had significant effects on computer learning performance. However, Yi and Im (2004) found a nonsignificant relationship between application

CSE and learning performance. They suggested that the predictive strength of application CSE seems to diminish rapidly as users gain experience with the technology.

Another plausible explanation for the nonsignificant relationship described above pertains, in part, to including personal goals as a determinant of learning performance. According to goal setting theories, individuals who set higher and more challenging goals for themselves expend more effort to achieve higher levels of performance than those who accept less challenging goals. Given the strong conceptual similarities between self-efficacy and goal setting (Bandura, 1986; Gist, 1987; Wood & Bandura, 1989), it is possible that the effects of CSE may have been captured by personal goals. This explanation is further supported by the indirect influence of application CSE on learning performance through its direct effect on personal goal.

TRAINING OUTCOMES

Kirkpatrick (1959) suggests that effective training should result in four types of outcomes: reactions, learning, behavior, and results. Reactions focus on trainees' feelings, attitudes, and opinions about training. Learning pertains to the skills and knowledge acquired in training. Behavior concerns the transfer of learned skills and knowledge to the workplace. Finally, results refer to the impact of training on the organization in terms of cost reduction, quality improvement, increases in quantity of work, and reduced absenteeism.

This study focuses on the first two groups of training outcomes, reactions and learning. Based on past studies of computer training (e.g., Agarwal et al., 2000; Davis & Bostrom, 1993; Hu, Clark, & Ma, 2003; Simon, Grover, Teng, & Whitcomb, 1996; Yi & Davis, 2001; Yi & Hwang, 2003), reactions are examined with respect to perceived ease of use and computer anxiety. Similarly, consistent with theories of learning (e.g., Ausubel, 1968), learning performance is examined in terms of near- and far-transfer learning.

Perceived Ease of Use

According to the technology acceptance model (TAM) (Davis, 1989; Davis et al., 1989), the ease of use and perceived usefulness constructs represent the key determinants of IS acceptance behavior. As defined by Davis (1989), perceived ease of use refers to the degree to which an individual believes that using a system would be free of effort.

Past research indicates that general CSE has a significant, positive effect on perceived ease of use (e.g., Hong et al., 2002; Venkatesh & Davis, 1996). For instance, Hu, Clark, and Ma (2003) found a positive relationship between general CSE and perceived ease of use before and after a 4-week training program on a computer system. Likewise, Agarwal et al. (2000) found that application CSE had a positive effect on perceived ease of use of Windows 95 and Yi and Hwang (2003) found that application CSE had a significant effect on perceived ease of use before and after a training program on a WWW-based system. Thus, based on the empirical studies cited above and Bandura's (1986) suggestion that individuals with higher self-efficacy believe that they can orchestrate their skills to perform successfully, both levels of CSE (general and application-specific) are posited to have positive effects on perceived ease of use. Hence, the following two hypotheses are presented.

H1a: General computer self-efficacy will have a positive effect on perceived ease of use.
H1b: Application computer self-efficacy will have a positive effect on perceived ease of use.

Computer Anxiety

Computer anxiety refers to the feeling of unease or apprehension about the consequences of using computers such as loss of important data or making mistakes (Thatcher & Perrewé, 2002). Past research has shown that computer anxiety had negative impact on various IS-related outcomes such as perceived ease of use (Venkatesh, 2000), computer use (Igbaria & Parasuraman, 1989), computing skills (Harrison & Rainer, 1992), and affect toward computers (Compeau & Higgins, 1995). These findings substantiate the notion that computer anxiety increases resistance to technology and represents a barrier to individuals' involvement with computers (Howard & Smith, 1986).

In computer training settings, Martocchio (1994) examined the influence of perceptions of ability as an acquirable skill or fixed entity on computer anxiety. Accordingly, conceptions of computer ability were introduced to one group of subjects as a fixed entity (i.e., subjects believed they would not be able to learn any new skills) and to the other group as acquirable skills (i.e., subjects believed they would be able to learn new skills). The results showed that subjects who received the acquirable skills induction demonstrated a significant decrease in computer anxiety than those who received the fixed entity induction.

Theoretical and empirical findings suggest a negative relationship between CSE and computer anxiety. According to social cognitive theory (Bandura, 1986), individuals with high efficacy beliefs experience lower anxiety levels because they believe that they can master the needed skills and accomplish their goals. Additionally, Thatcher and Perrewé (2002) maintain that individuals with more confidence in their abilities (i.e., high CSE) tend to exhibit lower levels of computer anxiety. Hackbarth, Grover, and Yi (2003) found that prior system experience had a strong, negative impact on computer anxiety ($\beta = -0.44$). Given the positive correlation between general and application

CSE (Agarwal et al., 2000; Hsu & Chiu, 2004), we suggest that application CSE will also have an inverse impact on computer anxiety. As such, the following two hypotheses are presented.

H2a: General computer self-efficacy will have a negative effect on computer anxiety.
H2b: Application computer self-efficacy will have a negative effect on computer anxiety.

Near-Transfer and Far-Transfer Learning

Learning transfer refers to the extent to which new learning can be applied to other situations (Haskell, 2001). Near-transfer learning refers to learning which cannot be applied to novel situations that are different from the training environment. In contrast, far-transfer learning refers to learning that can be applied to situations that are different from the training situation. The theoretical basis of near- and far-transfer learning is grounded in rote and meaningful learning of the assimilation theory of learning (ATL) (Ausubel, 1968). ATL posits that rote learning occurs when the learner memorizes the new information without connecting it to existing knowledge allowing the memorized knowledge to be recalled in situations that are similar to the learning environment. Conversely, meaningful learning occurs when new knowledge is completely understood and linked to existing knowledge structure. Thus, meaningful learning can be manipulated, extended, and applied to tasks and situations that are different from the training setting in which these skills were initially learned.

The type of learning (near- or far-transfer) that one accomplishes depends, in part, on the amount of effort he/she is willing to expend to understand and integrate the new information into existing knowledge (Novak, 2002). Since self-efficacy represents a key determinant of the amount of effort and persistence that people exert to perform successfully (Bandura, 1986),

individuals with higher CSE beliefs are expected to expend more effort to understand and learn the new skills and, as a result, will demonstrate higher levels of learning performance than those with lower CSE.

Martocchio and Hertenstein (2003) investigated the impact of application CSE on declarative knowledge (similar to near-transfer knowledge). They found that Access 97 CSE had a significant effect on declarative knowledge (i.e., specific knowledge about basic features of Access 97). Thus, based on the theoretical and empirical studies described above, general and application CSE beliefs are likely to have positive effects on near-transfer and far-transfer learning of computer skills.

H3a: General computer self-efficacy will have a positive effect on near-transfer learning.
H3b: Application computer self-efficacy will have a positive effect on near-transfer learning.
H4a: General computer self-efficacy will have a positive effect on far-transfer learning.
H4b: Application computer self-efficacy will have a positive effect on far-transfer learning.

METHOD

Procedure

Seventy-eight undergraduate juniors and seniors (28 females, 50 males) enrolled in two elective computer information systems courses at a Midwestern university participated in this study. All subjects indicated that IS was their major or minor. Subjects were given extra credit for their participation in the study. The mean age of subjects was 23.06 years (SD = 2.77).

Davis (1993) recommends using less familiar applications to allow users to form their beliefs based on their interaction with the technology rather than on their past experience with it. Thus, the Unix platform was selected for the purpose of the present study. To verify that subjects had little experience with the selected technology, subjects were asked to rate their prior experience with Unix on a 10-point scale ranging from 1 (*no experience*) to 10 (*very experienced*). The mean score was 3.15, indicating that subjects had little experience with Unix.

A field experiment was conducted to empirically test the research model and its hypothesized relationships. Prior to training, subjects completed a questionnaire containing measures of general and application (Unix) CSE along with some background and demographic questions. Next, subjects received about one-hour training on manipulating file and directory structures in the Unix environment. Examples of the skills presented in training included creating, renaming, copying, deleting files/directories, listing contents of a directory or subdirectory, searching for a file or a directory, identifying the location of the current (working) directory in the directory structure, and using absolute and relative directory paths.

Consistent with previous studies which used tutorials and self-paced manuals (e.g., Simon & Werner, 1996), subjects were also given a short tutorial explaining the training material and were encouraged to study and practice the illustrative examples included in the tutorial. Finally, based on past studies which used comprehension tests of computer learning (Bostrom, Olfman, & Sein, 1990; Lu et al., 2003; Simon et al., 1996), subjects took a comprehension test of the training material and completed a questionnaire regarding their perceptions of ease of use and computer anxiety.

Measures

Six items from the widely used instrument developed by Compeau and Higgins (1995) were used to measure general CSE. Items on this instrument asked subjects to rate their ability to perform a computing task using unfamiliar application. Responses were recorded on a10-point interval scale with end-points of 1 (*not at all confident*) and 10 (*totally confident*). Application CSE was measured by six items adapted from Johnson and Marakas (2000). These items asked subjects to indicate the extent to which they agreed or disagreed with six statements related to their ability to use Unix to manipulate files and directories. Responses were recorded on a 7-point Likert-type scale ranging from 1 (*strongly disagree*) to 7 (*strongly agree*).

Three items from Davis's (1989) instrument were used to measure perceived ease of use. Following the suggestion that computer anxiety has multiple dimensions including computer learning anxiety (e.g., Chua, Chen, & Wong, 1999), computer anxiety was measured with respect to Unix. Accordingly, four items from the instrument used by Venkatesh (2000) were used to measure computer anxiety. Items on this measure asked subjects to indicate the extent of their agreement or disagreement with statements about their uneasiness or nervousness toward learning and using Unix. Responses to perceived ease of use and computer anxiety items were recorded on a 7-point Likert-type scale ranging from 1 (*strongly disagree*) to 7 (*strongly agree*). A summary of all multi-item measures is presented in Appendix 1.

Simple or near-transfer tasks are usually used to measure rote or near-transfer learning (Davis & Bostrom, 1993; Simon et al., 1996). Near-transfer tasks are characterized as being simple tasks that are similar to the tasks presented in training. Accordingly, a five-question learning test was used to measure near-transfer learning. The skills included in the learning test were identical to the concepts and skills covered in training. The specific near-transfer skills included on the learning test were: (1) renaming a file in the current directory, (2) navigating to a parent directory, (3) creating a new subdirectory in the current directory, (4) listing the contents of the current directory, and (5) deleting a file from the current directory. Each question was worth 3 points. Completely correct answers were given 3 points and completely incorrect answers received 0 points. Answers that were neither entirely correct nor completely incorrect received 2 points. As such, possible scores on near-transfer learning test have a possible range of 0 to 15.

Complex or far-transfer tasks are often used to measure meaningful and far-transfer learning (Davis & Bostrom, 1993). Simon et al. (1996) suggest that far-transfer tasks comprise two or more near-transfer tasks, and it is left to the trainee to determine which and how the near-transfer tasks should be combined to perform the given far-transfer task. Thus, far-transfer learning was measured by a four-item learning test. Similar to the tasks used by Davis and Bostrom (1993), far-transfer tasks included on the learning performance test were: (1) creating a multilevel directory structure, (2) deleting a non-empty subdirectory, (3) copying a file from one directory to another directory in a different level in the directory structure, and (4) renaming files in another directory. Since performing a far-transfer task requires more mental and physical effort than performing a near-transfer task, each question was worth 6 points. Scoring of the far-transfer learning test followed the same procedure used in the near-transfer learning test with proportional points for partially correct answers.

The two learning tests were graded by two independent graders. Each grader was given written instructions to follow in grading the tests and assigning grades. The correlation between the grades obtained from the two graders was 0.94 (p < 0.001) for the near-transfer learning test and 0.91 (p <.001) for the far-transfer learning test. The average of the two scores awarded by the two graders for each test was used in the data analysis.

RESULTS

Although this study used previously validated instruments, a confirmatory analysis was performed on all multi-item measures. All items exhibited high loading on their intended constructs and all measures demonstrated high internal consistency reliability (coefficient alpha) as can be seen in Appendix 1.

The means, standard deviations, and correlations among the study variables are presented in Table 1. As can be seen in Table 1, although measured on different scales, general CSE beliefs are noticeably higher than application (Unix) CSE beliefs. This was expected because Unix is not a common technology that students interact with very often or use on a regular basis. The correla-

Table 1. Means, standard deviations, and correlations

Variable	Mean	SD	1	2	3	4	5
1. General CSE	40.63	11.62	--				
2. Software-specific CSE	28.43	9.32	0.62**	--			
3. Perceived ease of use	15.26	4.64	0.49**	0.34**	--		
4. Computer anxiety	13.68	6.44	-0.56**	-0.55**	-0.60**	--	
5. Near-transfer learning	10.82	2.74	0.20	0.56**	-0.02	-0.19	--
6. Far-transfer learning	15.79	5.45	0.53**	0.58**	0.30**	-0.34**	0.36**

** p < 0.01

tions were below the cutoff value of 0.8 suggested by Bryman and Cramer (1994) to suspect the presence of multicollinearity.

Regression analysis was used to test the research hypotheses. Accordingly, a separate regression test was performed for each dependent variable and the results of regression analyses are presented in Table 2. The regression results show that general CSE has significant effects on: (1) perceived ease of use ($\beta = 0.421, p = 0.003$); (2) computer anxiety ($\beta = -0.360, p = 0.004$); and (3) far-transfer learning ($\beta = 0.259, p = 0.033$). Thus, hypotheses 1a, 2a, and 4a were supported by the data. However, general CSE demonstrated a nonsignificant negative effect on near-transfer learning ($\beta = -0.229, p = 0.076$). Therefore, hypothesis 3a was not supported.

With respect to application CSE, the results in Table 2 show that application CSE has significant effects on: (1) computer anxiety ($\beta = -0.317, p = 0.012$); (2) near-transfer learning ($\beta = 0.683, p = 0.000$); and (3) far-transfer learning ($\beta = 0.447, p = 0.000$). Thus, hypotheses 2b, 3b, and 4b were supported by the data. Contrary to expectations, the effect of application CSE on perceived ease of use was small and nonsignificant ($\beta = 0.127, p = 0.345$). As such, hypothesis 1b was not supported. Moreover, Table 2 shows that general and application CSE explained about 25% of the variance in perceived ease of use; 37% for computer anxiety; 32% for near-transfer learning; and 41% for far-transfer learning.

DISCUSSION

The purpose of this study was to examine the impact of CSE on computer training effectiveness. A research model positing relationships among general and application CSE on perceived ease of use, computer anxiety, near-transfer learning, and far-transfer learning was developed and tested. Experimental results provided adequate support for the research model and supported six of the eight hypothesized relationships. As expected, general CSE demonstrated a significant positive effect on perceived ease of use. Accordingly, perceptions of ease of use of a given system are expected to be higher for individuals with higher CSE judgments than those with lower CSE. This finding is consistent with previous studies (e.g., Hong, Thong, Wong, & Tam, 2002; Hu et al., 2003; Igbaria & Iivari, 1995; Venkatesh & Davis, 1996) and further corroborates the relationship between general CSE and perceived ease of use.

In contrast to recent findings which showed a significant relationship between application CSE and perceived ease of use (Agarwal et al., 2000; Yi & Hwang, 2003), application CSE failed

Table 2. Results of regression testing

Training Outcome	R2	Level of CSE	β	t	Sig.	Hypothesis	Result
Perceived ease of use	0.256	General	0.421	3.123	0.003	1a	S
		Software-specific	0.127	0.950	0.345	1b	NS
Computer Anxiety	0.374	General	-0.360	-2.942	0.004	2a	S
		Software-specific	-0.317	-2.588	0.012	2b	S
Near-transfer learning	0.322	General	-0.229	-1.801	0.076	3a	NS
		Software-specific	0.683	5.356	0.000	3b	S
Far-transfer learning	0.412	General	0.259	2.182	0.033	4a	S
		Software-specific	0.447	3.769	0.000	4b	S
S: Supported, NS: Not Supported							

to demonstrate significant effect on perceived ease of use. Subjects' familiarity with the target technology may offer a possible explanation for this finding. According to innovation diffusion literature, greater visibility (the degree to which a technology is available and visible to users) and trialability (the degree to which an individual can experiment with a technology) of a technology enhance users' beliefs about that technology (Karahanna, Straub, & Chervany, 1999; Moore & Benbasat, 1991). Most studies that found a significant relationship between application CSE and perceived ease of use have used common and popular technologies such as Windows 95, Lotus 123, and Blackboard. Thus, it is possible that those technologies were more visible and available for trial by subjects than the technology examined in this study (Unix), which is not a very common or user-friendly technology.

The study also hypothesized that general and application CSE would have negative effects on computer anxiety. Consistent with prior studies (e.g., Johnson & Marakas, 2000; Thatcher & Perrewé, 2002) and providing additional support for the inverse relationship between CSE and computer anxiety, both levels of CSE exhibited significant negative effects on computer anxiety in this study. The results also showed that general and application CSE explained about 37% of the variance in computer anxiety. Given that general CSE alone explained about 25% of the variance in computer anxiety in previous studies (e.g., Compeau & Higgins, 1995), application CSE represents a valuable addition to predictors of computer anxiety.

Although general and application CSE were hypothesized to have positive effects on near-transfer learning, only application CSE demonstrated a significant effect on near-transfer learning. This is not surprising because performing a near-transfer computing task requires a specific set of skills that are usually captured by application CSE. In contrast, general CSE focuses on general computing skills and cross-domain tasks

that may not be directly linked to the specific task in question. Hence, it is plausible that application CSE efficacy beliefs may be more dominant in situations that require using the new knowledge in a standard manner to perform simple and similar computing tasks. Moreover, the lack of significant effect of general CSE on near-transfer learning is consistent with Bandura's (1997) assertion that performance in specific situations is better predicted by more specific assessments of self-efficacy because these measures focus on evaluations of abilities and requirements that are closely related to the task.

General and application CSE demonstrated significant positive effect on far-transfer learning. The assimilation learning theory suggests that meaningful (i.e., far-transfer) learning occurs when the learner fully understands the new knowledge and is able to recall this knowledge and apply it to execute a complex task. Likewise, self-efficacy theory suggests that competent and successful performance requires possession of necessary skills and strong confidence in ability to use these skills effectively.

IMPLICATIONS

Before discussing the implications of the study results, potential limitations of the present study should be acknowledged and recognized when interpreting the results. The first limitation pertains to the use of student subjects and the relatively small sample size used to test the research model. While similar studies have used student subjects (e.g., Torkzadeh et al., 2006) or have been conducted in educational settings (e.g., Tai, 2006), it is necessary to repeat this study using larger and more diverse samples in different settings to enhance the validity and generalizability of the results.

The use of a comprehension test rather than actual computing tasks to measure learning performance presents another possible limitation.

Therefore, future research should consider using actual near-transfer and far-transfer computing tasks and examine other technologies to enhance the validity of the results and increase their generalizability across technologies. Finally, learning performance was measured in a short period of time after training. Gist and Mitchell (1992) maintain that in the time span between assessments of self-efficacy and performance, many factors can influence actual performance. Thus, measuring learning performance in an extended period of time such as one or two months after training is needed to evaluate the long-term effects of CSE on learning performance.

From a research perspective, this study extended prior research on CSE and computer training and showed that CSE had general and application components. The study also demonstrated how the two components of CSE affect computer training outcomes. With respect to computer training, this study took a broader approach to evaluating the effectiveness of such training. More specifically, two key training outcomes (reactions and learning performance) from Kirkpatrick's (1959) model of training effectiveness were used to evaluate effectiveness of computer training. Based on past studies, reactions were examined with respect to perceived ease of use and computer anxiety. In addition, two types of learning (near-transfer and far-transfer) were considered as indicators of learning performance. Thus, this study represents an important attempt to enhance understanding of the impact of CSE on computer training outcomes.

Regarding practical and managerial implications, the results of this study could be useful in designing and administering computer training programs. For example, if near-transfer learning is the primary objective of training, then it may be more helpful to focus on enhancing on application CSE prior to training. Conversely, if far-transfer learning is the main objective, then it may be more useful to focus on enhancing both levels of CSE prior to training. Prior studies have

shown that increased experience with computers, implementing more user-friendly interfaces, and the availability of organizational support are helpful in improving users' computer efficacy beliefs (Igbaria & Iivari, 1995). Recent studies indicate that training framing (i.e., verbal persuasion or encouragement from managers and supervisors) is useful in enhancing trainees' CSE beliefs.

With respect computer anxiety, the results showed that both levels of CSE (general and application-specific) had inverse impact on computer anxiety. Since computer anxiety is a treatable state anxiety (Chua et al., 1999; Dyck, Gee, & Smither, 1998), organizational interventions designed to alleviate computer anxiety should focus on enhancing general and application CSE. Increasing organizational support (Igbaria & Iivari, 1995), increasing computer experience (Hackbarth, Grover, & Yi, 2003), and increasing awareness of user-friendly and easy-to-use applications that require little or no knowledge of mathematics or computer programming (Igbaria & Parasuraman, 1989) have also been found to be effective in reducing computer anxiety.

This study may have implications for teaching computer-related courses. Havelka, Beasley, and Broome (2004) indicate that attempts to reduce computer anxiety should improve students' experiences and enhance their attitudes towards their education. Given that general and application CSE play a significant role in reducing computer anxiety, approaches to increase students' CSE such as social encouragement or verbal persuasion from instructors may have positive effects on students' educational experiences and learning.

Finally, this study provides some implications for enhancing IS acceptance. For instance, perceived ease of use represents a key determinant of IS acceptance (Davis, 1989) and reviews of empirical studies found a positive relationship between ease of use and IS acceptance behavior (Mahmood, Hall, & Swanberg, 2001). Since general CSE was found to have a significant effect on perceived ease of use, enhancing users' general CSE should improve perceptions of ease of use of a target system and improve subsequent acceptance of the system.

FUTURE RESEARCH

In addition to research aimed at addressing the limitations described earlier, an interesting opportunity for future research would be to examine the antecedents of each level of CSE. Since this study demonstrated that the two levels of CSE had varying effects on computer training outcomes, it is important to understand factors that affect each level of CSE. Given that factors affecting general CSE had received extensive research attention, there is a genuine need for focusing on the antecedents of application CSE in future research.

Examining the four training outcomes identified in Kirkpatrick's (1959) training effectiveness model represents another valuable issue to consider in future research. As noted earlier, this study focused on the first two outcomes. That is, the other two outcomes in Kirkpatrick's model (trainee behavior and training results) were not examined in this study. Thus, evaluating all training outcomes suggested by Kirkpatrick's model rather than a subset of these outcomes represents a worthwhile issue to explore in future research and will certainly provide important practical implications.

REFERENCES

Agarwal, R., Sambamurthy, V., & Stair, R. (2000). The evolving relationship between general and specific computer self-efficacy: An empirical assessment. *Information Systems Research, 11*(4), 418-430.

Ausubel, D. P. (1968). *Educational psychology, a cognitive view*. New York: Holt, Rinehart and Winston, Inc.

Bandura, A. (1986). *Social foundations of thought and action: A social cognitive theory*. Upper Saddle River, NJ: Prentice Hall.

Bandura, A. (1997). *Self-efficacy: The exercise of control*. New York: Freeman.

Bostrom, R. P., Olfman, L., & Sein, M. K. (1990). The importance of learning style in end user training. *MIS Quarterly, 14*(1), 101-119.

Bryman, A., & Cramer, D. (1994). *Quantitative data analysis for social scientists*. New York: Routledge.

Chua, S. L., Chen, D., & Wong, A. (1999). Computer anxiety and its correlates: A meta-analysis. *Computers in Human Behavior, 15*(5), 609-623.

Compeau, D. R., & Higgins, C. A. (1995). Application of social cognitive theory to training for computer skills. *Information Systems Research, 6*(1), 118-143.

Cormier, S., & Hagman, J. (1987). *Transfer of learning: Contemporary research and applications*. San Diego: Academic Press, Inc.

Davis, F. D. (1989). Perceived usefulness, perceived ease of use, and user acceptance of information technology. *MIS Quarterly, 13*(3), 319-340.

Davis, F. D. (1993). User acceptance of information technology: System characteristics, user perceptions and behavioral impacts. *International Journal of Man-Machine Studies, 38*(3), 475-487.

Davis, F. D., Bagozzi, R. P., & Warshaw, P. R. (1989). User acceptance of computer technology: A comparison of two theoretical models. *Management Science, 35*(8), 982-1003.

Davis, S., & Bostrom, R. (1993). Training end users: An experimental investigation of the roles of the computer interface and training methods. *MIS Quarterly, 17*(1), 61-79.

Dyck, J. L., Gee, N. R., & Smither, J. A. (1998). The changing construct of computer anxiety for younger and older adults. *Computers in Human Behavior, 14*(1), 61-77.

Gist, M.E. (1987). Self-efficacy: Implications for organizational behavior and human resource management. *Academy of Management Review, 12*(3), 472-485.

Gist, M. E., Schwoerer, C., & Rosen, B. (1989). Effects of alternative training methods on self-efficacy and performance in computer software training. *Journal of Applied Psychology, 74*(6), 884-891.

Hackbarth, G., Grover, V., & Yi, M. Y. (2003). Computer playfulness and anxiety: Positive and negative mediators of the system experience effect on perceived ease of use. *Information & Management, 40*(3), 221-232.

Harrison, A. W., & Rainer, R. K. (1992). The influence of individual differences on skill in end-user computing. *Journal of Management Information Systems, 9*(1), 93-111.

Haskell, R. E. (2001). *Transfer of learning: Cognition, instruction and reasoning.* San Diego: Academic Press.

Havelka, D., Beasley, F., & Broome, T. (2004). A study of computer anxiety among business students. *Mid-American Journal of Business, 19*(1), 63-71.

Holladay, C. L., & Quiñones, M. A. (2003). Practice variability and transfer of training: The role of self-efficacy generality. *Journal of Applied Psychology, 88*(6), 1094-1103.

Hong, W. Y., Thong, J. Y. L., Wong, W. M., & Tam, K. Y. (2002). Determinants of user acceptance of digital libraries: An empirical examination of individual differences and system characteristics.

Journal of Management Information Systems, 18(3), 97-124.

Howard, G. S., & Smith, R. D. (1986). Computer anxiety in management: Myth or reality? *Communications of the ACM, 29*(7), 611-615.

Hsu, M.-H., & Chiu, C.-M. (2004). Internet self-efficacy and electronic service acceptance. *Decision Support Systems, 38*(3), 369-381.

Hu, P. J. H., Clark, T. H. K., & Ma, W. W. (2003). Examining technology acceptance by school teachers: A longitudinal study. *Information & Management, 41*(2), 227-241.

Igbaria, M., & Iivari, J. (1995). The effects of self-efficacy on computer usage. *OMEGA International Journal of Management Science, 23*(6), 587-605.

Igbaria, M., & Parasuraman, S. (1989). A path analytic study of individual characteristics, computer anxiety, and attitudes towards microcomputers. *Journal of Management, 15*(3), 373-388.

Jawahar, I. M., & Elango, B. (2001). The effects of attitudes, goal setting and self-efficacy on end user performance. *Journal of End User Computing, 13*(2), 40-45.

Johnson, R. D., & Marakas, G. M. (2000). The role of behavioral modeling in computer skills acquisition: Toward refinement of the model. *Information Systems Research, 11*(4), 402-417.

Karahanna, E., Straub, D., & Chervany, N. (1999). Information technology adoption across time: A cross-sectional comparison of pre-adoption and post-adoption beliefs. *MIS Quarterly, 23*(2), 183-213.

Kirkpatrick, D. L. (1959). Techniques for evaluating training programs. *Journal of the American Society of Training Directors, 13*(11-12), 3-26.

Lu, J., Yu, C., & Liu, C. (2003). Learning style, learning patterns, and learning performance in a WebCT-based MIS course. *Information & Management, 40*(6), 497-507.

Mahmood, M. A., Hall, L., & Swanberg, D. L. (2001). Factors affecting information technology usage: A meta-analysis of the empirical literature. *Journal of Organizational Computing & Electronic Commerce, 11*(2), 107-130.

Marakas, G. M., Yi, M. Y., & Johnson, R. (1998). The multilevel and multifaceted character of computer self-efficacy: Toward a clarification of the construct and an integrative framework for research. *Information Systems Research, 9*(2), 126-163.

Martocchio, J. J. (1994). Effects of conceptions of ability on anxiety, self-efficacy, and learning in training. *Journal of Applied Psychology, 79*(6), 819-825.

Martocchio, J. J., & Hertenstein, E. J. (2003). Learning orientation and goal orientation context: Relationships with cognitive and affective learning outcomes. *Human Resources Development Quarterly, 14*(4), 413-434.

Moore, G. C., & Benbasat, I. (1991). Development of an instrument to measure the perceptions of adopting an information technology innovation. *Information Systems Research, 2*(3), 192-222.

Novak, J. D. (2002). Meaningful learning: The essential factor for conceptual change in limited or inappropriate propositional hierarchies leading to empowerment of learners. *Science Education, 86*(4), 548-571.

Simon, S. J., Grover, G., Teng, J. T., & Whitcomb, K. (1996). The relationship of information system training methods and cognitive ability to end-user satisfaction, comprehension, and skill transfer: A longitudinal field study. *Information Systems Research, 7*(4), 466-490.

Simon, S. J., & Werner, J. M. (1996). Computer training through behavior modeling, self-paced, and instructional approaches: A field experiment. *Journal of Applied Psychology, 81*(6), 648-659.

Tai, W.-T. (2006). Effects of training framing, general self-efficacy and training motivation on trainees' training effectiveness. *Personnel Review, 35*(1), 51-65.

Thatcher, J. B., & Perrewé, P. L. (2002). An empirical examination of individual traits as antecedents to computer anxiety and computer self-efficacy. *MIS Quarterly, 26*(4), 381-395.

Torkzadeh, G., Chang, J. C. J., & Demirhan, D. (2006). A contingency model of computer and Internet self-efficacy. *Information & Management, 43*(4), 541-550.

Venkatesh, V. (2000). Determinants of perceived ease of use: Integrating perceived behavioral control, computer anxiety and enjoyment into the technology acceptance model. *Information Systems Research, 11*(4), 342-365.

Venkatesh, V., & Davis, F. D. (1996). A model of the antecedents of perceived ease of use: Development and test. *Decision Sciences, 27*(3), 451-481.

Wood, R., & Bandura, A. (1989). Social cognitive theory of organizational management. *Academy of Management Review, 14*(3), 361-384.

Yi, M.Y., & Davis, F. D. (2001). Improving computer training effectiveness for decision technologies: Behavior modeling and retention enhancement. *Decision Sciences, 32*(3), 521-544.

Yi, M. Y., & Davis, F. D. (2003). Developing and validating an observational learning model of computer software training and skill acquisition. *Information Systems Research, 14*(2), 146-169.

Yi, M. Y., & Hwang, Y. (2003). Predicting the use of Web-based information systems: Self-efficacy, enjoyment, learning goal orientation, and the technology acceptance model. *International Journal of Human-Computer Studies, 59*(4), 431-449.

Yi, M. U., & Im, K. S. (2004). Predicting computer task performance: Personal goal and self-efficacy. *Journal of Organizational and End User Computing, 16*(2), 28-37.

Chapter IV
Optimizing the ROI
of Enterprise Architecture
Using Real Options

David F. Rico
Independent Consultant, USA

ABSTRACT

This chapter illustrates how to optimize the return on investment (ROI) of enterprise architecture. Enterprise architecture is a blueprint for defining the structure and operation of organizations such as local, state, and federal agencies. Done well, enterprise architecture results in leaner and more effective information systems that satisfy organizational goals and objectives. This chapter introduces a suite of simple metrics and models for measuring the ROI of enterprise architecture. This chapter also introduces real options, which is a contemporary approach to measuring ROI. Whereas typical measures tend to underestimate ROI, real options have the ability to unearth business value hidden deep within the economics of investments in enterprise architecture.

OVERVIEW

Enterprise architecture is a comprehensive framework or taxonomy of systems analysis models for aligning organizational strategy with information technology. Strategies are plans to satisfy organizational goals and objectives by competing based on size, cost, variety, speed, quality, uniqueness, or innovation. Information technology refers to the computers, software, and networks used for safely storing, processing, retrieving, and transmitting data and information. John A. Zachman is credited with creating enterprise architecture, though its foundations date back to the early 1900s (Zachman, 1987).

Enterprise architecture has five major layers: (a) scope, (b) business model, (c) system model, (d) technology model, and (e) components as shown in Table 1. The purpose of the layers is to align an organization's strategy with its information technology. Two basic assumptions are that a strategy exists and the result is a functioning enterprise. A centralized strategy may not be defined for large organizations (e.g., enterprise of enterprises), though it should be, which makes developing models difficult. Enterprise architects often start building information technology from the bottom up, because they cannot see the relevance of strategy and modeling.

METRICS AND MODELS

The value of enterprise architecture may be measured using seven metrics: (a) costs, (b) benefits, (c) benefit to cost ratio, (d) return on investment, (e) net present value, (f) breakeven point, and (g) real options (Kodukula, 2006; Rico, 2004, 2005, 2006). Costs are the accumulation of expenses, such as labor, training, tools, verification, validation, and compliance or maturity assessment. Benefits are the monetization of increased efficiency, reduced operational costs and personnel numbers, increased customer satisfaction, and consolidated legacy computer systems. Costs and benefits are the basic inputs to benefit to cost ratio, return on investment, net present value, breakeven point, and real options.

COSTS AND BENEFITS

There are also five major classes of costs and benefits for enterprise architecture: (a) financial improvement, (b) constituent services, (c) reduced redundancy, (d) economic development, and (e) fostering democracy (Meskell, 2003). Financial improvements mean reducing the costs of organizations and enhancing revenue collection. Constituent services mean improved service to customers, suppliers, and key stakeholders. Reduced redundancy means consolidating, reducing, or eliminating un-needed legacy computer systems. Economic development means to grow local, state, and federal economies. Finally, fostering democracy may mean offering a consistent level of customer service to all stakeholders, regardless of political affiliation.

RETURN ON INVESTMENT EXAMPLES

Using enterprise architecture for aligning the strategy with the information technology of local, state, and federal agencies, and corporations has measurable return on investment (Meskell,

Table 1. John A. Zachman framework for enterprise architecture

Interrogatives	What?	How?	Where?	Who?	When?	Why?
Product (Form)	Data (Entity/Relation)	Function (Process/IO)	Network (Node/Line)	Organization (Agent/Work)	Schedule (Event/Cycle)	Strategy (End/Means)
Scope (Contextual)	Business Priorities	Business Processes	Business Locations	Business Organizations	Business Cycles	Business Goals
Business Model (Conceptual)	Semantic Model	Process Model	Logistics Model	Workflow Model	Schedule Model	Business Plan
System Model (Logical)	Logical Data Model	Application Architecture	Distributed System Architecture	Human Interface Architecture	Processing Structure	Business Rule Model
Technology Model (Physical)	Physical Data Model	System Design	Technology Architecture	Presentation Architecture	Control Structure	Rule Design
Components (Out-of-Context)	Data Definition	Computer Program	Network Architecture	Security Architecture	Timing Definition	Rule Specification

2003). The first priority is to collect detailed cost data for enterprise architecture. Next, it is very important to establish and monetize measurable performance improvement objectives. Finally, benefit to cost ratio, return on investment, net present value, breakeven point, and real options are determined from the cost and benefit data,

with no further data collection. The states in Table 3 estimated the costs of their e-government initiatives, identified their benefits, and then monetized them. B/CR, ROI%, NPV, breakeven, and real options were then estimated using the metrics from Table 2.

Table 2. A suite of simple of metrics and models for measuring the ROI of enterprise architecture

Costs (sum of costs)	Total amount of money spent on enterprise architecture	
Benefits (sum of benefits)	Total amount of money gained from enterprise architecture	$\sum_{i=1}^{n} Benefit_i$
B/CR (benefit to cost ratio)	Ratio of enterprise architecture benefits to costs	$\dfrac{Benefits}{Costs}$
ROI% (return on investment)	Ratio of adjusted enterprise architecture benefits to costs	$\dfrac{Benefits - Costs}{Costs} \times 100\%$
NPV (net present value)	Discounted cash flows of enterprise architecture	$\sum_{i=1}^{Years} \dfrac{Benefits_i}{(1 + Discount\ Rate)^{Years}} - Costs_0$
BEP (breakeven point)	Point when benefits exceed costs of enterprise architecture	$\dfrac{Costs}{NPV} \times 0\ Months$
ROA (real options analysis)	Business value realized from strategic delay due to risk	$N(d_1) \times Benefits - N(d_2) \times Costs \times e^{-Rate \times Years}$

d1 = [ln(Benefits ÷ Costs) + (Rate + 0.5 × Risk²) × Years] ÷ Risk × √ Years, d2 = d1 − Risk × √ Years

Figure 1. Cost and benefit categories and data from 75 state-level e-government initiatives

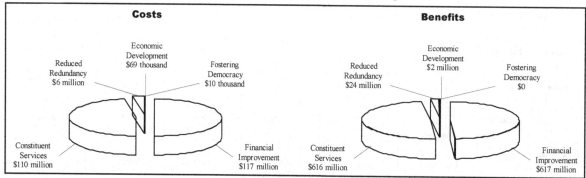

Table 3. Estimated cost and benefit data from 8 state-level e-government initiatives

State	Costs	Benefits	B/CR	ROI%	NPV	Breakeven	ROA
KY	$138,332	$24,740,000	179:1	17,785%	$21,283,919	0 Mos.	$24,632,267
FL	$211,200	$23,299,995	110:1	10,932%	$19,964,157	1 Mos.	$23,135,514
NC	$640,000	$20,000,000	31:1	3,025%	$16,677,907	2 Mos.	$19,501,956
WI	$400,000	$7,500,000	19:1	1,775%	$6,094,215	4 Mos.	$7,189,456
DC	$1,000,000	$9,000,000	9:1	800%	$6,793,058	9 Mos.	$8,234,368
NM	$167,550	$1,182,200	7:1	606%	$856,111	12 Mos.	$1,055,276
IA	$277,000	$1,320,000	5:1	377%	$865,982	19 Mos.	$1,116,054
ID	$1,770,000	$2,560,000	1:1	45%	$446,692	238 Mos.	$1,533,423
Average	$575,510	$11,200,274	45:1	4,418%	$9,122,755	36 Mos.	$10,799,789

The return on investment data in Table 3 were normalized and illustrated graphically in Figure 2. Return on investment is the simple ratio of benefits, less the costs of course, to the costs themselves. That is, benefits less the costs are the numerator and costs are the denominator. Return on investment is large if there were more benefits than costs. As shown in Figure 2, Kentucky had very low costs, high benefits, and thus very high return on investment. Idaho, on the other hand, had very high costs, low benefits, and little return on investment. This is seen by the increasing costs and decreasing return on investment from left to right. Some will assert that net present value is a conservative, smaller, and more realistic estimate of return on investment. However, Table 3 shows that measures such as real options improve the outlook substantially.

The benefit equation in Figure 3 was derived from actual cost and benefit data from 16 state-

Figure 2. Estimated costs and return on investment of 8 state-level e-government initiatives

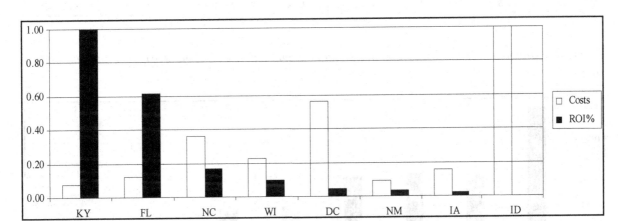

Figure 3. Log-linear benefit model derived from 16 state-level e-government initiatives

$$Benefits = 5853559.75792164 \times 1.000000023^{Costs}$$

level e-government initiatives (Meskell, 2003). It is based on a log-linear regression analysis of 16 actual cost and benefit data pairs. The 16 data pairs came from a database of 75 e-government initiatives. Only 21% of the e-government initiatives reported cost and benefit pairs. Others reported only costs or benefits, or only qualitative results. Valid cost data from eight federal enterprise architecture initiatives were combined with the e-government benefit model based on this log-linear equation (Hite, 2002). Then, benefit to cost ratio, return on investment, net present value, breakeven point, and real options were estimated for eight federal enterprise architecture initiatives shown in Table 4.

The return on investment data in Table 4 were normalized and illustrated graphically in Figure 4. The cost data in Table 4 were taken from a database of 45 federal enterprise architecture initiatives (Hite, 2002). As shown in Figure 4, the International Trade Administration had very low costs, and thus has the capability to yield a high return on investment. The federal agencies in Figure 4 have moderate costs and the potential to yield good results as well. There are some enterprise architecture initiatives with higher costs than those illustrated here. Some have yielded good, mediocre, and even no results. Once again, however, Table 4 demonstrates that real options may

Table 4. Estimated cost and benefit data from 8 federal-level enterprise architecture initiatives

Agency	Costs	Benefits	B/CR	ROI%	NPV	Breakeven	ROA
ITA	$120,000	$5,869,907	49:1	4,792%	$4,962,725	1 Mos.	$5,776,469
DLSA	$194,000	$5,880,011	30:1	2,931%	$4,897,474	2 Mos.	$5,729,052
FRA	$194,000	$5,880,011	30:1	2,931%	$4,897,474	2 Mos.	$5,729,052
FSA	$200,000	$5,880,831	29:1	2,840%	$4,892,184	2 Mos.	$5,725,215
BoP	$276,000	$5,891,227	21:1	2,035%	$4,825,186	3 Mos.	$5,676,759
CB	$285,000	$5,892,459	21:1	1,968%	$4,817,253	4 Mos.	$5,671,042
DCAA	$358,000	$5,902,465	16:1	1,549%	$4,752,917	5 Mos.	$5,624,860
OPM	$400,000	$5,908,229	15:1	1,377%	$4,715,908	5 Mos.	$5,598,466
Average	$253,375	$5,888,142	27:1	2,553%	$4,845,140	3 Mos.	$5,691,364

Figure 4. Estimated costs and return on investment of eight federal-level enterprise architecture initiatives

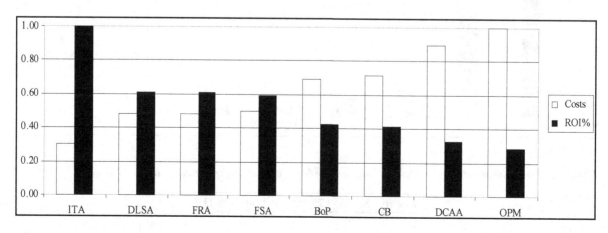

be the key to wringing out return on investment from stingy enterprise architecture initiatives.

PRINCIPLES FOR SUCCESSFUL ENTERPRISE ARCHITECTURE

Here are a few tips, tricks, and techniques for succeeding with enterprise architecture. They apply to enterprise architecture initiatives of all sizes, but have special meaning for large ones. The gist of the matter is to have a clear understanding of what one is trying to achieve. That is, what benefits does one expect? Some organizations may be doing enterprise architecture just to comply with government regulations. These principles apply whether the organization is trying to gain a competitive advantage, reign in information technology, or fulfilling an obligation.

- **Form a clear vision and stick to it:** It is important to have a clear vision of how to approach enterprise architecture. Survey the field of world class enterprise architecture initiatives, see the results for yourself, and use that as a basis to form your vision. The worst thing you can do is embark on a long and arduous enterprise architecture initiative without a clear vision.

- **Define early measurable objectives:** Determine highly measurable goals and objectives before starting enterprise architecture. Set measurable targets for operating efficiency, cost reductions, staff reductions, customer satisfaction, computing budgets, and economic growth. Enterprise architecture without measurable goals and objectives is a death march.

- **Think small, fast, and lean:** Whatever your scope, size, and objectives, think small, fast, and lean. Keep your scope well defined, use small teams of highly experienced experts, and set out to complete the enterprise architecture in small, frequent, and near term increments. Enterprise architecture means to design or architect, so you do not need an army of builders.

- **Manage like a well run project:** Apply project management principles to enterprise architecture. Devise work breakdown structures, activity network diagrams, and cost and resource estimates. Use earned value management, quality management, and return on investment track your progress. Do not treat enterprise architecture like an endless journey.

- **Apply top down systems analysis:** Stick to the business of developing enterprise architecture models. Remember what is in scope and out of scope. Enterprise architecture assumes an organization's strategic plan already exists. Enterprise architecture is about determining information technology needs, not implementing the infrastructure itself.

- **Create style guides and standards:** Establish crystal clear style guides and standards for enterprise architecture models very early. Consistency is of the utmost importance in enterprise architecture, especially on large projects. The goal is not to produce nonsensical models, but aesthetically pleasing models people can actually read, use, and understand.

- **Think outside-of-the-box for tools:** Try to identify a short list of best-in-class tools for enterprise architecture. It is best to choose a tool that does a few models really well, rather than one that does many models very poorly. Do not discard the notion of using separate tools for each model, especially for complex enterprises. There are too many mediocre tools in use.

Encroaching upon the task of strategic planning or information technology implementation is a common error. But, all is not well even for those who stay within the bounds of enterprise architecture. Oftentimes, the organization's strategy is not well defined, therefore insufficient data are available to proceed. Likewise, too many models are produced, which are inconsistent and incompatible. Finally, some models are completely unusable and poor tools often hinder completion of enterprise architecture.

PRINCIPLES FOR SUCCESSFUL RETURN ON INVESTMENT

Return on investment principles go hand in hand with the tips, tricks, and techniques for enterprise architecture. Some people feel measuring payback is a principle for the industrial age and some believe it is path towards the 21st century. Some say return on investment is irrelevant in lieu of net present value, the plethora of payback algorithms, or concepts in real options. The bottom line is that return on investment is a strategic approach to measuring the value of any activity, especially enterprise architecture. And, real options are a key to unlocking its benefits.

- **Use ROI as a success factor:** Use return on investment to drive enterprise architecture. By definition, the goal of enterprise architecture is to align an organization's strategy with its information technology. By implication, a strategy cannot be realized without this alignment. Set out to measure the costs and benefits of using enterprise architecture for this alignment.
- **Etch the desired benefits in stone:** Identify a core set of benefits that you wish to realize from enterprise architecture. Establish measurable goals for operating efficiency, cost reductions, staff reductions, customer satisfaction, computing budgets, and economic growth. Monetize the benefits early (e.g., convert improvements into money), which many do not do.
- **Establish early ROI objectives:** Establish ambitious return on investment objectives

for enterprise architecture based on tangible measures of costs and benefits. Use return on investment to establish safety margins. That is, given the risk of any project or initiative, ensure the payoff far exceeds the cost of enterprise architecture, lest you end up with none.

- **Operationalize a core set of metric:** Define a set of clear, measurable, and quantitative economic benefits for enterprise architecture. Examples include people, time, budgets, customers, throughput, volume, bandwidth, computers, and maintenance. Common mistakes are failing to define metrics, defining qualitative ones, or defining far too many metrics.
- **Continuously measure the payback:** Measure the return on investment of enterprise architecture early and frequently. Measure the payback at regular intervals along with normal project management activities, such as cost, time, and earned value reporting. Payback can be estimated similarly to cost and schedule performance indices before it is too late.
- **Use automated tools to do the work:** Use an integrated project management reporting system with built-in return on investment tracking and reporting. There is no sense in having to master all of the latest payback formulas or designating a return on investment manager. Instead, collect payback data automatically and have the computer system help you along.
- **Standardize ROI reporting:** Create a system for measuring and reporting measures for the return on investment of enterprise architecture. It is virtually impossible to do so with so many local, state, federal, and international enterprise architecture initiatives in existence. It is just too difficult to measure payback after the fact without a standard system in place.

The goal of enterprise architecture is to enable an organization to realize its strategic goals and objectives by streamlining its information technology infrastructure. And, strategic plans are simply a means of ensuring the operational efficiency and effectiveness of organizations and firms alike. The problem is that few people apply return on investment, and few apply it in a consistent manner. The way to avoid this is to elevate return on investment to center stage, identify measurable goals and objectives, and strive to achieve them in every way.

SUMMARY

The goal of this chapter was to introduce a suite of simple metrics for estimating the return on investment of enterprise architecture. This chapter was designed to feature a simple metric for applying contemporary measures of return on investment, such as real options. Traditional measures of payback are considered obsolete in some circles and net present value is often suggested as the most realistic measure of return on investment. Still others say all of these measures are simply obsolete in lieu of real options. Therefore, this chapter introduced a simple model of real options to show practitioners how to easily apply contemporary measures of ROI.

The goal of enterprise architecture is to improve organizational efficiency and effectiveness and return on investment is an excellent way to measure the business value of enterprise architecture. The goals and objectives of enterprise architecture were introduced because they are closely related to the principles of measuring payback. Metrics came next to show how to measure the return on investment of enterprise architecture. From this, we observed that the basic elements of payback are costs and benefits, and return on investment measures flow naturally from these.

The most challenging aspect of measuring the payback of enterprise architecture is not choosing measures of return on investment, but rather identifying, measuring, and monetizing its benefits. A critical element of this chapter was to broach the subject of how to identify the benefits of enterprise architecture, which is why there was a short, but important discussion of its benefits. With enterprise architecture costs and benefits as a foundation, we quickly solved the dilemma of how to illustrate the return on investment of eight federal-level enterprise architecture initiatives. Finally, we showed how real options may be used to optimize the ROI of enterprise architecture.

This chapter went beyond introducing a framework of metrics and models for measuring the return on investment of enterprise architecture. It identified tangible principles for successful enterprise architecture and return on investment itself. Successfully applying enterprise architecture is necessary to achieve return on investment, establishing measurable goals and objectives is necessary for measuring return on investment, and contemporary measures of return on investment such as real options may the key to getting payback from enterprise architecture.

REFERENCES

Hite, R. C. (2002). *Enterprise architecture use across the federal government can be improved* (GAO-02-6). Washington, DC: U.S. Government Accounting Office (GAO).

Kodukula, P. (2006). *Project valuation using real options*. Ft. Lauderdale, FL: J. Ross Publishing.

Meskell, D. (2003). *High payoff in electronic government: Measuring the return on e-government investment*. Washington, DC: U.S. General Services Administration (GSA).

Rico, D. F. (2004). *ROI of software process improvement: Metrics for project managers and software engineers*. Boca Raton, FL: J. Ross Publishing.

Rico, D. F. (2005). Practical metrics and models for return on investment. *TickIT International, 7*(2), 10-16.

Rico, D. F. (2006). A framework for measuring the ROI of enterprise architecture. *International Journal of End User Computing,18*(2), 1-12.

Zachman, J. A. (1987). A framework for information systems architecture. *IBM Systems Journal, 26*(3), 276-292.

Chapter V
An Extension of the Technology Acceptance Model to Determine the Intention to Use Biometric Devices

Tabitha James
Virginia Polytechnic Institute and State University, USA

Taner Pirim
Mississippi Center for Supercomputing Research, USA

Katherine Boswell
University of Louisiana - Monroe, USA

Brian Reithel
University of Mississippi, USA

Reza Barkhi
Virginia Polytechnic Institute and State University, USA

ABSTRACT

Protection of physical assets and digital information is of growing importance to society. The need for development and use of security technologies is ever increasing. As with any new technology, user acceptance of new software and hardware devices is often hard to gauge, and policies to introduce and ensure adequate and correct usage of such technologies are often lacking. Security technologies have widespread applicability to different organizational contexts that may present unusual and varied adoption considerations. This study adapts the technology acceptance model and extends it to study the intention to use security devices, more specifically biometrics, across a wide variety of organizational contexts. Due to the use of physiological characteristics, biometrics present unique adoption concerns. The extension of the technology acceptance model for biometrics is useful, as biometrics encompass many of the same adoption concerns as traditional security devices, but include a level of invasiveness that is obvious to the user. Through the use of vignettes, this study encompasses a systematically varied set of usage contexts for biometric devices to provide a generalizable view of the factors impacting intention to use over all categories of situational contexts of the device's use. The technology acceptance model is extended in this study to include constructs for perceived need for privacy, perceived need for security, and perceived physical invasiveness of biometric devices as factors that influence intention to use. The model is shown to be a good predictor of intention to use biometric devices and implications of the results for biometric and security technology acceptance is discussed.

INTRODUCTION

Property theft, violent crimes, theft, and misuse of digital information, terrorism, and threats to privacy, including identity fraud, in today's digitally connected, mobile society necessitate the development of tools to protect digital information and physical assets by both individuals and corporate entities. According to findings from the National Crime Victimization Survey, approximately 23 million U.S. residents were victims of crime in 2005, including both property crime and violent criminal acts (Bureau of Justice, 2005). The 2006 CSI/FBI Computer Crime and Security Survey reported that 52% of their participants reported unauthorized computer use. Out of the respondents that were willing or could quantify the financial implications, the amount of losses reported exceeded $52 million (Gordon, Loeb, Lucyshyn, & Richardson, 2006). The Federal Trade Commission reported 246,035 identity theft complaints in 2006 which accounted for 36% of all FTC complaints for the year (Federal Trade Commission, 2007). The most common form of identity theft reported was credit card fraud which accounted for 25% of the complaints, followed by phone or utilities fraud, bank fraud, and employment fraud (Federal Trade Commission, 2007).

The need to secure both digital and physical assets is apparent from these statistics, yet it is often difficult for technology to keep pace with the growing number of threats and the increasing number of vulnerabilities that exist in traditional methods of security. A method of identification that has been growing in popularity is the use of physical or behavioral traits, such as fingerprints or DNA, to identify and authenticate individuals. Certain physical and behavioral traits are unique to each individual and therefore may provide methods of identification that are more successful than traditional approaches. Technological devices that utilize these unique traits to identify and authenticate an individual are known as biometrics. These devices have the obvious advantage of not falling prey to many of the well known vulnerabilities of traditional methods. Since a biometric device uses a unique biological trait to distinguish an individual, it is very difficult and often impossible for the identifier to be lost, stolen, duplicated, or given away (Liu & Silverman, 2001). This advantage makes biometric devices an appealing option for individuals and corporations that wish to adopt a new security technology.

The technology acceptance model (TAM) has received wide acceptance for studying the usage behavior of new technologies (Davis, 1989). We extend TAM to determine the intention to use security technologies, specifically biometric devices. We utilize a vignette based survey design to study the user behavior towards biometrics and the intention to use these devices. This approach provides a general overview of individual's perceptions of biometrics regardless of the application area or device type, hence providing insight into possible barriers of adoption of biometric technologies for security purposes. By focusing on factors that influence an individual's intention to use biometric technologies, we can explore the possible modes of adoption that may smooth the transition to new forms of security and authentication technologies. The literature suggests that barriers to adoption of biometric devices can be grouped into the following categories: physical invasiveness, information invasiveness, ease of use, privacy, and the perceived level of benefit from the device (Deane, Barrelle, Henderson, & Mahar, 1995; Liu & Silverman, 2001; Woodward, 1997). We posit that an individual's need for privacy and security, along with the perceived invasiveness of the device and the original TAM constructs of perceived usefulness and ease of use, will impact the intention to use biometric devices. This model is generalizable to a wider range of security/privacy technologies which will aid in our understanding of barriers to adoption to these technologies so that appropriate policies and marketing strategies may be designed to aid in their implementation and use.

In the following section, the relevant literature is presented, along with the theoretical foundation for the proposed constructs. The third section discusses the methodology used to test the proposed model, and the fourth section presents the findings. The fifth section provides a discussion of the results, as well as the limitations and directions for future research, and the last section provides conclusions.

LITERATURE REVIEW AND RESEARCH MOTIVATION

Biometrics

Biometrics can be defined as "the application of computational methods to biological features,

especially with regard to the study of unique biological characteristics of humans" (Hopkins, 1999, p. 337). More generally, a biometric system can be referred to as "a pattern recognition system that makes a personal identification by establishing the authenticity of a specific physiological or behavioral characteristic possessed by the user" (Jain, Hong, & Pankanti, 2000, p.92). Interest in using biometrics is rising, and adoption of these technologies is penetrating corporations and governments. The International Biometric Group predicts the market for biometrics to rise from $1538 million in 2005 to $5749 million by 2010 (BTT, 2006). These numbers indicate that biometric devices will emerge as an important security tool over the next several years. Biometric devices fall into two main categories: physiological, which includes fingerprint, retinal, hand geometry, and facial scanners, and behavioral such as signature biometrics.

There are several areas of usage for biometric devices. These application areas can be loosely grouped into four categories: physical access, virtual access, e-commerce, and covert surveillance (Liu & Silverman, 2001). Applications in the physical access category include any situation where restricted availability of a facility or mode of transportation is necessary (Beiser, 1999; BTT, 2001; Liu & Silverman, 2001; McMillian, 2002; Wayman, 2000; Woodward, 1997). Physical access control holds the major share of the biometrics market, accounting for approximately 50% of the biometrics market (Norton, 2002).

Security devices used for this category have received increased scrutiny as the importance of authenticating individuals for security purposes grows, yet often conflicts with personal privacy issues. The trade-off between maintaining a desired level of security while maintaining a sufficient level of privacy for an individual has received a new level of importance. Privacy advocates often argue that new security infrastructures often encroach upon an individual's privacy by providing means by which characteristics and movements may be more easily tracked and information on individuals more easily exchanged. However, in light of heightened awareness in the United States and other countries due to recent security threats and breaches (e.g., September 11th plane high-jackings and London subway bombings), there has been a renewed interest in means of security that may better protect public places and transportation.

Virtual access includes biometric protection of information, that is, network and computer security. This provides protection of data that are stored on a company's computer systems and traverses the corporate network (Suydam, 2000). A major use of biometrics in the virtual access category is the replacement of passwords, or as an additional level of security on top of a password (Dean, 2002; Liu & Silverman, 2001). Since passwords can be easily forgotten or given away, this alternative may not only improve security, it may also ease administrative tasks.

Credit card, online banking, online trading, ATMs, and online purchasing provide many e-commerce applications to which biometrics may be applied (Liu & Silverman, 2001). Some companies hope that the use of biometric technologies for authentication may reduce the amount of money spent for fraud cases. Devices in this category can help prevent unlawful financial transactions, identity theft, and help provide security for an individual's credit cases (Arent, 1999; Herman, 2002; Jain et al., 2000; Jeffords, Thibadoux, & Scheidt, 1999; Liu & Silverman, 2001; Woodward, 1997).

Covert surveillance forms the last category. Devices in this category are intended to identify possible criminals. Applications in this area are often the most controversial, yet are growing in popularity due to increased interest in providing additional levels of security by monitoring, for example, passengers in public transportation, people attending large public events, buildings with public access, or traffic. Biometrics may be used, for example, to compare individuals against

databases of known criminal offenders in airports or casinos (Scheeres, 2001; Titsworth, 2002). Biometric devices are being used by several states in attempts to avoid issuance of fraudulent driver's licenses (Atkinson, 2002; Titsworth, 2002; Wayman, 2000). The use of mobile biometric devices by police departments are being explored as a way to decrease the number of fraudulent IDs used (Dale, 2001). As these systems advance, they should help provide personal security for individuals and help find criminals.

As with many security technologies, biometric devices have widespread applicability. Unlike many traditional technologies, they are not specialized in their usage setting or purpose and their usefulness is often associated with their function rather than their stand-alone implementation, as would be the case with a software package. Biometric devices may be adopted for use in a variety of settings for a myriad of functions by different types of entities. The adoption decision for biometrics, not unlike many security technologies, may be an individual decision or an organizational decision. That is, these devices may be marketed as devices that can be obtained by an individual for general purposes such as securing one's home or may be implemented as an additional security device on a vehicle which is then sold as a package. They may also be implemented by an organization where compliance for use is mandatory such as entry to a facility by employees or where the implementation and usage may be regarded as a choice. A determination of the general acceptance of the device is useful to any entity considering the adoption of these types of security devices regardless of context. The purpose of this study is to develop a general model of user acceptance for biometric devices, regardless of the context of their use or the physiological or behavioral traits they use for identification.

TECHNOLOGY ACCEPTANCE MODEL

Determining the factors influencing acceptance of technologies provides useful insight for entities both wishing to market a technology or those attempting to successfully adopt a technology. An understanding of possible barriers to successful adoption and usage of a technology can enable parties to put in place techniques that will aid the process, thus lessening possible financial losses from an unsuccessful adoption attempt. There have been significant advances in predicting usage and determining factors influencing adoption. The technology acceptance model, developed by Davis (1989), has gained much popularity in the literature due to its success in determining intention to use and usage of technologies (Venkatesh & Davis, 2000).

The TAM model is an adaptation of the theory of reasoned action (Ajzen & Fishbein, 1980) intended to focus on acceptance and usage behavior specifically for information systems. TAM postulates that the two most important determinants of user acceptance of computing technologies are ease of use and usefulness (Davis, 1989; Davis, Bagozzi, & Warshaw, 1989). The TAM model looks at these two determinants and their relationship to behavioral intention to use and actual system usage. Significant empirical research has shown positive results in using TAM to predict acceptance and usage behavior of end users in several areas. Application areas include end-user software adoption (Szajna, 1994), e-commerce (Chen, Gillenson, & Sherrell, 2002; Koufaris, 2002), digital libraries (Hong, Thong, Wong, & Tam, 2002), telemedicine technologies (Hu, Chau, Sheng, & Tam, 1999), smart cards (Plouffe, Hulland, & Vandenbosch, 2001), and building management systems (Lowry, 2002).

As has been shown in previous TAM studies, we expect perceived usefulness and perceived ease of use to positively impact intention to use. If an individual believes the device to be useful and

easy to use we assume that they will be likely to submit to the use of the device. We also expect the perceived ease of use of the technology to impact the perceived usefulness of the technology.

Hypothesis 1: The perceived usefulness of the security technology will have a positive impact an individual's intention to use the technology.
Hypothesis 2: The perceived difficulty/ease of use of the security technology will have a positive impact an individual's intention to use the technology.
Hypothesis 3: The perceived ease of use of the security technology will have a positive impact on the perceived usefulness of the technology.

The current research extends and adapts the original technology acceptance model to study security technology implemented as biometric devices. As the purpose of security technologies is to protect physical assets and digital information, the perception of the importance of securing digital and physical assets should influence the beliefs and behaviors of the participants. To study biometric technology, we need to extend the TAM model to account for the level of physical invasiveness that is not included in the original TAM model. While we focus on biometric technology, physical invasiveness is not completely unique to biometrics but also applicable to other security technologies such as microchip implantation. Approaches such as biometric identification and microchip implantations are technologies that avoid some of the well-known vulnerabilities in identification and authentication methods. Physical invasiveness adds a new dimension to the acceptance and use of security devices.

This study extends the TAM model with the addition of constructs for perceived need for security and privacy as well as perceived invasiveness to provide a robust model of technology acceptance for biometrics which could be easily adapted for any class of security device. These added constructs take into account the user's perceptions and beliefs in the areas of security, privacy, and physical invasiveness which are not captured in the original TAM model. The resulting model, therefore, provides further insight into the usage intentions of the end users or security technologies. Due to the rising importance of security and privacy in today's society, a closer examination of the acceptance of advanced technologies such as biometrics, is warranted. These extensions are further justified in the following sections. The resulting conceptual model developed for this study, including the hypothesized relationships, is shown in Figure 1.

Physical Invasiveness

The perception of physical invasiveness is relatively new to the computing technologies area. Invasiveness in the medical technologies area has been an area of concern, but the application for these technologies is drastically different in type (e.g., medical technologies for treatment purposes). Recent discussions of using implanted microchips for identification and tracking pur-

poses have raised some concerns. Although discussed, the use of this technology in humans has not currently reached the market.

Biometric devices require the use of physiological traits and in some cases may be perceived as physically invasive. Many biometric devices can be intimidating to use for many individuals, especially initially. Many people have a natural aversion to using devices that require a scan of their eyes and fingerprint biometrics can have negative associations (Kim, 1995). Due to the personal nature of this identification method, individuals may view the devices as invasive which may present an obstacle to user acceptance (Liu & Silverman, 2001). The use of fingerprint biometrics and especially retinal biometrics are often encumbered by the perception of physical invasiveness (Kim, 1995). Due to the newness of physical invasiveness to security devices, little research has been conducted to determine the impact of this characteristic on usage. Kim (1995) point out that certain biometric devices may be perceived as more physically invasive or hold a more negative connotation than others.

Figure 1. Conceptual model

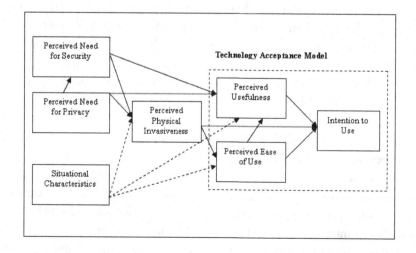

For example, fingerprint scanners may be associated with the criminal bookings. Similarly, due to the inherent self-protection of the eyes, most people are likely to feel uncomfortable with the idea of having a laser directed at their eye retina every time they want to make a financial transaction. In contrast, hand recognition where the palm is placed on the plate, appears not to bother people so much (probably because hand-shaking is common behavior). Also, dynamic signature verification would be acceptable to people of all ages and social groups who are literate, since signature is already widely used as a means of personal identification. (Kim, 1995)

The perception of physical invasiveness of biometric devices may affect the usage behavior for the technology as well as impact the perception of ease of use of the device. Invasiveness can be perceived as an intrusion or encroachment to one physically and/or from a privacy standpoint. As can be seen from the proceeding quote, biometric devices can have negative connotations as to their use as well as a level of physicality that may provide levels of discomfort (both physically and mentally) than traditional security devices. In this study, we are concerned with the physical invasiveness of the devices. That is, the perception of discomfort or fear from the physicality of the device use. The perceived physical invasiveness construct is defined for the current study as one's perception of the invasiveness of the technology to their person.

We expect the perceived invasiveness of the devices should negatively impact their perceived ease of use. If an individual perceives these technologies to be highly invasive, then they may think they are more difficult to use.

Hypothesis 4: The perceived physical invasiveness of the security technology will have a negative impact on the perceived ease of use of the technology.

The perceived invasiveness of the biometrics should also directly negatively impact an individual's intention to use. When they perceive the devices to be highly physically invasive, they should be more reluctant to submit to their use and more likely to avoid or object to their adoption or use.

Hypothesis 5: The perceived invasiveness of the security technology will have a negative impact an individual's intention to use the technology.

Security

Security in a broad sense encompasses the protection of assets, both physical and digital. These assets may be physical, a person or a building, or informational, a company's financial records or a person's medical records. Perceived need for security is therefore defined as one's perceived need for the safekeeping of physical or informational assets.

Physical asset security has long been protected by the use of traditional methods such as restricted entry to areas by the use of locks. Digital security has become increasingly important as the connectedness of society grows with the use of the Internet. Various security measures have been implemented in the attempt to thwart an ever-increasing number of threats from viruses or malicious invasions of digital information.

Traditionally, devices to assure that only authorized individuals can access restricted areas fall into two categories: something an individual has, such as a key or a smart card, or something the user knows, such as a pin or password (Jain et al., 2000). The major downfalls to these practices are the possibility of theft of the entry token or intentional (unintentional) compromise of the knowledge necessary to gain access. Physical asset security is often one measure used to protect digital information. Restricted access to areas that house the equipment used to store data has long been of primary concern for information security practitioners (Loch, Carr, & Warkentin, 1992).

The reliability and protection of data has long been an issue. Physical protection of data and the reduction of data errors have been compounded by the increased reliance on networks which frequently introduce new information security threats on top of the traditional ones. Threats to information security include accidental and intentional entry of bad data, accidental and intentional destruction of data, unauthorized access to data, inadequate control over media, poor control over manual I/O, access to data or systems by outsiders (both hackers and competitors), computer viruses/worms, weak or inadequate physical control, and natural disasters (i.e., fire, flood, power loss) (Loch et al., 1992). Development and adoption of new technologies to attempt to prevent and detect new types of information security breaches are extremely important in today's computing environment and the topic of much research.

There has been a lack of research to study an individual's perception of the importance of or need for security. Behavioral studies have focused on security awareness in information security (Siponen, 2000) or organizational security practices (Straub, 1990). However, of increasing importance is an individual's perception of the importance of securing their physical assets and digital information as this may impact their perception of the importance of security devices and thereby influence their usage behavior. As biometric devices by design are targeted towards securing digital and physical assets, an individual's perceived need for security should influence the perception of usefulness of the device. If an individual has a high perceived need for security, the perceived usefulness of a security tool to protect themselves as well as their assets should increase. This leads us to the following hypothesis:

Hypothesis 6: An individual's desire for the security of his/her person and personal information will have a positive impact on the perceived usefulness of the technology.

Although the requirements for use of biometric technologies may be perceived as more invasive than traditional security technologies, a high perceived need for security may counteract the perception of invasiveness and therefore have a negative impact on the perceived physical invasiveness of biometrics. If an individual places major importance on their security and/or the security of their assets, the physicality of using the biometrics may be perceived as less of a factor than otherwise.

Hypothesis 7: An individual's desire for the security of his/her person and personal information will have a negative impact on the perceived invasiveness of the technology.

Privacy

Privacy refers to the ability of an individual to "control the terms under which personal information is acquired and used" (Westin, 1967, p. 7). Information privacy has been defined as, "the ability of the individual to personally control information about one's self" (as quoted in Smith, Milberg, & Burke, 1996, p. 168). For the current study, perceived need for privacy will be defined as the importance to an individual of being able to control the acquisition and usage of personal information.

The reliance on the collection and use of data in today's technology dependent society has increased privacy concerns. Hence, privacy has been listed as one of the biggest ethical issues of the information age (Mason, 1986). Mason argues that there exist two major threats to an individual's right to privacy: an increased ability to collect data due to the growth of information technology in areas such as surveillance, communication, computation, storage, and retrieval and an increase in the value of this information for decision making (Mason, 1986). Henderson and Snyder (1999) describe three major forces driving an increased focus on personal information privacy: (1) new technological capabilities, (2) an increased value of information, and (3) confusion over what is ethically right and wrong.

Research in the information systems area on privacy has focused on organizational use of collected data. Smith et al. (1996) developed an instrument to measure an individual's concern over an organization's information privacy practices which was later re-examined by Stewart and Segars (2002). Their study identified four primary dimensions of an individual's concern of organizational information privacy practices: collection, unauthorized secondary use, improper access, and errors (Smith et al., 1996).

Security tools are often used as a means of protecting an individual's privacy, and therefore if an individual has a high perceived need for privacy, this should have a positive impact on the perceived usefulness of the devices. We propose that an individual's need for privacy will positively impact perceived usefulness.

Hypothesis 8: An individual's perceived need for privacy will have a positive impact on the perceived usefulness of the technology.

Security is often tied into privacy due to the use of security devices to protect personal information. The protection of information considered sensitive, especially in digital form, is a major concern for both individuals and corporations. The use and security of personal information released to a secondary party is also of rising concern in society due to the increased ability to collect and process such information. In many cases, however, the use of security devices raises its own set of privacy concerns. It is often necessary to collect data considered personal from individuals in order to enforce user authentication to facilities and digital information. Along with the possibility of perceived invasion of privacy from monitoring and surveillance security systems, the technologies themselves often give rise to privacy issues (Kim, 1995).

It has been shown that an individual's perception of the importance of privacy has a positive impact on the individual's need for security as shown in Pirim, James, Boswell, Reithel, and Barkhi (in press). If an individual places a high importance on privacy, that individual will place a high importance on securing privacy. Therefore, it is expected that an individual's need for privacy will positively impact the individual's perceived need for security.

Hypothesis 9: An individual's perceived need for privacy will have a positive effect on his/her need for security.

Complications for the use of security tools arise due to the fact that methods of providing security can be viewed as invasions of privacy. Identification and verification are the primary means of providing security. In order to protect assets and individuals, it is necessary to know the identity of the individuals who are granted access to physical locations as well as digital information and to be able to verify that an individual is who he/she claims to be. To accomplish this task, a certain amount of information that may be considered private is necessary. Privacy advocates often object to the collection of personal information and to appease society's need for privacy, it is necessary to collect the minimum amount of information necessary and to protect the information that is collected from misuse or theft. Biometrics present an even more unique characteristic in the collection of personal information as the data needed to implement the devices are physiological or behavioral traits of an individual, rather than typical data collected to identify an individual such as a name, birth date, or identification number.

Biometric devices may be viewed as invasions of privacy due to the personalized physical usage requirements. Therefore, the more private an individual perceives her/himself to be, the more invasive the biometric devices may be perceived.

This leads to the following hypotheses:

Hypothesis 10: An individual's desire for privacy will have a positive impact on the perceived invasiveness of the technology.

Methodology

Smith et al. (1996) developed a survey instrument to measure information privacy, focusing on corporate information privacy. The construct for perceived need for privacy utilized in our study is more general. This study uses an instrument developed to measure an individual's perceived need for privacy in a general context. The set of items to measure the perceived need for security are intended to look at an individual's general feelings on security. The instrument for both the perceived need for privacy (Appendix A, Questions 1-9) and perceived need for security constructs (Appendix A, Questions 10-18) was developed in prior research where it was pretested and refined (Pirim et al., 2004). Cronbach's Alphas obtained for the current study were 0.90 for the perceived need for security construct and 0.85 for the perceived need for privacy construct. The Cronbach's Alphas obtained for both constructs were higher than the recommended levels of 0.70. Table 1 shows the result of the confirmatory factor analysis for these instruments, and Table 2 provides means and standard deviations for the items.

Perceived physical invasiveness, perceived usefulness, perceived ease of use, and intention to use were examined through the use of a series of vignettes. The vignettes (see Appendix A) were designed to include a selection of various application areas for biometrics devices, along with a selection of different device types. The application areas include situations where biometric devices were used in each of the following categories: physical access, virtual access, e-commerce, and covert surveillance (Liu & Silverman, 2001). A variety of biometric devices were included in the

vignettes, from both the behavioral and physiological categories, including retinal scanners, fingerprint scanners, hand geometry scanners, signature biometrics, and facial recognition devices. The amount of time required to use the device was also varied slightly. Along with varying the device type, usage time, and application area, the vignettes were also varied as to the implementation. That is, the situations described not only had various purposes but various requirements as to choice of use. For example, in some situations, the adoption involved an individual choice, such as employing a device to enter one's home; in other situations, the adoption involved an organization where the usage requirement could be viewed as either mandatory (e.g., entrance into a corporate

Table 1. Factor loadings for the perceived need for privacy and security instrument (S1-S9 correspond to questions 1-9 in Appendix A, and P1-P9 correspond to questions 10-18 in Appendix A)

Item	Factor	
	1	2
S1	**.731**	.056
S2	**.761**	.086
S3	**.801**	.148
S4	**.753**	.119
S5	**.721**	.159
S6	**.631**	.223
S7	**.648**	.378
S8	**.652**	.384
S9	**.625**	.379
P1	.420	**.591**
P2	.444	**.616**
P3	.192	**.770**
P4	.473	**.571**
P5	.380	**.617**
P6	.305	**.619**
P7	-.077	**.725**
P8	-.034	**.688**
P9	.435	**.488**

facility) or not mandatory (e.g., use of a biometric at an ATM). The variations in security technology and the situations were an attempt to generalize the findings.

The purpose of the study was not to determine which contexts or device types impacted the attitudes of the users, but rather to develop a generalizable model of technology acceptance for this category of devices. In order to control for potential situational confounds and biases,

the vignettes were developed to include all of the application areas discussed above. In addition, we selected a sample of devices to represent both the behavioral and physiological categories. All vignettes were presented to each study participant to be able to generalize the findings of the research over all usage categories and device types. The subjects were asked the same questions after reading each of the vignettes (see Appendix A) and all vignettes were presented to each survey

Table 2. Descriptive statistics for perceived need for security and privacy

Item No.	Question	Mean	S.D.
S1	I feel that the safeguarding from potential external threats of my physical being is important to me.	1.56	.76
S2	I feel that my personal security at my home or in my vehicle is important to me.	1.39	.67
S3	I feel that my personal security at my place of work or other work related places is important to me.	1.51	.71
S4	My security at places of public access, such as a mall or airport, or special public events, such as the Olympics or the Super Bowl, is important to me.	1.48	.64
S5	I feel that the security of my tangible assets (such as my home, vehicle, etc.) is important to me.	1.53	.70
S6	I feel that keeping my personal possessions, such as jewelry, money, electronics, etc. safe is important to me.	1.66	.74
S7	I feel that the safekeeping of my informational assets contained in digital or paper format is important to me (such as financial records, medical records, etc.)	1.53	.72
S8	I feel that the security of my personal information, such as my PC files or personal records (financial, medical, etc.) is important to me.	1.56	.72
S9	I feel that the safekeeping of information I have provided to a corporation or other entity is important to me.	1.66	.78
P1	I feel my privacy is very important to me.	1.47	.68
P2	I feel that my control over my personal information is very important to me.	1.51	.69
P3	I feel that it is important not to release sensitive information to any entity.	1.92	.97
P4	I feel it is important to avoid having personal information released that I think could be financially damaging.	1.48	.70
P5	I feel it is important to avoid having personal information released that I think could be socially damaging to me.	1.65	.76
P6	I feel it is important to avoid having personal information about me released that may go against social morals and attitudes.	1.80	.86
P7	I feel that the release of personal information to individuals with whom I have a high comfort level is unacceptable.	2.62	1.19
P8	I feel that the release of personal information to entities where I feel as though I am anonymously providing the information is unacceptable.	2.27	1.11
P9	I feel that the use of personal information that has been released by me but is used in a manner not intended by me is unacceptable.	1.61	.86

participant. For each vignette, the same set of questions was asked for each of the following constructs: perceived physical invasiveness, perceived usefulness, perceived ease of use, and intention to use. All items were measured by a five point scale (1 = strongly agree, 5 = strongly disagree).

The survey was administered to faculty, staff, and students at the University of Mississippi. A total of 298 usable responses were collected. Table 3 shows the demographic information for the sample used.

To analyze the model, a series of linear regressions were performed to obtain path coefficients for the proposed model. Situational differences in the usage scenarios of the devices were introduced through the use of vignettes in the instrument. As described above, the vignettes were varied by changing the device type, usage context, and application area as well as the length of time as-

sociated with using the device. To test the impact of varying the situational characteristics on the model, dummy variables were introduced in some of the regressions. In this manner, we were able to observe if any vignette had an undue influence while the number of vignettes introduced to each subject and the variation of their contexts allowed for an overall view of the impact of the additional constructs. The regression equations (1 thru 3) for these tests are shown below.

Where PI = perceived invasiveness, P = perceived need for privacy, S = perceived need for security, PEU = perceived ease of use, PU = perceived usefulness, and D_1 through D_7 are dummy variables associated with the vignette scenarios (where D_i = 1 if vignette i is used, D_i = 0 otherwise).

The proposed relationship between perceived need for privacy and perceived need for security was found to be significant in prior research (Pirim

Table 3. Profile of survey participants

Total Number of Participants	298
Sex	
Male	144
Female	154
Age	
17-21	98
22-36	97
Over 36	103
Major	
CS	6
Engineering	16
Finance	31
Management	23
MIS	13
Marketing	47
Other	162
Highest Level of Education	
High School	78
2-Year Associates	51
4-Year Undergraduate	67
Masters	42
Ph.D.	60

et al., 2004). We tested this relationship again in the current study using a regression to obtain path coefficients for the constructs in the model related to intention to use. These regression equations (4 & 5) are shown below.

Where P = perceived need for privacy, S = perceived need for security, IU = intention to use, PU = perceived usefulness, PEU = perceived ease of use, and PI = perceived invasiveness.

RESULTS

The hypotheses were tested to determine the model's capability of predicting user acceptance of biometric devices and the operationalized model is presented in Figure 2. Table 4 presents the regression coefficients, t-values, and significance levels for the model.

Both perceived usefulness and perceived ease of use had significant effects on intention to use ($\beta = 0.50$; $\beta = 0.30$), supporting hypotheses 1 and 2. The implication here is that if the individual feels that the biometric device is useful in a particular situation, they will be more likely to use the technology. An individual may also be more likely to use the device if they feel that it is easy to use.

The perceived ease of use of the device was found to have a significant impact on perceived usefulness ($\beta = .65$), supporting hypothesis 3. An individual's perception of how easy the device will be to use may be a large determining factor on its perceived usefulness. This implies that the complexity of use of the device will significantly impact whether or not said device is perceived as being useful.

Perceived invasiveness has a negative significant impact on the ease of use of the device ($\beta = -.187$), supporting hypothesis 4. This result implies that the more invasive the biometric is perceived to be, the less easy it will be viewed to use.

Perceived physical invasiveness impacted negatively an individual's intention to use the biometric device ($\beta = -0.12$), supporting hypothesis 5. This implies that the more invasive a biometric is perceived to be, the less likely are the chances of the individual actually using the device if a choice is given.

An individual's perceived need for security was found to have a significant impact on perceived usefulness ($\beta = .12$), supporting hypothesis 6. The

Regression Equations

[1] $\quad PI = \beta_0 + \beta_1 P + \beta_2 S + \beta_3 D_1 + \beta_4 D_2 + \beta_5 D_3 + \beta_6 D_4 + \beta_7 D_5 + \beta_8 D_6 + \beta_9 D_7$

[2] $\quad PU = \beta_0 + \beta_1 P + \beta_2 S + \beta_3 PEU + \beta_4 D_1 + \beta_5 D_2 + \beta_6 D_3 + \beta_7 D_4 +$
$\beta_8 D_5 + \beta_9 D_6 + \beta_{10} D_7$

[3] $\quad PEU = \beta_0 + \beta_1 PI + \beta_2 D_1 + \beta_3 D_2 + \beta_4 D_3 + \beta_5 D_4 + \beta_6 D_5 + \beta_7 D_6 + \beta_8 D_7$

[4] $\quad S = \beta_0 + \beta_1 P$

[5] $\quad IU = \beta_0 + \beta_1 PU + \beta_2 PEU + \beta_3 PI$

Figure 2. Extended technology acceptance model for biometric technologies

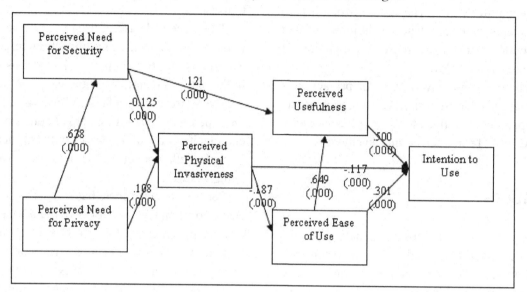

results of the regression imply that an individual's perceived need for security will positively impact how useful they feel the biometric device will be.

Perceived need for security has a negative significant impact on perceived invasiveness (β = -.125), supporting hypothesis 7. This implies that the more secure an individual feels he/she needs, the less invasive the technology will be viewed.

Perceived need for privacy did not have a significant impact as expected on perceived usefulness, therefore did not support hypothesis 8. However, perceived need for privacy impacts perceived need for security, thus indirectly affecting the perceived usefulness of the device.

The results obtained show a significant effect (β = 0.64) of perceived need for privacy on the perceived need for security. The implication of this relationship is that if an individual feels a high perceived need for privacy, the individual will have a high perceived need for security. This finding supports hypothesis 9.

Perceived need for privacy is shown to have a significant positive affect on perceived invasiveness of the device (β = .108), supporting hypothesis 10. Biometric devices may be viewed as invasions

of privacy due to the personalized physical usage requirements. Therefore, the implication of the results obtained is that the more private an individual perceives themselves to be, the more invasive the biometric device may be perceived.

DISCUSSION, LIMITATIONS, AND DIRECTIONS FOR FURTHER RESEARCH

The results of the statistical tests of the hypotheses indicate that the additional constructs do significantly impact the intention of a user towards biometric devices. Invasiveness is shown to have, as expected, a significant negative impact on ease of use as well as intention to use security technology. As was mentioned in previous research, negative connotations associated with biometric devices as well as the obvious physicality of using the technology will influence the adoption behaviors of the users. When examining the invasiveness construct, the influence of the situational contexts were more apparent. There was a noticeable impact from the vignettes where a retinal biometric device was employed and to the use of a biometric device in a public arena where identification could be viewed with a negative connotation. Although not explicitly tested for, this implies that there is the possibility that the eye may be viewed as a more sensitive or invasive area of a person than the areas subjected to other biometric devices.

Kim (1995) addressed this issue as described in the literature review. This indicates that further research as to the area of the body that is subject to appraisal by different device types may be an interesting avenue to explore.

Table 4. Regression coefficients for extended technology acceptance model

Dependent Variable	Construct	Standardized Coefficient	t	Sig
Security ($R^2 = .408$)	Privacy	.638	14.272	.000
Invasiveness ($R^2 = .027$)	Privacy	.108	4.087	.000
	Security	-.125	-4.753	.000
	D1	-.027	-.999	.318
	D2	-.116	-4.330	.000
	D3	-.126	-4.709	.000
	D4	-.071	-2.650	.008
	D5	-.078	-2.918	.004
	D6	-.070	-2.595	.010
	D7	-.128	-4.777	.000
EOU ($R^2 = .058$)	Invasiveness	-.187	-9.288	.000
	D1	.004	.170	.865
	D2	.018	.698	.486
	D3	.106	4.014	.000
	D4	-.024	-.901	.368
	D5	.001	.029	.977
	D6	.004	.148	.882
	D7	.095	3.591	.000
Usefulness ($R^2 = .471$)	EOU	.649	41.274	.000
	Security	.121	6.204	.000
	Privacy	-.006	-.301	.763
	D1	.082	4.160	.000
	D2	-.054	-2.731	.006
	D3	-.099	-4.980	.000
	D4	.011	.579	.562
	D5	-.016	-.820	.412
	D6	-.022	-1.110	.267
	D7	-.050	-2.534	.011
Intention ($R^2 = .595$)	EOU	.301	17.259	.000
	Usefulness	.500	28.472	.000
	Invasiveness	-.117	-8.678	.000

alpha = .05 for all regressions

The addition of the perceived physical invasiveness construct in the current model provides an important addition to the adoption literature as it has not been explored in terms of nonmedical technology in a rigorous way due to the lack of its presence in most mainstream technologies. With the development and exploration of technologies for identification that require unusual usage requirements (e.g., that a person must submit to a scan of a body part or to the implantation of a chip in order for the device to be used for its intended purpose), perceived physical invasiveness determining the impact of this construct on the adoption behaviors of end users will increase in importance. By gauging this impact, organizations considering implementing these types of devices for use by consumers or employees as well as companies marketing such tools will be able to carefully consider their device choice as well as develop informational and training sessions tailored to the concerns of the users that may help ease fears and smooth adopting.

Perceived need for security positively impacted the usefulness of the device, but perceived need for privacy did not. However, perceived need for privacy is shown to impact perceived need for security. These results imply that an individual's perception of their need for privacy did not directly impact the device's perceived usefulness but is closely tied to the individual's perceived need for security forming an indirect relationship. These results imply that security and privacy are strongly linked. An individual with a strong desire for privacy may therefore view security technologies as a means to protect this privacy. Privacy could thus be viewed as something an individual wishes to protect therefore providing additional utility to security devices. There does exist a conflicting issue, as can be seen with the impact of perceived need for privacy on perceived physical invasiveness, in that all security devices typically require some relinquishing of personal "data" in order to properly identify and verify (or secure) the individual, facility, or digital information.

The study was limited due to the number and variation of survey participants. The sample was restricted to faculty, staff, and students at one major university located in an area with a small population. While providing a good sample due to the variation of backgrounds, educational level, and employment opportunities that are present in a university environment, a larger sample size with greater variation in physical location and place of employment may be a direction for future research. Due to the substantial number of constructs, a larger number of subjects would be required to employ a technique such as structural equation modeling. The methodology employed in the current study provided key insights into the model being explored. However, the model could be further investigated in later studies utilizing methods such as structural equation modeling.

CONCLUSION

The model developed in this study is shown to be a good predictor for intention to use biometric devices. The instrument developed in this research could be used as an indicator of adoption success of biometric technologies for both an adoption company and entities wishing to market and sell these technologies for different security situations. Obtaining an idea of adoption success could be useful in preventing unsuccessful attempts to utilize a biometric technology prior to adoption and prevent or mitigate financial losses due to unsuccessful adoption attempts or underutilized technology.

The results of testing the model show that an individual's perceived need for security and the perceived ease of use of the device significantly impact the individual's perception of the usefulness of the biometric device. This would imply that the more security conscious an individual is the more likely they would be to accept the use of a biometric technology. This implies that they would perceive the device as being useful as a means to protect their security. Both perceived usefulness and perceived ease of use impact an individual's intention to use the biometric device. Perceived physical invasiveness of the device was shown to have a significant negative impact on intention to use. Perceived physical invasiveness of the device is also shown to have a significant negative impact on the ease of use of the technology. These results are especially important in the biometrics arena as several of the devices may produce strong feelings of physical invasiveness that many other technologies in the security environment are exempt from. They are also useful from the perspective of the choice of biometric type to implement. Since physical invasiveness is shown to have an impact, more attention may need to be paid to this concern in the decision making process.

The results outline two major areas of managerial significance related to the adoption of biometric devices. First, the careful consideration as to the specific biometric technology implemented is important as physical invasiveness may produce unwanted adoption behavior. This perceived invasiveness may also impact the perceived ease of use of the device in an unexpected way, possibly requiring the use of different approaches for adoption procedures or more extensive training on the technology. Second, it is also useful to note that an individual's perceived need for security plays an important role in the intention to use the biometric device. Therefore, as security concerns become more important in the current state of the world, adoption procedures that emphasize this benefit of the technology may aid in improving the adoption procedure.

The model proposed and tested in this project could be modified and applied to other technologies in the security area. As concern over privacy and security issues increase, the ability to obtain an overall picture of security technology adoption becomes more important not only to help increase the level of security of crucial assets but to aid in the prevention of unsuccessful attempts to adopt new technologies.

REFERENCES

Ajzen, I., & Fishbein, M. (1980). *Understanding attitudes and predicting social behavior*. Upper Saddle River, NJ: Prentice Hall.

Arent, L. (1999). ATM wants to be your friend. Retrieved August 6, 2007, from Wired News, http://www.wired.com

Atkinson, R. (2002, May). Biometrics drivers' licenses on the cards. *Biometric Technology Today, 10*(5), 1-2.

Beiser, V. (1999). Biometrics breaks into prisons. Retrieved August 6, 2007, from Wired News, http://www.wired.com

BTT. (2001). Biometrics secure Internet data centres worldwide. *Biometric Technology Today, 9*(2), 3.

BTT. (2006). Biometric statistics in focus. *Biometric Technology Today, 14*(2), 7-9.

Bureau of Justice. (2005). Bureau of Justice statistics: Criminal victimization. Retrieved August 6, 2007, from http://www.ojp.usdoj.gov/bjs/cvictgen. htm.

Chen, L., Gillenson, M., & Sherrell, D. (2002). Enticing online consumers: An extended technology acceptance perspective. *Information and Management, 39*, 705-719.

Dale, L. (2001). Mobile biometric devices help in law enforcement. *Biometric Technology Today, 9*(8), 6-7.

Davis, F. (1989, September). Perceived usefulness, perceived ease of use, and user acceptance of information technology. *MIS Quarterly*, pp. 319-340.

Davis, F., Bagozzi, R., & Warshaw, P. (1989). User acceptance of computer technology: A comparison of two theoretical models. *Management Science, 35*(8), 982-1003.

Dean, K. (2002). College seeks security in thumbs. Retrieved August 6, 2007, from Wired News, http://www.wired.com

Deane, F., Barrelle, K., Henderson, R., & Mahar, D. (1995). Perceived acceptability of biometric security systems. *Computers and Security, 14,* 225-231.

Federal Trade Commission. (2007). FTC issues annual list of top consumer complaints. Retrieved August 6, 2007, from the Federal Trade Commission, http://www.ftc.gov/opa/2007/02/top-complaints.htm

Gordon, L., Loeb, M., Lucyshyn, W., & Richardson, R. (2006). 2006 CSI/FBI computer crime and security survey. Retrieved August 6, 2007, from CSI, http://www.gocsi.com/

Henderson, S., & Snyder, C. (1999). Personal information privacy: Implications for MIS managers. *Information and Management, 36,* 213-220.

Herman, A. (2002). Major bank signs up for digital signature verification technology. *Biometric Technology Today, 10*(1), 1.

Hong, W., Thong, J., Wong, W., & Tam, K. (2002). Determinants of user acceptance of digital libraries: An empirical examination of individual differences and system characteristics. *Journal of Management Information Systems, 18*(3), 97-124.

Hopkins, R. (1999). An introduction to biometrics and large scale civilian identification. *International Review of Law Computer and Technology, 13*(3), 337-363.

Hu, P., Chau, P., Sheng, O., & Tam, K. (1999). Examining the technology acceptance model using physician acceptance of telemedicine technology. *Journal of Management Information Systems, 16*(2), 91-112.

Jain, A., Hong, L., & Pankanti, S. (2000). Biometric identification. *Communications of the ACM, 43*(2), 91-98.

Jeffords, R., Thibadoux, G., & Scheidt, M. (1999, March). New technologies to combat check fraud. *The CPA Journal, 69*(3), 30-34.

Kim, H. (1995). Biometrics, is it a viable proposition for identity authentication and access control? *Computers and Security, 14,* 205-214.

Koufaris, M. (2002). Applying the technology acceptance model and flow theory to online consumer behavior. *Information Systems Research, 13*(2), 205-223.

Liu, S., & Silverman, M. (2001, January/February). A practical guide to biometric security technology. *IT Professional,* pp. 27-32.

Loch, K., Carr, H., & Warkentin, M. (1992). Threats to information systems: Today's reality, yesterday's understanding. *MIS Quarterly, 16*(2), 173-186.

Lowry, G. (2002). Modeling user acceptance of building management systems. *Automation in Construction, 11,* 695-705.

Mason, R. (1986). Four ethical issues of the information age. *MIS Quarterly, 10*(1), 5-12.

McMillian, R. (2002). The myth of airport biometrics. Retrieved August 6, 2007 from Wired News, http://www.wired.com

Norton, R. (2002, October). The evolving biometric marketplace to 2006. *Biometric Technology Today,* pp. 7-8.

Pirim, T., James, T., Boswell, K., Reithel, B., & Barkhi, R. (in press). An empirical investigation of an individual's perceived need for privacy and security. *International Journal of Information Security and Privacy.*

Plouffe, C., Hulland, J., & Vandenbosch, M. (2001). Research report: Richness versus parsimony in modeling technology adoption decisions: Understanding merchant adoption of a smart card-based payment system. *Information Systems Research, 12*(2), 208-222.

Scheeres, J. (2001). Smile, you're on camera. Retrieved August 6, 2007, from Wired News, http://www.wired.com

Siponen, M. (2000). A conceptual foundation for organizational information security. *Information Management and Computer Security, 8*(1), 31-44.

Smith, H., Milberg, S., & Burke, S. (1996). Information privacy: Measuring individuals' concerns about organizational practices. *MIS Quarterly, 20*(2), 167-196.

Stewart, K., & Segars, A. (2002). An empirical examination of the concern for information privacy instrument. *Information Systems Research, 13*(1), 36-49.

Straub, D. (1990). Effective IS security: An empirical study. *Information Systems Research, 1*(3), 255-276.

Suydam, M. (2000, March). Taking (health) care. *Information Security,* p. 54.

Szajna, B. (1994). Software evaluation and choice: Predictive validation of the technology acceptance instrument. *MIS Quarterly, 18*(3), 319-324.

Titsworth, T. (2002). More than face value: Airports and multimedia security. *IEEE Multimedia, 9*(2), 11-13.

Venkatesh, V., & Davis, F. (2000). A theoretical extension of the technology acceptance model: Four longitudinal field studies. *Management Science, 46*(2), 186-204.

Wayman, J. (2000, February). Federal biometric technology legislation. *Computer,* pp. 76-80.

Westin, A. (1967). *Privacy and freedom.* New York: Atheneum Publishers.

Woodward, J. (1997). Biometrics: Privacy's foe or privacy's friend? *Proceedings of the IEEE, 85*(9), 1480-1492.

APPENDIX A

The following scale was presented for all questions (1-58):

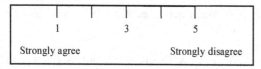

Choose the best response to the following statements by circling either a **1 (strongly agree)**, **2 (agree)**, **3 (neither agree nor disagree)**, **4 (disagree)**, or **5 (strongly disagree)**.

1. I feel that the safeguarding from potential external threats of my physical being is important to me.
2. I feel that my personal security at my home or in my vehicle is important to me.
3. I feel that my personal security at my place of work or other work related places is important to me.
4. My security at places of public access, such as a mall or airport, or special public events, such as the Olympics or the Super Bowl, is important to me.
5. I feel that the security of my tangible assets (such as my home, vehicle, etc.) is important to me.
6. I feel that keeping my personal possessions, such as jewelry, money, electronics, etc. safe is important to me.
7. I feel that the safekeeping of my informational assets contained in digital or paper format is important to me (such as financial records, medical records, etc.).
8. I feel that the security of my personal information, such as my PC files or personal records (financial, medical, etc.) is important to me.
9. I feel that the safekeeping of information I have provided to a corporation or other entity is important to me.
10. I feel my privacy is very important to me.
11. I feel that my control over my personal information is very important to me.

12. I feel that it is important not to release sensitive information to any entity.
13. I feel it is important to avoid having personal information released that I think could be financially damaging.
14. I feel it is important to avoid having personal information released that I think could be socially damaging to me.
15. I feel it is important to avoid having personal information about me released that may go against social morals and attitudes.
16. I feel that the release of personal information to individuals with whom I have a high comfort level is unacceptable.
17. I feel that the release of personal information to entities where I feel as though I am anonymously providing the information is unacceptable.
18. I feel that the use of personal information that has been released by me but is used in a manner not intended by me is unacceptable.

VIGNETTES

Please read the following vignettes and then respond to **each statement** below. Your responses should fall between **1 (strongly agree) and 5 (strongly disagree)**.

Vignette 1:

Jimmy returns home from work. To enter his residence, he places his hand on a biometric hand geometry scanner located by the door instead of using a key for entrance. He holds his hand on the pad for a few seconds.

1. I think this biometric device is useful.
2. I think this biometric device is easy to use.
3. I think one of the reasons this device is useful is because of its ease of use.

4. I think that this device would be physically invasive.
5. I think I would use this device.

Vignette 2:

Birsel goes to the airport to visit Turkey. A facial scanner is used upon entering the airport, where the image is compared against a database of known criminal offenders, to prevent the entry of undesirable persons to the sterile area of the airport. She has to step on a marked spot and look at a camera for a few seconds in order to have her face scanned to compare it with this database.

1. I think this biometric device is useful.
2. I think this biometric device is easy to use.
3. I think one of the reasons this device is useful is because of its ease of use.
4. I think that this device would be physically invasive.
5. I think I would use this device.

Vignette 3:

Ken works at a bio-chemical company where sensitive research on cloning practices is taking place. This area of the company contains computers and sensitive research information that is restricted to certain employees. He needs to be authorized to enter the area every time access is needed by using a retinal scanner at the door. He has to place his face in a frame, with his chin in a chin slot. He has to look in a scanning device for a few seconds without blinking.

1. I think this biometric device is useful.
2. I think this biometric device is easy to use.
3. I think one of the reasons this device is useful is because of its ease of use.
4. I think that this device would be physically invasive.
5. I think I would use this device.

Vignette 4:

Jane goes to the bank to get cash out of the ATM machine. In lieu of a passcode and ATM card, the transaction is authorized and her identity authenticated by the use of a fingerprint scanner. She has to press her thumb on a biometric device and the device scans her thumbprint instantaneously to access the records pertaining to her.

1. I think this biometric device is useful.
2. I think this biometric device is easy to use.
3. I think one of the reasons this device is useful is because of its ease of use.
4. I think that this device would be physically invasive.
5. I think I would use this device.

Vignette 5:

Peter works for a data center that contains highly sensitive information and expensive equipment. The data center tracks the times that the individual enters and exits the data center. Peter enters the data center by using a hand geometry scanner and to exit the data center he has to also use a hand geometry scanner. To use the device, Peter has to place his hand on the hand geometry scanner for a few seconds upon entry and exit to the data center.

1. I think this biometric device is useful.
2. I think this biometric device is easy to use.
3. I think one of the reasons this device is useful is because of its ease of use.
4. I think that this device would be physically invasive.
5. I think I would use this device.

Vignette 6:

Ken is one of the system administrators for a company. As a system administrator Ken has access to all files on the computer. The company tracks administrator access to the server. The company is implementing a fingerprint biometric to authenticate onto the server as administrator. Ken has to place his index finger on a biometric device, which instantly authenticates him into the server.

1. I think this biometric device is useful.
2. I think this biometric device is easy to use.
3. I think one of the reasons this device is useful is because of its ease of use.
4. I think that this device would be physically invasive.
5. I think I would use this device.

Vignette 7:

A hospital keeps medical records on all its patients. In the past, this information was protected by a password that was freely passed around when information was needed. For liability reasons, the hospital wants to restrict access to the medical records to only doctors and nurses. The hospital decides to implement a retinal scanner biometric device to ensure that only authorized individuals access the medical records. The doctor or nurse has to stand in front of the retinal scanner staring at a marked spot for a few seconds to authenticate into the system.

1. I think this biometric device is useful.
2. I think this biometric device is easy to use.
3. I think one of the reasons this device is useful is because of its ease of use.
4. I think that this device would be physically invasive.
5. I think I would use this device.

Vignette 8:

Katherine wants to use a credit card at a store to pay for her purchases. Normally, she would have to present an official photo id and sign a credit slip. To increase security, a digital signature device is used to authenticate the person. Katherine has to sign a digital pad instead of signing a credit slip.

1. I think this biometric device is useful.
2. I think this biometric device is easy to use.
3. I think one of the reasons this device is useful is because of its ease of use.
4. I think that this device would be physically invasive.
5. I think I would use this device.

Chapter VI
Intentions to Use Information Technologies:
An Integrative Model

Ron Thompson
Wake Forest University, USA

Deborah Compeau
University of Western Ontario, Canada

Chris Higgins
University of Western Ontario, Canada

Nathan Lupton
University of Western Ontario, Canada

ABSTRACT

An integrative model explaining intentions to use an information technology is proposed. The primary objective is to obtain a clearer picture of how intentions are formed, and draws on previous research such as the technology acceptance model (Davis, Bagozzi, & Warshaw, 1989) and the decomposed theory of planned behavior (Taylor & Todd, 1995a). The conceptual model was tested using questionnaire responses from 189 subjects, measured at two time periods approximately two months apart. The results generally supported the hypothesized relationships, and revealed strong influences of both personal innovativeness and computer self-efficacy.

INTRODUCTION

Understanding the process by which individuals adopt and use information technologies in the workplace and the factors that influence their decisions about what technologies to use to aid in the performance of their work tasks remains an important focus of IS research (Venkatesh, Morris, Davis, & Davis, 2003). While our ultimate interest is often in the achievement of organizational benefits from technology, the behavior of the individual represents a critical prerequisite for achieving these larger goals (Seddon, 1997).

Our review of current research on individual technology acceptance reveals, among other things, two overarching themes in the models. The first theme reflects the importance of pursuing parsimonious models. Parsimony is an important element in the development of theory and is one of the key contributions of the Technology Acceptance Model (TAM) (Davis, Bagozzi, & Warsaw, 1989). The second theme reflects the dominance of what we will refer to as an instrumental view of technology adoption decisions. Under this perspective, the dominant influences on intentions to use technologies are those involving beliefs about the degree to which using an information technology will result in objective improvements in performance.

The pursuit of parsimony and the focus on instrumental determinants have served the technology adoption stream well. The relative simplicity of TAM has made it a fertile ground for extensive study (Venkatesh & Davis, 2000). Similarly, the focus on an instrumental view of technology adoption has allowed us to explore this aspect of the influences on adoption in relatively deep fashion. On the other hand, both characteristics have had a limiting effect in other respects. Plouffe, Hulland, and Vandenbosch (2001) argue that an exclusive focus on parsimony, while sufficient if the research goal is prediction, may produce a narrower understanding of the phenomenon and perhaps limit our ability to influence it by not recognizing the myriad forces involved. Agarwal and Karahanna (2000) make a similar argument with respect to the focus on instrumental beliefs. They argue that a more holistic assessment of technology adoption is necessary, incorporating elements more related to intrinsic than extrinsic motivation. In part, they suggest this is necessary because of the nature of modern information technologies. What is also apparent, however, is the need to examine holistic perceptions in order to improve our understanding of the phenomenon of technology acceptance.

The purpose of this study, then, is to build on existing technology adoption theory in a more holistic and integrative fashion. Specifically, we seek to extend the Decomposed Theory of Planned Behavior (DTPB) (Taylor & Todd, 1995a). This theory was chosen as it represents a broader perspective, yet has enjoyed less ongoing development than TAM. Our extensions focus on three areas. First, we seek to explore the linkages among the independent variables proposed by Taylor and Todd (1995a). Second, we extend DTPB to be consistent with TAM. Third, we incorporate the trait of personal innovativeness with information technology (Agarwal & Prasad, 1998) into the model. This is a small step towards broadening our view from the more instrumental focus that has guided us to date. Finally, we seek, as have others (Agarwal, Sambamurthy, & Stair, 2000; Karahanna, Straub, & Chervany, 1999; Venkatesh & Davis, 2000) to understand the influence of experience within our model. While several previous authors have examined the role of experience within the context of TAM, to our knowledge, only one study (Taylor & Todd, 1995b) has done so within the TPB perspective. Before discussing the research design in more detail, we turn to the theoretical background and the research model to be tested.

THEORETICAL BACKGROUND AND RESEARCH MODEL

Decomposed Theory of Planned Behavior

The Theory of Planned Behavior (TPB) (Ajzen, 1991) was constructed as an extension to the Theory of Reasoned Action, or TRA (Fishbein & Ajzen, 1975) including, in addition to attitude and subjective norm, the construct of perceived behavioral control. Taylor and Todd (1995a) compared TAM with an adaptation of TPB, finding that perceived behavioral control and subjective norm added little in terms of explained variance in intentions to use technology. Taylor and Todd (1995a) went further, however, by proposing what they termed a decomposed theory of planned behavior (see Figure 1). Their intent was not to try to improve on TAM or TPB in terms of explaining variance in intentions or use of a technology, but rather to identify additional components of belief structures that would provide more explanation of the antecedents to attitude, subjective norm, and perceived behavioral control.

In an empirical test of their model, Taylor and Todd (1995a) found support for most of the hypothesized relations. Others have since built on the model, focusing on the constructs of technology and resource facilitating conditions (Mathieson, Peacock, & Chin, 2001), the interaction of age and gender to influence user perceptions and use (Morris, Venkatesh, & Ackerman, 2005) and applying the model to the adoption of IT by health

Figure 1. Decomposed theory of planned behavior (Taylor & Todd, 1995a)

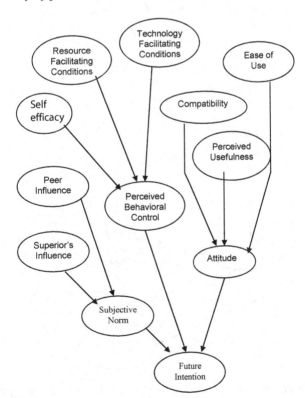

care professionals (Chau & Hu, 2001) and use of EDSS (Workman, 2005). Collectively, these studies suggest that the TPB perspective is reasonable, though it does not add significantly to explained variance except when fully integrated with TAM (Riemenschneider, Harris, & Mykytyn, 2003). Attitude and control beliefs are consistently and significantly related to adoption intention. The role of normative beliefs is mixed and suggests a weaker effect than the others.

Our extended conceptual model is shown in Figure 2. The model extends DTPB by including more concepts related to non-instrumental influences on technology adoption, and by including a more complex web of relationships among the antecedents. We adopted DTPB as the founda-

tion for our model, rather than TAM, as DTPB represents a more general theoretical model. To highlight the differences between DTPB and our model, we provide a brief overview of our model and then describe the rationale for the hypothesized relationships in more detail.

Intention to use Microsoft Access (the target system) is influenced by affect (attitude), social factors (subjective norms), and perceived behavioral control. Consistent with TAM (e.g., Davis et al., 1989; Taylor & Todd, 1995a), intention is also hypothesized to be influenced directly by perceived usefulness. Affect is influenced by three factors, two of which (perceived usefulness and perceived ease of use) were predicted in the original TAM (Davis et al., 1989) and in DTPB

Figure 2. Research model

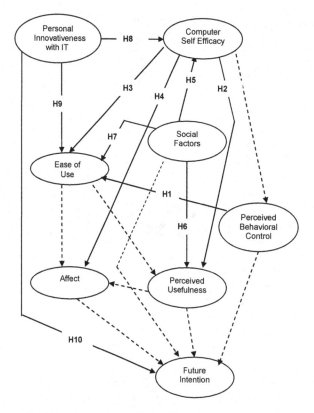

Note: *Dotted lines represent relationships previously established by DTPB (Taylor & Todd, 1995a) and TAM (Davis, et al, 1989)*

(Taylor & Todd, 1995a). The third influence on affect is self-efficacy. Perceived usefulness is hypothesized to be influenced by perceived ease of use, computer self-efficacy, and social factors, while perceived ease of use is hypothesized to be influenced by self-efficacy, social factors, perceived behavioral control, and personal innovativeness with IT. Perceived behavioral control is influenced by self-efficacy as well. Finally, self-efficacy is influenced by personal innovativeness with IT and social factors.

Our model builds on previous literature in several ways. First, we have opened up the paths across the avenues of behavioral, normative, and control beliefs. In earlier models (e.g., TAM, DTPB), these antecedents were viewed as separate and distinct influences, with no linkages among them. As we discuss in detail in the following section, however, there are theoretical reasons and empirical support for the existence of linkages across these influences.

Second, we have incorporated the personality trait of personal innovativeness with information technology as an attempt to begin the reintegration of general tendencies into our understanding of individual behavior with respect to IT. An explicit aim of TRA and TPB, when they were developed, was to move away from trying to associate general personality traits with behaviors. At the time, it was felt that such predictors were not as good as beliefs and attitudes (Ajzen, 1991). Yet now that we have begun to understand these specific beliefs and attitudes, there is a benefit to re-examining the role of personality variables in our models.

In addition, we consider the model at two time periods to examine the influence of experience in changing the model parameters. Other specific differences between our model and previous ones (e.g., TAM, DTPB) are discussed in later sections. The primary goal of the study is not to try and increase the amount of variance explained in intentions or use of an IT, but rather to obtain a clearer picture of the antecedent factors that influ-

ence attitudes, subjective norms, and perceived behavioral control, as well as the inter-relations among them.

CONSTRUCTS AND HYPOTHESES

For space reasons, we do not provide detailed definitions of the constructs employed in the model. Interested readers can refer to previous sources for intentions to use a specific information technology in the future (Davis et al., 1989; Venkatesh et al., 2003), affect (Compeau & Higgins, 1995a; Thompson, Higgins, & Howell, 1991), perceived usefulness (Davis et al., 1989), perceived ease of use (Davis et al., 1989), perceived behavioral control (Ajzen, 1991; Taylor & Todd, 1995a), computer self-efficacy (Compeau & Higgins, 1995a; Taylor & Todd, 1995a), social factors (Compeau & Higgins, 1995a), and personal innovativeness in the domain of information technology (Agarwal & Prasad, 1998). Explanations and working definitions for all constructs are also available from the authors upon request.

To avoid unnecessarily repeating the rationale for hypotheses and relationships that have been well established by previous research, we simply list relationships that are not considered controversial and then focus on those that are extensions to DTPB and TAM. Relationships that have been previously established (and represented with dotted lines on Figure 2) include:

- Affect toward using an information technology will have a positive influence on intentions to use the technology (DTPB, TAM).
- The perceived usefulness of an information technology will exert a positive influence on affect toward using the technology (DTPB, TAM).
- Perceived usefulness of an information technology will exert a positive influence on intentions to use the information technology (TAM).

- The perceived ease of use of an information technology will have a positive influence on affect toward using the technology (DTPB, TAM).
- Perceived ease of use of an information technology will exert a positive influence on perceived usefulness of the technology (TAM).
- Perceived behavioral control will exert a positive influence on intentions to use an information technology (DTPB).
- Computer self-efficacy will exert a positive influence on perceived behavioral control (DTPB).
- Social factors will exert a positive influence on intentions to use an information technology (DTPB).

In addition to a direct influence on intentions as depicted above, there may be additional roles for perceived behavioral control (PBC). In their study of technology adoption and use, Mathieson et al. (2001) argued that perceived resources (a subset of PBC) included personal assets such as an individual's expertise. In addition, they suggested that perceived ease of use would be influenced by expertise. As a result, Mathieson et al. (2001) concluded that perceived resources should influence perceived ease of use, and they observed empirical support for this relationship. The resulting hypothesis is:

H1: Perceived behavioral control will exert a positive influence on perceived ease of use of an information technology.

In addition to the potential influence of computer self efficacy (CSE) on PBC, there is evidence from other research that CSE might influence additional factors within the DTPB model. If an individual is confident in his or her ability to learn to use an information technology, he or she is more likely to believe that he or she will be able to put the technology to productive use.

Although we would anticipate that the influence of specific self-efficacy would be stronger than general CSE, general CSE has been shown to exert a positive influence on perceived usefulness of a specific IT (e.g., Compeau & Higgins, 1995a; Compeau, Higgins, & Huff, 1999). The associated hypothesis is:

H2: Computer self-efficacy will have a positive influence on perceived usefulness of an information technology.

Venkatesh and Davis (1996) posited that computer self-efficacy should act as a precursor to perceived ease of use. Individuals who are confident in their ability to learn to use information technologies are likely to view specific information technologies as easier to use than their counterparts who are less confident in their ability to learn. The results from their empirical testing provided support for this proposition. Agarwal et al. (2000) also observed a positive influence of self-efficacy on perceived ease of use, as did Venkatesh (2000). This leads to the following hypothesis:

H3: Computer self-efficacy will exert a positive influence on perceived ease of use of an information technology.

Compeau and Higgins (1995b) argued that computer self-efficacy should influence affect toward using an information technology. If an individual is confident in his or her ability to learn to use an information technology, he or she is more likely to have positive affective reactions to using the technology. In testing this relation, Compeau and Higgins (1995b) observed a statistically significant, though small, influence in a cross-sectional design. Compeau et al. (1999) further observed that self-efficacy measured at one point in time exerted an influence on affect measured one year later. From these findings, the associated hypothesis is:

H4: Computer self-efficacy will exert a positive influence on affect toward using an information technology.

There are possible influences for social factors beyond a direct effect on intentions, as well. Bandura (1997) argues that social persuasion is an important source of information that can influence the formation of self-efficacy judgments and expectations of outcomes. Encouragement by others in the reference group to use technology may carry with it a sense of encouragement regarding one's skills; in other words, you should use this technology *and you are capable of it.* Even if unspoken, this evaluation is implied; after all, why would a friend or colleague encourage you to do something wholly outside your capabilities? To the extent that this skills evaluation is present, social factors would be expected to influence self-efficacy. Compeau and Higgins (1995b) observed a positive influence of social persuasion on self-efficacy. These observations lead to the following hypothesis:

H5: Social factors will exert a positive influence on computer self-efficacy.

Social factors also influence perceived usefulness. Klein and Sorra (1996) argue that social influence operates through either a process of compliance or one of internalization. Compliance involves acting as the others desire because of perceived pressure. Internalization involves taking on the views of the other for oneself. Thus, an individual who feels persuaded to use technology by his or her reference group attributes the persuasion to a rational judgment on the part of the group; the group is encouraging the use of the technology because they see it as useful. Given that, the individual also decides that the technology is useful. Thus, through a process of internalization, the social factors result in increased perceptions of perceived usefulness.

H6: Social factors will exert a positive influence on perceived usefulness of an information technology.

Similarly, we anticipate that perceptions about ease of use of a technology could be influenced by social factors, especially in the absence of direct experience. In a training environment, for example, communication cues from the instructor regarding the relative ease (or difficulty) of learning to become proficient with the technology could influence initial perceptions on the part of the individual. This leads us to propose that:

H7: Social factors will exert a positive influence on perceived ease of use of an information technology.

Agarwal et al. (2000) argued for a direct influence of personal innovativeness on computer self-efficacy. Their rationale was that, consistent with the original formulation of social cognitive theory (Bandura, 1986), individual personality exerts an indirect influence on performance, through self-efficacy. Their empirical test found support for a positive influence of PIIT on general computer self-efficacy. The corresponding hypothesis is:

H8: Personal innovativeness will exert a positive influence on computer self-efficacy.

We also anticipate that personal innovativeness will influence perceived ease of use. If I am someone who is more innovative with respect to technology use, I will tend to view new technologies as being easier to use, above and beyond any indirect influence through self-efficacy. This is supported by learning theory (Ford, Smith, Weissbein, Gully, & Salas, 1998) that shows the ability to generalize skills across related domains. This hypothesis has also been verified in research based on TAM (Lu, Yao, & Yu, 2005; Yi, Fiedler, & Park, 2006). Since the underlying software structures (i.e., menus, concepts, functions) tend to be similar across technology domains, an individual who experiments actively with new technologies has the opportunity to engage in greater learning which can then be transferred to other domains. This results in perceptions of greater ease of use. The resulting hypothesis is:

H9: Personal innovativeness will exert a positive influence on perceived ease of use of an information technology.

Finally, since we are investigating intentions to use an information technology in the future, we would expect more innovative individuals to have stronger intentions (once again, above and beyond any indirect influences through intervening variables). This hypothesis reflects, at least to a degree, the influence of habit on behavior (Triandis, 1980) and the relationship between innovativeness and system use (Larsen & Sorebo, 2005). All things being equal, we would expect those who have habitually been ready adopters of technology in the past to continue to do so in the future, irrespective of specific attitudes and beliefs as they continue a set behavior pattern that has become habitual. Hence:

H10: Personal innovativeness will exert a positive influence on intentions to use information technology.

Experience

Considerable research has shown that computer experience influences many of the constructs and relations within a nomological network that involves intentions, use, and/or performance (e.g., Compeau & Higgins, 1995b; Compeau et al., 1999; Davis et al., 1989; Karahanna et al., 1999; Lippert & Forman, 2005; Szajna, 1996; Taylor & Todd, 1995b; Thompson, Higgins, & Howell, 1994; Venkatesh et al., 2003).

The experience level, or skill level, of an individual can be considered to fall across a continuum. When we assess experience and skill at specific points in time, we are essentially taking a snapshot of a potentially changing phenomenon (Marcolin, Compeau, Munro, & Huff, 1998). When an individual has no personal experience with a specific information technology, his or her attitudes, beliefs, and expectations toward using the technology may be influenced by factors such as social influences from peers and superiors, and personal experience with similar technologies. As the individual gains experience with the technology, he or she has objective outcomes (positive and/or negative) that are internalized, and which in turn influence beliefs about expected outcomes (Triandis, 1980), perceived usefulness (Bhattacherjee & Premkumar, 2004), and ease of use (Hackbarth, Grover, & Yi, 2003).

Thus, we expect that some of the constructs and the relations in the model will be influenced by the increased experience (skill level) of the respondent. As a result, we conducted supplemental analysis (described later) to examine the influence of experience in more detail.

RESEARCH METHODOLOGY

The data collection and analysis reported here is a subset of a larger research program that encompassed data collected in several related studies. For the overall research program, we wished to measure a relatively large number of constructs. In the interest of keeping the research questionnaire to a reasonable length (to increase participation rates and reduce the possibility of errors caused by respondent fatigue or declining interest), the number of items for most constructs was reduced to three. Although most of the individual items used here have been employed in previously published studies, some were developed or modified specifically for this research program.

The primary risks in using this approach were (1) some of the measures could prove to be unreliable, reducing the number of measures per construct even further; and (2) the limited number of measures might tap only a subset of a given construct. To reduce these risks, the choice of items was made partially on a face validity basis (in an effort to identify the most relevant measures), and partially from the results of a pilot study. The pilot study allowed us to refine the measures, resulting in the final set used in the main study. Note that most of the items used in this study were also included in the empirical work conducted by Venkatesh et al. (2003) as they tested for commonality across measures from previous work. Since Venkatesh et al. (2003) found that these measures were similar to others purporting to measure the same constructs (i.e., they loaded together in a factor analytic sense), we have more confidence that the measures selected for this study are in fact reasonable measures of the constructs (further details of the pilot study and a table showing the similarities between the measures used in this study and measures used in related work is available upon request from the authors).

SAMPLE AND PROCEDURES

Data were collected from junior and senior undergraduate students (business majors) completing a required course in management information systems (MIS). The respondents were required to use the Microsoft Access database management system for a group project (two students per group), representing 10% of their final grade. All students received some training with the software, and completed three individual assignments with it prior to completing the group project.

Measures were taken at two time periods approximately two months apart. At the time of the first measurement (T_1), the respondents had received a demonstration of the software and had completed one simple assignment using it. At the time of the second measurement (T_2), they had received additional training and had completed two additional (more complex) individual assignments as well as the group project (which required fairly extensive use of the software).

All students in five different sections of the course were asked to participate in the study. No inducements were offered, and students were given the option of not participating. All who were invited agreed to participate. Questionnaires were distributed in class to all students that were in attendance during specific class periods. 219 students completed the pretraining questionnaire, and 209 completed the postquestionnaire; those not completing both (i.e., those that were absent on one of the days) were removed from the sample. In total, 193 respondents completed both pre and postmeasures. Questionnaires from four respondents were removed due to missing data, leaving a net sample size of 189. The questionnaire responses were associated with an identification number, making it possible to match responses by respondent across the two time periods.

Of the 189 respondents, 117 were male and 72 were female. All respondents were traditional third and fourth year undergraduate students, and all had a reasonable level of familiarity with personal computers. We asked the respondents to rate their skill level with PC operating systems, word processing, spreadsheets, and e-mail using a 7-point scale with anchors of Novice (1), Intermediate (4), and Expert (7). We then summed across the four technologies to obtain a general measure of self-rated expertise. The scores ranged from 10 to 28 (out of a possible 28), with a mean of 19.3 and standard deviation of 3.3.

Although the generalizability of results will be constrained somewhat since the use of Access was mandatory for the students, many situations involving the use of information technologies by professionals are also mandatory. In addition, since our intention measure is focused on future, optional use by the respondent, the constraints on generalizability imposed by the mandatory nature of the task are mitigated somewhat.

RESULTS

The measures were tested using PLS-Graph (Chin & Frye, 2001) by running the full research model with the data collected at Time 1 and again with the data collected at Time 2. The first test of the measures was to examine the item loadings to assess individual item reliability. As in the pilot study, there were weaknesses evident in the loadings for the computer self-efficacy measures for the data collected at Time 1. These results were somewhat surprising, since the Compeau and Higgins measures of computer self-efficacy had demonstrated adequate psychometric properties in previous use (e.g., Compeau & Higgins, 1995a, 1995b; Compeau et al., 1999). Gundlach and Thatcher (2000) argue that the self-efficacy construct is multidimensional, reflecting human assisted vs. individual self-efficacy. This would be consistent with our findings. Factor analysis of the eight items also supported this view. A principal components analysis resulted in two factors, one of which included items 1, 2, 6, and 7 and the other which included 3, 4, 5, and 8. Since the variation was greater on the first set and there was less risk of a ceiling effect, we chose to retain those items.

The loadings for one measure of perceived behavioral control (PBC2) were low (below 0.5) for both time periods. In retrospect, this finding should not have been a surprise. PBC2 states that "the amount I use Access is within my control." Since the respondents were required to use Access to complete their projects, there was very little variation on this item. This issue was not a problem in the pilot study, since those respondents had the opportunity to use other software for completing the assigned task. We therefore decided to remove this item, and re-run the models. Table 1 shows the final list of items, including the means and standard deviations (at Time 1), and the item loadings obtained from the PLS run for Times 1 and 2.

Note that for social factors, both the weights and loadings (respectively) are displayed. Since the social factors construct was modeled as formative (Barclay, Higgins, & Thompson, 1995), the important indicators are the weights (not the loadings), and the criteria considered is whether or not the weights are statistically significant. In both models, and for all three social factor items, the weights were positive and significant at $p < 0.05$. For adequate item reliability for the reflective constructs, ideally loadings should be higher than 0.7 (Barclay et al., 1995). All observed loadings were close to or above the desired level (i.e., 0.67 or greater). We also examined the loadings and cross-loadings for all items at both time periods (see Table 2), and observed no violations (i.e., all loadings were greater than 0.65, and all cross-loadings were less than 0.60).

Table 3 shows the results of further tests for the reliability and validity of the measures. The average variance extracted (AVE) is shown for each construct, as is the Fornell and Larcker (1981) measure of composite reliability (CR). For adequate scale reliability, AVE should be greater than 0.5. CR may be interpreted similarly to Cronbach's alpha. That is, 0.70 may be considered an acceptable value for exploratory research, with 0.80 appropriate for more advanced studies. Table 3 also shows the correlations between constructs, and the diagonal, shaded cells display the square root of the average variance extracted. For adequate discriminant validity, the values on the diagonal (shaded cells) should be greater than the off-diagonal elements. The corresponding test results at Time 2 are not shown here (for space reasons) but the pattern of results was similar to those shown for Time 1.

At Time 1, all constructs have composite reliabilities in excess of 0.80, with the exception of social factors. Average variance extracted is above 0.50 for all constructs except social factors

Table 1. Item reliability: Time 1 and Time 2

Item	Description	Mean	S.D.	Loading T1	Loading T2
CSE1	I could complete the job using the software... ...if there was no one around to tell me what to do as I go	4.0	1.7	.87	.87
CSE2	...if I had only the software manuals available for reference	4.8	1.5	.86	.85
CSE6	...if I had a lot of time to complete the task for which the software was provided	5.6	1.2	.70	.67
CSE7	...if I had just the built-in help facility for assistance	4.4	1.7	.71	.81
PIIT1	Among my colleagues and peers, I will be among the first to try new computer tools and applications	4.4	1.6	.68	.77
PIIT2	I only use computer tools that fit a specific need; I seldom try new tools or applications just for the fun of it (R)	4.1	1.8	.87	.81
PIIT3	I must see other people using new computer tools before I will consider using them myself (R)	5.0	1.6	.74	.82
EOU1	Learning to use [software package] would be easy for me	4.3	1.5	.82	.86
EOU2	Working with [software package] is so complicated, it is difficult to understand what is going on (R)	4.9	1.4	.82	.69
EOU3	I would find it difficult to get [s/w pkg] to do what I need (R)	4.8	1.4	.81	.69
PU1	Using [software package] would... ...allow me to increase my productivity	5.2	1.3	.80	.87
PU2	...increase my quantity of output for the same amount of effort	4.9	1.4	.86	.88
PU3	...increase my effectiveness	5.4	1.2	.89	.93
PBC1	I have the resources to use [s/w package] whenever I wish	5.9	1.5	.78	.78
PBC3	I have the resources, the knowledge, and the ability to make effective use of [software package]	4.6	1.7	.87	.92
AFF 1	I really dislike using [software package] (R)	5.1	1.5	.84	.83
AFF 2	Working with [software package] is a lot of fun	3.8	1.5	.91	.91
AFF 3	I really enjoy working with [software package]	4.1	1.4	.94	.93
AFF 1	I really dislike using [software package] (R)	5.1	1.5	.84	.83
AFF 2	Working with [software package] is a lot of fun	3.8	1.5	.91	.91

Continued on following page

Table 1. continued

Item	Description	Mean	S.D.	Loading T1	Loading T2
AFF 3	I really enjoy working with [software package]	4.1	1.4	.94	.93
INT1	I predict that I will use [s/w pkg] on a regular basis in the future	4.7	1.3	.87	.90
INT2	Although I will likely use outputs from [software package] quite extensively, I don't see myself directly using [software package] in the future (R)	4.9	1.5	.85	.86
INT3	I expect that I will use [software package], or a similar type of software product, quite extensively in the future	5.1	1.5	.85	.88
SF1	My colleagues and peers expect me to learn how to use computers effectively	5.6	1.4	.45 .65	.30 .65
SF2	My instructor (or boss) is supportive of my use of computers	6.3	1.0	.54 .65	.53 .70
SF3	People whose opinions I value will perceive me as being competent if I use computers effectively	5.1	1.3	.51 .68	.57 .77

Note: For SF1, SF2 and SF3, the item weight is displayed on top, and the loading below.

(where again, such measures are not considered to be relevant given the formative nature of the construct). In all cases, the variance shared between a construct and its measures is greater than the variance shared among the constructs.

The PLS results for the structural model (path coefficients and R^2 values) for Time 1 are displayed in Figure 3, and for both time periods are shown in Table 4. The path coefficients (which can be interpreted similarly to standardized path coefficients from a regression model) are provided, along with an indication of whether or not a specific path is statistically significant. The t-statistics for testing statistical significance were obtained by

running a bootstrapping routine (Chin & Frye, 2001), with 500 samples, each containing 189 observations.

Table 4 shows the direct, indirect, and total effects for each of the hypothesized paths, as well as the amount of variance explained (R^2) for all of the endogenous constructs. Cohen (1988) defined strong, moderate, and weak effects for regression as corresponding to effect sizes of approximately 0.35, 0.15, and 0.02, respectively. Although similar statements have not been made specifically for PLS, since PLS uses regression in its analysis, these rules of thumb are most likely appropriate.

Table 2. Loadings and cross-loadings of indicators on constructs at Time 1

	CSE	PIIT	EOU	PU	PBC	AFF	INT
CSE1	**0.87**	0.46	0.38	0.22	0.43	0.37	0.31
CSE2	**0.86**	0.42	0.45	0.26	0.46	0.41	0.38
CSE6	**0.70**	0.26	0.20	0.34	0.29	0.30	0.34
CSE7	**0.71**	0.39	0.24	0.22	0.24	0.31	0.29
PIIT1	0.38	**0.68**	0.30	0.14	0.22	0.31	0.25
PIIT2	0.42	**0.87**	0.44	0.19	0.32	0.44	0.44
PIIT3	0.33	**0.74**	0.34	0.05	0.23	0.20	0.22
EOU1	0.44	0.37	**0.82**	0.26	0.44	0.54	0.32
EOU2	0.26	0.33	**0.82**	0.13	0.31	0.47	0.18
EOU3	0.31	0.45	**0.81**	0.11	0.27	0.49	0.29
PU1	0.27	0.13	0.14	**0.80**	0.32	0.34	0.41
PU2	0.30	0.15	0.25	**0.86**	0.31	0.40	0.45
PU3	0.26	0.16	0.14	**0.89**	0.37	0.34	0.50
PBC1	0.32	0.22	0.32	0.27	**0.78**	0.28	0.28
PBC3	0.44	0.33	0.38	0.37	**0.87**	0.47	0.34
AFF1	0.35	0.42	0.62	0.35	0.36	**0.84**	0.44
AFF2	0.39	0.33	0.48	0.39	0.38	**0.91**	0.44
AFF3	0.46	0.39	0.55	0.39	0.49	**0.94**	0.49
INT1	0.35	0.35	0.31	0.50	0.37	0.43	**0.87**
INT2	0.36	0.31	0.25	0.42	0.31	0.44	**0.85**
INT3	0.36	0.40	0.28	0.45	0.29	0.45	**0.85**

CSE – computer self-efficacy; PIIT – personal innovativeness in the domain of IT; EOU – ease of use; PU – perceived usefulness; PBC – perceived behavioral control; AFF – affect; INT – future intentions

As can be seen in Table 4, most of the relationships taken from DTPB and TAM received at least partial support, although there were exceptions. Affect was found to have a moderate and significant influence on long term intentions at both Time 1 and Time 2, suggesting that people will expect to do things that they enjoy doing. Perceived usefulness exerted a moderate and significant influence on affect and a moderate (Time 2) or strong (Time 1) influence on intentions. Thus, the influence of perceived usefulness was only partly mediated by affect.

Perceived ease of use exerted a strong influence on affect at both Times 1 and 2, but the relative influence declined somewhat at Time 2. This result is consistent with other studies that have found that the direct influence of EOU tends to decrease over time (e.g., Venkatesh et al., 2003). At Time 2, perceived ease of use exerted a moderate and significant influence on perceived usefulness; this effect was not significant (at the p < 0.05 level) at Time 1. This result is consistent with most prior research, suggesting that the influence of ease of use on usefulness becomes stronger with direct experience.

Perceived behavioral control showed no significant influence on intentions at Time 1, but a significant influence at Time 2. Thus, for this group of individuals, control beliefs have a stronger effect following greater experience with the behavior.

Table 3. Reliability and discriminant validity

(Revised Model at Time 1)

	CR	AVE
PIIT	.81	.59
SF	.70	.44
CSE	.87	.62
EOU	.86	.67
PU	.89	.73
PBC	.82	.69
AFF	.92	.80
INT	.89	.73

CR = Composite Reliability
AVE = Average Variance Extracted

	PIIT	SF	CSE	EOU	PU	PBC	AFF	INT
PIIT	**0.77**							
SF	0.21	**0.66**						
CSE	0.49	0.21	**0.79**					
EOU	0.47	-0.03	0.42	**0.82**				
PU	0.17	0.26	0.33	0.21	**0.85**			
PBC	0.34	0.13	0.46	0.42	0.39	**0.83**		
AFF	0.43	0.11	0.45	0.62	0.42	0.46	**0.89**	
INT	0.41	0.26	0.42	0.33	0.53	0.38	0.51	**0.85**

PIIT – personal innovativeness in the domain of IT; SF – social factors; CSE – computer self-efficacy; EOU – ease of use; PU – perceived usefulness; PBC – perceived behavioral control; AFF – affect; INT – future intentions

Diagonal elements represent the square root of the average variance extracted. Off diagonal elements represent correlations. For discriminant validity, the diagonal elements should be higher than the off-diagonal elements, indicating that the variance shared between a construct and its measures is higher than the variance shared between construct pairs.

The magnitude of the path ($\beta = 0.17$), however, still suggests a smaller effect than that of affect or perceived usefulness. No direct effect of social factors on intentions was found, although the total effects in Time 1 were substantive.

With respect to the hypotheses directly tested in this study, PBC was found to exert a moderate influence on perceived ease of use at Time 1, and a strong influence at Time 2 (H1). General computer self-efficacy exerted moderate but significant influences on both EOU and affect at both time periods (H3, H4). The influence on perceived usefulness was significant at Time 1 but not at Time 2 (H2). Interestingly, the effect on perceived ease of use was stronger at Time 2, resulting in an increased indirect effect of self-efficacy on perceived usefulness, partly compensating for the reduced direct effect. Thus, it appears that with direct experience, people can separate the potential of the software from their ability to realize that potential.

Table 4. Tests of hypotheses (direct effects), indirect and total effects for Time 1 and Time 2

Relationship	Time 1			Time 2		
	Total Effects	Direct Effects	Indirect Effects	Total Effects	Direct Effects	Indirect Effects
AFF - INT	0.24	0.24**	0.00	0.31	0.31**	0.00
PU - AFF	0.27	0.27**	0.00	0.25	0.25**	0.00
PU - INT	0.42	0.36**	0.06	0.32	0.24**	0.08
EOU - AFF	0.53	0.50**	0.03	0.39	0.35**	0.04
EOU - PU	0.12	0.12+	0.00	0.16	0.16**	0.00
PBC - INT	0.08	0.04	0.04	0.23	0.17**	0.06
CSE - PBC	0.46	0.46**	0.00	0.44	0.44**	0.00
SF - INT	0.19	0.09	0.10	0.09	-0.05	0.14
H1: PBC-EOU	0.25	0.25**	0.00	0.35	0.35**	0.00
H2: CSE-PU	0.25	0.23**	0.02	0.15	0.10	0.05
H3: CSE-EOU	0.17	0.17**	0.00	0.29	0.29**	0.00
H4: CSE-AFF	0.36	0.15**	0.21	0.41	0.21**	0.20
H5: SF-CSE	0.12	0.12+	0.00	0.12	0.12+	0.00
H6: SF-PU	0.24	0.21**	0.03	0.38	0.36**	0.02
H7: SF-EOU	-0.14	-0.17*	0.03	0.03	-0.02	0.05
H8: PIIT-CSE	0.47	0.47**	0.00	0.57	0.57**	0.00
H9: PIIT-EOU	0.47	0.34**	0.13	0.36	0.11	0.25
H10: PIIT-INT	0.37	0.22*	0.15	0.33	0.18**	0.15

Amount of Variance Explained (R^2)	Time 1	Time 2
Future intentions	44%	40%
Affect	49%	38%
Perceived Usefulness	15%	23%
Perceived Ease of Use	34%	35%
Perceived behavioral control	21%	19%
Computer self efficacy	26%	39%

$+ p < 0.10$; $* p < 0.05$; $** p < 0.01$

The influence of social factors was mixed. The influence of social factors on self-efficacy (H5) was positive but not significant at $p < 0.05$. Since social persuasion is one of the weaker sources of self-efficacy information and, more importantly, since the persuasion that was examined here was encouragement to use computers rather than specific encouragement about one's skills, this is not overly surprising. Social factors did exert a moderate influence on perceived usefulness (H6) at Time 1 and strong influence at Time 2. This is consistent with the notion of internalization suggested by Klein and Sorra (1996). The influence of social factors on perceived ease of use (H7) was surprising, with a significant negative influence at Time 1 and no influence at Time 2. This finding was unexpected and bears further consideration.

Figure 3. PLS results

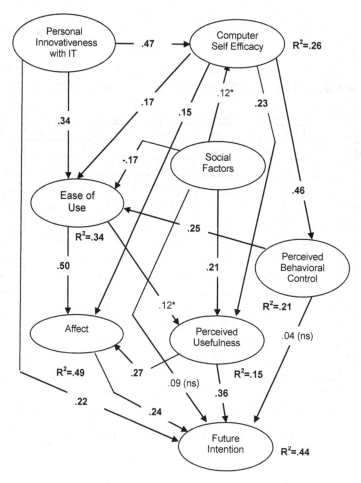

Note: **bolded** values are significant at p < .05; * at p < .10

Table 5. Comparison of construct means

	Mean (Std. Deviation)		
	Time 1	Time 2	p-value
GENERAL FACTORS			
Personal Innovativeness	13.5 (3.8)	13.2 (3.9)	.22
Computer Self-efficacy	18.8 (4.8)	19.2 (4.8)	.21
Social Factors	17.0 (2.5)	17.4 (2.4)	.01
SPECIFIC FACTORS			
Perceived Usefulness	15.5 (3.2)	16.3 (3.7)	.001
Perceived Ease of Use	14.1 (3.5)	14.6 (3.6)	.88
Affect	13.1 (3.9)	13.4 (4.1)	.005
Perceived Behavioral Control	10.5 (2.7)	11.6 (2.2)	.001
Future Intentions	14.7 (3.7)	14.4 (4.2)	.65

Personal innovativeness with information technology exerted a strong positive influence on computer self-efficacy (H8) at both time periods, and a strong positive influence on perceived ease of use (H9) at Time 1. At Time 2, there was no influence of personal innovativeness on perceived ease of use. This is consistent with the arguments of Venkatesh and Davis (1996) who suggest that through experience, ease of use perceptions become more rooted in specific features of the software and less influenced by general personal traits. Personal innovativeness also exhibited a direct influence on intentions at both time periods (H10).

Supplemental Analysis Concerning Experience

Our analysis, discussed above, suggests that experience moderates many of the relationships between constructs in technology acceptance models. As subjects gain in experience, their intentions are more strongly influenced by affect and perceived behavioral control and less influenced by perceived usefulness and personal innovativeness. Computer self-efficacy exerts a stronger influence on perceived ease of use and affect, but a weaker influence on perceived usefulness. Thus, individuals become able to separate the potential of the software from their ability to use it. Personal innovativeness exerts a stronger influence on self-efficacy following experience but becomes a nonsignificant predictor of perceived ease of use.

The findings that experience moderates some relationships in the model are important for researchers to understand as we attempt to comprehend the forces involved in technology adoption decisions. But it is equally important to understand the direct effects of experience on the constructs in the model. To examine this aspect of the role of experience, we conducted supplemental analyses, comparing the means of each of our model constructs across the two

month time period. We expected greater change in the software specific constructs (usefulness, ease of use, affect, perceived behavioral control) than in the more general constructs (social factors, personal innovativeness, self-efficacy). To perform this test, we computed a summed scale score for all constructs at Time 1 and Time 2, and then employed a t-test to see if the difference was statistically significant.

The results (shown in Table 5) partly support our expectation. Of the general factors, neither PIIT nor self-efficacy changed. However, the mean perception of social influence did increase from Time 1 to Time 2. For the specific factors, perceived usefulness, affect, and perceived behavioral control all increased. However, perceived ease of use did not change, nor did long term intentions.

DISCUSSION

In general, the results supported the hypothesized relations. The model explained 44% of the variance in intention at Time 1 and 40% at Time 2. While improving on prediction was not our primary aim in this chapter, examination of explained variance is nonetheless a critical element of PLS analysis. The R^2 values we obtained are less than some other models have explained (e.g., Taylor & Todd, 1995 explained more than 60% of the variance in intention). To provide an internally consistent basis of comparison, we ran a model at each time period based on TAM, using just PU, EOU, and Future Intentions. These models explained 34% and 30% of the variance in intention, compared to 44% and 40% for our expanded model.

We also ran models based on DTPB, eliminating the interlinkages among the independent constructs. These models explained 34% of the variance in intention (same at both time periods).

In general, then, an integrated model acknowledging the linkages between behavioral, control, and normative beliefs, and including general factors such as personal innovativeness, seems to be appropriate for describing technology adoption decisions. The areas where results were not as predicted, or where the paths changed from the first to second time periods, bear particular attention. First, perceived behavioral control exerted a positive influence on intentions at Time 2, but not Time 1. In addition, we noted that the responses to the perceived behavioral control items increased significantly from Time 1 to Time 2. Keeping in mind that one of the PBC items referred to having the "... resources, the knowledge, and the ability to make effective use of Access," this suggests that as the respondents gained experience with the software, they gained more confidence in their ability to control their decisions to use it.

This finding is not completely consistent with Taylor and Todd (1995b), who noted a positive influence of PBC on intentions for both inexperienced and experienced users. The influence was much stronger for experienced users, with path coefficients of 0.16 for inexperienced and 0.50 for experienced (Taylor & Todd, 1995b). In addition, Taylor and Todd (1995b) tested their model within a different context (use of a computer resource center), which could explain the discrepancy in results. In our study, respondents were required to use Access for a course project. Even though our questions focused on long-term, rather than short-term intentions, it is possible that the mandatory nature of the course project interfered with their perceptions of control, and resulted in intentions at Time 1 that were more based on the course requirement than on their future plans. If this were so, it is possible that there was both a negative and positive influence at play, and these cancelled each other.

Social factors did not exert an influence on intentions at either time period. Keeping in mind that the use of the software "in the future" would be completely voluntary for the respondents, these results are consistent with those of Venkatesh and Davis (2000), who observed an influence of social norms in mandatory, but not voluntary, settings. We observed another interesting finding with respect to the hypothesized influence of social factors on perceived EOU. Recall that the scores on the EOU scale did not change significantly from Time 1 to Time 2, while the increase in the scores on the social factors scale was statistically significant. In addition, we hypothesized three other factors as influencing EOU: self-efficacy, personal innovativeness, and perceived behavioral control. At Time 1, self-efficacy, personal innovativeness, and perceived behavioral control all had positive influences on EOU, while the path from social factors to EOU was negative. At Time 2, only the influences of self-efficacy and perceived behavioral control were statistically significant.

There were at least two additional observations worth noting. First, computer self-efficacy provided a strong, positive influence on PBC, EOU, Affect, and PU (at Time 2). These results show a much stronger role for self-efficacy than what Taylor and Todd (1995a) and Venkatesh et al. (2003) hypothesized in their models. In addition, CSE exerted a strong (indirect) influence on intentions to use technology. Second, personal innovativeness was also shown to exert an influence on intentions, both directly and indirectly through CSE and EOU (at Time 1).

IMPLICATIONS FOR RESEARCH AND PRACTICE

One limitation of the study was the use of student subjects, which limits the generalizability to some extent (Compeau, Marcolin, & Kelley, 2001). This provides an opportunity for future research, in that it would be very useful to replicate the study in an applied field setting with knowledge workers who are being asked to adopt and use a new information technology. A second limitation was the use of a limited number of items (generally three) to measure many of the constructs in the model. Future research should include the development and testing of more appropriate scales for each of the constructs.

The results of our analysis have several implications for research on technology adoption, as well as for organizational practice. The most important implication for research is to reinforce the arguments of authors such as Agarwal and Karahanna (2000) and Plouffe et al. (2001) who call for richer models of technology adoption. Moreover, the results suggest that integration, as well as richness, is of value to improving our understanding of an individual's technology adoption choice. Our integrative model shows multiple mechanisms through which personal innovativeness, self-efficacy, and social factors influence technology adoption choices, and adds to our understanding of how judgments of perceived usefulness and perceived ease of use are formed.

The results also show the influence of general factors on specific software beliefs, suggesting a degree of generality in perceptions relating to computers. Bandura (1997) and others (e.g., Agarwal et al., 2000) argue persuasively for the need to match self-efficacy judgments to the specific task. This makes sense from the standpoint of maximizing prediction, yet our results show that these general influences can also influence beliefs about specific software packages. Further study of the generalizability of self-efficacy perceptions (following the work of Agarwal et al., 2000) would be valuable in building this understanding.

In addition, the strong influence of personal innovativeness on self-efficacy and ease of use perceptions (as well as on future intentions) suggests that measuring personal innovativeness and self-efficacy perceptions could help in developing more effective training programs prior to the introduction of new information technologies. For example, knowing that a group of workers scored highly on personal innovativeness would suggest that less time and effort would be needed to ensure they had positive beliefs about the ease of use of a new information system. Further, the

relatively small influence of PBC at Time 1, followed by the medium influence at Time 2, suggests that the influence of PBC increases as users gain experience. This suggests that managers should ensure that potential users perceive they have adequate access to resources (including training) after they have had some initial experience with the technology, and not just when it is introduced to them.

Finally, the results confirm the importance of incorporating experience into models of technology acceptance. Several authors have shown changes in technology adoption models, and we confirm their findings. We further show that it is specific, more than general, measures that tend to change with experience. The conceptualization of experience is challenging however. As we noted earlier, experience partly reflects exposure to the tool and partly reflects the skills and abilities that one gains through using a technology. Experience also probably reflects habit to some extent. Our research findings, including previous authors and those in this study, do not clearly differentiate between these types of effects. Nonetheless, it seems reasonable that there might be different sorts of influences depending on the extent to which experience reflects habit, skill, or simply exposure. Thus, we believe it is important for future research to more fully examine the conceptualization of experience and its influence in technology adoption models.

CONCLUSION

In summary, our results provide support for an extended model based on the decomposed theory of planned behavior. They confirm existing findings within the technology adoption stream, but also show the possibility of a more holistic and integrative approach to our models. Such an approach allows for the inclusion of less instrumental beliefs (e.g., personal innovativeness with IT) as influences on technology adoption, demonstrates the complexity of the mechanisms through which general beliefs such as personal innovativeness and self-efficacy influence adoption intention, and aids in building our understanding of the antecedents of perceived usefulness and perceived ease of use, the critical constructs in the Technology Acceptance Model. We further echo the calls of other researchers (e.g., Sun & Zhang, 2006) to extend our conceptualization and understanding of the role of experience in the formation of judgments about information technologies.

While it has been argued that technology acceptance is a mature model (Venkatesh, 2006; Venkatesh et al, 2003), we believe there is substantial work to be done in further understanding the process of adoption. We agree with Jasperson, Carter, and Zmud (2005) that richer models are required which take into account the varying features of different technologies, the extent to which these features are used, and the individual differences of the users themselves. Initial research in this area has found that feature specific self-efficacy predicts usage above and beyond a more generalized operationalization of self-efficacy (Hasan, 2006; Hsu & Chiu, 2003). In addition to better prediction, richer models of adoption can better inform the design and support of information technologies in organizations.

REFERENCES

Agarwal, R., & Karahanna, E. (2000). Time flies when you're having fun: Cognitive absorption and beliefs about information technology usage. *MIS Quarterly, 24*(4), 665-694.

Agarwal, R., & Prasad, J. (1998, June). A conceptual and operational definition of personal innovativeness in the domain of information technology. *Information Systems Research, 9*(2), 204-215.

Agarwal, R., Sambamurthy, V., & Stair, R.M. (2000, December). Research report: The evolving relationship between general and specific computer self-efficacy: An empirical assessment. *Information Systems Research, 11*(4), 418-430.

Ajzen, I. (1991). The theory of planned behavior. *Organizational Behavior and Human Decision Processes, 50*, 179-211.

Bandura, A. (1986). *Social foundations of thought and action.* Englewood Cliffs, NJ: Prentice Hall.

Bandura, A. (1997). *Self-efficacy: The exercise of control.* New York: W.H. Freeman & Co.

Barclay, D.W., Higgins, C.A., & Thompson, R.L. (1995). The partial least squares approach to causal modeling: Personal computer adoption and use as an illustration. *Technology Studies: Special Issue on Research Methodology, 2*(2), 285-324.

Bhattacherjee, A., & Premkumar, G. (2004). Understanding changes in belief and attitude toward information technology usage: A theoretical model and longitudinal test. *Management Information Systems Quarterly, 28*(2), 229-254.

Chau, P., & Hu, P. (2001). Information technology acceptance by individual professionals: A model comparison approach. *Decision Sciences, 32*(4), 699-719.

Chin, W.W., & Frye, T. (2001). *PLS-Graph* (Version 03.00). Soft Modeling Inc.

Cohen, J. (1988). *Statistical power analysis for the behavioral sciences.* Hillside, NJ: L. Erlbaum Associates.

Compeau, D.R., & Higgins, C.A. (1995a). Application of social cognitive theory to training for computer skills. *Information Systems Research, 6*(2), 118-143.

Compeau, D.R., & Higgins, C.A. (1995b). Computer self-efficacy: Development of a measure and initial test. *MIS Quarterly, 19*(2), 189-211.

Compeau, D.R., Higgins, C.A., & Huff, S. (1999). Social cognitive theory and individual reactions to computing technology: A longitudinal study. *MIS Quarterly, 23*(2), 145-158.

Compeau, D., Marcolin, B., & Kelley, H. (2001). Generalizability of technology acceptance research using student subjects. In A. Ramirez (Ed.), *Proceedings of the Administrative Science Association of Canada, 22*(4), 35-47.

Davis, F.D., Bagozzi, R.P., & Warshaw, P.R. (1989, August). User acceptance of computer technology: A comparison of two theoretical models. *Management Science, 35*(8), 983-1003.

Fishbein, M., & Ajzen, I. (1975). *Belief, attitude, intentions and behavior: An introduction to theory and research.* Boston: Addison-Wesley.

Ford, J., Smith, E., Weissbein, D., Gully, S., & Salas, E. (1998). Relationships of goal orientation, metacognitive activity, and practice strategies with learning outcomes and transfer. *Journal of Applied Psychology, 83*, 218-233.

Fornell, C., & Larcker, D. (1981). Evaluating structural equation models with unobservable variables and measurement error. *Journal of Marketing Research, 18*, 39-50.

Gundlach, M.J., & Thatcher, J.B. (2000). *Examining the multi-dimensionality of computer self-efficacy: An empirical test.* Unpublished manuscript, Florida State University.

Hackbarth, G., Grover, V., & Yi, M.Y. (2003). Computer playfulness and anxiety: Positive and negative mediators of the system experience effect on perceived ease of use. *Information and Management, 40*, 221-232.

Hasan, B. (2006). Delineating the effects of general and system-specific computer self-efficacy beliefs on IS acceptance. *Information and Management, 43*, 565-571.

Hsu, M-H., & Chiu, C-M. (2004). Internet self-efficacy and electronic service acceptance. *Decision Support Systems, 38*, 369-381.

Jasperson, J., Carter, P.E., & Zmud, R.W. (2005). A comprehensive conceptualization of post-adoptive behaviors associated with information technology enabled work systems. *MIS Quarterly, 29*(3), 525-557.

Karahanna, E., Straub, D.W., & Chervany, N.L. (1999, June). Information technology adoption across time: A cross-sectional comparison of pre-adoption and post-adoption beliefs. *MIS Quarterly, 23*(2), 183-213.

Klein, K.J., & Sorra, J.S. (1996). The challenge of innovation implementation. *Academy of Management Review, 21*, 1055-1080.

Larsen, T.J., & Sorebo, O. (2005). Impact of personal innovativeness on the use of the Internet among employees at work. *Journal of Organizational and End User Computing, 17*(2), 43-63.

Lippert, S.K., & Forman, H. (2005). Utilization of information technology: Examining cognitive and experiential factors of post-adoption behavior. *IEE Transactions on Engineering Management, 52*(3), 363-381.

Lu, J., Yao, J.E., & Yu, C.-S. (2005). Personal innovativeness, social influences and adoption of wireless Internet services via mobile technology. *Strategic Information Systems, 14*, 245-268.

Marcolin, B.L., Compeau, D.R., Munro, M.C., & Huff, S.L. (2000, March). Assessing user competence: Conceptualization and measurement. *Information Systems Research, 11*(1), 37-60.

Mathieson, K., Peacock, E., & Chin, W.W. (2001). Extending the technology acceptance model: The influence of perceived user resources. *The DATA BASE for Advances in Information Systems, 32*(3), 86-112.

McFarland, D.J., & Hamilton, D. (2006). Adding contextual specificity to the technology acceptance model. *Computers in Human Behavior, 22*, 427-447.

Morris, M.G., Venkatesh, V., & Ackerman, P.L. (2005). Gender and age differences in employee decisions about new technology: An extension to the theory of planned behavior. *IEEE Transactions on Engineering Management, 52*(1), 69-84.

Plouffe, C.R., Hulland, J.S., & Vandenbosch, M. (2001). Richness versus parsimony in modelling technology adoption decisions: Understanding merchant adoption of a smart card-based payment system. *Information Systems Research, 12*(2), 208-222.

Riemenschneider, C.K., Harris, D.A., & Mykytyn, P.P., Jr. (2003). Understanding IT adoption decisions in small business: Integrating current theories. *Information and Management, 40*, 269-285.

Seddon, P.B. (1997). A respecification and extension of the DeLone and McLean model of IS success. *Information Systems Research, 8*(3), 240-253.

Sun, H., & Zhang, P. (2006). The role of moderating factors in user technology acceptance. *International Journal of Human-Computer Studies, 64*, 53-78.

Szajna, B. (1996, January). Empirical evaluation of the revised technology acceptance model. *Management Science, 42*(1), 85-92.

Taylor, S., & Todd, P.A. (1995a, June). Understanding information technology usage: A test of competing models. *Information Systems Research, 6*(2), 144-176.

Taylor, S., & Todd, P.A. (1995b). Assessing IT usage: The role of prior experience. *MIS Quarterly, 19*, 561-570.

Thompson, R.L., Higgins, C.H., & Howell, J.M. (1991, March). Towards a conceptual model of utilization. *MIS Quarterly, 15*(1), 125-143.

Thompson, R.L., Higgins, C.H., & Howell, J.M (1994). Influence of experience on personal computer utilization: Testing a conceptual model. *Journal of Management Information Systems, 11*, 167-187.

Triandis, H.C. (1980). Values, attitudes and interpersonal behavior. In H.E. Howe (Ed.), *Nebraska Symposium on Motivation, 1979: Beliefs, Attitudes and Values* (pp. 195-259). Lincoln, NE: University of Nebraska Press, 195-259.

Venkatesh, V. (2000). Determinants of perceived ease of use: Integrating control, intrinsic motivation and emotion into the technology acceptance model. *Information Systems Research, 11*(4), 342-365.

Venkatesh, V. (2006). Where to go from here? Thoughts on future directions for research on individual-level technology adoption with a focus on decision making. *Decision Sciences, 37*(4), 497-518.

Venkatesh, V., & Davis, F.D. (1996). A model of the antecedents of perceived ease of use: Development and test. *Decision Sciences, 27*(3), 451-482.

Venkatesh, V., & Davis, F.D. (2000). A theoretical extension of the technology acceptance model: Four longitudinal field studies. *Management Science, 46*, 186-204.

Venkatesh, V., Morris, M.G., Davis, G.B., & Davis, F.D. (2003). User acceptance of information technology: Toward a unified view. *MIS Quarterly, 27*, 425-478.

Workman, M. (2005). Expert decision system use, disuse and misuse: A study using the theory of planned behavior. *Computers in Human Behavior, 21*, 211-231.

Yi, M.Y., Fiedler, K.D., & Park, J.S. (2006). Understanding the role of individual innovativeness in the acceptance of IT-based innovations: Comparative analyses of models and measures. *Decision Sciences, 37*(3), 393-426.

Chapter VII
The Organization of End User Development in an Accounting Company

Anders I. Mørch
University of Oslo, Norway

Hege-René Hansen Åsand
University of Oslo, Norway

Sten R. Ludvigsen
University of Oslo, Norway

ABSTRACT

The chapter presents a case study following the activities of super users and local developers during the adoption of a new business application by an accounting firm in Scandinavia (referred to as the Company). The Company launched a program to train super users to help with this process because of the complexity of the new system, a generic, multipurpose application system replacing several older, non-integrated systems. The system, Visma Business (VB), is a comprehensive financial and accounting application delivered as a set of components that need to be configured for domain-specific tasks, depending on the clients the accountants will interact with. The super users and the local end user developer (also called the application coordinator) were asked to take part in this study. We documented their activities empirically and analytically, using interviews to gather data and drawing on aspects of activity theory for the conceptual framework for analysis. Our findings provide insight into end-user development (EUD) activities with VB: what roles were created by the Company, what roles emerged spontaneously during the process, what the various user groups (regular users, super users, and the application coordinator) did, and how EUD was coordinated between super users and the application coordinator. Our findings show that super users fill an important niche as mediators between regular users and local developers and can make a significant contribution to the success of EUD efforts in a nontechnical application domain.

INTRODUCTION

The concept of coworker competence has become a matter of interest in many companies in Scandinavia as well as elsewhere in the world. Work has become significantly more complex as workers confront the integration of traditional work with computer use. Employees in the modern workplace need to master new tools while continuing to employ older skills. In addition, the available task-relevant information has mushroomed. In knowledge intensive domains, such as accounting, this involves immediate access to large amounts of information (e.g., all the rules for income tax returns for various enterprises).

The development of coworker competence must keep pace with the introduction of new technology (Edwards, 1997; Ellström, Gustavsson, & Larsson, 1996). It raises the importance of how organizations employ information and communication technology (ICT) to adapt the workplace to the learning needs of diverse employees, or increase the flexibility of technical support (for example, using in-house expertise vs. buying software for adaptation; IT consultants vs. outsourcing). For the company in our study, we focused our observations and interviews on the technical and organizational infrastructures (Guribye, 2005) surrounding a new business application. This perspective enabled us to analyze activities associated with end user development (EUD) and learning at work, two important aspects in the adoption and use of generic (multipurpose) applications. We have chosen a framework for analysis based on activity theory (Engeström, 1987; Kaptelinin, 1996; Kuutti, 1996; Nardi, 1996). This framework provides analytic categories that allowed us to focus both on the integration of design and use and the integration of work and learning. We find that these four related activities need to be addressed when introducing complex application systems into an organization with a large and diverse user group. We focus in particular on the intereaction of the design and use activity systems. Furthermore, the support needs of the users (accountants) varied depending on the clients with whom they interact (from small and medium-sized businesses (SMBs) to large enterprises).

Previously the problem of introducing new technology into an organization has been addressed by bringing users and professional developers closer together (Grudin, 1991), for example, conducting user testing in developer laboratories; developing in-house software systems using participatory design techniques (Namioka & Schuler, 1993); and instituting companywide teaching programs. The case we analyzed had a different goal, namely to bridge the gap between developers and users by creating new user-developer roles. Furthermore, these roles were acknowledged and supported by management in the organization and they persisted after the technology had been put into use and the researchers had left the site.

We present a case study of "super users" who we define as *regular employees with in-depth knowledge of one or more of the organization's computer applications without being programmers.* Super users have both domain expertise and computer know-how, and they are trained to teach other users. They are not trained as programmers; instead they interact with regular users and with local developers in their daily work. We analyzed how an organization successfully initiates a program to train super users in conjunction with introducing a new software application, Visma Business (VB). Based on empirical material, we discuss our experiences and summarize our findings. Our research was formulated to address the following questions:

- How do super users engage in EUD activities in order to achieve an efficient use of a complex computer application?
- How are EUD activities organized (roles, division of labor, etc.)?

The questions are discussed throughout the chapter and specifically addressed in the empirical section. The rest of this chapter is organized as follows. We start by presenting the perspective and rationale of the study, followed by a brief survey of EUD and user design activities. Next, we present our conceptual framework, based on elements of activity theory. Then we provide background information of the company we studied and present the case in some detail, including an overview of the VB application. Next, we present the method for data analysis. The last part provides an empirical analysis of the data we collected. At the end, we summarize our findings and provide suggestions for further work.

PERSPECTIVE

Knowledge transfer and learning have always been a central factor in organizational implementation of ICT. When an organization chooses to implement a new application system, access to information will rapidly increase. As a consequence, few individuals are able to master all information relevant for their daily work. Instead, information becomes distributed among people and stored in databases, causing an information management problem (Ackermann, Pipek & Wulf, 2003; Gantt & Nardi, 1992; Hollan, Hutchins, & Kirsh, 2000). In this chapter, we address this information management problem at its most dramatic, in conjunction with the introduction of a new and different information system. The new system, a multipurpose application system, replaces several older, non-integrated systems. Two central issues need to be addressed to ensure a smooth transition from development to use: the integration of work and learning, and the integration of design and use. The former is about the task relevant information employees need access to while working in increasingly information rich environments and when interacting with collaborators who have different backgrounds

ands skills. The latter is about EUD. Although the four activities are intertwined, we focus on EUD in this chapter. We have also been involved in studies of the integration of work and learning in conjunction with other companies, describing similar adoption and use cases as the one reported here (Mørch, Engen, & Åsand, 2004a; Netteland, Wasson, & Mørch, 2007).

End User Development

The motivation for EUD in our study is as follows. Users of computer applications that interact heavily with customers as part of their work (e.g., accountants) operate in a variety of business contexts and scenarios that cannot always be predicted in advance. Thus, the line between "users" and "developers" becomes blurred as ICT spreads and as tailoring tools becomes available. The support for EUD in these settings is therefore fundamental in order to resolve the difference between a generic system and customer-specific needs. The generic system provides functionality for everyone, but can hamper productivity for individuals and work teams with excess information and functionality that is poorly adapted. On the other hand, the localized versions created as a result of tailoring generic systems address the specific needs of individual employees and work teams, but what enhances productivity at one local office may prove less useful in other parts of the company. These discrepancies are not easily resolved by conventional system development techniques, and generic systems with EUD support are one alternative to address the issues.

The introduction and gradual acceptance of EUD (Lieberman, Paterno, & Wulf, 2006; Mehandjiev & Bottaci, 1998), along with the related areas of human-computer interface design and recent trends in software engineering, can be seen as a result of software developers having succeeded in embedding easy-to-use customization tools in commercial off-the shelf (COTS) application systems, making generic applications programmable (Eisenberg, 1995), and supporting the evolution of generic applications into domain-specific ones (Mørch, 1996). The European end-user development network of excellence (http://giove.cnuce.cnr.it/eud-net.htm) has further developed these initiatives, studied the processes in detail, and proposes the following general definition of EUD: *End user development is a set of methods, activities, techniques, and tools that allow people who are nonprofessional software developers, at some point to create or modify a software artifact.*

Recent studies and system building efforts (e.g., Fischer, Giaccardi, Ye, Sutcliffe, & Mehandjiev, 2004; Nardi, 1996) have shown there is a growing need for new methods, activities, techniques, and tools for end user development. This is motivated by increased user diversity in organisations employing advanced information systems and a tendency in software houses to produce generic (multipurpose) software packages for a wide range of application domains. By user diversity, we mean users with different cultural, educational, training, and employment backgrounds. They are novice and experienced computer users, ranging from the young to the mature, and they have many different abilities and disabilities (Costabile, Foglia, Fresta, Mussio, & Piccinno, 2004). Generic means systems that can be configured to different organizational needs (Bansler & Havn, 1994) and can, for example, provide different user groups with different access rights to shared objects (Stevens & Wulf, 2002). In this chapter, we use the term "generic" synonymously with "multipurpose." A multipurpose computer application is an application with multiple functions, and one of the functions is EUD. The integration of EUD with conventional applications is motivated by EUD as a method for development that attempts to bring programming closer to the users, so that they can participate in the adaptation and further development of the applications in the context of use. Two approaches to this are (1) high-level

(user oriented) programming languages and (2) the components approach.

Creating high-level (user oriented) programming languages and related methods, activities, techniques, and tools to bridge the gap between using and creating or modifying a software application is no panacea. Indeed, the gradual steps from using an application to programming it are sometimes referred to as climbing a "programming mountain" (Fischer & Girgensohn, 1990; MacLean, Carter, Lövstrand, & Moran, 1990; Mørch, Stevens, Won, Klann, Dittrich, & Wulf, 2004b; Trigg & Moran, 1987). The increase in knowledge required for an end-user developer to move one step up this mountain should be proportional to complexity of the task to be accomplished with the system, and should take into account the benefits the task can provide to end users (including the pleasure of accomplishment and the satisfaction of learning to modify a computer application). Otherwise, the task should be left to professional developers. Tools such as customization forms, templates for frequently performed tasks, and easy-to-use programming languages like spreadsheet macros and scripting languages support EUD activities as a form of higher-level programming. These activities share characteristics with customization (Mackay, 1990) and local development (Gantt & Nardi, 1992).

The components approach to EUD differs from the "programming approach" in that end users interact with components in visual builders to select, modify, and connect components using high-level operations rather than writing program code in a text editor. However, components must be programmed before they can be deployed in visual builders; they might even be end-user programmable, making it difficult to draw a straight line between the two approaches. The important distinction for the purpose of EUD is the size of the programs and the complexity of the programming task. A component is part of an application and thus not a complete application program. Therefore, the task of programming or modifying a component at the code level will in most cases be considerably less demanding and less error prone than making changes to the entire application.

Programming a component is simplified with user-oriented languages (e.g., Visual Basic), but in most cases, end user developers using the components approach will not want to modify components by writing code. Instead they will choose techniques more appropriate to their background and skills (e.g., selection, editing attribute values, composition). Based on a survey of previous work, we suggest the following strategies for incorporating EUD functionality into generic applications using the components approach:

- **Under-design:** A EUD-enabled application framework or a set of components for a group of related tasks are examples of this. When first installed, the generic application is incomplete or not yet assembled. The architecture of the system defines a "family of applications," and specific applications are created as instantiations of the framework or as configurations of the set of components, which is brought about with the help of EUD techniques and tools. This strategy as viewed from software engineering defines flexible design spaces for end-use developers.
- **Over-design:** This strategy is modeled after multifunctional everyday physical objects, ranging from photocopiers to mobile phones, and notoriously represented by the Swiss army knife, providing a superset of required functionality. Other examples are minimalist furniture and household appliances that are both functional objects and works of art (Figure 1). Techniques such as graying-out, hiding, and deselection support this strategy in software applications.
- **Meta-design:** A design environment that supports an end-user developer in composing higher-level components from basic building blocks, which can be stored in a visual builder

and incorporated in future applications. A design environment might also allow an end user developer to descend to a lower level of abstraction in order to decompose a compound building block into smaller units in order to rearrange them into a modified, new component.

The three types of strategies of the components approach to EUD have been inspired by the work of Gerhard Fischer at the University of Colorado (Fischer et al., 2004; Fischer & Lemke, 1988). Further improvement and detailing of the components approach have been proposed in subsequent work (e.g., Mørch et al., 2004b; Won, Stiemerling, & Wulf, 2006). In the study reported here, we identified a set of EUD activities that were accomplished with techniques that range from deselecting redundant functionality to creating new functionality from a set of components (a design architecture). The EUD environment can

Figure 1. Josef Albers "Tea Glass," 1926, Bauhaus-Archive, Berlin. This is a minimalist example of the overdesign strategy to end-user development. Albers' teacup has two functions: a horizontal handle for the server and a vertical handle for the drinker.

be classified as a combination of under-design and over-design.

Previous Studies of Organization of EUD

In a study at MIT in the late 1980s, Mackay (1990) studied expert users of a UNIX windowing system (X-Windows). Many of the users in that study performed activities that went beyond regular use of the system. For example, they would engage in metalevel activities such as setting parameters for the position of the screen's user interface objects and storing them in a start-up file. Gantt and Nardi (1992) studied users of a CAD application (AutoCAD) and a spreadsheet application (Excel) to find how well users employed built-in tailoring tools. The authors found that users who tailored their applications very often worked in groups, and in those groups the authors identified one or more users described as "local developers." These particular users were sometimes referred to as "gardeners" to emphasize their ability to "nurture" a user organization and assist regular users to use the system more effectively. Other authors have used these terms to describe similar activities in other contexts (e.g., Christiansen, 1997; Kanstrup, 2004). A local developer, or gardener, is an expert in the professional domain who also has enough computer knowledge to tailor an application to domain-specific needs. In the context of AutoCAD, this meant adding new templates (e.g., domain-specific drawing symbols) and integrating them into the application. In the context of Excel, it meant adding computational depth to spreadsheet operations such as "sum" and "average" by creating small scripts and macros to operate across spreadsheet cells.

EUD goes beyond methods and techniques for human-computer interface design and software engineering and extends into user organizations as well. Volkoff, Strong, and Elmes (2002) introduced the term "boundary spanner" to designate individuals who can bridge the gap between domain

experts who have comprehensive knowledge of organizational processes and product experts who determine how the software operates. Boundary spanners serve as "brokers" between the two groups by employing various means to explain the practices of one community to the other (Volkoff et al., 2002). Mackay (1990) has used the term "translation" to explain a related phenomenon whereby a "gatekeeper" translates a user's problem into a technical solution. Local developers, gardeners, boundary spanners, and gate keepers are all roles assumed by super users.

The super users we studied in the Company engaged in the type of EUD activities just described, but they differ from the users described above. The main difference is that the super users we studied took on a contract-based role assigned to them by the company for which they work, whereas in the cases reported above, the EUD actors emerged out of the group of regular users as people who demonstrated proficiency in using a system and who showed an interest in helping other users learning to use it efficiently as well. In the study reported by Volkoff et al (2002), boundary spanners ended up taking on two roles even though there were few rewards for the extra role. The authors suggested the need for "system sponsors" to provide special incentives for boundary spanners in order to motivate them and help them maintain credibility in both communities, but in the companies reported on, this was not achieved.

User-Developer Continuum

Some organizations in Scandinavia use the term "super user" in conjunction with the above activities and have started to train super users to address the information overload problem associated with the introduction of advanced information systems. The term was first used, to the best of our knowledge, to name IT staff asked to provide technical assistance to other employees when a new system was introduced in the organization

(Kaasbøll & Øgrim, 1994). Supers users were selected to take part in this activity based on their skill in using the new system, knowledge of the application domain, and their ability to teach other employees to use the system effectively. In the case we studied, the Company defined the role of super users under a contract-based agreement with a group of accountants distributed across the organization.

EUD activities can be located along a continuum from regular use to professional development. The spectrum includes:

- **Regular users:** Workers who are not interested in tailoring a system, but who want to use the system's various productivity and computational tools to accomplish their required tasks.
- **Super users:** Domain-trained workers who are also skilled with computers, interested in exploring tools for tailoring if there is time set aside for this and who like to teach other user how to use the system. Super users are boundary spanners and translators between regular users and local developers.
- **Local developers:** Domain-trained workers who have more computer skill than super users. They know more about programming and have more responsibility than super users and will often be asked to coordinate the organization's EUD activities. They communicate directly with professional developers regarding development tasks that cannot be accomplished locally. In the company we report on, one person was assigned the position of "application coordinator." We see this person as a local developer in light of the EUD activities he performs. We will refer to him by the position he holds.
- **Professional developers:** IT workers who develop a new software application or a new version of an existing application. Developers work in software houses and are trained as software engineers and/or programmers.

Sociocultural Perspective

When the Company shifted from using several accounting applications to one core application, VB, it encountered the situation of a new system impacting an existing work process. The super user initiative that was launched as a result of this process created a subsidiary function in the organization that modified the conditions for individual and collaborative communication and problem solving. To understand the various roles and relationships that were created as a result of this intervention, we need a theoretical perspective and explanatory terms. A sociocultural perspective allows us to talk about how human development changes through interaction and collaboration with peers while mediated by artifacts such as ICT (Lave & Wenger, 1991; Vygotsky, 1978; Wertsch, 1998).

The sociocultural perspective can help us to understand the relationship between individuals and the artifacts they use and work with and the organizational units they belong to. It implies that artifacts, such as computer applications, mediate interactions between people. The introduction of new technology, such as an accounting application, creates a discontinuity between how tasks used to be carried and how they will be accomplished in the future using the new technology. From a sociocultural perspective, the concept of "artifact" is used in a broad sense but with a strong focus on its mediating function (Cole, 1996; Wertsch, 1998). Understanding artifact mediation gives us some insight into how knowledge is accumulated in the organization, for example, how it is represented in computers and distributed among individuals and processes that persist over time through transformations and discontinuous developments. In our case, knowledge concerning accounting was codified in the existing system in the form of rules and procedures and specialized client-specific business solutions. The new artifact (VB) creates opportunities and constraints on accomplishing required accounting tasks (often simplifying work). To understand the change in work as a result of the new technology, we must use a conceptual framework that provides a comprehensive set of analytic categories and explanatory terms for bridging technology and organization. For this purpose, we have chosen activity theory.

ACTIVITY THEORY

Activity theory (AT) provides a conceptual framework for understanding human and work-oriented developmental processes (Engeström, 1987; Kuutti, 1996). It is a powerful, descriptive tool rather than a predictive theory (Nardi, 1996). Whereas in many psychological theories human actions are used as the unit of analysis, AT takes action a step further by claiming that it is difficult to analyze real-life situations outside a laboratory without considering the context in which actions are taken. In AT, the unit of analysis is human action within its minimal meaningful context (Kuutti, 1996), which is encapsulated in the term "activity." Activity unites action and context into a conceptual whole (Engeström, 1987). We will not go into depth concerning the structure of the framework of activity theory here. Interested readers are encouraged to consult the sources (e.g., Engeström, 1987; Kaptelinin, 1996; Kuutti, 1996; Nardi, 1996). We give a brief overview of the relevant concepts we used in our analysis.

Studying human activity means understanding the artifact-mediated and object-oriented actions of humans as they interact and collaborate within a system, and examining how these actions relate to the transformation of the activity system over time (Engeström, 2001; Kaptelinin, 1996; Vygotsky, 1978). activity theory studies both individual activity systems and the interaction of multiple systems. According to the theory, individual systems are internally unstable. Interaction becomes important because it can lead to transformations of a system over time and further development

towards more stable systems (Kuutti, 1996). All activity systems are mediated by artifacts and objects, which provide the focal points of the activities. Together with subject, rules, community, and division of labor, these are the basic concepts of AT (e.g., Engeström, 1987). The objects define what the activities are aiming at and when multiple activity systems are interacting the objects are often referred to as "boundary objects." The boundary object concept originated with Star and Griesemer (1989). It is characterized as something that is common to more than one activity system and holds them together as well as separates them. Furthermore, a boundary object can be either a physical thing (the conventional meaning of the term object) or a pre-understanding of the thing, such as a plan or an objective (e.g., adapt VB to meet the needs of the accountants). It is both a given in the situation and something towards which the activity is directed, that is, something anticipated, projected, transformed, and achieved (Engeström, 1987; Kuutti, 1996). The subject in this context is the participant in the community at the workplace. The relationship between the subject and the object in an activity is mediated by the artifact or tool. A tool can be anything used in the process of transforming the object, whether material or conceptual. In our case, VB is the central tool, as well as its tailoring or metalevel features. We used concepts from AT to analyze the activities of super users and a local developer in the Company.

In addition to subject, object, and tool, the framework contains a fourth component, community. Community consists of all those who share or interact with the same object during a given activity. Furthermore, the relationship between subject and community is mediated by rules (e.g., tax rules, business logic), and the relationship between the community and the object is mediated by the division of labor. Division of labor is useful in analyzing how super users and the local developer share and divide tasks and how this relationship evolves. The division of labor is a fundamental part of how work and responsibility are organized in the Company. When this can be described in terms of community and objects operating in an activity system, the explanation of the organization of EUD can be put in a meaningful context.

For our purposes, the activity of the super users and local developers in the process of adapting VB to new needs forms our unit of analysis. In particular, we look at how EUD activities are mediated by artifacts such as VB, VB tailoring tools, accounting practice, and computer knowledge. Our analysis takes into account data sampled from the entire EUD community in the Company, and identifies the division of labor within the community according to what the various end user developers do. We see EUD activities as several activity systems (regular users, super users, local developer, professional programmers) in their effort of working together, and we try to relate this to the various work procedures (rules) in the workplace that constrain and enable EUD.

CASE

The case we have analyzed is part of the research and developmental project "Læring på ArbeidsPlassen" (LAP, learning and knowledge building at work). The LAP project, which started in May 2002 and ended in December 2004, was a consortium of six partners, with partial funding from the Research Council. The consortium had two industrial partners (an oil company and the accounting firm referred to as the Company), three research units, and one national federation of service companies. The project was classified as "user-oriented," a project category defined by the Research Council, meaning that the industry partners defined the research problems the three research units should work on, while the methods, techniques, and theories to address the problems were selected or developed by the research partners in collaboration. The effect of this was a division

of labor when it came to implementing changes proposed during the project. These were primarily undertaken by the industry partners based on research reports and knowledge dissemination seminars delivered by the research units.

One of the industry partners, the Company, figures in the case study we describe in this chapter. The Company is an accounting consulting company that is office-based, project-driven, and geographically distributed, with a long-term emphasis on competence development for its employees. To that end, it has started to include ICT in its agenda. Furthermore, the Company is interested in research and development activities that can produce useful results not only for its individual employees and its overall business goals, but also for other companies that have a similar organizational structure. The Company had decided to implement a new computer application, Visma Business, and this decision was made prior to conception of the LAP project.

The Company makes its revenues by undertaking accounting and tax consultancy services for SMBs and large enterprises in the Nordic region of Europe. It has around 1,000 employees distributed in 75 offices across Scandinavia. The Company has expanded in the last few years through the acquisition of new offices. Until recently, the Company had used a total of 13 different accounting systems to support the work of its accountants. A decision was made in 2001 that all offices should convert to one single application, called Visma Business. This is a large and complex generic computer application consisting of several modules covering all aspects of accounting. The employees in the Company work with different clients and therefore have different requirements regarding which functionality they need or do not need. After the completion of the adoption process, VB became the main tool for all employees in the company, and for most of them, this has had an impact on the tasks they perform. In anticipation of this expected interaction between tools and tasks, all of the employees had to go through an introductory course in VB. The course combined e-learning and face-to-face meetings in a classroom. In addition to regular users learning how to use the system, super users were also selected and given additional training. They would later play the dual role of teacher and local developer: to reinforce the training to colleagues in their office after the introductory course and to adapt VB to local client needs. The decision to cultivate super users was also made by the Company before they joined the LAP project. In this chapter, we take a closer look at the super user program, the role played by super users, the activities they carried out during adoption and use of VB, and the other employees they interacted with during EUD activities.

After completing the initial training, the super users went back to their offices with the new responsibility of helping their colleagues use the system, which in many cases meant adapting it to their needs using EUD techniques. They did not rely on a central technical support unit for this purpose. The Company already had an IT department, but they chose to position super users in the zone between technical support and employees. In case of technical difficulties, the super user could contact IT for technical assistance, but this channel was rarely used. One reason for this (on which we elaborate in the empirical part) is that while the IT department provides technical support, they do not know the profession-oriented language of accounting very well, which was a key to understanding the reason for many of the EUD activities with VB.

Super Users and the Application Coordinator

The Company, as mentioned above, chose to initiate a super user program in the hope of achieving a successful adoption of the new application (Åsand, Mørch, & Ludvigsen, 2004). They decided to have 1 super user for every 10 employees, and these were chosen from among the ordinary employees

in the local offices. The corporate management formalized the criteria for being a super user in form of a contract. Both the local office manager and each super user had to sign the contract. The contract lays out the duties and expectations of the super user role, as follows:

- The super user must be competent both professionally and technically, with the emphasis on mastery of the profession-oriented accounting language.
- The super user must set aside time for training, and for sharing knowledge, for example, conducting workshops for their office colleagues.
- The super user must provide all employees in their local office with the necessary training to use the new VB application for their specific accounting needs, and to manage a specific schedule for such training. The latter requirement was of great importance and was made explicit in the contract. Without scheduled presentations, the training may not be as effective.

By the use of this contract, the Company formalized the super user role, which conferred legitimacy and visibility on the time and effort invested by the super users. After they signed the contract, the super users received additional, more thorough training in VB that focused on the more technical aspects of the application, especially the EUD features.

In addition to the super users, the Company appointed one person to be responsible for coordinating all the super user activities and gave them training. This person, called the *application coordinator*, is the only appointed local developer in the Company. However, he is a trained accountant. He showed a special interest in the new application from the very beginning of the project, and was asked to manage the super users and the centralized EUD activities, in a full time position. He is also responsible for reporting problems to the software house that develops VB, including errors and adaptation tasks that could not be solved in the Company, based on feedback from the super users and their colleagues. The adaptation tasks handled by the application coordinator include adding new menus and new fields to existing applications in order to evolve them into domain-specific business solutions. The results are referred to as screens and resemble spreadsheet applications, and the method employed can be seen as an instance of evolutionary application development (Mørch, 1996). If new business rules required new functionality in the software, developers in the software house handled those modifications by writing new program code. A new solution typically starts with a request from an accountant for a change to an existing solution based on the specific needs of a client. The simpler tailoring tasks are handled locally by an office super user, but more complicated tasks are referred to the application coordinator. The application coordinator has enhanced access rights to the system, allowing him to distribute generally useful solutions to other offices as well. Through a centralized application system, a locally adapted business solution can be made "global" (generalized) and therefore accessible to everyone using VB. Due to the amount of work required to create specialized solutions, the application coordinator has gradually given access rights to some of the other super users as well so that they can help him to speed up the process. These super users evolved into the role of *local developer* because they showed more interest than the average super users in creating solutions with the tailoring tools in VB. These local developers collaborate closely with the other super users in their office, who are in a similar position, and with the application coordinator.

The Visma Business (VB) Application

Visma Business is a complex accounting application, consisting of several modules, providing a superset of the functionality of the old systems. This is why we call it a generic system (Bansler & Havn, 1994; Mørch, 1996, 2003) and it is an example of what we above referred to as over-design, providing a superset of required functionality. On a daily basis, much of the generic system is not used, since it includes too much information for any one accountant. The range of possible ways of doing things makes it very frustrating to learn. There are many functions and possibilities and only a few users can employ them all. Actually, 95% of the time spent in VB is spent in a few accounting modules. In addition, VB comes with a small set of business solutions for client-specific tasks available for everyone, and a set of tailoring tools (referred to as design mode) to create new specialized business solutions, to modify existing solutions, and to remove superfluous (un-needed) functionality. The initial configuration of VB is shown in Figure 2.

The business solutions are normally tailored for specific offices, depending on the clients the offices do business with. So even though VB starts as a generic application, end users can make changes and tailor it to their use. The changes are made locally, but those found to have companywide application could also be enabled "globally" by the application coordinator, as previously described, hence making them available for everyone. Possible changes include choosing which functions to make available and modifying or creating menus and fields. Much of this activity is similar to creating spreadsheets (see Figure 3). In fact, VB is closely related to the spreadsheet concept and can actually be connected with Excel sheets. New functionality can be defined in Excel cells and linked to VB, making them accessible through VB screens. Access to the tailoring tools is accomplished by switching to a *design mode*,

Figure 2. The Visma Business (start window): A multipurpose application system

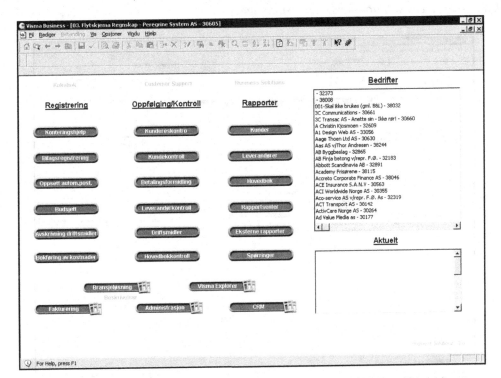

which applies to those users who have been given this access right. This provides the application coordinator and some super users with an expanded set of commands for making such changes. This mode is controlled by an administrative password that only the local developer and super users have access to. Simpler tailoring tasks, such as modifying the name of an existing field or menu, is also accomplished in design mode.

The screenshot in Figure 3 is an example of the design mode used by the local developer when making changes in the system. For regular users without appropriate rights, these choices are not available and appear as unavailable functions (i.e., presented on grayed-out menus).

Method

As a basis for the analysis, we conducted interviews with a broad sample of super users as well as with other employees in the Company. The main purpose was to identify various relationships that arose between super users and their colleagues as a result of the introduction of VB, and how these relationships fit into the larger context of professional development, learning, and EUD activities in the workplace.

The interviews were conducted from December 2002 through May 2003, and were grouped in three rounds. In total, 16 super users and 23 regular employees were interviewed. The respondents were distributed across nine offices and the selection criteria included gender, number of employees at a given location, geographical location, and phase of converting to VB. With the selected super users as a starting point, we selected the 23 regular employees based on their contact with these super users. The first 10 interviews were carried out by the researchers during visits to local offices, while the remaining interviews were per-

Figure 3. Tailoring VB provides access to an expanded command set. A field "Sum" has been created and added to a business solution for a real estate agent.

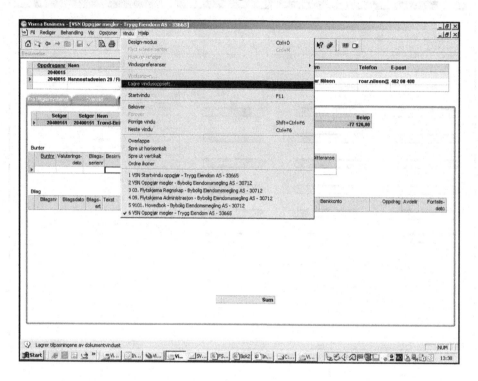

formed by telephone. Each interview started with an e-mail introduction from the management of the Company, followed by a more detailed e-mail about the procedure, sent out by the LAP-project researchers that would conduct the interviews (one Ph.D. student and two master students). Each interview took approximately 15 to 20 minutes. Confidentiality was of great importance, and all interviews were carried out by researchers and not by the Company. By focusing on the research as the agenda, we hoped to capture the variety in experiences related to being a super user or being a regular user interacting with a super user. In addition to these interviews, we conducted interviews with the director of competence, and the application coordinator. All interviews were taped and transcribed. These transcripts together with the contract the super users signed constitute the basis for the analysis we present next.

EMPIRICAL ANALYSIS

Activity theory provides a set of concepts that is helpful to analyze our case. The emphasis on *activity* brings certain features of a developmental process to the forefront that might otherwise be overlooked when studying interaction with technology. For example, there are different actors involved in EUD (regular users, super users, and application coordinator) with different goals and different artifacts to accomplish their work, regulated by different work procedures (rules). To explain how these phenomena are inter-related, we have chosen to use the concepts of subjects, community, objects, artifacts, and division of labor in our analysis. For example, the relationship between the artifact (VB or the professional domain) and the object (the reason for EUD or goal of tailoring) is reciprocal, creating a kind of task-artifact-task dependency relation (Carroll,

Kellogg, & Rosson, 1992). When the artifact changes, the object is likely to change as well. The professional domain is ambivalent in that it belongs to multiple categories and we treat it as a "boundary object" between two activity systems. But there are other dependency relationships and analytic categories as well. Subjects, artifacts, and objects are affected by the existing rules, the community in which the activity occurs, and the division of labor within this community. We analyze the following topics in more detail in the following subsections:

- The profession of accounting as a boundary object;
- The VB application as a meditating artifact;
- The division of labor among the different user groups and developers.

The first topic is of special importance in that it stands as a prerequisite for the other two. It concerns the process that leads up to EUD, whereas the other two show the results after a boundary object has been successfully established.

The Profession of Accounting as a Boundary Object

Star and Griesemer (1989) introduced boundary objects as objects that are both flexible enough to adapt to local needs and constrained enough to allow several parties to employ them for their own purposes. These objects are robust enough to maintain a common identity across communities (activity systems). Boundary objects can be both abstract and concrete and they have different meanings in different communities. The creation and management of boundary objects thus becomes a key task in order to develop and maintain coherence across interacting activity systems.

When regular users, super users, the application coordinator (local developer), and sometimes the professional developers talk about VB together, it is important that they have a shared object in mind or in front of them to ground the discussion. This can be the goal of the activity (e.g., tailoring VB) but more often it is the profession-oriented language of the domain. The latter provides the necessary pre-understanding for using and further developing the application. We see both of them as boundary objects (one concrete the other abstract). Previous studies have shown that both the "application system language" and the profession-oriented language of the domain have to be learned for collaboration between developers and users to succeed (Nygaard, 1984).

It was the opinion among all employees interviewed that it was positive to have a super user acting as the local expert at each office. This made it possible to have a professional discussion of accounting issues with the confidence that the super user could understand the problems the employees were experiencing. It was also commonly accepted that technical competence and the ability to grasp new knowledge quickly were very important requirements for being a super user. One of the super users put it this way:

I think it is important to have both. We noticed it at the same time we converted to VB, when we called the support unit. Many of them managed the technical bit, but nobody had any clue about accounting. It was a problem. When the super users are here in the house they use the same applications. We talk the same language.

The employee here points to the importance of a shared understanding (boundary object) by saying that the super users need to have the same common understanding of the problem as the person stating the problem. They interact within the same community of practice (Wenger, 1998) as the regular users, where the shared object represented by accounting constitutes the basis for the collective competence that develops. This is what, in the context of traditional system development,

Nygaard (1984) refers to as "profession-oriented language" or "user-oriented languages" and what, in the context of AT, Engeström (2001) calls a "shared repertoire." To develop a shared repertoire requires a reciprocal engagement regarding the task of solving problems (Wenger, 1998). When problems requiring EUD occur, an engagement is created by the involved parties in such a way that super users, the application coordinator, and regular users can all learn something new. The super user's motivation and learning potential is in generalizing from the situation to solve related problems in the future. The application coordinator sees an opportunity to improve the application with a new business solution that might apply across all local offices. The regular user wishes to solve a problem for a client (e.g., completing a budget on time). Hence, they all have a wish to understand the situation.

When a shared repertoire has been established, one can then start to close the gap between the multipurpose VB application and the specific requirements of a client solution. Examining what kind of knowledge is required to accomplish this is the next stage in the process. The emphasis on a shared object is maintained, and the additional application system knowledge required is built on this pre-understanding, gradually translating the understanding of the domain (a profession-oriented language) into an application system language. The bottom-up direction of competence development was stressed by all users interviewed. It starts with a foundation of knowledge that the IT support unit and the professional developers do not hold.

I pay bills directly for a customer and it is a sensitive operation, then the money goes directly out from the bank, and in this process I have used the super user a lot when I was insecure. The super user does the same operation for his clients and we have had a close collaboration in this part of VB, and it has been under construction, and I

have therefore been very careful. It's been good to have a super user.

Security is important when providing a service for a customer in the business the company is competing in, especially when one has the full responsibility for the clients' financial statements. It becomes even more important when providing a service while trying out a new accounting application. The above excerpt shows how important this security was as a reason for seeking assistance from an expert. The professional integrity required by an accountant in their interactions with colleagues and clients is something the IT staff and professional developers do not have the background to fully understand. The trust that exists among those who already know the profession is a very valuable resource when solving problems. Although developers have competence in technical solutions, they do not see the possibilities and constraints of various solutions from the user's point of view the way a super user can.

It is through their professional competence and ability to recommend solutions based on this competence that super users and the local developer have developed their skills as translators (Mackay, 1990) and boundary spanners (Volkoff et al., 2002). At the same time, it becomes important that the "translation" from a domain-specific problem to a technical solution be accomplished. What is central in the above excerpt is the fact that one has to take the client's perspective into account when solving the problem and be able to access other people's competence during the process. With the super users' knowledge of the new application, they can act as translators (Mackay, 1990) and boundary spanners (Volkoff et al., 2002) for the regular users, as, for example, when a super user assists in the process of finding the right functionality for a regular user based on their clients' needs. Furthermore, some of the super users make changes in VB to facilitate certain accounting processes by creating new menus and fields or renaming existing ones. This overview of the application is not something a regular user has.

The VB Application as a Mediating Artifact

Using VB to mediate the relationship between the subject (users) and the object is also a process aimed at closing the gap mentioned earlier. Adaptation of VB to domain-specific needs will be the task of the super users in collaboration with the application coordinator. The accountants have various clients they keep accounts for, and to offer good service to the clients, they depend on finding the right functions in VB, making them available and to ensure the workflow is optimal. By learning the proper way of working in VB, the super users tailor the application for each client by selecting and deselecting functionality. To be able to modify a function such as a button or field, they may have to get assistance from someone who has expertise in the underlying functionality in VB. This requires boundary spanning (Volkoff et al., 2002). The super users communicate with both regular users and the application coordinator, assisting the former in finding the right functions in VB, consulting the latter when the task is beyond their skill and training. One of the users described VB:

VB is not a completed program and may never be. It is a pile of Lego blocks that you have to put together to create an accounting system suiting the needs of the clients you keep accounts for. It's clearly a high threshold to cross.

This illustrates what we referred to above as the under-design strategy to end-user development (Fischer et al., 2004). VB is a generic system, represented by an architecture (set of components) that embodies a family of applications. To create an accounting system (a specific application) out of the "pile of Lego blocks" requires design work involving multiple actors. Furthermore, the ex-

cerpt as viewed under an AT framework defines mediation through an artifact. When a regular user and a super user discuss how to tailor VB to achieve the best result for working with a client's account, they use VB as a mediating artifact or tool for the purpose of accomplishing the object, which is to do accounting for the client. In this tailoring process, the super user helps the regular user to choose the options that best fit the task to be accomplished. This mediation can also be seen when the super user takes a more complex problem to the application coordinator. Together they discuss possible changes to be made to the application, and sometimes they end up with a new business solution tailored to a specific client or a branch of clients.

The changes we make are often tailor-made solutions for a particular group of clients, such as real-estate agents. When a group of clients is relatively large we produce shared solutions for them, which make doing their accounts more streamlined. The request for these kinds of solutions comes from those who do the accounts.

It is not always the super users who discover the solution to a problem. Often a regular user, through their position in the organization, is able to bring the solution to the attention of other VB users. This is achieved as a result of collaboration between local developers, super users, and regular users. This is also something Gantt and Nardi (1992) have explored, that user and local developers often collaborate to make adjustments that one person in the group cannot do on his or her own.

Figure 4 shows the development of a business solution for real estate agents. The application coordinator and a super user have developed this solution by tailoring VB. They have removed standard fields and added new ones to model their clients' accounts better. All fields in VB can be hidden and made visible again. They can also be sorted and selected using shortcuts.

Figure 4. A business solution for real estate agents

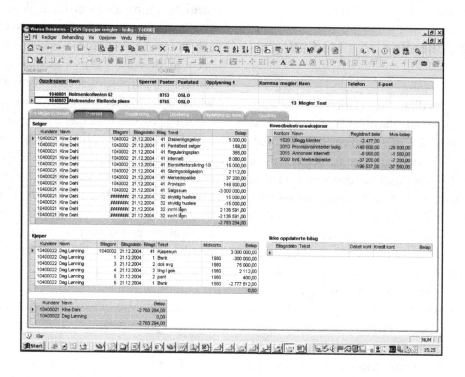

Much of the tailoring is done in design mode and the changes made in this mode can very easily be made global for all users of VB, which is a feature of VB's common base architecture. In the beginning of the implementation process of VB, the management and the application coordinator discussed how wide the access should be. They agreed to start with an open approach, by which all super users had access to the design mode and could thus save their changes globally in VB. After a period of testing, the access rights became restricted, and only the local developer and some chosen super users were allowed this access right. Having the access rights available to all super users became a problem because not every super user had the need to make their solutions global (shared by all). In fact, when this feature was overused, it tended to be disruptive to everyday work as regular users were overloaded with functionality they did not need. As it is now implemented, it works well. However, this still depends on good

communication between those super users who do not have full access rights and those who do, such as the application coordinator.

The Division of Labor Between the Different User Groups and Developers

We see that the various roles of regular user, super user, local developer, and professional developer differ in responsibilities regarding EUD activities. A typical difference is associated with multiple access rights required when making changes global as we just described. Another difference is related to making the local changes. Regular users cannot make persistent changes to the application, but have the option to select only those parts of the application they want to use, and the super users help them in doing this because they have a better overview of the VB functionality. One super user put it this way when asked about the division of labor between him and the others users in his office:

Regular users do not make changes in VB, I do it. Users notify me about needs for making changes or modifying modules in VB.

Modifications to VB are performed by the local developer and by some of the super users. When making modifications, there is an explicit organization in the community of users regarding the transformation of the object into outcome. The object is here to make VB work in interactions with their clients, and to achieve this they need to cooperate within their community in the local offices to make the changes in VB. A similar division of labor can be found between the application coordinator and the software house, in situations where he has to consult the developers to solve a EUD problem that involves application programming. The following comment from the application coordinator illustrates the situation:

I don't do any programming within VB (Visma Business). For that I need the professional developers. I report possible improvements, and maybe we see a result of it in the next version.

The EUD activities performed by the application coordinator include selecting modules to be part of a new business solution and modifying the menus and fields within new and existing solutions. The local developers cannot modify the program behind the menus and fields because this is written in a proprietary language. Programming of this kind is judged to be too complex for someone not trained as a programmer and is therefore left to professional developers in the software house. It is more complex than writing macros in Excel, which is a task most super users and even some regular users are quite familiar with, and sometimes workarounds are made by integrating VB with Excel functionality. It is illustrated with the following comment from the application coordinator:

As application coordinator, I have access to make and save changes to VB. These possibilities are not available to the regular users; it is only a few selected super users and me. This difference is made visible in VB in that the tailoring tools are "grayed out" in the regular users' interface.

Technologically, two levels of access rights to the system's tailoring features manifest the division of labor between local developers and regular users: *use mode* and *design mode* (see Figure 3). In this way, division of labor enables boundary objects, in this case, tailoring tools to serve as a link between the community of users and the community of developers. The Company experimented for a while before they decided to modify the access rights to these tools. This may be a result of the size of the company (close to 1,000 accountants) and the multitude of specialized solutions that were created with VB. To make the system manageable, it became necessary to restrict full tailoring rights to only a handful of super users. Finally, the technique of "graying out" is a feature of software components to make the tools that do not apply to certain users or in certain situations unavailable. It is associated with the over-design strategy to end-user development that was presented in the beginning of this chapter.

SUMMARY AND CONCLUSION

We have presented a case study of the organizational implementation of a complex (multipurpose) business application in an accounting Company. During this process, the Company chose to use super users and a local developer, referred to as application coordinator, to support the adoption and use of the system, including tailoring it to the needs of local offices. We observed the EUD activities and collected data by interviewing regular users, super users, and the application coordinator. In the analysis, we identified the importance of the professional language of accounting as a boundary object, as well as the VB application as a mediating artifact. The primary result of these activities is a tailored set of VB solutions. These local solutions are created with the help of super users and the application coordinator in collaboration, and professional developers are sometimes involved, but it is the regular users (accountants) who identify the need for the solutions. This is a bottom-up process of problem identification and problem solving, and a top-down process of spread of innovation (globalization), making generally useful local adaptations available throughout the Company. These processes span multiple activity systems (clients, regular users, super users, application coordinator, professional developers).

By taking a sociocultural approach (Wertsch, 1998), we have focused on the overall organization of EUD activity, and by applying basic concepts from activity theory (Engeström, 1987) (objects, mediating artifacts, communities, division of labor, multiple activity systems, rules), we are able to explain a set of inter-related phenomenon. The object of activity is the not-quite-ready generic application Visma Business, which is transformed into a user-oriented application supporting accountants in their interactions with clients and with the domain knowledge held by the experienced accountants (here VB serves as mediating artifact). The regular users, the super users, and the application coordinator are the community that shares these objects, occasionally joined by one or more professional developers. There is a certain division of labor within the community: (1) between the regular users and the super users, (2) between the super users and the application coordinator, and (3) between the application coordinator and the professional developers. There is also a set of rules, defined by tax laws and contractual agreements between the Company and the super users, or implicit by a general working

culture established in the Company as the users work together. The "business logic" programmed in VB components also provides rules at a more detailed level. In the application transformation process from problem identification to ICT solution, the professional language of the domain (accounting) and the application system language (e.g., application modules, tailoring tools, and business logic) interact. Various tools mediate this, VB, and the already established (physical and conceptual) tools used in the company.

Our main findings from the analysis are three criteria we believe important for an organization desiring the successful implementation of a complex computer application:

- **Institutionalization of super user initiative:** EUD became institutionalized in the Company with the strategic decision to involve super users in the implementation process. This was in response to the complexity of a large and multipurpose application system (VB). The role of super users was established through a contract, which guaranteed that the super users had time to perform the activities the role required.
- **Two-way grounding:** The Company chose to have a distributed network of super users located at all of its offices (1 super user for every 10 accountants). The grounding was accomplished in two ways: (1) geographical distribution of super users and (2) utilization of super users with a background in the same profession as the regular users.
- **Local developer as coordinator:** The Company chose to have one person holding the position as an application coordinator. This person's responsibility is primarily to perform EUD activities at a general level and work closely with some of the more experienced super users in the offices as well as communicating with the professional developers. This person generalizes the results of useful EUD activities and makes local solutions

available throughout the Company. This responsibility was also associated with access rights to the tools for accomplishing the task. This organization of responsibility enabled a smooth transition from everyday use and user requirements capture to development of new functionality.

- **End-user development using the components approach:** The EUD strategy supported in VB follows the "components approach" to EUD. Super users were not involved in programming, but in configuring applications by (de)selecting and modifying components in order to create specific solutions for the various accounting offices and their clients. The strategies of *under-design* and *over-design* were implicit in these activities. Future work should investigate how the meta-design strategy can be integrated with the two other strategies in order to provide increased flexibility for modification of components without sacrificing ease of use. Meta-design can provide design environments for modifying individual components (basic and compound) by part composition, a technique that might overcome shortcomings associated with modification of fixed attributes.

ACKNOWLEDGMENT

The case study was conducted while the second author was a Ph.D. student at the Faculty of Education, University of Oslo. We want to thank InterMedia, University of Oslo, for financing our work. We also thank the other members of the LAP project and the many employees in the company who took part in the study.

REFERENCES

Ackerman, M.S., Pipek, V., & Wulf, V. (2003). *Sharing expertise: Beyond knowledge management.* Cambridge, MA: The MIT Press.

Åsand, H.-R.H., Mørch, A., & Ludvigsen, S. (2004). Super users: A strategy for ICT-introduction. In A.M. Kanstrup, A.M. Roskilde, & D.K. Universitesforlag (Eds.), *E-learning at work* (pp. 131-147, in Danish).

Bansler, J.P., & Havn, E. (1994). Information systems development with generic systems. In W.R.J. Baets (Ed.), *Proceedings of the 2nd European Conference on Information Systems,* Nijenrode University (pp. 30-31). Breukelen: Nijenrode University Press.

Carroll, J.M., Kellogg, W.A., & Rosson, M.B. (1992). The task-artifact cycle. In J.M. Carroll (Ed.), *Designing interaction: Psychology at the human-computer interface* (Cambridge Series on Human-Computer Interaction, pp. 74-102). Cambridge University Press.

Christiansen, E. (1997). Gardening: A metaphor for sustainability in information technology-technical support. In J. Berleur & D. Whitehouse (Eds.), *An ethical global information society: Culture and democracy revisited.* London: Chapman & Hall.

Cole, M. (1996). *Cultural psychology: A once and future discipline.* Cambridge, MA: Harvard University Press.

Costabile, M.F., Foglia, D., Fresta, G., Mussio, P., & Piccinno, A. (2004). Software environments for end-user development and tailoring. *PsychNology Journal, 2*(1), 99-122.

Edwards, R. (1997). *Changing places: Flexibility, lifelong learning, and a learning society.* London: Routledge.

Eisenberg, M. (1995). Programmable applications: Interpreter meets interface. *SIGCHI Bulletin, 27*(2), 68-83.

Ellström, P.E., Gustavsson, B., & Larsson, S. (1996). *Livslångt lärande* [Lifelong learning]. Lund: Studentlitteratur.

Engeström, Y. (1987). *Learning by expanding: An activity-theoretical approach to developmental research.* Helsinki: Orienta-Konsultit.

Engeström, Y. (2001). Expansive learning at work: Towards an activity theoretical reconceptualization. *Journal of Education and Work, 14,* 133-156.

Fischer, G., & Girgensohn, A. (1990). End-user modifiability in design environments. In *Proceedings of the Conference on Human Factors in Computing Systems (CHI'90)* (pp. 183-192). New York: ACM Press.

Fischer, G., Giaccardi, E., Ye, Y., Sutcliffe, A.G., & Mehandjiev, N. (2004). Meta-design: A manifesto for end-user development. *Communications of the ACM, 47*(9), 33-37.

Fischer, G., & Lemke, A.C. (1988). Constrained design processes: Steps toward convivial computing. In R. Guindon (Ed.), *Cognitive science and its application for human-computer interaction* (pp. 1-58). Hillsdale, NJ: Lawrence Erlbaum.

Gantt, M., & Nardi, B. (1992). Gardeners and gurus: Patterns of cooperation among CAD users. In *Proceedings of the Conference on Computer-Human Interaction (CHI '92)* (pp. 107-117). New York: ACM Press.

Grudin, J. (1991). Interactive systems: Bridging the gaps between developers and users. *IEEE Computer, 24*(4), 59-69.

Guribye, F. (2005). *Infrastructures for learning: Ethnographic inquiries into the social and technical conditions for education and training.* Doctoral thesis, University of Bergen, Norway, Department of Information Science and Media Studies.

Hollan, J., Hutchins, E., & Kirsh, D. (2000). Distributed cognition: Toward a new foundation for human-computer interaction research. *ACM Transactions on Computer-Human Interaction, 7*(2), 174-196.

Kaasbøll, J., & Øgrim, L. (1994). Super-users: Hackers, management hostages or working class heroes? A study of user influence on redesign in distributed organizations. In *Proceedings of the 17th Information Systems Research Seminar in Scandinavia (IRIS-17)* (pp. 784-798). Department of Information Processing Science, University of Oulu, Finland.

Kanstrup, A-M. (2004). E-learning behind the facade: The value of local gardeners. In A.M. Kanstrup, A.M. Roskilde, & D.K. Universitesforlag (Eds.), *E-learning at work* (pp. 149-166, in Danish).

Kaptelinin, V. (1996). Activity theory: Implications for human-computer interaction. In B. Nardi (Ed.), *Context and consciousness: Activity theory and human-computer interaction* (pp. 103-116). Cambridge: MIT Press.

Kuutti, K. (1996). Activity theory as a potential framework for human-computer interaction research. In B. Nardi (Ed.), *Context and consciousness: Activity theory and human-computer interaction* (pp. 17-44). Cambridge: MIT Press.

Lave, J., & Wenger, E. (1991). *Situated learning: Legitimate peripheral participation.* Cambridge: University Press.

Lieberman, H., Paterno, F., & Wulf, V. (Eds.). (2006). *End-user development.* Berlin: Springer-Verlag.

Mackay, W.E. (1990). Patterns of sharing customizable software. In *Proceedings of the Conference on Computer Supported Cooperative Work (CSCW'90)* (pp. 209-221). New York: ACM Press.

MacLean, A., Carter, K., Lövstrand, L., & Moran, T. (1990). User-tailorable systems: Pressing the issue with buttons. In *Proceedings of the Conference on Human Factors in Computing Systems (CHI'90)* (pp. 175-182). New York: ACM Press.

Mehandjiev, N., & Bottaci, L. (Eds.). (1998). End-user development [Special issue]. *Journal of End User Computing, 10*(2).

Mørch, A. (1996). Evolving a generic application into a domain-oriented design environment. *Scandinavian Journal of Information Systems, 8*(2), 63-90.

Mørch, A.I. (2003). Aspect-oriented software components. In N. Patel (Ed.), *Adaptive evolutionary information systems* (pp. 105-123). Hershey, PA: Idea Group Publishing.

Mørch, A.I., Engen, B.K., & Åsand, H.-R.H. (2004a). The workplace as a learning laboratory: The winding road to e-learning in a Norwegian service company. In *Proceedings of PDC 2004* (pp. 142-151).

Mørch, A.I., Stevens, G., Won, M., Klann, M., Dittrich, Y., & Wulf, V. (2004b). Component-based technologies for end-user development. *Communications of the ACM, 47*(9), 59-62.

Nardi, B. (1996). Studying context: A comparison of activity theory, situated action models, and distributed cognition. In B. Nardi (Ed.), *Context and consciousness: Activity theory and human-computer interaction* (pp. 69-102). Cambridge, MA: MIT Press.

Netteland, G., Wasson, B., & Mørch, A.I. (2007). E-learning in a large organization: A study of the critical role of information sharing [Special issue]. *Journal of Workplace Learning, 19*(6), 392-411.

Nygaard, K. (1984). User-oriented languages. In *Proceedings of Medical Informatics Europe 84* (pp. 38-44). Berlin: Springer-Verlag.

Schuler, D., & Namioka, A. (1993). *Participatory design: Principles and practices.* Hillsdale, NJ: Erlbaum.

Star, S.L., & Griesemer, J.R. (1989). Institutional ecology, "translations" and boundary objects: Amateurs and professionals in Berkley's Museum of Vertebrate Zoology 1907- 39. *Social Studies of Science, 19*(3), 387-420.

Stevens, G., & Wulf, V. (2002). A new dimension in access control: Studying maintenance engineering across organizational boundaries. In *Proceedings of CSCW'92* (pp. 196-205). New York: ACM Press.

Trigg, R.H., Moran, T.P., & Halasz, F.G. (1987). Adaptability and tailorability in NoteCards. In H.-J. Bullinger & B. Shackel (Eds.), *Proceedings of INTERACT'87* (pp. 723-728). Amsterdam: North-Holland.

Volkoff, O., Strong, D.M., & Elmes, M.B. (2002, August 9-11). Between a rock and a hard place: Boundary spanners in an ERP implementation. *Proceedings of the Americas Conference on Information Systems*, Dallas, Texas (pp. 958-962).

Vygotsky, L.S. (1978). *Mind in society: The development of higher psychological processes.* Cambridge, MA: Harvard University Press.

Wenger, E. (1998). *Communities of practice: Learning, meaning and identity.* New York: Cambridge University Press.

Wertsch, J. (1998). *Mind as action.* New York: Oxford University Press.

Won, M., Stiemerling, O., & Wulf, V. (2006). Component-based approaches to tailorable systems. In H. Lieberman, F. Paterno, & V. Wulf (Eds.), *End-user development.* Berlin: Springer-Verlag.

Chapter VIII
End User Perceptions of the Benefits and Risks of End User Web Development

Tanya McGill
Murdoch University, Australia

Chris Klisc
Murdoch University, Australia

ABSTRACT

The development of applications by end users has become an integral part of organizational information provision. It has been established that there are both benefits and risks associated with end-user development, particularly in the areas of spreadsheets and databases. Web development tools are enabling a new kind of end user development. The fact that Web page creation may impact not only locally but also globally significantly raises the importance of this type of end user application development. This chapter reports on the extent of Web page development amongst end users and investigates their perceptions of the benefits and risks of end-user Web development relative to those associated with spreadsheet development and explores approaches to reducing the risks.

INTRODUCTION

End-user computing now dominates organizational use of information technology worldwide (Sutcliffe & Mehandjiev, 2004). Its growth has been driven by increasingly inexpensive hardware, increasingly powerful and easy to use software,

and user demand for control of information resources (McLean, Kappelman, & Thompson, 1993; Shayo, Guthrie, & Igbaria, 1999). Organizations also rely heavily on applications developed by end users (Ferneley, 2007). These applications support a wide range of information provision and decision-making activities and contribute to business processing in a wide range of tasks (Downey, 2004). Increasingly, the ability to develop small applications forms part of the job requirements for many positions (Jawahar & Elango, 2001). The study reported on in this chapter explores the expansion end-user developers are experiencing as they add the role of Web page developer to their repertoire of end-user development skills, and investigates end-user perceptions of the benefits and risks of end-user Web development relative to those of end-user spreadsheet development.

Although a wide range of tools is available for use by end-user developers, the most commonly used software tools have been spreadsheets (United States Bureau of the Census, 2003). The majority (88%) of the 34 organizations participating in Taylor, Moynihan, and Wood-Harper's (1998) study used spreadsheets for end-user development whereas only 35% used query languages and 12% used databases. Recently Web development tools have started to be used by end-user developers (Govindarajulu, 2003; Nelson & Todd, 1999; O'Brien, 2002; Ouellette, 1999), and it is anticipated that this use will increase rapidly in years to come (Goupil, 2000). Very little is known, however, about how end users acquire the skills necessary for successful development or about how and why they develop Web applications.

A substantial body of research has investigated the benefits and risks of development by end users and explored the factors that influence them (e.g., Alavi & Weiss, 1985-1986; e.g. Amoroso & Cheney, 1992; Benson, 1983; Brancheau & Brown, 1993; Davis, 1988; O'Donnell & March, 1987; Rivard & Huff, 1984, 1985). The benefits that have been claimed include improved decision making, improved productivity, and increased satisfaction of end users (Amoroso & Cheney, 1992). The risks that have been identified include mismatches between tools and applications (Alavi & Weiss, 1985-1986; Davis, 1988; O'Donnell & March, 1987), lack of testing (Alavi & Weiss, 1985-1986; Davis, 1988; O'Donnell & March,

1987; Panko, 2007), inability to identify correct and complete information requirements (Davis, 1988) and failure to back up data (Benson, 1983). The proposed benefits of user development of applications can be attributed to users having a better understanding of the problem to be solved by the application, and the proposed risks to users having less understanding of the process of system development than do information technology professionals.

Whilst problems with traditional end-user developed applications can have a large impact on organizational decision making, it has largely been believed that the possible negative impacts are limited to local effects, for example, workgroup or department (Nelson & Todd, 1999). Web development tools, however, are now enabling end users to develop applications that are accessible to vast numbers of people from all over the world (Ferneley, 2007; Nelson & Todd, 1999). This brings with it greater potential benefits and risks. These benefits and risks may affect business processes, customers, suppliers, and other organizations more than ever before. The study reported on in this chapter considers end-user perceptions of both the benefits and risks of end-user Web development and compares them to their perceptions of the benefits and risks of end-user spreadsheet development. This comparison will provide insight into areas where end-user developers are gaining new advantages due to their Web development practices, and into areas of risk that may require future attention from those responsible for end-user Web development.

Strategies for reducing the risks associated with end-user development have been presented in the literature and there is some evidence to suggest that employing them is effective. For example, Alavi, Nelson, and Weiss (1987-1988) presented a comprehensive framework of controls for addressing risks at different stages of the application life cycle, and several studies have demonstrated the value of introducing controls during the design and development of spreadsheets (Alavi, Phillips, & Freedman, 1990; Janvrin & Morrison, 2000). End-user training has also been shown to positively influence attitudes to technology (Igbaria, Guimaraes, & Davis, 1995; Simmers & Anandarajan, 2001) and to improve the quality of end-user developed applications (Kreie, Cronan, Pendley, & Renwick, 2000; Kruck, Maher, & Barkhi, 2003).

However, despite this evidence, organizations have done little to address the risks of end-user development (Panko & Halverson, 1996; Taylor et al., 1998). Nelson and Todd (1999) investigated what strategies organizations are using to reduce the risks of end-user development on the Web. They followed up on 18 risk reduction activities identified by Alavi, Nelson, and Weiss (1987-1988). Each of these activities was classified as being in one of three categories: standards setting, resource allocation, or management and support of application development. They found that organizations placed most emphasis on setting standards, followed by resource allocation, and that support of development was the least used type of approach. They also noted that there were large gaps between the perceived importance of some approaches to reducing the risks of end-user Web development and the degree to which they were currently being used.

RESEARCH AIMS

Despite the various largely anecdotal reports of the popularity of end-user Web development (e.g., O'Brien, 2002; Ouellette, 1999), there has been little empirical research on end-user Web development. In a recent survey of end-user development, Govindarajulu (2003) found that approximately 40% of his sample of end-user developers had created static Web pages and 25% had created dynamic Web pages; however, information about the levels of experience of these end-user Web developers or the training they had received was not available. Given the potential

importance of end-user Web development, more needs to be known about end-user Web developers and the preparation they receive. The first two aims of this study were therefore to:

1. Explore the extent of end-user Web development amongst current end-user developers.
2. Explore the training end users receive to prepare them to undertake end-user Web development.

As discussed above, Web development tools facilitate the development of applications that are more widely accessible than end-user developed applications have traditionally been (Nelson & Todd, 1999). End-user Web development has the potential to bring greater benefits to end users and their organizations, but also has the potential for increasing risks. The benefits and risks of end-user Web development may affect the various stakeholders more than ever before. As spreadsheet development has been the most common form of end-user development to date, the benefits and risks of Web development relative to spreadsheet development are of interest. The next aim of the study was therefore to:

3. Compare end-user developers' perceptions of the relative benefits and risks of end-user spreadsheet development and end-user Web development.

Despite research highlighting the risks of end-user development, organizations have done little to counter them (Panko & Halverson, 1996; Taylor et al., 1998). Given the potential for greater risks to be associated with end-user Web development, more research is required on approaches to addressing these risks. The only significant research to date on the risks of end-user Web development is the study by Nelson and Todd (1999) that surveyed predominantly information technology staff (28 out of 34) with the remainder being senior management. Given that end users themselves have a large degree of control over the success or otherwise of their applications, there is also a need to consider end users' perceptions of the various approaches to reducing risks. The final aim of this study was therefore to:

4. Investigate the perceptions of end-user developers as to the importance of various approaches to reducing the risks of end-user Web development.

THE PROJECT

This study was conducted via survey. The participants were a group of end users who were known to have developed spreadsheet applications, but whose experience with Web development was unknown. This group was targeted as it provided an opportunity to explore the uptake of end-user Web development amongst experienced end-user developers, and also to compare perceptions of the benefits and risks of the two types of development.

Participants

The sample for this study consists of 60 end-user developers who had previously participated in a study on end-user spreadsheet development. The participants in the previous study were active end-user developers from a wide range of business organizations. They had a wide range of experience and training (details of the original study can be found in McGill, 2004). 35% of the participants in the current study were males, and 65% were females. Ages ranged from 20 to 67 years with an average of 45 years.

Procedure

A summary of the results of the earlier spreadsheet study was mailed to all participants, along with a request to participate in the current study by completing an enclosed questionnaire. Some participants, for whom no postal address details were recorded, were initially contacted via e-mail and asked to participate in the current study before being mailed the questionnaire. Those who failed to return the questionnaire and for whom e-mail addresses were recorded were sent a reminder by e-mail after approximately 3 weeks. 167 questionnaires were mailed out and 60 completed questionnaires were received, giving a response rate of 36%.

The Questionnaire

The questionnaire consisted of several sections. The first section asked questions about the background and previous computing experience of participants. The second section asked specifically about Web page development experience and training, and where relevant, explored reasons for nondevelopment. The third and fourth sections included questions to be answered by all respondents about the potential benefits and risks of both spreadsheet development and Web page development. The final section addressed approaches to reducing the risks of end-user Web development. The draft questionnaire was pilot tested by four end users and slight changes made to clarify the questions.

Section 1: Background Information

The first section asked questions about the participants and their previous training and experience with computers, spreadsheets, and the Internet. Experience was measured in years. Questions relating to spreadsheet and Internet training asked about formal courses and self study separately using measures that were adapted from Igbaria

(1990) and are similar to those used by Simmers and Anandarajan (2001) in their study of Internet user satisfaction in the workplace. The items had a 5-point scale where (1) was labeled 'none' and (5) was labeled 'very intensive.'

Section 2: Web Development Experience

Levels of Web development training were also obtained for formal courses and self study separately, using items similar to those described above. In order to determine which Web development tools end users had used, a list of nine popular tools (see Table 4) was created based on information from a review of authoring tools (Moore, 2002). Respondents were asked whether they had used each of them and also given provision to name any other tools used. Reasons for non-development were explored via three items that were developed for this study. Respondents were asked to rate the importance of each reason for non-development on a 5 point scale where (1) was labelled 'not important' and (5) was labelled 'very important' (see Table 5 for the items).

Sections 3 and 4: Benefits and Risks

A list of the major benefits and a list of the major risks were developed from the literature on benefits and risks of development by end users (Alavi & Weiss, 1985-1986; Amoroso & Cheney, 1992; Benson, 1983; Brancheau & Brown, 1993; Davis, 1988; O'Donnell & March, 1987; Rivard & Huff, 1984, 1985). Each potential benefit and risk was

rated for importance on a 5-point scale measured from (1) 'not important' to (5) 'very important'. 12 questions addressed potential benefits and 12 questions addressed potential risks (see Table 6 and Table 7, respectively, for lists of the potential benefits and risks).

Section 5: Approaches to Reducing the Risks of End-user Web Development

The questionnaire included 14 items to measure the perceived importance of the major activities that can be undertaken to reduce the risks of end-user development on the Web. These items are from the Nelson and Todd (1999) instrument. Each approach was rated for importance on a 5-point scale measured from (1) 'not important' to (5) 'very important.'

RESULTS AND DISCUSSION

Spreadsheet, Internet, and Web Development Experience

Table 1 summarises how long the respondents had been using computers, spreadsheets, and the Internet. On average, they had been using computers for 14 years (ranging from 4 years to 30 years). Some participants had considerable experience, as 30 years of use indicates adoption very early in the personal computing revolution. The average length of spreadsheet use was just under 8 years (with a range of a few months through to 21 years). Respondents had been using the Internet

Table 1. Background characteristics of respondents

	Mean	Minimum	Maximum	Standard Deviation
Age (years)	44.68	20	67	10.32
Computing experience (years)	14.22	4	30	6.66
Spreadsheet experience (years)	7.85	0	21	5.40
Internet experience (years)	6.19	0	12	2.79

for an average of around 6 years (ranging from not having used it at all to 12 years). Considering the WWW came into practical existence around 1994, some of the respondents were obviously at the forefront of online communications, having used the Internet prior to the emergence of the WWW. However, most respondents appear to have used the Internet for between 3 and 9 years, indicating Internet use as being dependent upon the emergence of the WWW. Internet use appears to have coincided largely with spreadsheet use, with respondents having used spreadsheets for only about a year and a half longer on average than they have been using the Internet.

Reasons for spreadsheet and Internet use were also investigated, and the results are reported in Table 2. 90% of the respondents used spreadsheets for work purposes and 73% used them at home. The Internet was used even more heavily for both work and personal tasks (91.7% and 93.3%, respectively). It is worth noting that of the 60 respondents, only one reported not having used the Internet at all. These figures suggest a rapid increase in Internet usage in the workplace. In an Internet demographics survey in 1998, only 50% of Internet users were found to use the Internet at work (Commercenet, 1999).

Web page development was not as common. Just under half (27 or 45.0%) of the total sample of 60 spreadsheet end-user developers surveyed

had engaged in Web page development. Of these 27 end users, 55.5% (15 people) had created Web pages for work use and 66.7% (18 people) had done so for personal interests. It would be useful to further explore the nature of the Web development that the participants had undertaken. Simmer and Anandarajan's (2001) index of Web page experience would provide a starting point for future research on the nature of development undertaken.

Previous Training

Respondents had had little formal training in spreadsheets, Internet use, or Web page development. The average level of formal spreadsheet training was 1.98 (out of 5) and the average level of self study training was 2.69, so self study was the main source of spreadsheet training. This is consistent with previous research on spreadsheet users, which has reported that spreadsheet users generally receive little training (Taylor et al., 1998) and that the major means of training is self study (Chan & Storey, 1996; Hall, 1996).

The average level of formal Internet training was 1.63, and the average level of self study training was 2.61, so self study was again the main source of training. This is consistent with the findings of Simmer and Anandarajan (2001)

Table 2. Reasons for use

	Number	Percentage*
Spreadsheet		
Work purposes	54	90.0
Personal purposes	44	73.4
Internet		
Work purposes	55	91.7
Personal purposes	56	93.3
Web page development		
Any Web page development	27	45.0
Work purposes	15	25.0
Personal purposes	18	30.0
* Of total sample of 60 respondents		

in their study of Internet use in the workplace; however, it is unclear whether the relatively high level of self training is because end-user developers prefer self training or because other forms of training are not available. Over half (55%) had received no formal training and almost half (47%) indicated that they had either not undertaken any self study or had done very little. No respondents rated their formal Internet training as extremely intensive and only two (3.3%) rated their self study as extremely intensive.

Those respondents who had developed Web pages were asked to indicate their prior Web page development training. As can be seen from Table 3, levels of Web development training were relatively low but consistent with levels of spreadsheet training, with an average of 1.96 out of 5 for formal training and 2.58 out of 5 for self study. Self study was again the predominant method of training. 40% of those who had developed Web

pages had received no formal training. Again, the emphasis on self training is consistent with other forms of end-user development such as spreadsheet development (Chan & Storey, 1996; Hall, 1996), but may also indicate the 'fun' aspect of engaging in what is currently seen as 'hot' (Atkinson & Kydd, 1997). The role of self training in end-user Web page development should be investigated in further research.

It appears that a substantial proportion of Internet and Web development learning may be achieved via activities and interactions that are not perceived as training. This reinforces the popular image that 'people enjoy surfing the Web' (Atkinson & Kydd, 1997) and raises the issue of the role of communities of practice, where learning occurs by end-user developers doing and sharing with their peers (Stamps, 2000). The role of communities of practice in end-user Web development should be explored in future research.

Table 3. Levels of previous training

		Number	Mean	Minimum	Maximum	Standard Deviation
Spreadsheet						
	Formal	60	1.98	1	5	1.05
	Self study	59	2.69	1	5	1.21
Internet						
	Formal	60	1.63	1	4	0.80
	Self study	59	2.61	1	5	1.08
Web development						
	Formal	27	1.96	1	4	0.98
	Self study	26	2.58	1	5	1.03

Table 4. Web development tools used

	Number	Percentage
Microsoft Frontpage	15	55.6
Microsoft Word	13	48.1
Notepad	12	46.2
Macromedia Dreamweaver	11	40.7
HotDog Pro	2	7.4
Adobe GoLive	1	3.7
Macromedia Homesite	1	3.7
CoffeeCup HTML Editor	1	3.7
HotMetal Pro	0	0.0

Web Development Tools Used

As can been seen in Table 4, the most common tool used by the 27 respondents who had developed Web pages was Microsoft FrontPage (55.6%). This is consistent with the case study discussed in Ouellette (1999), where Microsoft FrontPage was used by 108 end users who contribute to an intranet. The second most commonly used tool was Microsoft Word (48.1%). The third most frequently used tool was Notepad (46.2%), which suggests some measure of familiarity with HTML code, and may indicate a desire on the part of users to 'understand' and have more control over Web page development, not just create the pages. The final tool of significance is Macromedia Dreamweaver, which had been used by 40.7% of users. As Dreamweaver is a rather expensive program for home use, perhaps it would be fair to say that this tool was primarily used in the workplace. No other tools were used by more than two respondents.

Nondevelopment

The reasons why almost one half of the sample of spreadsheet developers had not yet developed Web pages were also explored. 33 respondents (55.0%) reported not having created a Web page and their reasons are listed in Table 5. The most important reason for not creating Web pages was lack of knowledge despite wishing to do so (with an average importance of 2.50 out of 5), while lack of professional need and lack of personal need were rated as less important on average (1.45 and 1.58 respectively out of 5). It is worth noting that not one person strongly disagreed with 'no personal need for creating a Web page', indicating a recognition of the role that Web page development plays in many people's personal lives and possibly acknowledging the potential for it to enter their own. This subset of respondents was also asked if they anticipated developing Web pages in the future. 11 people (33%) indicated that they did not anticipate developing Web pages in the future and 5 (15%) indicated that they would create a Web page in the future, while 19 (58%) acknowledged the possibility of doing so. As it is very difficult to predict future needs, the high percentage in the 'possibly' category reflects acceptance of the rate of change that is associated with the Internet (Burn & Loch, 2001).

Benefits of End User Web Page Development and Spreadsheet Development

Table 6 presents the average perceived importance of each potential benefit for both Web development and spreadsheet development. The ratings of benefits are ranked by perceived importance for Web page development. The average importance of each potential benefit was compared between Web development and spreadsheet development using paired t-tests and the results are also reported in Table 6.

The most important perceived benefits of Web development relate to accessing and disseminating information. Improved accessibility of information was ranked most highly and was followed closely by improved communication of informa-

Table 5. Reasons for not developing Web pages

	Mean	Minimum	Maximum	Standard Deviation
No professional need (/5)	1.45	1	5	1.00
No personal need (/5)	1.58	1	4	0.89
Would like to, but do not know how (/5)	2.50	1	5	1.42

Table 6. Perceived importance of benefits

Benefits	Web Development		Spreadsheet Development		Sign.
	Mean Impt.	SD	Mean Impt.	SD	
Improved accessibility of information	4.25	1.07	4.27	0.96	0.922
Improved communication of information	4.12	1.08	4.05	1.02	0.759
Faster response to information requests	3.82	1.15	4.00	1.06	0.216
Direct control over information and applications	3.66	1.28	3.77	1.27	0.153
Better use of limited resources	3.54	1.24	3.62	1.08	0.262
Improved user computer literacy	3.30	1.25	3.07	1.31	0.151
Encourages experimentation and innovation	3.27	1.10	3.18	1.32	0.910
Reduction in development backlog	3.20	1.24	3.10	1.41	0.825
Increased user satisfaction	3.18	1.10	3.31	1.28	0.345
Improved productivity	3.12	1.31	3.97	0.94	<0.001***
Improved decision making effectiveness	3.02	1.26	3.90	1.12	<0.001***
Improved relationships with IT staff	2.46	1.19	2.55	1.94	0.416

*** < 0.01

tion. Faster response to information requests and direct control over information and applications were ranked third and fourth, respectively. End users recognise that Web page development gives them a unique opportunity to both provide and access information. Whilst increasing access to the Internet and the availability of user-friendly browsers has made accessing sites developed by information technology professionals a valuable information gathering approach, the development of user-friendly Web development tools has enabled end users to participate in information dissemination to a degree never before possible. These first four benefits were also rated highly as benefits of spreadsheet development, and no significant differences were found between their importance for Web development and their importance for spreadsheet development. Presumably Web development allows access to, and dissemination of, information over a wider domain, but spreadsheet development allows more focused specific addressing of information needs.

The middle ranked benefits appear to reflect personal benefits from end-user development. Better use of limited resources was ranked fifth followed by improved user computer literacy and encouragement of experimentation and innovation. End-user developers appear to place

moderate value on what they learn and gain from development beyond their specific task-oriented information needs. These results for end-user Web development are consistent with the literature on other kinds of end-user computing (Agarwal, 2000; Amoroso & Cheney, 1992; Davis, 1988; Pentland, 1989) and no significant differences were found between perceptions of their importance as benefits of Web development and spreadsheet development.

Reduction in development backlog was ranked fairly lowly at eighth in importance amongst the Web development potential benefits. This implies that end users are not developing applications that would otherwise be developed by information technology professionals. Their Web pages are in addition to those deemed necessary by their organizations and hence their development effort may not impact significantly on development backlogs. This is consistent with the perception of reduction of development backlog as a benefit of spreadsheet development as no significant difference was found between the ratings.

The ninth most important perceived benefit of end-user development was user satisfaction and its relatively low ranking suggests that whilst Web development tools have become more user-friendly, Web development is not yet a straightforward and satisfying experience. End users perceived the experience as one of learning and self-improvement rather than one that satisfies and/or results in applications that improve user satisfaction. The user satisfaction resulting from spreadsheet development was not significantly different from that resulting from Web development, suggesting that spreadsheet development is also not yet a straightforward and satisfying experience.

The tenth and eleventh ranked benefits of Web page development were improved productivity and improved decision making effectiveness. Thus, Web page development was not perceived as a particularly important source of productivity or decision making effectiveness. Web page development leads to information dissemination for the developer, but the participants in this study did not see this as improving their own productivity or decision making effectiveness, nor that accessing information provided from Web pages developed by other end users would play an important role in improving their own productivity. This raises questions about the purposes of user developed Web pages. Future research should explore more closely the reasons for which Web pages are developed by end users. Spreadsheet development was considered to be a significantly more important source of productivity benefits (t(55) = 4.97, p < 0.001) and of benefits resulting from improved decision making (t(55) = 6.46, p < 0.001).

The lowest ranked potential benefit for both Web development and spreadsheet development was improved relationships with information technology staff. The low ranking reinforces the idea that end-user Web development is an activity that is removed from organizational system development. End users do not perceive it as supporting organizational development. The low ranking may possibly reflect the introduction of additional tensions in relationships with information technology staff, brought about by the risks of end-user development.

No significant differences were found in the importance ratings of any benefits between those who had and those who had not previously developed Web pages.

Risks of End User Web Page Development and Spreadsheet Development

Table 7 presents the average perceived importance of each potential risk for both Web development and spreadsheet development. The ratings of risks are ranked by perceived importance for Web page development. The average importance of each potential risk was compared between Web development and spreadsheet development using paired t-tests.

All potential risks of Web development were rated fairly highly with averages above the midpoint of the scale, which implies a good awareness of the problems that can plague end-user development. Unreliable systems were perceived as being the most important risk, with lack of data security ranked closely behind. The potential for development of unreliable and insecure systems has long been recognised as one of the major problems with end-user development (Benson, 1983; Brancheau & Brown, 1993). Despite this recognition, organizations have done little to protect against it (Panko & Halverson, 1996). The high ranking of this risk with respect to end-user Web development reflects the increased level of importance of the problem due to the global accessibility of Web-based systems. The potential for damage to the reputation of an organization has increased as applications have become accessible by vast numbers of people from all over the world (Nelson & Todd, 1999). Unreliable systems were perceived to be a significantly less important risk for spreadsheet development (t(53) = -3.60, p = 0.001) and lack of data security was also rated as a less important risk for spreadsheet development (t(53) = -1.95, p = 0.057). This suggests that end-user developers are very aware of the increases in risk associated with Web development.

Table 7. Comparison of risks

Risks	Web Development		Spreadsheet Development		Sign.
	Mean Impt.	SD	Mean Impt.	SD	
Unreliable systems	4.24	1.03	3.61	1.21	<0.001***
Lack of data security	4.19	1.10	3.84	1.36	0.057^m
Incompatible end-user tools preventing sharing of applications and information	4.19	0.93	3.93	1.14	0.332
Inability to identify correct and complete information requirements	4.00	1.08	4.02	0.94	0.371
Lack of testing	3.96	1.04	3.77	1.13	0.455
Lack of documentation for applications	3.93	1.11	3.86	1.16	0.672
Mismatch between development tools and applications	3.87	1.10	3.68	1.18	0.667
Use of private systems when organizational systems would be more appropriate	3.83	1.10	3.60	1.12	0.411
Failure to backup data	3.81	1.16	4.16	1.15	<0.001***
Inefficient use of personnel time	3.79	1.04	3.44	1.16	0.225
Solving the wrong problem	3.51	1.28	3.68	1.09	0.044*
Redundant development effort	3.41	1.17	3.70	1.08	0.014*

*** < 0.01
* < 0.05
^{m} < 0.1

Incompatible end-user tools preventing sharing was ranked equal second in terms of importance as a risk of Web development. The last decade has been marked by great improvements in the compatibility of end-user software; hence this result was unanticipated and requires further research.

The midranked group of risks all focus on the ability of the end-user developer to undertake specific necessary development tasks such as identifying requirements, testing, documenting, and choosing appropriate development tools. The respondents appeared to recognise the importance of each of the activities and the risks that can result from lack of skills in these areas. No significant differences were found between the perceived importance of these risks between Web development and spreadsheet development.

Use of private systems when organizational systems would be more appropriate was ranked as the eighth most important risk of Web devel-

opment, and failure to backup data as the ninth. Both of these risks normally relate to use of user developed Web applications rather than the actual development process and their lower ranking suggests that the respondents recognise that the major risks result from development practices rather than from use of applications. Failure to back up data was rated as significantly less important a risk for Web development than for spreadsheet development (t(52) = 4.43, p < 0.001). In fact, failure to backup data was perceived as the most important of all the potential risks of spreadsheet development. This may be because the types of Web applications developed by end users are likely to involve static data, whereas the data in end-user developed spreadsheet applications is likely to be updated more often, and hence is more vulnerable and reliant on regular backup in case of problems. Further research on the types of Web applications developed by end users is required to understand the perceptions of these risks.

The lowest ranked risks of Web development were inefficient use of personnel time, followed by solving the wrong problem and lastly redundant development effort. However, none of these risks was discounted, with averages that indicate that the majority of respondents recognised them as risks of relative importance. Not one respondent rated inefficient use of personnel time as 'not important'; five (9.4%) rated solving the wrong problem as 'not important' and one (1.9%) rated redundant development effort as 'not important'. The participants considered solving the wrong problem and redundant development effort to be greater risks when undertaking spreadsheet development (t(52) = 2.06, p = 0.044; t(52) = 2.55, p = 0.014). This may reflect an increased sophistication of end-user developed spreadsheet applications compared to end-user developed Web applications.

It was interesting to note that the average importance of each risk was lower for the group who had previously developed Web pages than for the group who had not, although the differences were only significant for four risks: inability to identify correct and complete requirements (t(52) = 2.36, p = 0.022), use of private systems when organizational systems would be more appropriate (t(52) = 2.19, p = 0.033), solving the wrong problem (t(51) = 2.54, p = 0.014), and redundant development effort (t(52) = 2.70, p = 0.009). A reason for this difference could be that the development process has given them insight that allows them to discount the risks; however, this seems unlikely given the prevalence of problems with end-user developed applications. It would seem more likely that the satisfaction they derive from their own Web development allows an overshadowing of the perceptions of risks. This should be explored further in future studies.

Future research should also differentiate between different types of Web applications that might have different risks and benefits. For example, the risks associated with end-user developed Web pages that merely display informa-tion could be considered substantially less than those associated with applications that process information.

Approaches to Reducing the Risks of End User Web Development

The approaches to reducing the risks of end-user Web page development are ranked by perceived importance in Table 8. This table also includes the average importance of each of the approaches reported for the predominantly information technology staff in the Nelson and Todd (1999) study. The importance of each approach as perceived by the end-user developers in the current study is compared with the average obtained in Nelson and Todd's study using one sample t-tests and the results are also presented in Table 8. All of the approaches were rated fairly high by the end-user developers with averages above the midpoint of the scale. The highest ranked approach was training. As discussed above, previous studies have found that end-user developers receive very little train-ing and what they do get tends to be self-training rather than formal training (Chan & Storey, 1996; Hall, 1996). The results in this study regarding training for Web development are consistent with other forms of end-user development such as spreadsheet development. The acknowledgment of the importance of training is quite interest-ing, as despite having received little training themselves, the respondents considered training to be the most important approach to reducing the risks of end-user Web development. Nelson (1991) suggested that training is perhaps the most effective tool for minimising the risks associated with end-user development and the results of this study suggest that end users agree.

Policies for data management were considered to be the second most important approach. This was unexpected because end-user developers have traditionally been dissatisfied with approaches to the management of end-user computing that involved control rather than support (Bergeron & Berube, 1988; Bowman, 1988). However, this ranking is promising as it suggests that end-user Web developers recognise that Internet applications are particularly vulnerable to data security risks and that therefore these must be addressed.

The middle grouping consisted of a number of approaches of similar importance that include assignment of roles and responsibilities, standards for purchases of hardware and software, and scope of Web-related activities (i.e., clear distinctions between applications that are developed by end users and by information technology professionals) amongst others. The very consistent levels of importance given to these suggest that end users recognise that a variety of approaches is necessary, all of which are complementary.

Audit and review standards for end-user development and a requirement for documentation of Web applications were ranked towards the bot-

tom of the possible approaches. This is consistent with previous research that suggests that users are less satisfied when subject to greater application development control (Bergeron & Berube, 1988; Bowman, 1988). Nevertheless, a need for setting and enforcing organizational development standards for end users has been widely recognised (Cragg & King, 1993; Guimaraes, Gupta, & Rainer, 1999). Setting priorities was also not given a high importance ranking. This suggests that, as might be expected, end-user developers consider the Web development they do as an individual activity designed to support their own work rather than part of an organizational information technology strategy.

As can be seen in Table 8, the end-user developers who responded to this survey rated every approach to reducing the risks of end-user Web development more highly than did the information technology professionals and senior management who participated in Nelson and Todd's

Table 8. Approaches to reducing the risks of end-user Web development

Rank	Approaches to Reducing the Risks of End-user Web Page Development	This Study Mean	SD	N & T Study Mean	Sign.
1	Training	4.39	0.81	3.48	<0.001***
2	Policies on data management	4.39	0.71	4.25	0.157
3	Coordination across organizational boundaries	4.31	0.75	4.00	0.003***
4	Assignment of roles and responsibilities	4.28	0.81	3.61	<0.001***
5	Standards for purchases of hardware and software	4.19	0.83	3.76	<0.001***
6	Data access	4.17	0.86	3.85	0.009***
7	Planning for equipment, capacity, and manpower	4.17	0.77	3.97	0.066[m]
8	Scope of Web-related activities	4.15	1.02	3.03	<0.001***
9	Systems integration	4.11	0.86	3.36	<0.001***
10	Consulting	4.06	0.90	3.58	<0.001***
11	Audit and review	3.98	1.04	3.47	0.001***
12	Standards for end-user development	3.98	0.84	3.73	0.031*
13	Setting priorities	3.89	0.90	3.88	0.943
14	Documentation	3.83	1.00	3.18	<0.001***

*** < 0.001
* < 0.05
[m] < 0.1

(1999) study. These differences were significant for all except two of the approaches (policies on data management and setting priorities). The approaches on which opinion differed the most were training (t(53) = 8.24, p < 0.001) and scope of Web-related activities (t(53) = 8.08, p < 0.001). Information technology staff involved in managing end-user development should recognise the importance to end users of appropriate training to support their development activities and of the need for clear distinctions to be made to enable the confidence of end users in determining which projects are appropriate for them.

There have been previous calls for increased provision of training to Internet users (Aggarwal, 2003). The results of this study reinforce the importance of this. However, given the relative prevalence of self training in end-user Web development training, the role of self training should be further explored. It has been suggested that when end users are self taught, the emphasis is predominantly on how to use software rather than broader analysis and design considerations (Benham, Delaney, & Luzi, 1993). The many books that cover introductory Web development typically give a detailed, step-by-step coverage of examples that illustrate product features. Examples are presented as solutions to requirements without the design stages being made explicit. Thus, end users may have a narrow knowledge focused on software features but lacking in techniques for developing Web applications that are user-friendly, reliable, and maintainable. Taylor et al. (1998) found that few, if any, quality principles are applied in end-user development. Therefore, organizations that rely on self training must ensure that end users have materials available that will help provide all of the skills necessary for developing good quality Web applications. This is consistent with Shaw, DeLone, and Niederman's (2002) finding that documentation to support training was perceived as one of the most important information technology support factors in terms of user satisfaction. Given the current heavy reli-

ance on end-user developed applications and the increased risks associated with end-user development in the Internet domain, it is essential that organizations support end users as they strive to become proficient Web developers.

Guidelines on the kinds of applications that are suitable for end-user Web development should also be provided (Goupil, 2000). Several authors have proposed guidelines recommending what kinds of applications are appropriate for end-user development (Salchenberger, 1993), and what kinds are not (Bowman, 1990). These types of guidelines need to be researched further so that more detailed assistance can be provided to prospective end-user developers. In particular, the ability to tailor recommendations on what types of applications are appropriate to individual end users' backgrounds would be very valuable. Given the current heavy reliance on end-user developed applications and the increased risks associated with end-user development in the Internet domain, it is essential that organizations support end users as they strive to become proficient Web developers.

As discussed in the Introduction, each of the approaches to risk reduction was classified as relating to standards setting, resource allocation, or management and support of application development (Nelson & Todd, 1999). Nelson and Todd (1999) found that organizations in their study placed most emphasis on setting standards, followed by resource allocation, and that support of development was the least used type of approach. They noted that most firms in their study appeared to be relying on a monopolistic control strategy, as described by Gerrity and Rockart (1986) and Alavi et al. (1987-1988) and then concluded that while such a strategy may be the best approach given the relative infancy of Web technology, it could prove to be an unstable strategy in the future. The results of the study reported in this chapter suggest that end-user developers would support a change to the strategies used to manage end-user Web development with greater emphasis being placed on support of development via such mechanisms as training and clear definition of roles and responsibilities.

Those who had and those who had not previously developed Web pages were compared with respect to their perceptions of the importance of the approaches to reducing the risks of Web development. As with perceptions of risks, those who had previously developed Web pages tended to rate the importance of the approaches lower than did the end users who had not, although the differences were only significant for two approaches: standards for purchases of hardware and software activities ($t(52) = 2.80$, $p = 0.007$), and scope of Web-related activities ($t(52) = 2.22$, $p = 0.031$).

Main End User Web Development Issues

The study reported on in this chapter explored the nature of the emerging area of end-user Web development. A range of areas were investigated and Table 9 below summarises some of the main issues that emerged. The study highlighted that Web development is becoming popular amongst end users both as part of work responsibilities and in pursuing personal interests. This popularity is likely to increase. Yet, consistent with other kinds of end-user development, end users receive little formal training to prepare them for it. The end users surveyed recognised the importance of training and considered it to be the most important strategy for reducing the risks associated with end-user development of Web applications. This finding was not however mirrored in the Nelson and Todd (1999) study. The information technology staff in that study considered training to be one of the less important strategies. Given the potential impacts of end-user developed Web applications, organizations increase the risks by not adequately preparing end users.

The end users surveyed showed a good awareness of the risks of end-user Web development. All potential risks of Web development were rated fairly highly with averages above the midpoint of the scale, which implies a good awareness of the problems that can plague end-user development. It is reassuring that end users do not discount the

Table 9. Summary of main issues

Issue	The study found ...
Extent of Web development	Over half of the spreadsheet developers surveyed also develop Web pages.
End users receive little formal training	40% of end users who had developed Web pages had received no formal training.
End users consider training to be the most important strategy for reducing the risks of end-user Web development	The average importance rating for training was 4.39 (out of 5).
End users have a good awareness of the risks of end-user Web development	All potential risks of Web development had averages above the midpoint of the scale (i.e., were considered important).
End users recognise the need for complementary approaches to risk reduction	All strategies for risk reduction had averages above the midpoint of the scale (i.e., were considered important).
End users appear to be becoming more sophisticated in matching tools to applications.	Web development was rated very highly for improving accessibility of information, but significantly less important than spreadsheets for improving decision making effectiveness.

risks. This is also reflected in their recognition of the need for complementary approaches to risk reduction.

There has been concern expressed in the literature about the ability of end users to recognise what kinds of development tools are appropriate for different sorts of applications (Alavi & Weiss, 1985-1986; Davis, 1988; O'Donnell & March, 1987). The comparative rankings of the perceived benefits of Web development and spreadsheet development suggest that end users are becoming more sophisticated in matching tools to applications. For example, Web development was rated very highly for improving accessibility of information, but significantly less important than spreadsheets for improving decision making effectiveness.

CONCLUSION

Despite early concerns about its risks (e.g., Alavi & Weiss, 1985-1986; Davis, 1988), end-user development has become an integral part of organizational information provision (Downey, 2004; McLean, Kappelman, & Thompson, 1993; Shayo et al., 1999). End-user developers may now take advantage of user-friendly Web development tools to create Web applications, and the prevalence of these applications will only increase (Ouellette, 1999). The study reported on in this chapter investigated the extent of Web page development amongst end users and compared end-user perceptions of the benefits and risks of end-user Web development with their perceptions of those associated with spreadsheet development. Almost half of the sample of spreadsheet users studied had created Web pages, yet they had received little prior training in Web development. Microsoft Frontpage was the most common tool used for Web development; however, almost half had previously used Notepad indicating some familiarity with HTML code. This suggests a desire to 'understand' and have more control

over Web page development. The most important reason for not creating Web pages was lack of knowledge, and the majority of those who had not yet created Web pages acknowledged the possibility of doing so in the near future.

As can be seen from the discussion of the risks and benefits of end-user development, although end-user Web page development has many characteristics in common with traditional end-user development, there are many areas in which Web page development differs and it is important that research into these areas continue. It seems that end-user Web development is here to stay, and will have far-reaching consequences. Management of its risks will therefore be of increasing importance to organizations. The results of this study have practical implications for the management of end-user Web development in organizations. End-user developers are aware of both the benefits and risks of end-user Web development, and it will be essential to ensure their involvement in the development of approaches to control risks.

Previous research suggests that end-user developers respond better to approaches that emphasise support for development of high quality and appropriate applications rather than control of development (Bergeron & Berube, 1988; Bowman, 1988). The results of this study support this, with training being seen as the most important approach to the reduction of the risks of end-user Web development. Self training was found to be the most prevalent type of training, but it is unclear from this study whether this is because end-user developers prefer self training or because other forms of training are not available. Simmers and Anandarajan (2001, p. 55) recommended that 'formal training should be planned and implemented so that the positive attributes of self training (flexibility, moving at one's own pace, freedom and autonomy) can be blended with organizational requirements, creating a better training experience for both the individual and the organization.' This advice appears sound and meshes with the need to explore the role of communities of practice in end-user Web development.

Finally, the current study raises several potential areas for further study. As end-user Web development is likely to increase in the future, better guidelines are needed to help identify applications that are particularly suited for end users with a particular background. The different types of Web applications developed by end users carry different risks and so future studies should differentiate between types of applications in order to further clarify the associated risks. The participants of the present study identified training as one of the most significant factors in reducing the risk associated with end-user developed Web pages, yet users appear to be gaining their knowledge from self training rather than formal training. This role of self training should be further investigated. Additional studies are also needed to further examine the reasons for Web page development, as it appears that the satisfaction derived from end-user Web development may overshadow the risks associated with these applications that are accessible to vast numbers of people from all over the world.

REFERENCES

Agarwal, R. (2000). Individual acceptance of information technologies. In R. W. Zmud (Ed.), *Framing the domains of IT management: Projecting the future ... through the past* (pp. 85-104). Cincinnati, OH: Pinnaflex Educational Resources, Inc.

Aggarwal, A. K. (2003). Internetalization of end-users. *Journal of End User Computing, 15*(1), 54-56.

Alavi, M., Nelson, R. R., & Weiss, I. R. (1987-1988). Strategies for end user computing: An integrative framework. *Journal of Management Information Systems, 4*(3), 28-49.

Alavi, M., Phillips, J. S., & Freedman, S. M. (1990). An empirical investigation of two alternative approaches to control of end-user application development process. *Data Base, 20*(4), 11-19.

Alavi, M., & Weiss, I. R. (1985-1986). Managing the risks associated with end-user computing. *Journal of Management Information Systems, 2*(3), 5-20.

Amoroso, D. L., & Cheney, P. H. (1992). Quality end user-developed applications: Some essential ingredients. *Data Base, 23*(1), 1-11.

Atkinson, M., & Kydd, C. (1997). Individual characteristics associated with World Wide Web use: An empirical study of playfulness and motivation. *The DATA BASE for Advances in Information Systems, 28*(2), 53-62.

Benham, H., Delaney, M., & Luzi, A. (1993). Structured techniques for successful end user spreadsheets. *Journal of End User Computing, 5*(2), 18-25.

Benson, D. H. (1983). A field study of end user computing: Findings and issues. *MIS Quarterly, 7*(4), 35-45.

Bergeron, F., & Berube, C. (1988). The management of the end-user environment: An empirical investigation. *Information & Management, 14,* 107-113.

Bowman, B. (1988). *An investigation of application development process controls.* Unpublished doctoral dissertation, University of Houston.

Bowman, B. (1990). Controlling application development by end-users in a PC environment: A survey of techniques. *Information Executive, 32*(2), 70-74.

Brancheau, J. C., & Brown, C. V. (1993). The management of end-user computing: Status and directions. *ACM Computing Surveys, 25*(4), 450-482.

Burn, J. M., & Loch, K. D. (2001). The societal impact of the World Wide Web: Key challenges for the 21st century. *Information Resources Management Journal, 14*(4), 4-14.

Chan, Y. E., & Storey, V. C. (1996). The use of spreadsheets in organizations: Determinants and consequences. *Information & Management, 31*, 119-134.

Commercenet, N. M. R. (1999). Nielsen Media Research and Netrating to measure at-work Internet use. Retrieved August 6, 2007, from *http://www. nielsenmedia.com/newsreleases/releases/1999/ netratings3.html*

Cragg, P. G., & King, M. (1993). Spreadsheet modelling abuse: An opportunity for OR? *Journal of the Operational Research Society, 44*(8), 743-752.

Davis, G. B. (1988). The hidden costs of end-user computing. *Accounting Horizons, 2*(4), 103-106.

Downey, J. P. (2004). Towards a comprehensive framework: EUC research issues and trends (1990-2000). *Journal of Organizational and End User Computing, 16*(4), 1-16.

Ferneley, E. H. (2007). Covert end user development: A study of success. *Journal of Organizational and End User Computing, 19*(1), 62-71.

Gerrity, T. P., & Rockart, J. F. (1986). End-user computing: Are you a leader or a laggard? *Sloan Management Review, 27*(4), 25-34.

Goupil, D. (2000, June). End-user application development: Relief for IT. *Computing Channels*, pp. 2-4.

Govindarajulu, C. (2003). End users: Who are they? *Communications of the ACM, 46*(9), 152-159.

Guimaraes, T., Gupta, Y., & Rainer, K. (1999). Empirically testing the relationship between end-user computing problems and information center success factors. *Decision Sciences, 30*(2), 393-413.

Hall, M. J. J. (1996). A risk and control oriented study of the practices of spreadsheet application developers. *Proceedings of the 29th Hawaii International Conference on System Sciences*, (pp. 364-373). Maui, Hawaii.

Igbaria, M. (1990). End-user computing effectiveness: A structural equation model. *OMEGA, 18*(6), 637-652.

Igbaria, M., Guimaraes, T., & Davis, G. B. (1995). Testing the determinants of microcomputer usage via a structural equation model. *Journal of Management Information Systems, 11*(4), 87-114.

Janvrin, D., & Morrison, J. (2000). Using a structured design approach to reduce risks in end user spreadsheet development. *Information & Management, 37*(1), 1-12.

Jawahar, I. M., & Elango, B. (2001). The effect of attitudes, goal setting and self-efficacy on end user performance. *Journal of End User Computing, 13*(3), 40-45.

Kreie, J., Cronan, T. P., Pendley, J., & Renwick, J. S. (2000). Applications development by end-users: Can quality be improved? *Decision Support Systems, 29*(2), 143-152.

Kruck, S. E., Maher, J. J., & Barkhi, R. (2003). Framework for cognitive skill acquisition and spreadsheet training. *Journal of End User Computing, 15*(1), 20-37.

McGill, T. (2004). The effect of end user development on end user success. *Journal of Organizational and End User Computing, 16*(1), 41-58.

McLean, E. R., Kappelman, L. A., & Thompson, J. P. (1993). Converging end-user and corporate computing. *Communications of the ACM, 36*(12), 79-92.

Moore, P. (2002). Software test bench mega guide. *Australian PC User*, pp. 54-55.

Nelson, R. R. (1991). Educational needs as perceived by IS and end-user personnel: A survey of knowledge and skill requirements. *MIS Quarterly, 15*(4), 503-525.

Nelson, R. R., & Todd, P. (1999). Strategies for managing EUC on the Web. *Journal of End User Computing, 11*(1), 24-31.

O'Brien, J. A. (2002). *Management information systems: Managing information technology in the e-business enterprise* (5th ed.). New York: McGraw-Hill.

O'Donnell, D., & March, S. (1987). End user computing environments: Finding a balance between productivity and control. *Information & Management, 13*(1), 77-84.

Ouellette, T. (1999, July 26). Giving users the keys to their Web content. *Computerworld*, pp. 66-67.

Panko, R. R. (2007). Two experiments in reducing overconfidence in spreadsheet development. *Journal of Organizational and End User Computing, 19*(1), 1-23.

Panko, R. R., & Halverson, R. P. (1996). Spreadsheets on trial: A survey of research on spreadsheet risks. *Proceedings of the 29th Hawaii International Conference on System Sciences, 2*, 326-335.

Pentland, B. T. (1989). Use and productivity in personal computing: An empirical test. *Proceedings of the 10th International Conference on Information Systems* (pp. 211-222).

Rivard, S., & Huff, S. L. (1984). User developed applications: Evaluation of success from the DP department perspective. *MIS Quarterly, 8*(1), 39-49.

Rivard, S., & Huff, S. L. (1985). An empirical study of users as application developers. *Information & Management, 8*, 89-102.

Salchenberger, L. (1993). Structured development techniques for user-developed systems. *Information & Management, 24*, 41-50.

Shaw, N. C., DeLone, W. H., & Niederman, F. (2002). Sources of dissatisfaction in end-user support: An empirical study. *The DATA BASE for Advances in Information Systems, 33*(2), 41-55.

Shayo, C., Guthrie, R., & Igbaria, M. (1999). Exploring the measurement of end user computing success. *Journal of End User Computing, 11*(1), 5-14.

Simmers, C. A., & Anandarajan, M. (2001). User satisfaction in the Internet-anchored workplace: An exploratory study. *Journal of Information Technology Theory and Application, 3*(5), 39-61.

Stamps, D. (2000). Communities of practice: Learning is social. Training is irrelevant? In E. L. Lesser, M. A. Fontaine, & J. A. Slusher (Eds.), *Knowledge and communities* (pp. 53-64). Boston: Butterworth-Heinemann.

Sutcliffe, A., & Mehandjiev, N. (2004). End-user development. *Communications of the ACM, 47*(9), 31-32.

Taylor, M. J., Moynihan, E. P., & Wood-Harper, A. T. (1998). End-user computing and information systems methodologies. *Information Systems Journal, 8*, 85-96.

United States Bureau of the Census. (2003). *Computer use in the United States*. Washington, DC: Department of Commerce.

Chapter IX
Advancing End User Development Through Metadesign

Maria Francesca Costabile
Università degli Studi di Bari, Italy

Daniela Fogli
Università degli Studi di Brescia, Italy

Rosa Lanzilotti
Università degli Studi di Bari, Italy

Piero Mussio
Università degli Studi di Milano, Italy

Loredana Parasiliti Provenza
Università degli Studi di Milano, Italy

Antonio Piccinno
Università degli Studi di Bari, Italy

ABSTRACT

End-user development means the active participation of end users in the software development process. In this perspective, tasks that are traditionally performed by professional software developers at design time are transferred to end users at use time. This creates a new challenge for software engineers: designing software systems that can be evolved by end users. Metadesign, a new design paradigm discussed in this chapter, is regarded as a possible answer to this challenge. In this line, we have developed a metadesign methodology, called Software Shaping Workshop methodology, that supports user work practice and allows experts in a domain to personalize and evolve their own software environments. We illustrate the Software Shaping Workshop methodology and describe its application to a project in the medical domain. The work proposes a new perspective on system personalization, distinguishing between customization and tailoring of software environments. The software environments are customized by the design team to the work context, culture, experience, and skills of the user communities; they are also tailorable by end users at runtime in order to adapt them to the specific work situation and users' preferences and habits. The aim is to provide the physicians with software environments that are easy to use and adequate for their tasks, capable to improve their work practice and determine an increase in their productivity and performance.

INTRODUCTION

The increasing diffusion of the World Wide Web as the platform for a wide variety of applications creates many expectations about the possibilities offered by these interactive tools, but also raises many challenges about their effective design. In this chapter, we focus on Web applications that support professional people in their work practice. Such professional people are a particular class of end users; that is, they are not expert in computer science, nor willing to be (Cypher, 1993), but they are forced, by the evolution of the organizations in which they work and by the progress of information technology, to use computers and, increasingly often, to perform programming activities (Folmer, van Welie, & Bosch, 2005). In this chapter, by "end users," we denote these professionals and not end users in a wider meaning.

Nowadays, end users evolve from passive consumers of computer tools to a more active role of information and software artifacts producers (Fischer, 2002). This is also highlighted by the Shneiderman's (2002) claim: "the old computing was about what computers could do; the new computing is about what users can do" (p. 2).

The interaction dimension creates new challenges for system specification, design, and implementation. It is well known that "using the system changes the users, and as they change they will use the system in new ways" (Nielsen, 1993, p. 78).

These new uses of the system make the working environment and organization evolve, and force the designers to adapt the system to the evolved user, organization, and environment (Bourguin, Derycke, & Tarby, 2001). Moreover current techniques for software specification and design, such as UML, are very useful for software engineers, but they are often alien to users' experience, language, and background. A communication gap arises between application designers and users, which leads to design of software applications that are not usable (Folmer et al., 2005). To overcome these problems, software development life cycles that foresee participatory design (Schuler & Namioka, 1993) and open-ended design (Hartson & Hix, 1993) are invoked. The diversity of end users also calls for general, adaptive systems (Folmer et al., 2005). The temptation is to develop very general systems, thus falling in the Turing Tar Pit, in which *"everything is possible but nothing of interest is easy"* (Perlis, 1982, p. 10).

Actually, what software engineers should design are systems that can be used by end users in a dependable and easy way. Hence, the opposite temptation arises of creating specialized tools, focused on the activity of a well specified user, or a well specified and restricted community of users tied by similar practices or similar interests, working in a restricted context. Fischer (2006) warns about the perils of this tendency: beware of the inverse Turing Tar Pit, in which overspecialized tools permit only trivial and isolated activities that cannot be generalized or adapted and evolved.

We discuss a methodology to develop Web applications that do not fall in the Turing Tar Pit or in its inverse. The methodology stems from our experience in participatory design of several applications devoted to end users. It requires that a team of designers, including representatives of end users, that we call domain experts, develop and evolve an application to support professional people in their work practice. Karasti says that work practice consists of "unfolding activity in actual communities that is concrete and *situated*, complexly socially organized and technologically mediated" (Karasti, 2001, p. 16). In their work practice, professional people reason and communicate with each other through documents, expressed using notations, which represent abstract or concrete concepts, prescriptions, and results of activities. Often, dialects arise in a community, because the notation is used in different practical situations and environments. For example, mechanical drawings are organized according to rules, which are different in Europe and in the USA.

Professional people need to use computer systems to perform their work tasks exploiting all the communication and operation possibilities offered by these systems, but they are not and do not want to become computer experts. These end users often complain about the systems they use, and feel frustrated because of the difficulties they encounter interacting with them.

Our approach to system development starts from the observation of activities of domain experts during their daily work. The research we have developed in this field, and the experience gained has brought us to develop software environments that support users in performing activities in their specific domains, but also allow them to tailor these environments for better adapting to their needs, and even to create or modify software artifacts. The latter are defined activities of End-User Development (EUD), to which

a lot of attention is currently devoted by various researchers in Europe and all over in the world (Burnett, Cook, & Rothermel, 2004; Fischer & Giaccardi, 2006; Myers, Hudson, & Randy, 2003; Sutcliffe & Mehandjiev, 2004).

EUD can be considered a two-phase process, the first phase being designing the design environment, the second one being designing the applications using the design environment. These two phases are not clearly separated and are executed several times in an interleaved way, because the design environments evolve both as a consequence of the progressive insights the different stakeholders gain into the design process and as a consequence of the comments of end users at work. Note that this two-phase process requires a shift in the design paradigm, which must move from user-centered and participatory design to metadesign (Costabile, Fogli, Mussio, & Piccinno, 2005; Fischer, Giaccardi, Ye, Sutcliffe, & Mehandjiev, 2004). Through metadesign, design environments can be created that permit designing applications which can be evolved in the hands of end users.

The chapter is organized as follows. It first discusses EUD and the new design paradigm called metadesign. Then it presents the methodological assumptions underlying our work. Next it illustrates our (meta)design methodology and suggests some refinement to the definition of metadesign provided in the literature. Then it describes the application of the methodology to a project in the medical domain. Finally, a comparison with related works and the conclusions are provided.

END USER DEVELOPMENT AND METADESIGN

New technologies have created the potential to overcome the traditional separation between end users and software developers. New environments able to seamlessly move from using software to programming (or tailoring) can be designed. Advanced techniques for developing applications can be used by individuals as well as by groups or social communities or organizations.

The end-user population is not uniform, but it includes people with different cultural, educational, training, and employment backgrounds, novice and experienced computer users, the very young and the elderly, and people with different types of disabilities. Moreover, these users operate in various interaction contexts and scenarios of use, and they want to exploit computer systems to improve their work, but often complain about the difficulties in the use of such systems.

There are also important differences among end users, professional programmers, and software engineers. They are different in training, culture, skill, and technical abilities, in the scale of problems to be solved, in the processes, and so forth. However, there are some similarities. For instance, managing the successive versions of a piece of software is most probably a problem for software engineers as managing successive versions of documents with a word processor is a problem for end users. Reports or letters are often written in several phases; a businessman will write successive versions of a contract that must be proofread by all parties; a home user will reuse the same letter year after year when sending his or her tax report and just change some figures in the letter. In these cases, clever or appropriately educated users learn a simple technique aimed at helping them to manage the successive versions: assigning a number to each version. What about something of a greater complexity than the numeration of versions? One cannot expect an end user to apply the techniques provided within the software engineering field. Software engineering methods and tools require knowledge of abstract models that end users do not have and that require specific training. Consequently, an interesting line of research consists in identifying new sets of techniques and tools that would be the counterpart of software engineering for end users: *end-user development*.

Based on the activity performed within the thematic network on EUD funded by the European Commission during 2002-2003, the following definition of EUD has been proposed: "*End-User Development is a set of activities or techniques that allow people, who are non-professional developers, at some point to create or modify a software artifact*" (EUD-Net, http://giove.cnuce. cnr.it/eud-net.htm). EUD means the active participation of end users in the software development process. In this perspective, tasks that are traditionally performed by professional software developers are transferred to the users, who need to be specifically supported in performing these tasks. The active user participation in the software development process can range from providing information about requirements, use cases, and tasks, from participatory design to end user programming. Some EUD-oriented techniques have already been adopted by software for the mass market such as the adaptive menus in MS Word™ or some Programming by Example techniques in MS Excel™. However, we are still quite far from their systematic adoption.

All these techniques can be considered as belonging to a new design paradigm called metadesign (Fischer & Giaccardi, 2006; Fischer et al., 2004; Costabile et al., 2005). Metadesign goes beyond but includes user-centered design and participatory design. As defined in Fischer et al. (2004):

Meta-design characterizes objectives, techniques, and processes for creating new media and environments allowing "owners of problems" (that is, end users) to act as designers. A fundamental objective of meta-design is to create socio-technical environments that empower users to engage actively in the continuous development of systems rather than being restricted to the use of existing systems. (p. 35)

In this perspective, metadesign underlines a novel vision of interactive systems that is at the basis of our approach. All stakeholders of an interactive system are "owners" of a part of the problem and therefore they must all contribute to system design. Moreover, co-evolution of users and systems (Arondi, Baroni, Fogli, & Mussio, 2002; Bourguin et al., 2001; Costabile, Fogli, Marcante, & Piccinno, 2006c) forces all stakeholders in a continuous development of the system. This can be carried out, on one hand, by end users, who can perform tailoring activities to adapt the software environments they use to their evolved needs and habits. On the other hand, end users should collaborate with all other stakeholders in the evolution of the interactive system rather than just in the design. For these reasons, stakeholders need different software environments, specific to their culture, knowledge, and abilities, through which each stakeholder can contribute to shape software artifacts. They should also exchange among them the results of these activities, to converge into a common design or evolve an existing system.

Metadesign is a huge challenge in the current software engineering scenario. Somebody even thinks, for various reasons, that allowing end users to perform design activities is a utopian idea. Ben Shneiderman, introducing the Lieberman book on Programming by Example (Lieberman, 2001), states that there is magic and power in creating programs by direct manipulation activities, as opposed to writing code. The 18th-century scientists, such as Ben Franklin, experimented with electricity and found its properties quite amazing. Successively, Franklin and other scientists, such as Michael Faraday, laid the foundation for Thomas Edison's different applications, such as generators and electric lighting. Thus, in Shneiderman's opinion, also in the field of Programming by Example, there are a lot of researchers like Franklin and Faraday who are laying the foundation for the Thomas Edison still to come, but it is difficult at the moment to tell which idea will trigger broad dissemination or which insights will spark a new industry.

On the other hand, some drawbacks can affect EUD and metadesign: for example, if some situated practices of end users are inadequate, then they are replicated in the software environment obtained through EUD activities. However, end users are the owners of the problems, and the end user community is the referee of the adequacy of the work practice. The approach proposed in this chapter develops tools supporting end-user work practice. These tools force end users to externalize the decision process and to document it through annotations. These annotations allow a critical evaluation of the work practice by the whole community. If the work practice of the end user is inadequate within the professional domain, the inadequacies are made evident by the annotations and can be discussed at large by the community.

METHODOLOGICAL ASSUMPTIONS

Following Schön (1983), we assume that end users do perform their activity as competent practitioners, in that "they exhibit a kind of knowing in practice, most of which is tacit" and they "reveal a capacity for reflection on their intuitive knowing in the midst of action and sometimes use this capacity to cope with the unique, uncertain, and conflicted situations of practice" (pp. 8-9).

Tacit knowledge consists of habits and culture that we do not recognize in ourselves, but which can be used in performing our activities (Polanyi, 1967). End users, as competent practitioners, apply their tacit knowledge if the current context and the tools at hand support them to apply it.

Competent practitioners reason and communicate with each other through documents, expressed using notations, which represent abstract or concrete concepts, prescriptions, and results of activities. Such notations emerge from users' practical experiences in their specific domain of activity. As suggested in Petre (1995), they high-light those kinds of information users consider important for achieving their tasks, even at the expense of obscuring other kinds, and facilitate the problem solving strategies, adopted in the specific user community. Notations reflect tacit knowledge shared among users in the community. Authors build documents in the notation using their *tacit knowledge*, and the document can be understood by readers who possess a similar knowledge (Schön, 1983). The document conveys *implicit information*, which can be elicited only by readers in the community (Costabile et al., 2006c). Practitioners should be able to use their tacit knowledge while interacting with computer systems. The messages on which interaction is based should convey implicit information.

Users often complain about the system they use to perform their work tasks, but they are not and do not want to become computer experts. One of the reasons that interactive systems are unusable is because the system imposes strategies of task execution alien to users; it drives them to follow unfamiliar reasoning strategies and to adopt inefficient procedures. It is well known that "using the system changes the users, and as they change they will use the system in new ways" (Nielsen, 1993, p. 78). In turn, the designer must evolve the system to adapt it to its new usages; this phenomenon is called *co-evolution of users and systems* (Arondi et al., 2002; Costabile et al., 2006c). In Bourguin et al. (2001), it is observed that these new uses of the system determine the evolution of the user culture and of her or his models and procedures of task evolution, while the requests from users force the evolution of the whole technology supporting interaction.

In order to design a system that meets users' needs and expectations, we must take into account the following observations:

1. The notations developed by the user communities from their work practice are not defined according to computer science formalisms,

but they are concrete and situated in the specific context, in that they are based on icons, symbols, and words that resemble and schematize the tools and the entities that are to be operated in the working environment. Such notations emerge from users' practical experiences in their specific domain of activity. They highlight those kinds of information users consider important for achieving their tasks, even at the expense of obscuring other kinds, and facilitate the problem solving strategies, adopted in the specific user community.

2. Software systems are in general designed without taking into account the problem of implicit information, user articulatory skills, and tacit knowledge, so that they can be interpreted with high cognitive costs. Actually, these factors are among those determining the so-called *invisible work* (Nardi & Engeström, 1999). To design and manage organizations is therefore crucial to understand the nature and structure of invisible work. Implicit information, for example, the spatial location and the physical appearance of the objects of interest, is often significant only to users who possess the knowledge to interpret it. Most of this knowledge is not made explicit and codified but is tacit knowledge, namely it is knowledge that users possess and currently use to carry out tasks and to solve problems, but that they are unable to express in verbal terms and that they may even be unaware of. It is a common experience that in many application fields, users exploit mainly their tacit knowledge, since they are often more able to do that than to explain what they do. Thus, as suggested in Karasti (2001), "to make the invisible visible, to tease out the implicit, complex workplaces need to be investigated for the practical task-oriented activities" (p. 34). This implies the need of a close observation of everyday work practice settings, rather

than simply interviewing practitioners about their working activities.

3. A system acceptable by its users should have a gentle slope of complexity: this means it should avoid big steps in complexity and keep a reasonable trade-off between ease-of-use and functional complexity. Systems might offer users, for example, different levels of complexities in performing EUD activities, going from simply setting parameters to integrating existing components to extending the system by developing new components (Myers, Smith, & Horn, 1992; Myers et al., 2003). The system should then evolve with the users (co-evolution) (Arondi et al., 2002; Bourguin et al., 2001), thus offering them new functionalities when needed.

4. Co-evolution forces the design team in a continuous development of the system. This is carried out on one hand by end users who can perform a tailoring activity adapting the software environments they use to their own needs and habits. On the other hand, end users should collaborate with all other stakeholders both in the design and in the evolution of the whole interactive system.

SOFTWARE SHAPING WORKSHOP METHODOLOGY

Starting from the above observations, three principles are at the basis of our methodology to design interactive software systems (Costabile, Fogli, Mussio, & Piccinno, 2006a; Costabile, Fogli, Lanzilotti, Mussio, & Piccinno, 2006b): (1) the language in which the interaction with systems is expressed must be based on notations traditionally adopted in the domain; (2) systems must present all and only the tools necessary to perform the user work, without overwhelming users by unnecessary tools and information; and (3) systems must provide a layout conveying implicit information by simulating the traditional

layout of the tools employed in the domain such as mechanical machines or chapter-based tools.

Our methodology emphasizes a perspective on metadesign that goes beyond but includes user-centered design and participatory design: user-centered design relies on a deep study of the end users, their tasks, and their involvement in prototypes and system evaluation; participatory design means that representatives of end users participate in the design team. In our view, metadesign means that design environments are developed in a participatory way and provided to end users, permitting them to shape their application environments. Thus, end users play two main roles in the life cycle of the interactive software system: (1) they perform their working tasks; and (2) they participate in the development of software environments as stakeholders of the domain.

In the first role, as users performing working activities, end users can tailor the software environment to their current needs and context. Practitioners, such as mechanical engineers, geologists, and physicians, often work in a team to reach a common goal. The team might be composed by members of different subcommunities, each subcommunity with different expertise. Our approach to the design of a software system in a certain domain is to see the system as composed of various environments, each one for a specific subcommunity of end users. Such environments are organized in analogy with the artisans workshops, where the artisans find all and only the tools necessary to carry out their activities. Following the analogy, end users using a virtual workshop, called *Software Shaping Workshop* (SSW), find available all and only the tools required to develop their activities. A type of SSW which allows end users to perform their daily tasks are *application workshops*. End users may also perform EUD activities, for example, by using annotation tools permitting the definition of new widgets (Carrara, Fogli, Fresta, & Mussio, 2002): as a reaction to the annotation activity performed by the end user, the workshop may transform the annotated document area into a new widget, to which a computational meaning is associated. This widget is added to the common knowledge base and becomes accessible by other end users, each one accessing the data through his or her own workshop enriched by the new widget that is adapted to the specific context.

In the second role, as members of the design team, end users participate directly in the development of the workshops for their daily work. In fact, even if they are nonprofessional software developers, they are required to create or modify application workshops. To this end, different workshops (*system workshops*) are made available to them, which permit the customization of each application workshop to the end-user community needs and requirements. The concept of system workshop is more general: actually, system workshops exist that allow the members of any community involved in design and validation of the system to participate in this activity. For ex-

ample, system workshops for Human-Computer Interaction (HCI) experts and software engineers are used.

Each member of the design team can examine, evaluate, and modify an application workshop using tools shaped to his or her culture. In this way, this approach leads to a workshop network that tries to overcome the difference in language among the experts of the different disciplines (software engineering, HCI, application domain) who cooperate in developing computer systems customized to the needs of the user communities without requiring end users to become skilled in all the involved domains of knowledge.

The network is structured so that the different users can participate in the application workshops design, implementation, and use without being disoriented. Every user can access more than one workshop. For example, an end user as practitioner uses an application workshop, while as a member of the design team (representative of the user

Figure 1. The SSW network; dashed arrows indicate communication paths, and full arrows indicate generation and evaluation paths

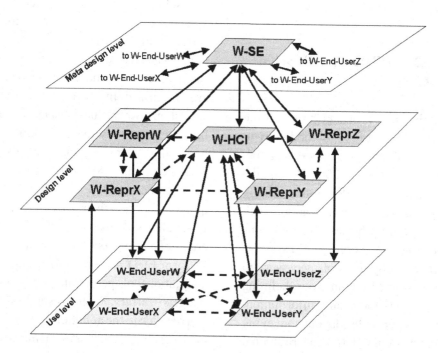

community), uses a system workshop; a software engineer uses a particular system workshop to produce the tools for the other members of the team and accesses other workshops to check their functionalities.

In general, a network is organized in levels. In each level, one or more workshops can be used, which are connected by communication paths. In the example in Figure 1, three levels exist: (a) the *metadesign level*, where software engineers use a system workshop called W-SE to prepare the tools to be used and to participate in the design, implementation, and validation activities; (b) the *design level*, where software engineers, HCI experts, and end-user representatives cooperate in the design, implementation, and validation activities; a design member belonging to the community X participates in the design using a system workshop W-ReprX customized to the needs, culture, and skills of community X; and (c) the *use level*, where practitioners of the different communities cooperate to achieve a task; similarly, practitioners belonging to the community X participate in the task achievement using the application workshop W-End-UserX customized to their needs, culture, and skills.

Software engineers are required (a) to provide the software tools necessary to the development of the overall application and (b) to participate in the design of application and system workshops. Therefore, from their workshops, software engineers may reach each system and/or application workshop.

Representatives of end users may work at two levels. At the design level, they use their own system workshop to participate in the design, and, at the bottom level, they use their own application workshop to carry out specific activities in their application domain.

HCI experts use their own system workshop to participate in the design and, at the bottom level, may access all application workshops to check their functionalities.

Practitioners can only use their own application workshop to perform their tasks.

At each level, communication paths exist that allow experts in a domain to communicate with experts in a different domain. A domain expert using his or her workshop W-ReprZ can send data or programs to a different domain expert. Data and programs are interpreted and materialized by the workshop W-ReprY, customized to the second domain expert. As we have discussed in detail in Costabile et al. (2006a), the main tool currently used for this kind of communication is electronic annotation.

It is important to notice that a communication exists from a lower level to the upper one and vice versa. In our approach, this capability is given by (a) allowing end users, interacting with an SSW, to annotate their usability problems and to communicate them to all the experts reachable in the network and (b) allowing designers to update the applications and propose the updated versions to end users. See Costabile et al. (2006c) for a detailed discussion about the communication paths in a SSW network and their role in supporting the co-evolution of users and systems.

Each SSW co-evolves in time with end users and the design team. Co-evolution is a long life process asking for a *continuous development* of the interactive system. This is different from the so-called Rapid Application Development (RAD) that foresees the possibility for programmers of quickly building working programs. RAD systems emphasize reducing development time, while the SSW focuses on user satisfaction, that is, (1) acceptability and usability of the application and (2) balancing the features of the tools on user needs and expectations. Moreover, RAD systems are development environments devoted to software engineers, but they are still far from being used easily and effectively by end users. The SSW approach stresses the role of representatives of end users as active members of the design team. To this end, system workshops at the design level, used by either HCI experts or representatives of end users, are customized to the user community to which they are devoted, speak user languages, and present all and only the tools necessary in that context for developing further workshops.

Refining Metadesign

Metadesign emerges from the practice of Computer Science, in particular from what is now called end-user development (Lieberman, Paternò, & Wulf, 2006). As already mentioned, recently a definition of metadesign has been given in Fischer et al. (2004):

Meta-design characterizes objectives, techniques, and processes for creating new media and environments allowing "owners of problems" (that is, end users) to act as designers. A fundamental objective of meta-design is to create socio-technical environments that empower users to engage actively in the continuous development of systems rather than being restricted to the use of existing systems. (p. 35)

In Fischer and Giaccardi (2006), the authors add that metadesign can be regarded "as an emerging conceptual framework aimed at defining and creating social and technical infrastructures in which new forms of collaborative design can take place" (p. 427).

We refine and clarify herein these definitions on the basis of our experimental activities.

End users are indeed the "owners of problems", and have a domain-oriented view of the processes to be automated. Moreover, they are not expert in HCI or software engineering, so they can act as designers contributing their experience on the domain of activity. In turn, software engineers have the knowledge about tools and techniques for system development, and the HCI experts have the knowledge on system usability and human behavior. HCI experts and software engineers are stakeholders whose contribution is necessary to the development of the system because they are

the only ones who can guarantee the usability and the performance of the system.

The SSW methodology offers to each stakeholder a software environment, a Software Shaping Workshop, by which the stakeholder can test and study a software artifact and contribute to its shaping and reshaping as any object or tool that can be easily created, manipulated, and modified. HCI experts, software engineers, and users acting as developers, each through his or her SSW, can access, test, and modify the system of interest according to his or her own culture, experience, needs, and skills. They can also exchange the results of these activities to converge to a common design.

In the light of these considerations, *metadesign is a design paradigm that includes end users as active members of the design team and provides all the stakeholders in the team with suitable languages and tools to foster their personal and common reasoning about the development of interactive software systems that support end users' work.*

End users must be in the situation to act as designers when they need and to act as end users when the tools match their needs. This twofold role of end users is discussed also by Fischer (2002), where he argues about the "consumer" and "designer" perspectives by saying "that the same person is and wants to be a consumer in some situations and in others a designer; therefore 'consumer/designer' is not an attribute of a person, but of a context" (p. 6).

Overall, the development of a system supporting the work practice in a specific domain of application results into the development of a network of system and application workshops. The design team is engaged in a continuous development of the system. This continuous development is carried out, on one hand, by end users of application workshops, who can perform a tailoring activity adapting the application workshops they use to their own needs and habits; on the other hand, all other stakeholders participate in system evolution, by customizing the application workshops using their system workshops.

In this organization, the personalization activities of application workshops can be performed by the design team or by the end users themselves. Thus, we classify personalization activities into customization and tailoring. *Customization* is the activity performed by the design team which generates application workshops for a specific community of users by exploiting users' notations, dialects, principles, and standard rules. *Tailoring* is the activity performed by end users to adapt an application workshop to the current activity and context of work. The idea is to permit tailoring of systems already specific and suitable to the needs of a specific community of users, thus allowing users a further step of individual personalization. We call this activity tailoring toward the individual (or *individual tailoring*), which is performed by the users through small incremental steps.

Different types of individual tailoring can be devised: *tailoring for individual work*, concerning the activities that the specialist can perform to adapt her or his environment during her or his own work; and *tailoring for cooperative work*, including those activities that the specialist performs to prepare the information that will be provided to another specialist to whom a consultation is requested.

An Application in the Medical Domain

In this section, we describe a project in the medical domain, to which we are currently applying the SSW methodology. The improvement of the quality of the medical diagnosis is the main goal of each physician. Thanks to the evolution of research and technology in the medical domain, each specialist may have the aid of medical examinations of different types, that is, laboratory examinations, X-rays, MRI (Magnetic Resonance Imaging), and so forth. A team of physicians with different specializations should analyze the

medical examinations giving their own contribution according to their "expertise". However, the increasing number of diagnostic tools and medical specializations as well as the increasing number of patients do not permit the team of specialists to meet as frequently as needed to analyze the clinical cases especially if they do not work in the same building or moreover they work in different towns or states.

The information technology has today the potential of overcoming this difficulty by providing software environments that allow a synchronous and/or asynchronous collaboration "at a distance". Thus, the specialists do not need to meet at the same moment for analyzing the clinical cases on which they collaborate. Software environments will give the possibility to each specialist of analyzing the medical cases of different patients and of formulating her or his own diagnosis, taking into account the opinions of the other colleagues without the need of a synchronous consultation.

There are already tools for supporting the physicians to formulate the medical diagnosis, for example, telemedicine, videoconference, and so forth. They are very sophisticated and often they need large system resources. Moreover, physicians complain that although these tools are very expensive, they are designed more for computer experts than for physicians. In the experience with physicians collaborating with us, these tools present personalization features very difficult to be learned and used by them. Our proposal of SSWs aims at providing the physicians with software tools that are first of all easy and adequate for the physicians' current tasks. This would determine an increase in end-user productivity and performance, with the achievement of competitive advantage for the organization they work in, by permitting consultations among physicians without constraints of time and place.

In the case study with radiologists and pneumologists (Costabile et al., 2006a), we adopted the SSW approach to provide physicians with software tools that are both usable and tailorable to their needs. The case study had the goal of supporting different communities of physicians, namely radiologists and pneumologists, in the analysis of chest radiographies and in the generation of the diagnosis. Radiologists and pneumologists represent two subcommunities of the physicians community: they share patient-related data archives, some models for their interpretation, some notations for their presentation, but they have also to perform different tasks, documented through different subnotations and tools. Therefore, their notations can be considered two (visual) dialects of the physicians' general notation. As a consequence, two different application workshops have been designed for these two communities of users. The pneumologist and the radiologist involved in the study of the pulmonary diseases, even if they are working in different wards or different hospitals, can define an agreed diagnosis using each one her/his application workshop tailored to her or his culture, skills, and articulatory abilities in an asynchronous and distributed way.

We are currently applying the same approach in a larger project in which we are involved, in collaboration with the physicians of the neurology department of the "Giovanni XXIII" Pediatric Hospital of Bari, Italy. In this project, different communities of physicians are involved, namely neurologists and neuroradiologists, in the analysis of clinical cases and in the generation of the diagnosis. Neurologists need to exchange consultations with other neurologists and/or neuroradiologists in order to make a better diagnosis for their children patients. These groups of physicians autonomously organized a procedure for the exchange of information (data, images, and text), using common network tools such as e-mail. However, the physicians were not satisfied with the quality and reliability of such a procedure, so that we started a collaboration with them with the objective of creating software environments that might satisfy their needs.

We developed a first version of the prototypes devoted to neurologists and neuroradiologists, on the basis of the experience gained in the previous project with radiologists and pneumologists (Costabile et al., 2006a). Then, usability evaluation of these prototypes was performed by applying different techniques, such as heuristic evaluation, cognitive walkthrough, and user testing. In parallel, we carried out an accurate field study in the neurology department of the hospital and we developed a second version of the prototypes. In particular, the field study was aimed at understanding and identifying the environmental and organization factors that influence the work of the physicians and the flow of activities, as well as the communities of end users involved and their main tasks, their common languages, and their specialized medical dialects. Various methods have been considered to perform this study, such as user observations, interviews, and analysis of users' documents and languages. From our previous experience with this particular community of users, we decided to perform the field study to deeply know the work practice of the physicians.

Prototypes of SSWs have been developed on the basis of the information collected during the field study. As previously discussed, the resulting interactive system is structured as a network of SSWs, each specific for a community of users. Being the network modular, we foresee the possibility in the future of extending it by creating other SSWs for other stakeholders, for example, clerks and managers dealing with management and billing systems.

The Field Study

The field study was mainly aimed at understanding how the physicians collaborate in the analysis of clinical cases. In accordance with the basic principles of our methodology, we also wanted to look at (a) the notations adopted in the specific domain, (b) the documents the various users exchange, and (c) the tools they usually use.

During the field study, the analysts periodically observed the physicians during their daily work in the hospital (about two to three visits per month since 2003). They observed meetings of physicians of the same departments and meetings of physicians with different specialization. Sometimes, they performed semistructured interviews for better understanding documents, tools, and languages. The information collected during the study has been used to identify the right requirements of the application.

The stakeholders identified through the field study are the neurologist; neuroradiologist; patient (the child with neurological troubles and her or his family); family doctor (knows the symptomatology of the patient and prepares a diagnostic question for the neurologist); internal laboratory (performs the examinations prescribed by the neurologist and is sited in the hospital in which the neurologist works); and external laboratory (performs examinations but is outside the hospital in which the neurologist works).

Usually, a patient with troubles first goes to her or his family doctor. The doctor suggests to the patient family to go to a neurologist and prepares a diagnostic question for the patient. The neurologist studies the symptomatology of the patient

and prescribes others medical analyses that can be performed in the internal laboratory, such as EEG (electroencephalogram), or in the external laboratory, such as blood test, magentic resonance image (MRI) and so on. When the neurologist has the analysis results of the patient, the neurologist studies them accurately and often identifies critical results and makes some annotations on them. Then, the neurologist defines a diagnosis and gives it to the patient or the patient's family. In particularly serious and difficult cases, before formulating a diagnosis, the neurologist needs to ask other physicians for a consultation to better reason through the pathology of the patient. For example, the neurologist can decide to refer to a neuroradiologist for a more detailed analysis through MRI. The neuroradiologist provides an opinion to the neurologist. Both neurologist and neuroradiologist can also ask for a consultation to another colleague, neurologist, or neuroradiologist respectively, specialized in particular pathologies. At the end of the consultations, the neurologist gives the diagnosis and the treatment to the patient. The information flow just described is represented in Figure 2, where the interaction among neurologists and neuroradiologists is highlighted, the one we investigated in this chapter.

Figure 2. The information flow: The interaction among neurologist and neuroradiologist is that one investigated in the chapter

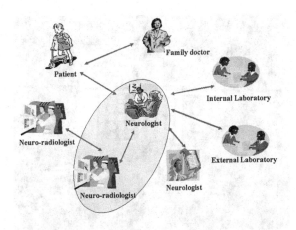

We now describe a scenario in which a neurologist asks for a consultation to a neuroradiologist to analyze clinical cases by studying MRI. In our scenario, both physicians are male.

Currently, consultations occur during a real meeting. Due to the busy schedule of the physicians, these consultations cannot be frequent; therefore, when meeting, they have to analyze several clinical cases. During the meeting, the cases are discussed one at a time and always with the same procedure. The neurologist chooses a case, gives the MRI plats to the neuroradiologist, and begins to tell the most relevant data about the patient history. The neuroradiologist puts three or four MRI plats on the diaphanoscope and begins to study them (Figure 3).

During the study of the MRI, neurologist, and neuroradiologist exchange information in order to clarify possible doubts and converge to an agreed opinion (Figure 4). At the end, the diagnosis on which the specialists agreed is written on the patient record and the next clinical case is considered.

If the physicians cannot physically meet, the consultations occur through e-mail. Obviously, in this case, some problems arise such as limited

Figure 3. A photo taken during the direct observation of a physician meeting: The neuroradiologist is examining an MRI

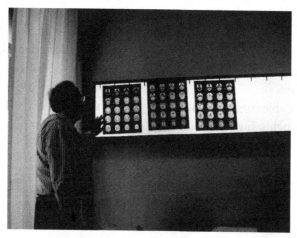

Figure 4. Another photograph of the same meeting: Neuroradiologist and radiologist are discussing a clinical case

capacity of the e-mail, connection problems, and so on.

The analysis of the information collected during the field study allowed us to develop the prototypes described in the next section.

System Customization and Tailoring

The described scenario is a typical case of co-operative work. We adopted the SSW methodology to build application workshops customized to the physicians' notation, language, culture, and background, that physicians themselves can further tailor according to their needs. These workshops allow the specialists to cooperate in virtual meetings. The specialists may use their own application workshops to perform their working tasks: for example, a specialist may analyze the available EEG or MRI, perform annotations and/or computations on them, select parts of them, define diagnoses, and/or consultation requests.

The observations collected during the field study are at the basis of the design of the application workshops to be used by the two different communities of physicians. Differently from the case of the pneumologists and radiologists (Costabile et al., 2006a), the application workshops designed for the physicians of the new project (neurologists and neuroradiologists) have an overview area on the top of the screen which may be used to browse MRI plats or EEG portions. The overview area is the electronic counterpart of the diaphanoscope used by the physicians in a real meeting (see Figure 5). During the observations, we noticed that neuroradiologists are only interested in MRI; thus, in their application workshop, they find only the MRI overview area together with tools to process the MRI and to formulate the diagnosis.

On the other hand, neurologists study primarily a great number of EEGs, but in some cases, they analyze MRI plats. Thus, in their application workshop there are two overview areas that are resizable (see Figure 6). In this way, the neurologists can reduce (or even close completely) the area containing the MRI plats, in order to expand the EEG overview area according to their needs.

Each workshop is designed to be equipped with a certain set of tools. Some are provided

Figure 5. The application workshop prototype devoted to the neuro-radiologist

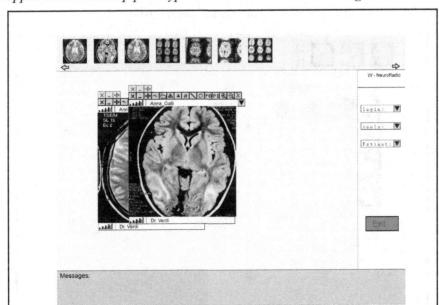

as default. Moreover, the workshop allows the physician to eliminate or add some tools, the workshop permits this. Adding or deleting tools and resizing the overview area are examples of *tailoring for individual work* activities.

As already mentioned in the previous section, tailoring for cooperative work refers to tailoring activities needed to communicate efficiently and effectively with colleagues, for example to shape software artifacts made available to another specialist of whom a consultation is requested. In the following, we describe how a neurologist may tailor the system in order to communicate with a neuroradiologist and request a consultation from the neuroradiologist.

As the field study revealed, in their daily work, neurologists and neuroradiologists highlight parts of EEG and/or MRI. As shown in Figure 6, in the neurologist application workshop, a portion of EEG can be selected from the EEG overview area and automatically loaded in a specific window, called *working bench*, which appears in the working area. The working bench is equipped with a toolbar hosting the tools to be used by the neurologist to study the EEG and prepare requests

of consultation to be sent to other specialists. According to the principles at the basis of SSW methodology, these tools resemble the real tools the physicians use in their work practice.

Moreover, neurologists and neuroradiologists request and provide consultations by indicating to their colleagues parts of EEG and/or MRI which may be of interest to formulate the diagnosis. This kind of activity is supported by the application workshops we have developed. For example, the neurologist may find in the working bench two different tools for selecting limited areas in the portion of EEG: (1) one allows the physician to circle the area of interest; and (2) the other permits the physician to identify, through two vertical red bars, a limited part of the selected portion of EEG concerning a certain period of time (see Figure 6).

A selected area can be annotated and the annotation exploited in supporting the collaboration between specialists that want to reach a common diagnosis. For example, if the neurologist needs to consult a neuroradiologist, he makes a request by opening a special type of annotation window, called *consulting window*. This window permits

Figure 6. The application workshop prototype devoted to the neurologist

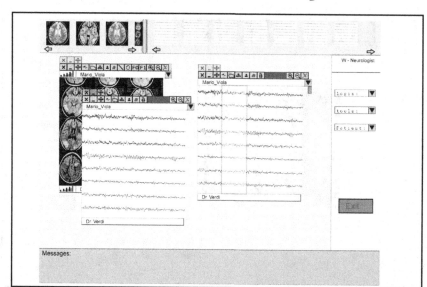

the physician to articulate the annotation into two parts: the *question* to be asked to the colleague and the *description* which summarizes information associated to the question. A third part can be tailored according to the addressee of the consultation request: if a physician needs more details about the clinical case, the sender may activate the *detailed description* and fill it, otherwise the sender can hide it. Examples of consulting windows are shown in Figure 7.

In other words, the physician who wants to ask for a consultation is allowed to prepare a tailored annotation specific to the physician he is consulting. In a similar way, a physician can make a different type of annotation in order to add a comment that can be stored and possibly viewed by his colleague. It is worth noting that both types of annotation never damage the original image. Back to the example of a consulting request of the neurologist for the neuroradiologist, the neurologist can save the annotation, that can be successively viewed by his colleagues. When the neuroradiologist starts working with his application workshop and finds the request

of the neurologist, he reads all the information and answers by filling the proper fields in the consulting window (see Figure 8).

Related Work

The SSW methodology has been influenced by the work performed within the EUD-Net thematic network. In literature, end-user programming and end-user computing are often used as interchangeable terms; for example, in Balaban, Barzilay, and Elhadad (2002, p. 640), the authors discuss "enhancing editors with *end-user programming capabilities*". They also say that "end-user computing is needed in domains or applications where the activity cannot be planned in advance" and that it should have the flavor of "on-the-fly" computing: that is, it should emerge during the user activity, when the user needs to tailor the environment or create a new software artifact, according to some concrete situation. Brancheau and Brown describe *end-user computing* as the adoption and use of information technology by people outside the information system department,

Figure 7. Examples of consulting windows: Leftmost image (a) is for a consultation request to a physician who does not need further details and rightmost image (b) is for a consultation request to a physician who needs details about the clinical case

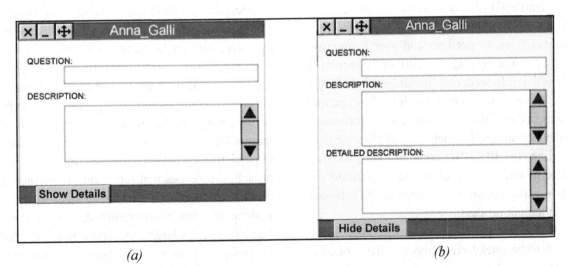

(a)   (b)

Figure 8. An example of consulting window for the neuro-radiologist who is answering to the neurologist's request

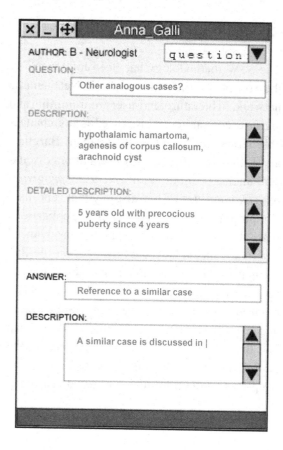

to develop software applications in support of organizational tasks (Brancheau & Brown, 1993). The organization in which such people work requires them to perform end-user computing and to assume the responsibility of the results of this activity. Indeed, one fundamental challenge is to develop environments that allow people without a particular background in programming to develop and tailor their own applications. In this line, the EUD-Net collaboration preferred the term end-user development to indicate the active participation of end users in the software development process.

Traditional participatory design approaches exploit techniques derived from social theories that support communication and collaboration within the interdisciplinary team: such techniques move from just system descriptions to collaborative construction of mock-ups, cooperative prototyping, and game-like design sessions. Most of these techniques use fantasy and imagined futures to study specific actions rather than just analyze solutions after setting up goals (Bødker, Grønbæk, & Kyng, 1993). In Greenbaum and Kyng (1991), the Future Workshop technique is discussed: it foresees group meetings run by at least two facilitators with the aim of analyzing common problematic situations, generating visions about the future, and discussing how to realize these visions. In our approach, the term "workshop" is used with a different meaning provided in every English dictionary: for example, "a small establishment where manufacturing or handicrafts are carried" (Merrian-Webster online, www.m-w.com). We speak about "Software Shaping Workshops", referring to software environments that enable users to "shape" virtual tools and data. In other words, the real workshop is the metaphor we adopt for the conceptual model of our software environments. Participatory design of visual interactive systems is performed through the interaction with SSWs customized to the needs, preferences, habits, and capabilities of each specific community of users belonging to the interdisciplinary team. A similar approach in participatory design literature is Cooperative Prototyping (Bødker & Grønbæk, 1991), in which prototyping is viewed like a cooperative activity between users and designers. Prototypes are developed by software engineers, then discussed with users, and possibly experienced by them in work-like situations. Prototype modifications may be immediately made by direct manipulation, also by users, during each session of participatory design. However, in such an approach, prototypes just represent an interactive digital evolution of chapter-based mock-ups: real systems are then reprogrammed, and all modifications require large programming efforts that are postponed and made by designers after each session. Our approach foresees the participation of all the stakeholders in the development of the final system, each one according to their own view, through the use of SSWs. Therefore, our SSWs can be regarded like a new technique supporting participatory design. In particular, the use of prototypes permits the participation of end users in the creation of software tools, that they can tailor, customize, and program themselves in line with *participatory programming* (Letondal & Mackay, 2004). Participatory programming is regarded like a way to transcend participatory design, but exploits traditional techniques of participatory design (in situ observations, interviews, workshops) to allow representatives of end users and software engineers to collaborate in developing and tailoring software tools.

Fischer et al. propose the SER (Seeding, Evolutionary growth, Reseeding) process model to design systems as seeds, with a subsequent evolutionary growth, followed by a reseeding phase. This model was used for the development and evolution of the so-called DODEs (Domain-Oriented Design Environments), which are "software systems that support design activities within particular domains and that are built specifically to evolve" (Fischer, 1998, p. 447). The SER model is currently adopted to support metadesign. For example, it is at the based of the work described in Carmien, Dawe, Fischer, Gorman, Kintsch, and Sullivan (2005), where a system is first created by metadesigners (software engineers) to be used by caregivers who design and create scripts supporting people with cognitive disabilities. As in our approach, particular attention is put on the kinds of users involved in the domain, and customized environments are provided to them. Co-evolution may also be sustained since tools for automatic feedback and remote observations are used to notify problems to the design team. Our SSW approach has some similarities with this work, but it emphasizes the need of providing personalized environments to all stakeholders, in terms of language, notation, layout, and interaction possibilities.

In our approach, end users play a role similar to handymen in MacLean, Kathleen, Lövstrand, and Moran (1990). The handyman bridges between workers (people using a computer application) and computer professionals; she or he is able to work alongside users and communicate their needs to programmers. Similarly, representatives of end users bridge between workers and computer professionals, but are end users themselves. To participate in SSWs development, they must be provided with environments that are adapted to their culture, skills, and articulatory abilities. Besides the projects in the medical domain already discussed in this chapter, in Costabile, Fogli, Fresta, Mussio, and Piccinno (2004), we describe an environment devoted to mechanical engineers who were the representatives of end users involved in the development of the application workshop devoted to assembly-line operators.

Karasti (2001) explores the integration of work practice and system design and insists on increasing the sensitivity of system design towards everyday work practice. She characterizes work practice by describing the complex social organization, technological mediation, knowledge and meaning as socially constructed, and the intertwined nature of the unfolding activities in which all these aspects are joined. Everyday work practice has historically been invisible in design. We agree that an understanding of current work practice is useful in the design of new technologies. Moreover, two different bodies of knowledge are explored in Karasti (2001) to make work practice visible and intelligible for system design: the actual work activities and knowledge of practitioners and what is considered relevant information for requirements analysis in system design. Thus, the challenge is to dissolve the barriers existing between designer and user knowledge, and to search for adequate methods to secure the inclusion of practitioner and work practice knowledge in design.

Research with similar interests in work practice has been carried out in studies that intertwine work practice and system design, especially within the field of Computer Support Cooperative Work (CSCW) (e.g., Suchman, Blomberg, Orr, & Trigg, 1999; Suchman & Trigg, 1991; Goodwin & Goodwin, 1997; Hughes, Randall, & Shapiro, 1992), and can also be found in other collections (Button, 1993; Chaiklin & Lave, 1993; Engeström & Middleton, 1996; Greenbaum & Kyng, 1991; Resnick, Saljo, Pontecorvo, & Burge, 1997).

In Penner and Steinmetz (2002) and Stary (2000), task-based and user-centered development approaches are presented to support the automation of user interface design. The TADEUS project (Stary, 2000) proposes a development methodology starting from a business intelligence model to generate user interfaces or portals by integrating a model-driven, task-based, user-oriented, and object-driven life cycle. Moreover, to cope with the complex and continuously changing needs of end users, Penner and Steinmetz propose a iteratively created operational prototype called DIGBE (Dynamic Interaction Generation for Building Environment) (Penner & Steinmetz, 2002). DIGBE is a multiplatform and generic building control system (heating, cooling, ventilation, access control, security, and so on). A domain expert, typically a building manager, starts up the DIGBE application and, through a simple dialog, sets the initial state of the system. In response, DIGBE creates a dedicated child application for the other domain experts (i.e., managers, operators, technicians), accessible through a log-on screen. After the domain expert successfully enters the new system, DIGBE designs and presents (in real time) a user interface dedicated to the underline task set of the logged user. Moreover, during the interaction, the system dynamically adapts the ongoing user interface. This methodology is similar to the SSW methodology, but it is simply user-centered and leads to a unique general suitable system that can be specialized according to the domain and user community needs.

Finally, other works focus on experience-centered domains, that is, domains requiring six to 12 years of intensive practice before practitioners achieve the most effective levels of skill (Hayes, 1985). In these domains (i.e., medical diagnosis, chess, professional design, planning tasks, etc.), one of the main challenges in building decision support is that users, at different levels of domain experience, have often very different needs. For example, a system designed to satisfy domain experts' specific needs may frustrate novices and vice versa. DAISY (Design Aid for Intelligent Support System) (Brodie & Hayes, 2002) is a design methodology for building decision support systems in complex, experience-centered domains. It provides a technique for identifying the specialized needs of users within a specific range of domain experience.

CONCLUSION

This chapter discusses a novel methodology, proposed to design interactive systems in which operations are easy to perform and many interesting activities can be carried out, thus avoiding a fall into the Turing Tar Pit and into its inverse.

To reach this goal, the software environments (application workshops) made available to end users the option to adopt a Visual Interaction Language tailored to end-user culture, in that it is defined by evolving the traditional end-user notations and systems of sign, with the constant support of domain experts, acting as designers in the design team. Each application workshop allows end users to develop a specific types of activities. Hence, it makes available to the end users all and only the tools to perform such activities. The data on which end users operate are however interoperable within a set of application workshops.

The domain experts contribute in the design team to the creation of the set of application workshops. Indeed, the methodology offers to each stakeholder a software environment (system workshop), by which the stakeholder contributes to the design and implementation of software artifacts, including application workshops. In this way, software engineers, HCI experts, and end users acting as developers, each one through his or her system workshop, can shape software artifacts by working with tools that are in accordance with his or her own culture, experience, needs, and skills; they can also exchange the results of these activities to converge to a common design. The proposed approach fosters the collaboration among communities of end users, managers, and designers, with the aim of increasing motivation and reducing cognitive and organizational cost, thus providing a significant contribution to the EUD evolution, as suggested in Fischer et al. (2004).

We have discussed how the SSW methodology exploits metadesign by requiring that software engineering actually design environments that allow representatives of end users to be involved in the design of the application workshops that will be used by all end users in the specific project domain. End users have then a twofold role: users and designers of their own software environment. Moreover, the work described introduces a perspective on system personalization, distinguishing between customization and tailoring of software environments. The software environments are customized by the design team to the work context, culture, experience, and skills of the user communities; they are also tailorable by end users at runtime in order to adapt them to the specific work situation and users preferences and habits. End-user development is thus sustained by these two kinds of personalization.

Because end users and systems evolve during time, the design team must evolve the set of application workshops as well as the visual interaction languages. To face this phenomenon, the design team must be maintained active for the whole life of the system. The SSW network is organized so that designers in the team receive the observations of end users at work (Costabile, Fogli, Mussio, & Piccinno, in press) and also can monitor end user usage of the application workshops (Arondi et al., 2002). Working at the design and metadesign level, the team can improve the application workshops whenever necessary to evolve it in response to the end-user evolution at the work level.

The application of the SSW methodology to a project in a medical context has been described. Physicians and their activities have been carefully examined through a field study, in order to understand their work practice and integrate it in the software design. Physicians are collaborating with enthusiasm to the development of the SSW prototypes. They understand and appreciate the novel approach of being involved in collaborative design processes, through which they can have a more active role than simple consumers of new technologies. Actually, available off-the-shelf software in the medical domain is designed to support specialized activities, such as image processing, clinical data organization, and statistical analysis. However, they do not support physicians in integrating these activities for diagnostic purpose. The Software Shaping Workshops designed for physicians allow them to carry out the activities that physicians are used to perform face-to-face (e.g., exchanging consultations) and that off-the-shelf software does not address yet. We are confident that this approach may determine an increase in end user productivity and performance, that is, a better quality of diagnosis and medical cure.

ACKNOWLEDGMENT

The authors wish to thank the physicians of the Hospital "Giovanni XXIII" in Bari for their collaboration. We are also grateful to Giuseppe Fresta for his contribution to the implementation of the prototypes presented in the chapter. This work was partially supported by the Italian MIUR and by EU and Regione Puglia under grant DIPIS.

REFERENCES

Arondi, S., Baroni, P., Fogli, D., & Mussio, P. (2002). Supporting co-evolution of users and systems by the recognition of interaction patterns. In M. De Marsico, S. Levialdi, & E. Panizzi (Eds.), *Proceedings of the International Conference Advanced Visual Interfaces (AVI 2002)*, Trento, Italy (pp. 177-189). New York: ACM Press.

Balaban, M., Barzilay, E., & Elhadad, M. (2002). Abstraction as a means for end-user computing in creative applications. *IEEE Transactions on Systems, Man, and Cybernetics: Part A, 32*(6), 640-653.

Bødker, S., & Grønbæk, K. (1991). Cooperative prototyping: Users and designers in mutual activity. *International Journal of Man-Machine Studies, 34*(3), 453-478.

Bødker, S., Grønbæk, K., & Kyng, M. (1993). Cooperative design: Techniques and experiences from the Scandinavian scene. In D. Schuler & A. Namioka (Eds.), *Participatory design: Principles and practices* (pp. 157-175). Hillsdale, NJ: Lawrence Erlbaum Associates.

Bourguin, G., Derycke, A., & Tarby, J.C. (2001). Beyond the interface: Co-evolution inside interactive systems: A proposal founded on activity theory. In Blandford, Vanderdonckt, Gray (Eds.), *Proceedings of the IHM-HCI 2001 Conference*, Lille, France (pp. 297-310). Berlin, Germany: Springer-Verlag.

Brancheau, J.C., & Brown, C.V. (1993). The management of end-user computing: Status and directions. *ACM Computing Surveys, 25*(4), 437-482.

Brodie, C.B., & Hayes, C.C. (2002). DAISY: A decision support design methodology for complex: Experience-centered domains. *IEEE Transactions on Systems, Man, and Cybernetics: Part A, 32*(1), 50-71.

Burnett, M., Cook, C., & Rothermel, G. (2004). End-user software engineering. *Communications of the ACM, 47*(9), 53-58.

Button, G. (Ed.) (1993). *Technology in working order: Studies of work, interaction and technology.* New York: Routledge.

Carmien, S., Dawe, M., Fischer, G., Gorman, A., Kintsch, A., & Sullivan, J.F. (2005). Socio-technical environments supporting people with cognitive disabilities using public transportation. *ACM Transactions on Computer Human Interaction, 12*(2), 233-262.

Carrara, P., Fogli, D., Fresta, G., & Mussio, P. (2002). Toward overcoming culture, skill and situation hurdles in human-computer interaction. *International Journal Universal Access in the Information Society, 1*(4), 288-304.

Chaiklin, S., & Lave, J. (Eds.). (1993). *Understanding practice: Perspectives on activity and context.* Cambridge, MA: Cambridge University Press.

Costabile, M.F., Fogli, D., Fresta, G., Mussio, P., & Piccinno, A. (2004). Software environments for end user development and tailoring. *Psychology, 2*(1), 99-122.

Costabile, M.F., Fogli, D., Mussio, P., & Piccinno, A. (2005). A meta-design approach to end-user development. In *Proceedings of the IEEE Symposium on Visual Languages and Human-Centric Computing (VL/HCC'05)* (pp. 308-310). Dallas, Texas: IEEE Computer Society.

Costabile, M.F., Fogli, D., Mussio, P., & Piccinno, A. (2006a). End user development: The software shaping workshop approach. In H. Lieberman, F. Paternò, & V. Wulf. (Eds.), *End user development* (pp. 183-205). Dordrecht, The Netherlands: Springer.

Costabile, M.F., Fogli, D., Lanzilotti, R., Mussio, P., & Piccinno, A. (2006b). Supporting work practice through end user development environments. *Journal of Organizational and End User Computing, 18*(4), 43-65.

Costabile, M.F., Fogli, D., Marcante, A., & Piccinno, A. (2006c). Supporting interaction and co-evolution of users and systems. In A. Celentano & P. Mussio (Eds.), *Proceedings of the International Conference on Advanced Visual Interfaces (AVI 2006)*, Venice, Italy (pp. 143-150). New York: ACM Press.

Costabile, M.F., Fogli, D., Mussio, P., & Piccinno, A. (in press). Visual interactive systems for end-user development: A model-based design methodology. *IEEE Transactions on Systems, Men and Cybernetics: Part A.*

Cypher, A. (Ed.). (1993). *Watch what I do: Programming by demonstration.* Cambridge, MA: The MIT Press.

Engeström, Y., & Middleton, D. (Eds.). (1996). *Cognition and communication at work.* Cambridge: Cambridge University Press.

Fischer, G. (1998). Seeding, evolutionary growth, and reseeding: Constructing, capturing, and evolving knowledge in domain-oriented design environments. *Automated Software Engineering, 5*(4), 447-468.

Fischer, G. (2002). Beyond "couch potatoes": From consumers to designers and active contributors. *FirstMonday, 7*(12). Retrieved from http://firstmonday.org/issues/issue7_12/fischer/index.html

Fischer, G. (2006). Beyond binary choices: Understanding and exploiting trade-offs to enhance creativity. *First Monday, 11*(4). Retrieved from http://firstmonday.org/issues/issue11_4/fischer/index.html

Fischer, G., & Giaccardi, E. (2006). Meta-design: A framework for the future of end-user development. In H. Lieberman, F., Paternò, & V. Wulf (Eds.), *End user development* (pp. 427-457). Dordrecht, The Netherlands: Springer.

Fischer, G., Giaccardi, E., Ye, Y., Sutcliffe, A.G., & Mehandjiev, N. (2004). Meta-design: A manifesto for end user development. *Communications of the ACM, 47*(9), 33-37.

Folmer, E., van Welie, M., & Bosch, J. (2005). Bridging patterns: An approach to bridge gaps between SE and HCI. *Journal of Information and Software Technology, 48*(2), 69-89.

Goodwin, C., & Goodwin, M.H. (1997). Seeing as a situated activity: Formulating planes. In Y. Engeström & D. Middleton (Eds.), *Cognition and communication at work* (pp. 61-95). Cambridge, MA: Cambridge University Press.

Greenbaum, J., & Kyng, M. (Eds.). (1991). *Design at work.* Hillsdale, NJ: Lawrence Erlbaum Associates.

Hartson, H.R., & Hix, D. (1993). *Developing user interfaces: Ensuring usability through product & process.* New York: John Wiley.

Hayes, J.R. (1985). *Three problems in teaching general skills.* Hillsdale, NJ: Lawrence Erlbaum Associates.

Hughes, J.A., Randall, D., & Shapiro, D. (1992). Faltering from ethnography to design. In M. Mantel & R. Baecher (Eds.), *Proceedings of the International Conference on Computer-Supported Cooperative Work (CSCW'92)*, Toronto, Canada (pp. 115-122). New York: ACM Press.

Karasti, H. (2001). *Increasing sensitivity towards everyday work practice in system design.* Doctoral thesis, University of Oulu, Oulu.

Letondal, C., & Mackay, W.E. (2004). Participatory programming and the scope of mutual responsibility: Balancing scientific, design and software commitment. In A. Clement & P. Van den Besselaar (Eds.), *Proceedings of the 8th Conference on Participatory Design Conference (PDC 2004)*, Toronto, Canada (pp. 31-41). New York: ACM Press.

Lieberman, H. (2001). *Your wish is my command: Programming by example.* San Francisco: Morgan Kaufman.

Lieberman, H., Paternò, F., & Wulf, V. (2006). *End-user development* (Human-Computer Interaction Series, Vol. 9). Dordrecht, The Netherlands: Springer.

MacLean, A., Kathleen, C., Lövstrand, L., & Moran, T. (1990). User-tailorable systems: Pressing the issues with buttons. In J. Carrasco & J. Whiteside (Eds.), *Proceedings of ACM CHI'90*, Seattle, Washington (pp. 175-182). New York: ACM Press.

Myers, B.A., Hudson, S.E., & Randy, P. (2003). Past, present, and future of user interface software tools. In J. Carroll (Ed.), *Human-computer interaction in the new millennium* (pp. 213-233). New York: ACM Press.

Myers, B.A., Smith, D.C., & Horn, B. (1992). *Report of the "end-user programming" working group: Languages for developing user interfaces* (pp. 343-366). Boston: Jones and Bartlett.

Nardi, B., & Engeström, Y.A. (Guest Eds.). (1999). Web on the wind: The structure of invisible work. *Computer-Supported Cooperative Work, 8*(1-2), 1-8.

Nielsen, J. (1993). *Usability engineering.* San Diego, CA: Academic Press.

Penner, R.R., & Steinmetz, E.S. (2002). Model-based automation of the design of user interfaces to digital control systems. *IEEE Transactions on Systems, Man, and Cybernetics: Part A, 32*(1), 41-49.

Perlis, A. (1982). Epigrams on programming. *SIGPLAN Notices, 17*(9), 7-13.

Petre, M. (1995). Why looking isn't always seeing: Readership skills and graphical programming. *Communication of ACM, 38*(6), 33-44.

Polanyi, M. (1967). *The tacit dimension.* London: Rouledge & Kegan Paul.

Resnick, L.B., Saljo, R., Pontecorvo, C., & Burge, B. (Eds.). (1997). *Discourse, tools, and reasoning: Essays on situated cognition.* Berlin, Germany: Springer-Verlag.

Schön, D. (1983). *The reflective practitioner: How professionals think in action.* New York: Basic Books.

Shneiderman, B. (2002). *Leonardo's laptop: Human needs and the new computing technologies.* Cambridge, MA: MIT Press.

Schuler, D., & Namioka, A. (Eds.). (1993). *Participatory design: Principles and practices.* Hillsday, NJ: Lawrence Erlbaum Associates.

Stary, C. (2000). TADEUS: Seamless development of task-based and user-oriented interfaces. *IEEE Transactions on Systems, Man, and Cybernetics: Part A, 30*(5), 509-525.

Suchman, L., Blomberg, J., Orr, J., & Trigg, R. (1999). Reconstructing technologies as social practice. *American Behavioral Scientist, 43*(3), 392-408.

Suchman, L., & Trigg, R.H. (1991). Understanding practice: Video as a medium for reflection and design. In J. Greenbaum & M. Kyng (Eds.), *Design at work: Cooperative design of computer systems* (pp. 65-89). Hillsdale, NJ: Lawrence Erlbaum.

Sutcliffe, A., & Mehandjiev, M. (Guest Eds.). (2004). End-user development. *Communications of the ACM, 47*(9), 31-32.

Wegner, P., & Goldin, D. (2003). Computation beyond turing machines. *Communications of the ACM, 46*(4), 100-102.

Chapter X
Semantic Composition of Web Portal Components

Jens H. Weber-Jahnke
University of Victoria, Canada

Yury Bychkov
University of Victoria, Canada

David Dahlem
University of Victoria, Canada

Luay Kawasme
University of Victoria, Canada

ABSTRACT

Many recently emerging component-based Web portal application platforms allow end users to compose dynamic Web dialogues on the fly. Experts predict that this paradigm will enable a class of new applications for Web-based content delivery in information-rich, agile business domains, such as health care. We present a conceptual analysis of the user-based composition paradigm currently used and argue that its usability is limited with respect to complex, dynamic applications. To overcome these limitations, we present an alternative composition paradigm, which is based on a semantic model of a portal's application domain. We evaluate this approach with an application scenario in the health care domain.

INTRODUCTION

With much ambiguity, the term "Web portal" has been used for years to refer to Web sites that provide "starting points" (or "gateways") for Web users of a particular service infrastructure (e.g., MSN, AOL, Yahoo) or for users interested in a particular subject (e.g., investment, health care, technology).

Early Web portals were little more than frequently updated or database-driven Web pages and users had only very limited options for personalising the information content provided. Since then, portals have become increasingly customisable. Many current portal sites provide the means to personalise information content and to customise the way in which this content is rendered on the screen.

Recently, there has been an increasing trend of employing Web portals within organisations to provide a unified and personalised user interface for all relevant information content, and to facilitate collaboration in virtual enterprises. The metaphor of a digital "dashboard" has been coined to describe such intranet portals, which enable users to choose from a gallery of information components in order to customise their individual information delivery (Harmon, Conroy, Emory, & Macfarlane, 2000). A number of dedicated portal server technologies have been developed by software vendors such as Sun Microsystems, Microsoft, IBM, Bea, and the open source community. Such portal servers implement extensible frameworks for a new kind of software component. We will refer to these components as *Web portal components* (WPCs) in order to avoid vendor specific terminology such as Web parts (Baron, 2003), portlets (Buckner, Hesmer, Fischer, & Schuster, 2003), or modules (DNN, Rainbow) (Schultes, 2003).

An innovative feature of WPC technology is based on *end-user composition* of Web sites. Moreover, in some WPC models, users not only visually compose pages of WPCs with their Web browsers but they can also create connections between the interfaces of these components in order to let them exchange data. This feature carries great promise because it empowers users, in principle, to construct *integrated* forms based on WPCs.

While current WPC technology is satisfactory for simple applications and relatively static portal pages (i.e., pages that are largely predefined and modified infrequently), a number of problems arise with complex, more frequently modified portal applications. As an example for such an application,

we have been studying the Web based delivery of electronic medical record (EMR) services to health care professionals. The challenge in developing EMR applications consists of the large variety of potentially important information dialogues and forms. Moreover, physicians have different specialisations and preferences about their interaction with EMR information content. At first glance, WPC technology appears to be an ideal platform for building EMR applications, because it enables caregivers to compose personalised medical patient records. However, "on-the-fly" composition of WPC-based pages turns out to be difficult and error-prone in practice.

The main cause for this limitation is that WPC event interfaces are not semantically typed. This may result in a confusingly large number of technically possible event connections offered to the user during WPC composition. In this chapter, we present an approach to overcoming this limitation by associating semantic concepts with WPC event interfaces. This approach allows us to shift the WPC composition paradigm from the technology domain (which is unfamiliar to most end users) to the actual application domain of the portal user. Rather than creating event connections among WPCs, the user can simply specify a domain-specific *context information model,* which serves as input for creating the connections among WPCs.

The next section will discuss how the new WPC paradigm relates to other component technologies for the Web. In the third section, we conceptualise the event composition model in current WPC platforms and discuss its limitations for dynamic applications, in which end users frequently need to compose new portal pages on-the-fly. The fourth section represents the technical core of this chapter: we present an approach to facilitating end-user-driven composition of portal pages by moving the WPC composition paradigm from a technological level to a domain-oriented level. A case study for applying this approach is discussed in the fifth section. The final two sections close with a comparison of related work, evaluation, and conclusions about the current state of this research and future directions.

COMPONENT MODELS FOR THE WEB: WPC TECHNOLOGY IN PERSPECTIVE

The emergence of Web portal component models can be considered the most recent milestone in a timeline of standards introduced over the last decade for the purpose of constructing component-based software for Web-centric applications (cf. Figure 1). However, WPC components are significantly different from earlier component models with respect to the fact that they cross-cut layers of the classical three-tier architecture for Web-centric information systems (presentation, application, and data layer) (Vidgen, Avison, Wood, & Wood-Harper, 2002). Component models introduced earlier target specific layers, for example, the middle-tier (EJB, COM+, etc.) and the presentation layer (ActiveX, JavaBeans, etc.). Another remarkable feature of WPC technology is that it enables end-user-based component composition. The potential impact of this technology is immense and might revolutionise the way Web applications will be developed and used in the future.

Prior to the introduction of WPC platforms, there have been little fundamental changes to the way Web applications are engineered and used during the last decade. While languages and component frameworks have evolved over time, underlying methodologies have not changed drastically. Even the introduction of Web service standards (Ferris & Farrel, 2003) has earned much of its furor from the political buy-in of major vendors, rather than from conceptual innovations.

Microsoft has introduced the first WPC platform with their Digital Dashboard initiative (Harmon et al., 2000). WPC components are called *Web parts* in this architecture. More recently, the WebPart model has been integrated with the .Net component framework and is now supported by Microsoft's product *Sharepoint Portal Server*. Similar WPC platforms have been developed by the .Net open source community, for example, *DNN* and *Rainbow*. Vendors involved in Java technology have released comparable platforms for Java WPCs called *Portlets,* for example, IBM's *Websphere Portal Server and* Sun's *Java System Portal Server.* Recently, the Java Community Process (JCP) has generated the final release of the Java Specification Request "JSR 168" for standardising the WCP model for Java (Introduction to JSR, 2003). While there are individual differences and variations among these WPC platforms, they share the objective of creating a market for user-composable visual components in Web applications.

A Composition Model for Web Portal Components

We now present a conceptual model for the event-based composition of WPCs, which serves as a

Figure 1. Component models for Web-based software

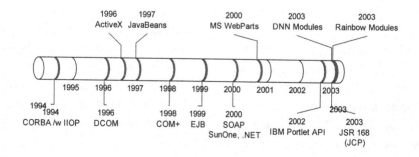

basis for our approach. While there are several technical development guides on how to implement WPCs for specific portal server platforms, there has been little systematic treatment of the common conceptual aspects of WPC models. In our research, we have concentrated on studying WPC component technologies that support event-based communication among components. In particular, we have concentrated on three specific technologies (Microsoft's *WebParts,* IBM's *Portlets,* and DNN's *Modules).*

All three platforms support event-based communication; however they vary with respect to technical details. To date, Microsoft's WebPart technology is arguably the most advanced, in that WebParts can exchange events on the client side in addition to the server-side events provided by all WPC models. The advantage of using client-side event communication is that it does not require a "post-back" operation involving the server, which

often causes undesired time delays during user interaction. Furthermore, WPC platforms differ with regard to the degree with which the data types of event payload are predefined. Microsoft's WebPart platform defines three standard data types for event payload, namely primitive values (cells), tuples of values (rows), and ordered relations (lists). The conceptual composition model shown in Figure 2 most closely reflects this WebPart platform. Still, it can also be realised based on the other WPC platforms mentioned in this section. However, these other platforms leave the definition of data types for event-based information exchange up to the portal developer.

The composition model in Figure 2 shows possible types of connections between outgoing event interfaces (event sources) and incoming interfaces (event sinks) belonging to different WPC components. Connections between event sources and sinks of the same physical data type are called

Figure 2. Composition model for Web portal components

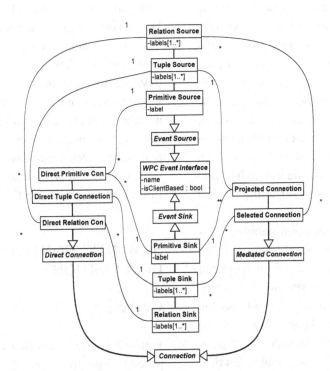

Direct Connections in this model. The right side of the model in Figure 2 shows that it is also possible to mediate between event sources and sinks of different types by using filter components implementing operations well known from the theory of relational algebra. For example, cell-sinks are connectable to tuple-sources by means of a *projection* operation (Projected Connection), and tuple-sinks can connect to relation-sinks through a selection operation (Selected Connection). Obviously, these operations can be nested to build more complex mediated connections that could be added to Figure 2. However, for reasons of simplicity, we do not consider such complex mediated connections in this chapter.

User-Driven WPC Composition: Criticism of the Current Paradigm

WPC platforms enable users to create connections between WPCs at runtime in an ad-hoc fashion using a Web browser. For this purpose, the browser would present to its user all possible (direct or mediated) connections for a given WPC. This set of possible connections can quickly become confusing for complex applications, for example, when composing a portal to enter electronic medical records. This is because event interfaces are not semantically typed with concepts from the application domain. Currently, semantics can be associated with event interfaces only informally, namely by giving human-understandable names to event sinks and sources (*labels*). This approach puts the cognitive load on the end user to interpret and match these labels and to select the desired connections.

We criticise this composition paradigm because it is error-prone and might require users to spend significant effort in configuring portal pages. Of course, the actual severity with which these drawbacks are perceived depends on the evolution frequency of portal pages. Users will be much more likely to accept the current composition paradigm if changes to the portal pages they compose are relatively rare. However, in more agile

domains (such as health care), portal users might frequently customise the information components and entry forms in their portal pages, for example, with respect to different patient treatment situations. In such cases, the cognitive load implied in the described WPC composition paradigm might become unacceptable.

Another problem is that the current WPC interface composition model is a *directed* one; that is, the user (who is typically not a software programmer) has to think in terms of event *sinks* and *sources* instead of just being able to decide that certain data entries in different components "should hold the same information." Besides being unnatural from a nonprogrammer's point of view, this directed approach to WPC composition also restricts the way users can interact with portal pages. For example, take a physician who composes a WPC-based page for examining and diagnosing a patient with particular symptoms. If the physician composes a patient encounter report based on three different examination forms (provided by a WPC component each), she should have to enter common data, such as the patient ID and symptoms, just once. Event connections can be used to propagate such contextual data among WPC components. However, the directed nature of the composition model described requires the physician to follow an implicit order when entering this information; that is, form components that act as data sources have to be filled out first. Having to think of this implicit order puts additional cognitive load on Web portal developers and users. We will now present an approach to overcoming the limitations addressed in this discussion.

SEMANTIC CONTEXT COMPOSITION

Overview

Figure 3 gives an overview of the approach proposed in order to lighten the cognitive load during

Figure 3. Semantic WPC composition: Overview

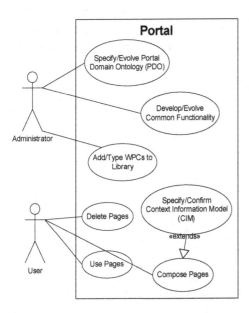

end-user-based WPC composition. In a nutshell, we employ a formal specification of the concepts in the application domain served by a particular portal, a so-called *Portal Domain Ontology* (PDO). The PDO is maintained by the portal administrator, in addition to normal activities, such as granting privileges for access control, maintaining WPC libraries, and evolving general portal functionality. Whenever the administrator adds WPCs to a library, the administrator ensures that their event interfaces are *semantically typed;* that is, they must be mapped to concepts in the PDO.

With this semantic knowledge about WPC component interfaces, the portal can provide end users with a simpler, more abstract composition paradigm, namely a paradigm that is grounded in the user's business domain. Composing portal pages in this new paradigm happens in two steps: first, the user selects the components to be presented on the page, and, second, the user associates a *Context Information Model* (CIM) with the composed portal page. Essentially, the CIM contains instances of the concepts in the PDO and relates them to the WPC

components chosen for the page. The information provided in the CIM is sufficient for the portal framework in order to generate the actual event connections between WPC interfaces.

The following subsections will provide a more detailed explanation of the approach sketched in this overview.

Portal Domain Ontology

An ontology is a predefined set of concepts, relationships among concepts, and constraints on those concepts that exist in a particular domain. Ontological specifications are meant to be shared. Their key benefit is to provide a common understanding and terminology for domains. Researchers and practitioners in the general area of knowledge engineering and specific disciplines, such as biology and medicine, have been using ontologies for many years. More recently, ontology engineering has increasingly been applied to software engineering, in particular for the purpose of business-to-business (B2B) data integration and the Semantic Web (McGuinnes, Fikes, Hendler, & Stein, 2002).

Many languages have been proposed for the formal specification of ontologies. In the areas of software engineering, W3C's standards proposal for the Ontology Web Language (OWL) arguably seems to have the best chances to achieve broad adoption (Heflin, 2004). The native representation of OWL specifications is textual, based on RDF (Resource Description Format) and XML. Such textual specifications are hard to comprehend and maintain. Therefore, our framework uses a graphical ontology development tool, *ezOWL,* which is based on Protege 2000 (Noy, Sintek, Decker, Crubezy, Fegerson, & Musen, 2001).

Figure 4 shows a simplified excerpt of a PDO for vision care, which could be used in a portal associated with a hospital department. Central conceptual abstractions are *entities* (e.g., persons, places, organisations, etc.), *acts* (e.g., observations, procedures), *roles* (e.g., nurses, patients), and *clinical documents* (e.g., cataract assessment, slit lamp examination). In addition to concept classes, ontologies can specify *properties,* which can be associated with concepts. To some extent, the notion of a property in ontologies resembles the notion of an attribute in object-oriented

specifications. In ontology languages such as OWL, however, the specification of properties, their semantics, domains, and ranges is significantly more expressive. A notable difference is, for example, that properties are defined independently

Figure 4. Portal domain ontology: Vision care (simplified)

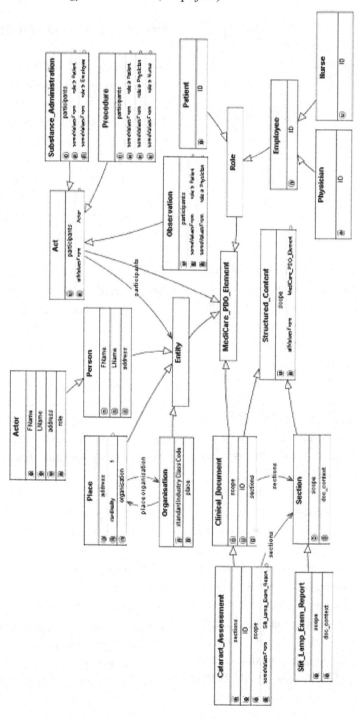

from the classes they are associated with. A full introduction to OWL is beyond the scope of this chapter. Therefore, we will restrict ourselves to explanations necessary for the purpose of gaining an intuitive understanding of Figure 4.

Inheritance relationships are rendered as arcs with large white arrow heads, whereas (instance) references are shown as arcs with small open arrow heads. References merely represent a special kind of property. Their range can be instances of classes as well as the concept classes themselves. Property *participants* of class Act is an example for an instance reference. While the base range of property *participants* covers all values (instances) of class *Entity*, its range has been restricted in class *Act* to values of class *Actor*. Further restrictions are shown in subclasses of *Act*. Note that in the ezOWL visualisation, inherited properties are repeatedly listed in subclasses.

We assume that the reader has an intuitive understanding of the concepts depicted in Figure 4 except, perhaps, for the part that deals with clinical documents. This part is based on the HL7 Clinical Document Architecture (CDA), which structures medical documents in terms of *sections* and *entries,* the latter not shown here. This model is based on the idea that the same type of section can appear in different types of documents; for example, the *slit lamp exam report* section can appear in documents other than a *cataract assessment.*

The part in Figure 4 that deals with clinical documents is most important from a portal administrator's point of view, because sections would be represented by WPC in the component library and clinical documents would be represented by portal pages composed by end users, such as physicians.

Semantic Typing of WPC Interfaces

With a PDO, it becomes possible for the administrator to attach semantic to interfaces of portal components. For simplification purposes, we will describe how this is done for primitive WPC interfaces only. The main idea is to attach to each (primitive) WPC interface a reference to a property of a PDO concept. Figure 5 illustrates this graphically by adding concepts for WPCs and their properties to the PDO from Figure 4. (Note that *Medicare_PDO_element* is the root concept in our PDO.) A primitive interface has now a semantic label consisting of two properties: PDO Element references a concept in the PDO and *Element property* references a property of this concept. Using the dot-shorthand to separate the two parts of a semantic label, an example would be "Patient.ID" for a WPC event interface that can accept or emit a patient identification.

Besides semantic typing, another notable feature of the model in Figure 5 is that it shows

Figure 5. Structure of semantic WPC interface

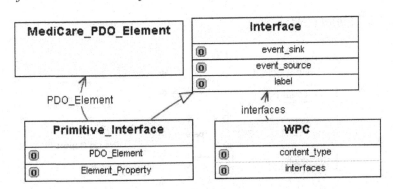

WPC interfaces as consisting of an event sink *and* an event source, rather than being a sink *or a* source, as modeled in current portal applications (cf. Figure 2). The reason for this way of modeling interfaces is to avoid the problem of enforcing a predefined order in which WPC components have to be arranged and filled out by the user (cf. discussion on directional composition in the User-Driven WPC Composition: Criticism of the Current Paradigm section).

Finally, we use the *content_type* property in Figure 5 to associate meaning with WPC components currently only informally. For example, the value of *content_type* for a WPC could be "Pre-Operative Assessment." It is, of course, possible and desirable to also use semantic typing for the content type of WPC components. In this case, property *content_type* became a reference to concepts contained in the *Structured Content* hierarchy in the PDO (Figure 4). For example, a given WPC could be typed as a *Slit Lamp Report* section .This further semantic typing would require a complete hierarchy of all possible content types for a given domain, which may not always be available.

Semantic WPC Composition

This section focuses on portal composition by end users. The semantic typing of WPC interfaces gives way to a composition paradigm that is more abstract (and easier to use) than the traditional connection-based programming described in the third section:

Rather than connecting syntactically-typed event sinks to event sources, the user completes a *Context Information Model,* which contains instances of domain concepts specified in the PDO. The following steps provide an overview on this user-centric component composition paradigm:

1. User creates a new page, selects and visually arranges WPCs to be displayed.
2. An initial CIM is generated automatically by instantiating PDO concepts according to the semantic types associated with the component interfaces chosen.
3. The user modifies the CIM identifying instances of PDO concepts that should be identical in the particular application context.
4. Interface connections among WPCs are generated automatically based on the refined CIM.
5. The user uses the new portal page and stores its configuration.

We will now elaborate on these steps. The first step is supported by standard functionality of current portal server platforms and does not require further explanation.

Automatic Construction of Initial CIM

The CIM is a relation between instances of PDO concepts and WPC components. In order to define the CIM more precisely, we denote the following conventions:

Figure 6. Example for initial CIM

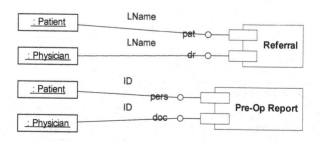

For a given portal P with PDO o, let *lib(P)* denote the set of all WPCs available in the component library of P. For any portal page p let *inst(p)* denote all component instances represented on p. Furthermore, for any component instance i⊠*inst(p)*, let *type(i)*⊠*lib(P)* denote the component (type) of i. Finally, let *inter(i)* denote the finite set of all interfaces of component i; each interface f⊠*inter(i)* is described by a tuple f:(l, e, a), where l is a string label, e is a concept specified in o, and a is a property of e.

Then we can define the initial CIM for a newly created page p as a finite relation defined as:

$$CIM(p) := \{(i, f) \mid i \in inst(p) \land c \in type(i) \land f \in inter(c)\}$$

Intuitively, an initial CIM relates component instances arranged on a portal page with instances of concepts in the corresponding PDO. As a simple example, let us assume that the user has arranged two WPC instances on a new portal page, the first (i_1) a "Referral" and the second (i_2) a "Pre-Operative Report". Let us further assume that both components have interfaces that reference a patient and a physician, for example:

inter(i_1)={(pat, Patient, LName), (dr, Physician, LName)}
inter(i_2)={(pers, Patient, ID), (doc, Physician, ID)}

In this case, the initial CIM for this new portal page will contain four instances of PDO concepts and two instances of WPC components, as shown on the left and right side of Figure 6.

Interactive Refinement of CIM

The initial CIM constructed in the previous step contains one instance of a PDO concept for each component instance interface. The purpose of the interactive refinement step is to specify which of these conceptual instances are in fact equivalent in the context of the page. In the above example, the user might want to specify that the referral document and the pre-op report are, in fact, dealing with the i patient. However, the referral was created by a physician different from the doctor who enters the pre-op report. In this case, the user would *fold* the two instances of concept *Patient*, which would result in the refined CIM in Figure 7. Formally, the refinement of a CIM m can be defined as an equivalence relation $\approx(m) \leq \prod_2(m) \times \prod_2(m)$, where $\prod_2$ denotes the relational projection on the second element of m.

Obviously, the user should only be allowed to merge operations that do not cause a contradiction with respect to the corresponding PDO. In order to formulate this restriction, we derive • as the set of equivalence classes, which is defined as:

$$\bullet(m) := \bigcup_{f \in \prod_2(m)} \left\{ x \mid (x, f) \in \approx^* (m) \lor (f, x) \in \approx^* (m) \right\}$$

Figure 7. Example of refined CIM

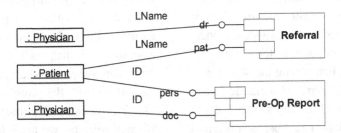

where $\approx^*(m)$ denotes the transitive closure over $\approx(m)$.

In order to avoid contradictions, we demand that

$$\forall k \in \bullet(m) : \exists c : \forall(l,e,a) \in k : \left(c \text{ isa } e \vee e \text{ isa c}\right) \wedge c \text{ has } a$$

, where "isa" and "has" are Boolean predicates; "isa" is true if and only if its first argument is a sub-concept of its second argument in the PDO; "has" is true if and only if its first argument is a concept that has its second argument as a property.

Generation of Event Connections

The conventional model for connections among WPCs is directional, as outlined in the third section. This means that any WPC event inter-face can function either as a source or a sink for events of a certain type. We have argued in the User-Driven WPC Composition: Criticism of the Current Paradigm section that this "directional" composition model limits the usability of portal applications in which pages are composed in an ad-hoc fashion. Our approach to resolving this issue is based on two ideas:

- **Symmetric interfaces:** WPCs for ad-hoc composition should be designed with sym-metric event interfaces for exchanging data with other WPCs. As shown in Figure 5, this means that there is a sink and a source for each event that carries application semantics. (Obviously, we do not consider housekeeping events such as redraw actions, etc.)
- **CIM blackboard:** Rather than connecting WPC event interfaces directly, we connect WPCs to a component that instantiates the CIM discussed earlier. This component functions as a "blackboard" for exchanging semantic information among the WPCs on a portal page. WPCs can post semantic data to the CIM blackboard as well as subscribe to changes to this data. This approach is based

on the idea or reactive tuple spaces (Cabri, Loeonardi, & Zambonelli, 1998).

Application Case Study

Health care is an agile environment with increasing demand to provide the right services at the right time with minimal user input. Health care professionals require efficient access to personalised Electronic Medical Records (EMRs) composed on-the-fly. At the outset, the idea of a digital "dashboard" for patient treatment cases sounds appealing because it enables users to customise the contents of their portal. However, offering a practical dashboard draws closer significant challenges to the average user, a clinician in our case, and to the designer of portal applications.

Together with domain experts, we have collab-oratively tested our approach with a case study from the vision health care field. Eye diseases and disorders vary from cases that require simple treat-ment with eye drops and patches to sophisticated surgeries. An example of a disease that requires a surgery is a cataract, which is a clouding of the eye's lens that causes loss of vision (National Eye Institute, 2006).

The large variety of diseases combined with individual specialisations of physicians impedes the development of a single, one-size-fits-all EMR application. Rather, a portal application that provides physicians with the ability to compose, organise, and link information based on "typical cases" appears more appropriate and powerful.

We will focus on one of these treatment cases, cataract, and illustrate our approach to customise a portal based on the underlying PDO. An ophthal-mologist might go through the following scenario when dealing with a new patient assessed with a cataract. First, the ophthalmologist performs an assessment of the patient's case. At this stage, the physician completes what is called an "Assessment Report," where the physician records the results of a few eye exams. For the purposes of simplicity we will refer to two tests: (a) a Corrected Vision

Figure 8. Initial and refined context information models

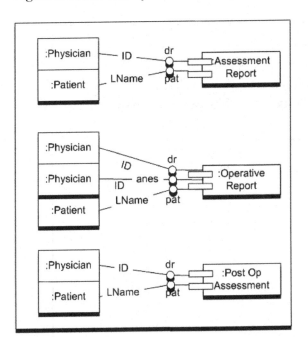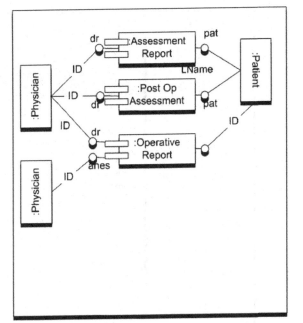

Test for each eye and (b) a Slit Lamp examination. Second, based on the assessment results, the ophthalmologist elects to perform a surgery, that is, cataract surgery, to one or both eyes. At this stage, the physician completes an "Operative Report," where the physician provides information about the surgery in addition to information about various participants in the surgery like the anaesthesiologist. Finally, after a successful completion of the surgery, the physician completes a "Post Operative Report," where the physician performs exams similar to the exams performed during the initial assessment phase.

In order for the physician to efficiently conduct work using information technology, the physician needs the ability to compose a patient EMR that will give access to the already-mentioned medical documents: Assessment Report, Operative Report, and Post-Operative Report. Additionally, the physician needs access to a library of exams that could be plugged into the medical report under consideration.

If we are using a portal application to realise the described functionality, the underlying PDO should provide the physician with the appropriate elements to compose the portal page. For example, the PDO for a vision health care application consists of a library of medical documents and exams. Each element in the library is available as a WPC that could be added to the portal and linked to other WPCs.

Once the physician selects those WPCs from the PDO, the system generates an initial CIM and displays a visual representation of all elements. The left side of Figure 8 illustrates the initial CIM of our case study. The initial CIM contains an Assessment Report, an Operative Report, and a Post-Op report. Each one of these elements is represented by a WPC on the portal page for this EMR. Also, the initial CIM contains three instances of the "Patient" concept. The physician can now refine the CIM by specifying that all instances of concept Patient refer to the same patient in this scenario. Hence, they are folded into one single instance.

Figure 9. Portal interaction

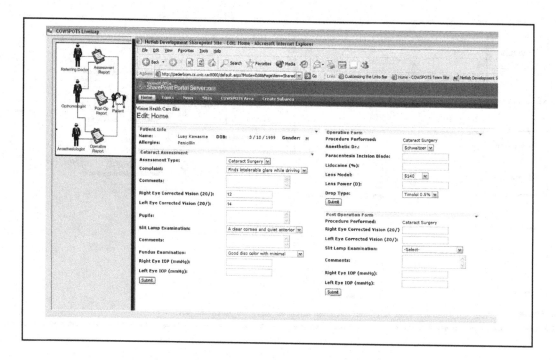

Additionally, the initial CIM generates five instances of the "Physician" concept. In this situation, the same ophthalmologist is in charge of all medical documents: Assessment, Operative, and Post-Op reports. Therefore, the user merges the three instances that are denoted with an "Ophthalmologist" link together. The other two "Physician" instances, the referring physician and the anaesthesiologist, represent different individuals in this situation. The right side of Figure 8 illustrates the final CIM after merging all the instances that refer to the same person. Note that the "Assessment Report" WPC and the "Post-Op Report" are linked to different instances of the "Corrected Vision Exam" element. This reflects the real life scenario because one of the exams is performed during the assessment phase while the other exam is performed after the completion of the surgery.

Figure 9 shows a screen capture of the actual sample application. For the purpose of customising the CIM, we have developed "smart browser"

that consists of a normal Web browser pane (right side) and a context customisation pane (left side). The context customisation pane is only necessary for the composition of new portal pages and can be hidden in case of portal page reuse.

EVALUATION

Since this work is still in the prototype stage and access to the domain experts is limited, an empirical evaluation of the usability of the new composition paradigm involving real clinicians cannot yet be undertaken. However, in the current section we will theoretically evaluate our approach using the well-known Cognitive Dimensions Framework (CDF) (Green, 1989).

The CDF has been developed for evaluating the usability of programming tools and systems (e.g., Kadoda, 2000). We have chosen CDF for this research mainly because, unlike many other usability evaluation tools, it is designed for nonspecialists and takes into account both the types of users working with the system and the environment it is being applied to. CDF examines a subject system with respect to 13 orthogonal concerns, that is, cognitive dimensions. We will now iterate through these concerns, describe them briefly, and use them to compare our approach to semantic Web portal composition with the traditional way of composing WPC components.

- **Abstraction gradient:** *What are the minimum and maximum levels of abstraction?* The traditional approach to composing Web portals uses three main kinds of abstractions: WPCs, WPC event interfaces, and portal pages. There are six different types of WPC event interfaces, namely primitive sinks, primitive sources, tuple sinks, tuple sources, relation sinks, and relation sources (cf. Figure 2). The only way new abstractions can be defined is by adding new WPCs to the component library. However, this is a complex activity, which involves a deep understanding of low-level programming techniques in the component framework architecture used (e.g., ASP.net, C#, MSQL, and SharePoint). This type of programming is not realistically considered doable for end users. Therefore, we may consider the number of abstractions in the traditional approach as fixed from the point of view of the end user. In our semantic composition approach, three kinds of abstractions exist: WPCs, portal pages, and domain concepts (defined within the PDO). Users can easily define new domain concepts by extending the PDO (e.g., using ezOwl). Users do not need to understand the different kinds of event interfaces. In particular, they do not have to worry about their directionality in terms of sources and sinks. WPC interface connections are generated automatically based on the user configuring domain instances in the CIM. Consequently, abstraction is higher and more extensible in our approach.

- **Closeness of mapping:** *Closeness of representation to domain.* In the traditional approach to portal composition, WPCs are the only abstractions that map close to the problem domain of the end user. For example, our case study contains WPCs for assessment reports, surgical reports, and so forth. Event interfaces, an important abstraction when it comes to portal composition, do not closely map to any end-user domain, posing significant cognitive load for portal composers. In our approach, WPCs and PDO concepts directly map to the end-user domain. Users do not directly have to deal with event interfaces during composition, reducing their cognitive load.

- **Consistency:** *Degree to which parts of the language can be inferred from other parts.* In traditional portal composition, there is a cognitive gap between the domain of WPCs (the end user's problem domain) and the domain of WPC interfaces (technical domain of event-based systems and data structures). This gap does not exist in the semantic composition approach. Users use the same concepts in the PDO as well as in the CIM. They stay on the level of the problem domain throughout the composition process. Therefore, the semantic approach to composition is more consistent.

- **Diffuseness:** *Number of symbols or graphical entities required to express the meaning.* The newly proposed semantic approach to composition is more diffuse since it uses additional graphical entities PDO concepts, instances of PDO concepts in the CIM. Still, all of these concepts map closely to the end user's domain knowledge. Therefore, we do not believe that this is a significant disadvantage.

- **Error-proneness:** *How likely are careless mistakes?* In the traditional approach, WPC interfaces are not semantically typed; for example, any (primitive, relation, tuple) event source can be connected to any (primitive, relation, tuple) event sink. It is easily possible to make semantic connection errors, for example, match a patient ID source with a clinician ID sink. Moreover, errors can be made with respect to the directionality of event connections, for example, cycles. The presented semantic approach is less error-prone with respect to careless mistakes in composing WPC pages since interfaces are semantically typed and users do not have to deal with directionality.

- **Hard mental operations:** *Are there places where the user needs to resort to fingers or penciled annotation to keep track of what is happening?* Hard mental operations may be necessary only for very complex and large portal pages that consist of many WPCs. In this case, the user of the traditional system may have to think deeply about how to connect event connections and how to design the event workflow. This operation is easier in the newly proposed solution, since the CIM provides an abstract representation of the concepts relevant in the composed portal page, and the user does not have to deal with setting up event connections manually.

- **Hidden dependencies:** *Is every dependency overtly indicated in both directions? Is the indication perceptual or only symbolic?* In the traditional approach, interface dependencies among WPC components are hidden from the user. The only way to make them visible is by inspecting them one by one. This is done by selecting a WPC on a browser page and invoking the interface context menu with the right mouse button. In the proposed semantic approach to composition, concrete interface dependencies are hidden in the same way. However, users do not need to understand them. It is sufficient to understand the abstract (domain-oriented) dependencies in the CIM, which are displayed as a graph.

- **Premature commitment:** *Do programmers have to make decisions before they have the information they need?* As argued earlier, the layout of WPCs on the portal page has ramifications on the wiring of the event connections and vice versa. This dependency may, in some cases, force users to prematurely commit to a specific interface wiring or layout. This dependency is not present in the semantic composition approach.

- **Progressive evaluation:** *Can a partially complete program be executed to obtain feedback on "How am I doing?"* The traditional composition approach has an advantage when it comes to progressive evaluation. Portal pages can be executed at any stage of the composition. This is also true for the semantic approach, except for cases where WPC components are deployed, where the interfaces have not yet been mapped to concepts in the PDO. (Of course, it would be possible to simply ignore these interfaces during portal execution.)

- **Role-expressiveness:** *Can the reader see how each component of a program relates to the whole?* There is no significant difference between the two approaches with respect to role-expressiveness.

- **Secondary notation:** *Can programmers use layout, color, or other cues to convey extra meaning?* Choosing appropriate identifiers for event interfaces and WPC components can be used as an informal way to convey semantics in the traditional approach. The same is possible using the semantic composition approach. Here, users do not deal with event interfaces directly; however, their names are exploited for deriving names of elements in the CIM.

- **Viscosity:** *Resistance to change.* We consider the following different categories of changes: (1) change to the visual layout of a portal page, (2) adding/removing WPCs to/from a page, (3) change to a WPCs realisation without impacting its interface, (4) change to a WPCs realisation impacting its interface, and (5) change to the end-user problem domain. In our approach, a change to the visual layout (Change category 1) does not have any impact on the functioning of the portal. In contrast, a visual layout change in the traditional approach may require further changes to event interface connections. The reason for this is the directionality of interface connections in the traditional approach. Users (in Western cultures) often fill out forms in an order influenced by their visual layout (top to bottom, left to right). Event sinks and sources should be connected in this direction to be able to propagate data between the WPCs that make up the form. If their visual arrangement is changed, the direction of these event connections should be changed to avoid counter-intuitive behaviour. This is not necessary in our approach, which has a lower viscosity to this category of change. A similar consideration is made for the second category of change (adding/deleting WPCs to/from portal pages). When a WPC is removed from a page using the traditional approach, its removal may cause a gap in a transitive event data propagation scheme, requiring changes to source/sink interface connections of the remaining WPCs. Moreover, adding a new WPC component to a page may change the page's layout causing further changes as described in category 1. Both effects are not present in our approach, leasing to lower viscosity in this category. Changes according to category 3 are fully encapsulated and the viscosity of both approaches is identical. Changes according to category 4 can be in one of four subcategories: (a) technical retyping of interfaces (e.g., the change from a primitive event interface to a tuple event interface); (b) adding event interfaces mapped to concepts existing in the PDO; (c) adding event interfaces mapped to

new concepts in the PDO; and (d) deleting event interfaces. The first subcategory of change requires end users to redefine interface connections in the traditional approach. This is not necessary in our approach, since end users deal with connections on a higher level of abstraction (domain concepts). The second subcategory of changes requires a change in the CIM only in those cases where the new WPC interface refers to a PDO concept not yet instantiated in the CIM. In the traditional approach, it always requires changes to interface connections. The third subcategory of changes (c) requires an extension of the PDO and the CIM in our approach vs. the definition of new interface connections in the traditional approach. The final subcategory of changes (d) requires changes only in the traditional approach according to the argument made for change category 1. In summary, the viscosity of the semantic approach to composition is lower than the traditional approach except for subcategory (c), in which case it may be higher, depending on the severity of the PDO update. Still, such updates should be rare.

- **Visibility and Juxtaposability:** *Ability to view components easily respectively to place any two components side by side.* Both the traditional approach and the semantic approach proposed in this chapter can visualise the graphical positioning of WPCs that reside on the same portal page. However, their event connections can only be visualised one connection at a time using a context menu invoked with the right mouse button. In addition to this, to semantic approach offers a graphical visualisation of the CIM that governs the wiring of any given portal page, resulting in a higher overall visibility.

In summary, the semantic composition approach described in this chapter has benefits in all but one cognitive dimension, namely *progressive evaluation*. This deficit can be compensated by allowing the execution of WPCs with semantically untyped event interfaces, that is, interfaces that have no mapping within the PDO. Moreover, the new approach exhibits higher viscosity with respect to a specific subcategory of changes, namely WPC additions that require the introduction of new concepts in the PDO. Still, we expect that once the PDO has gained some maturity, these types of changes will be rare. All other types of changes had lower viscosity in the new approach.

RELATED WORK

Our work combines two separate, but related areas of software engineering research, namely *component-based software composition* and *end-user programming*.

Two key problems in the area of component-based software are the definition of interfaces for reusable components and selection of an appropriate set of components needed to achieve the goal of the composition. Techniques various power and complexity have been developed to describe interfaces of components. These approaches range from abstract interface definition languages like the Balboa Interface Definition Language (BIDL) (Doucet, Shukla, Gupta, & Otsuka, 2002), over XML-based component description languages (Pahl & Ward, 2002) and logic-based specifications (Lammermann & Tyugu, 2001) to automata-based languages (de Alfaro & Henzinger, 2001) that also capture temporal aspects of component interfaces. While the goal of these techniques is to facilitate the composition of components, they generally require programming expertise and the knowledge of technical details and, as such, are not suitable for the end users. This issue started to be addressed with the emergence of the Semantic Web (W3C Semantic Web, 2001) paradigm. The use of ontologies to describe component interfaces allowed approaches (Fujii & Suda, 2004; Gomez, Han, Toma, Sapkota, & Garcia-Crespo, 2006; Medja-hed, Bouguettaya, & Elmagarmid, 2003) to make

interface descriptions understandable by humans and machine agents. This trend of semantically enriching component interfaces in order to facilitate their composition is now also being applied to the grid distributed computing environments (Pastore, 2007) and service-oriented architectures (Narayanan & McIlraith, 2002).

While many of the approaches referenced previously include algorithms for the component selection, this problem is outside the scope of our project, since we rely on the user's ability to select appropriate WPCs for a particular situation. It is important to note that the components we deal with in our research are mainly for the purpose of information content delivery and data input. In other words, they can primarily be characterised as data components, as opposed to computational components. As such, they comprise data-oriented interfaces involving very simple protocols only.

Several research and commercial projects leverage component composition concepts to promote end-user-initiated evolution of software systems. Won and Cremers (2002) describe the concept of interactive integrity checking in support end-user tailoring of component compositions. Integrity checks are used for ensuring the correctness of compositions and also to provide feedback information to end users on how to correct malformed component compositions. In our approach, a check-feedback-correction interaction is performed by the user who first uses a portal page.

Many workflow editors (e.g., Edge Diagrammed, 2006; VisiQuest, 2007) have been developed to allow non-expert users to develop end-to-end workflows by enabling user selection and composition of shared components. Congruent with our approach, Kim, Spraragen, and Gil (2004) seek to overcome problems associated with manual or user-directed component/workflow compositions by defining components in terms of a domain-specific ontology. The ontology is utilised as a means for evaluating the correctness of a component (or, more specifically, a workflow) composition and implicitly to support end-user comprehension of the workflows designed.

Similar to Won and Cremers (2002), the user is provided with information about how to correct malformed component compositions, which is not required with our approach. Our research has been influenced by advances in groupware technology. Our current prototypes for semantic portals are based on Microsoft Sharepoint 2003, a popular commercial groupware product. The CoCoWare .Net (Slagter & Hofte, 2002) project is designed to enable end-user-initiated adaptation of groupware interactions, based on component compositions. Such adaptations are accomplished by allowing end users to compose and extend the behaviour of the groupware system. To reduce the number of possible component interactions, the CoCoWare .Net architecture is limited to four groupware-specific component types. As in our approach, CoCoWare .Net users need not deal with low level details of building connections between components.

CONCLUSION AND RESEARCH DIRECTIONS

Information delivery and content management in dynamic, ad-hoc business domains such as health care have been recognised as a difficult challenge. The main problem behind the current poor adoption of EMR software is the high degree of variability of information content to be managed on a case-by-case basis. Web portal component (WPC) technology has great potential to address this problem, if it manages to provide end users with an efficient and easy way to compose pages from interacting WPC components. In this chapter, we have argued that the user-based component composition paradigm provided by current Web portal servers is too limited for applications that involve frequent changes to portal pages by end users. In fact, this argument is based on feedback we received from real domain experts using an early EMR portal application developed in our lab.

We have developed and presented an approach to overcoming this problem by shifting the compo-

sition paradigm to the actual application domain familiar to the end user. Therefore, it is fair to assume that the new composition paradigm will be more usable for our end users. We have successfully evaluated this assumption theoretically using the cognitive dimension framework. An empirical validation of this assumption that has statistical relevance will be difficult, though, since we currently have only limited access to domain experts (physicians). Our approach has been implemented in a prototype portal application in the domain of vision care. We are currently beginning to implement another portal application in a different health care domain (palliative care), since we have access to a larger group of test users. (We have started a collaborative research partnership with the Victoria Hospice Society.) Another future research focus will be on mechanisms supporting the evolution of portal domain ontologies with respect to existing portal pages and component libraries.

ACKNOWLEDGMENT

We would like to thank the anonymous reviewers of earlier versions of this chapter for their great support in helping us to improve its evaluation. We thank the National Science and Engineering Research Council (NSERC) for funding this research.

REFERENCES

Baron, A. (2003). *A developer's introduction to Web parts*. Retrieved August 10, 2007, from http://msdn. microsoft.com/library/

Buckner, T., Hesmer, S., Fischer, P., & Schuster, I. (2003). *Portlet development guide*. IBM. Retrieved August 10, 2007, from http://www-128. ibm.com/developerworks/websphere/zones/portal/portlet/portletdevelopmentguide.html

Cabri, G., Loeonardi, L., & Zambonelli, F. (1998). Reactive tuple spaces for mobile agent coordination. *LNCS, 1477*, 237-248. Springer.

de Alfaro, L., & Henzinger, T.A. (2001). Interface automata. In *Proceedings of the 8th European Software Engineering Conference held jointly with the 9th ACMSIGSOFT International Symposium on Foundations of Software Engineering,* Vienna, Austria (pp. 109-120). ACM Press.

Doucet, F., Shukla, S., Gupta, R., & Otsuka, M. (2002). An environment for dynamic component composition for efficient co-design. In *Proceedings of the Design, Automation, and Test in Europe Conference,* Paris (pp. 736-744). IEEE Computer Society.

Edge Diagrammed. (2006). Retrieved August 10, 2007, from http://www.pacestar.com/edge/

Ferris, C, & Farrel, J. (2003). What are Web services? *Communications of the ACM, 46*(6), 31-36.

Fujii, K., & Suda, T. (2004). Component service model with semantics (CoS-MoS): A new component model for dynamic service composition. In *Proceedings of the International Symposium on Applications and the Internet Workshops (SAINTW'04)* (pp. 321-327).

Gomez, J., Han, S.-K., Toma, I., Sapkota, B., & Garcia-Crespo, A. (2006). A semantically-enhanced component-based architecture for software composition. In *Proceedings of the International Multi-Conference on Computing in the Global Information Technology* (p. 43).

Green, T. (1989). Cognitive dimensions of notations. In *Proceedings of the HCI'89 Conference* (pp. 443-460). Cambridge University Press.

Harmon, B., Conroy, R., Emory, C, & Macfarlane, K. (2000). *Using digital dashboards.* Retrieved August 10, 2007, from http://www.microsoft.com/education/default.asp?ID=DigitalDashTutorial

Heflin, J. (2004). *OWL Web ontology language: Use cases and requirements.* World Wide Web Consortium. Retrieved August 10, 2007, from http://www.w3.org/TR/webont-req/

Introduction to JSR 168. (2003). *The Java Portlet specification.* Santa Clara, CA: Sun Microsystems.

Kadoda, G. (2000). A cognitive dimensions view of the differences between designers and users of theorem proving assistants. In *Proceedings of the 12th Annual Meeting of the Psychology of Programming Interest Group* (pp. 33-44).

Kim, J., Spraragen, M., & Gil, Y. (2004). An intelligent assistant for interactive workflow composition. In *Proceedings of the 9th International Conference on Intelligent User Interfaces,* Funchal, Portugal (pp. 125-135).

Lammermann, S., & Tyugu, E. (2001). A specification logic for dynamic composition of services. In *Proceedings of the Distributed Computing Systems Workshop, 2001 International Conference,* Mesa, Arizona, USA (pp. 157-162).

McGuinnes, D.L., Fikes, R., Hendler, J., & Stein, L.A. (2002). DAML+OIL: An ontology language for the semantic Web. *IEEE Intelligent Systems, 17*(5), 72-80.

Medjahed, B., Bouguettaya, A., & Elmagarmid, A.K. (2003). Composing Web services on the semantic Web. *The International Journal on Very Large Data Bases, 12*(A), 333-351.

Microsoft Sharepoint. (2003). Retrieved August 10, 2007, from http://www.microsoft.com/sharepoint

Narayanan, S., & Mcllraith, S.A. (2002). Simulation, verification and automated composition of Web services. In *Proceedings of the 11th International Conference on World Wide Web,* Honolulu, Hawaii (pp. 77-88).

National Eye Institute Resource Guide. (2006). Retrieved August 10, 2007, from http://www.nei.nih.gov/health

Noy, N.F., Sintek, M., Decker, S., Crubezy, M., Fegerson, R.W., & Musen, MA. (2001). Creating Semantic Web contents with Protege-2000. *IEEE Intelligent Systems, 16*(2), 60-71.

Pahl, C., & Ward, D. (2002). Towards a component composition and interaction architecture for the Web. *Electronic Notes in Theoretical Computer Science, 65*(A).

Pastore, S. (2007) Introducing semantic technologies in Web services-based application discovery within grid environments. In *Proceedings of the Fourth European Conference on Universal Multiservice Networks* (pp. 22-31).

Schultes, S. (2003). Create a Web portal module. *Visual Studio Magazine,* 13(14).

Slagter, R., & Hofte, H.T. (2002). *End-user composition of groupware behaviour: The CoCoWare .NET architecture.* Telematica Instituut. Retrieved August 10, 2007, from http://www.telin.nl/project. cfm?language=en&id=241

Vidgen, R., Avison, D., Wood, B., & Wood-Harper, T. (2002). *Developing Web information systems.* Butterworth-Heinemann.

VisiQuest. (2007). Retrieved August 10, 2007, from http://www.accusoft.com/products/visiquest/

W3C Semantic Web. (2001). Retrieved August 10, 2007, from http://www.w3.org/2001/sw/

Won, M., & Cremers, A.B. (2002). Supporting end-user tailoring of component-based software: Checking integrity of composition (TRNumber CLIP4/02.0) In *Proceedings of the Colognet,* Madrid, Spain.

Chapter XI
Privacy Statements as a Means of Uncertainty Reduction in WWW Interactions

Irene Pollach
Vienna University of Economics and Business Administration, Austria

ABSTRACT

Grounded in uncertainty reduction theory, the present study analyzes the content of 50 privacy policies from well-known commercial Web sites with a view to identifying starting points for improving the quality of online privacy policies. Drawing on traditional content analysis and computer-assisted textual analysis, the study shows that privacy policies often omit essential information and fail to communicate data handling practices in a transparent manner. To reduce Internet users' uncertainty about data handling practices and to help companies build stable relationships with users, privacy policies need to explain not only the data collection and sharing practices a company engages in but also those practices in which companies do not engage. Further, more exact lexical choice in privacy policies would increase the transparency of data handling practices and, therefore, user trust in World Wide Web (WWW) interactions. The results also call for less verbose texts and alternatives to the current narrative presentation format.

INTRODUCTION

The growth of information technology and its enhanced capacity for data mining have given rise to privacy issues for decades (Mason, 1986). The advent of the Internet and its unprecedented opportunities for communication, community building, commerce, and information retrieval have exacerbated this problem. Online retailers can track users' site behavior in order to create user profiles, enhance the functionality of their Web sites, and target offerings to customers on subsequent Web site visits (Caudill & Murphy, 2000). Although online retailers might use the information they obtain about visitors and customers solely to increase the system's convenience, they may misuse it as well to harass users with personalized advertising material or to pass on user information to third parties (Sama & Shoaf, 2002).

The same information practices that provide value to companies may raise privacy concerns among Internet users (Culnan & Armstrong, 1999). It is the asymmetric information between companies as data collectors and users as data providers coupled with the lack of user control over data collection that causes mistrust and concerns about electronic privacy (Reagle & Cranor, 1999), including, for example, identity theft or the receipt of unsolicited e-mails (Baumer et al., 2004). The most pervasive concern among users is that their information is used for purposes other than those for which it was collected (Turner & Dasgupta, 2003). Over the past decade, media coverage of consumer privacy issues has increased dramatically (Roznowski, 2003). Several highly publicized privacy breaches in recent years have sensitized and alerted the general public to potential data misuse. Cases in point of such incidents include Internet advertiser DoubleClick, which matched anonymous user profiles with personally identifying information and sold these data (Charters, 2002), and RealJukeBox, which collected personally identifying information, including musical preferences, matched it with the musical files that users had on their PCs, and sold these data (Turner & Dasgupta, 2003).

In view of these threats to information privacy, the winning companies in electronic commerce will be those who understand and respond to people's privacy concerns (Luo & Seyedian, 2004). Corporate privacy policies are capable of dispelling users' fears about privacy infringements by detailing when and how a company collects data. Given that users have been found to have more trust in privacy policies that they perceive as comprehensible (Milne & Culnan, 2004), companies might be able to build trusting

relationships with Internet users, if they manage to communicate their data handling practices in a clear and concise manner on their Web sites.

Grounded in Uncertainty Reduction Theory (Berger & Calabrese, 1975), the purpose of this article is to identify shortcomings of online privacy policies and to suggest ways of improving them with a view to easing people's concerns about data handling practices. More precisely, the article looks at the content of online privacy policies, examining systematically what data handling practices companies engage in, which ones they do not engage in, and whether they fail to address important areas of concern. The findings of this analysis together with the findings from a computer-assisted textual analysis provide starting points for enhancing the effectiveness of privacy policies as vehicles for uncertainty reduction in WWW interactions.

This article is divided into six sections. The first section reviews the relevant literature, the second describes the theoretical grounding, and the third focuses on the methodology. The following two sections present the findings of a content analysis and a computer-assisted textual analysis, respectively. Ultimately, the sixth section discusses the implications of the findings for practice and explores avenues for future research.

PRIVACY IN THE INTERNET AGE

Privacy is commonly defined as the right to be left alone (Turner & Dasgupta, 2003). Data privacy is understood as people's right to control information about themselves (Mason et al., 1995) and to control how others use it (Shaw, 2003). The concept of data privacy has become a major obstacle to the success of electronic business models, as the Internet has made it technically easier for companies to gather and disseminate personal, demographic, and behavioral consumer data (Dhillon & Moores, 2001). Although consumers may benefit from the collection of their data with improved customer service and personalized offerings, they may not want these personalized services to be imposed on them and actually may prefer data privacy to personalized offerings (Stead & Gilbert, 2001; Maury & Kleiner, 2002). This section discusses data collection methods on the Internet, the nature of people's privacy concerns, and the usefulness of privacy policies and other remedies against privacy concerns.

Data Collection on the Internet

The primary tool for data collection on the WWW is cookie files, which Web sites place on users' PCs. Every time a user connects to the site, the browser checks the cookies on the hard drive and uploads the cookie, if it matches the site's URL. Web sites place cookies to collect click-stream information when users navigate the site, personalize offerings, record purchases, target advertisements to users, and, most importantly, to eliminate the need for users to re-enter their names and passwords. Users could disable cookies, but usually this means that they do not have access to all features of a Web site anymore (Cunningham, 2002; Szewczak, 2002). However, Whitman, et al. (2001) have shown that Web users are largely unaware of the placement of cookies, which calls for more transparency as to the purpose and methods of data collection.

Another way of collecting user data on the Internet is Web beacons, also referred to as Web bugs, pixel tags, or clear GIFs. These transparent, single-pixel graphics are used to track users' site activities, to monitor how often an e-mail is read and forwarded, and to collect the Internet protocol (IP) address of the e-mail recipient. Web beacons and cookies can be synchronized to a particular e-mail address, allowing a Web site to identify people when they return to the site. Unlike cookies, Web beacons cannot be disabled or filtered and, thus, represent an even greater threat to privacy than cookies (Kay, 2004; Harding et al., 2001).

User Privacy Concerns

Users' information privacy concerns relate primarily to data collection, improper access to personal data, unauthorized secondary use of personal data, data sharing, and unsolicited marketing communications (Miyazaki & Fernandez, 2000; Smith et al., 1996). The nature of Internet users' privacy concerns has been explored in numerous academic studies, focusing on consumers' willingness to provide personal information to marketers (Phelps et al., 2000), their awareness of privacy protection strategies in direct marketing (Dommeyer & Gross, 2003), and the determinants of consumer trust in corporate data handling practices (Schoenbachler & Gordon, 2002). Further, previous research has looked at the impact of perceived privacy invasions on Internet users' online purchasing behaviors (Brown & Muchira, 2004), the implications of privacy concerns for customer relationship management (Fletcher, 2003), and the extent to which major privacy concerns have been incorporated into the Federal Trade Commission's privacy principles (Sheehan & Hoy, 2000).

In particular, online users have been found to have different thresholds toward information privacy and thus perceive potential privacy invasions with different levels of intensity (Culnan, 1993; Mitchell, 2003; Sheehan, 2002; Treiblmaier et al., 2004).) They are rather unconcerned about the collection of aggregate information but fear that companies misuse personally identifying information and share it with third parties or send unsolicited commercial e-mails to users (Han & Maclaurin, 2002). Therefore, users are more likely to provide information when they are not identified (Cranor et al., 1999). The reputation and trustworthiness of online merchants thus play an important role when consumers decide whether or not to divulge personally identifying information (Belanger et al., 2002). Stewart and Segars (2002) have tested a model of consumer concern for information privacy and found that people want more control over their personally identifying information. Similarly, Graeff and Harmon (2002) report that consumers who make purchases over the Internet are less concerned about information privacy than those who do not, but both groups have the desire to be better informed about data handling practices.

Olivero and Lunt (2004) found that users' risk awareness raises the demand for control and rewards. Because of their lack of control, consumers tend to provide false information, disable cookies, or abort transactions altogether when they are required to enter personal data (Eirinaki & Vazirgiannis, 2003; Milne & Boza, 1999). Hagel and Rayport (1997) hold that this unwillingness to divulge personally identifying information stems from people's perceptions that companies make use of the data they obtain but do not provide users with benefits in return. Such benefits may include better customer relationship management or refined products and services (Danna & Gandy, 2002). However, users have been found to be willing to make trade-offs and exchange personal information for benefits that are clearly visible. Monetary rewards, in particular, have been found to raise users' willingness to divulge personally identifiable information (Teo et al., 2004). This runs counter to the findings of Andrade et al. (2002), who report that solid corporate reputations and complete privacy policies decrease people's concerns about data privacy, whereas offering a reward in exchange for data intensifies people's concerns.

Privacy Policies

In the past few years, privacy policies on commercial Web sites have become *de rigueur*. In 1997, comprehensive privacy policies were still the exception rather than the rule, even among large corporations (Messmer, 1997). Two U.S. Federal Trade Commission Surveys and the Georgetown Internet Privacy Policy Survey have revealed that the percentage of Web sites disclosing their privacy practices was 14% in 1998 (Federal Trade Commission, 1998), 66% in 1999 (Culnan, 1999), and 88% in 2000 (Federal Trade Commission, 2000), indicating that companies seem to prefer self-regulation to legislation and have begun to disclose their privacy policies voluntarily before they were required to do so by law.

Privacy policies are capable of increasing user knowledge about data collection and dispelling users' fears about privacy infringements by detailing how data are collected and for what they are used. A problem inherent in privacy policies, however, is the paradox situation that data may have already been collected before users are able to access the privacy policy and learn when data are collected. Anther shortcoming of privacy policies is that users have no means to check whether companies fulfill the privacy commitments they make in their policies (Presler-Marshall, 2000). The dynamic nature of the WWW makes it particularly difficult for companies to comply with their own privacy policies. Every time a company adds new features, it risks invading users' privacy or violating its own privacy policy. Similar problems arise when companies have co-branded Web sites or when content and images are delivered by third parties, who collect data governed by their own privacy policies (Lynch, 2004).

Previous studies on privacy policies have examined the extent to which they address the U.S. Federal Trade Commission's privacy dimensions (Liu & Arnett, 2002; O'Connor, 2003; Ryker et al., 2002), the presence or absence of information on data collection and data sharing (Miyazaki & Fernandez, 2000), the evolution of online privacy disclosures posted by U.S. companies (Milne & Culnan, 2002), and cultural differences among privacy policies posted by companies in different countries (Johnson-Page & Thatcher, 2001).

Milne and Culnan's (2004) survey of when and why consumers read privacy policies reveals that Internet users read privacy policies to manage risk but are more likely to read them if they perceive them as comprehensible. In this case, they are also more likely to trust them. In general, the survey respondents indicated that they found privacy statements to be too long, too verbose, too legalistic, and all the same. The study also reports that consumers tend not to read privacy policies when they have prior experience with a company. These findings suggest that privacy policies are an important trust-building vehicle in initial interactions between companies and users. Therefore, improving their quality is a worthwhile effort that may result in stable relationships.

Additional Remedies Against Privacy Concerns

To enhance user trust in privacy practices, self-regulatory privacy certification schemes have emerged. These certification programs audit privacy practices in exchange for a fee and allow Web sites to display a privacy seal (trustmark), if their practices adhere to the program's guidelines (Sinrod, 2001). The two most prominent examples include seal pioneer TRUSTe, founded by the Electronic Frontier Foundation and CommerceNet (Cranor, 1998) and the Better Business Bureau's privacy seal BBBOnline (BBBOnline, 2004). Clearly, there is an inherent conflict of interest in paid third-party certification, as the certifying institutions are obviously interested in adding seals but might be reluctant to remove seals from sites that do not comply. The display of such a seal of approval may add trustworthiness and credibility to corporate Web sites, suggesting that the company is willing to have its privacy practices audited (Benassi, 1999). Miyazaki and Krishnamurthy (2002) examined the effectiveness of privacy seals and found that even the mere display of a trustmark increases user trust. Similarly, Nöteberg, et al. (2003) conclude that privacy seals have a significant effect when a company is not well known but are unnecessary for high-reputation companies.

Another attempt to make data collection and sharing more transparent is the Platform for Privacy Preferences (P3P) launched in 1997 by the World Wide Web Consortium in an attempt to give users more control over their own data (World Wide Web Consortium, 2003). The P3P privacy technology saves users the need to read online privacy policies, as P3P-enabled Web browsers compare privacy policies in the P3P format against users' preset privacy preferences when they enter a site, and determines whether a Web site's privacy policy reflects their personal wishes for privacy (Presler-Marshall, 2000). If implemented correctly, P3P theoretically renders it unnecessary for users to read privacy policies, as the browser notifies users in case of inconsistencies (Reagle & Cranor, 1999). As of 2003, only 10% of Web sites had P3P-based privacy policies (Cranor et al., 2003).

Reasons for its slow adoption include unresolved legal issues and the fact that companies find it hard to squeeze their complicated privacy policies into the more straightforward P3P scheme (Thibodeau, 2002). However, companies using P3P may project the image of an organization willing to make an investment of time and resources to increase the transparency of its data handling practices (Turner & Dasgupta, 2003). But, like conventional privacy policies, users with P3P-enabled Web browsers still cannot be sure whether companies adhere to what they state in their P3P privacy policies (Delaney et al., 2003). An additional hurdle is that users still are reluctant to fill out a form and set their privacy preferences in order to activate P3P (Ghosh, 2001). Thus, for the time being, privacy policies still have to be read by humans rather than Web browsers, and so their quality is critical to users' trust in Web sites.

THEORETICAL FOUNDATION

Originally put forward by Berger and Calabrese (1975), uncertainty reduction theory (URT) provides the framework for this study. Based on the

Table 1. Information-gathering strategies of Internet users and companies

Strategies	Users	Companies
Passive	Browsing Web site, Reading privacy policy	Cookies, Web beacons
Active	Consumer-to-consumer interaction (off-line or online)	Acquiring customer information from third parties
Interactive	E-mails, Feedback forms	Site registration, Surveys/feedback

notions that (1) humans have an innate need to reduce uncertainty about themselves and others and (2) they prefer predictable relationships with others, URT posits that reducing uncertainty by sharing social information is crucial to developing stable relationships (Berger, 1979; Berger & Bradac, 1982; Berger & Calabrese, 1975). Uncertainty is defined as a cognitive state resulting from an individual's assessment of the number of alternative predictions available for a stranger's future behavior" (Bradac, 2001, p. 464). This uncertainty in a relationship is perceived as unpleasant and motivates people to seek information about others (i.e., social information) to increase the predictability of their behavior in interactions. High levels of uncertainty in a relationship lead to low levels of self-disclosure and prompt information-seeking behavior. Thus, in initial interactions, both interactants in a relationship seek information about each other. Basically, people use three different strategies to gather social information about others: passive (observation from afar), active (acquisition of information from third parties), and interactive (direct contact) (Berger & Bradac, 1982). But only if both interactants are willing to divulge information about themselves can a relationship be built. In order for a stable relationship to develop, the amount of information disclosed to an interactant needs to correspond to the amount of information received from that interactant (Cragan & Shields, 1998).

URT has been applied to relationships in a variety of contexts, including organizational communication (Kramer, 1993), cross-cultural communication (Gudykunst et al., 1985; Hammer

& Martin, 1992; Olaniran & Williams, 1995), and computer-mediated communication (Grabowski & Roberts, 1998). It is also well suited as a framework for examining the usefulness of privacy policies for reducing Internet users' uncertainties about data privacy, since users have been found to read privacy policies to manage risk (Milne & Culnan, 2004). In WWW interactions between users and companies, both participants have the means to collect information about their business partners actively, passively, or interactively, as outlined in Table 1. Users may access company information on the company's Web site (passive), obtain information about the company from other customers (active), or contact the company directly via e-mail or feedback forms (interactive). To collect information on users, companies may employ cookies and Web beacons, acquire information from third parties (e.g., credit agencies, information brokers) or ask users for personal information when they register with the site or complete surveys and feedback forms.

Thus, users provide data to companies either consciously (e.g., when they order goods or complete surveys) or unconsciously (e.g., when their navigation behavior on the site is tracked). Companies collect these types of data not only to handle orders but also to improve and customize their Web sites and their products with a view to strengthening customer relationships. As illustrated in Figure 1, companies disclosing their data handling practices in the form of privacy policies may reduce users' uncertainties about data privacy. If companies communicate data handling practices in an unequivocal manner and

Figure 1. Data privacy and uncertainty reduction

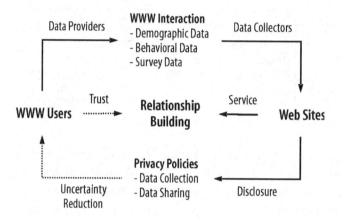

comply with what they stipulate in their policies, their data handling behavior is predictable, which may help them to build trusting relationships with users. Once a relationship of trust has been established between users and companies, users may be more willing to divulge personal information, which may lead to even more enhanced customer service, more customized Web sites, and eventually customer loyalty.

METHODOLOGY

To examine systematically (1) what data handling practices companies engage in, (2) which ones they do not engage in, and (3) whether they fail to address important areas of concern to users, a content analysis of privacy policies was conducted to scrutinize their content in a systematic manner, taking into account both what is in a text and what is not. Further, a computer-assisted textual analysis was performed to uncover lexical patterns that raise rather than reduce the level of uncertainty in privacy policies.

Sampling

The privacy policies of 50 well-known Web sites were used for the analysis (see Appendix A). This

sample size compares favorably with other content analysis studies (Daly et al., 2004; Döring, 2002; Kolbe & Burnett, 1991; O'Connor, 2003; Ryker et al., 2002). All Web sites included in the sample collect personally identifiable information when users register with the site or place orders. While being essentially a convenience sample, the selected privacy policies stem from companies covering a broad spectrum of business models and industries. They include companies selling goods and providers of services; pure e-brands and off-line brands with online outlets; and B2C online stores and C2C auctions. Also, they belong to four different industries, including retail, travel, Internet services, and news. This sampling method was adopted to ensure the inclusion of a diverse range of businesses to which WWW interactions are vital. However, the sample was not intended to be representative of commercial Web sites, as the purpose of this study was to identify starting points for improving existing privacy policies.

The sample companies were chosen on the basis of their commercial success, as successful Web sites were assumed to serve as lead innovators for other Web sites. The companies in the Retail category were taken from the top-performing companies of *Store* magazine's ranking of the most successful Internet retailers (Reda, 2000), ignoring Web sites of conglomerates, those co-branded on Amazon.com, and those not available at the time of data collection. The companies included in the Travel category were identified as successful travel sites by the business press (Ebenkamp, 2002; Forrester Research, 2002). The Web sites in the News and Internet Services categories were selected intuitively in an attempt to choose the most well-known Web sites in these industries. The sample contains a subsample of 19 companies that display one or more privacy seals and, henceforth, are referred to as *seal companies*.

Methods of Analysis

To analyze and compare what data handling practices the sample companies engaged in or did not engage in, a content analysis of the 50 privacy policies was conducted. The goal of content analyses was to examine message characteristics in an objective manner by applying consistent criteria rigorously (Neuendorf, 2002). The documents analyzed represent how the writer "naturally presents or projects itself to its normal audience, rather than to a researcher" (Kabanoff, 1996, p. 6). Essentially, content analysis reduces data by categorizing content into predefined categories, thereby quantifying qualitative data. The results obtained from content analyses are quantitative indices of textual content and, thus, categorical and descriptive in nature. They show not only what is in a text but also what is not (Kolbe & Burnett, 1991). Other analytic approaches, such as discourse analysis or critical theory, concentrate on what is said and how it is said but do not systematically assess what is not said (Lacity & Janson, 1994). Content analysis was chosen for this study, because its major strengths (i.e., the systematic analysis of textual data and the unobtrusive examination of naturally occurring data) prevent biases in the collection and analysis of the data.

To facilitate the analysis, each privacy policy was saved as a text file and as an image file to preserve the original layout. Together, the privacy policies of the 50 Web sites contained 108,570 words, with document lengths varying from 575 to 6,139 words. In a pilot study of the four longest privacy policies in the sample, a coding frame (see Appendix B) was developed, based on an inductive coding strategy applied to these four documents. Inductive coding refers to the close and thorough study of documents in an unrestricted manner to open up the inquiry and to identify relevant categories that fit the data (Strauss & Corbin, 1990). These inductively derived codes were factual rather than referential in nature. Factual codes condense the information contained in a text by denoting precisely defined facts, whereas referential codes represent only themes in a text (Kelle & Laurie, 1995). In this study, the factual codes referred to countable features or were closed-ended questions referring to data handling practices with the code values *yes*, *no*, or *no answer*.

After a pilot coding of five other privacy policies and subsequent amendments to the coding sheet, the coding frame consisted of 35 questions pertaining to general characteristics (11 codes), data collection (15 codes), marketing communications (one code), and data sharing (eight codes). The coding was based on the at-least-some rule, which considers practices true, even if they are carried out only occasionally. All 50 privacy statements were coded by the author in July 2003. Of the 35 questions applied to the 50 privacy policies, no answers were found to 22.86% of these questions; thus, their code values were *no answer*. This level was 19.55% for the seal companies and 24.88% for non-seal companies. Taking into account only those 24 questions focusing on specific data handling practices (see codes 12-35, Appendix B), these levels were 33.33% for the total sample, 28.51% for the seal companies, and 36.29% for the non-seal companies.

Clearly, the type of metric used has a bearing on the types of analyses that may be conducted (Bauer, 2000). The nominal scales used in the coding procedure achieve higher accuracy than ordinal scales, since the former do not require human judgment and interpretation, thus rendering the use of a second coder unnecessary. As a check on intracoder reliability and consistency (Bauer, 2000; Stempel & Wesley, 1981), all texts were recoded in August 2003 to eliminate the possibility of error. The agreement between the two codings was 98.71%.

Content analysis examines a text only in light of the questions included in the coding frame. However, since content analysis should not only be concerned with what a text is about but also with its vocabulary and, in particular, lexical patterns in the text corpus (Bauer, 2000), a word frequency list of the total text corpus was created to identify words of potential interest and to uncover patterns that otherwise may not be obvious (Wolfe et al., 1993). The most frequent words in a corpus were a clear indicator of those concepts and ideas that received special attention in the text (Krippendorff, 1980). The word frequency list was calculated with WordSmith Tools, a software tool for textual analysis. The initial list of 4,016 different words (representing 108,570 running words) was lemmatized automatically to remove inflectional suffixes (e.g., plural endings, -*ing* forms) and to separate contracted verb forms. In addition, all words of less than three letters and all words appearing only once were eliminated, as they were considered insignificant to the content of a text (Lebart et al., 1998). For the same reason, all grammatical words (e.g., the auxiliary verbs *be* and *have*, articles, conjunctions, prepositions), numbers, names (e.g., for cities, states, companies, months), and Internet domain extensions were excluded. The elimination of all non-content words produced a list of 1,637 content words, representing 52.15% of the running words.

This list was then used for the computer-assisted textual analysis. Typically, such frequency counts are subject to distortions. For one, words may have multiple meanings (polysemy), and for another, authors deliberately may vary the terms they use when they refer to the same concept (synonymy) (Weber, 1985). Therefore, frequency counts require human interpretation, which can be facilitated by keyword-in-context (KWIC) lists. These lists show all instances of a certain word in their immediate contexts, thus helping to identify lexical patterns (Stubbs, 2001).

RESULTS OF THE CONTENT ANALYSIS

General Characteristics

On average, a privacy policy consists of 1.12 Web pages and 2,157 words. Ninety percent of the privacy policies are accessible with just one click on a link on the bottom of the Web site's home page. Table 2 gives an overview of additional characteristics of these documents, including document name, contact information, and last update. Most commonly, the documents are referred to as *policies* or *statements*. Other documents bear titles like *notices, policy statements, information,* or have no titles at all. Almost all of them provide some form of contact information. A significant portion of the companies (44%) do not provide any indication of when they last updated their privacy policies. While 86% of the companies point out that their privacy policies are subject to change, only 20% promise to post a notice on the Web site prior to the change, and 14% notify registered users of significant changes by e-mail.

The majority of the companies (62%) do not display or refer to any privacy seal; 30% have one seal, and 8% have two seals. The seals displayed include TRUSTe (n = 11), BBB Online (n = 8), and AOL (n = 4). Only 12% of the companies have their privacy practices and the enforcement of their policies audited either by internal reviewers or as part of external reviews by experts or consulting firms.

Table 2. General document characteristics (n=50)

Document Name		Contact Information		Last Update	
Privacy policy	70%	Postal Address	56%	2003	32%
Privacy statement	18%	Phone number	34%	2002	20%
Other	12%	Email address	62%	2001	2%
		Email form	36%	2000	2%
		None	4%	No answer	44%

Data Collection

Clearly, the collection of personally identifiable information (PII) is necessary to complete business transactions and, thus, is collected by all companies. As Table 3 shows, only 68% provided information regarding users' control over their profiles, while 32% provide no information as to what users can do with the data they have provided to the company. All companies state explicitly (94%) or implicitly (6%) that they collect aggregate user data. Implicitly here means that they mention the use of cookies but do not say that the purpose of placing cookies on users' computers is data collection.

A total of 49 companies mention cookies, but only 35 companies draw attention to the fact that users may prevent this form of data collection and point out the consequences this entails. In addition to cookies, the sample companies use a variety of other techniques, including Web beacons, customer inquiries, surveys, and sweepstakes to gather customer information, especially demographic data. They also obtain customer information from unspecified other sources and match them with the data they have collected themselves. Another

Table 3. Collection of aggregate user data

User Control over PII (n = 50)	
Users have access to their PII	2%
Users can update it	34%
Users can update it or request its deletion	6%
Users can update and delete it	26%
No answer	32%
Collection of Aggregate User Data (n = 50)	
Use of cookies to collect aggregate data	92%
Collection of aggregate data (no indication of method)	2%
Use of cookies (no indication of purpose)	6%
Consequences of Disabling Cookies (n = 35)	
No restrictions	5.7%
Cannot use certain features but can still shop	65.7%
Cannot shop	17.1%
No answer	11.4%
Other Sources of Customer Data (n = 50)	
Web beacons	36%
Online surveys	62%
Sweepstakes	52%
Third parties	36%
Customer inquiries	18%

Table 4. Third-party data collection

	Total Sample (n = 34)	Seal Companies (n = 13)
TYPE OF DATA		
Aggregate information	55.88%	76.92%
Aggregate and PII	5.88%	7.69%
Type of data not specified	38.24%	15.38%
COLLECTION METHOD		
Cookies and Web beacons	47.06%	61.54%
Cookies only	38.24%	30.77%
Web beacons only	8.82%	7.69%
No answer	5.88%	0.00%
THIRD-PARTY PRIVACY AGREEMENT		
Yes	5.88%	17.69%
No	44.12%	46.15%
No answer	50.00%	46.15%

way of collecting customer data is storing e-mail addresses from customer inquiries, which 18% of the companies admit to doing, while 12% say explicitly that they do not do so.

The content analysis further examined data collection by third parties (e.g., advertising networks). Overall, 34 (68%) of the companies state that they allow third parties to collect data on their Web sites. The results for the 19 seal-companies echo those for the total sample, with 13 (68.42%) companies enabling third-party collection. Table 4 gives an overview of what kind of data third parties are allowed to collect, what methods these third parties use, and whether these third parties are required to sign a privacy agreement with the company enabling this third-party data collection. The results suggest that the seal companies have slightly more comprehensive policies, as the percentages of seal companies providing no answers or unspecific answers is always lower than those of the total sample.

As for opting out of third-party data collection, 61.67% of the companies enabling this form of data collection point to this possibility but merely refer users to the Web site of the third party collecting the data. Of the 13 seal companies

enabling third-party data collection, only 53.85% provide information on opting out of third-party data collection.

Unsolicited Marketing Communications

Sending commercial e-mails such as special offers, product updates, or newsletters to customers is common practice among the sample companies. While the majority (82%) offer opt-in or opt-out facilities for unsolicited e-mails to their customers, 14% send unsolicited e-mails without this option, and 4% do not disclose any information on this. Among the seal companies, 78.95% provide opt-in or opt-out facilities, while the remaining 21.05% send unsolicited e-mails without opt-in/opt-out. It often was not clear from the wording of the privacy policies whether opt-in or opt-out was offered (e.g., in phrases like "only when authorized," "with your permission," or "not without your consent." In other cases, companies offer opt-in only for certain types of communications and opt-out for others. Therefore, opt-in and opt-out were treated as one category in the analysis.

Data Sharing

Most companies (84%) point out that they share data with agents who either assist in completing orders (e.g., delivery companies) or perform other business services (e.g., customer communications or data analysis). While 28% of those companies who address data sharing with business agents (n = 42) do not specify whether these agents have to sign a privacy agreement with the company, 50% state that they have to, 4% state that only some agents are required to sign such agreements, and 2% say that agents are not required to sign any agreement.

Table 5 shows the companies' data sharing practices of aggregate and personally identifiable information with third parties and with what they call *affiliates*, which they fail to define. The exact nature of these affiliations is not explained in the privacy policies. The percentage of companies providing no information is alarming, particularly regarding the sharing of information with affiliates (66%). As for the sharing of aggregate data, the results obtained for the seal companies (36.8%) closely mirror those obtained for the total sample (34%). The high percentage of companies sharing PII with affiliates (42%) is also noteworthy, considering that these may maintain completely different privacy policies. The fact that relatively more seal companies provide specific information on PII sharing obviously results in a relatively higher number of companies sharing (52.6%) and not sharing (15.8%) data with affiliates,

compared to the total sample. Similarly, more seal companies (94.7%) provide information on PII sharing with third parties than companies in the total sample (88%). Notably, no seal company admits to sharing PII with third parties without the user's permission.

Another code in the analysis addressed the selling of customer data. Half of the companies say that they do not sell or rent customer data to third parties, and only one company admits to selling customer data. Interestingly, the percentage of companies promising not to sell PII (50%) is higher than those not sharing PII with third parties (42%). As for the seal companies, the percentage of those not selling and those not sharing PII is the same (57.89%).

Only nine companies say explicitly that they do not share e-mail addresses with third parties, while six admit to doing so, and 14 do so only with the user's permission. Of the 19 seal companies, two share e-mail addresses, and 10 offer opt-in or opt-out facilities, but not a single one claims that it does not share e-mail addresses. As mentioned earlier, 52% of the companies use sweepstakes as a means of collecting customer data, but only one of them promises not to share these data, while six state explicitly that they share these data, one shares only aggregate data and lets users opt out of sharing PII, and two share only aggregate data. The remaining companies do not provide any information as to what happens with data that users divulge when participating in a sweepstake.

Table 5. Data-sharing practices

	AGGREGATE		PERSONAL	
	Affiliates	Third Parties	Affiliates	Third Parties
yes	34% (36.8%)	62% (63.2%)	42% (52.6%)	6% (0%)
no	-	-	10% (15.8%)	42% (57.9%)
if authorized	-	-	-	38% (36.8%)
No answer	66% (63.2%)	38% (36.8%)	48% (31.6%)	12% (5.3%)

Note: Seal companies in brackets (n = 19)

RESULTS OF THE COMPUTER-ASSISTED TEXTUAL ANALYSIS

To gain additional insights into how companies communicate data handling practices, the vocabulary used in the privacy policies was examined. The 10 most frequent content words and their counts are (1) information (3,023); (2) use (1,339); (3) site (1,174); (4) may (948); (5) personal (902); (6) privacy (850); (7) service (811); (8) e-mail (777); (9) not (753); and (10) will (740). The first three words on the list — *information*, *use*, and *site* — account for almost 10% of all content words and the first 10 words for as much as 20%. Also, the 70 most frequent content words represent 50.10% of all content words. This suggests that the vocabulary used in privacy policies is rather homogenous, which explains why people consider them to be all the same (Milne & Culnan, 2004). *May* and *not* were the only surprising words among the 10 most frequent words and, thus, were subjected to KWIC analyses.

The modal verb *may* expresses either permission (intrinsic modality) or possibility (extrinsic modality) (Greenbaum & Quirk, 1990). Extrinsic modality adds intermediate degrees to the choice between *yes* and *no* either in terms of probability (maybe yes, maybe no) or in terms of frequency (sometimes yes, sometimes no). Thus, modal verbs like *may* cause a proposition to become arguable (Halliday, 1994), thereby lowering the degree of certainty of a text (Stillar, 1998). This is a strategy for speakers/writers to mitigate negative content in order to make it more acceptable to the audience (Callow, 1998). For a closer inspection of *may*, the words *might* and *will sometimes/occasionally* also were examined in view of their similar meanings. Table 6 shows all co-occurrences of *may, might,* and *will sometimes/occasionally* with verbs related to data handling practices. The results indicate that the policies contain a large number of vague and, to some extent, ambiguous statements that do not specify how user data are actually handled. They leave the reader in the unknown as to when and how data are collected or shared and whether users receive unsolicited marketing communications. This suggests that the companies use modal verbs strategically to downplay their questionable data handling practices and the frequency with which they occur.

A second KWIC analysis was conducted, examining *not* and *never* to identify the verbs with which they co-occur. They were most frequently found in combination with *collect* (72 times), *share* (51 times), *use* (44 times), and *sell* (33 times). In general, negative statements suggest that the speaker/writer is "taking issue with the corre-

Table 6. The use of modal verbs in privacy policies

	may	might	will sometimes will occasionally	TOTAL
collect	52	1	-	
gather	6	-	-	59
use	120	3	1	124
share	54	2	3	
disclose	27	-	-	
provide	24	-	-	
release	9	-	-	119
send	23	3	-	
receive	20	-	7	53
TOTAL	**335**	**9**	**11**	**355**

sponding positive assertions" (Fairclough, 2001, p. 128). When companies commit themselves, for example, to not selling or renting customer data, they implicitly contest the charge that they do. It thus seems that companies employ negations to raise the level of certainty and to dispel users' fears about privacy infringements.

DISCUSSION AND IMPLICATIONS

Discussion of Findings

Companies admit to data handling practices that disrespect user privacy, such as sharing e-mail addresses with third parties (12%), sharing personally identifiable information with affiliates (42%) or third parties (6%), forcing users to accept cookies to be able to shop at a site (17.1%), selling customer data (2%), sending unsolicited e-mails without opt-out facilities (14%), and allowing data collection by third parties who are not required to sign privacy agreements (44.12%). It also seems that some companies use sweepstakes as loopholes to obtain customer data that are not subject to the company's general privacy principles and, thus, may be shared or sold (18%). These findings suggest that users' privacy concerns outlined in the literature review are well founded, given that companies admit to the very practices about which consumers are concerned. The comparison of the total sample and the seal companies has shown that the latter also engage in questionable practices, such as third-party data collection or

the sharing of PII, suggesting that a privacy seal is no guarantee that Web sites do not infringe upon user privacy.

The study also has shown that privacy policies may not always tell readers what they want to know. As mentioned earlier, when coding the privacy policies, no answers were found for about one-third of all questions, either because the issues were not addressed in the privacy policies or because the information provided was not sufficient to answer the questions posed, thus leaving readers in the unknown as to whether a certain practice is carried out or not. Table 7 shows a breakdown of all unanswerable questions into the four coding categories, including only those 24 questions referring to specific data handling practices (codes 12 through 35, Appendix B). Comparing the results for seal companies and those for the total sample, it becomes evident that the disclosures of seal companies are slightly more comprehensive than those of the total sample, leaving fewer questions unanswered in all four categories. Third-party data collection is evidently an issue not dealt with sufficiently in privacy policies of both non-seal companies (48.39%) and seal companies (47.37%). The results for data sharing are considerably better for seal companies (27.63%) than for non-seal companies (43.55%) but still rank second in terms of unanswerable questions, followed by data collection. Unsolicited marketing communications, in turn, are well addressed in the privacy policies examined, although it has to be taken into consideration that only one code dealt with this issue.

Table 7. Breakdown of questions not addressed

Coding Category	Codes	Non-Seal Companies	Seal Companies	Total Sample
Third-Party Data Collection	4	48.39%	47.37%	48.00%
Data Sharing	8	43.55%	27.63%	37.50%
Data Collection	11	29.33%	24.88%	27.64%
Unsolicited Marketing	1	6.45%	0.00%	4.00%
OVERALL	**24**	**36.29%**	**28.51%**	**33.33%**

Overall, the results show that all privacy policies provided answers to roughly two-thirds of the questions, thus reducing users' uncertainties about data handling practices in WWW interactions only to a limited extent. Since interactants in initial interactions require information about each other to build relationships successfully, the privacy policies examined will not help users to gather enough information passively. Relationships thus will be established only if users have a high tolerance to uncertainty or obtain information actively by asking other users or interactively by contacting the company directly.

Also, these results are only indicative of what companies say but not necessarily of what they do. The assertions made in corporate privacy policies cannot be verified by anyone outside the company. Thus, for privacy policies to be worth reading, they would have to be supplemented with trustworthy privacy seals, so that Internet users have some assurance that companies abide at least by the certifying institution's guidelines, provided that the seal program enforces its guidelines rigorously.

Managerial Implications

The previous findings have three important implications for managerial practice that relate to shortcomings in the content, language, and presentation format of online privacy policies. First, companies need to be aware that even if they do not engage in certain data handling practices, these practices are worth mentioning in their privacy policies in order to reduce users' uncertainties. Although the computer-assisted textual analysis and the content analysis have shown that companies do mention things they do *not* do, more transparency is needed in communicating data handling practices. Companies probably do not see the need to mention certain practices if they do not engage in them, but users

are more likely to have trust in a company's Web site if they can learn from a privacy policy not only what the company does with user data but also what it does *not* do. Clearly, not mentioning something also may be a strategy for concealing practices consumers would find unacceptable.

Further, the examination of the content words has shown that companies obscure privacy infringements by downplaying their frequency or probability. More exact lexical choices in privacy policies would increase the transparency of data handling practices and would make them more capable of reducing uncertainties. If users were able to fully understand when data are collected and how they are used, they would be less concerned about data misuse and would have more trust in the company. The frequent use of *may*, for example, does not reduce uncertainties about data handling practices. Rather, companies should explain in detail under what circumstances a certain practice is carried out and when it is not. This, of course, would make privacy policies even longer, which shows the inappropriateness of text-based online privacy policies due to the complex nature of data handling in electronic commerce.

Therefore, companies should look for more user-friendly alternatives to the narrative presentation format of privacy policies. eBay was the only company among the 50 sample companies that offered such an alternative. In addition to the long version of its privacy policy, the company posts a tabular version and a short version, both of which give users a much better idea of how their data are collected, used, and shared. But similar to conventional privacy policies, this format also gives rise to the paradox situation that data already may have been collected before the user has viewed the privacy policy. This calls for a faster adoption of P3P-enabled privacy policies and the more widespread use of privacy seal programs to eliminate conventional privacy policies altogether.

Limitations of Findings

As pointed out, the sample is not representative of all Internet companies. Thus, the main findings are not the frequencies the content analysis has yielded but the fact that privacy policies are incomplete and, thus, unlikely to fulfill their purpose of uncertainty reduction. A second limitation is the nature of content analysis, which "neglects the rare and the absent" (Bauer, 2000, p. 148). Although in this study, the collective-level data provided by the content analysis are supplemented by textual data, both analyses focus on frequencies and are biased toward the presence. Only qualitative research such as discourse analysis could remedy this situation.

Avenues for Future Research

Further research is needed to understand the capabilities language has for disguising, deemphasizing, and obscuring privacy practices. As long as P3P policies do not catch on, language will play a crucial role in easing users' privacy concerns and building trust. Therefore, qualitative research is needed to examine privacy policies in light of their communicative action. In addition, research is needed to gain insight into how companies design privacy policies, whom they include in the design process, and what determines which issues they address in their privacy policies. Ultimately, future research also should look at how privacy policies differ across countries or continents in terms of scope and depth and in how far national legislation has a bearing on commercial privacy policies.

ACKNOWLEDGMENT

The author wishes to thank three anonymous reviewers and one associate editor for their thoughtful reviews of earlier versions of this manuscript.

REFERENCES

Andrade, E. B., Kaltechva, V., & Weitz, B. (2002). Self-disclosure on the Web: The impact of privacy policy, reward, and company reputation. *Advances in Consumer Research*, 29, 350-353.

Bauer, M. W. (2000). Classical content analysis: A review. In M.W. Bauer, & G. Gaskel (Eds.), *Qualitative researching with text, image and sound* (pp. 131-151). London: Sage.

Baumer, D. L., Poindexter, J. C., & Earp, J. B. (2004). Meaningful and meaningless choices in cyberspace. *Journal of Internet Law, 7*(11), 3-11.

BBBOnline. (2004). Retrieved from http://www.bbbonline.org/privacy/

Belanger, F., Hiller, J.S., & Smith, W. J. (2002). Trustworthiness in electronic commerce: The role of privacy, security, and site attributes. *The Journal of Strategic Information Systems, 11*(3/4), 245-270.

Benassi, P. (1999). TRUSTe: An online privacy seal program. *Communications of the ACM, 42*(2), 56-59.

Berger, C. R. (1979). Beyond initial interactions: Uncertainty, understanding and the development of interpersonal relationships. In H. Giles, & R. Sinclair (Eds.), *Language and social psychology* (pp. 122-144). Oxford: Basil Blackwell.

Berger, C. R., & Bradac, J.J. (1982). *Language and social knowledge: Uncertainty in interpersonal relations.* London: Arnold.

Berger, C. R., & Calabrese, R. J. (1975). Some explorations in initial interaction and beyond: Toward a developmental theory of interpersonal communication. *Human Communication Theory, 1*, 99-112.

Bradac, J. J. (2001). Theory comparison: Uncertainty reduction, problematic integration, uncertainty management, and other curious constructs. *Journal of Communication, 51*(3), 456-476.

Brown, M., & Muchira, R. (2004). Investigating the relationship between Internet privacy concerns and online purchase behavior. *Journal of Electronic Commerce Research, 5*(1), 62-70.

Callow, K. (1998). *Man and message. A guide to meaning-based text analysis.* Boston: University Press of America.

Caudill, E. M., & Murphy, P. E. (2000). Consumer online privacy: Legal and ethical issues. *Journal of Public Policy & Marketing, 19*(1), 7-19.

Charters, D. (2002). Electronic monitoring and privacy issues in business-marketing: The ethics of the DoubleClick experience. *Journal of Business Ethics, 35*, 243-254.

Cragan, J. F., & Shields, D. C. (1998). *Understanding communication theory. The communicative forces for human action.* Boston: Allyn and Bacon.

Cranor, L. F. (1998). Internet privacy: A public concern. *netWorker: The Craft of Network Computing, 2*(2), 13-18.

Cranor, L. F., Byers, S., & Kormann, D. (2003). *An analysis of P3P deployment on commercial, government, and children's Web sites as of May 2003* (Technical Report prepared for the 14 May 2003 Federal Trade Commission Workshop on Technologies for Protecting Personal Information). Retrieved from http://www.research.att.com/projects/p3p/

Cranor, L. F., Reagle, J., & Ackerman, M. S. (1999). *Beyond concern: Understanding net users' attitudes about online privacy* (AT&T Labs-Research Technical Report TR 99.4.3). Retrieved from http://www.research.att.com/projects/privacystudy/

Culnan, M. J. (1993). How did they get my name? An exploratory investigation of consumer attitudes toward secondary information use. *MIS Quarterly, 17*(3), 341-361.

Culnan, M. J. (1999). *Georgetown Internet privacy policy survey: Report to the Federal Trade Commission.* Retrieved from http://www.msb.edu/faculty/culnanm/gippshome.html

Culnan, M. J., & Armstrong, P. K. (1999). Information privacy concerns, procedural fairness, and impersonal trust: An empirical investigation. *Organization Science, 10*(1), 104-115.

Cunningham, P. J. (2002). Are cookies hazardous to your privacy? *Information Management Journal, 36*(3), 52-54.

Daly, J. P., Pouder, R. W., & Kabanoff, B. (2004). The effects of initial differences in firms' espoused values on their postmerger performance. *The Journal of Applied Behavioral Science, 40*(3), 323-343.

Danna, A., & Gandy, O. H., Jr. (2002). All that glitters is not gold: Digging beneath the surface of data mining. *Journal of Business Ethics, 40*, 373-386.

Delaney, E. M., Goldstein, C. E., Gutterman, J., & Wagner, S. N. (2003). Automated computer privacy preferences slowly gain popularity. *Intellectual Property & Technology Law Journal, 15*(8), 17.

Dhillon, G. S., & Moores, T. T. (2001). Internet privacy: Interpreting key issues. *Information Resources Management Journal, 14*(4), 33-37.

Dommeyer, C. J., & Gross, B. L. (2003). What consumers know and what they do: An investigation of consumer knowledge, awareness, and use of privacy protection strategies. *Journal of Interactive Marketing, 17*(2), 34-51.

Döring, N. (2002). Personal home pages on the Web: A review of research. *Journal of Computer-*

Mediated Communication, 7(3). Retrieved from http://www.ascusc.org/jcmc/vol7/issue3/doering.html

Ebenkamp, B. (2002). Brand keys to travel sites. *Brandweek, 43*(25), 19.

Eirinaki, M., & Vazirgiannis, M. (2003). Web mining for Web personalization. *ACM Transactions on Internet Technology, 3*(1), 1-27.

Fairclough, N. (2001). *Language and power* (2nd ed.). London: Longman.

Federal Trade Commission. (1998). *Privacy online: A report to Congress.* Retrieved from http://www.ftc.gov/reports/privacy3/priv-23a.pdf

Federal Trade Commission. (2000). *Privacy online: Fair information practices in the electronic marketplace* (A Report to Congress). Retrieved from http://www.ftc.gov/reports/privacy2000/privacy2000.pdf

Fletcher, K. (2003). Consumer power and privacy: The changing nature of CRM. *International Journal of Advertising, 22*(2), 249-272.

Forrester Research. (2002, August 29). US eCommerce — The next five years. *M2 Presswire.*

Ghosh, A. (2001). *Security and privacy for e-business.* New York: Wiley.

Grabowski, M., & Roberts, K. (1998). Risk mitigation in virtual organizations. *Journal of Computer-Mediated Communication, 3*(4). Retrieved from http://jcmc.huji.ac.il/vol3/issue4/grabowski.html

Graeff, T. R., & Harmon, S. (2002). Collecting and using personal data: Consumers' awareness and concerns. *The Journal of Consumer Marketing, 19*(4/5), 302-318.

Greenbaum, S., & Quirk, R. (1990). *A student's grammar of the English language.* Harlow: Longman.

Gudykunst, W. B., Yang, S. M., & Nishida, T. (1985). A cross-cultural test of uncertainty reduction theory: Comparisons of acquaintances, friends, and dating relationships in Japan, Korea, and the United States. *Human Communication Research, 11*, 407-454.

Hagel, J., & Rayport, J. F. (1997). The coming battle for customer information. *Harvard Business Review, 75*(1), 53-65.

Halliday, M. A. K. (1994). *Introduction to functional grammar* (2nd ed.). London: Edward Arnold.

Hammer, M. R., & Martin, J. N. (1992). The effects of cross-cultural training on American managers in a Japanese-American joint venture. *Journal of Applied Communication Research, 20*, 161-182.

Han, P., & Maclaurin, A. (2002). Do consumers really care about online privacy? *Marketing Management, 11*(1), 35-38.

Harding, W. T., Reed, A. J., & Gray, R. L. (2001). Cookies and Web bugs: What they are and how they work together. *Information Systems Management, 18*(3), 17-24.

Johnson-Page, G. F., & Thatcher, R. S. (2001). B2C data privacy policies: Current trends. *Management Decision, 39*(4), 262-271.

Kabanoff, B. (1996). Computers can read as well as count: How computer-aided text analysis can benefit organizational research. *Journal of Organizational Behavior, 3*, 1-21.

Kay, R. (2004, March 15). Quick study: Privacy glossary. *Computerworld*, 41.

Kelle, U., & Laurie, H. (1995). Computer use in qualitative research and issues of validity. In U. Kelle (Ed.), *Computer-aided qualitative data analysis. Theory, methods and practice* (pp. 19-28). London: Sage.

Kolbe, R. H., & Burnett, M. S. (1991). Content-analysis research: An examination of applications with directives for improving research reliability and objectivity. *Journal of Consumer Research, 18*(2), 243-250.

Kramer, M. W. (1993). Communication and uncertainty reduction during job transfers: Leaving and joining processes. *Communication Monographs, 60*, 178-198.

Krippendorff, K. (1980). *Content analysis. An introduction to its methodology.* Beverly Hills, CA: Sage.

Lacity, M. C., & Janson, M. A. (1994). Understanding qualitative data: A framework of text analysis methods. *Journal of Management Information Systems, 11*(2), 137-155.

Lebart, L., Salem, A., & Berry, L. (1998). *Exploring textual data.* Dordrecht: Kluwer Academic Publishers.

Liu, C., & Arnett, K. P. (2002). An examination of privacy policies in Fortune 500 Web sites. *Mid-American Journal of Business, 17*(1), 13-21.

Luo, X., & Seyedian, M. (2004). Contextual marketing and customer-orientation strategy for e-commerce: An empirical analysis. *International Journal of Electronic Commerce, 8*(2), 95-118.

Lynch, B. (2004, March). Web-privacy management increases in importance. *Wall Street & Technology*, 48-49.

Mason, R. O. (1986). Four ethical issues of the information age. *MIS Quarterly, 10*(1), 5-12.

Mason, R. O., Mason, F. M., & Culnan, M. J. (1995). *Ethics of information management.* Thousand Oaks, CA: Sage.

Maury, M. D., & Kleiner, D. S. (2002). E-commerce, ethical commerce? *Journal of Business Ethics, 36*, 21-31.

Messmer, E. (1997, June 16). Group slams Web sites for lack of privacy policies. *Network World.*

Milne, G. R., & Boza, M.-E. (1999). Trust and concern in consumers' perceptions of marketing information management practices. *Journal of Interactive Marketing, 13*(1), 5-24.

Milne, G. R., & Culnan, M. J. (2002). Using the content of online privacy notices to inform public policy: A longitudinal analysis of the 1998-2001 US Web surveys. *The Information Society, 18*(5), 345-359.

Milne, G. R., & Culnan, M. J. (2004). Strategies for reducing online privacy risks: Why consumers read (or don't read) online privacy notices. *Journal of Interactive Marketing, 18*(3), 15-29.

Mitchell, S. (2003). The new age of direct marketing. *Journal of Database Management, 10*(3), 219-229.

Miyazaki, A. D., & Fernandez, A. (2000). Internet privacy and security: An examination of online retailer disclosures. *Journal of Public Policy & Marketing, 19*(1), 54-61.

Miyazaki, A. D., & Krishnamurthy, S. (2002). Internet seals of approval: Effects of online privacy policies and consumer perceptions. *The Journal of Consumer Affairs, 36*(1), 28-49.

Neuendorf, K. A. (2002). *The content analysis guidebook.* Thousand Oaks, CA: Sage.

Nöteberg, A., Christiaanse, E., & Wallage, P. (2003). Consumer trust in electronic channels: The impact of electronic commerce assurance on consumers' purchasing likelihood and risk perceptions. *e-Service Journal, 2*(2), 46-67.

O'Connor, P. (2003). What happens to my information if I make a hotel booking online: An analysis of on-line privacy policy use, content and compliance by the international hotel companies. *Journal of Services Research, 3*(2), 5-28.

Olaniran, B. A., & Williams, D. E. (1995). Communication distortion: An intercultural lesson from the visa application process. *Communication Quarterly, 43,* 225-240.

Olivero, N., & Lunt, P. (2004). Privacy versus willingness to disclose in e-commerce exchanges: The effect of risk awareness on the relative role of trust and control. *Journal of Economic Psychology, 25*(2), 243-262.

Phelps, J., Nowak, G., & Ferrell, E. (2000). Privacy concerns and consumer willingness to provide personal information. *Journal of Public Policy & Marketing, 19*(1), 27-41.

Presler-Marshall, M. (2000). Web privacy and the P3P standard. *IBM Raleigh Lab.* Retrieved from http://www7.software.ibm.com/vad. nsf/Data/Document2363?OpenDocument&p =1&BCT=1Footer=1

Reagle, J., & Cranor, L. F. (1999). The platform for privacy preferences. *Communications of the ACM, 42*(2), 48-55.

Reda, S. (2000). VeriFone and Russell Reynolds Associates Top 100 Internet retailers. *Stores.* Retrieved September 2000, from https://www. stores.org/archives/00top100int_1.asp

Roznowski, J. A. (2003). A content analysis of mass media. Stories surrounding the consumer privacy issue 1990-2001. *Journal of Interactive Marketing, 17*(2), 52-69.

Ryker, R., Lafleur, E., McManis, B., & Cox, K. C. (2002). Online privacy policies: An assessment of the Fortune E-50. *The Journal of Computer Information Systems, 42*(4), 15-20.

Sama. L. M., & Shoaf, V. (2002). Ethics on the Web: Applying moral decision-making to the new media. *Journal of Business Ethics, 36,* 93-103.

Schoenbachler, D. D., & Gordon, G. L. (2002). Trust and customer willingness to provide information in database-driven relationship marketing. *Journal of Interactive Marketing, 16*(3), 2- 16.

Shaw, T. R. (2003). The moral intensity of privacy: An empirical study of Webmasters' attitudes. *Journal of Business Ethics, 46*(4), 301-318.

Sheehan, K. B. (2002). Toward a typology of Internet users and online privacy concerns. *The Information Society, 18,* 21-32.

Sheehan, K. B., & Hoy, M. G. (2000). Dimensions of online privacy concerns among online consumers. *Journal of Public Policy & Marketing, 19*(1), 62-73.

Sinrod, E. J. (2001). The future of Internet privacy. *Journal of Internet Law, 4*(9), 22-25.

Smith, H. J., Milberg, S. J., & Burke, S. J. (1996). Information privacy: Measuring individuals' concerns about organizational practices. *MIS Quarterly, 20*(2), 167-196.

Stead, B. A., & Gilbert, J. (2001). Ethical issues in electronic commerce. *Journal of Business Ethics, 34*(2), 75-85.

Stempel, G. H., & Wesley, B. H. (Eds.). (1981). *Research methods in mass communication.* Englewood Cliffs, NJ: Prentice-Hall.

Stewart, K. A., & Segars, A. H. (2002). An empirical examination of the concern for information privacy instrument. *Information Systems Research, 13*(1), 36-49.

Stillar, G. F. (1998). *Analyzing everyday texts. Discourse, rhetoric, and social perspectives.* Thousand Oaks, CA: Sage.

Strauss, A. L., & Corbin, J. (1990). *Basics of qualitative research: Grounded theory procedures and techniques.* Newbury Park, CA: Sage.

Stubbs, M. (2001). *Words and phrases. Corpus studies of lexical semantics.* Oxford: Blackwell.

Szewczak, E. (2002). Beware the cookie monster. *Information Resources Management Journal, 15*(1), 3-4.

Teo, H. H., Wan, W., & Li, L. (2004). Volunteering personal information on the Internet: Effects of reputation, privacy initiatives, and reward on online consumer behavior. In *Proceedings of the 37th Hawaii International Conference on System Sciences*. Retrieved from http://csdl. computer.org/comp/proceedings/hicss/2004/ 2056/07/205670181c.pdf

Thibodeau, P. (2002). P3P supporters struggle to increase adoption of data privacy standard. *Computerworld, 36*(47), 20.

Treiblmaier, H., Madlberger, M., Knotzer, N., & Pollach, I. (2004). The ethics of personalization and customization on the Internet: An empirical study. In *Proceedings of the 37th Hawaii International Conference on System Sciences*. Retrieved from http://csdl.computer.org/comp/proceedings/ hicss/2004/2056/07/205670181b.pdf

Turner, E. C., & Dasgupta, S. (2003, Winter). Privacy on the Web: An examination of user concerns, technology, and implications for business organizations and individuals. *Information Systems Management*, 8-18.

Weber, R. P. (1985). *Basic content analysis*. Newbury Park, CA: Sage.

Whitman, M. E., Perez, J., & Beise, C. (2001). A study of user attitudes toward persistent cookies. *The Journal of Computer Information Systems, 41*(3), 1-7.

Wolfe, R. A., Gephart, R. P., & Johnson, T. E. (1993). Computer-facilitated qualitative data analysis: Potential contributions to management research. *Journal of Management, 19*(3), 637-660.

World Wide Web Consortium. (2003). *Platform for privacy preferences (P3P) project*. Retrieved from http://www.w3.org/P3P/

This work was previously published in the Journal of Organizational and End User Computing, edited by M. Adam Mahmood, pp. 23-49, copyright 2006 by IGI Publishing, formerly known as Idea Group Publishing (an imprint of IGI Global).

Chapter XII
Examining User Perception of Third–Party Organization Credibility and Trust in an E–Retailer

Robin L. Wakefield
Hankamer School of Business, Baylor University, USA

Dwayne Whitten
Mays School of Business, Texas A&M University, USA

ABSTRACT

Despite the fact that over half of U.S. residents are now online, Internet users hesitate to enter into transactions with e-retailers in the absence of certain assurances. Recent IS research shows that institution-based assurance structures, such as Web seals, are drivers of online trust. We extend the research in online trust to include the effect of third-party organization (TPO) credibility on both Internet users' perceptions of assurance structures and purchase risk. Findings indicate that TPO credibility is positively related to the value that Internet users assign to assurance structures and negatively related to perceptions of purchase risk. Furthermore, perceptions of TPO credibility are strongly associated with users' trusting attitudes toward the e-retailer. For some online consumers, trust may have less to do with privacy and security and more to do with the reputation of the TPO. These findings have important implications for the design of Web sites, the selection of assurance providers and services, and the reputation of both e-retailers and providers.

INTRODUCTION

Compared to the 130-plus-years existence of telephone communications in the United States, the development of the Internet is still in its infancy. Today, more people go online to communicate via e-mail than to send first-class letters. The U.S. Census Bureau reports that more than 54% of Americans have access to the Internet, with 84% of Internet users engaging in e-mail, 67% searching for information, and 39% purchasing products (NTIA, 2002). The Internet is changing not only the way people communicate but how they shop, invest, and gather information. By overcoming barriers of time, place, and distance, the Internet renders considerable economic benefits. Yet, significant numbers of Internet users hesitate to transact online and, thus, forgo the economic efficiencies of the medium.

Empirical research confirms the significance of trust in order for e-commerce transactions to occur between buyers and unknown sellers (Hoffman, Kalsbeek, & Novak, 1999; Shankar, Urban, & Sultan, 2002). Since trust is an important component of e-commerce, understanding the antecedents to trusting attitudes should be of major concern to e-retailers. Often, Internet users decline to enter into transactions with e-retailers in the absence of certain assurances. IS research reveals a positive relationship between institution-based structures (e.g., Web assurance seals), online trust, and intent to purchase (Houston & Taylor, 1999; Kovar, Gladden-Burke, & Kovar, 2000; Lala, Arnold, Sutton, & Guan, 2002; Odom, Kumar, & Saunders, 2002; Wakefield, 2001). Institution-based structures are significant trust drivers that mitigate perceived risks and allow Internet users to believe that they are supported externally (McKnight, Cummings, & Chervany, 1998). Researchers (Shankar et al., 2002) believe it is important to continue to identify the salient assurance needs of online stakeholders in order to implement and to enhance the dominant drivers of trust in an e-business strategy.

One objective of this study is to extend the IS trust research in order to encompass Internet user perceptions of the role of institution-based assurance structures in e-commerce. Online trust is a complex and multi-dimensional concept related to the success of e-retailers, and the role of assurance mechanisms may be perceived differently by e-retailers and Internet users. For example, e-retailers utilize assurance service providers such as BBB Online or TRUSTe in order to convey legitimacy, among other things, to online consumers. However, research shows that online shoppers rarely consult the privacy and security statements of the assurance provider or differentiate among providers (Odom et al., 2002). Nevertheless, third-party assurances are shown to promote trust in the electronic environment. It is likely that online consumers consider other aspects of the assurance provider apart from the actual assurances before entering into electronic transactions. The specific attributes of assurance providers that convey trust is generally unknown and unexamined. This dearth of knowledge has significant implications for e-retailers in their selection of a provider and in the scope of services that they purchase. This study contributes to the online trust literature by examining additional antecedents of trust in the online marketplace.

Specifically, a model is constructed that examines user attitudes toward third-party organization (TPO) assurance providers and the effect of those attitudes on trust in the e-retailer. We propose that TPO credibility is an important factor in the value that users assign to the institution-based assurance (i.e., Web site seal) associated with the TPO. Credibility factors are important antecedents of trust in tradition buyer-seller exchanges (Harmon & Coney, 1982; Moore, Hausknecht, & Thamodaran, 1988; Sternthal, Dholakia, & Leavitt, 1978) but have not been applied yet to the electronic marketplace. It is our goal to better understand the mechanisms by which institutional assurance structures shape the trusting attitudes that are necessary for successful e-commerce activities.

We begin this article with a brief background discussion of Internet assurance providers, market signaling, and TPO credibility. The conceptual framework and hypotheses sections precede a discussion of the research methodology and the measures. The article concludes with the results of data analysis and a discussion of the findings.

BACKGROUND

Web Assurance Providers

E-commerce assurance services created in the 1990s address issues of privacy and trust related to online transactions. Internet users indicate that a main concern with e-commerce transactions is related to security (Crowell, 2001; Hoffman et al., 1999; Urban, Sultan, & Qualls, 2000). Security and privacy issues continue to hinder electronic transactions, thus promoting a stream of IS research investigating the operationalization of trust in the electronic environment (Shankar et al., 2002).

TPOs (e.g., Better Business Bureau, American Institute of Certified Public Accountants, Electronic Frontier Foundation) address user security concerns by providing assurance services to online businesses. Their goal is to promote trusting attitudes that allow electronic transactions to proceed unhindered. E-retailers that display a TPO's Web assurance seal signal to the consumer certain affirmations such as legitimacy, security of transactions, privacy, and integrity. Research shows that Web seals promote feelings of security and trust (Houston & Taylor, 1999; Schneiderman, 2000; Palmer, Bailey, & Faraj, 2000) and influence users' intents to purchase online (Kovar et al., 2000; Mauldin & Arunachalam, 2001; Wakefield, 2001).

Empirical research also relates the positive effects of third-party certification to the likelihood of online purchases and trusting attitudes (Houston & Taylor, 1999; Kovar et al., 2000; Mauldin & Arunachalam, 2001). However, only a few studies examine user perceptions of Web seals. Lala, et al. (2002) find that respondents prefer WebTrust compared to BBB On-line, and Odom, et al. (2002) examine how the brand awareness of Verisign, TRUSTe, Good Housekeeping, and WebTrust relates to purchase intentions. It is not our objective to evaluate individual TPOs but rather to identify the mechanisms by which they convey trust in the electronic marketplace.

Four of the more prominent assurance providers are included in this study: BBB OnLine, TRUSTe, WebTrust, and Verisign. We focus on the relationships between the perceived credibility of the TPO (Better Business Bureau, TRUSTe, American Institute of Certified Public Accountants, and Verisign) and user value perceptions and purchase risk perceptions. Moreover, we identify the influence of these variables on trusting attitudes and intent to purchase.

Market Signaling

The information economics approach to the effects of information in a market channel is based on the different parties being privy to disparate amounts of information related to the transaction. Specifically, "when one party lacks information that the other party has, the first party may make inferences from the information provided by the second party, and this inference formation should play a role in the information the second party chooses to provide" (Kirmani & Rao, 2000, p. 66). Disparity in information levels has been shown to exist in a variety of settings (Rothschild & Stiglitz, 1976; Spence, 1973), including organization buyers' uncertainties regarding vendor abilities (Stump & Heide, 1996). Information disparity in e-commerce encourages the use of institution-based assurances, because they are a signal to the user of legitimacy and trustworthiness. Firms often employ signals, "which are actions that parties take to reveal their true types" (Kirmani & Rao, 2000), in order to minimize the uncertainty associated with information asymmetry in a market exchange. Market signaling is one way to pass on information to others in a marketplace (Spence, 1973), and theory posits that a rational consumer expects a firm to honor the implicit commitment suggested by the signal.   Signaling is best suited for situations in which a good or service must be experienced before the gap between perceptions and expectations is evaluated (Kirmani & Rao, 2000). In other words, signaling is most useful when the product or service of a vendor is unknown, as often occurs between Internet users and e-retailers. Signaling also lends a certain amount of credibility and assurance when the actual qualities of the transaction are unobservable. Research has studied the effects of market signals such as advertising (Kihlstrom & Riordan, 1984; Ippolito, 1990), price (Wolinsky, 1983; Milgrom & Roberts, 1986), quality (Boulding & Kirmani, 1993), and switching costs (Anderson & Weitz, 1992; Eliashberg & Robertson, 1988). Since a TPO's Web seal is often the only indication of an institution-based assurance structure, it is an important market signal for online consumers. Prior research shows that these signals (i.e., Web site seals) are important mechanisms to promote trust in electronic exchanges.

TPO Credibility

In consumer behavior literature, endorser credibility influences both consumer attitudes and behavioral intentions (Harmon & Coney, 1982; Moore et al., 1988; Sternthal et al., 1978), since endorser credibility is related to trustworthiness and expertise. Consumers often transfer the perceptions of trust and expertness generated in response to the endorser onto the product, service, or organization that is being recommended (Hawkins, Best, & Coney, 1998). Thus, the importance of endorser credibility should not be underestimated. Endorsers are perceived

to hold credible information and to be unbiased communicators of information (Dean & Biswas, 2001). A message delivered by a highly credible source is accepted more readily by the receiver and is more likely to lead to a change in attitude (Miller & Baseheart, 1969; Schulman & Worrall, 1970).

TPOs offering e-commerce assurance services may be perceived in the electronic marketplace as third-party endorsers. The signals generated by a Web seal may enhance perceptions of trust for the e-retailer, based on the trustworthiness or expertise of the third party, regardless of the actual assurance services provided. For example, online consumers may believe that the TPO's Web seal signals greater product quality or service quality rather than serving as an indicator of the assurance services that are rendered. We contend that online consumers assign value to assurance symbols in direct relation to their TPO credibility beliefs rather than to their beliefs about the assurances. This possible misconception of the market signal has important implications for e-retailers, assurance providers, and online consumers.

CONCEPTUAL FRAMEWORK AND HYPOTHESES

Shankar et al. (2002) outline a broad framework to motivate and to elicit research in online trust. From relevant literature, they identify three groups of antecedent factors to online trust. These groups include Web site characteristics, user characteristics, and other characteristics. Web site characteristics include factors such as user friendliness, error-freeness, privacy, brand, presentation, and Web assurance seals. User characteristics encompass variables such as past shopping experience, Internet savvy, predisposition to technology, and feelings of control. The third group includes a broad range of other characteristics such as perceived size of the firm, perceived reputation of the firm, communication, and personalization.

Figure 1. Proposed model

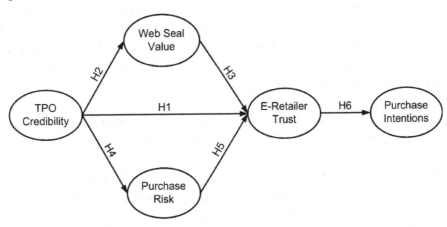

Apart from user traits, the antecedents to online trust represent user perceptions upon review of an e-retailer's Web site.

We utilize this framework to construct a model in order to examine the relationship between certain Web site characteristics (i.e., Web seals) and users' perceptions of TPO credibility, Web seal value, purchase risk, and trust. Furthermore, as illustrated in Figure 1, we model behavioral intentions to purchase from the e-retailer.

Research in the marketing literature shows that third-party endorsements function similarly to expert endorsements (Dean & Biswas, 2001). Expert endorsements persuade through the process of internalization whereby the receiver adopts a certain attitude, either because it is useful for problem solving or is demanded by the receiver's value system (Friedman & Friedman, 1979). Research also relates the ability of expert endorsements to change opinions (McGinnies & Ward, 1980) and to positively influence purchase intentions (Ohanian, 1991). E-retailers purchase assurance services to reduce consumer uncertainty, reduce risk perceptions, and persuade, based on the credibility of the third party and the services they provide. Thus, consumers that regard the TPO as highly credible are likely to have greater trust for the e-retailer.

H1: TPO credibility is positively related to trust in the e-retailer.

TPO endorsements are regarded as value signals that are significant in market transactions (Dean & Biswas, 2001). In e-commerce, Internet users initially are aware of a TPO assurance provider by the presence of the TPO's Web seal on the e-retailer's Web site. Internet users implicitly assign value to a market signal when they explicitly choose an unknown vendor with an assurance seal over an unknown vendor without a seal (Lala et al., 2002). Thus, Internet users likely assign higher levels of value to seals from TPOs that they consider highly credible, trustworthy, or expert. In signaling research, signals tend to be effective when the signaling firm maintains a high reputation (Hoxmeier, 2000). Furthermore, organizational credibility plays a role in influencing attitudes and purchase intentions (Goldsmith, Lafferty, & Newell, 2000; Lafferty, Goldsmith, & Newell, 2002) and is an important component of reputation (Keller, 1998). Hence, the seal of a credible TPO is likely to be more influential in an online purchase decision. In contrast, the value of a seal from a TPO with low perceived credibility is not likely to be highly valued.

H2: TPO credibility is positively related to the value of a Web assurance seal.

Endorser credibility impacts both consumer attitudes and purchase intentions (Lafferty & Goldsmith, 1999; Goldsmith et al., 2000; Lafferty et al., 2002). A credible source reduces situational complexity that allows for greater trust (Luhmann, 1988). Therefore, a credible TPO is likely to lessen user perceptions of uncertainty and risk, leading to positive, trusting attitudes. The appearance of a Web seal on the e-retailer's site is often the only signal of TPO involvement with the e-retailer. Thus, the importance and value assigned to this signal relates to the formation of trust toward the e-retailer. This leads to the following hypothesis:

H3: The value of a Web assurance seal is positively related to trust in the e-retailer.

Organizational credibility includes the dimension of trustworthiness (DeSarbo & Harshman, 1985), and trust reduces consumer uncertainty and perceptions of risk (Fukuyama, 1995; Morgan & Hunt, 1994). Therefore, the greater the perception of TPO credibility, the less purchase risk is likely to be associated with an unknown e-retailer.

H4: TPO credibility is negatively related to perceptions of purchase risk.

Consumers often hesitate to transact with unknown e-retailers due to uncertainty about vendor behavior and perceived technology risks (e.g., viruses, spam). The nature and complexity of the electronic environment are related directly to the importance of trust. When one is vulnerable to the misconduct of others, they have a greater need to trust (Rousseau, Sitkin, Burt, & Camerer, 1998). Research shows that high degrees of risk in electronic sales transactions lead to attitudes of distrust and unwillingness to purchase online (Jarvenpaa, Tractinsky, & Vitale, 2000). However,

when trusting attitudes are present, consumers are more comfortable sharing personal information and purchasing online (McKnight, Choudhury, & Kacmar, 2002). This suggests that as purchase risk is mitigated, greater trust in the e-retailer is attained.

H5: The perception of purchase risk is negatively related to trust in the e-retailer.

Trust literature suggests that trust acts to eliminate complexity in a transaction and, thus, has a positive influence on decisions (Luhmann, 1988). Essentially, trust rules out undesirable future actions of other parties. Gefen (2000) shows that trust in an Internet vendor positively influences intentions to purchase from that vendor, and Jarvenpaa, et al. (2000) support this relationship, as well. According to the well-known theory of reasoned action (TRA) (Ajzen & Fishbein 1980) from social psychology, attitude formation leads to an intention, and intention has a direct effect on actual behavior. In terms of consumer behavior, the main predictor variable in a purchase decision is the consumer's attitude or intention toward purchasing. Thus, based on TRA and past IS research, we hypothesize the following:

H6: Trust in the e-retailer is positively related to purchase intentions.

RESEARCH METHODOLOGY

In this study, the subjects evaluated an actual Web site for an online computer store that was renamed Laptop King (Appendix A). Six separate home pages were created and stored on a Web server managed by one of the researchers. Four home pages prominently displayed one of the institution-based assurances being tested (i.e., BBB OnLine, TRUSTe, Verisign, or WebTrust); one home page displayed all four Web seals; and one page was created without any assurance structure. Links remained active to all pages on the site, including the privacy and security statements accessible by clicking on the Web seal. Since the home pages were based on an actual Internet site, a check on whether subjects had ever visited the site resulted in one subject indicating the affirmative.

A group of 121 undergraduate students at a large southwestern university evaluated Laptop King's Web site. Students serve as reasonable surrogates for online users, because most Internet users are younger and more highly educated (NTIA, 2002). Students also tend to make decisions that approximate the general population for information processing and decision-making tasks (Ashton & Kramer, 1980), and research demonstrates that attitudes toward Internet shopping are not affected by demographic characteristics such as age (Jarvenpaa & Todd, 1996). Furthermore, Odom, et al. (2002) find no differences in responses between student and non-student samples evaluating different brands of Web seals. All subjects completed the questionnaire in a computer lab setting, where they were given the option of participating in the research. Extra class credit was given in order to motivate the desire to participate.

A scenario was created in which the subjects were told that they intended to purchase a laptop computer online with money they earned during the summer break (Appendix B). The scenario was created in order to represent a realistic purchase situation for student subjects. Furthermore, the purchase simulation is relatively high-risk in financial terms as well as in familiarity with the e-retailer. The subjects were directed to one of the six home pages created for Laptop King and asked to review it for two minutes. The two-minute time limit eliminates variability and allows for ample review of the site, considering that the average time spent on a site is 1.01 minutes (Nielsen/Net Ratings, 2003). Instructions directed the subjects to exit the site after two minutes and to respond to the questionnaire.

Measures

The dimensions of expertise and trustworthiness underlie endorser credibility and contribute to the persuasion effect. Expertise reflects the idea that the endorser has expert knowledge, and trustworthiness refers to the unbiased communication of knowledge (Dean & Biswas, 2001). The credibility scale (see Appendix B) is adapted from Ohanian (1991) and measures the perceived trustworthiness and expertise of an endorser. The items measuring credibility include the terms *credible, trustworthy*, and *reliable*. One item reflects perceptions of the TPO's expert knowledge. Semantic differentials are used to measure the items, and the reliability coefficient of the scale is .98.

Four items measuring the construct of value ask the subjects to indicate the extent to which the Web seal matters, is important, is valuable, and means a lot. Respondents indicated their (dis)agreement with the statements on a seven-point Likert scale. The value construct was computed as the average of the four scale items. Higher (lower) value corresponds to higher (lower) scores. The reliability coefficient of the value scale is .98.

Perceptions of e-retailer trustworthiness were measured using four items adapted from Larzelere and Huston's (1980) trust scale. The scale exploits the major dimensions of trust, including reliability, integrity, and confidence. This scale has successfully measured interorganizational trust (Morgan & Hunt, 1994) and is also highly reliable (alpha = .92). Responses were indicated on a seven-point scale that ranged from strongly disagree to strongly agree. E-retailer trust is computed as the average of the scale items, with higher (lower) trust corresponding with higher (lower) scores.

Purchase risk is measured with four items from Jarvenpaa et al. (2000). The construct addresses risky choice, high potential for loss, significant risk, and risk in the product not meeting customer expectations. Subjects related the extent of their agreement with the statements on a seven-point

Likert scale. The reliability coefficient of the scale was .90. Purchase intentions are measured with a five-item scale using semantic differentials to assess the likelihood of purchasing from the site. The reliability coefficient of the scale is .93.

RESULTS AND DISCUSSION

Descriptive Statistics

Of the 121 subjects, 46% were female, and 54% were male. A majority (75%) was between 20 and 25 years of age, with 19% below 20 years and 6% over 25 years. Among the respondents who had made prior Internet purchases, 27% indicated that they buy things on the Internet all the time, and 35% revealed that they were very likely to buy something online in the current month. About half of the subjects (49%) felt secure sending personal information over the Internet. Only 20% of the subjects indicated that they clicked the Web seal to view the assurances. This result is consistent with prior findings, indicating the majority of

online shoppers do not review TPO disclosures (Odom et al., 2002) and suggests that the sample is representative of online consumers.

Evaluation of the Model

Structural equations modeling (SEM) was used to evaluate the hypotheses and to estimate the relationships among the variables in the proposed model. Sample size plays an important role in the estimation and interpretation of SEM results. There is no single factor that determines adequate sample size, as it is impacted by model misspecification, model size, departures from normality, and estimation procedures. However, prior research supports the proposed model, and the number of variables incorporated does not imply an overly large or complex model. Based on these factors, Hair, Anderson, Tatham, and Black (1998) recommend a sample size of 100 to 200 in order to ensure valid results using maximum likelihood estimations.

A structural equations application (AMOS 4.0) was used to test the model. A two-step process

Table 1. Confirmatory factor analysis

	Factor 1	Factor 2	Factor 3	Factor 4	Factor 5
Credibility1	.884				
Credibility2	.936				
Credibility3	.785				
Credibility4	.823				
Seal Value1		.887			
Seal Value2		.918			
Seal Value3		.953			
Seal Value4		.880			
Trust1			.772		
Trust2			.814		
Trust3			.854		
Trust4			.895		
Risk1				.843	
Risk2				.836	
Risk3				.923	
Risk4				.721	
Intent1					.912
Intent2					.953
Intent3					.767
Intent4					.910
Intent5					.914

$X^2 = 132.16$, p = .012
GFI = .863

Figure 2. SEM model with standardized estimates

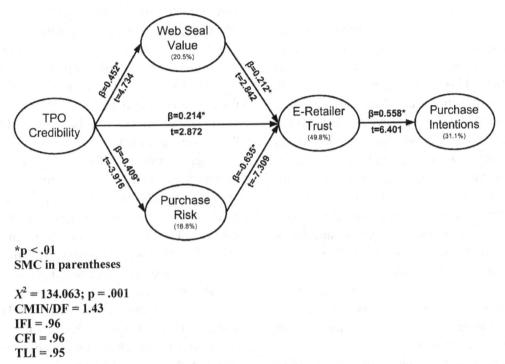

*p < .01
SMC in parentheses

X^2 = 134.063; p = .001
CMIN/DF = 1.43
IFI = .96
CFI = .96
TLI = .95

was applied that tested the measurement model and then evaluated the structural model. The measurement model included all the items underlying the constructs of TPO credibility, purchase risk, value, e-retailer trust, and purchase intentions. The confirmatory factor analysis indicated an acceptable fit to the data (x^2 =132.17, p = .012) with a goodness-of-fit (GFI) index of .863. An acceptable fit of the model to the data provides strong evidence of both discriminant and convergent validity among the constructs (Anderson & Gerbing, 1988).

The structural model containing the hypothesized relationships among TPO credibility, purchase risk, value, trust, and purchase intentions then was tested. The model fit the data well (x^2 = 134.063, p = .001). The fit measures (i.e., IFI = .96; TLI = .95; CFI = .96) provide different perspectives on the acceptability of the model and indicate good support for the model with all indices above the generally accepted mark of .90 (Hair et al., 1998).

All hypothesized paths are supported at the p < .01 level of significance. Results indicate that TPO credibility is positively related to both seal value and trust in the e-retailer while negatively related to purchase risk. Seal value, in turn, relates to trusting attitudes in the e-retailer, while purchase risk is negatively related to trust. As expected, trust in the e-retailer is positively related to purchase intentions.

The squared multiple correlation (SMC) is equivalent to the more familiar R^2 and is an indicator of the explanatory power of the model. The SMC reveals the amount of variance of a dependent variable that is explained by a set of predictor variables. The explanatory power of the model is fairly high, indicating that the model explains 49.8% of the variance for trusting the e-retailer as well as 31.1% of the variance in purchase intentions.

DISCUSSION

Web assurance services were created to address online consumers' security concerns in order to generate the trust necessary to complete electronic transactions. This study confirms prior research, showing that institution-based assurances enhance trust perceptions. This research also extends the concept by identifying an additional mechanism through which assurances influence user trust. We show that trust may originate in a credibility dimension related to the reputation of the assurance organization. Thus, for some consumers, trust may have less to do with their online privacy and security needs and more to do with what they believe about the TPO identified on a Web site. This has important implications for the design of Web assurance services, the selection of assurance providers and services, and the reputation of both e-retailers and providers.

For example, assurance service firms often attempt to differentiate in the market by enlarging their scope of services. What began as a service to users to establish the legitimacy of e-businesses (e.g., BBB OnLine Reliability) has grown in scope to examining e-retailers' business practices, electronic control mechanisms, and systems integrity (e.g., WebTrust). If institutional assurances are viewed as recommendations not associated with these specific assurance services, then expanding the range of services may have little value in attracting consumers. This is an important topic for future investigation.

Furthermore, the selection of the TPO becomes an important consideration, if perceived credibility is an important factor for consumers. Most assurance providers are selected by e-retailers based on cost (Craig, 2000), not reputation. This study indicates that the value of individual Web seals is related to what users believe about the trustworthiness, reliability, integrity, and expert knowledge of the TPO. TPO credibility may have more impact on perceptions of purchase risk and trusting attitudes than anticipated. Further

research is necessary in order to evaluate the extent to which users may depend on the reputation of the TPO to influence purchase decisions. For example, the credibility of the TPO may be more influential in high-risk purchases vs. low-risk purchases or in relation to familiarity with the e-retailer. Additionally, credibility may be a useful strategy in order to differentiate TPOs in the assurance market.

In applying signaling theory and the economics of information to this study, the findings suggest that credibility factors influence the value of the assurance signal. In high-risk purchase situations with an unknown e-retailer, consumers are likely to look for assurances of a positive outcome. Thus, the assurance symbol becomes important for the completion of the transaction, and users are likely to value the symbols of highly credible TPOs to a greater extent. Consequently, if value signals are appropriate mechanisms to convey trust, it is essential that e-retailers employ the symbols of highly credible organizations.

In traditional buyer-seller relationships, TPO endorsement is distinguished by the characteristics of trustworthiness and expertise attributed to the endorsing organization. This study indicates that online consumers may be making a similar application of endorsement mechanisms in the electronic marketplace. Also, TPO endorsements in the traditional marketplace often are perceived as product quality signals (Dean & Biswas, 2001). Assurance service organizations typically make no claim as to product quality, yet consumers often perceive that they do (Houston & Taylor, 1999). E-commerce would benefit from additional research, identifying the aspects of the e-retailer that users believe the TPO is sanctioning (e.g., the Web site, the transaction, the e-retailer, or product/service quality).

Endorsement perceptions have a variety of implications for e-retailers and assurance providers. Reputations may be affected by numerous variables such as consumer satisfaction with products or services, quality, business operations, and dispute resolution. Furthermore, some types of assurance organizations (i.e., AICPA) may generate greater trust for certain e-retailers (e.g., online trading, banking, mortgage brokers) due to enhanced perceptions of expertise, since expert endorsers are most effective for products high in financial, performance, or physical risk (Friedman & Friedman 1979). Additional research may discern if well-known consumer advocates (i.e., BBB) generate trust for specific types of products, e-retailers, or Internet shoppers.

CONCLUSION

It appears that Internet consumers may intermingle assurance organizations and e-retailers in ways that have not been considered. This study contributes to the online trust literature and provides important questions for future research, as the findings have important implications for the future and scope of e-commerce assurance services. Understanding how users perceive assurance organizations and symbols can aid in the creation of services that more effectively address users' online concerns. The success of e-commerce depends on identifying stakeholders, understanding and addressing assurance needs, and enhancing the dominant drivers of trust.

As the generalizability of any research is always a concern, the results of this study should be interpreted within the factors that limit the study. First, the study uses a single Web site and a single product category with a constant review time. While this controls variation and aids reliability, it also limits the generalizability of the results to other populations and/or products. Further studies are necessary to evaluate the research findings in different situations. Second, the study simulates a potential online purchase situation and a significant financial risk to the respondents. While realistic purchase simulations have been used extensively in online trust research, an extension

of the study might test the findings in an actual purchase situation. It is our hope that this research motivates further inquiry into an important area in the success of e-commerce.

REFERENCES

Ajzen, I., & Fishbein, M. (1980). *Understanding the attitudes and predicting social behavior.* Englewood Cliffs, NJ: Prentice-Hall.

Anderson, E., & Weitz, B. (1992). The use of pledges to build and sustain commitment in distribution channels. *Journal of Marketing Research, 29*(1), 18-34.

Anderson, J., & Gerbing, D. (1988). Structural equation modeling in practice: A review and recommended two-step approach. *Psychological Bulletin, 103*(3), 411-423.

Ashton, R., & Kramer, S. (1980). Students as surrogates in behavioral accounting research: Some evidence. *Journal of Accounting Research, 18*(1), 1-3.

Boulding, W., & Kirmani, A. (1993). A consumer-side experimental examination of signaling theory. *Journal of Consumer Research, 20*(1), 111-123.

Craig Jr., J. (2000). AICPA modifies WebTrust to respond to marketplace. *The Trusted Professional, 6,* 3-4.

Crowell, W. (2001). Trust, the e-commerce difference. *Credit Card Management, 14*(5), 80.

Dean, H., & Biswas, A. (2001). Third-party organization endorsement of products: An advertising cue affecting consumer pre-purchase evaluation of goods and services. *Journal of Advertising, 30*(4), 41-57.

DeSarbo, W., & Harshman, R. (1985). Celebrity brand congruence analysis. *Current Issues and Research in Advertising, 8*(1), 17-52.

Eliashberg, J., & Robertson, T. (1988). New product preannouncing behavior: A market signaling study. *Journal of Marketing Research, 25*(3), 282-292.

Friedman, H., & Friedman, L. (1979). Endorser effectiveness by product type. *Journal of Advertising, 19*(5), 63-71.

Fukuyama, R. (1995). *Trust: Social virtues and the creation of prosperity.* New York: The Free Press.

Gefen, D. (2000). E-commerce: The role of familiarity and trust. *Omega, 28,* 725-737.

Goldsmith, R., Lafferty, B., & Newell, S. (2000). The impact of corporate credibility and endorser celebrity on consumer reaction to advertisement and brands. *Journal of Advertising, 29*(3), 43-54.

Hair, J., Anderson, R., Tatham, R., & Black, W. (1998). *Multivariate data analysis.* Upper Saddle River, NJ: Prentice Hall.

Harmon, R., & Coney, K. (1982). The persuasive effects of source credibility in buy and lease situations. *Journal of Marketing Research, 19*(2), 255-260.

Hawkins, D., Best, R., & Coney, K. (1998). *Consumer behavior: Building marketing strategy.* Boston, MA: McGraw Hill.

Hoffman, D., Kalsbeek, W., & Novak, T. (1999). Internet and Web use in the U.S. *Communications of the ACM, 39*(12), 36-46.

Houston, R., & Taylor, G. (1999). Consumer perceptions of CPA WebTrust assurances: evidence of an expectation gap. *International Journal of Auditing, 3*(2), 89-105.

Hoxmeier, J. (2000). Software preannouncements and their impact on customer's perceptions and vendor reputation. *Journal of Management Information Systems, 17*(1), 115-139.

Ippolito, P. (1990). Bonding and nonbonding signals of product quality. *Journal of Business, 63*(1), 41-60.

Jarvenpaa, S., & Todd, P. (1996). Consumer reactions to electronic shopping on the World Wide Web. *International Journal of Electronic Commerce, 1,* 59-88.

Jarvenpaa, S., Tractinsky, N., & Vitale, M. (2000). Consumer trust in an Internet store. *Information Technology and Management, 1*(1-2), 45-71.

Keller, K. (1998). *Strategic brand management.* Upper Saddle River, NJ: Prentice Hall.

Kihlstrom, R., & Riordan, M. (1984). Advertising a signal. *Journal of Political Economy, 92*(3), 427-450.

Kirmani, A., & Rao, A. (2000). No pain, no gain: A critical review of the literature on signaling unobservable product quality. *Journal of Marketing, 64*(2), 66-79.

Kovar, S., Gladden-Burke, K., & Kovar, B. (2000). Consumer responses to the CPA WebTrust assurance. *Journal of Information Systems, 14*(1), 17-35.

Lafferty, B., & Goldsmith, R. (1999). Corporate credibility's role in consumers' attitudes and purchase intentions when a high versus a low credibility endorser is used in the ad. *Journal of Business Research, 44*(2), 109-116.

Lafferty, B., Goldsmith, R., & Newell, S. (2002). The dual credibility model: The influence of corporate and endorser credibility on attitudes and purchase intentions. *Journal of Marketing Theory and Practice, 10*(3), 1-12.

Lala V., Arnold, V., Sutton, S., & Guan L. (2002). The impact of relative information quality of e-commerce assurance seals on Internet purchasing behavior. *International Journal of Accounting Information Systems, 3*(4), 237-253.

Larzelere, R., & Huston, T. (1980). The dyadic trust scale: Toward understanding interpersonal trust in close relationships. *Journal of Marriage and Family, 42*(3), 595-604.

Luhmann, N. (1988). Familiarity, confidence, trust: Problems and alternatives. In D. Gambetta (Ed.), *Trust* (pp. 94-107). New York: Basil Blackwell.

Mauldin, E., & Arunachalam, V. (2001). An experimental examination of alternative forms of Web assurance for business-to-consumer e-commerce. *Journal of Information System, 16*(1), 33-54.

McGinnies, E., & Ward, C. (1980). Better liked than right: Trustworthiness and expertise as factors in credibility. *Personality and Social Psychology Bulletin, 6*(1), 467-472.

McKnight, H., Choudhury, V., & Kacmar, C. (2002). Developing and validating trust measures for e-commerce: An integrative typology. *Information Systems Research, 13*(3), 334-359.

McKnight, H., Cummings, L., & Chervany, N. (1998). Initial trust formation in new original relationships. *Academy of Management Review, 23*(3), 473-490.

Milgrom, P., & Roberts, J. (1986). Price and advertising signals of product quality. *Journal of Political Economy, 94*(4), 796-821.

Miller, G., & Baseheart, J. (1969). Source trustworthiness, opinionated statements, and response to persuasive communication. *Speech Monographs, 36*(1), 1-7.

Moore, D., Hausknecht, D., & Thamodaran, K. (1988). Time compression, response opportunity and persuasion. *Journal of Consumer Research, 13*(1), 12-24.

Morgan, R., & Hunt, S. (1994). The commitment-trust theory of relationship marketing. *Journal of Marketing Research, 29*(3), 20-38.

Nielsen/Net Ratings. (2003). Retrieved from www.nielsen-netratings.com.

NTIA. National Telecommunications and Information Administration. (2002). *A nation online: How Americans are expanding their use of the Internet.* Washington, DC: U.S. Department of Commerce.

Odom, M., Kumar, A., & Saunders, L. (2002). Web assurance seals: How and why they influence consumers' decisions. *Journal of Information Systems, 16*(2), 231-250.

Ohanian, R. (1991). The impact of celebrity spokespersons' image on consumers' intention to purchase. *Journal of Advertising, 31*(1), 46-54.

Palmer, J., Bailey, J., & Faraj, S. (2000). The role of intermediaries in the development of trust on the WWW: The use and prominence of trusted third parties and privacy statements. *Journal of Computer Mediated Communication, 5*(3). Retrieved from *http://www.ascusc.org/jcmc/vol5/issue3/palmer.html*

Rothschild, M., & Stiglitz, J. (1976). Equilibrium in competitive insurance markets: An essay on the economics of imperfect information. *Quarterly Journal of Economics, 90*(3), 630-649.

Rousseau D., Sitkin, S., Burt, R., & Camerer, C. (1998). Not so different after all: A cross-discipline view of trust. *Academy of Management Review, 23*(3), 393-404.

Schneiderman, B. (2000). Designing trust into online experiences. *Communications of the ACM, 43*(12), 57-59.

Schulman, G., & Worrall, C. (1970). Salience patterns, source credibility, and the sleeper effect. *Public Opinion Quarterly, 34*(3), 371-382.

Shankar, V., Urban, G., & Sultan, F. (2002). Online trust: A stakeholder perspective, concepts, implications, and future directions. *The Journal of Strategic Information Systems, 11*(34), 325-344.

Spence, M. (1973). Job market signaling. *Quarterly Journal of Economics, 87*(3), 355-374.

Sternthal, B., Dholakia, R., & Leavitt, C. (1978). The persuasive effects of source credibility: Tests of cognitive response. *Journal of Consumer Research, 4*(4), 252-260.

Stump, R., & Heide, J. (1996). Controlling supplier opportunism in industrial relationships. *Journal of Marketing Research, 33*(4), 431-441.

Urban, G., Sultan, F., & Qualls, W. (2000). Placing trust at the center of your Internet strategy. *Sloan Management Review, 42*(1), 39-48.

Wakefield, R. (2001). *A determination of the antecedents of online trust and an evaluation of current Web assurance seals.* Doctoral dissertation, University of Mississippi, University, MS.

Wolinsky, A. (1983). Prices as signals of product quality. *Review of Economic Studies, 50*(163), 647-658.

This work was previously published in the Journal of Organizational and End User Computing, edited by M. Adam Mahmood, pp. 1-19, copyright 2006 by IGI Publishing, formerly known as Idea Group Publishing (an imprint of IGI Global).

Chapter XIII
Supporting Distributed Groups with Group Support Systems:
A Study of the Effect of Group Leaders and Communication Modes on Group Performance

Youngjin Kim
Fordham University, USA

ABSTRACT

The leadership role facilitates group process by structuring group interaction. How leadership affects group performance in GSS settings remains one of the least investigated areas of GSS research. In this study, the presence of a group leader is found to make a significant difference in objective decision quality and satisfaction with the decision process. At the same time, perceived decision quality and consensus are not significantly different in groups with a leader and those without one. A content analysis of comments by group leaders shows that group leaders are effective when making comments on clear group objectives and interaction structure in the early stages of group interaction. In the later stages, however, it becomes more important for group leaders to offer comments encouraging interaction and maintaining group cohesion.

INTRODUCTION

Group support systems (GSS) are information technology-based environments to support group activities that may be distributed geographically and temporally (Dennis, George, Jessup, Nuna-maker, & Vogel, 1988). The objective of GSS is to increase the effectiveness and efficiency of group interaction by facilitating the interactive sharing of information among group members (Nuna-maker, Dennis, Valacich, Vogel, & George, 1991). These objectives are accomplished by augmenting the group's information-processing capability, increasing participation, and improving communication by structuring the interaction with technology (Ho & Raman, 1991). In this respect, there are clear parallels between GSS studies and structured group interaction techniques, such as the nominal group technique and the Delphi method (Turoff, Hiltz, Baghat, & Rana, 1993), in which leadership and structured communication have been found to exert a significant influence on group outcomes. In fact, GSS research has a strong tradition of studying the effects of structuring group communication (Fjermestad & Hiltz, 1998-1999). Investigation into the impact of leadership on group performance, however, is seldom part of GSS studies (Briggs, Nunamaker, & Sprague, 1997-1998; Parent & Gallupe, 2001). Out of about 230 published papers on GSS, only 6% investigated the effect of leadership in GSS environments (Fjermestad & Hiltz, 1999).

Another little-explored area is the effect of distributed group support systems (DGSS) on dispersed groups, where all group members are geographically and/or temporally dispersed and interact asynchronously through computer-mediated communication systems (CMCS) (Turoff et al., 1993). Although there has been considerable research on communication behavior in face-to-face groups with GSS, there have been few efforts to verify the generalizability of face-to-face communication behaviors in distributed group settings or to investigate factors of computer-mediated communication that uniquely affect the performance of distributed groups (Fjermestad, 2004).

Synthesizing previous studies, Bordia (1997) reports several behavioral differences between groups with CMCS and those with face-to-face communication. The main reason for these differences is that in computer-mediated communication, the lack of social presences (Short, Williams, & Christie, 1976) affects the perception and interpretation of the meaning of the messages exchanged (Rice, 1984), making exchange of information among dispersed group members difficult (Hightower & Sayeed, 1996). This implies that communication support for distributed groups is necessary to overcome the potential problems with limited bandwidth and lack of social presences in CMCS (Hiltz & Johnson, 1990). In addition, the support for asynchronous communication with CMCS should include ways to support larger decision groups, improve the participation of uncooperative subgroups, and deal with critical mass activity phenomena (Turoff et al., 1993). To this end, this study was designed to look into the effects of leadership and communication structuring on group performance in asynchronously interacting distributed groups with CMCS. In the following sections, the literature on leadership and GSS is briefly reviewed, research design and methodology are explained, and research findings are discussed.

LEADERSHIP AND GROUP SUPPORT SYSTEMS

Leadership, by its very nature, is the process of directing and coordinating group interaction (Jago, 1982). According to path-goal theory (House, 1971), a leader affects group performance by clarifying the path to the group's goals, reducing obstacles that prevent the group from reaching these goals, and trying to increase the group's satisfaction as it works toward achieving its goals. In doing so, a leader may define objectives, maintain goal direction, provide the means for goal attainment, provide and maintain group structure, facilitate group action and interaction, maintain group cohesiveness and member satisfaction, and facilitate group task performance (Roby, 1961; Schutz, 1961). Leaders also establish and maintain the link between satisfaction and group performance by employing different leadership styles whose effectiveness can be moderated by the nature of the task, which may account for variance in group performance of more than 50% (Hirokawa & Poole, 1986).

The study of leadership in GSS research also sees leadership as the process of directing and coordinating group interaction. In this research, leadership is considered to be another layer of the group interaction structure (George, Easton, Nunamaker, & Northcraft, 1990; Hiltz, Johnson, & Turoff, 1991) that uses GSS tools to dictate who can say what and when. But the effect of leadership in GSS still remains largely unexplored (Ho & Raman, 1991; Briggs et al., 1997-1998; Parent & Gallupe, 2001), particularly in DGSS settings. In fact, leadership effects have been investigated in just under 10% of the GSS studies (Fjemestad & Hiltz, 1998-1999). One reason is the lack of GSS software tools to support leadership functions. Since GSS research depends on software tools, as Turoff, et al. (1993) argue, there should be more efforts to develop GSS software tools to support the roles of leaders in GSS-supported groups. However, it is difficult to develop software tools that may replace/support the leadership role without understanding the behavior of leaders in GSS settings.

The majority of GSS leadership studies argue that leadership alone rarely affects group outcomes, although it may do so in group performance in interaction with other variables. This is probably the case, because the effect of a group leader is offset by the GSS tools used, where leadership itself is another GSS tool for interaction facilitation (Hiltz et al., 1991; Briggs et al., 1997-1998). This means that leadership alone does not have a significant impact on group performance. Rather, leadership in GSS settings is a moderating variable that affects group outcomes in conjunction with other variables such as anonymity (George et al., 1990; Sosik, Avolio & Kahai, 1997), communication channel (Barkhi, Jacob, Pipino, & Pirkul, 1998), and other GSS tools used (Ho & Raman, 1991; Lim, Raman, & Wei, 1994). Therefore, caution should be exercised when adopting leadership as a complement to GSS

tools in GSS-supported groups. When care is not taken, it could negatively affect group performance by creating too restrictive of an interaction structure (Kim, Hiltz, & Turoff, 2002). One case study, in fact, does report the failure of the use of GSS when the leadership style collides with the GSS arrangement (Parent & Gallupe, 2001). A few other studies demonstrate the mediating effect of leadership in a GSS environment. Hiltz, et al. (1991) find that when statistical feedback is given by the system, groups without leaders perform better, while groups with leaders are less able to reach consensus. Ho and Raman (1991) corroborate that a leader in GSS settings may be effective only when a group needs to establish an interaction structure, because this structure is already available as a GSS tool. George, et al. (1990) observe that anonymous groups with leaders are significantly more satisfied with the decision process. Equal participation and consensus are more likely to be achieved, since leaders are highly influential and dominant over group members and their interaction (Ho & Raman, 1991; Lim et al., 1994).

What do these findings mean to asynchronously interacting groups through CMCS? Can these findings be extended to distributed groups in order to improve their performance? The answer may be no. All these findings are context-specific, not replicated in other studies, and found mostly with face-to-face groups. Still, the way leaders work in CMC settings remains unstudied (George & Sleeth, 2000). To date, Kim et al. (2002) is the only GSS leadership study with fully distributed groups with CMCS. Although Hiltz et al. (1991) and Barkhi et al. (1998) investigated the leadership effect with distributed groups, the group distribution was limited to groups meeting at the same time but in different places. In this regard, a study was designed, as in Figure 1, to investigate how leadership would affect the performance of distributed groups in conjunction with communication modes.

Figure 1. Research design

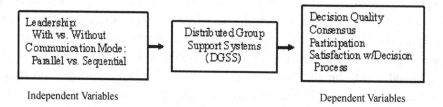

HYPOTHESES DEVELOPMENT

Decision Quality

GSS research has shown clearly that the communication mode has a positive impact on a group's decision quality. The impact of leadership in previous GSS studies, however, is inconsistent. The impact either was not measured (Ho & Raman, 1991; Lim et al., 1994), tested insignificant (George et al., 1990), or reported significant (Hiltz et al., 1991; Tan, Wei, & Lee-Partridge, 1999). In GSS research, because most tasks chosen for studies are preference tasks, decision quality generally is measured using either the perceptions of a panel of experts or the responses to a questionnaire. Perceived decision quality, however, rarely measures decision quality itself. Tan, et al. (1999) assert that perceived decision quality measures decision confidence, which is the degree to which group members are sure that they have arrived at an appropriate group decision. The nature of the experimental task in this study, however, allows objective decision quality as well as perceived decision quality to be measured.

Objective Decision Quality

H1a: Groups with a leader will make better decisions than groups without a leader.
H1b: Parallel communication groups will make better decisions than sequential communication groups.

Perceived Decision Quality

H2a: Groups with a leader will perceive that their decisions are better than groups without a leader.
H2b: Parallel communication groups will perceive that their decisions are better than sequential communication groups.

Consensus

Consensus refers to the degree of support among group members in synthesizing divergent and mutually conflicting ideas during interaction. The level of consensus indicates what happens during group interaction. Consensus also measures the degree of the acceptance of a decision and the commitment to it (Dess & Orieger, 1987; McGrath, 1984) and the level of effective completion of preferred tasks (Tan et al., 1999). Thus, when implementing a decision is more important than reaching a correct decision, consensus as the measure of the acceptance of a decision should take precedence over objective decision quality (Dickson, Lee-Partridge, & Robinson, 1993).

Leadership in GSS settings generally shows no significant impact on consensus. Ho and Raman (1991) indicate that a leader in an unsupported or unstructured group has more influence on consensus, but the leader's effectiveness may be canceled out when another process structuring mechanism is present (Hiltz et al., 1991). These findings suggest that leadership may be more important when a group needs to establish a structure for interaction. Hiltz et al. (1991) also found that asynchronously interacting groups through CMCS tend to be more task-oriented and, therefore, generate a lower level of consensus than face-to-face communication groups. This suggests that the influence of leadership on consensus in dispersed groups should be significant, because asynchronous interaction through CMCS requires more structure in order to coordinate its activities (Turoff et al., 1993).

With regard to the communication mode, the sequential communication mode is likely to show a higher level of consensus, because it provides a more focused interaction than the parallel communication mode. In interacting through CMCS, where social presences already are missing, groups interacting in the parallel communication mode, by allowing discussion on all topics, may have difficulty maintaining group cohesion (Turoff et al., 1993), which easily could lead to a low level of consensus.

H3a: Groups with a leader will show a higher level of consensus than groups without a group leader.
H3b: Sequential communication groups will show a higher level of consensus than parallel communication groups.

Participation

One or a small number of individuals generally dominate a discussion when there is unsupported group interaction. This may lead to lower decision quality and less effective group performance (Hiltz et al., 1991; Tan et al., 1999). GSS generally can ensure equal participation (Fjermestad, 2004). This is because GSSs diminish the potential for dominance by an informal leader by filtering out certain interpersonal cues and regulating the frequency and duration of speaking, which is linked empirically to the emergence of an informal leader (Culnan & Markus, 1987). Therefore, group leadership in GSS is likely to have a positive influence on equal participation. At the same

time, participation is expected to be less equal with the parallel communication mode, because when group members are allowed to discuss any of the topics when they see them, individuals may speak with greater frequency and for longer periods of time.

H4a: Participation will be more equal in groups with a leader than in groups without a leader.
H4b: Participation will be more equal in sequential communication groups than in parallel communication groups.

Satisfaction with the Decision Process

Satisfaction refers to morale, loyalty, or any other manifestation of individual contentment with group outcomes and processes. It is important to measure the level of satisfaction, because it clearly is related to group consensus, productivity, general performance, and effectiveness. Satisfaction also includes attitudinal changes, either positive or negative, toward GSS and the willingness of members to work again.

Findings on satisfaction with the decision process in GSS-supported groups are mixed. Some research results report higher satisfaction with the decision processes in GSS-supported groups (Easton, George, Nunamaker, & Pendergast, 1990). In other studies, however, either no difference or lower satisfaction is found in GSS-supported groups (Chidambaram & Jones, 1993). Findings on the impact of a group leader on satisfaction with the decision process also are inconsistent. While George et al. (1990) find no impact, Hiltz et al. (1991) and Tan et al. (1999) observe that satisfaction with the decision process is significantly higher in groups with leaders.

H5a: Satisfaction with the decision process will be higher in groups with a leader than in groups without a leader.

H5b: Satisfaction with the decision process will be higher in parallel communication groups than in sequential communication groups.

RESEARCH METHODOLOGY: CONTROLLED EXPERIMENT WITH 2X2 FACTORIAL DESIGN

Operationalization of Independent Variables

A group leader selected by group members during a training session is given the flexibility to change any interaction rules or structure, as necessary. In groups with a group leader, these rules and structure thus are not adhered to strictly during the experiment. Groups without a leader, however, are asked simply to adhere to the given interaction rules and structure; they do not have flexibility to modify them.

Communication structuring is arranged in two different modes: parallel and sequential. Generally, research on the impact of communication structuring compares the parallel communication mode through CMCS in GSS-supported groups and the sequential communication mode of turn-taking in face-to-face groups. What is different in this study is the control of human parallel processing (Gray, 1988). With human parallel processing, all group members contribute at the same time in an effort to eliminate communication inefficiencies, such as airtime fragmentation or production blocking (Nunamaker et al., 1991) of sequential face-to-face communication. In both the parallel and sequential communication modes in this study, human parallel processing always is allowed, because all communication takes place through CMCS. The difference between the parallel and sequential communication mode, as operationalized for the experiment, is the difference in the number of discussion items open for group discussion at a time. In the paral-lel communication mode, all discussion items are open concurrently to the group from the very beginning, until the experiment is completed. All group members concurrently discuss any topic at any time in any order throughout the experiment. In the sequential communication, when the experiment begins, groups are informed of all of the topics to discuss during the experiment. However, groups discuss one topic at a time sequentially. Once a group moves to the next discussion topic, it may not revisit previously discussed topics. This step-by-step communication leaves no freedom to deviate from a system-defined linear interaction procedure.

Experimental Task

The task developed for the study is the Investment Club Task (Kim et al., 2002). In performing this task, participants attempt to maximize their portfolio value by agreeing to invest in at least one but no more than three stocks out of 15 candidate stocks to be held for at least six months. Basic information about each stock is provided, and group members are free to gather additional information from any source. The task in a GSS experiment study is usually one of McGrath's Circumplex Task Types (McGrath, 1984). The problem with this task classification is its insistence upon the mutually exclusive categorization of tasks based on performance processes (Rana et al., 1997). The investment club task, however, has characteristics of both Intellective and decision-making task types (McGrath, 1984). It has the characteristics of a decision-making task, because when a decision is made at the end of the experiment, there is no way to have objective knowledge of the decision quality. On the other hand, after the decision horizon is reached (at least six months after the experiment), objective decision quality can be evaluated by measuring actual changes in stock prices.

Table 1. Subjects' backgrounds

Number of Subjects:	212		
Majors:		**Experience with EIES:**	
Information Systems	43%	Frequent Users	52%
Management	54%	Occasional Users	28%
Others	3%	Never Used	20%
Degree Enrolled:		**Investment Experience:**	
BA/BS	30%	Yes	43%
MS/MBA	68%	No	57%
Ph.D.	2%		

Subjects

There were 212 subjects in 47 groups in this experiment. The subjects were recruited from universities in the New York area. All subjects were enrolled in undergraduate or graduate-level MIS classes. During the recruiting session, the subjects filled out preexperiment questionnaires; were assigned to groups of five; and were scheduled for a one-hour, face-to-face training session. After the training session, groups were assigned randomly to experimental conditions. In a few groups, however, the experiment was conducted with three or four subjects due to dropouts during the training session. The subjects' backgrounds are summarized in Table 1.

Nunamaker, Briggs, Mittleman, Vogel, and Balthazard (1996-1997) argue that established groups of managers perform far better than the student subjects used in most GSS experiment studies. An advantage of using student groups, however, is the accessibility to a larger pool of subjects with little variances in their ages, education, or business experience that would enhance the statistical power in testing hypotheses. The use of student subjects can be justified, because when training is given to ad hoc groups before an experiment, ad hoc groups seem to perform as well as established groups (Mennecke, Hoffer, & Wayne, 1992).

Technology and Training

Electronic Information Exchange System 2 (EIES 2) was used for this experiment and modified to add experiment-specific procedures and rules. EIES 2 is one of the major GSS research tools (Fjermestad & Hiltz, 1998-1999) and is used frequently in conducting asynchronous experiments for DGSS research. It is similar to many group communication support systems now available for use through the Internet. To minimize the problems associated with student subjects, a week-long asynchronous online training session with EIES 2 was given to all subjects, beginning with a one-hour, face-to-face session. All the subjects in a training group were assigned to the same experimental group. During training, all subjects were introduced to the system's features and experimental formats. Each group then selected a group leader, who would serve as the group leader if the group were assigned to the with-a-group-leader condition in the experiment.

Administration of the Experimental Procedure

The experiment continued for two weeks. The experimental procedures were constructed by arranging discussion items, and the details are summarized in Table 2. There was no face-to-face session during the experiment. Each group mem-

Table 2. Summary of administration of experimental conditions

Communication Mode

		Sequential	Parallel
Presence of Group Leader	**With Leader**	• Discussion Items Presentation: Sequential • Transition: Sequentially as decided by leaders one item at a time • Leader: Allowed to modify procedures • Revisit: Not allowed for previously discussed items	• Discussion Items Presentation: Parallel • Transition: No transition required; all items open throughout the experiment • Leader: Allowed to modify procedures • Revisit: Allowed for all items at any time
	Without Leader	• Discussion Items Presentation: Sequential • Transition: Sequentially by timetable, one item at a time • Leader: No group leader • Revisit: Not allowed for previously discussed items	• Discussion Items Presentation: Parallel • Transition: No transition required; all items are open throughout the experiment • Leader: No group leader • Revisit: Allowed for all items at any time

Table 3. The results of the statistical analysis

Independent Variable: Group Leader

Dependent Variables	Means		SS	F	Pr > F
	With	Without			
Objective Decision Quality (H1)					
After Six Months *	27,992	25,580	66,330,15	4.690	0.0360
After One Year **	31,702	29,515	55,524,8	3.240	0.0789
Perceived Decision Quality (H2)	27.32	26.84	2.766	0.400	0.5293
Consensus (H3)	11.57	10.90	4.727	2.19	0.1463
Satisfaction with Decision Process (H6) *	6.62	7.70	12.367	6.400	0.0152

Independent Variable: Communication Structuring

Dependent Variables	Means		SS	F	Pr > F
	Parallel	Sequential			
Objective Decision Quality (H1)					
After Six Months	26,994	26,638	1,290,644	0.094	0.7461
After One Year	30,818	30,454	1,290,661	0.070	0.7918
Perceived Decision Quality (H2) *	27.94	26.29	36.160	5.260	0.0268
Consensus (H3)	11.66	10.85	7.716	3.57	0.0655
Satisfaction with Decision Process (H6) *	6.67	7.61	10.368	5.350	0.0255

* Significant at $\alpha= 0.05$; ** Marginally significant at $\alpha= 0.10$
Degree of Freedom: Model = 1; Error = 43

Table 4. Summary of hypotheses testing

	Group Leader	Communication Mode	Interaction
Objective Decision Quality	W > O (6 months) W > O (1 year)	-	-
Perceived Decision Quality	-	P > S	PO > SO
Consensus	-	P > S	-
Participation	W > O	-	PW>SW>SO >PO
Satisfaction	W > O	P>S	SW>SO

Communication Structuring: P - Parallel   S - Sequential
Group Leader: W- With a Leader O - withOut a Leader
- Marginally Significant

ber had to respond to each topic before seeing the responses of others or joining the discussion on the topic. All interactions took place asynchronously through EIES 2.

FINDINGS AND DISCUSSION

Statistical Measures

Except for the objective decision quality, all other dependent variables were measured by composite variables of multiple questionnaire items. A composite variable was used to test a hypothesis only when Cronbach's Coefficient Alpha was higher than 0.8. Because of the unequal number of subjects and groups for each experimental condition, the General Linear Model procedure was used instead of ANOVA for hypothesis testing. Whenever an interaction effect was significant, Fisher's Least Significant Difference Test (LSD) was used for pair-wise comparison of means among all experimental conditions. The results of the statistical analysis are summarized in Table 3, and a summary of the hypothesis testing is in Table 4.

Discussion

Objective decision quality was measured twice by comparing the dollar values of portfolios in six months and one year after the experiment, and perceived decision quality at the end of the experiment with the questionnaire. Although it did not play any significant role in perceived decision quality, the presence of a group leader significantly improves the objective decision quality after six months and after one year. The leadership variable was expected to have an impact on group performance in interaction with another variable (George et al., 1990; Hiltz et al., 1991; Ho & Raman, 1991)—communication mode in this study. However, there was no interaction ef-

fect with the communication mode on objective decision quality.

Although it made no significant difference in objective decision quality, the communication mode had a significant impact on perceived decision quality. Parallel communication groups felt that they made significantly better decisions than sequential communication mode groups (F=5.26 and p=0.0268). This finding can be explained by the preference for procedural order construct (Putnam, 1979), which states that individuals enter groups with a predisposition for particular work habits, ranging from tightly organized procedures to loosely structured ones. In making a decision in a group, all group members have implicit cognitive maps for structuring group activity that interacts with the group's contingency factors that influence group performance. These cognitive maps are relatively inflexible, regardless of their previous success or failure. Satisfaction with the decision process may have resulted from the fact that in the parallel communication mode, group members were able to rearrange the sequence of topics in a way that was compatible with their cognitive maps. Hence, they gave a high rating to perceived decision quality, which is correlated highly with satisfaction with the decision process. Indeed, perceived decision quality was found to correlate highly with satisfaction with the decision process (ρ=0.7718). On the other hand, group members with the sequential communication mode might have had a conflict with a GSS-enforced decision procedure, if it was not their preference. This preference for procedural order also was confirmed in the study of how group members appropriate and react to GSS technology and structured heuristics (Wheeler & Mennecke, 1992).

Another finding on decision quality is the relationship between objective and perceived decision quality. Although objective and perceived decision qualities were not expected to be different (Gopal, Bostrom, & Chin, 1992-1993), Pearson's Correlation Coefficient Rho between perceived and objective decision qualities was −0.0604. This simply indicates no correlation between them. The significance of this finding is that perceived decision quality cannot be used as a surrogate measure for objective decision quality in all situations. It must be used with caution. Any study that measures only perceived decision quality must make clear why objective decision quality cannot be measured. It also should state how perceived decision quality can be used as a surrogate measure for objective decision quality. Otherwise, the findings of studies will be misleading. Failure to distinguish clearly between perceived and objective decision quality may have contributed to inconsistent findings on decision quality in previous GSS research.

With regard to satisfaction with the decision process, there are significant differences in the communication mode and the presence of a group leader. Parallel communication mode groups reported a higher level of satisfaction with decision process than sequential communication groups, while groups with a leader reported a higher level of satisfaction with decision process than groups without a leader. Further analysis with Fisher's LSD indicates that sequential communication groups with a leader report a higher level of satisfaction with the decision process than sequential communication groups without a leader.

One important finding in satisfaction measure is that parallel communication groups generally indicate a higher level of satisfaction than sequential communication groups. The results of satisfaction with the decision process are particularly interesting. Because of novelty effect (Watson, DeSanctis, & Poole, 1988), parallel communication groups were expected to show a lower level of satisfaction with the decision process. These groups, however, reported higher satisfaction than sequential communication groups with more commonly used face-to-face interaction. It appears that as the use of multiple topics and multiple-participant CMCS such as e-mail or instant messengers becomes pervasive, sequential com-

munication no longer may be the preferred mode of communication, thereby dissipating the novelty effect. This opens up a new avenue for the use of GSS in different settings where it may be used as a knowledge management tool or organizational memory and not be limited to task-oriented groups or decision-making groups.

The equality of participation was measured objectively, by counting the number of groups in which an informal leader emerged, and subjectively with a questionnaire. The emergence of an informal leader was used as a surrogate measure for equal participation because it is linked to participation rate (Mullen, Sales, & Drisekll, 1987), and the rule of 50% or more comments than the group's average was used to determine the emergence of an informal leader (Hiltz, Johnson, & Turoff, 1982). The communication mode made no significant difference in either case. However, the number of groups where informal leaders emerged was significantly lower in groups with a leader than in groups without a leader. Ho and Raman (1991) and Lim et al. (1994) argue that the emergence of informal leaders is low in groups with a formal leader who tends to dominate the group process. This may impede a group member from accumulating idiosyncrasy credits that eventually can confer leadership status (Hollander, 1974). For the subjective measure of equal participation, neither the communication mode nor the presence of a group leader made any difference. All groups felt that participation was equal. This finding is in line with previous findings that CMCS increases the level of equal participation by reducing or eliminating the social influence of communication (Steiner, 1972).

The simple presence of a leader, however, did not make much difference. What was more important was whether leaders properly performed their leadership roles. To investigate the group leaders' performances, the contents of the group leaders' comments were analyzed to determine whether they were task-related or leadership-related, as summarized in Table 5. In doing so, all

Table 5. Average number of comments by group leader by content

Condition	Content Category				N. Items	N. CMT.	T.CMT	Percent
	DFN	SRT	FCT	MTN				
Sequential	1.3	3.8	6.1	2.3	11.6	10.8	25.3	41.7%
Parallel	3.3	5.2	6.3	3.2	13.6	12.3	24.8	51.1%

- Content Category:
  - DFN: the number of comments on defining objectives
  - SRT: the number of comments on providing structure
  - FCT: the number of comments on facilitating interaction
  - MTN: the number of comments on maintaining the group
- N. Items: the sum of the number of DFN, SRT, FCT, and MTN
- N.NMT: the number of comments where content category appeared
- T.CMT: the total number of comments generated by a group leader
- Percent: the percentage of N.NMT over T.CMT

leadership-related comments were classified as being in one of the content categories based on previous studies of leadership functions (Roby, 1961; Schutz, 1961): defining objectives, providing interaction structures, facilitating interaction, or maintaining group cohesion.

Of these, the category *providing interaction structure* shows the greatest difference in terms of the average number of comments between group leaders in parallel communication groups (5.2 comments) and those in sequential communication groups (3.8 comments). It appears that for groups interacting through CMCS, there is a need to provide a certain number of interaction requirements. In parallel communication groups, group leaders were effective in dealing with what could have been chaotic interaction due to the lack of social presences and concurrent discussion. They did so by providing more interaction structure, such as initiating further discussion on some topics or summarizing and pointing out explicit differences in the underlying assumptions of group members. Indeed, Ho, and Raman (1991) found that leadership in GSS settings appears more effective when there is a need to bring structure into group interaction. In sequential communication groups, where the interaction structure of what to discuss and when was known throughout the experiment, additional leader-initiated interaction requirements might have created too restrictive of an interaction structure, which negatively affects group performance (Kim et al., 2002).

The timing of each content category is also worth mentioning. In both sequential and parallel communication groups, group leaders tended to generate more comments on defining group objectives and providing interaction structure in the early stages of the experiment. The frequency of these comments diminished toward the middle of the experiment. On the other hand, group leaders started making comments on facilitating interaction and on maintaining a group shortly before the middle of the experiment and continued through the later stages of the experiment. It seems that in asynchronous interaction through CMCS, the role of a group leader in the early stages is to make clear the decision strategy by which group interaction is coordinated. As all group members come to understand the interaction requirements of the decision strategy, however, the role of a group leader tends to change to that of a facilitator. This facilitation encourages uncooperative members to improve their participation in order to increase group cohesiveness and to deal with the critical mass activity phenomenon associated with negative feedback, if the participation rate is too low (Turoff et al., 1993).

LIMITATION AND FUTURE RESEARCH

One limitation of the study was the training of groups before the experiment. The task given to all the training groups was the selection of a group leader to serve as a leader in the experiment. The selected leader was announced to groups in *with-a-leader* conditions at the beginning of the experiment. In groups in *without-a-leader* conditions, the selected leader was never announced. However, it is suspected that by selecting a group leader during the training session, the subjects in without-a-leader conditions may have participated in the experiment, subconsciously feeling the presence of a group leader. A different training task could have prevented this feeling in groups in without-a-leader conditions. Fortunately, however, not many of the leaders selected in training sessions emerged as informal leaders in groups in without-a-leader conditions.

This study can be extended further to examine the impact of different leadership styles in GSS settings. Leadership is a very complex construct for which a stronger theoretical basis is needed to develop software support for leadership and facilitation roles in DGSS and GSS, in general. Leadership might not be affected by GSS; however, the use of GSS may be affected by a leader, particularly by leadership style (Parent & Gallupe, 2001). For example, one study found that while interaction-oriented transformational leadership positively has amplified the effect of GSS anonymity on group potency and effectiveness, outcome-oriented transactional leadership did not (Sosik et al., 1997). Unfortunately, in this study, leadership styles were not controlled. Groups in the same experimental condition could have had different interaction environments because of the different leadership styles used by group leaders. In a future study with the group leader variable, it may be necessary to control different leadership styles rather than simply to adopt the with-and-without-a-group-leader conditions.

REFERENCES

Barkhi, R., Jacob, V. S., Pipino, L., & Pirkul, H. (1998). A study of the effect of communication channel and authority on group decision processes and outcomes. *Decision Support Systems, 23*(3), 205-226.

Bordia, P. (1997). Face-to-face versus computer-mediated communication: A synthesis of the experimental literature. *Journal of Business Communication, 34*(1), 99-120.

Briggs, R. O., Nunamaker, J. F., & Sprague, R. H. (1997-1998). 1001 unanswered research questions in GSS. *Journal of Management Information Systems, 14*(3), 3-21.

Chidambaram, L., & Jones, B. (1993). Impact on communication medium and computer support on group perceptions and performance: A comparison of face-o-face and dispersed meetings. *MIS Quarterly, 17*(4), 465-491.

Culnan, M. J., & Markus, M. L. (1987). Information technologies. *Handbook of Organizational Communication*, 420-443.

Dennis, A. R., George, J. F., Jessup, L. M., Nunamaker, J. F., & Vogel, D.R. (1988). Information technology to support electronic meetings. *MIS Quarterly, 12*(4), 591-616.

DeSanctis, G., & Gallupe, R. (1987). A foundation for the study of group decision support systems. *Management Science, 33*(5), 589-609.

Dess, G. G., & Orieger, N. K. (1987). Environment structure and consensus in strategy formulation: A conceptual integration. *Academy of Management Review, 12*(2), 313-330.

Dickson, G. W., Lee-Partridge, J., & Robinson, L. H. (1993). Exploring ,modes of facilitative support for GDSS technology. *MIS Quarterly, 17*(2), 173-194.

Easton, A., George, J. F., Nunamaker, J. F., & Pendergast, M. O. (1990). Using two different electronic meeting system tools for the same task: An experimental comparison. *Journal of Management Information Systems, 7*(1), 85-100.

Fiedler, F. E. (1974). The contingency model—New directions for leadership utilization. *Journal of Contemporary Business*, 65-79.

Fjermestad, J. (2004). An analysis of communication mode in group support systems research. *Decision Support Systems, 37*(2), 239-266.

Fjermestad, J., & Hiltz, S. R. (1998-1999). An assessment of group support systems experimental research: Methodology and results. *Journal of Management Information System, 15*(3), 7-149.

George, G., & Sleeth, R. G. (2000). Leadership in computer-mediated communication: Implications and research directions. *Journal of Business and Psychology, 15*(2), 287-310.

George, J. F., Easton, G. K., Nunamaker, J. F., & Northcraft, G. B. (1990). A study of collaborative group work with and without computer-based support. *Information Systems Research, 1*(4), 394-415.

Gopal, A. R., Bostrom, O., & Chin, Y. (1992-1993). Applying adaptive structuration theory to investigate the process of group support systems use. *Journal of Management Information Systems, 9*(3), 45-69.

Gray, P. (1988). *The* user interface in group decision support systems. In *Proceedings of the Eighth International Conference on Decision Support Systems*, Boston, MA (pp. 203-225).

Griffith, T. L., & Northcraft, G. B. (1994). Distinguish between the forest and trees: Media, features, and methodology in electronic communication research. *Organizational Science, 5*(2), 272-285.

Hightower, R., & Sayeed, L. (1996). Effects of communication mode and prediscussion information distribution characteristics on information exchange in groups. *Information Systems Research, 7*(4), 451-465.

Hiltz, S. R., & Johnson, K. (1990). User satisfaction with computer-mediated communication systems. *Management Science, 36*(6), 739-764.

Hiltz, S. R., Johnson, K., & Turoff, M. (1982). *The effects of formal human leadership and computer-generated decision aids on problem solving via computer: A controlled experiment* [Research Report No. 18]. Computerized Conferencing and Communication Center, New Jersey Institute of Technology.

Hiltz, S. R., Johnson, K., & Turoff, M. (1991). Group decision support: The effects of designated human leaders and statistical feedback in computerized conferences. *Journal of Management Information System, 8*(2), 81-108.

Hiltz, S. R., & Turoff, M. (1978-1993). *The Network Nation: Human Communication via Computer*. Reading, MA: Addison-Wesley.

Hirokawa, R. Y., & Poole, M. S. (Eds.). (1986). *Communication and group decision-making*. Beverly Hills, CA: Sage Publications.

Ho, T. H., & Raman, K. S. (1991). The effect of GDSS and elected leadership on small group meetings. *Journal of Management Information Systems, 8*(2), 109-133.

Hollander, E. P. (1974). Processes of leadership emergence. *Journal of Contemporary Business*, Autumn, 19-33.

House, R. J. (1971). A path goal theory of leader effectiveness. *Administrative Science Quarterly, 16*, 321-338.

Jago, A. G. (1982). Leadership: Perspectives in theory and research. *Management Science, 28*, 315-336.

Kim, Y. J., Hiltz, S. R., & Turoff, M. (2002). Coordination structures and system restrictiveness in distributed group support systems. *Group Decision and Negotiation, 11*(5), 379-404.

Lim, L. H., Raman, K. S., & Wei, K. K. (1994). Interacting effects of GDSS and leadership. *Decision Support Systems, 12*, 199-211.

McGrath, J. E. (1984). *Groups: Interaction and performance.* Englewood Cliffs, NJ: Prentice-Hall.

Mennecke, B. E., Hoffer, H. A., & Wynne, B. E. (1992). The implications of group development and history for group support system theory and practice. *Small Group Research, 23*(4), 524-572.

Mullen, B., Salas, E., & Drisekll, J. E. (1987). Salience, motivation, and artifact as contribution to the relation between participation rate and leadership. *Journal of Experimental Social Psychology, 25*, 809-826.

Nunamaker, J. F., Briggs, R., Mittleman, D. D., Vogel, D. R., & Balthazard, P. A. (1996-1997). Lessons from a dozen years of group support systems research: A discussion of lab and field findings. *Journal of Management Information Systems, 13*(3), 163-207.

Nunamaker, J. F., Dennis, A. R., Valacich, J. S., Vogel, D. R., & George, J. F. (1991). Electronic meeting systems to support group work. *Communications of the ACM, 34*(7), 40-59.

Parent, M., & Gallupe, R. B. (2001). The role of leadership in group support systems failure. *Group Decision and Negotiation, 10*(5), 405-422.

Putnam, L. L. (1979). Preference for procedural order in task-oriented small groups. *Communication Monographs, 46*, 193-218.

Rana, A. R., Turoff, M, & Hiltz, R. (1997). *Task and technology interaction (TTI): A theory of technological support for group tasks.* Proceedings of the Thirtieth Hawaii International Conference on System Sciences, 2, 66-75.

Rice, R. E. (1984). Mediated group communication. In R. E. Rice and Associates (Eds.), *The new media: Communication, research, and technology* (pp. 129-156). Beverly Hills, CA: Sage.

Roby, T. B. (1961). The executive function in small groups. In L. Petrullo, & B. Bass (Eds.), *Leadership and interpersonal behavior.* New York: Holt, Rinehart and Winston.

Schutz, W. C. (1961). On group composition. *Journal of Abnormal Social Psychology, 62*, 275-281.

Short, J., Williams, E., & Christie, B. (1976). *The social psychology of telecommunications.* New York: John Wiley.

Sosik, J. J., Avolio, B. J., & Kahai, S. S. (1997). Effects of leadership style and anonymity on group potency and effectiveness in a group decision support system environment. *Journal of Applied Psychology, 82*(1), 89-103.

Steiner, I. D. (1972). *Group process and productivity.* New York: Academic Press.

Tan, B., Wei, K., & Lee-Partridge, J. E. (1999). Effects of facilitation and leadership on meeting outcomes in a group support system environment. *European Journal of Information Systems, 8*, 223-246.

Turoff, M., Hiltz, S. R., Baghat, A., & Rana, A. (1993). Distributed group support systems. *MIS Quarterly, 17*(4), 399-417.

Watson, R. T., DeSanctis, G., & Poole, M. C. (1988). Using a GDSS to facilitate group consensus: Some intended and unintended consequences. *MIS Quarterly, 12*(3), 463-477.

Wheeler, B. C., & Mennecke, B. E. (1992). The effects of restrictiveness and preference for procedural order on the appropriation of group decision heuristics in a GSS environment. In *Proceedings of the Thirteenth Annual International Conference on Information Systems,* Dallas Texas (pp. 274-275).

ENDNOTE

[1]   A previous version of this article was published in the Proceedings of 15th International Conference of Information Resources Management Association, 2004.

Chapter XIV
Evaluating Group Differences in Gender During the Formation of Relationship Quality and Loyalty in ISP Service

Chieh-Peng Lin
Vanung University, Taiwan

Cherng G. Ding
National Chiao Tung University, Taiwan

ABSTRACT

This study examines the moderating role of gender during the formation of relationship quality and loyalty in the context of IT service. In the proposed model, expertise, relational selling behavior, perceived network quality, and service recovery indirectly influence a customer's loyalty through mediation of relationship quality. Gender moderates each model path. The moderating effects are examined simultaneously using data from customers of Taiwan's leading Internet service provider. Test results indicate that the influences of perceived network quality on relationship quality and of relationship quality on loyalty are stronger for males than females, while relational selling behavior influences relationship quality more for females than for males. Furthermore, service recovery influences relationship quality for both the male and female groups, but its influence does not differ significantly between the two groups. Finally, expertise exerts an insignificant influence on relationship quality for both groups. Implications of the empirical findings also are discussed.

INTRODUCTION

A battle for e-commerce is rising rapidly in Taiwan, one of the most competitive markets around the globe. Many emerging e-commerce companies, especially those that focus on B2C (business-to-consumer) are struggling to get more customers. These companies devote a large amount of their investment to state-of-the-art infrastructure and promotion, and extensively to outright customer subsidies. For instance, many ISPs (Internet service providers) are offering giveaways (e.g., MP3 players) or price discounts for new customers who sign up during a specific period of time.

There is no question that a focused approach to establishing the strengths and unique competitive edge of a company is necessary for survival, given the intense competition. Notably, the continuance of IT usage at the individual user level is crucial to many business-to-customer electronic commerce firms, such as ISPs, online retailers, online banks, online brokerages, online travel agencies, and so forth (Bhattacherjee, 2001). However, such continuance relies on achieving relationship quality and customer loyalty. As indicated by Chen and Hitt (2002), the expectation of B2C companies is that early investments in customer acquisition will result in a long-term stream of profits from loyal customers, which will offset the costs. Previous studies have demonstrated the importance of relationship quality and loyalty and their impact on firm profitability and customer retention (Crosby, Evans, & Cowles, 1990; Tam & Wong, 2001), but the first step in effectively managing relationship quality and customer loyalty in IT service contexts is identifying their antecedents. This study identifies the critical customer loyalty determinants from the perspective of users and also clarifies their importance in loyalty formation.

This study differs from previous works in two important ways. First, this work focuses on the study of relationship quality in the marketing of an intangible ISP service. The reason that intangible services (e.g., ISP services) should be treated differently from tangible goods is that consumers have more difficulty evaluating the quality of intangible services than physical goods prior to, during, and after consumption (Grove, Pickett, & Laband, 1995; Rushton & Carson, 1989). It has been suggested that the advertising and promotion for intangible services should differ from those of physical goods (Rushton & Carson, 1989). This study investigates customers using an ISP service and, through an examination of gender differences, brings implications for IT marketers. Second, gender generally is neglected in IT behavioral research (Gefen & Straub, 1997). This study is one of the earliest to conceptualize and to test a model of IT relationship quality that includes gender as a moderator. Since gender generally is acknowledged to influence profoundly one's response to marketing strategies (Brady & Robertson, 1999; Laroche, Saad, Cleveland, & Browne, 2000; Mattila, Grandey, & Fisk, 2003; Maxwell, 1999), specifying the moderating impacts of gender can guide IT service providers to design different strategies for different customers and, consequently, achieve high relationship quality and customer loyalty.

RESEARCH FRAMEWORK AND HYPOTHESIS DEVELOPMENT

The conceptual model, displayed in Figure 1, is a direct modification of those given by Crosby et al. (1990) and Lin and Ding (2005). The model not only includes relational selling behavior and expertise (Crosby et al., 1990) but also integrates two key variables specific to the IT service field: perceived network quality (Kettinger & Lee, 1994) and service recovery (Bob, 1989), which are rarely tested in IT service contexts.

In the proposed model, expertise, relational selling behavior, perceived network quality, and service recovery indirectly influence customer loyalty through the mediation of relationship

Figure 1.

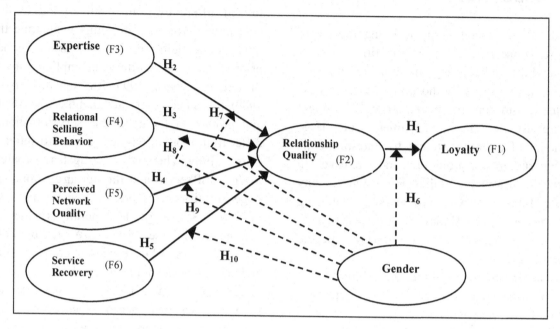

quality. Gender moderates each path in the model. While a similar work (Lin & Ding, 2005) puts emphasis on the prior experience of Internet users as a moderator, this study focuses on a different moderator—gender.

Lin and Ding (2005) gave reviews for loyalty, relationship quality and their antecedents, and tested for the path significance. We will first summarize their reviews and the relevant hypotheses, and then introduce gender as a moderator.

Relationship Quality

The relationship quality is a general evaluation of relationship strength and the extent to which a relationship meets the needs and expectations of the parties involved, based on a history of successful or unsuccessful encounters or events (Crosby et al., 1990). Even though no consensus exists concerning the constructs that form relationship quality (Kumar, Scheer, & Steenkamp, 1995), it often is conceptualized as involving

trust between relaters and their satisfaction with a relationship. In other words, relationship quality is regarded as a construct comprising at least two components: (1) trust in a sales agent and the service (Swan, Trawick, & Silva, 1985); and (2) satisfaction with a sales agent and the service (Crosby & Stephens, 1987).

Satisfaction is an emotional status that occurs in response to an assessment of buyer-seller interaction experiences (Westbrook, 1981). A practicing business concept entails the pursuit of customer satisfaction as the chief goal of any organization. Not only can customer satisfaction legitimately be an end in itself for business organizations, but it is considered a means to such ends as competitive advantages, customer loyalty, and consequently survival (Gopalakrishna & Mummalaneni, 1993).

Trust usually is considered necessary for successful relationships (Berry, 1995; Moorman, Deshpande, & Zaltman, 1993). From the existing literature (Moorman et al., 1993), trust can be viewed as a customer's confidence in the reliability and integrity of a seller. Previous works have proposed that an expectation of trustworthiness is created by ability (expertise), reliability, and intentionality (Crosby et al., 1990; Busch & Wilson, 1976; Swan et al., 1985). Furthermore, several scholars consider perceived trustworthiness and trusting behavior as two distinct but related aspects of trust (Crosby et al., 1990; Dwyer, Schurr, & Oh, 1987; Swan et al., 1985). Whereas trustworthiness describes a belief or confidence, trusting behavior is related to a willingness to engage in risk-taking and reflects reliance on a partner (Smith & Barclay, 1997).

Loyalty

In this study, loyalty to a service provider is conceptualized in terms of repeat patronage, switching behavior, and word-of-mouth recommendations. Empirical evidence has been found for a positive relationship between relationship quality (comprising satisfaction and trust) and customer loyalty. On the one hand, positive paths from relationship satisfaction to both relationship duration and purchase intentions are indicators of customer loyalty (Wulf, Oderkerken-Schroder, & Lacobucci, 2001). That is, customers who have experienced recent service problems and have received a satisfactory recovery and services had significantly more positive behavioral intentions than those with unresolved problems (Zeithaml, Berry, & Parasuraman, 1996), leading to increased loyalty. On the other hand, trust positively affects forbearance from opportunism (Smith & Barclay, 1997). It has been suggested that customers who trust a relationship might be more likely to act, owing to their need to maintain that trust, consequently leading to stronger customer loyalty. In summary, given that relationship quality is viewed as a construct comprising satisfaction and trust, the following hypothesis based on the above findings can be derived:

H1: Relationship quality positively influences loyalty.

Expertise

Expertise is a subjective term based on customer perceptions that service providers have valuable knowledge, experience, skills, or qualifications in a specific service domain (Shamdasani & Balakrishnan, 2000). Additionally, expertise frequently has been noted as attempts to influence a given target customer (Busch & Wilson, 1976). Customer perceptions of staff expertise reflect the identification of relevant competencies related to goods or service transactions, such as product knowledge, and generally are displayed in the form of staff-provided information. The role of staff expertise in IT service contexts has received limited attention in the MIS and marketing literature, but some evidence suggests that staff expertise enhances relationship quality (trust in and satisfaction with staff). Busch and Wilson (1976) found that staffs with high levels of perceived expertise and referent power are considered more trustworthy by customers, with expert power influencing perceptions of trustworthiness more than referent power. Similarly, Swan et al. (1985) noted that sales agent professionalism significantly influences perceived trust of customers in that sales agent. Therefore, staff expertise is hypothesized to positively influence relationship quality.

H2: Expertise positively influences relationship quality.

Relational Selling Behaviors

The difference between content and style in communication has been discussed before by Sheth (1975), who also recognizes the importance of ritualistic behavior patterns in shaping the outcomes of buyer/seller interactions. Therefore, relational selling behavior can be described as a behavioral tendency displayed by some staff to cultivate and maintain the buyer-seller relationship via mutual communications. Furthermore, the influence of such behavior on the buyer-seller relationship also depends on customer expectations regarding the role(s) of the staff (Solomon, Surprenant, Czepiel, & Gutman, 1985). For example, Soldow and Thomas (1984) suggested that successful selling depends heavily on the interaction between the buyer and the seller, as defined by their level of relational communication. Similarly, relational selling reflects an effort on the part of the salesperson to keep efficient communication channels for the purpose of maintaining a good relationship with consumers (Crosby et al., 1990; Williamson, 1983). Efforts to establish a good selling relationship with customers have been discussed as a key determinant of relationship maintenance in life insurance (Crosby et al., 1990), wholesale banking (Greenwich Associates, 1987), and so forth. Hence, relational selling behavior takes the form of an exogenous construct in the proposed model and is hypothesized to positively influence relational quality.

H3: The relational selling behavior has a positive influence on the relationship quality.

Perceived Network Quality

The stability of a causal attribution associated with network quality influences customer evaluations and future attitudes. From the previous literature, the perception of stable network quality should boost customer satisfaction and trust (Kettinger & Lee, 1994; Woo & Fock, 1999), thus improving relationship quality. Some of the dominant models relating to customer satisfaction describes satisfaction as a function of expectations and confirmation resulting from a comparison between expectation and actual performance perception (Oliver, 1980), and perceived network quality is the strongest influence on actual performance and, thus, on customer perceptions. Consequently,

perceived network quality should be the main focus of ISP marketers.

H4: Perceived network quality positively influences relationship quality.

Service Recovery

However much Internet quality is driven, ISPs inevitably need to deal with customer dissatisfaction following service failures. Service recovery is defined as specific actions taken to ensure that a customer receives a reasonable level of service following the disruption of normal service (Lewis & Spyrakopoulos, 2001). Service recovery is especially important in ISP service, because there exist some complex issues of service failure during the usage of ISP service. These issues may be caused by any change of hardware or software; the internal setup of the computer; or even a missing password, either deliberately or accidentally. They also could result from the infection of a computer virus. Whenever Internet service failure happens for any of these reasons, most customers will argue with their ISP and ask for help rather than figure out the technical difficulty by themselves (sometimes it is just too difficult for customers to solve complicated issues by themselves). Under this circumstance, which has nothing to do with network quality, ISPs still have to deal with the issue of service failure with efficient service recovery by debugging the service failure for customers. That is also why service recovery becomes much more critical in ISP service than in other service sectors.

From the theory of disconfirmation paradigm (Oliver, 1980), relationship quality is the outcome of an evaluation process, whereby customers compare their expectations of how the service recovery should be offered to the actual experience with the service recovery. Either a negative or positive confirmation of expectations will change the current levels of customers' trust in and satisfaction with the ISP. A negative disconfirmation is said to happen when the service recovery cannot be performed promptly and properly. Conversely, for example, by recording service failure in a database and establishing guidelines and standards, Chunghwa Telecom performs efficient service recovery and, consequently, establishes a positive confirmation of customers.

In fact, good service recovery can create more trust than if things had gone smoothly in the first place (Hart, Heskett, & Sasser, 1990). Additionally, satisfaction with service recovery markedly enhances the overall customer satisfaction and willingness to recommend the firm and consequently increases loyalty. Therefore, the hypothesis is stated as follows.

H5: Service recovery positively influences relationship quality.

Gender as a Moderator

Customer-perceived value is critical to understanding the choices of marketing management in setting up how to improve relationship quality and customer loyalty, because relationship quality may be established via customer perceived value in the areas of expertise, relational selling behavior, perceived network quality, and service recovery. However, customer-perceived value is a complex element instead of a univariate element, and it displays significant gender differences (Hall, Shaw, Lascheit, & Robertson, 2000). Extensive research (Granzin, 1976; Holbrook, 1986; Palmer & Bejou, 1995) has investigated the formation of satisfaction and trust (relationship quality) across gender during buying processes. Individuals with stronger feminine or masculine identities make repeated purchases (regarded as loyalty) based on different service choices accordingly (Costa, 1994), as certain services are perceived to be gender-specific (Hall et al., 2000) and are satisfactory and trustworthy (regarded as relationship quality) in different ways sensitively across gender. Consequently, an important area

in gender differences has emerged; namely, that the connection from customer relationship quality to loyalty differs across gender.

H6: Gender moderates the influence of relationship quality on loyalty.

A good case for why women and men respond differently to IT service can be established via the literature on circumstances analogous to those involved in IT perception and use (Gefen & Straub, 1997). For example, extensive work (Hofstede, 1980) offers insight into the basis of sex differences in thinking and behavior, suggesting, in turn, why underlying IT gender differences may exist. Furthermore, it has been suggested that, compared to males, females are more likely to conform (Sistruck & McDavid, 1971), to be convinced, and to be more influenced by experts (Aronson, 1972). Worchel and Cooper (1976) suggested that these differences in conformity rates may be attributable to gender socialization processes; while males are taught to be independent thinkers and to assert themselves, females are not similarly encouraged and, consequently, are influenced by the expertise of a professional salesperson. Hence, this implies strongly that the influence from expertise to relationship quality differs between males and females.

H7: Gender moderates the influence of expertise on relationship quality.

The role of gender in market segment establishment has been well documented. Hofstede (1991) summarized the general nature of male-female differences based on previous research. Briefly, feminine traits reflect care for others, the importance of relationships (or relational exchanges), as well as compromise and negotiation with others for conflict resolution. Fournier (1998) concluded that females put more emphasis on interpersonal relationships with service providers than males. In particular, the theory on prescriptive stereotypes

(Deaux & Kite, 1993) suggests that because females valuing strong social relationships are more friendly to others than males (Eagly, 1987), they may be expected to emerge with a more sensitive response toward relationship quality to a greater extent than males, given that the level of their perceived relational selling behavior is similar to that of males. Consequently, the previous review indicates that the influence from relational selling behavior to relationship quality may differ across gender, given that females rate interpersonal aspects more highly than males during services provided.

H8:   Gender moderates the influence of relational selling behavior on relationship quality.

While females rate interpersonal aspects highly during services provided, a strong pattern is found in males rating material advancement and success highly (Hofstede, 1980). Therefore, male traits reflecting advancement and success lead to a more sensitive response (caused by network quality) on relationship quality, given that good network quality represents certain technical advancement. Accordingly, males, who are more impatient, also are more likely to respond sensitively to relationship quality, whenever the issue of service recovery arises. More specifically, people consider qualities such as patient, kind, understanding, considerate, and thoughtful to others as more typical of females than males (De Beauvoir, 1952; Flax, 1983). This *other* focus typically is associated with an understanding of the situations of service recovery performed by others during service failure and exemplified by feminine stereotypes (De Beauvoir, 1952; Flax, 1983). Consequently, females being more patient and more thoughtful to the situations of others (Bridges, 1989) suggests that the response (caused by service recovery) on relationship quality may be less sensitive than that of males. The previous review consequently indicates that the influences from perceived network quality and service re-

covery to relationship quality may differ across gender.

H9: Gender moderates the influence of perceived network quality on relationship quality.
H10: Gender moderates the influence of service recovery on relationship quality.

In conclusion, gender may moderate the relationships between relationship quality and its antecedents based on the previous review and inferences. Given this, determining the differences between male and female users in ISP services is important, although little research has been undertaken to explore such moderating effects in ISP service. More importantly, the differences in terms of gender may suggest alternative ways to effectively achieve high customer loyalty with the ISP.

RESEARCH METHODS

Subjects

The general approach used for empirically testing the relationships implied by the research model and research hypotheses is a field study using a survey methodology for data collection. Data were obtained from a large cross-sectional sample of ADSL customers of Taiwan's largest ISP, Chunghwa Telecom. Nowadays, Taiwan has more than 29 ISPs offering a variety of network services, such as ADSL, cable modem, and so forth. Despite Taiwan having a population of only 22 million, there are already approximately 8.59 million Internet users in Taiwan (Institute for Information Industry, 2002). The Internet broadband market penetration rate of Taiwan ranks second internationally, trailing South Korea (Institute for Information Industry, 2002). Among these ISPs, the network service provided by Chunghwa Telecom occupies a market share of more than 60% countrywide. Using the sample from a developed

Table 1. Characteristics of the sample

Characteristic	Male (N = 209)	Female (N = 130)
Age		
20 years or less	23 (11%)	17 (13%)
21-30 years	45 (22%)	41 (32%)
31-40 years	43 (21%)	25 (19%)
41-50 years	77 (37%)	37 (28%)
51 years or above	21 (9%)	10 (8%)
Education		
Non-college graduate	42 (20%)	36 (28%)
Four-year degree	138 (66%)	84 (65%)
Graduate education or degree	29 (14%)	10 (7%)
Marriage		
Single	83 (40%)	64 (49%)
Married	126 (60%)	66 (51%)
ADSL experience		
6 months or less	39 (19%)	22 (17%)
7-12 months	46 (22%)	27 (21%)
13-24 months	61 (29%)	51 (39%)
25-36 months	47 (22%)	22 (17%)
37 months or over	16 (8%)	8 (6%)

county—Taiwan—is one of the advantages that this study has, because college education is very popular in Taiwan, regardless of gender. In other words, such a similar context across gender in a modern society may dampen unpredictable inequality (e.g., educational inequality), leading to a better insight for the moderating role of gender.

Sampling was conducted in two stages: the proportional stratified sampling was first performed by area and then followed the systematic sampling from Chunghwa Telecom's customer phone numbers. Systematic sampling is appropriate, since the phone numbers in the database are neither serial nor acyclic. Eight hundred questionnaires were mailed, and a follow up was performed by telephone. Three hundred and thirty-nine completed questionnaires were returned to the researchers (response rate of 42%), comprising male and female groups as displayed in Table 1, which also lists the characteristics of the two groups.

Measures

The constructs in this study are measured using five-point Likert scales drawn and modified from the existing literature, and three common steps are employed to choose items for measurement. First, the items from the existing literature were translated into Chinese. Second, a university professor and a senior Chunghwa Telecom staff, who are proficient in English and familiar with IT, were asked to provide assistance in examining the appropriateness of the Chinese version of the scale, translated from the original English measurement items. Any inappropriate items were eliminated. Third, a reexamination for the measurements was repeated throughout the pretest process.

These steps ensure that the questionnaire satisfies the content validity. Loyalty (F1) is measured using seven items modified from Zeithaml et al. (1996); a sample item: I will continue using the service offered by [name of company]. Two facets of relationship quality (F2) are as follows: satisfaction, with three items adapted from Tam and Wong (2001); a sample item: I am satisfied with the service provided by [name of company]. Trust, with seven items modified from Crosby et al. (1990); a sample item: [name of company] is a reliable company. Expertise (F3) with five items is modified from Crosby et al. (1990); a sample

Table 2. Standardized loadings and reliabilities across gender

Construct	Indicators retained in the model	Total (N = 339) Standardized loading (*t* value)	Male (n_1 = 209) Standardized loading (*t* value)	Female (n_2 = 130) Standardized loading (*t* value)
Loyalty (F1)	1	0.88 (19.85)	0.89 (16.10)	0.84 (11.47)
	2	0.86 (19.12)	0.85 (14.96)	0.86 (11.81)
	4	0.85 (19.00)	0.86 (15.23)	0.84 (11.48)
	7	0.66 (13.24)	0.63 (9.88)	0.73 (9.34)
Cronbach's alpha		**0.88**	**0.88**	**0.89**
Relationship quality (F2)	8	0.90 (20.90)	0.89 (16.39)	0.90 (12.92)
	9	0.89 (20.46)	0.92 (17.22)	0.83 (11.32)
	11	0.83 (18.51)	0.84 (14.80)	0.82 (11.19)
Cronbach's alpha		**0.90**	**0.92**	**0.89**
Expertise (F3)	19	0.79 (16.85)	0.82 (13.95)	0.73 (9.31)
	20	0.85 (18.83)	0.87 (15.42)	0.81 (10.71)
	21	0.80 (17.17)	0.77 (12.68)	0.88 (12.21)
	22	0.78 (16.39)	0.80 (13.53)	0.74 (9.50)
Cronbach's alpha		**0.88**	**0.89**	**0.87**
Relational selling behavior (F4)	23	0.80 (16.62)	0.84 (14.14)	0.70 (8.39)
	24	0.75 (15.14)	0.77 (12.51)	0.71 (8.58)
	25	0.63 (12.09)	0.62 (9.46)	0.65 (7.70)
Cronbach's alpha		**0.77**	**0.78**	**0.73**
Perceived network quality (F5)	30	0.78 (15.26)	0.80 (12.35)	0.76 (9.06)
	32	0.78 (15.19)	0.78 (12.01)	0.77 (9.25)
Cronbach's alpha		**0.76**	**0.77**	**0.74**
Service recovery (F6)	35	0.79 (16.73)	0.79 (13.26)	0.77 (9.95)
	36	0.81 (17.42)	0.81 (13.79)	0.80 (10.57)
	37	0.84 (18.22)	0.82 (13.87)	0.88 (12.18)
Cronbach's alpha		**0.85**	**0.85**	**0.86**

item: my agent is highly skilled. Relational selling behavior (F4) with five items also is modified from Crosby et al. (1990); a sample item: my agent offers appropriate information according to my situation. Moreover, perceived network quality (F5) with four items is modified from the ideas of Jun and Cai (2001); a sample item: ADSL connection quality is reliable. Finally, service recovery (F6) is measured using four items modified from Andreassen (2000) and Boshoff and Leong (1998);

a sample item: my agent has tried to solve my problems promptly.

Measurement Model and Reliability

Following data collection, SEM (structural equation modeling) is applied to conduct data analysis. SEM is a multivariate statistical technique used to confirm the causal relations among latent variables. This study follows a two-step

Table 3. Goodness-of-fit indices for the measurement model

Group	χ^2	df	p-value	NFI	NNFI	CFI	GFI	AGFI	RMR
Total	249.98	137	.0001	.94	.97	.97	.93	.90	.03
Male	201.63	137	.0001	.93	.97	.98	.91	.88	.03
Female	202.78	137	.0002	.88	.95	.96	.86	.81	.03

procedure proposed by Anderson and Gerbing (1988). The first step involves developing an effective measurement model with confirmatory factor analysis, while the second step analyzes the structural model. Both SAS and AMOS are adopted as the tools for analyzing the data for reconfirmation.

MI (modification index) is the index for reference used to select indicator variables (Jöreskog & Sorbom, 1986). Through repeated filtering, some indicator variables have been removed. The indicators retained in each model (total group, male group, and female group) are identical. Every construct in the final measurement models is measured, using at least two indicator variables as in Table 2. The overall goodness-of-fit indices shown in Table 3 (chi-square/d.f. smaller than 2.0; RMR smaller than 0.05; CFI, NNFI, CFI, GFI, and AGFI greater than 0.9 except four values slightly lower than 0.9) indicate that the fits of the three models are all satisfactory.

Reliability can reflect the internal consistency of the indicators measuring a given factor. As shown in Table 2, reliabilities for all constructs exceed 0.7 for all three models, satisfying the general requirement of reliability for research instruments.

Convergent Validity and Discriminant Validity

Convergent validity is achieved, if different indicators used to measure the same construct obtain strongly correlated scores. In SEM, convergent validity can be assessed by reviewing the t tests for the factor loadings (Hatcher, 1994). Here, for all three models, all factor loadings for indicators measuring the same construct are statistically significant, showing that all indicators effectively measure their corresponding construct (Anderson & Gerbing, 1988). Hence, this supports convergent validity.

Discriminant validity is achieved, if the correlations between different constructs, measured with their respective indicators, are relatively weak. The chi-square difference test can be used to assess the discriminant validity of two constructs by calculating the difference of the chi-square statistics for the constrained and unconstrained measurement models (Hatcher, 1994). The unique and critical advantage of the chi-square difference test is that it allows for simultaneous pair-wise comparisons (based on the Bonferroni method) for the constructs. The constrained model is identical to the unconstrained model, in which all constructs are allowed to covary, except that the correlation between the two constructs of interest is fixed at 1.

Discriminant validity is demonstrated, if the chi-square difference (with 1 df) is significant, meaning that the model in which the two constructs are viewed as distinct (but correlated) factors is superior. Since we need to test the discriminant validity for every pair of five constructs, we should control the experiment-wise error rate (the overall significance level). By using the Bonferroni method under the overall 0.05 and 0.01 levels, the critical values of the chi-square

Table 4. Chi-square difference tests for examining discriminant validity

Construct Pair	Total (Unconstrained) $\chi2(d.f.=137) = 249.98$		Male (Unconstrained) $\chi2(d.f.=137) = 201.63$		Female (Unconstrained) $\chi2(d.f.=137) = 202.78$	
	Constrained χ (d.f.=138)	χ difference	Constrained χ (d.f.=138)	χ difference	Constrained χ (d.f.=138)	χ difference
(F1, F2)	456.50	206.52***	293.15	91.52***	313.11	110.33***
(F1, F3)	718.65	468.67***	467.78	266.15***	406.13	203.35***
(F1, F4)	374.76	124.78***	290.31	88.68***	238.29	35.51***
(F1, F5)	334.14	84.16***	248.53	46.9***	239.00	36.22***
(F1, F6)	476.10	226.12***	300.52	98.89***	332.84	130.06***
(F2, F3)	507.31	257.33***	390.55	188.92***	285.01	82.23***
(F2, F4)	312.89	62.91***	254.37	52.74***	212.02	9.24**
(F2, F5)	303.92	53.94***	233.48	31.85***	225.71	22.93***
(F2, F6)	337.90	87.92***	253.50	51.87***	239.62	36.84***
(F3, F4)	306.77	56.79***	235.87	34.24***	227.30	24.52***
(F3, F5)	343.37	93.39***	266.98	65.35***	229.71	26.93***
(F3, F6)	405.93	155.95***	298.46	96.83***	266.56	63.78***
(F4, F5)	329.71	79.73***	260.70	59.07***	219.76	16.98***
(F4, F6)	299.78	49.8***	231.88	30.25***	220.64	17.86***
(F5, F6)	301.25	51.27***	238.08	36.45***	216.34	13.56***

Notes:
F1 = Loyalty; F2 = Relationship quality; F3 = Expertise; F4 = Relational selling behavior; F5 = Perceived network quality; F6 = Service recovery.
*** significant at the 0.01 overall significance level by using the Bonferroni method.
** significant at the 0.05 overall significance level by using the Bonferroni method.

test are, respectively, $\chi^2(1, 0.05/15) = 9.14$ and $\chi^2(1, 0.01/15) = 10.83$. Since the chi-square difference statistics for every two constructs exceed 9.14 for each model (see Table 4), discriminant validity is successfully achieved.

Testing for the Moderating Effects

This study uses the analytical strategy of Singh (1995) to examine the existence of the moderating effect on the structural model. First, an unconstrained model is estimated, in which path coefficients are allowed to vary across the cross-group datasets. Next, a fully constrained model is estimated by requiring that all path coefficients are constrained to be equal for cross-group datasets. The fully constrained model, thus, is based on the notion of cross-group variance in model relationships. Comparing the goodness-of-fit statistics for the unconstrained and fully constrained models by using a χ^2 difference test will yield evidence for examining our hypotheses. The χ^2 statistics for the unconstrained and constrained models are 415.62 (df = 137) and 426.65 (df = 142), respectively. Their difference is 11.03, with 5 degrees of freedom. The significant difference (at the 10% level) indicates that moderating effects do exist. The χ^2 difference test is used again to test for the moderating effects of individual paths, as displayed in Figure 1. However, the χ^2 statistics for the unconstrained and the partially constrained models are compared herein. *Partially constrained* means that only the target path coefficients are set to be equal for cross-group datasets.

Empirical Results

Based on good model fitness as described previously, Table 5 lists the empirical testing results. Based on the entire sample (total group), one path is not supported (H_2 is not supported), while the remaining paths are all significant at the 0.01 level (H_1, H_3, H_4, and H_5 are supported).

Figure 2 and Table 6 list the further test of the moderating effect for individual paths. From Table 6, the test results indicate that the influences of perceived network quality on relationship quality and of relationship quality on loyalty are stronger for the male group than for the female group (H_6

and H_9 are supported), while the influence of relational selling behavior on relationship quality is stronger for the female group than for the male group (H_8 is supported). The influences of expertise and service recovery on relationship quality are similar for both the male and female groups (H_7 and H_{10} are not supported). The above results supporting H_6, H_8, and H_9 show weak moderating effects (statistically significant at the 0.1 level). Finally, Table 7 summarizes the test results.

Hypotheses H_2 and H_7 are not supported, maybe because of the virtual quality of Internet services. Unlike in other industries, ISP customers face difficulty distinguishing the expertise of different service providers. Moreover, the unsupported H_{10} may unveil an interesting phenomenon in that the influence of service recovery on relationship quality might be non-gender-specific, indicating it is equally important for both genders.

DISCUSSION AND MANAGERIAL IMPLICATIONS

A key challenge for research on relationship quality is identifying and understanding how managerially controlled antecedent variables

Table 5. Path coefficients and t values for three models

Hypothesis	Total		Male		Female	
	Standardized coefficient	*t* value	Standardized coefficient	*t* value	Standardized coefficient	*t* value
H_1	0.79***	14.99	0.85***	13.94	0.66***	7.17
H_2	0.03	0.36	0.05	0.49	0.03	0.28
H_3	0.36***	3.13	0.26*	1.70	0.58***	3.11
H_4	0.30***	3.97	0.36***	3.95	0.01	0.03
H_5	0.30***	2.78	0.33**	2.30	0.33*	1.92

Notes:
*** significant at the 0.01 overall significance level.
** significant at the 0.05 overall significance level.
* significant at the 0.10 overall significance level.

Figure 2.

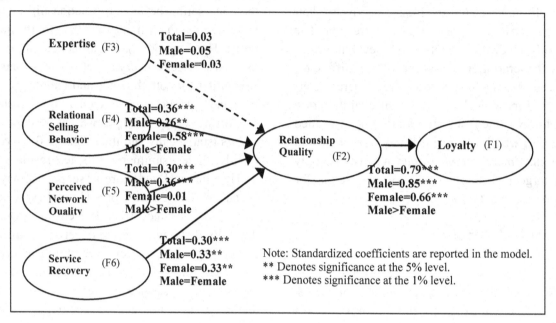

Table 6. Hypothesis testing results

Hypothesis	χ²			Male vs. Female	Conclusion
	Unconstrained	Constrained	difference		
H_6	415.62	419.22	3.60*	Male > Female	Supported
H_7	415.62	415.62	0.00	Male = Female	Not Supported
H_8	415.62	418.93	3.31*	Male < Female	Supported
H_9	415.62	418.84	3.22*	Male > Female	Supported
H_{10}	415.62	415.62	0.00	Male = Female	Not Supported

Notes:
1. The d.f. for the unconstrained and constrained models are respectively 282 and 283.
2. In the constrained models, The target path coefficients are set to be equal for cross-group datasets.
* Denotes significance at the 10% level.

Table 7. Summary of hypothesis testing results

Hypotheses	Results
H_1: Relationship quality positively influences loyalty. (F2→F1)	Supported
H_2: Expertise positively influences relationship quality. (F3→F2)	Not supported
H_3: The relational selling behavior positively influences relationship quality. (F4→F2)	Supported
H_4: Perceived network quality positively influences relationship quality. (F5→F2)	Supported
H_5: Service recovery positively influences relationship quality. (F6→F2)	Supported
H_6: Gender moderates the influence of relationship quality on loyalty.	Supported
H_7: Gender moderates the influence of expertise on relationship quality.	Not supported
H_8: Gender moderates the influence of relational selling behavior on relationship quality.	Supported
H_9: Gender moderates the influence of perceived network quality on relationship quality.	Supported
H_{10}: Gender moderates the influence of service recovery on relationship quality.	Not supported

influence relationship quality and loyalty. This study finds that relationship quality significantly and positively influences loyalty, while relational selling behavior, perceived network quality, and service recovery simultaneously influence relationship quality. This study offers additional support for Bhattacherjee's (2001) contention that user satisfaction with an IS determines continuance intention. Moreover, the present results also support the findings of Bagozzi (1995) and Kang and Ridgway (1996), who argued that customers feel obligated to reciprocate the investments of sellers in a seller-buyer relationship by increasing their loyalty to the seller. This finding implies that investment in customer relationship quality benefits service providers in the form of increased loyalty. Additionally, the findings of this study indicate that IT service providers should realize the importance of service-related factors, including relational selling behavior, perceived network quality, and service recovery, in shaping relationship quality.

Whatever trouble service providers take to increase relationship quality and loyalty, the effects of their efforts remain subject to the influence of customer gender. Although the path between expertise and relationship quality do not differ significantly between the male and female groups, most of the test results have critical implications for IT service practices.

A stronger link between relationship quality and loyalty in the male group (H_6) indicates that males are more likely to switch brand immediately in response to declining relationship quality. Such a phenomenon may be caused by the intrinsic male traits, as evidenced by the use of strongly aggressive actions to resolve conflict or dissatisfaction (Costa, 1994; Fischer & Arnold, 1994; Scherhorn, Reisch, & Raab, 1990). Therefore, agents must put increased emphasis on market surveys on perceived relationship quality, particularly for male customers. Once male customers perceiving low relationship quality are identified, agents should visit them immediately to understand the problem and to strengthen their confidence regarding perceived network quality and service recovery via a detailed introduction of product advantages, since male customers who trust and are satisfied with their ISP undoubtedly will stick to the same ISP longer and more actively broadcast positive messages via word of mouth. Of course, it would be inaccurate to say that the influence of relationship quality on loyalty does not matter for all females. However, research on gender stereotypes has discussed that acting so violently to external events often violates feminine gender role norms (De Beauvoir, 1952; Flax, 1983), and therefore, the influence of females' relationship quality on loyalty is not as strong as that of males.

The stronger relationship between relational selling behavior and relationship quality for the female group compared to the male group (H_8) alternatively indicates that female customers are more sensitive than male customers to relational selling behavior efforts. This difference suggests that females display more intense interpersonal relationships, and it is consistent with the argument that higher levels of computer anxiety and lower computer aptitude among females (Felter, 1985; Rosen & Maguire, 1990; Venkatesh & Morris, 2000) may necessitate the increased use of support services, making the influence of relational selling behavior on relationship quality more salient for females. Again, this difference has important implications for IT service providers, who should attempt to increase their appeal to females in their efforts to stimulate relationship quality. Such results also support the use of marketing tactics to enhance the perceptions of female customers regarding their relationships with firms, particularly by personifying the firm through developing closer customer-agent relationships (Iacobucci & Ostrom, 1996).

Firms seeking to obtain the true confidence of female customers may have to place greater emphasis on interpersonal relationships or find innovative ways to make individual-to-firm relationships more closely resemble interpersonal relationships. Although asking employees to establish social relationships with customers is a difficult demand to make from a managerial perspective, it is relatively easy to achieve in cyberspace via mass mailings. For example, an ISP can effectively strengthen relationship quality with female customers by sending Internet greeting cards or mailing discount coupons more frequently. Of course, managers seeking to cultivate closer relationships with female customers should be aware of some key considerations in order to avoid negative customer reactions. These principles include providing emotional support, respectful handling

of customers' private details, and tolerance of other relationships (Fournier, Dobscha, & Mick, 1998). The finding of a stronger link between relational selling behavior and relationship quality for the female group compared to the male group (H_8) brings on another implication. That is, since ISPs usually run other Internet-related businesses, such as online movie services, auctions, cosmetics marketing, and so forth, online advertising of these businesses to female customers as targets should be well tailored to demonstrate concern for the relationship with the targeted customers.

Another additional approach to strengthening the relational selling behavior with female customers could be tried by the creation of further contact possibilities via virtual communities (e.g., chat rooms, discussion forums, and expert forums), in which contexts concerning customers' needs and more updated service packages of the ISP can be exchanged.

The test result of a stronger link between perceived network quality and relationship quality for males than for females (H_9) is consistent with the natural male traits of concern with material advancement; namely, network quality. This finding provides additional support for the statement of Venkatesh and Morris (2000) that task-oriented (instrumental) factors are more important for males than females, given the network being regarded as an instrumental tool. Thus, surveys of network quality on males are more important to ISP providers than those on females; internal data are inadequate for understanding the views of male customers in this area. Since males are more impatient than females and more likely to resolve a conflict by confrontation, dissatisfaction with network quality would damage more dramatically the perceived relationship quality of male customers.

To keep a good network quality, ISPs should upgrade infrastructure and implement network management devices in order to maintain smooth network traffic flow. The main weakness of network management solutions is that they address problems only after they arise, by which time service already has suffered. Therefore, software or hardware with more advanced and predictive techniques should be applied in order to prevent technical difficulties or traffic overloading. In case male customers are dissatisfied with network quality, the firm should assign highly competent and senior staff to work on the problem. Competent and senior staff not only are likely to be able to fix the problem but also have more authority to give some type of compensation for any inconvenience or other lost experience by male customers, playing to the male gender trait of having a materialistic orientation. Moreover, as gender is also an effective positioning variable reflecting the prototypes of essential expression in commercials (Bartsch, Burnett, Diller, & Rankin-Williams, 2000; Goffman, 1979), promoting superior network quality via e-mail advertising to male customers may work to significantly boost customer confidence in network quality and, thus, to improve relationship quality.

Finally, since service recovery influences relationship quality equally for both genders (H_{10}), service recovery is substantial and fundamental to IT service value and is not gender-specific. This is not to suggest that service recovery is not important, but on the contrary, given that managers have to seriously justify their resources in service quality improvements, IT service providers should organize sufficient support for service recovery. Growing numbers of users of IT services also mean growing dependence on IT services, which, in turn, means that support for service recovery is critical. This IT support crisis (McClure, Smith, & Sitko, 1997) is really a crisis of knowledge; namely, knowledge management and the key components of knowledge transfer. Successful service recovery requires the rapid and comprehensive identification of user problems. Consequently, applying efficient databases combined with Web sites and call centers to go through a complaint-handling process assists service providers in achieving good service recovery.

Slow and inefficient service recovery causes dissatisfaction and perceptions of untrustworthiness among all customers. Online support delivered via e-mail and self-service from the knowledge base and expert system is inexpensive and can help to reduce the need for direct and personal contact with service units. These tools also can be used to accelerate service recovery.

Since different customers interpret the same words differently, staff communication techniques are also important. In fact, it is important for the frontline staff to listen and to respond to individual problems. Frontline staff thus should be taught the importance of displaying empathy and concern for users during service recovery, and they must avoid complacent attitudes and a lack of understanding. Finally, the employee who receives the complaint from the customer should be the one who stays with the matter from start to finish, if none of the other employees can take over the mission. At any rate, if the employee cannot actually do anything, he or she at least has to remain with the customer throughout the recovery process. This ensures that the service failure always is taken care of in a professional manner, since the customer has a consistent point of contact from the employee and will feel that the ISP is doing its utmost to solve the problem.

In conclusion, IT service providers must use a multifaceted approach in order to maintain relationship quality and strong loyalty in the long term. Simply applying a single approach to all customers without considering gender is not only inadequate but also inefficient. Specifically, genders have been observed to differ in the characteristics they consider important when assessing products (Holbrook, 1986; Meyers-Levy & Sternthal, 1991). Therefore, specialized training for understanding the influence of gender on the relationships between loyalty and relationship quality and their antecedents may be required to help frontline staff to promote good relationship quality and loyalty. Service providers may find it useful to examine how more effective gender-based market segmentation strategies can associate relational selling behavior and network quality with relationship quality. Segmenting the market in such a manner and modifying appeals and strategies to fit these segments may assist ISPs in competing in this increasingly crowded market.

LIMITATIONS AND FUTURE RESEARCH DIRECTIONS

This study suffers from some limitations. The first limitation relates to the measurement of customer loyalty. True customer loyalty may be reflected partially, given that it was based on self-reports. Database relating to actual purchasing history can be used as an input for measuring customer loyalty. The second limitation is the possibility of common method bias. The third limitation is that the results cannot be construed to be representative of all consumers of ISPs from all countries around the world due to the highly delimited nature of the sample. Indeed, cultural psychologists suggest that national cultural differences may influence consumer evaluations (Crotts & Erdmann, 2000) and decision making (Dann, 1993). For example, it has been commented that loyalty is a key concept in collectivist Eastern cultures, and such cultures are highly loyal because of their greater reliance on word of mouth about a service (Usunier, 1996). From a cross-cultural perspective, it was found that gender differences between males and females go along with the masculinity dimension (Brady & Robertson, 1999; Hofstede, 1980). Therefore, without further research from the cultural perspective (especially in the dimension of masculinity), it is far too premature to make a generalization that applies to all circumstances. Instead, the focus of this study should be limited to a test of theory examining the influence of four different antecedents on consumers' evaluations of a service as well as their loyalty. Future researchers can take note of these shortcomings by directly observing

the subjects over time and using larger sample sizes so that the genuine relationships of loyalty may then be more transparently revealed.

ACKNOWLEDGMENT

This work was supported partially by the National Science Council, Republic of China. The authors wish to thank Kang Chuang Chen of Chunghwa Telecom, Taiwan, for providing the data.

REFERENCES

Anderson, J. C., & Gerbing, D. W. (1988). Structural equation modeling in practice: A review and recommended two-step approach. *Psychological Bulletin, 103*(3), 411-423.

Andreassen, T. W. (2000). Antecedents to satisfaction with service recovery. *European Journal of Marketing, 34*(1/2), 156-175.

Aronson, E. (1972). *The social animal.* San Francisco, CA: W. H. Freeman and Company.

Bagozzi, R. P. (1995). Reflections on relationship marketing in consumer markets. *Journal of the Academy of Marketing Science, 23*(4), 272-277.

Bartsch, R. A., Burnett, T., Diller, T. R., & Rankin-Williams, E. (2000). Gender representation in television commercials: Updating and update. *Sex Roles, 43*(9/10), 735-743.

Berry, L. L. (1995). Relationship marketing of services—Growing interest, emerging perspectives. *Journal of the Academy of Marketing Science, 23*(4), 236-245.

Bhattacherjee, A. (2001). Understanding information systems continuance: An expectation-confirmation model. *MIS Quarterly, 25*(3), 351-370.

Bob, B. (1989). IBM offers customers new disaster recovery services. *Network World, 6*(14), 4.

Boshoff, C., & Leong, J. (1998). Empowerment, attribution, and apologising as dimensions of service recovery: An experimental study. *International Journal of Service Industry Management, 9*(1), 24-47.

Brady, M. K., & Robertson, C.J. (1999). An exploratory study of service value in the U.S.A. and Ecuador. *International Journal of Service Industry Management, 10*(5), 469-486.

Bridges, J. S. (1989). Sex differences in occupational values. *Sex Roles, 20*(2), 205-211.

Busch, P., & Wilson, D. (1976). An experimental analysis of a salesman's expert and referent bases of social power in the buyer-seller dyad. *Journal of Marketing Research, 13*(1), 3-11.

Chen, P. Y., & Hitt, L. M. (2002). Measuring switching costs and the determinants of customer retention in Internet-enabled business: A study of the online brokerage industry. *Information Systems Research, 13*(3), 255-274.

Costa, J. A. (1994). *Gender issues and consumer behavior.* London: Sage.

Crosby, L. A., Evans, K. R., & Cowles, D. (1990). Relationship quality in services selling: An interpersonal influence perspective. *Journal of Marketing, 54*(3), 68-81.

Crosby, L. A., & Stephens, N. (1987). Effects of relationship marketing on satisfaction, retention, and prices in the life insurance industry. *Journal of Marketing Research, 24*(4), 404-411.

Crotts, J. C., & Erdmann, R. (2000). Does national culture influence consumers' evaluation of travel services? A test of Hofstede's model of cross-cultural differences. *Managing Service Quality, 10*(5), 410-419.

Dann, G. (1993). Limitations in the use of nationality and country of residence variables. In D. Pearce, & R. Butler (Eds.), *Tourism research: Critiques and challenges* (pp. 88-112). London: Routledge.

Deaux, K., & Kite, M. E. (1993). Gender stereotypes. In F. Denmark, & M. Paludi (Eds.), *Handbook on the psychology of women* (pp. 107-139). Westport, CT: Greenwood Press.

De Beauvoir, S. (1952). *The second sex.* New York: Vintage Books.

Dwyer, F. R., Schurr, P. H., & Oh, S. (1987). Developing buyer-seller relationships. *Journal of Marketing, 51*(2), 11-27.

Eagly, A. H. (1987). *Sex differences in social behavior: A social-role interpretation.* Hillsdale, NJ: Erlbaum.

Felter, M. (1985). Sex differences on the California statewide assessment of computer literacy. *Sex Roles, 13*(2), 181-192.

Fischer, E., & Arnold, S.J. (1994). Sex, gender identity, gender role attitudes and consumer behavior. *Psychology and Marketing, 11*(2), 163-182.

Flax, J. (1983). Political philosophy and the partriarchal unconscious: A psychoanalytic perspective on epistemology and metaphysics. In S. Harding, & M. Hintikka (Eds.), *Discovering reality: Feminist perspectives on epistemology, metaphysics, methodology, and philosophy of science* (pp. 245-281). London: D. Reidel Publishing.

Fournier, S. (1998). Consumers and their brands: Developing relationship theory in consumer research. *Journal of Consumer Research, 24*(2), 343-373.

Fournier, S., Dobscha, S., & Mick, D.G. (1998). Preventing the premature death of relationship marketing. *Harvard Business Review, 76*(1), 42-51.

Gefen, D., & Straub, D. W. (1997). Gender differences in the perception and use of e-mail: An extension to the technology acceptance model. *MIS Quarterly, 21*(4), 389-400.

Goffman, E. (1979). *Gender advertisement.* New York: Harper and Row.

Gopalakishna, P., & Mummalaneni, V. (1993). Influencing satisfaction for dental services. *Journal of Health Care Marketing, 13*(1), 16-22.

Granzin, P. J. (1976). Profiling the male fashion innovator another step. In B. Anderson (Ed.), *Advances in consumer research* (Vol. 3) (pp. 40-45). Ann Arbor, MI: Association for Consumer Research.

Greenwich Associates. (1987). *Large corporate banking survey.* Greenwich, CT: Greenwich Associates.

Grove, S. J., Pickett, G. M., & Laband, D. N. (1995). An empirical examination of factual information content among service advertisements. *The Service Industries Journal, 15*(2), 216-233.

Hall, J. E., Shaw, M. R., Lascheit, J., & Robertson, N. (2000). Gender differences in a modified perceived value construct for intangible products. In *Proceedings of the ANZMEC Conference 2000,* Melbourne.

Hart, C. W. L., Heskett, J. L., & Sasser, W. E. (1990). The profitable art of service recovery. *Harvard Business Review, 68*(4), 148-156.

Hatcher, L. (1994). *A step-by-step approach to using the SAS system for factor analysis and structural equation modeling.* Cary, NC: SAS Institute.

Hofstede, G. (1980). *Culture's consequences: International differences in work related values.* London: Sage.

Hofstede, G. (1991). *Culture and organizations.* New York: McGraw-Hill.

Holbrook, M. (1986). Aims, concepts and methods for the representation of individual differences in aesthetic response to design features. *Journal of Consumer Research, 13*(3), 337-347.

Iacobucci, D., & Ostrom, A. (1996). Commercial and interpersonal relationships: Using the structure of interpersonal relationships to understand individual-to-individual, individual-to-firm, and firm-to-firm relationships. *International Journal of Research in Marketing, 13*(1), 53-72.

Institute for Information Industry. (2002). Retrieved January 6, 2002, from http://www.find.org. tw /0105/howmany/howmany_disp.asp?id=49", (in Chinese).

Jöreskog, K. G., & Sorbom, D. (1986). *LISREL VI: Analysis of linear structural relationships by maximum likelihood, instrumental variables, and least squares methods* (4th ed.). Mooresville, IN: Scientific Software.

Jun, M., & Cai, S. (2001). The key determinants of Internet banking service quality: A content analysis. *International Journal of Bank Marketing, 19*(7), 276-291.

Kang, Y. S., & Ridgway, N. M. (1996). The importance of consumer market interactions as a form of social support for elderly consumers. *Journal of Public Policy & Marketing, 15*(1), 108-117.

Kettinger, W., & Lee, C. C. (1994). Perceived service quality and user satisfaction with the information services function. *Decision Science, 25*(5/6), 737-766.

Kumar, N., Scheer, L. K., & Steenkamp, J. B. (1995). The effects of supplier fairness on vulnerable resellers. *Journal of Marketing Research, 32*(1), 54-65.

Laroche, M., Saad, G., Cleveland, M., & Browne, E. (2000). Gender differences in information search strategies for a Christmas gift. *Journal of Consumer Marketing, 17*(6), 500-524.

Lewis, B. R., & Spyrakopoulos, S. (2001). Service failures and recovery in retail banking: The customers' perspective. *The International Journal of Bank Marketing, 19*(1), 37-48.

Lin, C. P., & Ding, C. G. (2005). Opening the black box: Assessing the mediating mechanism of relationship quality and the moderating effects of prior experience in ISP service. *International Journal of Service Industry Management, 16*(1), 55-80.

Mattila, A. S., Grandey, A. A., & Fisk, G. M. (2003). The interplay of gender and affective tone in service encounter satisfaction. *Journal of Service Research, 6*(2), 136-143.

Maxwell, S. (1999). Biased attributions of a price increase: Effects of culture and gender. *Journal of Consumer Marketing, 16*(1), 9-23.

McClure, P. A., Smith, J. W., & Sitko, T. D. (1997). *The crisis in information technology support: Has our current model reached its limits?* Boulder, CO: CAUSE.

Meyers-Levy, J., & Sternthal, B. (1991). Gender differences in the use of message cues and judgments. *Journal of Marketing Research, 28*(1), 84-96.

Moorman, C., Deshpande, R., & Zaltman, G. (1993). Factors affecting trust in market relationships. *Journal of Marketing, 57*(1), 81-101.

Oliver, R. L. (1980). A cognitive model of the antecedents and consequences of satisfaction decisions. *Journal of Marketing Research, 17*(4), 460-469.

Palmer, A., & Bejou, D. (1995). The effects of gender on the development of relationships between clients and financial advisers. *The International Journal of Bank Marketing, 13*(3), 18-27.

Rosen, L. D., & Maguire, P. D. (1990). Myths and realities in computerphobia: A meta-analysis. *Anxiety Research, 3*(2), 175-191.

Rushton, A., & Carson, D. J. (1989). Services—Marketing with a difference. *Marketing Intelligence & Planning, 5*(5/6), 12-17.

Scherhorn, G., Reisch, L. A., & Raab, G. (1990). Addictive buying in West Germany: An empirical study. *Journal of Consumer Policy, 13*(4), 355-387.

Shamdasani, P. N., & Balakrishnan, A. A. (2000). Determinants of relationship quality and loyalty in personalized services. *Asia Pacific Journal of Management, 17*(3), 399-422.

Sheth, J. N. (1975). Buyer-seller interaction: A conceptual framework. In B. B. Anderson (Ed.), *Advances in consumer research* (Vol. 3) (pp. 382-386). Cincinnati, OH: Association for Consumer Research.

Singh, J. (1995). Measurement issues in cross-national research. *Journal of International Business Studies, 26*(3), 597-619.

Sistruck, F., & McDavid, J. W. (1971). Sex variable in conforming behavior. *Journal of Personality and Social Psychology, 17*(2), 200-207.

Smith, J. B., & Barclay, D. W. (1997). The effects of organizational differences and trust on the effectiveness of selling partner relationships. *Journal of Marketing, 61*(1), 3-21.

Soldow, G. F., & Thomas, G. P. (1984). Relational communication: From versus content in the sales interaction. *Journal of Marketing, 48*(1), 84-93.

Solomon, M. R., Surprenant, C., Czepiel, J. A., & Gutman, E. G. (1985). A role theory perspective on dyadic interactions: The service encounter. *Journal of Marketing, 49*(1), 99-111.

Swan, J. E., Trawick, I. F., & Silva, D. W. (1985). How industrial salespeople gain customer trust. *Industrial Marketing Management, 14*(3), 203-211.

Tam, J. L. M., & Wong, Y. H. (2001). Interactive selling: A dynamic framework for services. *Journal of Services Marketing, 15*(5), 379-396.

Usunier, J. (1996). *Marketing across cultures.* Englewood Cliffs, NJ: Prentice Hall.

Venkatesh, V., & Morris, M. G. (2000). Why don't men ever stop to ask for directions? Gender, social influence, and their role in technology acceptance and usage behavior. *MIS Quarterly, 24*(1), 115-139.

Westbrook, R. A. (1981). Sources of consumer satisfaction with retail outlets. *Journal of Retailing, 57*(3), 68-85.

Williamson, O. E. (1983). Credible commitments: Using hostages to support exchange. *American Economic Review, 73*(4), 519-540.

Woo, K. S., & Fock, H. K. Y. (1999). Customer satisfaction in the Hong Kong mobile phone industry. *The Service Industries Journal, 19*(3), 162-174.

Worchel, S., & Cooper, J. (1976). *Understanding social psychology.* Homewood, IL: Dorsey Press.

Wulf, K. D., Odekerken-Schroder, G., & Lacobucci, D. (2001). Investments in consumer relationships: A cross-country and cross-industry exploration. *Journal of Marketing, 65*(4), 33-50.

Zeithaml, V. A., Berry, L. L., & Parasuraman, A. (1996). The behavioral consequences of service quality. *Journal of Marketing, 60*(2), 31-46.

This work was previously published in the Journal of Organizational and End User Computing, edited by M. Adam Mahmood, pp. 38-62, copyright 2006 by IGI Publishing, formerly known as Idea Group Publishing (an imprint of IGI Global).

Chapter XV

The Importance of Ease of Use, Usefulness, and Trust to Online Consumers:
An Examination of the Technology Acceptance Model with Older Consumers

Donna Weaver McCloskey
Widener University, USA

ABSTRACT

This research examines electronic commerce participation and attitudes by older Americans. Questionnaires were distributed at a large retirement community and several senior centers located in Pennsylvania. The sample of 110 respondents ranged in age from 52 to 87. Fifty-nine percent reported purchasing an item online in the last 6 months. The Technology Acceptance Model (TAM) was used and modified to examine the impact attitudes concerning ease of use, usefulness and trust had on electronic commerce usage. Usefulness and trust were found to have a positive, direct affect on usage. Ease of use had significant impacts on usefulness and trust had a significant impact on both ease of use and usefulness. The chapter concludes with a discussion of these results, study limitations, and directions for future research.

INTRODUCTION

Older adults comprise a large and growing segment of the population. According to the U.S. Census Bureau (2002), the global population aged 65 and over was estimated to be 420 million people as of midyear 2000, an increase of 9.5 million since midyear 1999. Growth in this segment of the population is expected to continue rapidly. In 2000 12.6% of the North American population was age 65 or above. By 2015 it is estimated that 14.9% of the North American population will be in this age bracket. By 2030, this segment of the population will nearly double, with over 20% of the entire population over the age of 65 (U.S. Census Bureau, 2002). The graying of America will have a dramatic impact on the workforce, retirement age, healthcare, and elderly support services. This segment of the population will also be a lucrative market with low debt, higher disposable incomes, and additional leisure time due to retirement and reduced family commitments. The increased influence of seniors will require marketers to pay more attention to this segment of the population (Burnett, 1991; Moschis & Mathur, 1993; Schiffman & Sherman, 1991). What is not clear is whether older adults will be active participants in the online community.

Unlike prior generations, older Americans are extremely active and more likely to learn new skills. Perhaps contrary to the common perception, there has been a dramatic increase in the use of technology by seniors. A national survey done by the American Association of Retired People (AARP) found that 81% of the participating computer users used the Internet. The participants spent an average of five hours per week using e-mail and an additional nine hours using the Internet. Fifty one percent used the Internet to comparison shop and 39% had made purchases online (AARP, 2000). From January 2002 to 2003, AARP had a 70% increase in new and renewing memberships processed online (Kelleher, 2003). According to Nielson//NetRatings (2003), older Americans are the fastest growing segment using high-speed Internet access. The number of American aged 55-64 accessing the Internet via cable, DSL, ISDN, or other high-speed connections surged 78% from 2001 to 2002 (Nielson// NetRatings, 2003).

Researchers have explored some aspects of technology use by the elderly, including the psychological benefits of using the computer for communication and learning (Billipp, 2001; Ogozalek,

1991) and the effectiveness of computer training (Groves, 1990; Marquie, Jourdan-Boddaert, & Huet, 2002; Temple & Gavillet, 1990). There has also been a considerable amount written with regard to the elderly using technology to enable continued independent living (Finn, 1997). For example, robotics can be used to assist in routine household chores such as opening jars and artificial intelligence applications can include health monitoring (Raymond, 2002; Shellenbarger, 2002), and memory aids (Eisenberg, 2001). Research on the antecedents to online shopping participation by older adults is limited. Given the growth of this demographic and the attention marketers are placing on them as consumers, exploration of the motivators and barriers to electronic commerce participation by older adults is a critical area of examination.

MODEL

The acceptance of new technologies has long been an area of inquiry in the MIS literature. The acceptance of personal computer applications (Doll, Hendrickson, & Deng, 1998; Henry & Martinko, 1997; Igbaria, Guimaraes, & Davis, 1995), telemedicine (Hu, Chau, Sheng, & Tam, 1999), e-mail (Karahanna & Straub, 1999), broker workstations (Lucas & Spitler, 1999) and the WWW (Lederer, Maupin, Senca, & Zhuang, 2000; Lin & Lu, 2000; Moon & Kim, 2001) are a few examples of technologies that have been investigated. The model most widely used is the Technology Acceptance Model (TAM), developed by Davis (1989). TAM was specifically developed to measure the determinants of computer usage. The model states that perceived usefulness and perceived ease of use impact attitude towards use, which impacts behavioral intentions, which in turn impacts actual usage. As other researchers have done (Adams, Nelson, & Todd, 1992; Davis, 1989; Gefen, Karahanna, & Straub, 2003) this research drops the intermediate variable, attitudes towards use. This more parsimonious model hypothesizes that ease of use and usefulness will have a direct affect on usage. To adequately address electronic commerce participation by older consumers, three modifications were made to the traditional TAM. Electronic commerce participation is defined in four ways and age and trust have been added as both direct and indirect variables. The proposed model is depicted in Figure 1. The numbers in the figure correspond to the numbered hypotheses, which are detailed in the following section.

The issue of electronic commerce usage needs to be defined. There are two distinct ways that consumers can "use" or participate in e-commerce. The obvious use would be to purchase items via the Internet. Consumers shop, check prices, choose shipping methods and then pay and complete the transaction online. For some products and industries, such as houses, cars, and financial services, data gathering or browsing may take place over the Internet, but the actual purchase or transaction is made in another way. Since the motivation and barriers for participation would conceivably differ for buying and browsing

online, this model will address only purchases of products online. Additionally, there are a number of ways that the usage of online shopping can be addressed. This research will address usage from four perspectives, whether it has been used, how many times, how frequently and the amount of money spent online. As many other researchers have validated, ease of use and usefulness are critical precursors to system usage.

H1: Ease of use will be a significant factor in the four measures of electronic commerce participation for older consumers.
H2: Usefulness will be a significant factor in the four measures of electronic commerce participation for older consumers.

Additionally, perceived ease of use impacts usefulness to the extent that a system or application must be easy to use for people to use it and thus realize its' usefulness. This relationship has been strongly supported by prior research (Adams et. al., 1992; Chen, Gillenson, & Sherrell, 2002; Gefen, 2003; Gefen et al., 2003; Segars & Grover, 1993).

Figure 1. TAM adapted for electronic commerce acceptance

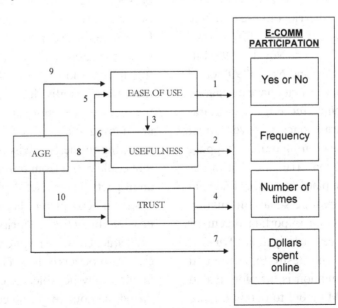

H3:   Ease of use will affect usefulness for older consumers.

To form a more complete picture regarding the antecedents to electronic commerce participation, the addition of trust was made to the traditional technology acceptance model. Trust has been defined, examined and operationalized in many ways. Researchers have addressed the importance of trust in business-to-business (Ratnasingam, Gefen, & Pavlou, 2005), consumer-to-consumer (Pavlou & Gefen, 2004) and and business-to-consumer (Pennington, Wilcox, & Grover, 2003) electronic commerce relationships. Research has examined the way individuals assess trustworthiness (Van Slyke, Belanger, & Comunale, 2004) as well as ways organizations can build trust online (Koufaris & Hampton-Sosa, 2004; Patton & Josang, 2004). Universally, trust has been found to be an important antecedant to electronic commerce usage (Gefen et al., 2003; Liu, Marchewka, Lu, & Yo, 2005; Yoon, 2002). This research focuses on trusting the ability of the online merchant to protect personal and financial data and their integrity in using that data appropriately. These dimensions were selected because credit card security and the disclosure of personal information are the greatest concerns to consumers and are believed to be frequent barriers to e-commerce usage (Bellman, Lohse, & Johnson, 1999; Brown & Muchira, 2004; Hoffman & Novak, 1999; Pitkow & Kehoe, 1996). Han and Noh (1999) found that lower levels of data security have a negative impact on electronic commerce usage. Vijayasarathy (2004) found security concerns have a direct impact on attitudes concerning online shopping in the general population. Trusting that the e-vendor has controls in place to protect financial information and will treat personal information legally and ethically is an important precursor to electronic commerce participation. Trust in the e-vendors' ability and desire to secure and protect personal information is therefore added to the traditional TAM model to obtain a more complete understanding of the factors contributing to e-commerce acceptance. It is hypothesized that trust will have both direct and indirect affects on electronic commerce participation.

Concerns about sending financial and other personal information over the Internet may be a direct reason individuals elect not to purchase items on line. If individuals perceive shopping online to be risky, they won't use this channel. As prior research has established (Lee & Turban, 2001; Liu et al., 2005; Van Slyke et al., 2004; Yoon, 2002) trust has a significant impact on electronic commerce participation.

H4: Trust will have a positive affect on the four dimensions of electronic commerce participation for older consumers.

Trust may also impact e-commerce usage through perceived ease of use and usefulness. The popular press has run a number of articles on protecting privacy online (Branscum, 2000; Cohen, 2001; Foster, 2003; Hawkins & Mannix, 2000; Jones, 2005; Tynan, 2002), raising the attention of the perils of online transactions. As these articles point out, individuals interested in vigilantly protecting their privacy may set their browser to reject third party cookies, run encryption and privacy protection software, install a firewall and read and understand privacy and security statements on Web sites before providing information. While these methods would increase and individual's privacy and decrease the chance of identity theft, they are also time consuming and may decrease the ease of use of shopping online. Likewise, the potential problems that could result from online shopping may have an impact on how useful an individual perceives electronic commerce. For some, the threat of a possible breech of security and the subsequent consequences may negate the usefulness of purchasing products online. The possibility that your identity may be stolen or credit record compromised may outweigh the convenience of having a book delivered to your door.

H5: Trust will have a positive affect on ease of use for older consumers.

H6: Trust will have a positive affect on usefulness for older consumers.

To what extent does age impact electronic commerce directly or indirectly through perceived ease of use, usefulness and trust? Although there are many older Americans who are active Internet users, the common perception is that the elderly are less likely to use technology and would therefore not shop online. Individuals in their 50s and 60s are more likely to have used computers in their work and would, perhaps be more likely to use the Internet and make purchases online. We hypothesize that electronic commerce usage will be the lowest for oldest respondents.

H7: Age will have a negative affect on the four dimensions of electronic commerce participation.

Shopping can be physically burdensome. The physical exertion required to shop, such as driving, walking and carrying packages, can make shopping difficult for the elderly. Going from store to store for price comparisons or availability can be trying on healthy adults, let alone those who are in poor health or are frail. Because it allows for the elimination of the physical nature of shopping, online shopping could be the most beneficial to this demographic.

H8: Older respondents will perceive online shopping to be more useful.

The physical deterioration that makes shopping more difficult could conceivably make the act of online shopping challenging as well. Online shopping requires both manual dexterity, to use the mouse, and strong vision to see small links and read the type. Older users may find shopping online to be more difficult than younger users.

H9: Older respondents will perceive online shopping to be less easy to use.

The elderly are often the victims of financial exploitation and fraud (O'Neill & Flanagan, 1998). Zeithaml and Gilly (1987) found older consumers were quite concerned with safety issues related to adopting technological innovations. It is hypothesized that the elderly, aware of the potential for fraud and abuse on the Internet, will view online shopping more skeptically and will have less trust concerning online purchases.

H10: Older respondents will have less trust concerning online purchases.

METHOD

Measures

Respondents were first asked some demographic questions, including age, gender and highest level of education attained. Respondents were then asked if they had access to the Internet. Those respondents who indicated they did not have access to the Internet were excluded from all analyses. As other researchers have done to improve reliability (Igbaria et. al., 1995; Igbaria, Zinatelli, Cragg, & Cavaya, 1997; Straub, Limayem, & Karahanna-Evaristo, 1995), usage was assessed in different ways. Respondents were asked to indicate the number of times they purchased products online over the last 6 months. Frequency of use was assessed with a 6-point scale ranging from (1) *not at all* to (6) *daily*. Additionally, those respondents who made online purchases were asked to estimate the total dollar amount of their purchases for the last 6 months. This timeframe was elected because it was thought to be long enough to be comprehensive but not so long as to make usage estimates uncertain.

Davis (1989) developed a set of six items to assess ease of use, which focus on whether the system was easy to learn, use, and control. Other research has addressed the ease of use of particular Web sites (Gefen et. al., 2003; Lederer et. al., 2000; Lin & Lu, 2000). Since it is not the purpose of this paper to assess the ease of using one particular site, issues of color and link placement were not relevant. The developed perceived ease of use items therefore focus on the ease of the entire transaction, including placing an order, making payment and rectifying any problems. Five items, contained in Table 2, were designed to address

the ease of use of buying online. A 5-point scale was used ranging from (1) *strongly agree* to (5) *strongly disagree*.

Since most applications of the technology acceptance model have addressed systems in an organizational context, prior usefulness measures have focused on work factors such as job performance and productivity. Since this study is addressing electronic commerce outside of an organizational perspective, most of the conventional measures were inappropriate. Using earlier

Table 1. Demographics on total sample and sub-groups

	Total Sample (N = 110)	Electronic Commerce Participants (N = 65)	Electronic Commerce Non-Participants (N = 45)	Chi Square
Gender	46 male (42%) 63 female (58%)	22 male (34%) 42 female (65%)	24 male (53%) 21 female (47%)	
Highest level of education completed	Middle school 1 (1%) Some high school 6 (6%) Completed H.S. 42 (38%) Some college 23 (21%) Completed college 13 (12%) Advanced degree 24 (22%)	Middle school 0 (0%) Some high school 3 (5%) Completed H.S. 24 (37%) Some college 12 (19%) Completed college 7 (11%) Advanced degree 18 (28%)	Middle school 1 (2%) Some high school 3 (7%) Completed H.S. 18 (40%) Some college 11 (24%) Completed college 6 (13%) Advanced degree 6 (13%)	
				Indep Mean t-test
Average Age	66 years	64 years	70 years	
Average number of hours spent using the internet and email per week	10.7 hours	10.2 hours	6.9 hours	**
Average number of hours spent using the Internet (excluding e-mail) per week	5.7 hours	7.1 hours	3.7 hours	**
Average number of hours spent using e-mail per week	4.9 hours	5.6 hours	3.8 hours	
Amount spent online in the past six months	$374	$635	$0	***

*p < .05   **p < .01   ***p < .001

Table 2. Frequency of purchasing products online

How many times have you purchased something over the Internet in the last 6 months?	TOTAL SAMPLE (N = 110)	Age 50-59 (N = 32)	Age 60-69 (N = 37)	Age 70-79 (N = 30)	Age 80+ (N = 11)
0	45 (40%)	7 (22%)	14 (38%)	17 (53%)	7 (58%)
1-5	38 (34%)	14 (44%)	13 (35%)	9 (28%)	2 (17%)
6-10	19 (17%)	9 (28%)	5 (14%)	4 (13%)	1 (8%)
11-15	2 (2%)	1(3%)	1(3%)	0 (0%)	0 (0%)
16-20	3 (3%)	1(3%)	2(5%)	0 (0%)	0 (0%)
21-25	1 (1%)	0(0%)	1(3%)	0 (0%)	0 (0%)
25+	2 (2%)	0(0%)	1(3%)	0 (0%)	1 (8%)

items as a guide, five items were developed to assess the usefulness of purchasing products over the Internet. The items, contained in Table 3, focus on convenience, efficiency and saving time. Responses to each item ranged from (1) *strongly agree* to (5) *strongly disagree*.

Concerns about security and privacy have been identified as barriers to electronic commerce participation (Hoffman et al., 1999; Pitkow & Kehoe, 1996). Five items, also contained in Table 3, were designed to assess the extent to which the respondent trusts that the personal and financial information they provide online to a vendor will be secure. The 5-item scale ranged from (1) *strongly agree* to (5) *strongly disagree*.

Sample

A large retirement community and several senior centers located in Pennsylvania made the questionnaires and postage-paid return envelopes available. Questionnaires were received from 150 respondents over the age of fifty. Since the questionnaires were not distributed to individuals, the response rate can not be calculated. Twenty-two responses were eliminated because the respondents indicated they did not have access to the Internet and another 18 responses were eliminated due to incomplete answers. This resulted in useable responses from 110 individuals. The average

age of the respondents was 66 years and ranged from 52 to 87. The sample was highly educated. Twelve percent had completed college and an additional 22% completed an advanced degree. The respondents reported having spent an average of $374 online in the last 6 months.

Data Analysis

Participants were asked to indicate how many times they had bought something online in the last 6 months. Sixty five respondents (59%) indicated they had made one or more online purchases in this time period. These individuals were categorized as electronic commerce participants. The 45 respondents (41%) who indicated they had not made an online purchase in the last 6 months were categorized as nonparticipants. Table 1 presents the demographics on the total sample and these subgroups. Chi-square analysis reveals that there was not a significant difference in the distribution of gender or education for the e-commerce participants and nonparticipants. Independent samples *t* test indicated the two groups did not differ significantly in terms of age or number of hours using e-mail. There was, however, a significant difference in the amount of time e-commerce participants and non-participants spent using the Internet. Electronic commerce participants spent an average of 3.4 more hours

Table 3. Factor analysis

	Ease of Use Alpha = .608	Usefulness Alpha = .865	Trust Alpha = .808
Questions and problems can easily be addressed when making purchases over the Internet.	.802		
Payment or delivery problems can easily be rectified with an online vendor.	.604		
It is easy to purchase items over the Internet.	.590		
Internet shopping makes my life easier.		.806	
Placing an order online is easy to do.		.594	
Shopping on the Internet saves me time.		.859	
Buying products over the Internet is easier than purchasing them from a store.		.637	
Buying things over the Internet is more convenient		.873	
*I worry about providing financial information when shopping online.			.786
Online retailers have adequate controls to keep my personal and financial data secure.			.728
*I worry about providing personal information when purchasing items on the Internet.			.766
It is safe to use a credit card when purchasing items over the Internet.			.590
Personal information about me and my buying habits are kept private when purchasing items over the Internet.			.706

*1 = strongly agree; 2 = agree; 3 = neutral; 4 = disagree; 5 = strongly disagree. * reverse scored*

using the Internet per week than those who have not made a purchase online. It will be important to control for this difference when evaluating the proposed model.

The National Service Framework for Older People makes a clear delineation between segments of the older community. The active 50 year old has little in common with the frail and inactive 80 year old. For this reason, the data was analyzed in aggregate and also by age subgroups. Table 2 shows the frequency of online purchases for the total sample and in age subgroups. Fifty-nine percent of the sample had made at least one online purchase in the last 6 months. The group of respondents in their 70s and 80s were the only two subgroups in which the majority of the

respondents had not made an Internet purchase in the last 6 months.

Before testing the proposed model it was first necessary to assess the validity of the multi-item scales. A total of fifteen questions were asked to assess attitudes concerning the ease of use, usefulness and trust related to buying products online. Two questions regarding ease of use ("Buying products online is confusing and risky" and "Internet shopping is useful because products can be easily found and purchased") caused spurious results. When those items were dropped, factor analysis with VARIMAX rotation indicated there were three distinct factors. Table 3 contains the loadings of the questions on each of the three factors.

Table 4. Correlation matrix of study variables

	Age	Educ	Hours using Internet and e-mail	Trust	Ease of Use	Usefulness	Use (1 = Y 0 = N)	Buy # of times	Buy freq	Spent Online
Age	1									
Education	.198*	1								
Hours using Internet and e-mail	.022	-.064	1							
Trust	.033	.011	-.365**	1						
Ease of Use	.234*	-.064	-.221*	.386***	1					
Usefulness	.242*	-.070	-.290**	.441***	.568***	1				
Use (1 = Y 0 = N)	-329***	.153	.275**	-.336***	-.193*	-.565***	1			
Buy # of times	-.148	.122	.317***	.287**	-.180	-.527***	.533***	1		
Buy frequency	-.367***	.066	.444***	-.449***	-.299**	-.654***	.795***	.742***	1	
Spent online	-.230*	.020	.079	-.111	-.282**	-.339***	.287**	.293**	.280**	1

$*p < .05; **p < .01; ***p < .001.$

Cronbach's alpha was calculated for each multi-item scale to assess the internal reliability. Nunnally (1978) suggests that alphas near .9 represent highly consistent scales, those near .7 reflect a moderate level of consistency and alphas below .3 indicate that the items have little in common. As shown in Table 3, the alpha scores are within the guidelines for research (Kerlinger, 1986; Nunnally, 1978). Table 4 contains the correlation matrix for the studied variables.

Given the sample size, structural equation modeling (SEM) was not advisable. Kelloway (1998) recommends that SEM, a method of examining the quality of the measurement and examining predictive relationships simultaneously, only be conducted when sample sizes are a minimum of 200. Since the sample size was only 110, multiple regression was used to see if there was support for the proposed model. It was necessary to include, and therefore control, demographic variables that may cause spurious effects. The choice of control variables was governed by theory and prior empirical studies as well as dictated by the current data. The number of hours spent using the Internet and e-mail were significantly correlated with the study variables and have been suggested as determinants of online shopping (Bellman et al., 1999). It was therefore necessary to control these characteristics. The number of hours spent per week using the Internet and e-mail were included as having a direct effect on the use of electronic commerce and an indirect effect via the three independent variables, ease of use, perceived usefulness and trust. Since electronic commerce participation (Y or N) is dichotomous, logistic regression was used to assess the affect of the study variables on this outcome. The results are presented in Table 5a and 5b and the supported relationships are shown in Figure 2. As summarized in Table 6, the proposed model was partially supported. Trust only had a direct impact on one of the four dimensions of usage but did have a positive impact on ease of use and usefulness. Ease of use did not

Table 5a. Hierarchical regression results

Adjusted	Coefficient	t(Sig)	R2
TRUST			
Age	.003	.411	.119
Hours spent using internet and email	-.028	-4.052***	
EASE OF USE			
Age	.015	2.733**	.192
Hours spent using internet and email	-.006	-1.037	
Trust	292	3.667***	
USEFULNESS			
Age	.010	1.921	.395
Hours spent using internet and email	-.011	-1.878	
Trust	.202	2.511*	
Ease of Use	.453	4.872***	
BUY (Frequency)			
Age	-.031	-4.325***	.584
Hours spent using internet and email	.033	4.293***	
Ease of Use	-.316	2.405*	
Usefulness	-.797	-6.349***	
Trust	-.243	-2.309*	
BUY (Number of time)			
Age	-.038	-.718	.302
Hours spent using internet and email	.123	2.125*	
Ease of Use	1.940	1.965	
Usefulness	-4.823	-5.111	***
Trust	-.406	-.512	
BUY (Dollar amount)			
Age	-14.326	-1.249	.102
Hours spent using internet and email	-3.501	-.277	
Ease of Use	-232.227	-1.037	
Usefulness	-435.649	-2.120*	
Trust	73.235	.436	

*p < .05, **p < .01, ***p < .001

have a direct affect on two dimensions of usage, had unexpected affects on two other dimensions and had a direct affect on usefulness. Usefulness had a significant impact on all four dimensions of electronic commerce participation. Age had a direct affect on two dimensions of usage and on ease of use.

DISCUSSION

Ease of use, quite surprisingly, does not appear to be a factor that contributes to the level of electronic commerce participation. It did not have a significant affect on the number of times individuals shopped online nor how much they spent. The relationship between ease of use and online shopping frequency and whether the individual had shopped online in the last 6 months was significant, but the reverse of what would be expected. Respondents who reported that online shopping was easy to use were less likely to shop online or to do so less frequently than those who reported online shopping was not easy to use. Given the substantial evidence that ease of use

Table 5b. Hierarchical regression results

Coefficient	S.E.	Sig
BUY (Y or N)		
Age	-.086	.030**
Hours spent using internet and email	.040	.038
Ease of Use	1.495	.686*
Usefulness	-2.904	.757**
Trust	-.778	.472

Figure 2. TAM adapted for electronic commerce acceptance—supported relationships

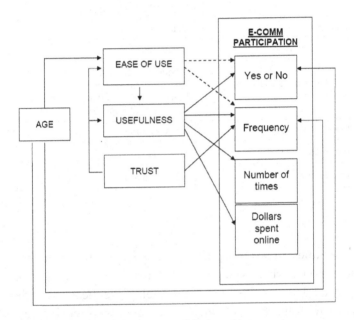

Dotted line indicated a significant relationship that is reverse of the hypothesis

impacts technology adoption, this result is quite surprising. Certainly there could be issues with the operalization of the ease of use measure or causality between ease of use and level of electronic commerce participation. The ease of use measure used in this research addressed the ease of placing and paying for an order as well as rectifying problems. Perhaps those individuals who are more frequent online shoppers have encountered difficulties, which has contributed to lower attitude towards ease of use

Prior research has found that convenience is an important factor in technology adoption by older adults (Smither & Braun, 1994; Zeithaml & Gilly, 1987). Likewise, these results indicate that usefulness has a significant affect on all four of the measures of electronic commerce participation: whether it was used, frequency, number of times purchases were made and amount spent online. Convenience and time saving are frequently cited as online shopping advantages and this is no exception for older consumers. Driving and shopping can be physically challenging for older

Table 6. Summary of hypotheses

H1	EOU → 4 dimensions of participation	Frequency – Significant, reverse of hypothesis Number of times – Not supported Dollar amount – Not supported Yes or No – Significant, reverse of hypothesis
H2	Usefulness → 4 dimensions of participation	Frequency – Supported Number of times – Supported Dollar amount – Supported Yes or No – Supported
H3	EOU → usefulness	Supported
H4	Trust → 4 dimensions of participation	Frequency – Supported Number of times – Not supported Dollar amount – Not supported Yes or No – Not supported
H5	Trust → EOU	Supported
H6	Trust → usefulness	Supported
H7	Age → 4 dimensions of participation	Frequency - Supported Number of times – Not supported Dollar amount – Not supported Yes or No – Supported
H8	Age → usefulness	Not supported
H9	Age → ease of use	Supported
H10	Age → trust	Not supported

adults. Marketing the usefulness of this shopping channel would be appropriate when trying to capture this very important demographic.

As other researchers have found (Gefen et al., 2003; Lin & Lu, 2000; Lucas & Spitler, 1999; Venkatesh & Davis, 2000) perceived ease of use was found to have a direct effect on perceived usefulness. Online shopping needs to be easy enough for people to try so that they can discover its usefulness. This is particularly important for older consumers. The deterioration of vision and manual dexterity can make it difficult to navigate Web pages when they are cramped and the font size is small. Electronic vendors should ensure that their Web sites are designed with font and link sizes that are easy for older adults to navigate and use.

Trust had only a significant direct affect on frequency of use. It did not have a significant impact on whether an individual shopped online, the number of times or the dollar amount spent. Being skeptical about the ability and desire of e-vendors' securing and protecting personal information doesn't necessarily impact whether an individual will shop online but will affect how often they shop this way. Additionally, trust has a significant, positive affect on ease of use and usefulness. The more a respondent trusted that their financial and personal data would be safe, the higher their belief that online shopping was easy to use and useful. Perhaps those consumers who are more trusting are able to take advantage of features that make shopping online even easier. One-Click by Amazon may be a useful example of this phenomenon. If the consumer trusts that their information is safe, they can set up a profile and save their address and payment information so that future purchases can be authorized, paid for and shipped with only one click. Higher levels of trust allow users to take advantage of ease of use options. Trusting that personal information will be secure and used appropriately may also make online shopping more useful. Recommendations based on prior purchases, being able to save items in a shopping cart and even saving your measurements via a virtual model, like at LandsEnd.com, may make it faster and more convenient for users to get to the products that they are interested in.

Our respondents ranged in age from 52 to 87. This is a large age range and it is likely that there would be significant differences in usage and attitudes within this age group. Age has a direct affect on two dimensions of electronic commerce participation. Older respondents were less likely to have made a purchase online and participate in electronic commerce transactions less often. Age also has an indirect affect through ease of use. Older respondents had more negative attitudes concerning ease of use. Older computer users have reported difficulties using the mouse and reading small print online (Licht, 1999; Opalinski, 2001). Practitioners need to be cognizant of this when designing Web sites. Age did not have a significant impact on usefulness. The impact of age on usefulness is not necessarily surprising but is disconcerting since online shopping could be of most use to the elderly. Clearly this segment of the population needs to be made more aware of this channel. Surprisingly, age did not have a significant impact on trust. Again, contrary to common perception, the elderly do not appear to be any more concerned with security and privacy in online transactions.

DIRECTIONS FOR FUTURE RESEARCH

This study sought to examine the impact trust, ease of use and usefulness had on electronic commerce participation by older Americans. The partici-

pants in this study were from affluent areas and were highly educated. Thirty-four percent of the respondents reported earning at least a bachelors degree. Clearly, the sample does not represent a cross section of older American consumers. The respondents are likely at the higher end of the socioeconomic scale. Since income is an important determinant of Internet usage (Bucy, 2000) and online shopping (Eastman, 2004) electronic commerce participation is probably higher for this sample than for this age group in general. Future research should reexamine the proposed model with a larger and broader sample.

The operationalization of ease of use and trust should be examined. The ease of use items in this study addressed the ease of buying online, not necessarily of using the Internet. Online transactions virtually require the use of the mouse. Research has found that older users have more difficulty with mouse control (Riviere & Thakor, 1996; Walker, Philbin, & Fisk, 1997) and tasks, such as clicking and double clicking (Smith, Sharit, & Czaja, 1999). Given that older adults have less manual dexterity and more vision difficulties, this measure could be broadened to include ease of use issues such as link placement, font size and navigation with the mouse versus the keyboard.

As others have done (Liu et al., 2005), this research operationalized trust by assessing the confidence people had with the security and confidentiality of personal and financial information. Since the design of this study, numerous researchers (Grabner-Kraeuter, 2002; Mukherjee & Nath, 2003; Strader & Ramaswami, 2002; Torkzadeh & Dhillon, 2002) have attempted to examine and operationalize the issue of trust in online transactions. Gefen and Straub (2002) propose that trust is multidimensional, comprised of integrity, benevolence and ability. Tan and Sutherland (2004) review the definitions and dimensionality of trust and propose that intention to trust impacts online purchase behavior and is comprised of dispositional, institutional and interpersonal trust. Additional research should address the multidimensional nature of trust and the ways in which it contributes to electronic commerce participation by this very important demographic.

There are many variants of electronic commerce. This research focused on buying products on the Internet. A number of services, including banking, investments and insurance are other forms of electronic commerce participation. A similar model could be tested looking at engaging in services online. Additionally, consumers can use the Internet to browse and then engage in a transaction offline. For example, reading descriptions and reviews and comparing pricing online is common when shopping for a new car, however the purchase is rarely made online. Although browsing was a key component to the decision to purchase, the actual purchase was made offline. Gefen and Straub (2000) propose that the importance of perceived ease of use will vary with the type of task being addressed. They hypothesize that ease of use will not have a significant impact on usage for something that is task oriented, such as making a purchase online, but will be significant in a task that is more intrinsic, such as gathering information. Additional research could address the concepts of browsing, including its importance, use and the impact on purchases.

It has been suggested that technology adoption differs between men and women. One study found that men perceived usefulness to be more influential in making a decision to use a new technology whereas women perceived ease of use to be more important (Venkatesh & Morris, 2000). Exploratory studies have found men to be more satisfied with online shopping than women (Rodgers & Harris, 2003). Given that there may be differences in the motivation, duration and enjoyment of shopping between genders, it may have an impact on the proposed model. In an attempt to better understand the adoption of electronic commerce by older consumers; future research should also examine gender differences.

Given the number of questions that still re-main concerning the acceptance of electronic commerce and the growth of the older segment of our population, it is expected that research in this area will continue. Expanding the modified TAM to include purchasing services, a more comprehensive definition and operationalization of ease of use and trust, browsing for products and services and gender differences would presumably provide more understanding as to why electronic commerce is used and what factors contribute to usage. These are issues that e-tailers will find critical for future growth.

REFERENCES

AARP. (2000). National survey on consumer preparedness and e-commerce: A study of computer users age 45 and older. Retrieved August 28, 2003, from *http://research.aarp.prg/consume.ecomerce1.html*

Adams, D. A., Nelson, R. R., & Todd, P. A. (1992). Perceived usefulness, ease of use and usage of information technology: A replication. *MIS Quarterly, 16*(2), 227-247.

Bellman, S., Lohse, G. L., & Johnson, E. J. (1999). Predictors of online buying behavior. *Communications of the ACM, 42*(12), 32-38.

Billipp, S. (2001). The psychological impact of interactive computer use within a vulnerable elderly population: A report on a randomized prospective trial in a home health care setting. *Public Health Nursing, 18*(2), 138-145.

Branscum, D. (2000). Guarding online privacy. *Newsweek, 135*(23), 77-78.

Brown, M., & Muchira, R. (2004). Investigating the relationships between Internet privacy concerns and online purchase behavior. *Journal of Electronic Commerce Research, 5*(1), 62-82.

Bucy, E. P (2000). Social access to the Internet. *Harvard International Journal of Press/Politics, 5*(1), 50.

Burnett, J. (1991). Examining the media habits of the affluent elderly. *Journal of Advertising Research, 31*(5), 33-41.

Chen, L., Gillenson, M. & Sherrell, D. (2002). Enticing online consumers: An extended technology acceptance perspective. *Information & Management, 39*(8), 705-719.

Cohen, A. (2001). Internet insecurity. *Time, 157*(26), 44-51.

Davis, F. D. (1989). Perceived usefulness, perceived ease of use and user acceptance of information technology. *MIS Quarterly, 13*(3), 319-339.

Doll, W. J., Hendrickson, A., & Deng, X. (1998). Using Davis's perceived usefulness and ease-of-use instruments for decision making: A confirmatory and multigroup invariance analysis. *Decision Sciences, 29*(4), 839-869.

Eastman, J., & Iyer, R. (2004). The elderly's uses and attitudes towards the Internet. *The Journal of Consumer Marketing, 21*(2/3), 208-220.

Eisenberg, A. (2001, April 5). A 'smart' home, to avoid the nursing home. *New York Times*, pp. G.1.

Finn, J. (1997). Aging and information technology: The promise and the challenge. *Generations, 21,* 5-6.

Foster, E. (2003). "Caught you!" *InfoWorld, 25*(12), 60.

Gefen, D. (2003). TAM or just plain habit: A look at experienced online shoppers. *Journal of End User Computing, 15*(3), 1-13.

Gefen, D., Karahanna, E., & Straub, D. (2003). Trust and TAM in online shopping: An integrated model. *MIS Quarterly, 27*(1), 51-90.

Gefen, D., & Straub, D. (2000). The relative use of perceived ease of use in IS adoption: A study of e-commerce adoption. *Journal of the Association for Information Systems, 1*(8), 1-28.

Grabner-Kraeuter, S. (2002). The role of consumers' trust in online-shopping. *Journal of Business Ethics, 39*(1/2), 43-50.

Groves, D. L. (1990). Computer assisted instruction with senior citizens. *Journal of Instructional Psychology, 17*(3), 172-177.

Han, K. S., & Noh, K. (1999). Critical failure factors that discourage the growth of electronic commerce. *International Journal of Electronic Commerce, 4*(2), 25-43.

Hawkins, D., & Mannix, M. (2000). Privacy is under siege at work, at home and online. *U.S. News and World Report, 129*(13), 62-68.

Henry, J. W., & Martinko, M. J. (1997). An attributional analysis of the rejection of information technology. *Journal of End User Computing, 9*(4), 3-17.

Hoffman, D. L., & Novak, T. P. (1999). Building consumer trust online. *Communications of the ACM, 42*(4), 80-85.

Hu, P. J, Chau, P., Sheng, O., & Tam, K. Y. (1999). Examining the technology acceptance model using physician acceptance of telemedicine technology. *Journal of Management Information Systems, 16*(2), 91-113.

Igbaria, M., Guimaraes, T., & Davis, G. B. (1995). Testing the determinants of microcomputer usage via a structural equation model. *Journal of Management Information Systems, 11*(4), 87-102.

Igbaria, M., Zinatelli, N., Craig, P., & Cavaya, A. (1997). Personal computing acceptance factors in small firms: A structural equation model. *MIS Quarterly, 21*(3), 279-305.

Jones, K. (2005). Pharming your identity; identity theft is on the rise, and phishing e-mail scams disguised as legitimate correspondence has risen to epidemic proportions. *PC Magazine, 24*(8), 19.

Karahanna, E., & Straub, D. W. (1999). The psychological origins of perceived usefulness and ease of use. *Information & Management, 35*(4), 237-250.

Kelleher, L. (2003). Breaking the stereotypes of older adults online. *AARP*. Retrieved August 21, 2003, from *http://www.aarp.org/olderwiserwired/Articles/a2003-02-20-oww-barriers.html*

Kelloway, E. K. (1998). *Using Lisrel for structural equation modeling: A researcher's guide.* Thousand Oaks, CA: Sage.

Kerlinger, F. N. (1986). *Foundations of behavioral research.* TX: Harcourt Brace College.

Koufaris, M., & Hampton-Sosa, W. (2004). The development of initial trust in an online company by new customer. *Information & Management, 41*(3), 377-388.

Lederer, A. L., Maupin, D. J., Seneca, M. P., & Zhuang, Y. (2000). The technology acceptance model and the World Wide Web. *Decision Support Systems, 29*(3), 269-282.

Lee, M. K. O., & Turban, E. (2001). A trust model for consumer Internet shopping. *International Journal of Electronic Commerce, 6*(1), 75-91.

Licht, J. (1999, August 31). Seniors assess a deluge of data: Operators of Web sites reach out to a growing audience of older people. *The Washington Post*, p. Z15.

Lin, J. C.-C., & Lu, H. (2000). Towards an understanding of the behavioural intention to use a Web site. *International Journal of Information Management, 20*(30), 197-208.

Liu, Chang, Marchewka, Jack T., Lu, June & Yu, Chun-Sheng. (2005). Beyond concern - A privacy-trust-behavioral intention model of electronic commerce. *Information & Management, 42*(1), 289-304.

Lucas, H., & Spitler, V. K. (1999). Technology use and performance: A field study of broker workstations. *Decision Sciences, 30*(2), 291-311.

Marquie, J. C., Jourdan-Boddaert, L., & Huet, N. (2002). Do older adults underestimate their actual computer knowledge? *Behavior and Information Technology, 21*(4), 273-280.

Moon, J., & Kim, Y. (2001). Extending the TAM for a World Wide Web context. *Information and Management, 38*(4), 217-230.

Moschis, G. P., & Mathur, A. (1993). How they're acting their age. *Marketing Management, 2*(2), 40-51.

Mukherjee, A., & Nath, P. (2003). A model of trust in online relationships banking. *The International Journal of Bank Marketing, 21*(1), 5-16.

Nielson//NetRatings. (2003). Broadband access grows 59 percent, while narrow band use declines, according to Nielson//NetRatings. Retrieved February 15, 2006, from http://www.nielsen-netratings.com/pr/pr_030115.pdf

Nunnally, J. C. (1978). *Psychometric theory.* New York: McGraw-Hill.

O'Neill, P., & Flanagan, E. (1998). Elderly consumers are a significant market - But may need special protection. *Journal of Retail Banking Services, 20*(1), 25-33.

Opalinski, L. (2001). Older adults and the digital divide: Assessing results of a Web-based survey. *Journal of Technology in Human Services, 18*(3/4), 203-221.

Ogozalek, V. (1991). The social impacts of computing: Computer technology and the graying of America. *Social Science Computer Review, 9*(4). 655-666.

Patton, M. A., & Josang, A. (2004). Technologies for trust in electronic commerce. *Electronic Commerce Research, 4*(1/2), 9-21.

Pavlou, P. A., & Gefen, D. (2004). Building effective online marketplaces with institution-based trust. *Information Systems Research, 15*(1), 37-60.

Pennington, R., Wilcox, H. D., & Grover, V. (2003). The role of system trust in business-to-consumer transactions. *Journal of Management Information Systems, 20*(3), 197.

Pitkow, J. E., & Kehoe, C. M. (1996). Emerging trends in the WWW user population. *Communications of the ACM, 39*(6), 106-108.

Ratnasingam, P., Gefen, D., & Pavlou, P. A. (2005). The role of facilitation conditions and institutional trust in electronic marketplaces. *Journal of Electronic Commerce in Organizations, 3*(1), 69-83.

Raymond, J. (2002). Gray market for gadgets. *Newsweek, 140*(13), 52.

Riviere, C. N. & Thakor, N. V. (1996). Effects of age and disability on tracking tasks with a computer mouse: Accuracy and linearity. *Journal of Rehabilitation Research and Development, 33*(1), 6-15.

Rodgers, S., & Harris, M. A. (2003). Gender and e-commerce: An exploratory study. *Journal of Advertising Research, 43*(3), 322-333.

Schiffman, L., & Sherman, E. (1991). Value orientations of new-age elderly: The coming of an ageless market. *Journal of Business Research, 22*(2), 187-194.

Segars, A. H., & Grover, V. (1993). Re-examining perceived ease of use and usefulness: A confirmatory factor analysis. *MIS Quarterly, 17*(4), 517-527.

Shellenbarger, S. (2002, July 25). Technology holds promise for easing families' worries over the elderly. *Wall Street Journal*, p. D1.

Smith, M., Sharit, J., & Czaja, S. (1999). Aging, motor control and the performance of computer mouse tasks. *Human Factors, 41*(3), 388-396.

Smither, A., & Braun, C. (1994). Technology and older adults: Factors effecting the adoption of au-

tomatic teller machines. *The Journal of General Psychology, 121*(4), 381-389.

Straub, D., Limayem, M., & Karahanna-Evaristo, E. (1995). Measuring system usage: Implications for IS theory testing. *Management Science, 41*(8), 1328-1342.

Strader, T., & Ramaswami, S. (2002). The value of seller trustworthiness in C2C online markets. *Communications of the ACM, 45*(12), 45-49.

Tan, F., & Sutherland, P. (2004). Online consumer trust: A multi-dimensional model. *Journal of Electronic Commerce in Organizations, 2*(3), 40-59.

Temple, L., & Gavillet, M. (1990). The development of computer confidence in seniors: An assessment of changes in computer anxiety and computer literacy. *Activities, Adaptation and Aging, 14*(3), 63-76.

Torkzadeh, G., & Dhillon, Gu (2002). Measuring factors that influence the success of Internet commerce. *Information Systems Research, 13*(2), 187-204.

Tynan, D. (2002). How to take back your privacy. *PC World, 20*(6), 103-107.

U. S. Census Bureau. (2002). U. S. Census 2000. Retrieved February 15, 2006, from *http://www.census.gov*

Van Slyke, C., Belanger, F., & Comunale, C. (2004). Factors influencing the adoption of Web-based shopping: The impact of trust. *Databases for Advances in Information Systems, 35*(2), 32-50.

Venkatesh, V., & Davis, F. (2000). A theoretical extension of the technology acceptance model: Four longitudinal field studies. *Management Science, 46*(2), 186-204.

Venkatesh, V., & Morris, M. (2000). Why don't men ever stop to ask for directions? Gender, social influence and their role in technology acceptance and usage behavior. *MIS Quarterly, 24*(1), 115-139.

Vijayasarathy, L. R. (2004). Predicting consumer intentions to use online shopping: The case for an augmented technology acceptance model. *Information & Management, 41*(6), 747-762.

Walker, N., Philbin, D. A., & Fisk, A. D. (1997). Age-related differences in movement control: Adjusting sub movement structure to optimize performance. *Journal of Gerontology, 52B,* 40-52.

Yoon, S.-J. (2002). The antecedents and consequences of trust in online purchase decisions. *Journal of Interactive Marketing, 16*(2), 47-63.

Zeithaml, V. A., & Gilly, M. C. (1987). Characteristics affecting the acceptance of retailing technologies: A comparison of elderly and nonelderly consumers. *Journal of Retailing, 63*(1), 49-68.

This work was previously published in the Journal of Organizational and End User Computing, Vol. 18, Issue 3, edited by M. Adam Mahmood, pp. 47-65, copyright 2006 by IGI Publishing, formerly known as Idea Group Publishing (an imprint of IGI Global).

Chapter XVI
End User Computing Ergonomics:
Facts or Fads?

Carol Clark
Middle Tennessee State University, USA

ABSTRACT

Until recent years, the end user computing ergonomic focus has primarily been on stationary computer use. A new trend for the end user is mobile computing. An increasing number of end users are working outside of the traditional office. Mobile computing devices allow for these workers to perform job functions while in the field, at home, or while traveling. The organizational and end user benefits abound for the use of such enabling technology. However, the mobile computing environment introduces a new area of ergonomic concerns. Are businesses and end users monitoring the use of these devices from an ergonomic perspective? The good news is the outcome can be influenced and/or determined with intentional efforts on the part of both end users and managers. This paper includes an in depth review of the current and emerging issues, especially the mobile end user environment, that is important to the end user, manager, and organization as a whole. It also provides end user ergonomic suggestions and resources and addresses the management challenges rising from ergonomic issues.

INTRODUCTION

A casual perusal of the current information technology (IT) literature supports the notion that interest in computing ergonomics is relatively low. Design improvements and technological advances have helped to reduce and even eliminate many of the early computing ergonomic problems.

However, any perception that computer ergonomics is yesterday's news overlooks two important computer use trends: expanding variety of use, especially as related to mobile computing and alternative office arrangements, and extended volume of use. These trends suggest that IT managers can expect a resurgence in ergonomic related challenges in the near future.

Expanding variety in the type of computer use is likely to be the real culprit in precipitating a rise in ergonomic challenges. PDAs (personal digital assistants), mobile computing, "hot desking" (Hanson, 2004), and telecommuting are introducing new ergonomic challenges daily.

Until recent years, the computing ergonomic focus has primarily been on stationary computer use. Mobile computing is an exploding trend for end users working outside of the traditional office. Mobile computing devices allow for these workers to perform job functions while in the field, at home, or while traveling. Benefits abound for the use of such enabling technology.

For example, mobile devices allow salespeople to more efficiently perform the sales process from start to finish. With wireless connections and a laptop, up to date data regarding a particular product (availability, price, delivery options, etc.) are readily accessible for immediate use. Handheld devices, such as PDAs, improve business processes by increasing portability. Data accessibility, immediate processing, and virtual office capabilities provide positive returns.

However, the mobile computing environment introduces a new area of ergonomic concerns. Is the ergonomic impact of the use of mobile devices being carefully monitored? Is the work environment while on the airplane suitable? What about the size of the keyboard on laptops or handhelds, especially as it relates to posture and vision? Is that so called "lightweight laptop" (including accessories) really lightweight? How are "shared workstations" designed to meet the specific needs of different users? Is the "home office" properly designed or is it "lowest cost furnishings" used in leftover space? Are mobile end users "making do" by adjusting themselves to fit the technology? If so, then an ergonomic dilemma may be just around the corner.

The extended volume of computer use is driven by three factors: the growing number of people using computers at work (Bureau of Labor Statistics, 2005), the expanding computing component in existing jobs, and increasing work day length. To paraphrase, more people are using computers to do more things and escalating productivity demands are adding hours to the work day. One survey reports that 9 out of 10 computer users say that workstation setup ergonomic issues directly affect their productivity. Since almost half of the survey respondents use a computer for work 8 or more hours per day, it is clear that any impact on productivity has the potential to be significant. (The Comfort Connection, 2004) Even with design improvements and technology advances the shear volume of use will extract a toll on workers.

This article includes a review of the important current and emerging ergonomic issues, especially in the mobile end user environment. It also provides suggestions and resources and addresses management challenges rising from ergonomic issues.

WHY ERGONOMICS NOW?

Historically, the computer ergonomic emphasis found in research and the media was on musculoskeletal disorders (MSD), vision problems, and radiation effects, especially on pregnancy. (Clark, 2001) The research produced useful awareness of advice and products that reduced, or in some cases even eliminated, ergonomic concerns. Even with improvements, some of these problems, such as repetitive stress injuries (RSI) like carpel tunnel syndrome (CTS), muscle fatigue and neck and shoulder pain, remain a source of concern. Are businesses paying attention to these issues today? Should they be? Or is computer ergonomics an outdated fad?

A tight economy and the demise of federal regulations (Tahmincioglu, 2004), rather than resolved problems, may be key contributing factors to the reduced ergonomic emphasis. Does this mean that the potentially negative consequences have disappeared and are no longer of concern?

The answer is no. Improving the user work environment, reducing health risks, improving end user productivity, and reducing the loss of work days are just a few of the reasons for addressing ergonomic issues.

Ergonomic problems continue to abound. A survey showed that 17% of office workers reported they had been diagnosed with CTS (Timm, 2005). In 2000, data entry workers missed an average of 10 days a year due to injuries at work, according to the Bureau of Labor Statistics. This group of workers missed more work days than the manufacturing, precision production, and service industry laborers (Timm, 2005). The importance of ergonomics is heightened by the aging U.S. workforce and the increased demand for productivity and output that leads to longer work hours (Timm, 2005). Additionally, ergonomics has the potential to impact long term health issues such as disability and early retirement. So whether the goal is to provide a safe, healthy end user computer working environment or to improve the company's bottom line, or both, an organization can reap benefits from effective ergonomic practice.

MOBILE COMPUTING AND ALTERNATIVE WORKSPACES

Mobility describes the contemporary workforce. Mobile tools, shared workspaces, and multiple locations increasingly characterize today's work environment. These factors elevate the need for ergonomic consideration.

Laptops

Laptops enable end users to work on the go. The benefits are apparent for both the end user and the organization. However, their special ergonomic issues should be addressed. For example, laptops do not adjust (Beharie, 2003). The fact that the monitor height cannot be changed is a potential problem. A laptop docking station is suggested by the Canadian Standards Association (CSA) for use on a daily basis (Beharie, 2003).

Some laptop keyboards are less comfortable to use. A separate keyboard and mouse can be provided to allow for more flexibility in adjusting the workstation setup (Hanson, 2004).

The weight of a laptop is usually reasonable. However, end users must consider the additional weight of peripherals, such as a laptop pad, an extra battery, and so forth, and the corresponding strain on the shoulder.

Heat generated from laptops has received attention, resulting in products available to end users. These products include laptop desks that help to reduce leg heat (Tucker, 2005). These products may help air to circulate, provide a fan to cool the laptop, or provide a barrier between the computer and the end user.

PDAs

Managers and end users should be aware of potential ergonomic issues when using PDAs. PDAs with small screens and simulated on-screen keyboards may pose health problems that need to be monitored. End users have complained of eye strain connected to the use of a small PDA screen and complaints of muscle fatigue have also been reported when using the on-screen keyboard and stylus (Briggs, 2003).

An additional keyboard may be used with the PDA. Voice activated capabilities may be used to reduce problems related to the use of the small onscreen keyboard (Hanson, 2004). Using a stylus with an ergonomic grip may be helpful to address the issue of related finger pain (Auty, 2004; Healthy Computing, 2002).

Other suggestions include being intentional about the type of screen on the PDA. Consider the type of lighting that will be used, that is, outdoor versus indoor lighting. A jog wheel, which allows the user to scroll through long documents rather than tapping the stylus many times, can also be helpful. Also, keeping the screen clean for better viewing will reduce eye strain (Healthy Computing, 2002).

Workstation Sharing

Some organizations provide technology to be shared among end users. The workspace is setup for multiple workers to use at various times. This is a practical approach to the efficient use of computing resources. Even though repetitive stress injuries are not usually an issue with shared workstations, posture may be an area of concern. Adjustability may need to be a priority in the case of shared workstations (Briggs, 2003; Hanson, 2004).

Hot-desking is a term used when end users do not have a dedicated workstation. In hot-desking situations, it is especially important for the workstation (including the chair and monitor) to be adjustable to suit the end users individually. The users must also be taught how to adjust the equipment and why it needs to be done (Hanson, 2004). The "importance" of adjusting the workstation components is essential. But just providing the "adjustability" may not be enough to get the ergonomic job done. Training and communication are key.

Telecommuting and Home Offices

Telecommuting is a growing business phenomenon. A survey conducted by the International Telework Association and Council showed a total of 23.5 million telecommuters (reported in September 2003). The number of telecommuters doubled from 1997 to 2003 (Karr, 2003). Given this data, it is reasonable to assume that the number of telecommuters today is dramatically greater. Questions arise as to how ergonomic issues are being addressed in this type of work environment.

The environment may be complicated by the fact that the desk area may be one that is shared by others at home. One source suggests a proper adjustable chair that fits the user. In fact it may be the most important piece in the ergonomic puzzle. Choosing furniture and equipment that maintains good posture is crucial (Karr, 2003). Telecommuters often overlook ergonomic issues, especially in "secondary" workspaces.

Future Technology and Ergonomics

Currently, the trend in office technology seems to center around smaller, transportable computing devices mentioned earlier. What could be next? Is it possible that end users may be performing computing tasks via "wearable computers?"

What exactly is a wearable computer? Venture Development Corp. (VDC) describes it as including a microprocessor and software (either user defined or specific task oriented). It is worn by an end user (creating a hands free environment) and is accessible and connected to a communication network. It may include Geographic Positioning Systems (GPS) or radio frequency (RF) as well as other sensors that can help to perform user tasks. Some companies now use voice based systems with headsets in warehouse situations. It is not clear how businesses will embrace this type of wearable technology; however, a market growth rate of over 50%, compounded annually, is expected (Shea & Gordon, 2003).

Wearable computers may seem science fiction based. However, with technologies like voice recognition and microphone headsets already available, it is really not difficult to imagine that wearable computers could be common equipment for computer end users. Only time will tell what kind of ergonomic issues will be emerging because of this type of computer equipment. Managers and end users should be attentive for proactive advice from ergonomic specialists as well as experiences from individual end users as they arise.

UPDATING HISTORIC ERGONOMIC ISSUES

Addressing mobile computing ergonomic issues is vital. However, some historically significant computing ergonomic issues, such as musculoskeletal problems and vision problems, remain important workplace considerations.

Musculoskeletal Problems

Musculoskeletal disorders (MSD), as they relate to keyboard and mouse use, continue to be the focus of some research. The studies look at the relationship between these devices and the occurrence of some type of MSD. For example, CTS, a repetitive stress injury, affects the medial nerve in the hand. It occurs when the nerve is pinched and may subsequently cause pain, as well as numbness, tingling, and weakness in the fingers (Rempel, 2001).

The mouse is a focal point for much of the current ergonomic concerns. It has been heralded as a keystroke reducer and as a more user friendly type of input device. Most end users assume that no special instructions are needed beyond "point and click."

The mouse is now one of the most common input devices used today. In the last 10 years, the use of the mouse has gone up drastically (Hanson, 2004). Most software packages require or expect the use of a mouse. The mouse's point and click approach is an efficient way to interact with the computer. It is, in many ways, easy for the end user. But is its use "easy on the user?" No, it is not necessarily easier on the user's musculoskeletal system.

According to researchers, a computer mouse causes more hand and arm pain than a keyboard does. Improper use of a mouse, like reaching, can lead to arm and shoulder strain (LaGesse, 2003).

"Mouse shoulder" is shoulder discomfort caused by stretching to reach the mouse. This occurs many times due to the placement of the keyboard in relation to the mouse. When the keyboard is in the center, oftentimes the mouse is over to the side. Thus, the user has to reach for the mouse (Goodwin, 2004; Hanson, 2004).

Jensen, Finsen, Sogaard, and Christensen (2002) studied the relationship between musculoskeletal symptoms and duration of computer and mouse use among a large number of Danish workers. A greater number of musculoskeletal symptoms were found among the computer users using a computer and mouse for long periods of time per day when compared to those using a computer for a shorter duration. The authors indicated there may be a risk of musculoskeletal symptoms associated with the repetitive nature of computer work (Jensen et al., 2002).

A study reported in the *Journal of the American Medical Association* (JAMA), was conducted to determine the relationship between computer use and CTS. The study results concluded a connection between a risk of possible CTS and using a mouse for greater that 20 hours per week (Andersen et al., 2003)

A study prepared at Cornell University addressed the effects of an electric height adjustable work surface (EHAW) on computer users' musculoskeletal discomfort and productivity. An EHAW allows the computer user to switch between a sitting and standing posture at work (Hedge, 2004). The study found "minor increases in the frequency of experiencing some musculoskeletal discomfort" (Hedge, 2004, p. 29). But it also found "substantial decreases in the severity of many upper body MSD symptoms after working at the EHAWs" (Hedge, 2004, p. 29). In addition, the computer users almost unanimously preferred the EHAW arrangement (Hedge, 2004).

Vision Issues

The American Optometric Association has identified a vision condition related to computer use called computer vision syndrome (CVS). It can include the following symptoms: headaches, dry or irritated eyes, blurred vision, eyestrain, slow refocusing, neck and/or backaches, double vision, and color distortion (Anshel, 2001).

However, there appears to be good news related to vision issues on the horizon for computer users. A more pervasive use of LCD screens on computers as opposed to CRT screens has caused a downturn in interest in radiation concerns. LCDs do not emit VLF/ELF electromagnetic radiation. LCDs should reduce some symptoms of CVS because they are flicker free, have reduced glare, and have a reduced occulomotor effort. However, research is needed to confirm that prediction (Hedge, 2003b).

Screen glare from lights or windows can be a problem. Glare can cause eyestrain and headaches. Having the monitor positioned too high can also increase glare that can cause headaches (Healthy Computing, 2001).

Eye strain and muscle fatigue may also be associated with small screens such as those found on PDAs. These issues are being monitored (Briggs, 2003).

Eye fatigue and dryness can also result from computer use. Extended viewing time can lead to discomfort. End users tend to blink less frequently when looking at a computer monitor (U. S. Department of Labor, 2004).

ECONOMICALLY JUSTIFYING ERGONOMICS

Some are interested in ergonomics either wholly or partially from a cost perspective. Some ergonomic computing issues can be addressed with little or no cost. But some require expenditures such as new workstation devices and furniture. Managers are looking to justify costs associated with ergonomic implementations.

How much will a new chair cost the company? When the cost is multiplied by a larger number of employees, the budget can expand rapidly. One source suggests analyzing ergonomically correct furniture from several perspectives that include (1) increasing time on task, (2) lowering employee "churn" rate, (3) fitting more people more often (adjustable furniture for multiple users over time), (4) saving space, and (5) reducing injury costs (Reiland, 2003).

One example uses a fictitious company with 100 computer operators and a potential purchase of adjustable workstations that are $500 more that a standard, fixed-type cube. The following questions can be asked. What if a comfortable workstation helps an employee to increase productivity by 2% more per day? If the employee earns $30,000 per year, that's a $600 savings per workstation (Reiland, 2003). Managers can ask: "Can we identify the ways that we already pay for a poor office environment?" "Can we afford to keep paying?" (Reiland, 2003, p. 117). This provides new insight for looking at and justifying ergonomic related costs.

SUGGESTIONS AND RESOURCES FOR END USERS

End users should become knowledgeable about ergonomic computer use. This knowledge can be helpful when providing input to managers regarding computer use and workstation design. Suggestions were given in previous discussions regarding mobile ergonomic computing issues. The following sections provide additional suggestions for addressing end user ergonomic issues.

Taking Breaks

Taking a break from computer work is widely stressed. Software is available to help remind end users to take breaks. "Stretch Break Pro" even shows "on the screen" stretches that can be done (Mikusch, 2003). There are other software packages available as well.

Ergonomic Chairs and Features

Having a good ergonomically designed chair is also commonly suggested. An end user needs to have a chair that fits correctly. For example, lumbar support, seat and back height adjustability, tilt ability and tilt lock are important features to have in an ergonomically sound chair (Kanarek, 2005).

According to ergonomic specialists, a neutral posture should be maintained when using the computer. "Ergonomics research shows that computer users often adopt poor wrist postures, and working in deviated postures is thought to increase the risks of injury" (Hedge, 2003a). Good posture plays an important role in preventing musculoskeletal disorders.

Monitor Related Concerns

The height of the monitor on the workstation should be addressed. The end user view towards the monitor should be slightly downward, according to Brian Weir of the CSA (Beharie, 2003). A similar suggestion made by the Occupational Safety and Health Administration (OSHA) is that the monitor should be positioned so that the middle of the screen is 15 to 20 degrees below the end user's horizontal eye level. This prevents the end user from having to tilt his or her head back which can cause muscle fatigue (U. S. Department of Labor, 2004).

If the monitor cannot be lowered, the user chair height may be adjusted, which could lead to the need to use a footrest or to raise the keyboard or both (U. S. Department of Labor, 2004). Another source recommends a similar monitor setup that prevents tilting the head forward or backward. It suggests positioning the monitor so that the eyes are level with a line about 2 to 3 inches below the top of the monitor (Healthy Computing, 2001).

Positioning the monitor, taking into consideration the previous suggestions, can decrease glare. However, an anti-glare screen may be warranted in some situations (Monitor Setup and Usage, 2001).

Tilting the head back can occur when end users wear bifocals. These end users need to take care not to strain neck muscles. Therefore, single vision glasses may be necessary for computer work (U. S. Department of Labor, 2004).

Some of the suggestions for dealing with computer related vision problems include seeing an eye doctor, taking breaks, using artificial tears, getting appropriate glasses, correcting posture, cleaning the screen, and so forth (Anshel, 2001). The solution depends of course on the actual symptoms experienced by the user. However, many of the solutions are not time consuming or costly. But communication regarding the symptoms by the end user and the precautions or solutions to the end user is important.

Mouse Use Modifications

To address "mouse shoulder," shorter keyboards can be used. The user would not have to reach for the mouse (Goodwin, 2004). An independent number pad can also be used with a shorter keyboard. (Hanson, 2004)

Another suggestion is to use two mouse devices simultaneously, one by the dominant hand and the other by the non-dominant hand when interacting with the computer. This, according to the source, would provide a safer ergonomic solution (Golden, 2004).

Using a mouse for interacting with a computer, is likely here to stay, at least for quite awhile. Professional suggestions for use can help to prevent muscle strain. If posture is being negatively impacted by mouse use, assess the workstation layout and modify it.

General Ergonomic Support

Resources are available that cover a variety of topics from computer workstation design to posture issues. The following sites provide detailed information that is accessible to end users: www. healthycomputing.com, http://ergo.human.cornell.edu/, and http://www.osha.gov/SLTC/etools/computerworkstations/.

An end user should consider his or her individual work tasks and environment when addressing work place ergonomics. While there are some suggestions that may apply across the board for all end users, others will be specific to each end user.

SUGGESTIONS AND RESOURCES FOR MANAGERS

Managers should consider the areas of ergonomic concern as they relate to end users both generally and specifically. Creating a healthy work environment can payoff in multiple ways. How can managers get feedback regarding the ergonomic issues in the work place?

Johnson & Johnson has begun to use a filtering tool that can evaluate end user computer workstations. If the evaluation indicates a high risk situation, then ergonomic specialists will evaluate the computer workstation (Tahmincioglu, 2004). This would provide information needed to ensure a more ergonomically sound computer workstation for the end user.

A software package by Niche Software in conjunction with The Netherlands Organisation for Applied Scientific Research is being tested in The Netherlands. It evaluates an employee's computer use and work habits over a period of one month. It assesses fitness and posture and relates this information with data from well-known research studies. It then provides a risk profile for the employee. If an employee is deemed at high risk, an individualized ergonomic program is developed that addresses things like posture, fitness, and number of breaks needed (Coming to Grips with OOS, 2005).

The reality of creating an ergonomically correct work environment for end users can be over-whelming. The information provided in previous sections is useful to managers in contemplating this issue. The web sites mentioned earlier for end users can be equally helpful for managers trying to be proactive or for those trying to resolve problematic ergonomic situations.

CONCLUSION

According to Marvin J. Dainoff, Director of the Center for Ergonomic Research at Miami University in Oxford, Ohio, "ergonomics is not about gadgets. It's about problem solving and getting into good work postures that are efficient, healthy, and pleasant" (Tahmincioglu, 2004).

End users are more "computer savvy" today, but they are not necessarily more "ergonomic savvy." End users need to be actively involved in creating and maintaining an ergonomically correct computer work environment. Resources are available. End users should take advantage of these resources.

Managers need to be proactive to create a healthier, more productive end user work environment. Therefore, communicating the importance of ergonomic issues is essential. Training is critical. Do not assume that the end user knows the correct sitting posture for computer work. Do not assume that the end user knows the correct viewing height for the monitor on his or her desk. Do not assume that the telecommuter has ergonomically correct furniture at home. Even if end users are aware of potential ergonomic risks associated with computer use, do not assume that they are implementing that knowledge on a regular basis.

Simply identifying work tasks to be completed, schedules to be followed, and technology to be used is not enough to ensure a productive and healthy work environment for telecommuters. Information and awareness regarding the importance of ergonomics are vital.

Ergonomics is not a fad. Ergonomics is an important organizational consideration especially given the growth of mobile computing including "hot-desking" (Hanson, 2004), telecommuting, and using mobile computing devices, like hand-held computers. End user ergonomic issues can have a dramatic effect on the work environment. The question is whether the effect will be positive or negative. The good news is the outcome can be influenced, and sometimes determined, with intentional efforts on the part of both end users and managers.

REFERENCES

Andersen, J. H., Thomsen, J. F., Overgaard, E., Lassen, C. F., Brandt, L. P. A., Vilstrup, I., Krugger, A. I. et al. (2003). Computer use and carpal tunnel syndrome: A 1-year follow-up study. *JAMA, 289*(22), 2963-2969.

Anshel, J. (2001). *Computer vision syndrome.* Retrieved from http://www.healthycomputing. com/articles/computer_vision_syndrome.html

Auty, S. (2004, May). Why is ergonomics important? *GP*, p. 41.

Beharie, N. (2003, April/May). Monitor height: How low should you go? *OH & S Canada, 9*(3), 52.

Briggs, B. (2003). Ergonomics: Looking for good fit. *Health Data Management, 11*(8), 44.

Bureau of Labor Statistics. (2005). *MLR: The editor's desk.* Retrieved February 15, 2006, from http://www.bls.gov/opub/ted/2005/aug/wk1/art03. htm

Clark, C. (2001). VDT health hazards: A guide for end users and managers. *Journal of End User Computing, 13*(1), 34-39.

The Comfort Connection. (2004). *Industrial Engineer, 36*(8), 16.

Coming to Grips with OOS. (2005). *NZ Business, 19*(2), 30.

Golden, J. (2004). Two-fisted mousing: Not just a macho thing! *Occupational Health & Safety, 73*(1), 44.

Goodwin, B. (2004, March). Take a break from your mouse: IT workers warned of RSI danger. *Computer Weekly*, p. 54.

Hanson, M. (2004). Not just a part of the furniture: Organisations can face a bewildering choice when selecting the right equipment to meet the requirements of the DSE regulations. *The Safety & Health Practitioner, 22*(2), 36-39.

Healthy Computing. (2001). *Monitor setup and usage.* Retrieved February 15, 2006, from http:// www.healthycomputing.com/office/setup/monitor

Healthy Computing. (2002). *PDA ergonomics.* Retrieved February 15, 2006, from http://www. healthycomputing.com/mobile/pda/

Hedge, A. (2003a). *Carpal tunnel syndrome and computer use – is there a link?* Retrieved February 15, 2006, from http://ergo.human.cornell. edu/JAMAMayoCTS.html

Hedge, A. (2003b). *Ergonomics considerations of LCD versus CRT displays.* Retrieved February 15, 2006, from http://ergo.human.cornell. edu/Pub/LCD_vs_CRT_AH.pdf

Hedge, A. (2004). *Effects of an electric height-adjustable worksurface on self-assessed musculoskeletal discomfort and productivity in computer workers* (Tech. Rep. 0904). Cornell University Human Factors and Ergonomics Research Laboratory .

Jensen, C., Finsen, L., Sogaard, K., & Christensen, H. (2002). Musculoskeletal symptoms and duration of computer and mouse use. *International Journal of Industrial Ergonomics, 30*, 265-275.

Kanarek, L. (2005). Avoiding a pain in the neck. *Office Solutions, 22*(3), 51.

Karr, A. R. (2003, September). An ergo-unfriendly home office can hurt; first buy a good chair; it could cost hundreds, but may keep doctor away. *Wall Street Journal*, p. 6.

LaGesse, D. (2003, October). Five tips for taming your mouse. *U.S. News & World Report.*

Mikusch, R. (2003). With more and more computer users suffering. *Beyond Numbers, 424,* 18.

Reiland, J. (2003). Justifying the cost of height-adjustable office work surfaces. *Occupational Health & Safety, 72*(6), 117.

Rempel, D. (2001). *Carpal tunnel syndrome.* Retrieved February 15, 2006, from http://www.healthycomputing.com/articles/carpal_tunnel_101.html

Shea, T., & Gordon, J. (2003). Wireless wearables—Where's the technology headed: The military's investing, industry's watching, and before long it could be what you put on in the morning. *Sensors Magazine, 20*(11), 40-42.

Tahmincioglu, E. (2004). Ergonomics is back on the radar screen for both business and regulators. *Workforce Management, 83*(7), 59.

Timm, D. (2005). How long can you stand to sit? *Occupational Health & Safety, 74*(9), 162-166.

Tucker, D. M. (2005, March). Ergonomics remains sore spot. *Knight Ridder Tribune Business News*, p. 1.

U. S. Department of Labor. (2004). *OSHA* computer workstations etool-components-monitors. Retrieved February 15, 2006, from http://www.osha.gov/SLTC/etools/computerworkstations/components_monitors.html

This work was previously published in the Journal of Organizational and End User Computing, Vol. 18, Issue 3, edited by M. Adam Mahmood, pp. 66-74, copyright 2006 by IGI Publishing, formerly known as Idea Group Publishing (an imprint of IGI Global).

Compilation of References

Ackerman, M.S., Pipek, V., & Wulf, V. (2003). *Sharing expertise: Beyond knowledge management.* Cambridge, MA: The MIT Press.

Adams, J.S. (1963). Towards an understanding of inequity. *Journal of Abnormal and Normal Social Psychology, 67,* 422-436.

Adams, J.S. (1965). Inequity in social exchange. In L. Berkowitz (Ed.), *Advances in experimental social psychology* (vol. 2, pp. 267-299). New York: Academic Press.

Agarwal, R., Sambamurthy, V., & Stair, R. (2000). The evolving relationship between general and specific computer self-efficacy: An empirical assessment. *Information Systems Research, 11*(4), 418-430.

Agarwal, R., & Karahanna, E. (2000). Time flies when you're having fun: Cognitive absorption and beliefs about information technology usage. *MIS Quarterly, 24*(4), 665-694.

Agarwal, R., & Prasad, J. (1998, June). A conceptual and operational definition of personal innovativeness in the domain of information technology. *Information Systems Research, 9*(2), 204-215.

Agarwal, R. (2000). Individual acceptance of information technologies. In R. W. Zmud (Ed.), *Framing the domains of IT management: Projecting the future ... through the past* (pp. 85-104). Cincinnati, OH: Pinnaflex Educational Resources, Inc.

Aggarwal, A. K. (2003). Internetalization of end-users. *Journal of End User Computing, 15*(1), 54-56.

Ajzen, I. (1991). The theory of planned behavior. *Organizational Behavior and Human Decision Processes, 50*(1), 179-211.

Ajzen, I. (2002). Residual effects of past on later behavior: Habituation and reasoned action perspectives. *Personality and Social Psychology Review, 6*(2), 107-122.

Ajzen, I., & Fishbein, M. (1977). Attitude-behavior relation: A theoretical analysis and review of empirical research. *Psychological Bulletin, 84*(5), 888-918.

Ajzen, I., & Fishbein, M. (1980). *Understanding attitudes and predicting social behavior.* Upper Saddle River, NJ: Prentice Hall.

Ajzen, I. (1991). The theory of planned behavior. *Organizational Behavior and Human Decision Processes, 50,* 179-211.

Aladwani, A.M. (2002). Organisational actions, computer attitudes, and end-user satisfaction in public organisations: An empirical study. *Journal of End User Computing, 14*(1), 42-50.

Alavi, M., Nelson, R. R., & Weiss, I. R. (1987-1988). Strategies for end user computing: An integrative framework. *Journal of Management Information Systems, 4*(3), 28-49.

Alavi, M., Phillips, J. S., & Freedman, S. M. (1990). An empirical investigation of two alternative approaches to control of end-user application development process. *Data Base, 20*(4), 11-19.

Alavi, M., & Weiss, I. R. (1985-1986). Managing the risks associated with end-user computing. *Journal of Management Information Systems, 2*(3), 5-20.

Allport, G. (1935). Attitudes. In C. Murchison (Ed.), *Handbook of social psychology* (pp. 798-844). Worcester, MA: Clark University Press.

Al-Rafee, S., & Cronan, T.P. (2005). *Digital piracy: Factors that influence attitude toward behavior* (Working Paper). Information Systems Department, University of Arkansas, Fayetteville, AR.

Amoroso, D. L., & Cheney, P. H. (1992). Quality end user-developed applications: Some essential ingredients. *Data Base, 23*(1), 1-11.

Anderson, E., & Weitz, B. (1992). The use of pledges to build and sustain commitment in distribution channels. *Journal of Marketing Research, 29*(1), 18-34.

Anderson, J. C., & Gerbing, D. W. (1988). Structural equation modeling in practice: A review and recommended two-step approach. *Psychological Bulletin, 103*(3), 411-423.

Andrade, E. B., Kaltechva, V., & Weitz, B. (2002). Self-disclosure on the Web: The impact of privacy policy, reward, and company reputation. *Advances in Consumer Research, 29*, 350-353.

Andreassen, T. W. (2000). Antecedents to satisfaction with service recovery. *European Journal of Marketing, 34*(1/2), 156-175.

Arent, L. (1999). ATM wants to be your friend. Retrieved August 6, 2007, from Wired News, http://www.wired.com

Armstrong, H.L., & Forde, P.J. (2003). Internet anonymity practices in computer crime. *Information Management & Computer Security, 11*(5), 209-215.

Arondi, S., Baroni, P., Fogli, D., & Mussio, P. (2002). Supporting co-evolution of users and systems by the recognition of interaction patterns. In M. De Marsico, S. Levialdi, & E. Panizzi (Eds.), *Proceedings of the International Conference Advanced Visual Interfaces (AVI 2002)*, Trento, Italy (pp. 177-189). New York: ACM Press.

Aronson, E. (1972). *The social animal.* San Francisco, CA: W. H. Freeman and Company.

Åsand, H.-R.H., Mørch, A., & Ludvigsen, S. (2004). Super users: A strategy for ICT-introduction. In A.M.

Kanstrup, A.M. Roskilde, & D.K. Universitesforlag (Eds.), *E-learning at work* (pp. 131-147, in Danish).

Ashton, R., & Kramer, S. (1980). Students as surrogates in behavioral accounting research: Some evidence. *Journal of Accounting Research, 18*(1), 1-3.

Atkinson, R. (2002, May). Biometrics drivers' licenses on the cards. *Biometric Technology Today, 10*(5), 1-2.

Atkinson, M., & Kydd, C. (1997). Individual characteristics associated with World Wide Web use: An empirical study of playfulness and motivation. *The DATA BASE for Advances in Information Systems, 28*(2), 53-62.

Australian Bureau of Statistics. (2001). *Use of the Internet by householder: Australia* (Catalogue: 8147.0). Canberra, Australia: Government Printing Office.

Australian Bureau of Statistics. (2004). *Measures of a knowledge-based economy and society: Australia information and communications technology indicators.* Retrieved August 4, 2007, from http://www. abs.gov.au

Ausubel, D. P. (1968). *Educational psychology, a cognitive view.* New York: Holt, Rinehart and Winston, Inc.

Bagozzi, R. P. (1995). Reflections on relationship marketing in consumer markets. *Journal of the Academy of Marketing Science, 23*(4), 272-277.

Balaban, M., Barzilay, E., & Elhadad, M. (2002). Abstraction as a means for end-user computing in creative applications. *IEEE Transactions on Systems, Man, and Cybernetics: Part A, 32*(6), 640-653.

Bandura, A. (1986). S*ocial foundations of thought and action: A social cognitive theory.* Upper Saddle River, NJ: Prentice Hall.

Bandura, A. (1997). *Self-efficacy: The exercise of control.* New York: W.H. Freeman & Co.

Banerjee, D., Cronan, T.P., & Jones, T.W. (1998). Modeling IT ethics: A study in situational ethics. *MIS Quarterly, 22*(1), 31-60.

Bansler, J.P., & Havn, E. (1994). Information systems development with generic systems. In W.R.J. Baets (Ed.), *Proceedings of the 2nd European Conference on*

Information Systems, Nijenrode University (pp. 30-31). Breukelen: Nijenrode University Press.

Barclay, D.W., Higgins, C.A., & Thompson, R.L. (1995). The partial least squares approach to causal modeling: Personal computer adoption and use as an illustration. *Technology Studies: Special Issue on Research Methodology, 2*(2), 285-324.

Barkhi, R., Jacob, V. S., Pipino, L., & Pirkul, H. (1998). A study of the effect of communication channel and authority on group decision processes and outcomes. *Decision Support Systems, 23*(3), 205-226.

Baron, A. (2003). *A developer's introduction to Web parts.* Retrieved August 10, 2007, from http://msdn.microsoft.com/library/

Bartsch, R. A., Burnett, T., Diller, T. R., & Rankin-Williams, E. (2000). Gender representation in television commercials: Updating and update. *Sex Roles, 43*(9/10), 735-743.

Bauer, M. W. (2000). Classical content analysis: A review. In M.W. Bauer, & G. Gaskel (Eds.), *Qualitative researching with text, image and sound* (pp. 131-151). London: Sage.

Baumer, D. L., Poindexter, J. C., & Earp, J. B. (2004). Meaningful and meaningless choices in cyberspace. *Journal of Internet Law, 7*(11), 3-11.

BBBOnline. (2004). Retrieved from http://www.bbbonline.org/privacy/

Beiser, V. (1999). Biometrics breaks into prisons. Retrieved August 6, 2007, from Wired News, http://www.wired.com

Belanger, F., Hiller, J.S., & Smith, W. J. (2002). Trustworthiness in electronic commerce: The role of privacy, security, and site attributes. *The Journal of Strategic Information Systems, 11*(3/4), 245-270.

Bellman, S., Johnson, E., Kobrin, S., & Lohse, G. (2004). International differences in information privacy concerns: A global survey of consumers. *Information Society, 20*(5), 313-324.

Benassi, P. (1999). TRUSTe: An online privacy seal program. *Communications of the ACM, 42*(2), 56-59.

Benham, H., Delaney, M., & Luzi, A. (1993). Structured techniques for successful end user spreadsheets. *Journal of End User Computing, 5*(2), 18-25.

Benson, D. H. (1983). A field study of end user computing: Findings and issues. *MIS Quarterly, 7*(4), 35-45.

Berger, C. R. (1979). Beyond initial interactions: Uncertainty, understanding and the development of interpersonal relationships. In H. Giles, & R. Sinclair (Eds.), *Language and social psychology* (pp. 122-144). Oxford: Basil Blackwell.

Berger, C. R., & Bradac, J. J. (1982). *Language and social knowledge: Uncertainty in interpersonal relations.* London: Arnold.

Berger, C.R., & Calabrese, R.J. (1975). Some explorations in initial interaction and beyond: Toward a developmental theory of interpersonal communication. *Human Communication Theory, 1,* 99-112.

Bergeron, F., & Berube, C. (1988). The management of the end-user environment: An empirical investigation. *Information & Management, 14,* 107-113.

Berry, L. L. (1995). Relationship marketing of services—Growing interest, emerging perspectives. *Journal of the Academy of Marketing Science, 23*(4), 236-245.

Bhatnagar, A., Misra, S., & Rao, H.R. (2000). On risk, convenience and Internet shopping behaviour. *Communications of the ACM, 43,* 98-105.

Bhattacharjee, S., Gopal, R.D., & Sanders, G.L. (2003). Digital music and online sharing: Software piracy 2.0? *Communication of the ACM, 46*(7), 107-111.

Bhattacherjee, A., & Premkumar, G. (2004). Understanding changes in belief and attitude toward information technology usage: A theoretical model and longitudinal test. *Management Information Systems Quarterly, 28*(2), 229-254.

Bhattacherjee, A. (2001). Understanding information systems continuance: An expectation-confirmation model. *MIS Quarterly, 25*(3), 351-370.

Bob, B. (1989). IBM offers customers new disaster recovery services. *Network World, 6*(14), 4.

Bødker, S., & Grønbæk, K. (1991). Cooperative prototyping: Users and designers in mutual activity. *International Journal of Man-Machine Studies, 34*(3), 453-478.

Bødker, S., Grønbæk, K., & Kyng, M. (1993). Cooperative design: Techniques and experiences from the Scandinavian scene. In D. Schuler & A. Namioka (Eds.), *Participatory design: Principles and practices* (pp. 157-175). Hillsdale, NJ: Lawrence Erlbaum Associates.

Bommer, M., Gratto, C., Gravander, J., & Tuttle, M. (1987). A behavioral model of ethical and unethical decision making. *Journal of Business Ethics, 6*(4), 265-280.

Bordia, P. (1997). Face-to-face versus computer-mediated communication: A synthesis of the experimental literature. *Journal of Business Communication, 34*(1), 99-120.

Boshoff, C., & Leong, J. (1998). Empowerment, attribution, and apologising as dimensions of service recovery: An experimental study. *International Journal of Service Industry Management, 9*(1), 24-47.

Bostrom, R. P., Olfman, L., & Sein, M. K. (1990). The importance of learning style in end user training. *MIS Quarterly, 14*(1), 101-119.

Boulding, W., & Kirmani, A. (1993). A consumer-side experimental examination of signaling theory. *Journal of Consumer Research, 20*(1), 111-123.

Bourguin, G., Derycke, A., & Tarby, J.C. (2001). Beyond the interface: Co-evolution inside interactive systems: A proposal founded on activity theory. In Blandford, Vanderdonckt, Gray (Eds.), *Proceedings of the IHM-HCI 2001 Conference*, Lille, France (pp. 297-310). Berlin, Germany: Springer-Verlag.

Bowman, B. (1988). *An investigation of application development process controls.* Unpublished doctoral dissertation, University of Houston.

Bowman, B. (1990). Controlling application development by end-users in a PC environment: A survey of techniques. *Information Executive, 32*(2), 70-74.

Bradac, J. J. (2001). Theory comparison: Uncertainty reduction, problematic integration, uncertainty management, and other curious constructs. *Journal of Communication, 51*(3), 456-476.

Brady, M. K., & Robertson, C.J. (1999). An exploratory study of service value in the U.S.A. and Ecuador. *International Journal of Service Industry Management, 10*(5), 469-486.

Brancheau, J.C., & Brown, C.V. (1993). The management of end-user computing: Status and directions. *ACM Computing Surveys, 25*(4), 437-482.

Bridges, J. S. (1989). Sex differences in occupational values. *Sex Roles, 20*(2), 205-211.

Briggs, R. O., Nunamaker, J. F., & Sprague, R. H. (1997-1998). 1001 unanswered research questions in GSS. *Journal of Management Information Systems, 14*(3), 3-21.

Brodie, C.B., & Hayes, C.C. (2002). DAISY: A decision support design methodology for complex: Experience-centered domains. *IEEE Transactions on Systems, Man, and Cybernetics: Part A, 32*(1), 50-71.

Brown, M., & Muchira, R. (2004). Investigating the relationship between Internet privacy concerns and online purchase behavior. *Journal of Electronic Commerce Research, 5*(1), 62-70.

Bryman, A., & Cramer, D. (2001). *Quantitative data analysis with SPSS Release 10 for Windows: A guide for social scientists.* London: Routledge.

Bryman, A., & Cramer, D. (1994). *Quantitative data analysis for social scientists.* New York: Routledge.

BTT. (2001). Biometrics secure Internet data centres worldwide. *Biometric Technology Today, 9*(2), 3.

BTT. (2006). Biometric statistics in focus. *Biometric Technology Today, 14*(2), 7-9.

Buchanan, T., Paine, C., Joinson, A.N., & Reips, U. (2007). Development of measures of online privacy concern and protection for use on the Internet. *Journal of the American Society for Information Science and Technology, 58*(2), 157-165.

Buchholz, R.A., & Rosenthal, S.B. (2002). Internet privacy: Individual rights and the common good. *SAM Advanced Manangement Journal, 67*(1), 34-41.

Buckner, T., Hesmer, S., Fischer, P., & Schuster, I. (2003). *Portlet development guide.* IBM. Retrieved August 10, 2007, from http://www-128.ibm.com/developerworks/websphere/zones/portal/portlet/portletdevelopment-guide.html

Bureau of Justice. (2005). Bureau of Justice statistics: Criminal victimization. Retrieved August 6, 2007, from http://www.ojp.usdoj.gov/bjs/cvictgen.htm.

Burn, J. M., & Loch, K. D. (2001). The societal impact of the World Wide Web: Key challenges for the 21st century. *Information Resources Management Journal, 14*(4), 4-14.

Burnett, M., Cook, C., & Rothermel, G. (2004). End-user software engineering. *Communications of the ACM, 47*(9), 53-58.

Busch, P., & Wilson, D. (1976). An experimental analysis of a salesman's expert and referent bases of social power in the buyer-seller dyad. *Journal of Marketing Research, 13*(1), 3-11.

Button, G. (Ed.) (1993). *Technology in working order: Studies of work, interaction and technology.* New York: Routledge.

Cabri, G., Loeonardi, L., & Zambonelli, F. (1998). Reactive tuple spaces for mobile agent coordination. *LNCS, 1477,* 237-248. Springer.

Callow, K. (1998). *Man and message. A guide to meaning-based text analysis.* Boston: University Press of America.

Campbell, M.C., & Goodstein, R.C. (2001). The moderating effect of perceived risk on consumers' evaluations of product incongruity: Preference for the norm. *Journal of Consumer Research, 28*(3), 439-450.

Cappel, J.J., & Windsor, J.C. (1998). A comparative investigation of ethical decision making: Information systems professionals versus students. *Database for Advances in Information Systems, 29*(2), 20-34.

Carmien, S., Dawe, M., Fischer, G., Gorman, A., Kintsch, A., & Sullivan, J.F. (2005). Socio-technical environments supporting people with cognitive disabilities using public transportation. *ACM Transactions on Computer Human Interaction, 12*(2), 233-262.

Carrara, P., Fogli, D., Fresta, G., & Mussio, P. (2002). Toward overcoming culture, skill and situation hurdles in human-computer interaction. *International Journal Universal Access in the Information Society, 1*(4), 288-304.

Carroll, J.M., Kellogg, W.A., & Rosson, M.B. (1992). The task-artifact cycle. In J.M. Carroll (Ed.), *Designing interaction: Psychology at the human-computer interface* (Cambridge Series on Human-Computer Interaction, pp. 74-102). Cambridge University Press.

Caudill, E. M., & Murphy, P. E. (2000). Consumer online privacy: Legal and ethical issues. *Journal of Public Policy & Marketing, 19*(1), 7-19.

Chaiklin, S., & Lave, J. (Eds.). (1993). *Understanding practice: Perspectives on activity and context.* Cambridge, MA: Cambridge University Press.

Chan, Y. E., & Storey, V. C. (1996). The use of spreadsheets in organizations: Determinants and consequences. *Information & Management, 31,* 119-134.

Charters, D. (2002). Electronic monitoring and privacy issues in business-marketing: The ethics of the double click experience. *Journal of Business Ethics, 35*(4), 243-255.

Chau, P., & Hu, P. (2001). Information technology acceptance by individual professionals: A model comparison approach. *Decision Sciences, 32*(4), 699-719.

Chen, L., Gillenson, M., & Sherrell, D. (2002). Enticing online consumers: An extended technology acceptance perspective. *Information and Management, 39,* 705-719.

Chen, P. Y., & Hitt, L. M. (2002). Measuring switching costs and the determinants of customer retention in Internet-enabled business: A study of the online brokerage industry. *Information Systems Research, 13*(3), 255-274.

Chidambaram, L., & Jones, B. (1993). Impact on communication medium and computer support on group perceptions and performance: A comparison of face-o-face and dispersed meetings. *MIS Quarterly, 17*(4), 465-491.

Chin, W.W., & Frye, T. (2001). *PLS-Graph* (Version 03.00). Soft Modeling Inc.

Christensen, A.L., & Eining, M.M. (1991). Factors influencing software piracy: Implications for accountants. *Journal of Information Systems, 5*(1), 67-50.

Christiansen, E. (1997). Gardening: A metaphor for sustainability in information technology-technical support. In J. Berleur & D. Whitehouse (Eds.), *An ethical global information society: Culture and democracy revisited.* London: Chapman & Hall.

Chua, S. L., Chen, D., & Wong, A. (1999). Computer anxiety and its correlates: A meta-analysis. *Computers in Human Behavior, 15*(5), 609-623.

Cohen, J. (1988). *Statistical power analysis for the behavioral sciences.* Hillside, NJ: L. Erlbaum Associates.

Cole, M. (1996). *Cultural psychology: A once and future discipline.* Cambridge, MA: Harvard University Press.

Commercenet, N. M. R. (1999). Nielsen Media Research and Netrating to measure at-work Internet use. Retrieved August 6, 2007, from *http://www.nielsenmedia.com/newsreleases/releases/1999/netratings3.html*

Compeau, D. R., & Higgins, C. A. (1995). Application of social cognitive theory to training for computer skills. *Information Systems Research, 6*(1), 118-143.

Compeau, D.R., & Higgins, C.A. (1995a). Application of social cognitive theory to training for computer skills. *Information Systems Research, 6*(2), 118-143.

Compeau, D.R., & Higgins, C.A. (1995b). Computer self-efficacy: Development of a measure and initial test. *MIS Quarterly, 19*(2), 189-211.

Compeau, D.R., Higgins, C.A., & Huff, S. (1999). Social cognitive theory and individual reactions to computing technology: A longitudinal study. *MIS Quarterly, 23*(2), 145-158.

Compeau, D., Marcolin, B., & Kelley, H. (2001). Generalizability of technology acceptance research using student subjects. In A. Ramirez (Ed.), *Proceedings of the Administrative Science Association of Canada, 22*(4), 35-47.

Conner, K., & Rumlet, R. (1991). Software piracy: An analysis of protection strategies. *Management Science, 37*(2), 125-139.

Consumer Reports Organization. (2002). *Big browser is watching you.* Retrieved August 4, 2007, from http://www.consumerreports/org/main/detailv2. jsp?CONTENT%3C%Ecnt_id=18207&FOLDER%3C %3Efolder_id=18151&bmUID=1057810848320

Cook, D.L., & Coupey, E. (1998, March). Consumer behavior and unresolved regulatory issues in electronic marketing. *Journal of Business Research, 41*(3), 231-238.

Cormier, S., & Hagman, J. (1987). *Transfer of learning: Contemporary research and applications.* San Diego: Academic Press, Inc.

Costa, J. A. (1994). *Gender issues and consumer behavior.* London: Sage.

Costabile, M.F., Foglia, D., Fresta, G., Mussio, P., & Piccinno, A. (2004). Software environments for end-user development and tailoring. *PsychNology Journal, 2*(1), 99-122.

Costabile, M.F., Fogli, D., Mussio, P., & Piccinno, A. (2005). A meta-design approach to end-user development. In *Proceedings of the IEEE Symposium on Visual Languages and Human-Centric Computing (VL/HCC'05)* (pp. 308-310). Dallas, Texas: IEEE Computer Society.

Costabile, M.F., Fogli, D., Mussio, P., & Piccinno, A. (2006a). End user development: The software shaping workshop approach. In H. Lieberman, F. Paternò, & V. Wulf. (Eds.), *End user development* (pp. 183-205). Dordrecht, The Netherlands: Springer.

Costabile, M.F., Fogli, D., Lanzilotti, R., Mussio, P., & Piccinno, A. (2006b). Supporting work practice through end user development environments. *Journal of Organizational and End User Computing, 18*(4), 43-65.

Costabile, M.F., Fogli, D., Marcante, A., & Piccinno, A. (2006c). Supporting interaction and co-evolution of users and systems. In A. Celentano & P. Mussio (Eds.), *Proceedings of the International Conference on Advanced Visual Interfaces (AVI 2006)*, Venice, Italy (pp. 143-150). New York: ACM Press.

Costabile, M.F., Fogli, D., Mussio, P., & Piccinno, A. (in press). Visual interactive systems for end-user development: A model-based design methodology. *IEEE Transactions on Systems, Men and Cybernetics: Part A*.

Cragan, J. F., & Shields, D. C. (1998). *Understanding communication theory. The communicative forces for human action*. Boston: Allyn and Bacon.

Cragg, P. G., & King, M. (1993). Spreadsheet modelling abuse: An opportunity for OR? *Journal of the Operational Research Society, 44*(8), 743-752.

Craig Jr., J. (2000). AICPA modifies WebTrust to respond to marketplace. *The Trusted Professional, 6*, 3-4.

Cranor, L. F. (1998). Internet privacy: A public concern. *netWorker: The Craft of Network Computing, 2*(2), 13-18.

Cranor, L. F., Byers, S., & Kormann, D. (2003). *An analysis of P3P deployment on commercial, government, and children's Web sites as of May 2003* (Technical Report prepared for the 14 May 2003 Federal Trade Commission Workshop on Technologies for Protecting Personal Information). Retrieved from http://www.research.att.com/projects/p3p/

Cranor, L. F., Reagle, J., & Ackerman, M. S. (1999). *Beyond concern: Understanding net users' attitudes about online privacy* (AT&T Labs-Research Technical Report TR 99.4.3). Retrieved from http://www.research.att.com/projects/privacystudy/

Cronan, T.P., & Al-Rafee, S. (2007). Factors that influence the intention to pirate software and media. *Journal of Business Ethics*.

Cronan, T.P., Leonard, L.N.K., & Kreie, J. (2005). An empirical validation of perceived importance and behavior intention in IT ethics. *Journal of Business Ethics, 56*(3), 231-238.

Crosby, L. A., Evans, K. R., & Cowles, D. (1990). Relationship quality in services selling: An interpersonal influence perspective. *Journal of Marketing, 54*(3), 68-81.

Crosby, L. A., & Stephens, N. (1987). Effects of relationship marketing on satisfaction, retention, and prices in the life insurance industry. *Journal of Marketing Research, 24*(4), 404-411.

Crotts, J. C., & Erdmann, R. (2000). Does national culture influence consumers' evaluation of travel services? A test of Hofstede's model of cross-cultural differences. *Managing Service Quality, 10*(5), 410-419.

Crowell, W. (2001). Trust, the e-commerce difference. *Credit Card Management, 14*(5), 80.

Culnan, M.J. (1995). Consumer awareness of name removal procedures: Implications for direct marketing. *Journal of Direct Marketing, 9*(2), 10-20.

Culnan, M.J., & Bies, R. (2003). Consumer privacy: Balancing economic and justice considerations. *Journal of Social Issues, 59*(2), 323-342.

Culnan, M. J. (1993). How did they get my name? An exploratory investigation of consumer attitudes toward secondary information use. *MIS Quarterly, 17*(3), 341-361.

Culnan, M. J. (1999). *Georgetown Internet privacy policy survey: Report to the Federal Trade Commission*. Retrieved from http://www.msb.edu/faculty/culnanm/gippshome.html

Culnan, M. J., & Armstrong, P. K. (1999). Information privacy concerns, procedural fairness, and impersonal trust: An empirical investigation. *Organization Science, 10*(1), 104-115.

Culnan, M. J., & Markus, M. L. (1987). Information technologies. *Handbook of Organizational Communication*, 420-443.

Cunningham, P. J. (2002). Are cookies hazardous to your privacy? *Information Management Journal, 36*(3), 52-54.

Cypher, A. (Ed.). (1993). *Watch what I do: Programming by demonstration.* Cambridge, MA: The MIT Press.

Dale, L. (2001). Mobile biometric devices help in law enforcement. *Biometric Technology Today, 9*(8), 6-7.

Daly, J. P., Pouder, R. W., & Kabanoff, B. (2004). The effects of initial differences in firms' espoused values on their postmerger performance. *The Journal of Applied Behavioral Science, 40*(3), 323-343.

Dann, G. (1993). Limitations in the use of nationality and country of residence variables. In D. Pearce, & R. Butler (Eds.), *Tourism research: Critiques and challenges* (pp. 88-112). London: Routledge.

Danna, A., & Gandy, O. H., Jr. (2002). All that glitters is not gold: Digging beneath the surface of data mining. *Journal of Business Ethics, 40,* 373-386.

Davis, F. D. (1993). User acceptance of information technology: System characteristics, user perceptions and behavioral impacts. *International Journal of Man-Machine Studies, 38*(3), 475-487.

Davis, F. D., Bagozzi, R. P., & Warshaw, P. R. (1989). User acceptance of computer technology: A comparison of two theoretical models. *Management Science, 35*(8), 982-1003.

Davis, S., & Bostrom, R. (1993). Training end users: An experimental investigation of the roles of the computer interface and training methods. *MIS Quarterly, 17*(1), 61-79.

Davis, F. (1989, September). Perceived usefulness, perceived ease of use, and user acceptance of information technology. *MIS Quarterly*, pp. 319-340.

Davis, G. B. (1988). The hidden costs of end-user computing. *Accounting Horizons, 2*(4), 103-106.

de Alfaro, L., & Henzinger, T.A. (2001). Interface automata. In *Proceedings of the 8th European Software Engineering Conference held jointly with the 9th ACMSIGSOFT International Symposium on Foundations of Software Engineering,* Vienna, Austria (pp. 109-120). ACM Press.

De Beauvoir, S. (1952). *The second sex.* New York: Vintage Books.

De Vaus, D. (2001). *Research design in social research.* London: Sage Publications.

Dean, K. (2002). College seeks security in thumbs. Retrieved August 6, 2007, from Wired News, http://www.wired.com

Dean, H., & Biswas, A. (2001). Third-party organization endorsement of products: An advertising cue affecting consumer pre-purchase evaluation of goods and services. *Journal of Advertising, 30*(4), 41-57.

Deane, F., Barrelle, K., Henderson, R., & Mahar, D. (1995). Perceived acceptability of biometric security systems. *Computers and Security, 14,* 225-231.

Deaux, K., & Kite, M. E. (1993). Gender stereotypes. In F. Denmark, & M. Paludi (Eds.), *Handbook on the psychology of women* (pp. 107-139). Westport, CT: Greenwood Press.

Delaney, E. M., Goldstein, C. E., Gutterman, J., & Wagner, S. N. (2003). Automated computer privacy preferences slowly gain popularity. *Intellectual Property & Technology Law Journal, 15*(8), 17.

Dennis, A. R., George, J. F., Jessup, L. M., Nunamaker, J. F., & Vogel, D.R. (1988). Information technology to support electronic meetings. *MIS Quarterly, 12*(4), 591-616.

Department of Communications Information Technology and the Arts. (2002). Consumer privacy fact sheet. Retrieved August 4, 2007, from http://www.dcita.gov.au

DeSanctis, G., & Gallupe, R. (1987). A foundation for the study of group decision support systems. *Management Science, 33*(5), 589-609.

DeSarbo, W., & Harshman, R. (1985). Celebrity brand congruence analysis. *Current Issues and Research in Advertising, 8*(1), 17-52.

Dess, G. G., & Orieger, N. K. (1987). Environment structure and consensus in strategy formulation: A conceptual integration. *Academy of Management Review, 12*(2), 313-330.

Dhillon, G. S., & Moores, T. T. (2001). Internet privacy: Interpreting key issues. *Information Resources Management Journal, 14*(4), 33-37.

Dickson, G. W., Lee-Partridge, J., & Robinson, L. H. (1993). Exploring ,modes of facilitative support for GDSS technology. *MIS Quarterly, 17*(2), 173-194.

Dinev, T., Bellotto, M., Hart, P., Russo, V., Serra, I., & Colautti, C. (2006). Internet users' privacy concerns and beliefs about government surveillance: An exploratory study of differences between Italy and the United States. *Journal of Global Information Management, 14*(4), 57-93.

Dommeyer, C. J., & Gross, B. L. (2003). What consumers know and what they do: An investigation of consumer knowledge, awareness, and use of privacy protection strategies. *Journal of Interactive Marketing, 17*(2), 34-51.

Döring, N. (2002). Personal home pages on the Web: A review of research. *Journal of Computer-Mediated Communication, 7*(3). Retrieved from http://www.ascusc.org/jcmc/vol7/issue3/doering.html

Doucet, F., Shukla, S., Gupta, R., & Otsuka, M. (2002). An environment for dynamic component composition for efficient co-design. In *Proceedings of the Design, Automation, and Test in Europe Conference,* Paris (pp. 736-744). IEEE Computer Society.

Douglas, D.E., Cronan, T.P., & Behel, J.D. (2006). *Equity perceptions as a deterrent to software piracy behavior* (Working Paper). Information Systems Department, University of Arkansas, Fayetteville, AR.

Dowling, G.R., & Staelin, R. (1994). A model of perceived risk and intended risk handling activity. *Journal of Consumer Research, 21*(1), 119-154.

Downey, J. P. (2004). Towards a comprehensive framework: EUC research issues and trends (1990-2000). *Journal of Organizational and End User Computing, 16*(4), 1-16.

Dubinsky, A., & Loken, B. (1989). Analyzing ethical decision making in marketing. *Journal of Business Research, 19*(2), 83-107.

Dwyer, F. R., Schurr, P. H., & Oh, S. (1987). Developing buyer-seller relationships. *Journal of Marketing, 51*(2), 11-27.

Dyck, J. L., Gee, N. R., & Smither, J. A. (1998). The changing construct of computer anxiety for younger and older adults. *Computers in Human Behavior, 14*(1), 61-77.

Eagly, A. H. (1987). *Sex differences in social behavior: A social-role interpretation.* Hillsdale, NJ: Erlbaum.

Easton, A., George, J. F., Nunamaker, J. F., & Pendergast, M. O. (1990). Using two different electronic meeting system tools for the same task: An experimental comparison. *Journal of Management Information Systems, 7*(1), 85-100.

Ebenkamp, B. (2002). Brand keys to travel sites. *Brandweek, 43*(25), 19.

Edge Diagrammed. (2006). Retrieved August 10, 2007, from http://www.pacestar.com/edge/

Edwards, R. (1997). *Changing places: Flexibility, lifelong learning, and a learning society.* London: Routledge.

Eirinaki, M., & Vazirgiannis, M. (2003). Web mining for Web personalization. *ACM Transactions on Internet Technology, 3*(1), 1-27.

Eisenberg, M. (1995). Programmable applications: Interpreter meets interface. *SIGCHI Bulletin, 27*(2), 68-83.

Eliashberg, J., & Robertson, T. (1988). New product pre-announcing behavior: A market signaling study. *Journal of Marketing Research, 25*(3), 282-292.

Ellström, P.E., Gustavsson, B., & Larsson, S. (1996). *Livslångt lärande* [Lifelong learning]. Lund: Student-litteratur.

Engeström, Y. (1987). *Learning by expanding: An activity-theoretical approach to developmental research.* Helsinki: Orienta-Konsultit.

Engeström, Y. (2001). Expansive learning at work: Towards an activity theoretical reconceptualization. *Journal of Education and Work, 14*, 133-156.

Engeström, Y., & Middleton, D. (Eds.). (1996). *Cognition and communication at work.* Cambridge: Cambridge University Press.

Fairclough, N. (2001). *Language and power* (2nd ed.). London: Longman.

Federal Trade Commission. (1996). *Consumer information privacy hearings.* Retrieved August 4, 2007, from http://www.ftc.gov

Federal Trade Commission. (1998). *Privacy online: A report to Congress.* Retrieved from http://www.ftc.gov/reports/privacy3/priv-23a.pdf

Federal Trade Commission. (2000). *Privacy online: Fair information practices in the electronic marketplace* (A Report to Congress). Retrieved from http://www.ftc.gov/reports/privacy2000/privacy2000.pdf

Federal Trade Commission. (2000a). *FTC sues failed Website, Toysmart.com, for deceptively offering for sale personal information of Website visitors.* Retrieved August 4, 2007, from http://ftc.gov/opa/2000/07/toysmart.htm

Federal Trade Commission. (2000b, July 21). *FTC announces settlement with bankrupt Website, Toysmart. Com, regarding alleged privacy violations.* Retrieved August 4, 2007, from http://www.ftc.gov/opa/2000/07/toysmart2.htm

Federal Trade Commission. (2007). FTC issues annual list of top consumer complaints. Retrieved August 6, 2007, from the Federal Trade Commission, http://www.ftc.gov/opa/2007/02/topcomplaints.htm

Felter, M. (1985). Sex differences on the California statewide assessment of computer literacy. *Sex Roles, 13*(2), 181-192.

Ferneley, E. H. (2007). Covert end user development: A study of success. *Journal of Organizational and End User Computing, 19*(1), 62-71.

Ferris, C, & Farrel, J. (2003). What are Web services? *Communications of the ACM, 46*(6), 31-36.

Festerand, T.A., Snyder, D.R., & Tsalikis, J.D. (1986). Influence of catalog versus store shopping and prior satisfaction on percieved risk. *Journal of the Academy of Marketing Science, 14*(4), 28-36.

Fiedler, F.E. (1974). The contingency model—New directions for leadership utilization. *Journal of Contemporary Business*, 65-79.

First Annual BSA and IDC Global Software Piracy Study. (2004). Retrieved August 3, 2007, from *http://www.bsa.org/globalstudy/*

Fischer, G., & Girgensohn, A. (1990). End-user modifiability in design environments. In *Proceedings of the Conference on Human Factors in Computing Systems (CHI'90)* (pp. 183-192). New York: ACM Press.

Fischer, G., Giaccardi, E., Ye, Y., Sutcliffe, A.G., & Mehandjiev, N. (2004). Meta-design: A manifesto for end-user development. *Communications of the ACM, 47*(9), 33-37.

Fischer, G., & Lemke, A.C. (1988). Constrained design processes: Steps toward convivial computing. In R. Guindon (Ed.), *Cognitive science and its application for human-computer interaction* (pp. 1-58). Hillsdale, NJ: Lawrence Erlbaum.

Fischer, G. (1998). Seeding, evolutionary growth, and reseeding: Constructing, capturing, and evolving knowledge in domain-oriented design environments. *Automated Software Engineering, 5*(4), 447-468.

Fischer, G. (2002). Beyond "couch potatoes": From consumers to designers and active contributors. *First Monday, 7*(12). Retrieved from http://firstmonday.org/issues/issue7_12/fischer/index.html

Fischer, G. (2006). Beyond binary choices: Understanding and exploiting trade-offs to enhance creativity. *First Monday, 11*(4). Retrieved from http://firstmonday.org/issues/issue11_4/fischer/index.html

Fischer, G., & Giaccardi, E. (2006). Meta-design: A framework for the future of end-user development. In H. Lieberman, F., Paternò, & V. Wulf (Eds.), *End user development* (pp. 427-457). Dordrecht, The Netherlands: Springer.

Fischer, G., Giaccardi, E., Ye, Y., Sutcliffe, A.G., & Mehandjiev, N. (2004). Meta-design: A manifesto for end user development. *Communications of the ACM, 47*(9), 33-37.

Fischer, E., & Arnold, S.J. (1994). Sex, gender identity, gender role attitudes and consumer behavior. *Psychology and Marketing, 11*(2), 163-182.

Fishbein, M., & Ajzen, I. (1975). *Attitude, intention, and behavior: An introduction to theory and research.* Reading, MA: Addison-Wesley.

Fishbein, M., & Ajzen, I. (1975). *Belief, attitude, intentions and behavior: An introduction to theory and research.* Boston: Addison-Wesley.

Fjermestad, J. (2004). An analysis of communication mode in group support systems research. *Decision Support Systems, 37*(2), 239-266.

Fjermestad, J., & Hiltz, S. R. (1998-1999). An assessment of group support systems experimental research: Methodology and results. *Journal of Management Information System, 15*(3), 7-149.

Flannery, B., & May, D. (2000). Environmental ethical decision making in the U.S. metal-finishing industry. *Academy of Management Journal, 43*(4), 642-662.

Flax, J. (1983). Political philosophy and the partriarchal unconscious: A psychoanalytic perspective on epistemology and metaphysics. In S. Harding, & M. Hintikka (Eds.), *Discovering reality: Feminist perspectives on epistemology, metaphysics, methodology, and philosophy of science* (pp. 245-281). London: D. Reidel Publishing.

Fletcher, K. (2003). Consumer power and privacy: The changing nature of CRM. *International Journal of Advertising, 22*(2), 249-272.

Folmer, E., van Welie, M., & Bosch, J. (2005). Bridging patterns: An approach to bridge gaps between SE and HCI. *Journal of Information and Software Technology, 48*(2), 69-89.

Ford, J., Smith, E., Weissbein, D., Gully, S., & Salas, E. (1998). Relationships of goal orientation, metacognitive activity, and practice strategies with learning outcomes and transfer. *Journal of Applied Psychology, 83*, 218-233.

Fornell, C., & Larcker, D. (1981). Evaluating structural equation models with unobservable variables and measurement error. *Journal of Marketing Research, 18*, 39-50.

Forrester Research. (2002, August 29). US eCommerce — The next five years. *M2 Presswire.*

Fournier, S. (1998). Consumers and their brands: Developing relationship theory in consumer research. *Journal of Consumer Research, 24*(2), 343-373.

Fournier, S., Dobscha, S., & Mick, D.G. (1998). Preventing the premature death of relationship marketing. *Harvard Business Review, 76*(1), 42-51.

Frewer, L., Shepherd, R., & Sparks, P. (1994). The interrelationship between perceived knowledge, control and risk associated with a range of food related hazards targeted at the self, other people and society. *Journal of Food Safety, 14*, 19-40.

Friedman, H., & Friedman, L. (1979). Endorser effectiveness by product type. *Journal of Advertising, 19*(5), 63-71.

Fujii, K., & Suda, T. (2004). Component service model with semantics (CoS-MoS): A new component model for dynamic service composition. In *Proceedings of the International Symposium on Applications and the Internet Workshops (SAINTW'04)* (pp. 321-327).

Fukuyama, R. (1995). *Trust: Social virtues and the creation of prosperity.* New York: The Free Press.

Gantt, M., & Nardi, B. (1992). Gardeners and gurus: Patterns of cooperation among CAD users. In *Proceedings of the Conference on Computer-Human Interaction (CHI '92)* (pp. 107-117). New York: ACM Press.

Gefen, D. (2000). E-commerce: The role of familiarity and trust. *Omega, 28,* 725-737.

Gefen, D., & Straub, D. W. (1997). Gender differences in the perception and use of e-mail: An extension to the technology acceptance model. *MIS Quarterly, 21*(4), 389-400.

George, G., & Sleeth, R. G. (2000). Leadership in computer-mediated communication: Implications and research directions. *Journal of Business and Psychology, 15*(2), 287-310.

George, J. F., Easton, G. K., Nunamaker, J. F., & Northcraft, G. B. (1990). A study of collaborative group work with and without computer-based support. *Information Systems Research, 1*(4), 394-415.

Gerrity, T. P., & Rockart, J. F. (1986). End-user computing: Are you a leader or a laggard? *Sloan Management Review, 27*(4), 25-34.

Ghosh, A. (2001). *Security and privacy for e-business.* New York: Wiley.

Gist, M.E. (1987). Self-efficacy: Implications for organizational behavior and human resource management. *Academy of Management Review, 12*(3), 472-485.

Gist, M. E., Schwoerer, C., & Rosen, B. (1989). Effects of alternative training methods on self-efficacy and performance in computer software training. *Journal of Applied Psychology, 74*(6), 884-891.

Glass, R., & Wood, W. (1996). Situational determinants of software piracy: An equity theory perspective. *Journal of Business Ethics, 15*(11), 1189-1198.

Goffman, E. (1979). *Gender advertisement.* New York: Harper and Row.

Goldsmith, R., Lafferty, B., & Newell, S. (2000). The impact of corporate credibility and endorser celebrity on consumer reaction to advertisement and brands. *Journal of Advertising, 29*(3), 43-54.

Gomez, J., Han, S.-K., Toma, I., Sapkota, B., & Garcia-Crespo, A. (2006). A semantically-enhanced component-based architecture for software composition. In *Proceedings of the International Multi-Conference on Computing in the Global Information Technology* (p. 43).

Goodwin, C. (1991). Privacy: Recognition of a consumer right. *Journal of Public Policy and Marketing, 10*(1), 149-167.

Goodwin, C., & Goodwin, M.H. (1997). Seeing as a situated activity: Formulating planes. In Y. Engeström & D. Middleton (Eds.), *Cognition and communication at work* (pp. 61-95). Cambridge, MA: Cambridge University Press.

Gopal, R., & Sanders, L. (1997). Preventive and deterrent controls for software piracy. *Journal of Management Information Systems, 13*(4), 29-47.

Gopal, A. R., Bostrom, O., & Chin, Y. (1992-1993). Applying adaptive structuration theory to investigate the process of group support systems use. *Journal of Management Information Systems, 9*(3), 45-69.

Gopalakishna, P., & Mummalaneni, V. (1993). Influencing satisfaction for dental services. *Journal of Health Care Marketing, 13*(1), 16-22.

Gordon, L., Loeb, M., Lucyshyn, W., & Richardson, R. (2006). 2006 CSI/FBI computer crime and security survey. Retrieved August 6, 2007, from CSI, http://www.gocsi.com/

Goupil, D. (2000, June). End-user application development: Relief for IT. *Computing Channels*, pp. 2-4.

Govindarajulu, C. (2003). End users: Who are they? *Communications of the ACM, 46*(9), 152-159.

Grabowski, M., & Roberts, K. (1998). Risk mitigation in virtual organizations. *Journal of Computer-Mediated Communication, 3*(4). Retrieved from http://jcmc.huji.ac.il/vol3/issue4/grabowski.html

Grace, D. (2007). How embarrassing! An exploratory study of critical incidents including affective reactions. *Journal of Service Research, 9*(3), 271-284.

Graeff, T. R., & Harmon, S. (2002). Collecting and using personal data: Consumers' awareness and concerns. *The Journal of Consumer Marketing, 19*(4/5), 302-318.

Granzin, P. J. (1976). Profiling the male fashion innovator another step. In B. Anderson (Ed.), *Advances in consumer research* (Vol. 3) (pp. 40-45). Ann Arbor, MI: Association for Consumer Research.

Gray, P. (1988). The user interface in group decision support systems. In *Proceedings of the Eighth International Conference on Decision Support Systems,* Boston, MA (pp. 203-225).

Green, T. (1989). Cognitive dimensions of notations. In *Proceedings of the HCI'89 Conference* (pp. 443-460). Cambridge University Press.

Greenbaum, J., & Kyng, M. (Eds.). (1991). *Design at work.* Hillsdale, NJ: Lawrence Erlbaum Associates.

Greenbaum, S., & Quirk, R. (1990). *A student's grammar of the English language.* Harlow: Longman.

Greenspan, R. (2004). *Three-quarters of Americans have access from home.* (Click Z News Formerly Internet Advertising Report). Retrieved August 4, 2007, from http://www.clickz.com/news/article.php/3328091

Greenwich Associates. (1987). *Large corporate banking survey.* Greenwich, CT: Greenwich Associates.

Griffith, T. L., & Northcraft, G. B. (1994). Distinguish between the forest and trees: Media, features, and methodology in electronic communication research. *Organizational Science, 5*(2), 272-285.

Grove, S. J., Pickett, G. M., & Laband, D. N. (1995). An empirical examination of factual information content among service advertisements. *The Service Industries Journal, 15*(2), 216-233.

Grudin, J. (1991). Interactive systems: Bridging the gaps between developers and users. *IEEE Computer, 24*(4), 59-69.

Gudykunst, W. B., Yang, S. M., & Nishida, T. (1985). A cross-cultural test of uncertainty reduction theory: Comparisons of acquaintances, friends, and dating relationships in Japan, Korea, and the United States. *Human Communication Research, 11*, 407-454.

Guimaraes, T., Gupta, Y., & Rainer, K. (1999). Empirically testing the relationship between end-user computing problems and information center success factors. *Decision Sciences, 30*(2), 393-413.

Gundlach, M.J., & Thatcher, J.B. (2000). *Examining the multi-dimensionality of computer self-efficacy: An empirical test.* Unpublished manuscript, Florida State University.

Guribye, F. (2005). *Infrastructures for learning: Ethnographic inquiries into the social and technical conditions for education and training.* Doctoral thesis, University of Bergen, Norway, Department of Information Science and Media Studies.

Hackbarth, G., Grover, V., & Yi, M. Y. (2003). Computer playfulness and anxiety: Positive and negative mediators of the system experience effect on perceived ease of use. *Information & Management, 40*(3), 221-232.

Hagel, J., & Rayport, J. F. (1997). The coming battle for customer information. *Harvard Business Review, 75*(1), 53-65.

Hagger, M., Chatzisarantis, N., & Biddle, S. (2002). A meta-analytic review of the theories of reasoned action and planned behavior in physical activity: Predictive validity and the contribution of additional variables. *Journal of Sport & Exercise Psychology, 24*(1), 3-32.

Hair, J., Anderson, R., Tatham, R., & Black, W. (1998). *Multivariate data analysis.* Upper Saddle River, NJ: Prentice Hall.

Hall, M. J. J. (1996). A risk and control oriented study of the practices of spreadsheet application developers. *Proceedings of the 29th Hawaii International Conference on System Sciences,* (pp. 364-373). Maui, Hawaii.

Hall, J. E., Shaw, M. R., Lascheit, J., & Robertson, N. (2000). Gender differences in a modified perceived value construct for intangible products. In *Proceedings of the ANZMEC Conference 2000*, Melbourne.

Halliday, M. A. K. (1994). *Introduction to functional grammar* (2nd ed.). London: Edward Arnold.

Hammer, M. R., & Martin, J. N. (1992). The effects of cross-cultural training on American managers in a Japanese-American joint venture. *Journal of Applied Communication Research, 20*, 161-182.

Han, P., & Maclaurin, A. (2002). Do consumers really care about online privacy? *Marketing Management, 11*(1), 35-38.

Harder, J.W. (1991). Equity theory versus expectancy theory: The case of major league baseball free agents. *Journal of Applied Psychology, 76*(3), 458-464.

Harding, W. T., Reed, A. J., & Gray, R. L. (2001). Cookies and Web bugs: What they are and how they work together. *Information Systems Management, 18*(3), 17-24.

Harmon, B., Conroy, R., Emory, C, & Macfarlane, K. (2000). *Using digital dashboards.* Retrieved August 10, 2007, from http://www.microsoft.com/education/default.asp?ID=DigitalDashTutorial

Harmon, R., & Coney, K. (1982). The persuasive effects of source credibility in buy and lease situations. *Journal of Marketing Research, 19*(2), 255-260.

Harrington, S.J. (1996). The effects of codes of ethics and personal denial of responsibility on computer abuse judgments and intentions. *MIS Quarterly, 20*(3), 257-278.

Harrison, A. W., & Rainer, R. K. (1992). The influence of individual differences on skill in end-user computing. *Journal of Management Information Systems, 9*(1), 93-111.

Hart, C. W. L., Heskett, J. L., & Sasser, W. E. (1990). The profitable art of service recovery. *Harvard Business Review, 68*(4), 148-156.

Hartson, H.R., & Hix, D. (1993). *Developing user interfaces: Ensuring usability through product & process.* New York: John Wiley.

Hasan, B. (2006). Delineating the effects of general and system-specific computer self-efficacy beliefs on IS acceptance. *Information and Management, 43*, 565-571.

Haskell, R. E. (2001). *Transfer of learning: Cognition, instruction and reasoning.* San Diego: Academic Press.

Hatcher, L. (1994). *A step-by-step approach to using the SAS system for factor analysis and structural equation modeling.* Cary, NC: SAS Institute.

Havelka, D., Beasley, F., & Broome, T. (2004). A study of computer anxiety among business students. *Mid-American Journal of Business, 19*(1), 63-71.

Hawkins, D., Best, R., & Coney, K. (1998). *Consumer behavior: Building marketing strategy.* Boston, MA: McGraw Hill.

Hayes, J.R. (1985). *Three problems in teaching general skills.* Hillsdale, NJ: Lawrence Erlbaum Associates.

Heflin, J. (2004). *OWL Web ontology language: Use cases and requirements.* World Wide Web Consortium. Retrieved August 10, 2007, from http://www.w3.org/TR/webont-req/

Henderson, S., & Snyder, C. (1999). Personal information privacy: Implications for MIS managers. *Information and Management, 36*, 213-220.

Herman, A. (2002). Major bank signs up for digital signature verification technology. *Biometric Technology Today, 10*(1), 1.

Hightower, R., & Sayeed, L. (1996). Effects of communication mode and prediscussion information distribution characteristics on information exchange in groups. *Information Systems Research, 7*(4), 451-465.

Hiltz, S. R., & Johnson, K. (1990). User satisfaction with computer-mediated communication systems. *Management Science, 36*(6), 739-764.

Hiltz, S. R., Johnson, K., & Turoff, M. (1982). *The effects of formal human leadership and computer-generated decision aids on problem solving via computer: A controlled experiment* [Research Report No. 18]. Computerized Conferencing and Communication Center, New Jersey Institute of Technology.

Hiltz, S. R., Johnson, K., & Turoff, M. (1991). Group decision support: The effects of designated human leaders and statistical feedback in computerized conferences. *Journal of Management Information System, 8*(2), 81-108.

Hiltz, S. R., & Turoff, M. (1978-1993). *The Network Nation: Human Communication via Computer*. Reading, MA: Addison-Wesley.

Hirokawa, R. Y., & Poole, M. S. (Eds.). (1986). *Communication and group decision-making*. Beverly Hills, CA: Sage Publications.

Hite, R. C. (2002). *Enterprise architecture use across the federal government can be improved* (GAO-02-6). Washington, DC: U.S. Government Accounting Office (GAO).

Ho, S.S.M., & Ng, V. (1994). A study of consumers risk perception of electronic payment systems. *International Journal of Bank Marketing, 12*(4), 26-38.

Ho, T. H., & Raman, K. S. (1991). The effect of GDSS and elected leadership on small group meetings. *Journal of Management Information Systems, 8*(2), 109-133.

Hoffman, D., Kalsbeek, W., & Novak, T. (1999). Internet and Web use in the U.S. *Communications of the ACM, 39*(12), 36-46.

Hofstede, G. (2003). *Culture's consequences, comparing values, behaviors, institutions, and organizations across nations* (2nd ed.). Newbury Park, CA: Sage Publications.

Hofstede, G. (1980). *Culture's consequences: International differences in work related values*. London: Sage.

Hofstede, G. (1991). *Culture and organizations*. New York: McGraw-Hill.

Holbrook, M. (1986). Aims, concepts and methods for the representation of individual differences in aesthetic response to design features. *Journal of Consumer Research, 13*(3), 337-347.

Holladay, C. L., & Quiñones, M. A. (2003). Practice variability and transfer of training: The role of self-efficacy generality. *Journal of Applied Psychology, 88*(6), 1094-1103.

Hollan, J., Hutchins, E., & Kirsh, D. (2000). Distributed cognition: Toward a new foundation for human-computer interaction research. *ACM Transactions on Computer-Human Interaction, 7*(2), 174-196.

Hollander, E. P. (1974). Processes of leadership emergence. *Journal of Contemporary Business*, Autumn, 19-33.

Hong, W., Thong, J., Wong, W., & Tam, K. (2002). Determinants of user acceptance of digital libraries: An empirical examination of individual differences and system characteristics. *Journal of Management Information Systems, 18*(3), 97-124.

Hopkins, R. (1999). An introduction to biometrics and large scale civilian identification. *International Review of Law Computer and Technology, 13*(3), 337-363.

House, R. J. (1971). A path goal theory of leader effectiveness. *Administrative Science Quarterly, 16*, 321-338.

Houston, R., & Taylor, G. (1999). Consumer perceptions of CPA WebTrust assurances: evidence of an expectation gap. *International Journal of Auditing, 3*(2), 89-105.

Howard, G. S., & Smith, R. D. (1986). Computer anxiety in management: Myth or reality? *Communications of the ACM, 29*(7), 611-615.

Hoxmeier, J. (2000). Software preannouncements and their impact on customer's perceptions and vendor reputation. *Journal of Management Information Systems, 17*(1), 115-139.

Hoy, M.G., & Phelps, J. (2003). Consumer privacy and security protection on church Web sites: Reasons for concern. *Journal of Public Policy & Marketing, 22*(1), 58-70.

Hsu, M.-H., & Chiu, C.-M. (2004). Internet self-efficacy and electronic service acceptance. *Decision Support Systems, 38*(3), 369-381.

Hu, P. J. H., Clark, T. H. K., & Ma, W. W. (2003). Examining technology acceptance by school teachers: A longitudinal study. *Information & Management, 41*(2), 227-241.

Hu, P., Chau, P., Sheng, O., & Tam, K. (1999). Examining the technology acceptance model using physician acceptance of telemedicine technology. *Journal of Management Information Systems, 16*(2), 91-112.

Hughes, J.A., Randall, D., & Shapiro, D. (1992). Faltering from ethnography to design. In M. Mantel & R. Baecher (Eds.), *Proceedings of the International Conference on Computer-Supported Cooperative Work (CSCW'92)*, Toronto, Canada (pp. 115-122). New York: ACM Press.

Huizingh, E.K.R.E., & Hoekstra, J.C. (2003). Why do consumers like Websites? *Journal of Targeting, Measurement and Analysis for Marketing, 11*(4), 350.

Iacobucci, D., & Ostrom, A. (1996). Commercial and interpersonal relationships: Using the structure of interpersonal relationships to understand individual-to-individual, individual-to-firm, and firm-to-firm relationships. *International Journal of Research in Marketing, 13*(1), 53-72.

Igbaria, M., & Iivari, J. (1995). The effects of self-efficacy on computer usage. *OMEGA International Journal of Management Science, 23*(6), 587-605.

Igbaria, M., & Parasuraman, S. (1989). A path analytic study of individual characteristics, computer anxiety, and attitudes towards microcomputers. *Journal of Management, 15*(3), 373-388.

Igbaria, M. (1990). End-user computing effectiveness: A structural equation model. *OMEGA, 18*(6), 637-652.

Igbaria, M., Guimaraes, T., & Davis, G. B. (1995). Testing the determinants of microcomputer usage via a structural equation model. *Journal of Management Information Systems, 11*(4), 87-114.

Im, J., & Van Epps, P. (1991). Software piracy and software security in business schools: An ethical perspective. *The DATABASE for Advances in Information Systems, 22*(3), 15-21.

Institute for Information Industry. (2002). Retrieved January 6, 2002, from http://www.find.org.tw/0105/howmany/howmany_disp.asp?id=49", (in Chinese).

Jöreskog, K. G., & Sorbom, D. (1986). *LISREL VI: Analysis of linear structural relationships by maximum likelihood, instrumental variables, and least squares methods* (4th ed.). Mooresville, IN: Scientific Software.

Jun, M., & Cai, S. (2001). The key determinants of Internet banking service quality: A content analysis. *International Journal of Bank Marketing, 19*(7), 276-291.

Kang, Y. S., & Ridgway, N. M. (1996). The importance of consumer market interactions as a form of social support for elderly consumers. *Journal of Public Policy & Marketing, 15*(1), 108-117.

Kettinger, W., & Lee, C. C. (1994). Perceived service quality and user satisfaction with the information services function. *Decision Science, 25*(5/6), 737-766.

Kumar, N., Scheer, L. K., & Steenkamp, J. B. (1995). The effects of supplier fairness on vulnerable resellers. *Journal of Marketing Research, 32*(1), 54-65.

Laroche, M., Saad, G., Cleveland, M., & Browne, E. (2000). Gender differences in information search strategies for a Christmas gift. *Journal of Consumer Marketing, 17*(6), 500-524.

Lewis, B. R., & Spyrakopoulos, S. (2001). Service failures and recovery in retail banking: The customers' perspective. *The International Journal of Bank Marketing, 19*(1), 37-48.

Lin, C. P., & Ding, C. G. (2005). Opening the black box: Assessing the mediating mechanism of relationship quality and the moderating effects of prior experience in ISP service. *International Journal of Service Industry Management, 16*(1), 55-80.

Mattila, A. S., Grandey, A. A., & Fisk, G. M. (2003). The interplay of gender and affective tone in service encounter satisfaction. *Journal of Service Research, 6*(2), 136-143.

Maxwell, S. (1999). Biased attributions of a price increase: Effects of culture and gender. *Journal of Consumer Marketing, 16*(1), 9-23.

McClure, P. A., Smith, J. W., & Sitko, T. D. (1997). *The crisis in information technology support: Has our current model reached its limits?* Boulder, CO: CAUSE.

Meyers-Levy, J., & Sternthal, B. (1991). Gender differences in the use of message cues and judgments. *Journal of Marketing Research, 28*(1), 84-96.

Moorman, C., Deshpande, R., & Zaltman, G. (1993). Factors affecting trust in market relationships. *Journal of Marketing, 57*(1), 81-101.

Oliver, R. L. (1980). A cognitive model of the antecedents and consequences of satisfaction decisions. *Journal of Marketing Research, 17*(4), 460-469.

Palmer, A., & Bejou, D. (1995). The effects of gender on the development of relationships between clients and financial advisers. *The International Journal of Bank Marketing, 13*(3), 18-27.

Rosen, L. D., & Maguire, P. D. (1990). Myths and realities in computerphobia: A meta-analysis. *Anxiety Research, 3*(2), 175-191.

Rushton, A., & Carson, D. J. (1989). Services—Marketing with a difference. *Marketing Intelligence & Planning, 5*(5/6), 12-17.

Scherhorn, G., Reisch, L. A., & Raab, G. (1990). Addictive buying in West Germany: An empirical study. *Journal of Consumer Policy, 13*(4), 355-387.

Shamdasani, P. N., & Balakrishnan, A. A. (2000). Determinants of relationship quality and loyalty in personalized services. *Asia Pacific Journal of Management, 17*(3), 399-422.

Sheth, J. N. (1975). Buyer-seller interaction: A conceptual framework. In B. B. Anderson (Ed.), *Advances in consumer research* (Vol. 3) (pp. 382-386). Cincinnati, OH: Association for Consumer Research.

Singh, J. (1995). Measurement issues in cross-national research. *Journal of International Business Studies, 26*(3), 597-619.

Sistruck, F., & McDavid, J. W. (1971). Sex variable in conforming behavior. *Journal of Personality and Social Psychology, 17*(2), 200-207.

Smith, J. B., & Barclay, D. W. (1997). The effects of organizational differences and trust on the effectiveness of selling partner relationships. *Journal of Marketing, 61*(1), 3-21.

Soldow, G. F., & Thomas, G. P. (1984). Relational communication: From versus content in the sales interaction. *Journal of Marketing, 48*(1), 84-93.

Solomon, M. R., Surprenant, C., Czepiel, J. A., & Gutman, E. G. (1985). A role theory perspective on dyadic interactions: The service encounter. *Journal of Marketing, 49*(1), 99-111.

Swan, J. E., Trawick, I. F., & Silva, D. W. (1985). How industrial salespeople gain customer trust. *Industrial Marketing Management, 14*(3), 203-211.

Tam, J. L. M., & Wong, Y. H. (2001). Interactive selling: A dynamic framework for services. *Journal of Services Marketing, 15*(5), 379-396.

Usunier, J. (1996). *Marketing across cultures.* Englewood Cliffs, NJ: Prentice Hall.

Venkatesh, V., & Morris, M. G. (2000). Why don't men ever stop to ask for directions? Gender, social influence, and their role in technology acceptance and usage behavior. *MIS Quarterly, 24*(1), 115-139.

Westbrook, R. A. (1981). Sources of consumer satisfaction with retail outlets. *Journal of Retailing, 57*(3), 68-85.

Williamson, O. E. (1983). Credible commitments: Using hostages to support exchange. *American Economic Review, 73*(4), 519-540.

Woo, K. S., & Fock, H. K. Y. (1999). Customer satisfaction in the Hong Kong mobile phone industry. *The Service Industries Journal, 19*(3), 162-174.

Worchel, S., & Cooper, J. (1976). *Understanding social psychology.* Homewood, IL: Dorsey Press.

Wulf, K. D., Odekerken-Schroder, G., & Lacobucci, D. (2001). Investments in consumer relationships: A cross-country and cross-industry exploration. *Journal of Marketing, 65*(4), 33-50.

Zeithaml, V. A., Berry, L. L., & Parasuraman, A. (1996). The behavioral consequences of service quality. *Journal of Marketing, 60*(2), 31-46.

AARP. (2000). National survey on consumer preparedness and e-commerce: A study of computer users age 45 and older. Retrieved August 28, 2003, from *http://research.aarp.prg/consume.ecomerce1.html*

Adams, D. A., Nelson, R. R., & Todd, P. A. (1992). Perceived usefulness, ease of use and usage of information technology: A replication. *MIS Quarterly, 16*(2), 227-247.

Bellman, S., Lohse, G. L., & Johnson, E. J. (1999). Predictors of online buying behavior. *Communications of the ACM, 42*(12), 32-38.

Billipp, S. (2001). The psychological impact of interactive computer use within a vulnerable elderly population: A report on a randomized prospective trial in a home health care setting. *Public Health Nursing, 18*(2), 138-145.

Branscum, D. (2000). Guarding online privacy. *Newsweek, 135*(23), 77-78.

Brown, M., & Muchira, R. (2004). Investigating the relationships between Internet privacy concerns and online purchase behavior. *Journal of Electronic Commerce Research, 5*(1), 62-82.

Bucy, E. P (2000). Social access to the Internet. *Harvard International Journal of Press/Politics*, 5(1), 50.

Burnett, J. (1991). Examining the media habits of the affluent elderly. *Journal of Advertising Research, 31*(5), 33-41.

Chen, L., Gillenson, M. & Sherrell, D. (2002). Enticing online consumers: An extended technology acceptance perspective. *Information & Management, 39*(8), 705-719.

Cohen, A. (2001). Internet insecurity. *Time, 157*(26), 44-51.

Davis, F. D. (1989). Perceived usefulness, perceived ease of use and user acceptance of information technology. *MIS Quarterly, 13*(3), 319-339.

Doll, W. J., Hendrickson, A., & Deng, X. (1998). Using Davis's perceived usefulness and ease-of-use instruments for decision making: A confirmatory and multigroup invariance analysis. *Decision Sciences, 29*(4), 839-869.

Eastman, J., & Iyer, R. (2004). The elderly's uses and attitudes towards the Internet. *The Journal of Consumer Marketing, 21*(2/3), 208-220.

Eisenberg, A. (2001, April 5). A 'smart' home, to avoid the nursing home. *New York Times*, pp. G.1.

Finn, J. (1997). Aging and information technology: The promise and the challenge. *Generations, 21*, 5-6.

Foster, E. (2003). "Caught you!" *InfoWorld, 25*(12), 60.

Gefen, D. (2003). TAM or just plain habit: A look at experienced online shoppers. *Journal of End User Computing, 15*(3), 1-13.

Gefen, D., Karahanna, E., & Straub, D. (2003). Trust and TAM in online shopping: An integrated model. *MIS Quarterly, 27*(1), 51-90.

Gefen, D., & Straub, D. (2000). The relative use of perceived ease of use in IS adoption: A study of e-commerce adoption. *Journal of the Association for Information Systems, 1*(8), 1-28.

Grabner-Kraeuter, S. (2002). The role of consumers' trust in online-shopping. *Journal of Business Ethics, 39*(1/2), 43-50.

Groves, D. L. (1990). Computer assisted instruction with senior citizens. *Journal of Instructional Psychology, 17*(3), 172-177.

Han, K. S., & Noh, K. (1999). Critical failure factors that discourage the growth of electronic commerce. *International Journal of Electronic Commerce, 4*(2), 25-43.

Hawkins, D., & Mannix, M. (2000). Privacy is under siege at work, at home and online. *U.S. News and World Report, 129*(13), 62-68.

Henry, J. W., & Martinko, M. J. (1997). An attributional analysis of the rejection of information technology. *Journal of End User Computing, 9*(4), 3-17.

Hoffman, D. L., & Novak, T. P. (1999). Building consumer trust online. *Communications of the ACM, 42*(4), 80-85.

Hu, P. J, Chau, P., Sheng, O., & Tam, K. Y. (1999). Examining the technology acceptance model using physician acceptance of telemedicine technology. *Journal of Management Information Systems, 16*(2), 91-113.

Igbaria, M., Guimaraes, T., & Davis, G. B. (1995). Testing the determinants of microcomputer usage via a structural equation model. *Journal of Management Information Systems, 11*(4), 87-102.

Igbaria, M., Zinatelli, N., Craig, P., & Cavaya, A. (1997). Personal computing acceptance factors in small firms: A structural equation model. *MIS Quarterly, 21*(3), 279-305.

Jones, K. (2005). Pharming your identity; identity theft is on the rise, and phishing e-mail scams disguised as legitimate correspondence has risen to epidemic proportions. *PC Magazine, 24*(8), 19.

Karahanna, E., & Straub, D. W. (1999). The psychological origins of perceived usefulness and ease of use. *Information & Management, 35*(4), 237-250.

Kelleher, L. (2003). Breaking the stereotypes of older adults online. *AARP.* Retrieved August 21, 2003, from *http://www.aarp.org/olderwiserwired/Articles/a2003-02-20-oww-barriers.html*

Kelloway, E. K. (1998). *Using Lisrel for structural equation modeling: A researcher's guide.* Thousand Oaks, CA: Sage.

Kerlinger, F. N. (1986). *Foundations of behavioral research.* TX: Harcourt Brace College.

Koufaris, M., & Hampton-Sosa, W. (2004). The development of initial trust in an online company by new customer. *Information & Management, 41*(3), 377-388.

Lederer, A. L., Maupin, D. J., Seneca, M. P., & Zhuang, Y. (2000). The technology acceptance model and the World Wide Web. *Decision Support Systems, 29*(3), 269-282.

Lee, M. K. O., & Turban, E. (2001). A trust model for consumer Internet shopping. *International Journal of Electronic Commerce, 6*(1), 75-91.

Licht, J. (1999, August 31). Seniors assess a deluge of data: Operators of Web sites reach out to a growing audience of older people. *The Washington Post*, p. Z15.

Lin, J. C.-C., & Lu, H. (2000). Towards an understanding of the behavioural intention to use a Web site. *International Journal of Information Management, 20*(30), 197-208.

Liu, Chang, Marchewka, Jack T., Lu, June & Yu, Chun-Sheng. (2005). Beyond concern - A privacy-trust-behavioral intention model of electronic commerce. *Information & Management, 42*(1), 289-304.

Lucas, H., & Spitler, V. K. (1999). Technology use and performance: A field study of broker workstations. *Decision Sciences, 30*(2), 291-311.

Marquie, J. C., Jourdan-Boddaert, L., & Huet, N. (2002). Do older adults underestimate their actual computer knowledge? *Behavior and Information Technology, 21*(4), 273-280.

Moon, J., & Kim, Y. (2001). Extending the TAM for a World Wide Web context. *Information and Management, 38*(4), 217-230.

Moschis, G. P., & Mathur, A. (1993). How they're acting their age. *Marketing Management, 2*(2), 40-51.

Mukherjee, A., & Nath, P. (2003). A model of trust in online relationships banking. *The International Journal of Bank Marketing, 21*(1), 5-16.

Nielson//NetRatings. (2003). *Broadband access grows 59 percent, while narrow band use declines, according to Nielson//NetRatings.* Retrieved February 15, 2006, from http://www.nielsen-netratings.com/pr/pr_030115.pdf

Nunnally, J. C. (1978). *Psychometric theory*. New York: McGraw-Hill.

O'Neill, P., & Flanagan, E. (1998). Elderly consumers are a significant market - But may need special protection. *Journal of Retail Banking Services, 20*(1), 25-33.

Opalinski, L. (2001). Older adults and the digital divide: Assessing results of a Web-based survey. *Journal of Technology in Human Services, 18*(3/4), 203-221.

Ogozalek, V. (1991). The social impacts of computing: Computer technology and the graying of America. *Social Science Computer Review, 9*(4). 655-666.

Patton, M. A., & Josang, A. (2004). Technologies for trust in electronic commerce. *Electronic Commerce Research, 4*(1/2), 9-21.

Pavlou, P. A., & Gefen, D. (2004). Building effective online marketplaces with institution-based trust. *Information Systems Research, 15*(1), 37-60.

Pennington, R., Wilcox, H. D., & Grover, V. (2003). The role of system trust in business-to-consumer transactions. *Journal of Management Information Systems, 20*(3), 197.

Pitkow, J. E., & Kehoe, C. M. (1996). Emerging trends in the WWW user population. *Communications of the ACM, 39*(6), 106-108.

Ratnasingam, P., Gefen, D., & Pavlou, P. A. (2005). The role of facilitation conditions and institutional trust in electronic marketplaces. *Journal of Electronic Commerce in Organizations, 3*(1), 69-83.

Raymond, J. (2002). Gray market for gadgets. *Newsweek, 140*(13), 52.

Riviere, C. N. & Thakor, N. V. (1996). Effects of age and disability on tracking tasks with a computer mouse: Accuracy and linearity. *Journal of Rehabilitation Research and Development, 33*(1), 6-15.

Rodgers, S., & Harris, M. A. (2003). Gender and e-commerce: An exploratory study. *Journal of Advertising Research, 43*(3), 322-333.

Schiffman, L., & Sherman, E. (1991). Value orientations of new-age elderly: The coming of an ageless market. *Journal of Business Research, 22*(2), 187-194.

Segars, A. H., & Grover, V. (1993). Re-examining perceived ease of use and usefulness: A confirmatory factor analysis. *MIS Quarterly, 17*(4), 517-527.

Shellenbarger, S. (2002, July 25). Technology holds promise for easing families' worries over the elderly. *Wall Street Journal*, p. D1.

Smith, M., Sharit, J., & Czaja, S. (1999). Aging, motor control and the performance of computer mouse tasks. *Human Factors, 41*(3), 388-396.

Smither, A., & Braun, C. (1994). Technology and older adults: Factors effecting the adoption of automatic teller machines. *The Journal of General Psychology, 121*(4), 381-389.

Straub, D., Limayem, M., & Karahanna-Evaristo, E. (1995). Measuring system usage: Implications for IS theory testing. *Management Science, 41*(8), 1328-1342.

Strader, T., & Ramaswami, S. (2002). The value of seller trustworthiness in C2C online markets. *Communications of the ACM, 45*(12), 45-49.

Tan, F., & Sutherland, P. (2004). Online consumer trust: A multi-dimensional model. *Journal of Electronic Commerce in Organizations, 2*(3), 40-59.

Temple, L., & Gavillet, M. (1990). The development of computer confidence in seniors: An assessment of changes in computer anxiety and computer literacy. *Activities, Adaptation and Aging, 14*(3), 63-76.

Torkzadeh, G., & Dhillon, Gu (2002). Measuring factors that influence the success of Internet commerce. *Information Systems Research, 13*(2), 187-204.

Tynan, D. (2002). How to take back your privacy. *PC World, 20*(6), 103-107.

U. S. Census Bureau. (2002). U. S. Census 2000. Retrieved February 15, 2006, from *http://www.census.gov*

Van Slyke, C., Belanger, F., & Comunale, C. (2004). Factors influencing the adoption of Web-based shopping: The impact of trust. *Databases for Advances in Information Systems, 35*(2), 32-50.

Venkatesh, V., & Davis, F. (2000). A theoretical extension of the technology acceptance model: Four longitudinal field studies. *Management Science, 46*(2), 186-204.

Venkatesh, V., & Morris, M. (2000). Why don't men ever stop to ask for directions? Gender, social influence and their role in technology acceptance and usage behavior. *MIS Quarterly, 24*(1), 115-139.

Vijayasarathy, L. R. (2004). Predicting consumer intentions to use online shopping: The case for an augmented technology acceptance model. *Information & Management, 41*(6), 747-762.

Walker, N., Philbin, D. A., & Fisk, A. D. (1997). Age-related differences in movement control: Adjusting sub movement structure to optimize performance. *Journal of Gerontology, 52B*, 40-52.

Yoon, S.-J. (2002). The antecedents and consequences of trust in online purchase decisions. *Journal of Interactive Marketing, 16*(2), 47-63.

Zeithaml, V. A., & Gilly, M. C. (1987). Characteristics affecting the acceptance of retailing technologies: A comparison of elderly and nonelderly consumers. *Journal of Retailing, 63*(1), 49-68.

Andersen, J. H., Thomsen, J. F., Overgaard, E., Lassen, C. F., Brandt, L. P. A., Vilstrup, I., Krugger, A. I. et al. (2003). Computer use and carpal tunnel syndrome: A 1-year follow-up study. *JAMA, 289*(22), 2963-2969.

Anshel, J. (2001). *Computer vision syndrome*. Retrieved from http://www.healthycomputing.com/articles/computer_vision_syndrome.html

Auty, S. (2004, May). Why is ergonomics important? *GP*, p. 41.

Beharie, N. (2003, April/May). Monitor height: How low should you go? *OH & S Canada, 9*(3), 52.

Briggs, B. (2003). Ergonomics: Looking for good fit. *Health Data Management, 11*(8), 44.

Bureau of Labor Statistics. (2005). *MLR: The editor's desk*. Retrieved February 15, 2006, from http://www.bls.gov/opub/ted/2005/aug/wk1/art03.htm

Clark, C. (2001). VDT health hazards: A guide for end users and managers. *Journal of End User Computing, 13*(1), 34-39.

The Comfort Connection. (2004). *Industrial Engineer, 36*(8), 16.

Coming to Grips with OOS. (2005). *NZ Business, 19*(2), 30.

Golden, J. (2004). Two-fisted mousing: Not just a macho thing! *Occupational Health & Safety, 73*(1), 44.

Goodwin, B. (2004, March). Take a break from your mouse: IT workers warned of RSI danger. *Computer Weekly*, p. 54.

Hanson, M. (2004). Not just a part of the furniture: Organisations can face a bewildering choice when selecting the right equipment to meet the requirements of the DSE regulations. *The Safety & Health Practitioner, 22*(2), 36-39.

Healthy Computing. (2001). *Monitor setup and usage*. Retrieved February 15, 2006, from http://www.healthy-computing.com/office/setup/monitor

Healthy Computing. (2002). *PDA ergonomics*. Retrieved February 15, 2006, from http://www.healthycomputing.com/mobile/pda/

Hedge, A. (2003a). *Carpal tunnel syndrome and computer use – is there a link?* Retrieved February 15, 2006, from http://ergo.human.cornell.edu/JAMAMayoCTS.html

Hedge, A. (2003b). *Ergonomics considerations of LCD versus CRT displays*. Retrieved February 15, 2006, from http://ergo.human.cornell.edu/Pub/LCD_vs_CRT_AH.pdf

Hedge, A. (2004). *Effects of an electric height-adjustable worksurface on self-assessed musculoskeletal discomfort and productivity in computer workers* (Tech. Rep. 0904). Cornell University Human Factors and Ergonomics Research Laboratory .

Jensen, C., Finsen, L., Sogaard, K., & Christensen, H. (2002). Musculoskeletal symptoms and duration of computer and mouse use. *International Journal of Industrial Ergonomics, 30,* 265-275.

Kanarek, L. (2005). Avoiding a pain in the neck. *Office Solutions, 22*(3), 51.

Karr, A. R. (2003, September). An ergo-unfriendly home office can hurt; first buy a good chair; it could cost hundreds, but may keep doctor away. *Wall Street Journal*, p. 6.

LaGesse, D. (2003, October). Five tips for taming your mouse. *U.S. News & World Report.*

Mikusch, R. (2003). With more and more computer users suffering. *Beyond Numbers, 424,* 18.

Reiland, J. (2003). Justifying the cost of height-adjustable office work surfaces. *Occupational Health & Safety, 72*(6), 117.

Rempel, D. (2001). *Carpal tunnel syndrome.* Retrieved February 15, 2006, from http://www.healthycomputing.com/articles/carpal_tunnel_101.html

Shea, T., & Gordon, J. (2003). Wireless wearables—Where's the technology headed: The military's investing, industry's watching, and before long it could be what you put on in the morning. *Sensors Magazine, 20*(11), 40-42.

Tahmincioglu, E. (2004). Ergonomics is back on the radar screen for both business and regulators. *Workforce Management, 83*(7), 59.

Timm, D. (2005). How long can you stand to sit? *Occupational Health & Safety, 74*(9), 162-166.

Tucker, D. M. (2005, March). Ergonomics remains sore spot. *Knight Ridder Tribune Business News*, p. 1.

U. S. Department of Labor. (2004). *OSHA computer workstations etool-components-monitors.* Retrieved February 15, 2006, from http://www.osha.gov/SLTC/etools/computerworkstations/components_monitors.html

Internet World Stats. (2007). Internet growth statistics. Retrieved August 4, 2007, from http://www.Internetworldstats.com/emarketing.htm

Introduction to JSR 168. (2003). *The Java Portlet specification.* Santa Clara, CA: Sun Microsystems.

Ippolito, P. (1990). Bonding and nonbonding signals of product quality. *Journal of Business, 63*(1), 41-60.

Jago, A. G. (1982). Leadership: Perspectives in theory and research. *Management Science, 28,* 315-336.

Jain, A., Hong, L., & Pankanti, S. (2000). Biometric identification. *Communications of the ACM, 43*(2), 91-98.

Janvrin, D., & Morrison, J. (2000). Using a structured design approach to reduce risks in end user spreadsheet development. *Information & Management, 37*(1), 1-12.

Jarvenpaa, S., & Tractinsky, N. (1999). Consumer trust in an Internet store: A cross-cultural validation. *JCMC, 5*(2).

Jarvenpaa, S., & Todd, P. (1996). Consumer reactions to electronic shopping on the World Wide Web. *International Journal of Electronic Commerce, 1,* 59-88.

Jarvenpaa, S., Tractinsky, N., & Vitale, M. (2000). Consumer trust in an Internet store. *Information Technology and Management, 1*(1-2), 45-71.

Jasperson, J., Carter, P.E., & Zmud, R.W. (2005). A comprehensive conceptualization of post-adoptive behaviors associated with information technology enabled work systems. *MIS Quarterly, 29*(3), 525-557.

Jawahar, I. M., & Elango, B. (2001). The effects of attitudes, goal setting and self-efficacy on end user performance. *Journal of End User Computing, 13*(2), 40-45.

Jawahar, I. M., & Elango, B. (2001). The effect of attitudes, goal setting and self-efficacy on end user performance. *Journal of End User Computing, 13*(3), 40-45.

Jeffords, R., Thibadoux, G., & Scheidt, M. (1999, March). New technologies to combat check fraud. *The CPA Journal, 69*(3), 30-34.

Johnson, R. D., & Marakas, G. M. (2000). The role of behavioral modeling in computer skills acquisition: Toward refinement of the model. *Information Systems Research, 11*(4), 402-417.

Johnson-Page, G. F., & Thatcher, R. S. (2001). B2C data privacy policies: Current trends. *Management Decision, 39*(4), 262-271.

Jones, T.W. (1991). Ethical decision making by individuals in organizations: An issue-contingent model. *Academy of Management Review, 16*(2), 366-395.

Joshi, K. (1989). The measurement of fairness or equity perception of management information systems users. *MIS Quarterly, 13*(3), 343-358.

Kaasbøll, J., & Øgrim, L. (1994). Super-users: Hackers, management hostages or working class heroes? A study of user influence on redesign in distributed organizations. In *Proceedings of the 17th Information Systems Research Seminar in Scandinavia (IRIS-17)* (pp. 784-798). Department of Information Processing Science, University of Oulu, Finland.

Kabanoff, B. (1996). Computers can read as well as count: How computer-aided text analysis can benefit organizational research. *Journal of Organizational Behavior, 3*, 1-21.

Kadoda, G. (2000). A cognitive dimensions view of the differences between designers and users of theorem proving assistants. In *Proceedings of the 12th Annual Meeting of the Psychology of Programming Interest Group* (pp. 33-44).

Kanstrup, A-M. (2004). E-learning behind the facade: The value of local gardeners. In A.M. Kanstrup, A.M. Roskilde, & D.K. Universitesforlag (Eds.), *E-learning at work* (pp. 149-166, in Danish).

Kaplan, L., Szybillo, G.J., & Jacoby, J. (1974). Components of perceived risk in product purchase: A cross validation. *Journal of Applied Psychology, 59*, 287-291.

Kaptelinin, V. (1996). Activity theory: Implications for human-computer interaction. In B. Nardi (Ed.), *Context and consciousness: Activity theory and human-computer interaction* (pp. 103-116). Cambridge: MIT Press.

Karahanna, E., Straub, D., & Chervany, N. (1999). Information technology adoption across time: A cross-sectional comparison of pre-adoption and post-adoption beliefs. *MIS Quarterly, 23*(2), 183-213.

Karahanna, E., Straub, D.W., & Chervany, N.L. (1999, June). Information technology adoption across time: A cross-sectional comparison of pre-adoption and post-adoption beliefs. *MIS Quarterly, 23*(2), 183-213.

Karasti, H. (2001). *Increasing sensitivity towards everyday work practice in system design*. Doctoral thesis, University of Oulu, Oulu.

Katz, J.E., & Rice, R.E. (2002). *Social consequences of Internet use: Access, involvement, and interaction*. Cambridge, MA: MIT Press.

Kay, R. (2004, March 15). Quick study: Privacy glossary. *Computerworld*, 41.

Kelle, U., & Laurie, H. (1995). Computer use in qualitative research and issues of validity. In U. Kelle (Ed.), *Computer-aided qualitative data analysis. Theory, methods and practice* (pp. 19-28). London: Sage.

Keller, K. (1998). *Strategic brand management*. Upper Saddle River, NJ: Prentice Hall.

Kihlstrom, R., & Riordan, M. (1984). Advertising a signal. *Journal of Political Economy, 92*(3), 427-450.

Kim, H. (1995). Biometrics, is it a viable proposition for identity authentication and access control? *Computers and Security, 14*, 205-214.

Kim, J., Spraragen, M., & Gil, Y. (2004). An intelligent assistant for interactive workflow composition. In *Proceedings of the 9th International Conference on Intelligent User Interfaces*, Funchal, Portugal (pp. 125-135).

Kim, Y. J., Hiltz, S. R., & Turoff, M. (2002). Coordination structures and system restrictiveness in distributed group support systems. *Group Decision and Negotiation, 11*(5), 379-404.

Kirkpatrick, D. L. (1959). Techniques for evaluating training programs. *Journal of the American Society of Training Directors, 13*(11-12), 3-26.

Kirmani, A., & Rao, A. (2000). No pain, no gain: A critical review of the literature on signaling unobservable product quality. *Journal of Marketing, 64*(2), 66-79.

Klein, K.J., & Sorra, J.S. (1996). The challenge of innovation implementation. *Academy of Management Review, 21,* 1055-1080.

Kodukula, P. (2006). *Project valuation using real options.* Ft. Lauderdale, FL: J. Ross Publishing.

Kohlberg, L. (1969). Stages and sequence: The cognitive-developmental approach to socialization. In D. Grosling (Ed.), *Handbook of socialization theory and research.* Chicago: Rand McNally.

Kolbe, R. H., & Burnett, M. S. (1991). Content-analysis research: An examination of applications with directives for improving research reliability and objectivity. *Journal of Consumer Research, 18*(2), 243-250.

Koufaris, M. (2002). Applying the technology acceptance model and flow theory to online consumer behavior. *Information Systems Research, 13*(2), 205-223.

Kovar, S., Gladden-Burke, K., & Kovar, B. (2000). Consumer responses to the CPA WebTrust assurance. *Journal of Information Systems, 14*(1), 17-35.

Kramer, M. W. (1993). Communication and uncertainty reduction during job transfers: Leaving and joining processes. *Communication Monographs, 60,* 178-198.

Kreie, J., Cronan, T. P., Pendley, J., & Renwick, J. S. (2000). Applications development by end-users: Can quality be improved? *Decision Support Systems, 29*(2), 143-152.

Krippendorff, K. (1980). *Content analysis. An introduction to its methodology.* Beverly Hills, CA: Sage.

Kruck, S. E., Maher, J. J., & Barkhi, R. (2003). Framework for cognitive skill acquisition and spreadsheet training. *Journal of End User Computing, 15*(1), 20-37.

Kuutti, K. (1996). Activity theory as a potential framework for human-computer interaction research. In B. Nardi (Ed.), *Context and consciousness: Activity theory and human-computer interaction* (pp. 17-44). Cambridge: MIT Press.

Lacity, M. C., & Janson, M. A. (1994). Understanding qualitative data: A framework of text analysis methods.

Journal of Management Information Systems, 11(2), 137-155.

Lafferty, B., & Goldsmith, R. (1999). Corporate credibility's role in consumers' attitudes and purchase intentions when a high versus a low credibility endorser is used in the ad. *Journal of Business Research, 44*(2), 109-116.

Lafferty, B., Goldsmith, R., & Newell, S. (2002). The dual credibility model: The influence of corporate and endorser credibility on attitudes and purchase intentions. *Journal of Marketing Theory and Practice, 10*(3), 1-12.

Lala V., Arnold, V., Sutton, S., & Guan L. (2002). The impact of relative information quality of e-commerce assurance seals on Internet purchasing behavior. *International Journal of Accounting Information Systems, 3*(4), 237-253.

Lammermann, S., & Tyugu, E. (2001). A specification logic for dynamic composition of services. In *Proceedings of the Distributed Computing Systems Workshop, 2001 International Conference,* Mesa, Arizona, USA (pp. 157-162).

Larkin, J., McDermott, J., Simon, D.P., & Simon, H.A. (1980). Models of competence in solving physics problems. *Cognitive Science, 208,* 317-345.

Larsen, T.J., & Sorebo, O. (2005). Impact of personal innovativeness on the use of the Internet among employees at work. *Journal of Organizational and End User Computing, 17*(2), 43-63.

Larzelere, R., & Huston, T. (1980). The dyadic trust scale: Toward understanding interpersonal trust in close relationships. *Journal of Marriage and Family, 42*(3), 595-604.

Lau, E. (2003). An empirical study of software piracy. *Business Ethics, 12*(3), 233-245.

Lave, J., & Wenger, E. (1991). *Situated learning: Legitimate peripheral participation.* Cambridge: University Press.

Lavidge, R.J., & Steiner, G.A. (1961). A model for predictive measurements of advertising effectiveness. *Journal of Marketing, 25,* 59-62.

Lebart, L., Salem, A., & Berry, L. (1998). *Exploring textual data*. Dordrecht: Kluwer Academic Publishers.

Leonard, L.N.K., Cronan, T.P., & Kreie, J. (2004). What influences IT ethical behavior intentions: Planned behavior, reasoned action, perceived importance, or individual characteristics? *Information and Management, 42*(1), 143-158.

Letondal, C., & Mackay, W.E. (2004). Participatory programming and the scope of mutual responsibility: Balancing scientific, design and software commitment. In A. Clement & P. Van den Besselaar (Eds.), *Proceedings of the 8th Conference on Participatory Design Conference (PDC 2004)*, Toronto, Canada (pp. 31-41). New York: ACM Press.

Lieberman, H., Paterno, F., & Wulf, V. (Eds.). (2006). *End-user development*. Berlin: Springer-Verlag.

Lieberman, H. (2001). *Your wish is my command: Programming by example*. San Francisco: Morgan Kaufman.

Lieberman, H., Paternò, F., & Wulf, V. (2006). *End-user development* (Human-Computer Interaction Series, Vol. 9). Dordrecht, The Netherlands: Springer.

Lim, L. H., Raman, K. S., & Wei, K. K. (1994). Interacting effects of GDSS and leadership. *Decision Support Systems, 12*, 199-211.

Lin, C., & Ding, C.G. (2003). Moderating information ethics: The joint moderaing role of locus of control and job insecurity. *Journal of Business Ethics, 48*(4), 335-346

Lippert, S.K., & Forman, H. (2005). Utilization of information technology: Examining cognitive and experiential factors of post-adoption behavior. *IEE Transactions on Engineering Management, 52*(3), 363-381.

Liu, S., & Silverman, M. (2001, January/February). A practical guide to biometric security technology. *IT Professional*, pp. 27-32.

Liu, C., & Arnett, K. P. (2002). An examination of privacy policies in Fortune 500 Web sites. *Mid-American Journal of Business, 17*(1), 13-21.

Loch, K., Carr, H., & Warkentin, M. (1992). Threats to information systems: Today's reality, yesterday's understanding. *MIS Quarterly, 16*(2), 173-186.

Lowry, G. (2002). Modeling user acceptance of building management systems. *Automation in Construction, 11*, 695-705.

Lu, J., Yu, C., & Liu, C. (2003). Learning style, learning patterns, and learning performance in a WebCT-based MIS course. *Information & Management, 40*(6), 497-507.

Lu, J., Yao, J.E., & Yu, C.-S. (2005). Personal innovativeness, social influences and adoption of wireless Internet services via mobile technology. *Strategic Information Systems, 14*, 245-268.

Luhmann, N. (1988). Familiarity, confidence, trust: Problems and alternatives. In D. Gambetta (Ed.), *Trust* (pp. 94-107). New York: Basil Blackwell.

Luo, X., & Seyedian, M. (2004). Contextual marketing and customer-orientation strategy for e-commerce: An empirical analysis. *International Journal of Electronic Commerce, 8*(2), 95-118.

Lwin, M.O., & Williams, J.D. (2003). Model integrating the multidimensional developmental theory of privacy and theory of planned behaviour to examine fabrication of information online. *Marketing Letters, 14*(4), 257-272.

Lynch, B. (2004, March). Web-privacy management increases in importance. *Wall Street & Technology*, 48-49.

Mackay, W.E. (1990). Patterns of sharing customizable software. In *Proceedings of the Conference on Computer Supported Cooperative Work (CSCW'90)* (pp. 209-221). New York: ACM Press.

MacLean, A., Carter, K., Lövstrand, L., & Moran, T. (1990). User-tailorable systems: Pressing the issue with buttons. In *Proceedings of the Conference on Human Factors in Computing Systems (CHI'90)* (pp. 175-182). New York: ACM Press.

MacLean, A., Kathleen, C., Lövstrand, L., & Moran, T. (1990). User-tailorable systems: Pressing the issues with buttons. In J. Carrasco & J. Whiteside (Eds.), *Proceedings of ACM CHI'90*, Seattle, Washington (pp. 175-182). New York: ACM Press.

Mahmood, M. A., Hall, L., & Swanberg, D. L. (2001). Factors affecting information technology usage: A meta-analysis of the empirical literature. *Journal of Organizational Computing & Electronic Commerce, 11*(2), 107-130.

Malhotra, N.K., Kim, S.S., & Agarwal, J. (2004). Internet users' information privacy concerns (IUIPC): The construct, the scale and a causal model. *Information Systems Research, 15*, 336-355.

Marakas, G. M., Yi, M. Y., & Johnson, R. (1998). The multilevel and multifaceted character of computer self-efficacy: Toward a clarification of the construct and an integrative framework for research. *Information Systems Research, 9*(2), 126-163.

Marcolin, B.L., Compeau, D.R., Munro, M.C., & Huff, S.L. (2000, March). Assessing user competence: Conceptualization and measurement. *Information Systems Research, 11*(1), 37-60.

Marshall, K.P. (1999). Has technology introduced new ethical problems? *Journal of Business Ethics, 19*(1), 81-90.

Martocchio, J. J. (1994). Effects of conceptions of ability on anxiety, self-efficacy, and learning in training. *Journal of Applied Psychology, 79*(6), 819-825.

Martocchio, J. J., & Hertenstein, E. J. (2003). Learning orientation and goal orientation context: Relationships with cognitive and affective learning outcomes. *Human Resources Development Quarterly, 14*(4), 413-434.

Mascarenhas, O.A.J., Kesavan, R., & Bernacchi, M.D. (2003). Co-managing online privacy: A call for joint ownership. *The Journal of Consumer Marketing, 20*(7), 686-702.

Mason, R.O. (1986). Four ethical issues of the information age. *MIS Quarterly, 10*(1), 4-12.

Mason, R. (1986). Four ethical issues of the information age. *MIS Quarterly, 10*(1), 5-12.

Mason, R. O. (1986). Four ethical issues of the information age. *MIS Quarterly, 10*(1), 5-12.

Mason, R. O., Mason, F. M., & Culnan, M. J. (1995). *Ethics of information management.* Thousand Oaks, CA: Sage.

Mathieson, K., Peacock, E., & Chin, W.W. (2001). Extending the technology acceptance model: The influence of perceived user resources. *The DATA BASE for Advances in Information Systems, 32*(3), 86-112.

Mauldin, E., & Arunachalam, V. (2001). An experimental examination of alternative forms of Web assurance for business-to-consumer e-commerce. *Journal of Information System, 16*(1), 33-54.

Maury, M. D., & Kleiner, D. S. (2002). E-commerce, ethical commerce? *Journal of Business Ethics, 36*, 21-31.

McCloskey, H. (1980). Privacy and the right to privacy. *Philosophy, 55*(211), 17-38.

McFarland, D.J., & Hamilton, D. (2006). Adding contextual specificity to the technology acceptance model. *Computers in Human Behavior, 22*, 427-447.

McGill, T. (2004). The effect of end user development on end user success. *Journal of Organizational and End User Computing, 16*(1), 41-58.

McGinnies, E., & Ward, C. (1980). Better liked than right: Trustworthiness and expertise as factors in credibility. *Personality and Social Psychology Bulletin, 6*(1), 467-472.

McGrath, J. E. (1984). *Groups: Interaction and performance.* Englewood Cliffs, NJ: Prentice-Hall.

McGuinnes, D.L., Fikes, R., Hendler, J., & Stein, L.A. (2002). DAML+OIL: An ontology language for the semantic Web. *IEEE Intelligent Systems, 17*(5), 72-80.

McKnight, H., Choudhury, V., & Kacmar, C. (2002). Developing and validating trust measures for e-commerce: An integrative typology. *Information Systems Research, 13*(3), 334-359.

McKnight, H., Cummings, L., & Chervany, N. (1998). Initial trust formation in new original relationships. *Academy of Management Review, 23*(3), 473-490.

McLean, E. R., Kappelman, L. A., & Thompson, J. P. (1993). Converging end-user and corporate computing. *Communications of the ACM, 36*(12), 79-92.

McMillian, R. (2002). The myth of airport biometrics. Retrieved August 6, 2007 from Wired News, http://www.wired.com

Medjahed, B., Bouguettaya, A., & Elmagarmid, A.K. (2003). Composing Web services on the semantic Web. *The International Journal on Very Large Data Bases, 12*(A), 333-351.

Mehandjiev, N., & Bottaci, L. (Eds.). (1998). End-user development [Special issue]. *Journal of End User Computing, 10*(2).

Mennecke, B. E., Hoffer, H. A., & Wynne, B. E. (1992). The implications of group development and history for group support system theory and practice. *Small Group Research, 23*(4), 524-572.

Meskell, D. (2003). *High payoff in electronic government: Measuring the return on e-government investment.* Washington, DC: U.S. General Services Administration (GSA).

Messmer, E. (1997, June 16). Group slams Web sites for lack of privacy policies. *Network World.*

Microsoft Sharepoint. (2003). Retrieved August 10, 2007, from http://www.microsoft.com/sharepoint

Milgrom, P., & Roberts, J. (1986). Price and advertising signals of product quality. *Journal of Political Economy, 94*(4), 796-821.

Miller, G., & Baseheart, J. (1969). Source trustworthiness, opinionated statements, and response to persuasive communication. *Speech Monographs, 36*(1), 1-7.

Milne, G.R., & Rohm, A.J. (2000). Consumer privacy and name removal across direct marketing channels: Exploring opt-in and opt-out alternatives. *Journal of Public Policy & Marketing, 19*(2), 238-249.

Milne, G.R, Rohm, A.J, & Bahl, S. (2004). Consumers protection of online privacy and identity. *The Journal of Consumer Affairs, 38*(2), 217-232.

Milne, G. R., & Boza, M.-E. (1999). Trust and concern in consumers' perceptions of marketing information management practices. *Journal of Interactive Marketing, 13*(1), 5-24.

Milne, G. R., & Culnan, M. J. (2002). Using the content of online privacy notices to inform public policy: A longitudinal analysis of the 1998-2001 US Web surveys. *The Information Society, 18*(5), 345-359.

Milne, G. R., & Culnan, M. J. (2004). Strategies for reducing online privacy risks: Why consumers read (or don't read) online privacy notices. *Journal of Interactive Marketing, 18*(3), 15-29.

Mitchell, V.-W. (1999). Consumer perceived risk: Conceptualisations and models. *European Journal of Marketing, 33*(1/2), 163-195.

Mitchell, S. (2003). The new age of direct marketing. *Journal of Database Management, 10*(3), 219-229.

Miyazaki, A., & Fernandez, A. (2001). Consumer perceptions of privacy and security risks for online shopping. *The Journal of Consumer Affairs, 35*(1), 27-44.

Miyazaki, A. D., & Fernandez, A. (2000). Internet privacy and security: An examination of online retailer disclosures. *Journal of Public Policy & Marketing, 19*(1), 54-61.

Miyazaki, A. D., & Krishnamurthy, S. (2002). Internet seals of approval: Effects of online privacy policies and consumer perceptions. *The Journal of Consumer Affairs, 36*(1), 28-49.

Moore, G. C., & Benbasat, I. (1991). Development of an instrument to measure the perceptions of adopting an information technology innovation. *Information Systems Research, 2*(3), 192-222.

Moore, P. (2002). Software test bench mega guide. *Australian PC User*, pp. 54-55.

Moore, D., Hausknecht, D., & Thamodaran, K. (1988). Time compression, response opportunity and persuasion. *Journal of Consumer Research, 13*(1), 12-24.

Mørch, A. (1996). Evolving a generic application into a domain-oriented design environment. *Scandinavian Journal of Information Systems, 8*(2), 63-90.

Mørch, A.I. (2003). Aspect-oriented software components. In N. Patel (Ed.), *Adaptive evolutionary information systems* (pp. 105-123). Hershey, PA: Idea Group Publishing.

Mørch, A.I., Engen, B.K., & Åsand, H.-R.H. (2004a). The workplace as a learning laboratory: The winding road to e-learning in a Norwegian service company. In *Proceedings of PDC 2004* (pp. 142-151).

Mørch, A.I., Stevens, G., Won, M., Klann, M., Dittrich, Y., & Wulf, V. (2004b). Component-based technologies for end-user development. *Communications of the ACM, 47*(9), 59-62.

Morgan, R., & Hunt, S. (1994). The commitment-trust theory of relationship marketing. *Journal of Marketing Research, 29*(3), 20-38.

Morris, M.G., Venkatesh, V., & Ackerman, P.L. (2005). Gender and age differences in employee decisions about new technology: An extension to the theory of planned behavior. *IEEE Transactions on Engineering Management, 52*(1), 69-84.

Moseley, O., & Whitis, R. (1995, December). Preventing software piracy. *Management Accounting*, pp. 42-47.

MPAA Report. (2003). Thoughts on the digital future of movies, the threat of piracy, the hope of redemption. Encino, CA: Motion Picture Association of America.

Mullen, B., Salas, E., & Drisekll, J. E. (1987). Salience, motivation, and artifact as contribution to the relation between participation rate and leadership. *Journal of Experimental Social Psychology, 25*, 809-826.

Myers, B.A., Hudson, S.E., & Randy, P. (2003). Past, present, and future of user interface software tools. In J. Carroll (Ed.), *Human-computer interaction in the new millennium* (pp. 213-233). New York: ACM Press.

Myers, B.A., Smith, D.C., & Horn, B. (1992). *Report of the "end-user programming" working group: Languages for developing user interfaces* (pp. 343-366). Boston: Jones and Bartlett.

Myspace.com. (2007). *Privacy policy.* Retrieved August 4, 2007, from http://www.myspace.com/Modules/Common/Pages/Privacy.aspx

Narayanan, S., & McIlraith, S.A. (2002). Simulation, verification and automated composition of Web services. In *Proceedings of the 11th International Conference on World Wide Web*, Honolulu, Hawaii (pp. 77-88).

Nardi, B. (1996). Studying context: A comparison of activity theory, situated action models, and distributed cognition. In B. Nardi (Ed.), *Context and consciousness: Activity theory and human-computer interaction* (pp. 69-102). Cambridge, MA: MIT Press.

Nardi, B., & Engeström, Y.A. (Guest Eds.). (1999). Web on the wind: The structure of invisible work. *Computer-Supported Cooperative Work, 8*(1-2), 1-8.

National Eye Institute Resource Guide. (2006). Retrieved August 10, 2007, from http://www.nei.nih.gov/health

Nelson, R. R. (1991). Educational needs as perceived by IS and end-user personnel: A survey of knowledge and skill requirements. *MIS Quarterly, 15*(4), 503-525.

Nelson, R. R., & Todd, P. (1999). Strategies for managing EUC on the Web. *Journal of End User Computing, 11*(1), 24-31.

Netteland, G., Wasson, B., & Mørch, A.I. (2007). E-learning in a large organization: A study of the critical role of information sharing [Special issue]. *Journal of Workplace Learning, 19*(6), 392-411.

Neuendorf, K. A. (2002). *The content analysis guidebook.* Thousand Oaks, CA: Sage.

Nielsen, J. (1993). *Usability engineering.* San Diego, CA: Academic Press.

Nielsen/Net Ratings. (2003). Retrieved from www.nielsen-netratings.com.

Nijboer, J. (2004). Big brother versus anonymity on the Internet: Implications for Internet service providers. *New Library World, 105*(7/8), 256-261.

Norton, R. (2002, October). The evolving biometric marketplace to 2006. *Biometric Technology Today*, pp. 7-8.

Nöteberg, A., Christiaanse, E., & Wallage, P. (2003). Consumer trust in electronic channels: The impact of electronic commerce assurance on consumers' purchasing likelihood and risk perceptions. *e-Service Journal, 2*(2), 46-67.

Novak, J. D. (2002). Meaningful learning: The essential factor for conceptual change in limited or inappropriate propositional hierarchies leading to empowerment of learners. *Science Education, 86*(4), 548-571.

Nowak, G.J., & Phelps, J. (1995). Direct marketing and the use of individual-level consumer information: Determining how and why privacy matters. *Journal of Direct Marketing, 9*(3), 46-60.

Noy, N.F., Sintek, M., Decker, S., Crubezy, M., Fegerson, R.W., & Musen, MA. (2001). Creating Semantic Web contents with Protege-2000. *IEEE Intelligent Systems, 16*(2), 60-71.

NTIA. National Telecommunications and Information Administration. (2002). *A nation online: How Americans are expanding their use of the Internet.* Washington, DC: U.S. Department of Commerce.

Nua Internet Surveys. (2002). How many online? Retrieved August 4, 2007, from http://Www.Nua.Com/Surveys/How_Many_Online/Index.html

Nua Internet Surveys. (2003). Nielsen Netratings: Global net population increases. Retrieved August 4, 2007, from http://www.Nua.Com/Surveys/Index

Nunamaker, J. F., Briggs, R., Mittleman, D. D., Vogel, D. R., & Balthazard, P. A. (1996-1997). Lessons from a dozen years of group support systems research: A discussion of lab and field findings. *Journal of Management Information Systems, 13*(3), 163-207.

Nunamaker, J. F., Dennis, A. R., Valacich, J. S., Vogel, D. R., & George, J. F. (1991). Electronic meeting systems to support group work. *Communications of the ACM, 34*(7), 40-59.

Nygaard, K. (1984). User-oriented languages. In *Proceedings of Medical Informatics Europe 84* (pp. 38-44). Berlin: Springer-Verlag.

O'Brien, J. A. (2002). *Management information systems: Managing information technology in the e-business enterprise* (5th ed.). New York: McGraw-Hill.

O'Connor, P. (2003). What happens to my information if I make a hotel booking online: An analysis of on-line privacy policy use, content and compliance by the international hotel companies. *Journal of Services Research, 3*(2), 5-28.

O'Donnell, D., & March, S. (1987). End user computing environments: Finding a balance between productivity and control. *Information & Management, 13*(1), 77-84.

Odom, M., Kumar, A., & Saunders, L. (2002). Web assurance seals: How and why they influence consumers' decisions. *Journal of Information Systems, 16*(2), 231-250.

Office of the Federal Privacy Commissioner. (2001a). Privacy and the community (Roy Morgan Research). Retrieved August 4, 2007, from http://www.privacy.gov.au/publications/rcommunity.pdf

Ohanian, R. (1991). The impact of celebrity spokespersons' image on consumers' intention to purchase. *Journal of Advertising, 31*(1), 46-54.

Olaniran, B. A., & Williams, D. E. (1995). Communication distortion: An intercultural lesson from the visa application process. *Communication Quarterly, 43*, 225-240.

Olivero, N., & Lunt, P. (2004). Privacy versus willingness to disclose in e-commerce exchanges: The effect of risk awareness on the relative role of trust and control. *Journal of Economic Psychology, 25*(2), 243-262.

Olson, J., & Zanna, M. (1993). Attitudes and attitude change. *Annual Review of Psychology, 44*(1), 117-154.

Orwell, G. (1951). *Nineteen eighty-four.* London: Secker and Warburg.

Ouellette, T. (1999, July 26). Giving users the keys to their Web content. *Computerworld*, pp. 66-67.

Pahl, C., & Ward, D. (2002). Towards a component composition and interaction architecture for the Web. *Electronic Notes in Theoretical Computer Science, 65*(A).

Paine, C., Reips, U.-D., Stieger, S., Joinson, A.N., & Buchanan, T. (2006). *Internet users' perceptions of "privacy concerns" and "privacy actions."* Manuscript submitted for publication.

Palmer, J., Bailey, J., & Faraj, S. (2000). The role of intermediaries in the development of trust on the WWW: The use and prominence of trusted third parties and privacy statements. *Journal of Computer Mediated Communication, 5*(3). Retrieved from *http://www.ascusc. org/jcmc/vol5/issue3/palmer.html*

Panko, R. R. (2007). Two experiments in reducing overconfidence in spreadsheet development. *Journal of Organizational and End User Computing, 19*(1), 1-23.

Panko, R. R., & Halverson, R. P. (1996). Spreadsheets on trial: A survey of research on spreadsheet risks. *Proceedings of the 29th Hawaii International Conference on System Sciences, 2*, 326-335.

Parent, M., & Gallupe, R. B. (2001). The role of leadership in group support systems failure. *Group Decision and Negotiation, 10*(5), 405-422.

Pastore, S. (2007) Introducing semantic technologies in Web services-based application discovery within grid environments. In *Proceedings of the Fourth European Conference on Universal Multiservice Networks* (pp. 22-31).

Pavlou, P. (2003). Consumer acceptance of electronic commerce: Interrating trust and risk with the technology acceptance model. *International Journal of Electronic Commerce, 7*(3), 101-134.

Peace, A., Galletta, D., & Thong, J. (2003). Software piracy in the workplace: A model and empirical test. *Journal of Management Information Systems, 20*(1), 153-177.

Penner, R.R., & Steinmetz, E.S. (2002). Model-based automation of the design of user interfaces to digital control systems. *IEEE Transactions on Systems, Man, and Cybernetics: Part A, 32*(1), 41-49.

Pentland, B. T. (1989). Use and productivity in personal computing: An empirical test. *Proceedings of the 10th*

International Conference on Information Systems (pp.211-222).

Perlis, A. (1982). Epigrams on programming. *SIGPLAN Notices, 17*(9), 7-13.

Perri 6. (2002). Who wants privacy protection and what do they want? *Journal of Consumer Behaviour, 2*(1), 80-100.

Peslak, A.R. (2006). Internet privacy policies of the largest international companies. *Journal of Electronic Commerce in Organisations, 4*(3), 46-62.

Petre, M. (1995). Why looking isn't always seeing: Readership skills and graphical programming. *Communication of ACM, 38*(6), 33-44.

Phelps, J., Nowak, G., & Ferrell, E. (2000). Privacy concerns and consumer willingness to provide personal information. *Journal of Public Policy & Marketing, 19*(1), 27-41.

Pirim, T., James, T., Boswell, K., Reithel, B., & Barkhi, R. (in press). An empirical investigation of an individual's perceived need for privacy and security. *International Journal of Information Security and Privacy.*

Plouffe, C., Hulland, J., & Vandenbosch, M. (2001). Research report: Richness versus parsimony in modeling technology adoption decisions: Understanding merchant adoption of a smart card-based payment system. *Information Systems Research, 12*(2), 208-222.

Plouffe, C.R., Hulland, J.S., & Vandenbosch, M. (2001). Richness versus parsimony in modelling technology adoption decisions: Understanding merchant adoption of a smart card-based payment system. *Information Systems Research, 12*(2), 208-222.

Polanyi, M. (1967). *The tacit dimension.* London: Rouledge & Kegan Paul.

Presler-Marshall, M. (2000). Web privacy and the P3P standard. *IBM Raleigh Lab.* Retrieved from http://www7. software.ibm.com/vad.nsf/Data/Document2363?OpenD ocument&p =1&BCT=1Footer=1

Putnam, L. L. (1979). Preference for procedural order in task-oriented small groups. *Communication Monographs, 46*, 193-218.

Rainie, L., & Kohut, A. (2000). Tracking online life: How women use the Internet to cultivate relationships with family and friends.

Rana, A. R., Turoff, M, & Hiltz, R. (1997). *Task and technology interaction (TTI): A theory of technological support for group tasks.* Proceedings of the Thirtieth Hawaii International Conference on System Sciences, *2*, 66-75.

Randall, D., & Gibson, A. (1991). Ethical decision making in the medical profession: An application of the theory of planned behavior. *Journal of Business Ethics, 10*(2), 111-122.

Reagle, J., & Cranor, L. F. (1999). The platform for privacy preferences. *Communications of the ACM, 42*(2), 48-55.

Reda, S. (2000). VeriFone and Russell Reynolds Associates Top 100 Internet retailers. *Stores.* Retrieved September 2000, from https://www.stores.org/archives/00top100int_1.asp

Reid, R., Thompson, J., & Logston, J. (1992). Knowledge and attitudes of management students toward software piracy. *Journal of Computer Information Systems, 33*(1), 46-51.

Resnick, L.B., Saljo, R., Pontecorvo, C., & Burge, B. (Eds.). (1997). *Discourse, tools, and reasoning: Essays on situated cognition.* Berlin, Germany: Springer-Verlag.

Rest, J. (1986). *Moral development: Advances in research and theory.* New York: Praeger.

Retsky, M.L. (2001). Just posting cookies agreement not enough. *Marketing News, 35*(20), 12-13.

Rice, R. E. (1984). Mediated group communication. In R. E. Rice and Associates (Eds.), *The new media: Communication, research, and technology* (pp. 129-156). Beverly Hills, CA: Sage.

Rico, D. F. (2004). *ROI of software process improvement: Metrics for project managers and software engineers.* Boca Raton, FL: J. Ross Publishing.

Rico, D. F. (2005). Practical metrics and models for return on investment. *TickIT International, 7*(2), 10-16.

Rico, D. F. (2006). A framework for measuring the ROI of enterprise architecture. *International Journal of End User Computing, 18*(2), 1-12.

Riemenschneider, C.K., Harris, D.A., & Mykytyn, P.P., Jr. (2003). Understanding IT adoption decisions in small business: Integrating current theories. *Information and Management, 40*, 269-285.

Rivard, S., & Huff, S. L. (1984). User developed applications: Evaluation of success from the DP department perspective. *MIS Quarterly, 8*(1), 39-49.

Rivard, S., & Huff, S. L. (1985). An empirical study of users as application developers. *Information & Management, 8*, 89-102.

Roby, T. B. (1961). The executive function in small groups. In L. Petrullo, & B. Bass (Eds.), *Leadership and interpersonal behavior.* New York: Holt, Rinehart and Winston.

Rodgers, S., & Sheldon, K.M. (2002). An improved way to characterize Internet users. *Journal of Advertising, 42(5), 85-84*

Roselius, T. (1971, January). Consumer rankings of risk reduction methods. *Journal of Marketing, 35*, 56-61.

Rothschild, M., & Stiglitz, J. (1976). Equilibrium in competitive insurance markets: An essay on the economics of imperfect information. *Quarterly Journal of Economics, 90*(3), 630-649.

Rousseau D., Sitkin, S., Burt, R., & Camerer, C. (1998). Not so different after all: A cross-discipline view of trust. *Academy of Management Review, 23*(3), 393-404.

Roznowski, J. A. (2003). A content analysis of mass media. Stories surrounding the consumer privacy issue 1990-2001. *Journal of Interactive Marketing, 17*(2), 52-69.

Rust, R.T., Kannan, P.K., & Peng, N. (2002). The customer economics of Internet privacy. *Academy of Marketing Science Journal, 30*(4), 455-464.

Ryker, R., Lafleur, E., McManis, B., & Cox, K. C. (2002). Online privacy policies: An assessment of the Fortune E-50. *The Journal of Computer Information Systems, 42*(4), 15-20.

Salchenberger, L. (1993). Structured development techniques for user-developed systems. *Information & Management, 24*, 41-50.

Sama. L. M., & Shoaf, V. (2002). Ethics on the Web: Applying moral decision-making to the new media. *Journal of Business Ethics, 36*, 93-103.

Sappington, D., & Silk, A. (2003). Marketing's information technology revolution: Implications for consumer welfare and economic performance: Overview of the special issue. *Journal of Public Policy and Marketing, 22*(1).

Saythe, M. (1999). Adoption of Internet banking by Australian consumers. *International Journal of Bank Marketing, 17*(7), 324-334.

Scheeres, J. (2001). Smile, you're on camera. Retrieved August 6, 2007, from Wired News, http://www.wired.com

Schiffman, L.G., Schus, S., & Winer, L. (1976). Risk perception as a determinant of in-home consumption. *Journal of the Academy of Marketing Science, 4*(4), 753-763.

Schneiderman, B. (2000). Designing trust into online experiences. *Communications of the ACM, 43*(12), 57-59.

Schoenbachler, D. D., & Gordon, G. L. (2002). Trust and customer willingness to provide information in database-driven relationship marketing. *Journal of Interactive Marketing, 16*(3), 2-16.

Schön, D. (1983). *The reflective practitioner: How professionals think in action.* New York: Basic Books.

Schuler, D., & Namioka, A. (1993). *Participatory design: Principles and practices.* Hillsdale, NJ: Erlbaum.

Schuler, D., & Namioka, A. (Eds.). (1993). *Participatory design: Principles and practices.* Hillsday, NJ: Lawrence Erlbaum Associates.

Schulman, G., & Worrall, C. (1970). Salience patterns, source credibility, and the sleeper effect. *Public Opinion Quarterly, 34*(3), 371-382.

Schultes, S. (2003). Create a Web portal module. *Visual Studio Magazine, 13*(14).

Schutz, W. C. (1961). On group composition. *Journal of Abnormal Social Psychology, 62*, 275-281.

Seddon, P.B. (1997). A respecification and extension of the DeLone and McLean model of IS success. *Information Systems Research, 8*(3), 240-253.

Shah, J.R., White, G.L., & Cook, J.R. (2007). Privacy protection overseas as perceived by USA-based IT professionals. *Journal of Global Information Management, 15*(1), 68-81.

Shankar, V., Urban, G., & Sultan, F. (2002). Online trust: A stakeholder perspective, concepts, implications, and future directions. *The Journal of Strategic Information Systems, 11*(34), 325-344.

Shaw, N. C., DeLone, W. H., & Niederman, F. (2002). Sources of dissatisfaction in end-user support: An empirical study. *The DATA BASE for Advances in Information Systems, 33*(2), 41-55.

Shaw, T. R. (2003). The moral intensity of privacy: An empirical study of Webmasters' attitudes. *Journal of Business Ethics, 46*(4), 301-318.

Shayo, C., Guthrie, R., & Igbaria, M. (1999). Exploring the measurement of end user computing success. *Journal of End User Computing, 11*(1), 5-14.

Sheehan, K.B. (2002). Toward a typology of Internet users and online privacy concerns. *The Information Age, 18*, 21-32.

Sheehan, K.B., & Hoy, M.G. (2000). Dimensions of privacy concern among online consumers. *Journal of Public Policy and Marketing, 19*(1), 62-73.

Sheehan, K. B. (2002). Toward a typology of Internet users and online privacy concerns. *The Information Society, 18*, 21-32.

Sheehan, K. B., & Hoy, M. G. (2000). Dimensions of online privacy concerns among online consumers. *Journal of Public Policy & Marketing, 19*(1), 62-73.

Shin, S.K., Gopal, R.D., Sanders, G.L., & Whinston, A.B. (2004). Global software piracy revisited. *Communications of the ACM, 47*(1), 103-107.

Shneiderman, B. (2002). *Leonardo's laptop: Human needs and the new computing technologies.* Cambridge, MA: MIT Press.

Short, J., Williams, E., & Christie, B. (1976). *The social psychology of telecommunications.* New York: John Wiley.

Simmers, C. A., & Anandarajan, M. (2001). User satisfaction in the Internet-anchored workplace: An exploratory study. *Journal of Information Technology Theory and Application, 3*(5), 39-61.

Simon, H. (1960). *The new science of management decisions.* New York: Harper and Row.

Simon, S. J., Grover, G., Teng, J. T., & Whitcomb, K. (1996). The relationship of information system training methods and cognitive ability to end-user satisfaction, comprehension, and skill transfer: A longitudinal field study. *Information Systems Research, 7*(4), 466-490.

Simon, S. J., & Werner, J. M. (1996). Computer training through behavior modeling, self-paced, and instructional approaches: A field experiment. *Journal of Applied Psychology, 81*(6), 648-659.

Sinrod, E. J. (2001). The future of Internet privacy. *Journal of Internet Law, 4*(9), 22-25.

Siponen, M. (2000). A conceptual foundation for organizational information security. *Information Management and Computer Security, 8*(1), 31-44.

Slagter, R., & Hofte, H.T. (2002). *End-user composition of groupware behaviour: The CoCoWare .NET architecture.* Telematica Instituut. Retrieved August 10, 2007, from http://www.telin.nl/project.cfm?language=en&id=241

Smith, H., Milberg, S., & Burke, S. (1996). Information privacy: Measuring individuals' concerns about organizational practices. *MIS Quarterly, 20*(2), 167-196.

Smith, H. J., Milberg, S. J., & Burke, S. J. (1996). Information privacy: Measuring individuals' concerns about organizational practices. *MIS Quarterly, 20*(2), 167-196.

Solomon, S., & O'Brien, J. (1990). The effect of demographic factors on attitudes toward software piracy. *The Journal of Computer Information Systems, 30*(3), 45-45.

Sosik, J. J., Avolio, B. J., & Kahai, S. S. (1997). Effects of leadership style and anonymity on group potency and effectiveness in a group decision support system environment. *Journal of Applied Psychology, 82*(1), 89-103.

Spence, M. (1973). Job market signaling. *Quarterly Journal of Economics, 87*(3), 355-374.

Stamps, D. (2000). Communities of practice: Learning is social. Training is irrelevant? In E. L. Lesser, M. A. Fontaine, & J. A. Slusher (Eds.), *Knowledge and communities* (pp. 53-64). Boston: Butterworth-Heinemann.

Star, S.L., & Griesemer, J.R. (1989). Institutional ecology, "translations" and boundary objects: Amateurs and professionals in Berkley's Museum of Vertebrate Zoology 1907- 39. *Social Studies of Science, 19*(3), 387-420.

Stary, C. (2000). TADEUS: Seamless development of task-based and user-oriented interfaces. *IEEE Transactions on Systems, Man, and Cybernetics: Part A, 30*(5), 509-525.

Stead, B. A., & Gilbert, J. (2001). Ethical issues in electronic commerce. *Journal of Business Ethics, 34*(2), 75-85.

Steiner, I. D. (1972). *Group process and productivity.* New York: Academic Press.

Stempel, G. H., & Wesley, B. H. (Eds.). (1981). *Research methods in mass communication.* Englewood Cliffs, NJ: Prentice-Hall.

Sternthal, B., Dholakia, R., & Leavitt, C. (1978). The persuasive effects of source credibility: Tests of cognitive response. *Journal of Consumer Research, 4*(4), 252-260.

Stevens, G., & Wulf, V. (2002). A new dimension in access control: Studying maintenance engineering across organizational boundaries. In *Proceedings of CSCW'92* (pp. 196-205). New York: ACM Press.

Stewart, K., & Segars, A. (2002). An empirical examination of the concern for information privacy instrument. *Information Systems Research, 13*(1), 36-49.

Stillar, G. F. (1998). *Analyzing everyday texts. Discourse, rhetoric, and social perspectives*. Thousand Oaks, CA: Sage.

Stone, R.N., & Winter, F.W (1987). Risk: It is still uncertainty times consequences? In R.W. Belk et al. (Eds.), *Proceedings of the American Marketing Association* (pp. 261-265).

Straub, D.W., & Nance, W.D. (1990). Discovering and disciplining computer abuse in organizations: A field study. *MIS Quarterly, 14*(1), 45-60.

Straub, D. (1990). Effective IS security: An empirical study. *Information Systems Research, 1*(3), 255-276.

Strauss, A. L., & Corbin, J. (1990). *Basics of qualitative research: Grounded theory procedures and techniques*. Newbury Park, CA: Sage.

Stubbs, M. (2001). *Words and phrases. Corpus studies of lexical semantics*. Oxford: Blackwell.

Stump, R., & Heide, J. (1996). Controlling supplier opportunism in industrial relationships. *Journal of Marketing Research, 33*(4), 431-441.

Suchman, L., Blomberg, J., Orr, J., & Trigg, R. (1999). Reconstructing technologies as social practice. *American Behavioral Scientist, 43*(3), 392-408.

Suchman, L., & Trigg, R.H. (1991). Understanding practice: Video as a medium for reflection and design. In J. Greenbaum & M. Kyng (Eds.), *Design at work:*

Cooperative design of computer systems (pp. 65-89). Hillsdale, NJ: Lawrence Erlbaum.

Sun, H., & Zhang, P. (2006). The role of moderating factors in user technology acceptance. *International Journal of Human-Computer Studies, 64*, 53-78.

Sutcliffe, A., & Mehandjiev, M. (Guest Eds.). (2004). End-user development. *Communications of the ACM, 47*(9), 31-32.

Suydam, M. (2000, March). Taking (health) care. *Information Security*, p. 54.

Sweat, J. (2001). Earthlink: An ISP that customers can trust? *InformationWeek, 851*, 36.

Syke, C., Shim, J.T., Johnson, R., & Jiang, J. (2006). Concern for information privacy and online consumer purchasing. *Journal of the Association for Information Systems, 7*(6), 415-444.

Szajna, B. (1994). Software evaluation and choice: Predictive validation of the technology acceptance instrument. *MIS Quarterly, 18*(3), 319-324.

Szajna, B. (1996, January). Empirical evaluation of the revised technology acceptance model. *Management Science, 42*(1), 85-92.

Szewczak, E. (2002). Beware the cookie monster. *Information Resources Management Journal, 15*(1), 3-4.

Tai, W.-T. (2006). Effects of training framing, general self-efficacy and training motivation on trainees' training effectiveness. *Personnel Review, 35*(1), 51-65.

Tan, B., Wei, K., & Lee-Partridge, J. E. (1999). Effects of facilitation and leadership on meeting outcomes in a group support system environment. *European Journal of Information Systems, 8*, 223-246.

Taylor, S., & Todd, P.A. (1995a, June). Understanding information technology usage: A test of competing models. *Information Systems Research, 6*(2), 144-176.

Taylor, S., & Todd, P.A. (1995b). Assessing IT usage: The role of prior experience. *MIS Quarterly, 19*, 561-570.

Taylor, M. J., Moynihan, E. P., & Wood-Harper, A. T. (1998). End-user computing and information systems methodologies. *Information Systems Journal, 8,* 85-96.

Teo, H. H., Wan, W., & Li, L. (2004). Volunteering personal information on the Internet: Effects of reputation, privacy initiatives, and reward on online consumer behavior. In *Proceedings of the 37th Hawaii International Conference on System Sciences.* Retrieved from http://csdl.computer.org/comp/proceedings/hicss/2004/2056/07/205670181c.pdf

Thatcher, J. B., & Perrewé, P. L. (2002). An empirical examination of individual traits as antecedents to computer anxiety and computer self-efficacy. *MIS Quarterly, 26*(4), 381-395.

Thibodeau, P. (2002). P3P supporters struggle to increase adoption of data privacy standard. *Computerworld, 36*(47), 20.

Thompson, R.L., Higgins, C.H., & Howell, J.M. (1991, March). Towards a conceptual model of utilization. *MIS Quarterly, 15*(1), 125-143.

Thompson, R.L., Higgins, C.H., & Howell, J.M (1994). Influence of experience on personal computer utilization: Testing a conceptual model. *Journal of Management Information Systems, 11,* 167-187.

Titsworth, T. (2002). More than face value: Airports and multimedia security. *IEEE Multimedia, 9*(2), 11-13.

Torkzadeh, G., Chang, J. C. J., & Demirhan, D. (2006). A contingency model of computer and Internet self-efficacy. *Information & Management, 43*(4), 541-550.

Trafimow, D., & Finlay, K. (1996). The importance of subjective norms for a minority of people: Between-subjects and within-subjects analyses. *Personality & Social Psychology Bulletin, 22*(8), 820-829.

Treiblmaier, H., Madlberger, M., Knotzer, N., & Pollach, I. (2004). The ethics of personalization and customization on the Internet: An empirical study. In *Proceedings of the 37th Hawaii International Conference on System Sciences.* Retrieved from http://csdl.computer.org/comp/proceedings/hicss/2004/2056/07/205670181b.pdf

Trevino, L.K. (1986). Ethical decision making in organizations: A person-situation interactionist model. *Academy of Management Review, 11*(3), 601-617.

Triandis, H.C. (1980). Values, attitudes and interpersonal behavior. In H.E. Howe (Ed.), *Nebraska Symposium on Motivation, 1979: Beliefs, Attitudes and Values* (pp. 195-259). Lincoln, NE: University of Nebraska Press, 195-259.

Trigg, R.H., Moran, T.P., & Halasz, F.G. (1987). Adaptability and tailorability in NoteCards. In H.-J. Bullinger & B. Shackel (Eds.), *Proceedings of INTERACT'87* (pp. 723-728). Amsterdam: North-Holland.

Turner, E. C., & Dasgupta, S. (2003, Winter). Privacy on the Web: An examination of user concerns, technology, and implications for business organizations and individuals. *Information Systems Management,* 8-18.

Turoff, M., Hiltz, S. R., Baghat, A., & Rana, A. (1993). Distributed group support systems. *MIS Quarterly, 17*(4), 399-417.

United States Bureau of the Census. (2003). *Computer use in the United States.* Washington, DC: Department of Commerce.

Urban, G., Sultan, F., & Qualls, W. (2000). Placing trust at the center of your Internet strategy. *Sloan Management Review, 42*(1), 39-48.

Venkatesh, V., Morris, M.G., Davis, G.B., & Davis, F.D. (2003). User acceptance of information technology: Towards a unified view. *MIS Quarterly, 27*(3), 425-478.

Venkatesh, V. (2000). Determinants of perceived ease of use: Integrating perceived behavioral control, computer anxiety and enjoyment into the technology acceptance model. *Information Systems Research, 11*(4), 342-365.

Venkatesh, V., & Davis, F. D. (1996). A model of the antecedents of perceived ease of use: Development and test. *Decision Sciences, 27*(3), 451-481.

Venkatesh, V., & Davis, F. (2000). A theoretical extension of the technology acceptance model: Four longitudinal field studies. *Management Science, 46*(2), 186-204.

Venkatesh, V. (2000). Determinants of perceived ease of use: Integrating control, intrinsic motivation and emotion into the technology acceptance model. *Information Systems Research, 11*(4), 342-365.

Venkatesh, V. (2006). Where to go from here? Thoughts on future directions for research on individual-level technology adoption with a focus on decision making. *Decision Sciences, 37*(4), 497-518.

Vidgen, R., Avison, D., Wood, B., & Wood-Harper, T. (2002). *Developing Web information systems.* Butterworth-Heinemann.

VisiQuest. (2007). Retrieved August 10, 2007, from http://www.accusoft.com/products/visiquest/

Volkoff, O., Strong, D.M., & Elmes, M.B. (2002, August 9-11). Between a rock and a hard place: Boundary spanners in an ERP implementation. *Proceedings of the Americas Conference on Information Systems*, Dallas, Texas (pp. 958-962).

Vygotsky, L.S. (1978). *Mind in society: The development of higher psychological processes.* Cambridge, MA: Harvard University Press.

W3C Semantic Web. (2001). Retrieved August 10, 2007, from http://www.w3.org/2001/sw/

Wakefield, R. (2001). *A determination of the antecedents of online trust and an evaluation of current Web assurance seals.* Doctoral dissertation, University of Mississippi, University, MS.

Walster, E., Berscheid, E., & Walster, G.W. (1973). New directions in equity research. *Journal of Personality and Social Psychology, 25*, 151-176.

Walster, E., Walster, G.W., & Berscheid, E. (1978). *Equity theory and research.* Boston: Allyn & Bacon

Warren, S.D., & Brandeis, L.D. (1890, December). The right for privacy. *Harvard Law Review, 4*, 193-220.

Watson, R. T., DeSanctis, G., & Poole, M. C. (1988). Using a GDSS to facilitate group consensus: Some intended and unintended consequences. *MIS Quarterly, 12*(3), 463-477.

Wayman, J. (2000, February). Federal biometric technology legislation. *Computer*, pp. 76-80.

Weber, R. P. (1985). *Basic content analysis.* Newbury Park, CA: Sage.

Wegner, P., & Goldin, D. (2003). Computation beyond turing machines. *Communications of the ACM, 46*(4), 100-102.

Wenger, E. (1998). *Communities of practice: Learning, meaning and identity.* New York: Cambridge University Press.

Wertsch, J. (1998). *Mind as action.* New York: Oxford University Press.

Westin, A. (1967). *Privacy and freedom.* New York: Atheneum Publishers.

Wheeler, B. C., & Mennecke, B. E. (1992). The effects of restrictiveness and preference for procedural order on the appropriation of group decision heuristics in a GSS environment. In *Proceedings of the Thirteenth Annual International Conference on Information Systems,* Dallas Texas (pp. 274-275).

Whitman, M. E., Perez, J., & Beise, C. (2001). A study of user attitudes toward persistent cookies. *The Journal of Computer Information Systems, 41*(3), 1-7.

Wolfe, R. A., Gephart, R. P., & Johnson, T. E. (1993). Computer-facilitated qualitative data analysis: Potential contributions to management research. *Journal of Management, 19*(3), 637-660.

Wolinsky, A. (1983). Prices as signals of product quality. *Review of Economic Studies, 50*(163), 647-658.

Won, M., Stiemerling, O., & Wulf, V. (2006). Component-based approaches to tailorable systems. In H. Lieberman, F. Paterno, & V. Wulf (Eds.), *End-user development.* Berlin: Springer-Verlag.

Won, M., & Cremers, A.B. (2002). Supporting end-user tailoring of component-based software: Checking integrity of composition (TRNumber CLIP4/02.0) In *Proceedings of the Colognet,* Madrid, Spain.

Wood, R., & Bandura, A. (1989). Social cognitive theory of organizational management. *Academy of Management Review, 14*(3), 361-384.

Woodward, J. (1997). Biometrics: Privacy's foe or privacy's friend? *Proceedings of the IEEE, 85*(9), 1480-1492.

Workman, M. (2005). Expert decision system use, disuse and misuse: A study using the theory of planned behavior. *Computers in Human Behavior, 21*, 211-231.

World Wide Web Consortium. (2003). *Platform for privacy preferences (P3P) project.* Retrieved from http://www3.org.P3P

Wyatt, S., Thomas, G., & Terranova, T. (2002). They came, they surfed, they went back to the beach: Conceptualizing use and new use of the Internet. In S. Woolgar (Ed.), *Virtual society? Technology, cyberbole, reality.* Oxford: Oxford University Press.

Yi, M.Y., & Davis, F. D. (2001). Improving computer training effectiveness for decision technologies: Behavior modeling and retention enhancement. *Decision Sciences, 32*(3), 521-544.

Yi, M. Y., & Davis, F. D. (2003). Developing and validating an observational learning model of computer software training and skill acquisition. *Information Systems Research, 14*(2), 146-169.

Yi, M. Y., & Hwang, Y. (2003). Predicting the use of Web-based information systems: Self-efficacy, enjoyment, learning goal orientation, and the technology acceptance model. *International Journal of Human-Computer Studies, 59*(4), 431-449.

Yi, M. U., & Im, K. S. (2004). Predicting computer task performance: Personal goal and self-efficacy. *Journal of Organizational and End User Computing, 16*(2), 28-37.

Yi, M.Y., Fiedler, K.D., & Park, J.S. (2006). Understanding the role of individual innovativeness in the acceptance of IT-based innovations: Comparative analyses of models and measures. *Decision Sciences, 37*(3), 393-426.

Zachman, J. A. (1987). A framework for information systems architecture. *IBM Systems Journal, 26*(3), 276-292.

About the Contributors

Steve Clarke received a BSc in economics from the University of Kingston Upon Hull, an MBA from the Putteridge Bury Management Centre, The University of Luton, and a PhD in human centered approaches to information systems development from Brunel University, all in the United Kingdom. He is professor of information systems in The University of Hull Business School. Clarke has extensive experience in management systems and information systems consultancy and research, focusing primarily on the identification and satisfaction of user needs and issues connected with knowledge management. His research interests include: social theory and information systems practice; strategic planning; and the impact of user involvement in the development of management systems. Major current research is focused on approaches informed by critical social theory.

* * *

Hege-René Hansen Åsand (heas@statoil.com)is a system analyst at Statoil ASA, Global Business Services in the Collaboration Competence Centre in Hammerfest, Norway. She received an MS in information science from the University of Bergen, Norway. Her thesis was on teachers' facilitator role when ICT is introduced in the classroom. Her general interests are computer-supported workplace learning, human-computer interaction, and information management. Her specific interests include computer-supported collaborative work and learning, end-user development, super users, and end-user tailoring. Currently, she is working towards a PhD on super users' dual role as end-user developers and knowledge activators at InterMedia, University of Oslo.

Reza Barkhi is an associate professor and faculty research fellow of information systems in the Department of Accounting and Information Systems, Pamplin College of Business, at Virginia Polytechnic Institute and State University. His current research interests are in the areas of collaborative technologies and problem solving, and topological design of telecommunication networks. Dr. Barkhi has published in journals such as *Location Science, European Journal of Operational Research, Computers & OR, Group Decision and Negotiation, Decision Support Systems,* and *Journal of Management Information Systems.* He received a BS in computer information systems, and an MBA, MA, and PhD in business focusing on information systems all from Ohio State University.

Katherine Boswell is an assistant professor at Middle Tennessee State University. She received her PhD in business administration in the area of management information systems from the University of Mississippi. Her minor areas of study were marketing and production operations management. She received her bachelor's in accounting in 1990, and her master's degree in business administration in 1991 from Mississippi State University. Katherine has publications in the areas of system development/strategy and in appropriate use policies. Her current research interests lie in the following areas: e-commerce, security, and privacy.

Yury Bychkov has received a Bachelor of Science (Honors, with distinction) in computer science from the University of Victoria in 1999 and a Master of Science in computer science at the University of Victoria, Canada in 2004 for the thesis entitled "Transformation-based Approach to Resolving Data Heterogeneity," which proposed a novel method of specifying the translation between heterogeneous XML document types. His other research interests include medical informatics, context-aware systems, intelligent systems, and management of uncertain knowledge. He is currently working as IT analyst at LGL Limited in Sidney, Canada.

Deborah Compeau is an associate professor of management information systems in the Richard Ivey School of Business Administration at the University of Western Ontario. Her research focuses on the individual user of information and communications technologies, viewed from a social cognitive perspective. In particular, she is interested in understanding what organizations can do to facilitate individual adoption of and learning about information technologies. Her research has been published in *Information Systems Research* and *MIS Quarterly* as well as other journals. Dr. Compeau has served as a member of the editorial boards of *MIS Quarterly* and *Information Systems Research*.

Maria Francesca Costabile is full professor at the Computer Science Department of the University of Bari, Italy, where she teaches courses for the computer science curriculum. She is currently the coordinator of computer science curricula at the University of Bari. She has been visiting scientist in several foreign universities in the USA and Germany. Her current research interests are in both theoretical and application oriented aspects of visual formalisms for information representation and querying, adaptive interfaces, user models, multimodal and multimedia interaction, Web interfaces, and system usability. She has published over 150 papers in scientific journals, books, and proceedings of international conferences on the above topics, and edited seven books. Professor Costabile is regularly in the program committees of international conferences and workshops; she has been program co-chair of INTERACT 2005 and is program co-chair of CHI 2008. She is on the steering committee of the AVI Conferences, that are organized in cooperation of ACM SIGCHI. She is senior member of IEEE and member of ACM and ACM SIGCHI. She was founding member of the Italian Chapter of ACM SIGCHI (SIGCHI Italy) and served as chair from 1996 to 2000.

Timothy Paul Cronan is professor and MD Matthews chair in information systems at the University of Arkansas, Fayetteville. Dr. Cronan received the DBA from Louisiana Tech University and is an active member of the Decision Sciences Institute and The Association for Computing Machinery. He has served as regional vice president and on the board of directors of the Decision Sciences Institute and as president of the Southwest Region of the Institute. In addition, he has served as associate editor for *MIS Quarterly*. His research interests include information systems ethical behavior, piracy and privacy, work groups, change management, data warehouse development, performance analysis and effectiveness, and end-user computing. Publications have appeared in *MIS Quarterly, Decision Sciences, Journal of Business Ethics, Information and Management, OMEGA The International Journal of Management*

Science, The Journal of Management Information Systems, Communications of the ACM, Journal of Organizational and End User Computing, Database, Journal of Research on Computing in Education, Journal of Financial Research, as well as in other journals and proceedings of various conferences.

David Dahlem is a Master of Science student in the Department of Computer Science at the University of Victoria, Canada. His thesis topic involves using pragmatics as a means for extracting context information from human to human conversations for use within context-aware systems. His other research interests include XML Web services, software security, data integration, and mobile device software development. He received a Bachelor of Arts in history from the University of Victoria in 1995. His Web site can be accessed at http://software-engineering.ca/Members/ddahlem.

David E. Douglas holds the rank of university professor in the Information Systems Department, Sam M. Walton College of Business, at the University of Arkansas. Dr. Douglas received his PhD in industrial engineering at the University of Arkansas. He teaches in a wide variety of information systems areas including programming, systems development, database management systems, enterprise systems, and business intelligence/knowledge management. Dr. Douglas is an active member in the Decision Sciences Institute, the Federation of Business Disciplines (FBD), and the Global Information Technology Management Association. He serves on the editorial board of several academic publications including the *Journal of Computer Information Systems.* Publications have appeared various journals including *Communications of the ACM, The Journal of Computer Information Systems, The Journal of Management Information Systems,* as well as international, national, and regional proceedings of various conferences.

Judy Drennan, PhD, is a senior lecturer in the School of Advertising, Marketing and Public Relations at the Queensland University of Technology. Her qualifications include a PhD from Deakin University focusing on information technology networks and small business, and a Master of Education from the University of Melbourne. Dr Drennan's research specialization is in electronic marketing, and she has published her work in the *Journal of Marketing Management, Journal of Macromarketing, Journal of Services Marketing,* and *Journal of Organizational and End User Computing.*

Daniela Fogli received the Laurea degree in computer science from the University of Bologna, Italy, in 1994 and PhD in information engineering from the University of Brescia, Italy, in 1998. From 1998 to 2000, she was a post-doc grant holder at the Joint Research Centre of the European Commission, Institute for Systems, Informatics and Safety. Since 2000, she has been assistant professor at the University of Brescia, Department of Electronics for Automation. In 2005, she was visiting scholar at the Center for LifeLong Learning & Design (L3D), University of Colorado at Boulder, USA. She served as short papers co-chair of the ACM Conference Advanced Visual Interfaces (AVI06). Her current research interests include specification and design of visual interactive systems, W3C technologies supporting the implementation of visual interactive systems, metadesign, and end-user development.

Bassam Hasan is an associate professor of management information systems in the College of Business Administration at the University of Toledo. He holds a PhD in MIS from the University of Mississippi and an MBA from Missouri State University. His research work has been published in various IS journal. He has also presented his research at various regional, national, and international conferences.

Chris Higgins is a professor at the Ivey School of Business, University of Western Ontario, London, Canada. Higgins' research focuses on the impact of technology on individuals, including such areas as computerized performance monitoring in the service sector; champions of technological innovation; alternative work arrangements; and, most recently, work and family issues and their impact on individuals and organizations. Higgins has published articles in several top journals, including the *Journal of Applied Psychology, Communications of the ACM, Administrative Sciences Quarterly, Sloan Management Review, Information Systems Research,* and *Management Information Systems Quarterly.* He is a former associate editor for *Information Systems Research.* Three of Higgins' doctoral students (Rebecca Grant, Betty Vandenbosch, Deb Compeau) have won major awards for their dissertation research. Higgins major expertise is in statistical analyses of large databases. He has expertise in standard statistical techniques (ANOVA, MANOVA, regression, contingency tables) as well as analyzing structural equation models (e.g., AMOS, LISREL, partial least squares) and hierarchical models using HLM.

Tabitha James is an assistant professor in the Department of Business Information Technology, Pamplin College of Business, at Virginia Polytechnic Institute & State University. Her current research interests are in the areas of security and privacy in information technology, combinatorial optimization, heuristics, parallel computing, and social networks. She received a BBA in management information systems and a PhD in business administration with a major in management information systems and a minor in productions and operations management from the University of Mississippi.

Luay Kawasme is a Master of Science student in the Department of Computer Science at the University of Victoria, Canada. His primary research interest focuses on the storage and retrieval of context patterns. His research includes leveraging multidimensional databases and data mining approaches to extract context patterns. He has 10 years experience in software development. He is currently a software engineer at Pivotal Corporation, a Vancouver-based software company. His work is focused on developing business intelligence solutions for the customer relationship management (CRM) industry. He received a Bachelor of Electrical Engineering from the University of Jordan, Jordan in 1994. His Web site can be accessed at http://www.cs.uvic.ca/~lkawasme.

Chris Klisc is a lecturer in the School of Information Technology at Murdoch University in Western Australia. She is currently undertaking postgraduate research in computer mediated communication and is interested in e-learning and end-user computing. She has taught undergraduate students information technology literacy, multimedia, and systems analysis and design.

Rosa Lanzilotti received the Laurea degree in computer science in April 2001 and the PhD in computer science in May 2006, both from the University of Bari, Italy. Since April 2002, she has been assistant researcher. She is currently assistant researcher at the Department of Computer Science, University of Bari. Her research interests focus on human-computer interaction, user-centered design, usability engineering, accessibility, evaluation methods, Web and e-learning systems interfaces. Dr. Lanzilotti served in the scientific secretariat of AVI 2004 Conference, Gallipoli (LE), May 25-28, 2004, and of the workshop "eLearning and Human Computer Interaction: Exploring Design Synergies for More Effective Learning," at INTERACT 2005 Conference, Rome, September 12-16, 2005. She is member of ACM SIGCHI (ACM's Special Interest Group on Computer-Human Interaction).

Sten R. Ludvigsen (sten.ludvigsen@intermedia.uio.no)is a professor at InterMedia, University of Oslo, Norway, where he currently is the director and scientific leader. He received his PhD in educational sciences (education psychology) based on a study of learning in medical institutions. His general areas of expertise are ICT and learning and sociocultural theory. His specific interests include how to use digital learning resources in teaching and learning, the relationship between co-located and distributed settings, and applications of this in the educational sector and workplaces. Professor Ludvigsen leads the PhD program in learning, communication, and ICT at the Faculty of Education, University of Oslo. At InterMedia, he leads the research group on sociocultural studies in ICT and learning. He is Scientific Manager (2007-2009) of the Kaleidoscope European Network of Excellence in Technology-enhanced Learning.

Nathan Lupton received his MBA from the Eric Sprott School of Business at Carleton University in 2006 and is currently a PhD student at the Richard Ivey School of Business at the University of Western Ontario. His research interests include IT adoption in health care, as well as trust and affect in technology mediated collaborative work arrangements.

Tanya McGill is a senior lecturer in the School of Information Technology at Murdoch University in Western Australia. She has a PhD from Murdoch University. Her major research interests include end-user computing and information technology education. Her work has appeared in various journals including *Decision Support Systems, European Journal of Psychology of Education, Journal of the American Society for Information Science, Journal of Organizational and End User Computing,* and *Information Resources Management Journal.*

Anders I. Mørch (anders.morch@intermedia.uio.no.)is an associate professor at InterMedia, University of Oslo, Norway. He received a PhD ininformatics from the University of Oslo (thesis on end-user tailoring of object-oriented application). He has worked in industry for three years at the NYNEX Science and Technology Center, New York. His general interests are computers in education and workplace learning, human-computer interaction, and participatory design. His specific interests include computer-supported collaborative work and learning, introduction of groupware and Web portals in organizations, and end-user development. Dr. Mørch was a member of the European Network of Excellence on End-User Development, and currently he is a Senior Researcher in the European Knowledge-Practices Laboratory (KP-Lab) integrated project.

Gillian Sullivan Mort, PhD, is an associate professor in marketing at Griffith Busienss School, Griffith University, Nathan campus, Australia. She holds her PhD from the University of Queensland as well as an MBA, BSc, BA, and Dip Psych with a Dip Ed. She researches in the areas of online and mobile marketing, nonprofits, and born globals. Her work has been published in such journals as *Journal of World Business, International Marketing Review,* and *Journal of Operations Management.*

Piero Mussio was a researcher at the Laboratory of Cosmic Physics, National Research Council of Italy, Milan (LFCTR). At the LFCTR, he was data reduction officer in European collaborations and in charge of the Group of Data Analysis. In 1983, he joined the Department of Physics, Milan University, as associate professor of computer science, where he was responsible for the Image Processing and Interpretation Group. From 1996 to 2003, he was at the University of Brescia, Italy, as professor of computer science. He is presently full professor at the Department of Informatics and Communication,

Milan University. His research interests evolved from pattern recognition in images and complex system behaviors to pattern recognition in human computer interaction, visual computing, and in visual language and visual computing environment design, formal specification, and experimental validation. He is associate editor of the *Journal of Visual Languages and Computing.* He served as president of the Italian Chapter of IAPR. He served as program chair for the 1999 IEEE Workshop on Visual Languages Tokio, 1999; general co-chair of 2000 IEEE Workshop on VL, Seattle, 2000; and program co-chair of ACM Conference AVI'06, Venezia, 2006. Prof. Mussio is an IAPR fellow, a member of ACM, and member of SIGCHI Italy (the Italian Chapter of ACM SIGCHI). He is/was program committee member for conferences, schools, and workshops on visual languages, pattern recognition, machine vision, and human computer interaction.

Loredana Parasiliti Provenza received the Laurea degree in mathematics from the University of Messina, Italy, in 2001 and a master's degree in information and communication security from the University of Milano, Italy, in 2002. She took the PhD in computer science at the University of Milano in 2006. Since May 2002, she is a research grant holder at the University of Milano, Department of Information and Communication. Her current research interests include specification, design and development of visual interactive systems, theory of visual languages, W3C technologies, and XML security and privacy preserving data mining.

Antonio Piccinno received the Laurea degree in computer science with full marks and honors in July 2001 and the PhD in computer science in March 2005, both from the University of Bari, Italy. Dr. Piccinno served in the scientific secretariat of the International Conference AVI 2004 (Advanced Visual Interfaces). He is member of ACM, ACM SIGCHI, and SIGCHI Italy (the Italian Chapter of ACM SIGCHI). Since April 2005, he has been assistant researcher at the Computer Science Department of the University of Bari. His research interests focus on human-computer interaction, visual interactive systems, theory of visual languages, end-user development, metadesign, component-based software development, WWW interfaces, multimodal and multimedia interaction, and adaptive interfaces.

Taner Pirim has a BS in environmental engineering from Marmara University in Istanbul and an MS in civil engineering emphasizing river hydraulics from the University of Mississippi. He has worked as an instructor and researcher in both the Engineering and Business Schools of the University of Mississippi. Since 2001, he has been working as a supercomputer consultant for the Mississippi Center for Supercomputing Research and as an adjunct professor for the Department of MIS/POM at the University of Mississippi.

Josephine Previte, PhD, is currently a postdoctoral fellow in the School of Advertising, Marketing and Public Relations at the Queensland University of Technology. Her doctoral research examined the role of the Internet in social marketing, applying a multidisciplinary approach that encompassed the sociology of technology, communication, and social marketing theory. In addition to a strong focus in marketing and society research, Josephine is also interested in a critical marketing analysis of consumption and e-marketplace behaviors and has other interests in the study of government and nonprofit marketing strategy.

Brian J. Reithel, PhD, is the dean of the School of Business Administration and a professor of MIS at the University of Mississippi. Previously, he served as MIS/POM department chair and as associate vice chancellor for University Relations. He has received numerous awards for excellence in teaching, research, and service over the past 20 years. He is the author of more than 70 research articles and papers that have appeared in leading journals and conference proceedings. He has also appeared in major practitioner magazines, including *ComputerWorld, PCWorld,* and *Inc.* He is currently the national executive-vice presidentpresident-elect of the Association of Information Technology Professionals. His research interests revolve around emerging technologies as well as factors that impact the success of systems development efforts, particularly in the area of strategic information systems.

David F. Rico has been in the field of computer programming since 1983. He worked on NASA's $20 billion space station in the 1980s, he worked for a $40 billion Japanese corporation in Tokyo in the early 1990s, and he worked on U.S. Navy fighters such as the F-18, F-14, and many others. He is also supported the U.S. Defense Advanced Research Projects Agency (DARPA), Defense Information Systems Agency (DISA), Space and Naval Warfare Center (SPAWAR), Air Force, and Army. He has been an international keynote speaker, published numerous articles on three continents, and written a textbook on computer science. He holds a bachelor's degree in computer science, a master's degree in software engineering, and is completing a doctoral degree in information technology.

Ron Thompson is associate professor of management in the Babcock Graduate School of Management at Wake Forest University. His research has been published or is forthcoming in a variety of journals, including *MIS Quarterly, Information Systems Research, the Journal of Management Information Systems,* and *Information & Management,* and he has given presentations at national and international conferences. Ron's current research interests include communication misreporting in IS projects, multi-attribute decision making, and the use of second-generation data analysis techniques. Ron is a former associate editor of *MIS Quarterly.*

Jens H. Weber-Jahnke is an associate professor in the Department of Computer Science at the University of Victoria, Canada. He holds a PhD in natural sciences (summa cum laude) from the University of Paderborn, Germany. He has authored more than 80 peer-reviewed publications and received several prestigious awards, including the German Software Engineering Prize (Ernst-Denert Stiftung) and a fellowship of the Advanced Systems Institute of British Columbia. His research interests lie in the area of medical informatics, pervasive computing, software security, and interoperability

Index